ACCORDING TO THEIR LIGHTS

STORIES OF IRISHMEN IN THE BRITISH ARMY, EASTER 1916

GW00982551

NEIL RICHARDSON studied philosophy in University College, Dublin, before writing his first book, *A Coward If I Return, A Hero If I Fall: Stories of Irishmen in World War I*, which won the Argosy Irish Non-Fiction Book of the Year award at the 2010 Irish Book Awards. This was followed by *Dark Times, Decent Men: Stories of Irishmen in World War II*. A member of the Reserve Defence Forces, Neil has also written and produced plays with a Great War theme and has made several national television and radio appearances, including as consultant historian on RTÉ television's centenary programme *My Great War*. He is also the historian with the Irish Military War Museum (www.imwm.ie).

For Caroline, and for all of history's forgotten Irish soldiers.

With very special thanks to David, Joan, Justin and Richard.

ACCORDING TO THEIR LIGHTS

STORIES OF IRISHMEN IN THE BRITISH ARMY, EASTER 1916

NEIL RICHARDSON

The Collins Press

FIRST PUBLISHED IN 2015 BY
The Collins Press
West Link Park
Doughcloyne
Wilton
Cork

A CIP record for this book is available from the British Library.

Paperback ISBN: 978-1-84889-214-9
PDF eBook ISBN: 978-1-84889-494-5
EPUB eBook ISBN: 978-1-84889-495-2
Kindle ISBN: 978-1-84889-496-9

Typesetting by Carrigboy Typesetting Services
Typeset in Garamond
Printed in Malta by Gutenberg Press Limited

Contents

'I will say a prayer for all brave men who do their duty according to their lights.'

James Connolly, when asked to pray for the British army soldiers about to carry out his execution, 12 May 1916.

Preface

Some years ago Patrick Hogarty, a member of the Royal Dublin Fusiliers' Association, was contacted by a priest who was interested in finding some information about a relative who had died during the Easter Rising, the armed rebellion by Irish republicans against British rule in Ireland that took place from 24 to 30 April 1916. The priest's two elderly aunts had told him about an uncle of theirs, Patrick Leen, a member of a British army lancers regiment, who had apparently been executed by the British for taking a pro-republican stance and refusing to fight against the rebels. In the eyes of the priest's aunts their uncle was a true Irish hero.

Patrick Hogarty's interest was piqued and he began to do some digging. What he discovered, as happens so often with family traditions about relatives who served in the British army during the Rising, was that the story was far from true. On 24 April 1916 a troop of cavalrymen from the 6th Reserve Cavalry Regiment, which included men drawn from the 5th Royal Irish Lancers, were despatched from Marlborough Barracks (now McKee Barracks) and ordered to proceed down Sackville Street (now O'Connell Street). Disturbances had been reported in the area, and at 12:10 p.m. the Dublin Metropolitan Police contacted the army and asked for troops to be sent immediately. The cavalrymen were quickly despatched to investigate; however, they had no idea that armed rebels had occupied several positions around Dublin, including the General Post Office in Sackville Street, which they were using as their headquarters, and so the lancers were riding straight into danger.

The scene was recorded in the *Sinn Fein Rebellion Handbook,* published by the *Weekly Irish Times* a year later. (It was incorrectly believed for a time that the nationalist political party Sinn Féin had been involved in the Rising, and the erroneous terms 'Sinn Féin Rebellion' and 'Sinn Féiners' came to be widely used.) The lancers, it reported,

> came into Sackville Street from the north end. As soon as they got in front of the Post Office they were met with a volley from the occupants of that building. The shots came for the most part from men who had got on the

roof, from which position they had a great advantage over the lancers. Four of the latter were shot, and the horse of one of them fell dead on the street. The dead bodies of these men were taken to Jervis street hospital. The Lancers withdrew to the Parnell Monument, where they remained for a short while before returning to barracks.

The lancers, commanded by a Colonel Hammond, were jeered by a crowd for not trying again to assault the rebel position, and were also pursued by two *Irish Independent* reporters, Maurice Linnane and Michael Knightly, looking for an interview. A company of Irish Volunteers from Rathfarnham were still making their way into the GPO when the fighting began.

The event has sometimes been referred to as the 'Charge of the Lancers', but, as this account shows, it was nothing of the sort. The insurgents in the GPO simply waited for the lancers to trot past, and opened fire. They had been ordered by Commandant-General James Connolly to hold their fire until the lancers were closer, but some of them opened fire early, and so their comrades fired too. A second volley caused no casualties.

In his autobiographical account *On Another Man's Wound* (1936), Ernie O'Malley, then a medical student (who later joined the IRA and fought in the War of Independence and the Civil War), described the scene:

> I walked up the street. Behind Nelson's Pillar lay dead horses, some with their feet in the air, others lying flat. 'The Lancers' horses,' an old man said, although I had not spoken. 'Those fellows,' pointing with his right hand towards the GPO, 'are not going to be frightened by a troop of Lancers. They mean business.' Seated on a dead horse was a woman ...

The English actor Sir Henry Lytton, who was in Dublin with the D'Oyly Carte Opera Company and was due to appear at the Gaiety Theatre on the day the Rising began, wrote about the event in his book *A Wandering Minstrel* (1933):

> The whole of the little cavalcade, except one horse, was shot to the ground, and I remember seeing the animal standing helplessly by the soldier who had fallen from its back, pushing its nose against the lifeless body, wondering why its master did not get up and remount. While it stood there it too was shot and fell to the ground dead. The terrible little heap remained there for many days, it being impossible for anyone to go out and get the soldiers to bury them, or to remove the carcasses of the dead horses.

Only three of the four lancers who were shot were killed outright. They were twenty-year-old Private Frederick Hughes from Kingston-upon-Thames, a member of the 12th (Prince of Wales's) Royal Regiment of Lancers, twenty-year-old Corporal James Headland from London, a member of the 5th Royal Irish Lancers, and forty-year-old Sergeant Thomas Henry 'Harry' Shepherd from Plymouth, also of the 5th Royal Irish Lancers (his wife, Mary O'Halloran, was from Ballincollig, Co. Cork, and his eldest son had been born there). The fourth lancer who was shot lingered on before dying on 1 May. This was 22-year-old Private Patrick Leen from Abbeyfeale, Co. Limerick, whose body lies in the cemetery of the Royal Hospital, Kilmainham, Dublin. Ironically, while Leen was part of his regiment's depot squadron, stationed at home, the bulk of his regiment, then serving on the Western Front, were relaxing far behind the front lines throughout the period. If Leen had been with them at war he would have been perfectly safe.

When Patrick Hogarty contacted the priest and told him the truth about his relative's death, the priest replied that his two aunts would not be happy with the story: it would shatter their long-held belief that their uncle was a republican hero who refused to fight against the rebels. Hogarty argued that Patrick Leen was indeed a hero: he died doing his duty as a soldier. It is not known whether the priest ever passed on the truth to his aunts.

When I looked into the history of Patrick Leen myself I discovered some more interesting facts about him. His father died when he was still a boy, and he was raised by his mother, Margaret, who ran a shop and a pub in Abbeyfeale. He was still living at home at the time of the 1901 census but by 1911 he was a boarder at Rockwell College, the private Catholic secondary school in Co. Tipperary.

Rockwell has its own better-known connections with the Easter Rising. Thomas MacDonagh, commandant of the 2nd Battalion of the Dublin Brigade of the Irish Volunteers, who was shot by firing squad in Kilmainham Jail on 3 May 1916 (two days after Patrick Leen died), was a former pupil; and Éamon de Valera, another rebel leader and future Taoiseach and President of Ireland, was a teacher there for a time.

My introduction to the fact that Irishmen had served in British army uniform during the Rising came in 2008 when I was researching for my first book, *A Coward If I Return, A Hero If I Fall: Stories of Irishmen in World War I*. Richard Moles, a former British army regimental sergeant-major turned military researcher, was assisting me with part of the book and mentioned that he had recently been asked to find the service file of an Irishman who, his descendants believed, had died on the Somme in 1916. He discovered that the man had indeed been killed during 1916, but not on the Somme: he had been killed on the streets of Dublin during the Easter Rising, one of the many Irishmen in British army uniform who fought and died that week.

When Richard contacted his clients to pass on the news, they were less than happy to learn that their relative had fought against the 1916 insurgents. Serving in British army uniform was apparently one thing, but fighting against the insurgents was an entirely different matter.

Later, when visiting my grandfather's grave in Mount Jerome Cemetery in Harold's Cross I came across a Commonwealth War Graves Commission headstone. This was not unusual. Many cemeteries in Irish towns, especially in

Dublin, contain the distinctive graves of British war dead from both world wars, although predominantly from the First World War. During the period 1914–18 men wounded at the front and transported to Irish hospitals to recover often succumbed to their injuries and were buried locally. Others died from disease, while sailors who perished at sea and whose bodies were either washed ashore or recovered from the water were also interred in Irish soil. However, I was also aware that many of the British war graves in the main Dublin cemeteries – Mount Jerome, Glasnevin, Deansgrange and Grangegorman Military Cemetery – contained the bodies of British army and Commonwealth soldiers killed during the Easter Rising. The grave I had come across was one of these.

Part of the inscription made me stop and take a closer look. It read: *140229 Private N. N. Fryday 75th Bn. Canadian Inf. 30th April 1916.* I was intrigued that a Canadian soldier – obviously on leave or in Ireland recovering from a wound – had managed to die in the Rising. Something told me to research him further, and my investigation into Private Fryday produced a surprise: Neville Nicholas Fryday was Irish. Also, he was only seventeen years old when he died. And he was the only man in Canadian army uniform to die during the Rising.

Born in Upperchurch, near Thurles, Co. Tipperary, Neville Fryday was living with his family in Aughvallydeag, just outside the village of Milestone, Co. Tipperary, at the time of the 1901 census. Some time after 1911 he emigrated to Canada, where several of his siblings had already gone, and began work as a labourer in Toronto. He joined the 9th Mississauga Horse, a local reserve cavalry unit, in which his eldest brother, William, was also serving.

In November 1914 another of Neville's older brothers, Henry 'Harry' Fryday, enlisted in the Canadian Expeditionary Force (CEF) that would sail to Europe and enter the war, and on 16 July 1915 Neville's eldest brother, 26-year-old William, also enlisted. Three days later Neville followed William and joined the same unit, the 75th (Mississauga) Battalion of the CEF. While Neville claimed to be twenty-one at the time he was in fact only seventeen. The ruse worked, and the two brothers were soon training together in Niagara and Toronto; they then sailed back to Europe when their battalion set out for the war, landing at Liverpool on 9 April 1916.

Records show that the two brothers were immediately given leave to visit their mother, Elizabeth, who was living in St Malachy's Road in Glasnevin, Dublin. They were still on leave when the Rising began and were called on to help defeat it. But on 30 April 1916 Neville Fryday received a gunshot wound in the abdomen. He was taken to Mercer's Hospital but soon died of his wounds. (At the same time his maternal uncle Dr Robert Wayland was working not far away in the improvised hospital set up in the High School in Harcourt Street.)

This book is not in any way an attempt to diminish the courage shown and the suffering and sacrifices endured by the insurgents of Easter Week, 1916. It was acknowledged by the British forces that – for the most part – they fought bravely and honourably, and their rebellion ultimately led to the formation of the modern Irish state. However, there is another aspect to the story of 1916, one that has never truly been told. By a twist of fate, the rebels ended up fighting against many Irishmen who also supported the ideal of an independent Ireland, albeit in the form of Home Rule.

Many others have written extensively about the experiences of the rebels during the Rising, and this book will not deal directly with those. It is my aim to tell the forgotten side of the story. (Even so, it is not an exhaustive account of all Irishmen who served in British army uniform during the Rising, and it deals with the Rising in Dublin only.)

All these Irishmen in the British army were ordinary men – the same as the rebels against whom they found themselves fighting – and their lives also deserve to be remembered. Like their republican counterparts, the Irishmen in the British army suffered greatly during the Rising. Many lost friends, many were wounded, and some even lost their lives, dying in a battle that would make their memory for ever unpalatable to the independent Ireland that was soon to come about. But they were Irishmen all the same, and this is their story.

1

Introduction

I had always believed, perhaps because it was never clarified in my school history books, that those who took part in the Easter Rising had fought against exclusively English troops. But, as it turns out, this is simply not so. When used with regard to the history of the Rising, the words 'British soldiers' – while completely accurate insofar as all men wearing a khaki uniform were soldiers of the British army – can conjure up the notion that all these men were from Great Britain. They were not.

In April 1916 the Great War, as it was called, was nearly two years old. Added to the 20,000 Irishmen already in the British army when the war began, and the 30,000 ex-regular reservists or special reservists who had been recalled or activated for full-time service, 95,000 Irish civilian volunteers had already enlisted, bringing the total number of Irishmen in the British army to 145,000. A further 55,000 would join up before the conflict ended.

The Royal Irish Rifles recruited from Cos. Antrim, Down and Louth, the Royal Irish Fusiliers from Cos. Armagh, Monaghan and Cavan, the Royal Inniskilling Fusiliers from Cos. Donegal, Derry, Tyrone and Fermanagh, the Royal Irish Regiment from Cos. Kilkenny, Tipperary, Waterford and Wexford, and the Leinster Regiment from Cos. Longford, Meath, Westmeath, Offaly and Laois. Despite its name, the Royal Dublin Fusiliers recruited from Cos. Dublin, Carlow, Kildare and Wicklow. Battalions from all of these regiments were involved in the Easter Rising in Dublin, meaning that men from nearly everywhere in Ireland served in British army uniform during the rebellion.

Stationed throughout the country were various battalions of the Irish infantry regiments of the British army, their ranks primarily filled with Irish-born soldiers. Some of these were 'reserve', 'extra reserve' or 'garrison' battalions – units that would never be sent to the battlefields of Europe or beyond; instead the reserve battalions trained new recruits, while the garrison battalions did exactly as their name suggests, so helping to free other units for service. In this way the military could retain a presence on the home front and train new recruits at the same time – fresh soldiers who could then be sent in groups or drafts to replace losses in the front-line battalions.

In Dublin in April 1916 two such reserve units were the 3rd (Reserve) Battalion of the Royal Irish Rifles, stationed in Portobello Barracks (now Cathal Brugha Barracks), Rathmines, with a complement of 21 officers and 650 other ranks, and the 3rd (Reserve) Battalion of the Royal Irish Regiment in Richmond Barracks (later Keogh Barracks), Inchicore, which comprised 18 officers and 385 other ranks.

There were also two garrison battalions in Dublin: the 2nd Garrison Battalion of the Royal Irish Regiment, based at Beggarsbush Barracks in Haddington Road, and the 2nd Garrison Battalion of the Royal Irish Fusiliers. (Both these battalions were very small in number, as they had been created only in March and April 1916, respectively.)

Meanwhile at the Curragh Camp in Co. Kildare were the 5th (Extra Reserve) Battalion of the Royal Dublin Fusiliers and 5th (Extra Reserve) Battalion of the Leinster Regiment. The 3rd (Reserve) Battalion of the Royal Dublin Fusiliers was based in Victoria Barracks (now Collins Barracks), Cork, while the 4th (Extra Reserve) Battalion of the same regiment was stationed in Templemore, Co. Tipperary. Finally, many soldiers in the Ulster-based reserve battalions of the Royal Irish Rifles, Royal Irish Fusiliers and Royal Inniskilling Fusiliers would also be summoned to the capital during the rebellion.

A problem with these units was that, because their primary roles were garrison and training duties, and their soldiers were never expected to see combat unless they travelled overseas to join a fighting unit, the ranks of reserve and garrison battalions often contained men unsuitable for the front, whether too young or too old, or – certainly in the case of the garrison battalions – medically unfit for active military service. Others were recovering from wounds received in the war.

Under-age recruits were often sent to these units. They may have lied about their age to sign up; experienced recruiting sergeants often saw through the ruse but enlisted them anyway, in the knowledge that they could be sent to danger-free battalions stationed at home, where they could gain a few years in age before being sent overseas and in the meantime would release an older man to head to the front. Similarly, older men – those who claimed to be younger so that they could enlist, or veterans who returned to the colours on the outbreak of war but who were past their fighting best – were sent to reserve or garrison units. Sadly, the same men would also soon appear on wounded and killed-in-action lists after the Rising.

The other type of British army infantry unit stationed in Ireland was the 'service battalion'. The first service battalions had been created at the start of the war so that the British army could expand to meet the demands of such a large-scale conflict. Their ranks were filled with citizen volunteers, but these battalions were to be sent to the battlefields as cohesive units. Every so often new service battalions of a given regiment were created, and in April 1916 one such unit was

British army lancers, Dublin, 1916 (from *Dublin and the Great War, 1914–1918*)

stationed in Dublin awaiting orders to travel overseas. This was the 10th (Service) Battalion of the Royal Dublin Fusiliers – also known as the 'Commercial Pals' – stationed in the Royal Barracks (later Collins Barracks), which comprised 37 officers and 430 other ranks.

Irishmen also served in the various cavalry, artillery and other corps of the British army in Ireland (as well as in the Royal Navy), while elsewhere around the country other Irish units would become involved with the Rising, such as the 3rd (Reserve) Battalion of the Connaught Rangers – which recruited from Cos. Galway, Leitrim, Mayo, Roscommon and Sligo – a battalion that aided in defeating the rebels at Enniscorthy, Co. Wexford, and the 3rd (Reserve) Battalion and 4th (Extra Reserve) Battalion of the Leinster Regiment and the 4th (Extra Reserve) Battalion of the Royal Irish Regiment, which were all involved in dealing with the uprising in Limerick.

Altogether, between the 6th Reserve Cavalry Regiment (which had 35 officers and 851 other ranks), the 3rd Royal Irish Regiment, the 3rd Royal Irish Rifles and the 10th Royal Dublin Fusiliers, the British army had 120 officers and 2,265 other ranks stationed in Dublin when the Rising began. However, this figure omits the soldiers in the 2nd Garrison Battalion of the Royal Irish Regiment and the

2nd Garrison Battalion of the Royal Irish Fusiliers, along with Dublin University Officers' Training Corps at Trinity College, the men of other OTCs, such as the Inns of Court OTC and Royal College of Surgeons OTC, the 1st (Dublin) Battalion of the Irish Association of Volunteer Training Corps – a home defence force – and the instructors and students attached to the Army School of Musketry at Dollymount and Elm Park Bombing School at Mount Merrion.

Ignoring all the additional smaller units and concentrating on the four main ones, the 6th Reserve Cavalry Regiment was not predominantly Irish, so if we take their numbers away from the total of British army troops in Dublin this still leaves 76 officers and 1,465 other ranks between the 3rd Royal Irish Regiment, the 3rd Royal Irish Rifles and the 10th Royal Dublin Fusiliers. Even if we allow for a third of these men to have been away on leave for the Easter holiday this still gives approximately 1,000 Irishmen in the British army who were present on the first day of the Rising in Dublin. (It is true that not all men who served in Irish regiments were Irish, but when the numbers of Irishmen serving in the 6th Reserve Cavalry Regiment and the additional smaller units throughout Dublin are taken into account the number would certainly return to at least the 1,000 mark.)

In comparison, Max Caulfield in *The Easter Rebellion* (1963) states that, 'according to insurgent calculations made on the actual morning of the insurrection (these have been amended over the years until they now amount to something like twice this number), there were just seven hundred rebels out in Dublin altogether.' If Caulfield is correct, Irishmen in the British army outnumbered the insurgents on the first day of the Rising. As Caulfield mentioned, other writers suggest a higher figure: as many as 1,200 to 1,400. This higher figure is now generally accepted to refer to the number of insurgents fighting in Dublin by the end of the Rising, meaning that as many as 700 later joined the 700 who set out on the first day. As several additional Irish regiments of the British army were summoned to Dublin after the outbreak of the Rising – an 'Ulster Composite Battalion' from the north, along with the 3rd, 4th and 5th Royal Dublin Fusiliers and the 5th Leinster Regiment, the majority of them Irishmen – it is unlikely that insurgent numbers ever exceeded the number of Irishmen in British army uniform in Dublin at any time.

So why did these Irishmen enlist in the British army for service during the Great War? Unfortunately, this is a loaded question. Too often the explanation is merely an attempt to remove 'blame' from them for having done so. When researching for *A Coward If I Return, A Hero If I Fall,* I often found that some families – perhaps less than proud that their ancestor had 'taken the King's shilling' – mistakenly believed that their relatives had either been under age (too young to know any better) or conscripted (had no choice but to serve); there was even the unusual response that they served with the 'Irish army' in the trenches.

Conscription was never introduced in Ireland; and I often discovered – by using several non-military sources, such as birth and baptism records and census returns – that the allegedly under-age soldier was nothing of the sort. As for serving with the Irish army in the trenches, Ireland was still a part of the United Kingdom during the whole of the period; there was no Irish army until 1922, and arguably if there had been it would never have taken part in the war. The confusion was perhaps a result of the fact that several regiments of the British army had the word 'Irish' in their names, leading some relatives to assume later that these must have been Irish army units.

Of course one of the main – and genuine – reasons for enlisting at the time was poverty. The average Irish person, going by general opinion, could be forgiven for thinking that all Irishmen who ever wore a British army uniform must have been previously starving or destitute, particularly about the time of the First World War, and that those few who were not must have been either 'West Brits' (supporters of the King and Empire and so not really Irish in the true sense) or fools (who fought on the wrong side or in the wrong war).

The truth was that, while poverty was a motivating factor for many – as it certainly was for many Dublin tenement-dwellers, and for my own great-grand-father, who enlisted to escape the harsh life of an unskilled labourer in his home town of Athlone – many signed up to better themselves. Through the army they could be educated or trained and find discipline, status and career progression through the rank structure. Some joined to stay close to their friends, or because of a tradition of soldiering in the family. Others signed on so that they could be part of something greater than themselves as individuals and 'make a difference', as they saw it, while many actually enlisted for politically idealistic reasons, including the cause of Ulster unionism or Irish nationalism. It is the latter of these two political motivations that makes the story of the Irishmen who served in the British army during the Easter Rising a particularly tragic and poignant one.

By 1912 many Irish politicians had been fighting for decades to secure 'Home Rule' for Ireland. The country would remain within the British Empire but would be granted its own parliament and government. On 11 April that year the third Home Rule Bill was introduced in the House of Commons. Previously, in 1893, the House of Lords had vetoed the second Home Rule Bill, but now it could only postpone a bill for two years; and so it appeared that by 1914 Home Rule would finally be introduced.

Many people in Ulster, however, refused to accept Home Rule. Ulster was predominantly Protestant, whereas in the rest of the country the people were mostly Catholic. Furthermore, the Ulster economy relied more on industry and manufacturing while most in the south lived off agriculture. Many people in Ulster feared, therefore, becoming a religious minority, and that their livelihood would be destroyed by the economic policies of any independent government. They insisted on remaining a part of the United Kingdom, and swore that they would resist Home Rule, by force if necessary. The Ulster Volunteers (later Ulster Volunteer Force) – a paramilitary force containing tens of thousands of men – was soon set up throughout Ulster to defend unionist ideals.

In response to this, the following year those who wanted to see the introduction of Home Rule set up their own paramilitary force, the Irish Volunteers. Tensions between the UVF and Irish Volunteers grew as both sides trained, prepared and steadily built up supplies of weapons. The assassination of Archduke Franz Ferdinand, heir to the Austro-Hungarian throne, in Sarajevo on 28 June 1914, and the subsequent outbreak of the First World War, probably stopped the UVF and Irish Volunteers from starting a civil war over the issue of Home Rule.

Though Home Rule was formally granted on 18 September 1914, when war broke out it was announced that its implementation would be postponed until the end of the war (or for one year if the war turned out to be short). As a result, leaders of the Home Rule movement, and in particular the leader of the Irish Party (also known as the Irish Parliamentary Party), John Redmond, began urging the Irish Volunteers to enlist in the British army to protect Home Rule. If the Irish people refused to support Britain in the war, perhaps Home Rule would be denied to them afterwards. (The UVF had a similar idea and began enlisting in the British army to defend their own goal.)

This call produced a split in the Irish Volunteers. The great majority – 180,000 out of 190,000 – agreed with Redmond's policy of supporting the British war effort. The dissenting minority had been influenced by the hard-line Irish Republican Brotherhood, a secret society that wanted to see the establishment of an Irish republic, totally free and independent of Britain. Those who supported Redmond renamed themselves the Irish National Volunteers, and thousands soon began enlisting in the British army – 22,000 by February 1916 and 32,000 by the end of the war – the majority of them Dubliners or Ulster Catholics, while those who wanted to bring about an independent republic kept the original name and began to plan a war of their own.

Ultimately this would become the Easter Rising of 1916. As fate would have it, the Irish Volunteers would fight their rebellion – along with their comrades in the Irish Citizen Army, Cumann na mBan, the Hibernian Rifles (a small military force organised by the Ancient Order of Hibernians) and Fianna Éireann – against many Irishmen in the British army who had been their comrades before the Irish Volunteers split.

An estimated 31,000 members of the UVF also enlisted. When this is added to the 32,000 Irish National Volunteers who enlisted, it means that 63,000 out of Ireland's 150,000 wartime citizen volunteers, or 43 per cent, enlisted for politically idealistic reasons.

As for the Rising itself, this was organised by the seven members of the IRB's Military Council. Planning had begun in September 1914, with the goal of raising rebellion before the end of the Great War, on the old principle that 'England's difficulty is Ireland's opportunity'; but the chief of staff of the Irish Volunteers, Prof. Eoin MacNeill, wanted to go ahead with a rising only after an increase in public support for its aims, or following an increase in unpopular wartime moves by the British government, and so the Military Council began to bypass his authority. Contact was also made with the German government, which agreed to send arms.

Patrick Pearse, director of military organisation for the Volunteers, organised 'parades and manoeuvres' for 23 April 1916 – Easter Sunday; but when MacNeill learnt that this was code for an actual rebellion he threatened to ensure that it was called off. As a result the IRB Military Council was forced to tell him that arms from Germany were already on their way and that, as events were already in motion, if the British found the arms the Irish Volunteers would be suppressed, rising or no rising. MacNeill agreed to go ahead. However, after Sir Roger Casement was captured returning from Germany, and the ship carrying the arms, the *Aud,* was scuttled after encountering the Royal Navy, MacNeill decided to call it off. He issued a countermanding order, announcing that all 'parades and manoeuvres' had been cancelled.

The Military Council rearranged the rising for the following day; but because of MacNeill's countermanding order only a minority of Volunteers in the Dublin area turned up at their assembly areas. But even with their ranks severely diminished, the rebels went ahead.

All in all, the 200,000 Irishmen who ultimately served in the British army during the Great War enlisted for many different reasons, and they continued to do so long after the brutally long lists of casualties became common in the newspapers after the battles of 1914 and 1915, so they were well aware of what they were letting themselves in for; but universally, they enlisted to fight Germany. They could not have imagined that, instead of finding themselves charging across a French or Belgian no man's land they would be fighting from building to building and room to room – a type of urban combat they knew nothing about – in Dublin against fellow-Irishmen. They certainly did not enlist to suppress Irish independence (although the unionist recruits definitely did not enlist to aid it), but they were ultimately remembered as having done so.

Despite the fact that the Irish people were at first outraged at the rebels during and immediately after the Rising – many Dubliners suffered near-starvation, the destruction of their homes and even the death of family members, while the *Irish Independent* and *Irish Times* demanded the execution of the leaders – on 3 May 1916, only four days after they surrendered, the first of the leaders were executed. The executions continued until 12 May, when Seán Mac Diarmada and the badly wounded James Connolly were shot by firing squad. In accordance with British army regulations, each prisoner was first blindfolded – James Connolly was also strapped to a chair – to face the firing squad. Fourteen men were ultimately executed in Kilmainham Jail; a fifteenth, Thomas Kent, was shot in Cork Detention Barracks, and a sixteenth, Sir Roger Casement, was hanged in Pentonville Prison, London, on 3 August.

The speed with which the death sentences were carried out shocked the public and resulted in the beginning of a change in attitude that ultimately led to the War of Independence of 1919–1921. However, this also had the effect of sealing the fate of all those Irishmen who had joined the British army and who supported Home Rule. By the end of the war many people had forgotten why these men had gone to war, while public opinion now favoured an independent republic, not 'Home Rule'. Ireland began to view its First World War soldiers as enemies – servants of a foreign oppressor.

Thomas Kettle, poet and Irish Party MP, had enlisted at the outbreak of the war to fight for the cause of Home Rule. After the Rising he remarked that the rebels 'will go down to history as heroes and martyrs, and I will go down – if I go down at all – as a bloody British officer.' He was killed on 9 September 1916 at the Battle of Ginchy on the Somme, aged thirty-six, while serving as a lieutenant with the 9th Royal Dublin Fusiliers. With no known grave, today his name is commemorated on the Thiepval Memorial.

Kettle was right to wonder 'if I go down at all', as the experiences of the vast majority of Irishmen in the British army during the period 1914–18 were forgotten in the years after the War of Independence. Many returning veterans were treated with hostility, were shunned and made to feel ashamed, and many never spoke about what they had been through; but in 21st-century Ireland the nation is well on its way to accepting and acknowledging the suffering of these men in the trenches. But what about the Irishmen whose battlefield was not France, Belgium or Gallipoli but Dublin? What about those whose enemy was not German or Turk but fellow-Irishman? First World War veterans may have suffered a stigma for having worn a British army uniform, but the Irishmen who actually fired at, and even killed, the soldiers of the Irish Volunteers or Irish Citizen Army were as good as cursed.

The truth is that they were there, and their role in modern Ireland's most pivotal historical event equally deserves to be told. After all, it is simply a part of our history.

So who were these Irishmen who served in the British army in Dublin during the Easter Rising? They were Catholics, Church of Ireland men, Presbyterians, Methodists, Episcopalians, Quakers, Unitarians and Jews. Some would go on to become TDs or senators, others became judges of the High Court or Supreme Court after the formation of the Irish Free State. Some would die in the trenches of the First World War, others would lose their lives in the Second World War. Many of the Dublin University OTC cadets who helped to defend Trinity College would become doctors, dentists, architects, lawyers or businessmen, respected members of post-independence Irish society. One man would later be awarded the Victoria Cross (the highest British award for bravery), while after the war some would fight on both sides in the War of Independence – some as policemen with the Royal Irish Constabulary or British army intelligence agents, others as guerrilla fighters with the IRA flying columns.

Finally, along with the Irishmen who fought and died while serving with the British army it must not be forgotten that many policemen, members of the Royal Irish Constabulary or Dublin Metropolitan Police, were also killed during the Rising, while Irish doctors and nurses of the Royal Army Medical Corps, Queen Alexandra's Imperial Military Nursing Service or the Red Cross struggled to cope with the influx of British army wounded, along with captured rebel prisoners or civilians, who began flowing into Dublin hospitals during the fighting.

The Rising resulted in the deaths of approximately 134 members of the British forces and RIC or DMP men, and approximately 387 more were wounded. Deducting the police figures for a moment (17 killed and 30 wounded), we see that Irishmen therefore made up 35 per cent of the British military fatalities incurred during the Rising

5th Royal Irish Lancers cap badge
(Author's Collection)

(41 out of the 117 military deaths) and 29 per cent of the wounded (106 out of the 357 military wounded). The insurgents lost 64 killed during the fighting and an unknown number of wounded, while 254 civilians were killed and a further 2,217 injured.

The truth is that the links between Irish rebels and Irish soldiers in the British army during the Easter Rising are stronger than the reader might first imagine. Aside from the fact that many of the insurgents and many of the Irishmen in the British army had been members of the Irish Volunteers before the 1914 split, many of the executed leaders had some link to Britain or service in the British army. Michael Mallin served for thirteen years in the Royal Scots Fusiliers between 1889 and 1902, mostly in India, while James Connolly, under the alias Reid, served for seven years in the British army, as did his brother John. (John Connolly died of natural causes in Edinburgh on 22 June 1916, aged fifty-two, while serving as a corporal in the Scots Guards, six weeks after his brother was executed in Dublin.) Tom Clarke's father, James Clarke from Co. Leitrim, had served for twenty-one years in the British army. He fought at the Battles of Alma, Inkerman and Sebastopol during the Crimean War and was later stationed in South Africa, where young Tom lived with him for six years. Sir Roger Casement's father, also Roger Casement, had been a captain in the 1st (Royal) Regiment of Dragoons. Joseph Plunkett was a member of the Officers' Training Corps while studying at Stonyhurst College, a Jesuit private school in Lancashire. Robert Erskine Childers, whose yacht, the *Asgard,* was involved in the Howth gun-running on 26 July 1914, had fought in the Anglo-Boer War and was then awarded the Distinguished

Service Cross while an officer in the Royal Navy during the First World War. Commandant Éamonn Ceannt (born Edmund Kent) of the 4th Battalion of the Dublin Brigade of the Irish Volunteers had a brother – Anglo-Boer War veteran Company Sergeant-Major William Kent of the 1st Royal Dublin Fusiliers – who was killed in France on the first anniversary of the Rising, 24 April 1917. With no known grave, today he is commemorated on the Arras Memorial.

Finally, after the execution of Thomas MacDonagh the poet Francis Ledwidge from Slane, Co. Meath, a supporter of Home Rule and a lance-corporal in the 1st Royal Inniskilling Fusiliers, wrote a 'Lament for Thomas MacDonagh'. Ledwidge himself was killed in action just over a year later in Belgium on 31 July 1917 and now lies in Artillery Wood Cemetery at Boezinge, near Ypres.

2

Unarmed Soldiers During the Early Hours of the Rising

Before the British army began to respond in force, or really knew what was going on in Dublin, Irish soldiers in British army uniform came under fire from the rebels, often while unarmed. One such was Private Patrick Conway of the 3rd Royal Dublin Fusiliers, who had joined up in July 1915. Thirty years old and from Donnybrook in Dublin, Conway was based in Cork and had gone home on leave not long before the Rising.

Private Conway's leave was due to end at midnight on 24 April, and that morning he made his way to Kingsbridge Station (now Heuston Station) to take the train back to the Royal Dublin Fusiliers' depot at Naas, Co. Kildare. While in the vicinity of Kingsbridge he was shot in the back and right lung by a rebel. He would have been in uniform at the time but unarmed. He was brought to the nearby King George V Military Hospital (now St Bricin's Military Hospital) but was soon reported dead. A month later, however, on 24 May, Conway's sister Hannah Gray, in response to a letter from a Captain Mooney, records officer with the Royal Dublin Fusiliers, wrote: 'Dear Sir, In answer to your letter of sympathy as regards the death of 22711 Private Patrick Conway 3rd Batt. R. D. Fusiliers I am very glad to let you no [sic] that he is in the City of Dublin Hospital Baggots Street where he is progressing favourably and expects to be up soon.'

Conway had survived his injuries and was discharged from hospital on 28 August and shortly afterwards returned to his battalion. Later in the year he was posted overseas, joining C Company of the 9th Battalion in France. He was still with this battalion when they took part in the disastrous Battle of Frezenberg Ridge on 16 August 1917. He miraculously survived the battle, but the following day he was admitted to the Boulogne Field Hospital suffering from a gunshot wound (listed as 'mild') to his left forehead and left eye.

By May 1918 he was back with the 3rd Battalion, now stationed in Grimsby, Lincolnshire, as part of the Humber Garrison, but on 3 June he returned to

France and joined the 2nd Battalion. But his various wounds had taken their toll, and within nine days he was found unfit for infantry service. He was transferred to the Labour Corps, and ultimately survived the war. He was demobilised in July 1919, now aged thirty-three, and returned to live with his sister in Donnybrook.

Private David Brady had a similar experience. Originally from Tyrrellspass, Co. Westmeath, he had been living in Lower Kevin Street, Dublin, for many years and working as a labourer. He was attached to the 3rd Royal Irish Rifles and was forty-one when the Rising began. Not long after the Rising a report entitled *Unarmed Persons Shot by Rebels* was compiled by the DMP, and it records that Private Brady was 'shot at Stephens Green with buck-shot [shotgun] when returning unarmed off furlough.' He was treated first at the nearby Mercer's Hospital and was later transferred to King George V Military Hospital. He ultimately recovered from his wounds and went on to serve with the 19th Battalion, a reserve battalion stationed in Newcastle, Co. Down, and later at Larkhill, Wiltshire, before finally transferring to the Army Ordnance Corps. He too survived.

Sailors in the Royal Navy and unarmed DMP men were also targets. One sailor who was home on leave when the Rising began was nineteen-year-old Stoker Neil Bowie. Born in Dublin in 1897 to Scottish parents, he lived at West Road in the north docks area of Dublin. He joined the Royal Navy as a stoker in November 1913 at the age of sixteen (claiming to be eighteen), having previously worked as an office boy and more recently as a dockyard packer. He was posted to the Royal Naval Air Service base at Eastchurch on the Isle of Sheppey, Kent, and on 31 December received a 'very good' character rating. The following year, on 1 April 1914, he joined the crew of the scout cruiser *Blanche*. He was convicted of theft while serving on this vessel and sentenced to ninety days' hard labour, after which he was discharged from the navy. Less than a month later, Britain declared war on Germany.

Despite having been discharged for a crime, Bowie managed to re-enlist, this time in the Royal Naval Reserve in Dublin on 20 October 1915 (and in fact now aged eighteen). He was posted to a shore establishment in the Crystal Palace, London, and just before the Rising went home to Dublin on leave.

On Monday 24 April, as recorded in his service file, Bowie was 'fired at by rebels while cycling in uniform at Fairview, Dublin ... & wounded in right thigh.' He was taken to Jervis Street Hospital and in mid-May was transferred to King George V Military Hospital. On 26 September 1916, now recovered from his wounds, Bowie received a 'very good' character rating and was transferred to the cruiser *Vindictive*, then stationed in the White Sea on the north-west coast of Russia. He was punished for not obeying orders relating to the upkeep of his hammock, and in 1918, while serving on the minesweeper *Tedworth*, he deserted for nearly fifteen months but returned and in January 1921 was discharged from the navy. He later married and emigrated to the United States but returned during the Great Depression. He settled in Leicester and died there in 1974, aged seventy-seven.

As for the unarmed DMP men who came under fire on 24 April 1916, the *Sinn Fein Rebellion Handbook* records that Constable Thomas Donohue, 'while passing on duty through Christ-church place between 12 noon and 1 p.m., 24th April, received a gunshot wound on the left forearm. He was medically treated at Bridewell Station, and was on sick report from his injuries for 27 days.' *Unarmed Persons Shot by Rebels* adds that Constable Donohue was 'unarmed. Shot in arm by rebel in motor car in Winetavern St.' Donohue, a native of Co. Cavan,

Royal Dublin Fusiliers cap badge
(Author's Collection)

was forty-seven and had served in the DMP for twenty-five years. He lived in Geraldine Street with his wife and their four children.

Later the same day near the Bridewell Police Station another DMP constable was wounded. The *Sinn Fein Rebellion Handbook* records that Constable Charles Hales, 'while passing on duty along Church street between 2 p.m. and 3 p.m., 24th April, was stopped by rebels one of whom fired at him with a revolver and wounded him slightly on the back of the left hand. He was then arrested by rebels and brought into the Four Courts, where one of them dressed his hand. He was released shortly after, and was nothing the worse for his slight injury.' Constable Hales, who was fifty-four, had served in the DMP for thirty years and, like Constable Donohue, was from Co. Cavan. He lived in Ard Righ Place, off Arbour Hill.

* * *

On 24 April 1916 Lieutenant Edward Halpin of the 3rd Sherwood Foresters (Nottinghamshire and Derbyshire Regiment), a reserve battalion, was home on leave. He was twenty-eight and a native of Limerick. Having just stepped off the ship from Holyhead at Kingstown (Dún Laoghaire), he took a tram into Dublin, intending to catch the 3:15 p.m. train from Kingsbridge Station to Limerick. The tram was delayed, so Halpin – not knowing the reason – got off and managed to find a cab along the quays when some members of the 1st Battalion of the Irish Volunteers opened fire on it near the Four Courts.

Halpin was then taken prisoner by the insurgents. One account of his capture was later recorded by Liam Tobin of the Irish Volunteers (later major-general and director of intelligence for the IRA during the War of Independence):

> I think it was on Easter Monday, when all the barricades had already been erected and such like, that I noticed a row going on at the barricade at the

far side of Church Street Bridge. ... A British officer in uniform was in the midst of our own men who were at that barricade, and a number of women – wives of British soldiers – were endeavouring to rescue him from our fellows. I succeeded in getting him away from the crowd – most of the women were hostile to us except one or two who were not. We got him across the bridge and over the barricades. He was our prisoner. He turned out to be a Lieutenant on his way home from England to Limerick on furlough. He was rather upset. He thought that he was going to be shot, and showed me his rosary beads. I assured him that he would not be shot, and that if I had the ill-luck to be taken prisoner, I hoped I would get as good treatment as I was sure he would receive from us. I brought him into the Four Courts, where he was put along with the other prisoners there.

Halpin remained in the Four Courts for the rest of the Rising, being released at 2 a.m. on Sunday 30 April. On 3 May he appeared as a witness at the court-martial of Commandant Edward 'Ned' Daly of the 1st Battalion of the Irish Volunteers, who had commanded the rebel garrison in the Four Courts. Halpin stated: 'I was arrested opposite the Four Courts on Monday 24 April and I was taken into the Four Courts and detained in Custody until the following Saturday. I first saw the accused on Thursday 27 April, he was armed and in uniform. I don't know if he was in authority. There was firing from the Four Courts while I was there.' Daly cross-examined Halpin, who admitted that he had been well treated while held as a prisoner.

Lieutenant Halpin later entered the war in October 1916. He survived the conflict and by 1923 was living in Patrick's Hill, Cork. He died in 1954 in Youghal, aged sixty-six.

At least one unarmed Irishman in the British army escaped being shot by the insurgents thanks to his neighbours. When the war broke out John 'Jack' Davin Power from Kimmage, Dublin, was thirty-three. He was working as a clerk for the London, Midland and Scottish Railway while living in Lower Beechwood Avenue in Ranelagh, Dublin, with his wife and their two daughters. In February 1915 he enlisted in the British army and, unusually, was immediately given the rank of staff sergeant-major in the Army Service Corps (responsible for transport, administration, and supplies) – perhaps because of his experience working for the railway – and quickly sent overseas. He landed in France on 18 February 1915, two weeks after enlisting. He served during the Gallipoli campaign against the Turkish army before developing severe influenza and being evacuated; in a postcard to his family he wrote that that 'this influenza has left me just skin and bone.' He was treated in Cape Town – a photograph taken at the time shows a thin, gaunt man – before being sent back to Ireland. According to the family, he returned to Dublin on 24 April 1916, now aged thirty-five, and was nearly shot by a member of the Irish Volunteers but, miraculously, a neighbour recognised him and made the Volunteer hold his fire.

Sergeant-Major John Davin
Power from Kimmage, Dublin,
photographed in Basingstoke, 1915
(David Davin-Power)

In 1919, the war now over, Jack Davin Power was discharged from the army, having reached the rank of regimental sergeant-major. However, he was mentally scarred from his experiences. He separated from his wife, leaving her and their three children and moving in with his brother Nick, who lived at Harold's Cross. Returning to his job with the railway, he later went on Mediterranean cruises and travelled around Europe alone. He was almost certainly suffering from what today would be diagnosed as post-traumatic stress disorder. In the 1920s and 30s, however, there were no counselling or other services available to men like Jack Davin Power.

In 1940, during the Second World War, now aged fifty-nine, he left Ireland for good. He moved to England, working first for a company in London and later as an official with St Pancras Borough Council. He also joined the National Fire Service as a firefighter. Having survived the Western Front and Gallipoli, influenza and the Easter Rising, he was killed by a German bomb on 14 March 1944.

However, not all the unarmed Irishmen shot by insurgents in the early hours of the Rising were members of the British army. At least one was a civil servant who simply lived in a building owned by the military.

Just after midday on 24 April 1916 a group of insurgents were sent to destroy the stockpile of ammunition stored in the Magazine Fort in the Phoenix Park. In their way was a small garrison, together with the resident Playfair family.

George Playfair was a captain in the Army Ordnance Corps who had been serving in France since August 1914. The Playfairs lived in the Magazine Fort, because George Playfair was also Assistant Commissary for Ordnance in Ireland. His 23-year-old son George Alexander 'Alec' Playfair worked as a clerk with the Commissioners of Inland Revenue.

That afternoon, just after 12:15 p.m., about thirty rebels under the command of Paddy Daly – who had worked with a building firm inside the fort six months earlier and so knew its layout and the routine of the guards – gathered at the foot of the hill below the fort. One of the rebels was a member of Fianna Éireann, Garry Holohan, who later recorded:

> After a few minutes chat together, as if we were a football team with followers, we moved around to the front of the Fort in a casual way, some of the lads kicking the ball from one to the other. When we got near the gate they rushed the sentry who was standing outside, and then another party rushed in and took the guardroom completely by surprise. I was detailed off with Barney Mellows to take the sentry on the parapet. I rushed straight through the Fort ... I rushed towards him, calling on him to surrender. He came towards me with his bayonet pointed towards me. I fired a shot and he fell, and at that moment Barney came along the parapet. The poor sentry was crying, 'Oh, sir, sir, don't shoot me. I'm an Irishman and the father of seven children.' Barney tried to stand him up but his leg must have been broken. We told him not to be afraid as we would do him no harm and we would send his companions to attend to him.

The rebels had brought five bags of gelignite with them. They intended to open the high-explosive storeroom, set the charges inside and then evacuate, blowing the fort sky-high. However, the key to the store, which should have been in the guardroom, was missing; by chance, the officer in charge had taken it with him to the bank holiday races at Fairyhouse. They were forced to lay their charges in the small-arms store next door, placing them against the wall that divided this from the high-explosive storeroom, hoping that the explosion might get through the wall and detonate everything.

Before lighting the fuses they rounded up the Playfair family – Alec's mother, Georgina, his seventeen-year-old brother Harold, his fifteen-year-old brother Gerald, and his six-year-old sister Marjorie – and let them go free, with instructions to get clear. Then they lit the fuses, took the Lee-Enfield rifles from the gun racks in the guardroom, and evacuated the fort. They brought their British army prisoners outside, under orders not to pursue them or try to raise the alarm once they were set free.

As they began to withdraw, however, one of them spotted someone running towards the exit at the nearby Islandbridge Gate. It was Alec Playfair. At some point during the attack he had managed to make it out of the fort in order to raise the alarm. Paddy Daly shouted at Garry Holohan, who was on a bicycle, 'That's young Playfair. Stop him!' (He clearly knew the Playfair family.) Holohan set off in pursuit on his bicycle, and he later recorded what happened: 'He [Playfair] stopped and spoke to the policeman who was in the middle of the road directing the traffic, and then ran away ... When he got to the corner of Islandbridge Road he ran towards one of the big houses, evidently with the intention of giving the alarm. I jumped off my bicycle, and just as the door opened I shot him from the gate. At that moment ... two large explosions took place in the Fort.'

The explosions were in fact quite small, the gelignite having failed to destroy the dividing wall and the high-explosive storeroom. The Magazine Fort was soon reoccupied by soldiers from Marlborough Barracks, who quickly put out the fire.

Alec Playfair had run to number 1 Park Place, the home of 56-year-old Joseph Higgins from Co. Offaly, a major in the Army Service Corps. Though Higgins was not at home, his wife was. She later gave a statement to the DMP for their report *Unarmed Persons Shot by Rebels,* to the effect that 'he asked if he could telephone for assistance ... Almost immediately afterwards a rough looking man came up to the house wheeling a bicycle; as he came up he drew a revolver and discharged three shots at Mr. Playfair, fatally wounding him. He died 24 hours later ... at 11 a.m.'

In his account of the Rising, Garry Holohan said that 'we were to take the Fort, blow it up, but we were not to hold it and we were not to take life if possible.' Alec's father, serving on the Western Front, could have had no idea that in April 1916 his son would be in worse danger back home in Ireland.

Alec Playfair was not the only person shot for attempting to let the military know what was going on at the Magazine Fort. *Unarmed Persons Shot by Rebels* records that William Hughes, a 61-year-old master bootmaker in Sarah Place – a street next to Park Place, where Alec Playfair was mortally wounded – was also 'wounded by rebels when attempting to phone re their attack on magazine.'

Finally, for 24 April 1916 *Unarmed Persons Shot by Rebels* reports 'a young soldier, unarmed, shot by two rebels in uniform on top of a tram car at Sandymount because he refused to fight for them ... Extracted from a letter from Rev. W. Corkey, Belfast, to the Provost Trinity College. The former states [that] this case came under the notice of four ladies from Belfast who were present.'

Word that republicans had started a rebellion on the streets of Dublin was slow to spread. Even the following day Irishmen in the British army – travelling around in uniform and unarmed – were unwittingly making themselves targets (despite an order issued by Pearse on the evening of the 24th that no unarmed person, in British army uniform or otherwise, was to be fired on).

On the morning of the 25th Captain Rowland Scovell, a doctor in the Royal Army Medical Corps, was on his way into the city. Born in Killiney, Co. Dublin, and now living in nearby Shankill, Scovell was forty-nine. He and his wife had one son. Scovell was giving a lift to a friend, Richard Waters from Blackrock, a bank official on his way into work at the Bank of Ireland in College Green. Their route would take them through Ballsbridge, along Northumberland Road and across Mount Street Bridge. Unknown to the two men, a detachment of the 3rd Battalion of the Irish Volunteers, commanded by Lieutenant Michael Malone, had occupied the area to stop British reinforcements advancing into Dublin from Kingstown. Despite Pearse's order not to fire on unarmed soldiers – specifically issued because Malone's men had fired the day before on a home defence force who had rifles but no ammunition – when Scovell and Waters drove across Mount Street Bridge at 8:30 a.m. a group of Volunteers in nearby Clanwilliam House opened fire. It was later noted that the rebels made no attempt to challenge Scovell or ask him to stop. They were clearly aiming for Scovell, who was in uniform though unarmed; but their fire hit Richard Waters.

Scovell managed to drive on through the rebel fire and get beyond Clanwilliam House. He then rushed Waters to Sir Patrick Dun's Hospital in Grand Canal Street. Waters, however, succumbed to his wounds and died later that day. As for Captain Scovell, he survived the Rising and the war, later moving to live in Farnham, Surrey, where he died in February 1939, aged seventy-four.

* * *

The same morning another Irishman knew there was some sort of civil disturbance going on in Dublin but had no idea how serious the situation was. Captain Edward Plunkett, eighteenth Baron Dunsany, an officer in the Royal Inniskilling Fusiliers, drove into Dublin to see if he could help with what he believed was a local riot. Born in London in 1878 into a Norman family who were also cousins of the seventeenth-century saint Oliver Plunkett, Dunsany was the son of a politician and mechanical engineer, John Plunkett, who had installed the first Irish telephone system and invented his own X-ray machine, while his uncle was Sir Horace Plunkett, founder of the Irish agricultural co-operative movement. His grandfather was an admiral in the Royal Navy, and his brother Reginald later became an admiral also. Dunsany was related also to Joseph Plunkett, one of the leaders of the Easter Rising, who would be executed on 4 May 1916.

Dunsany grew up in the family residences of Dunstall Priory and Ivy Cottage, both in Shoreham, Kent, and in London before coming to Ireland and settling in the main family home, Dunsany Castle in Co. Meath. The family also owned Trim Castle.

In 1896 Dunsany, aged eighteen, entered the Royal Military Academy at Sandhurst in Berkshire and later was commissioned into the Coldstream Guards. In 1899 he travelled to South Africa to take part in the Anglo-Boer War, fighting at Belmont and Modder River. He returned to Ireland in 1901. In 1904 he married Beatrice Child-Villers, and the following year his first book was published, *The Gods of Pegana,* a collection of fantasy short stories. W. B. Yeats asked Dunsany to write a play for the Abbey Theatre, and the result was *The Glittering Gate,* which opened to critical acclaim.

When the First World War broke out Dunsany, now thirty-six, rejoined the British army as a captain in the Royal Inniskilling Fusiliers. He continually requested to be sent to the front, but the authorities refused, saying that he was needed to train troops at home, probably because of his experience in the Anglo-Boer War.

On the morning of 25 April 1916 he set off for Dublin, intending to help out in any way he could. Travelling with Lieutenant A. P. Lindsay of the 5th Royal Inniskilling Fusiliers, a Gallipoli veteran, he drove straight into the rebel barricade in Church Street, near the Four Courts. Lieutenant Seán Kennedy of C Company, 1st Battalion, Irish Volunteers, later recorded what happened next:

> During my visit to the courtyard some short time afterwards, I found my Company Captain, Frank Fahy, speaking to a British officer in uniform who was wounded and whom I learned later was Lord Dunsany. Dunsany was accompanied by another British officer, Colonel [sic] Lindsay. They had been captured some time previously driving, from the Phoenix Park in the direction of O'Connell Bridge. They had approached our barricade at Church Street and had apparently attempted to crash it [other accounts say that Dunsany simply attempted to reverse and drive away]. Our people on the barricade opened fire and Dunsany was wounded in the cheek. As far as I could gather the outcome of the parley between Captain Fahy and Lindsay resulted in Dunsany giving his parole not to escape if he was permitted to go to the Richmond Hospital for medical attention. As his greatcoat was lying in the car some short distance up the Quays on the Park side of the barricade, and between it and Arran Quay chapel, I was detailed to go and get it for him. I went out on to the Quays and over to the car. While I was collecting his greatcoat, I noticed that there was a revolver and some ammunition in a small box also in the car, which I took possession of.

Dunsany went to the Richmond Hospital and later returned to the Four Courts, true to his word. Before he left for the hospital, as recorded by Liam Tobin of the Irish Volunteers, 'as he was being brought to the Four Courts [he] kept shouting and speaking loudly about the brave men he regarded us to be, and so on.' After returning to the Four Courts, Dunsany and Lindsay would have joined others, including Lieutenant Edward Halpin, who were taken prisoner the previous day.

Pauline Keating, née Morkan, a member of Cumann na mBan who was in the Four Courts during the Rising, recorded that 'Lord Dunsany was a prisoner there too, although I never saw him. The first day we laid an ordinary tray for him, but the next day the girl who did it decked it out in great style to show what we could do. We thought it good fun. I think she was able to produce some silver implements to make a splash.'

Dunsany and his fellow-officers remained as prisoners in the Four Courts until the Rising ended. When he was released he is reported to have said: 'Although in different uniforms, we are all Irishmen and you are all gentlemen.' After the Rising he finally got his wish and went on to serve in France from

September 1917. He served in the trenches for a time before being attached to General Headquarters.

Dunsany had been a patron of Francis Ledwidge and had opposed his enlistment, even offering him a stipend to support him if he stayed out of uniform, and in 1917 arranged for the publishing of two collections of his works. Ledwidge was killed in action on 31 July that year.

In February 1920, during the War of Independence, Dunsany was back at Dunsany Castle, which was raided by British forces in February 1921. A number of undisclosed shotguns and sporting weapons as well as ammunition were discovered, and Dunsany was arrested and subsequently court-martialled for 'the keeping of firearms and ammunition not under effective military control.' Clearly the authorities felt that these weapons might have been destined for the IRA, and that perhaps Dunsany was a republican sympathiser. During his trial he insisted that he was 'loyal to the Crown' and reminded the prosecution that he had been wounded and held prisoner by rebels during the Easter Rising; though he pleaded guilty, he stated that the weapons were merely curios or for sporting purposes. He was offered a choice between a fine of £25 and three months in prison. He chose to pay the fine.

Constable Eugene Bratton of the RIC recorded the incident in later years, recalling that

> Lord Dunsany, was not liked by the police, especially the officers, as he was wont to give them a rough time of it when they came up for cross-examination as witnesses. One day, while discussing game shooting at the Kildare St. Club, he made a foolish statement that he could always go shooting, as the I.R.A. provided a protection party for him. This was reported, and Dunsany Castle was raided. It was never even suggested that he had any contact with the I.R.A.

Despite living in the middle of the city, Peter Ennis knew nothing about a disturbance. He had emigrated to Scotland before the outbreak of the war and was working as a labourer in Glasgow. On 4 September 1914, at the age of thirty, he enlisted in the Scots Guards. Sent to the 3rd Battalion in London for his training, he was posted to the 1st Battalion on 6 March 1915. He landed in France the following day and soon joined his new battalion on the Western Front.

During September 1915 the battalion was involved in the Battle of Loos, and on the 30th Private Ennis was admitted to No. 3 General Hospital in Le Tréport with a gunshot wound to the hand. By early October he had returned from France to a hospital in Manchester and was again posted to the 3rd Battalion in London.

In April 1916, now aged thirty-two, he again came home on leave and stayed with his mother at her home in Queen's Square (now Pearse Square). This was not far from where the 3rd Battalion of the Dublin Brigade of the Irish Volunteers was based, its headquarters being in Boland's bakery in Lower Grand Canal Street (not Boland's Mill at Grand Canal Dock, as frequently stated).

On the morning of 25 April, Private Ennis had no idea what was going on in Dublin. In uniform but unarmed, he went for a walk along the canal. *Unarmed Persons Shot by Rebels* records what happened next: 'When coming along canal bank, unarmed, a shot was fired at him, and he was killed, the shot having passed through the heart.' This statement was signed by three witnesses in Sir Patrick Dun's Hospital, where Ennis's body was taken.

Peter Ennis is buried in Deansgrange Cemetery, where his headstone faces that of two Irish Volunteers: Lieutenant John Costello, who was killed in the vicinity of Boland's Mill on 26 April, and Volunteer Andrew Byrne, who was killed on 27 April. Also in the same plot are three civilians who died of gunshot wounds during the Rising: John Kenyon, Joseph Clarke and William Carrick.

3

3rd Royal Irish Regiment
From the South Dublin Union to the GPO

On the morning of 24 April 1916 the 3rd (Reserve) Battalion of the Royal Irish Regiment, comprising eighteen officers and 385 other ranks, was stationed in Richmond Barracks in Inchicore. During the Easter Rising the battalion would fight against the Irish Volunteers in the South Dublin Union (a workhouse and hospital operated by a union of parishes, now St James's Hospital), after which they would man the barricades in Sackville Street and the surrounding area, forming part of the military cordon around the GPO. An Irish officer and another Irish soldier of the battalion would later secure the Irish Republic flag from the top of the GPO, and it was to Richmond Barracks that the prisoners were taken after the Rising. During the fighting the regiment would lose six men killed, all Irish, and fifteen wounded, twelve of them Irish.

The 3rd Battalion was commanded by 56-year-old Lieutenant-Colonel Robert Owens, a soldier with a long and varied career. Born in Dublin in 1860, he enlisted as a private when he was about twenty-one. After serving for six years in the ranks – and obviously showing the potential for leadership – he was commissioned into the Bedfordshire Regiment as a second-lieutenant in May 1887. He was promoted to lieutenant the following December, and from 1890 to 1895 he was adjutant of the Indian Volunteers before joining the Royal Irish Regiment and being promoted to captain. He fought in the Anglo-Boer War with the 21st Battalion of the Imperial Yeomanry before returning to the Royal Irish Regiment. In 1908 – now a major, aged forty-eight, and with twenty-seven years' service – he retired from the regular army but stayed on in the reserve. By 1911 he and his family were living with his father-in-law in Slieveroe, near Carrigaline, Co. Cork. In April 1913 he was promoted to lieutenant-colonel and appointed commanding officer of the 3rd Royal Irish Regiment. One of his soldiers would later describe him as 'a shrewd man and a just one, but at times very bitter and uncouth.'

Owens had recently had a run-in with the anti-army and anti-recruitment Catholic Archbishop of Dublin, William Walsh. Father Michael Joseph Curran,

secretary to Archbishop Walsh from 1906 to
1919, later recorded that

on one particular occasion in 1914
the Archbishop peremptorily refused
a request of the military to allow
recruiting posters to be placed on the
railings of the Catholic Churches in
Dublin and, as the recruiting became
more active, he caused it to be known
that this procedure met with his strong
disapproval. He went so far as to
discountenance war hospital and Red
Cross collections. He believed that

Royal Irish Regiment cap badge
(Author's Collection)

these activities should be financed by the Government and that the appeals
were being used for recruiting purposes.

I wrote in my diary under the 31st March, 1915 'Father Mooney Parish
Priest, Ringsend and Chaplain to the Beggar's Bush Barracks received a
very curt letter this morning from Lieutenant-Colonel Owens, Officer
Commanding the 3rd Battalion of the Royal Irish Regiment at Beggar's
Bush, intimating "the intention of the military authorities to hold a military
parade on Easter Sunday, with a religious service in the Cathedral," and
asking him to arrange an hour with the cathedral authorities.' This was
announced also in the papers of Thursday. On Fr. Mooney visiting Fr. Bowden
(administrator of the Pro-Cathedral), the latter rang up Archbishop's House
and then sent up the letter. The Archbishop at once scribbled out the draft of
an equally curt reply for Fr. Mooney to sign: 'I have, of course, no authority
to interfere in arrangements for services in the Pro-Cathedral. The matter
has been brought to the notice of His Grace, the Archbishop, who directs
me to express his surprise that the military authorities, without having
even applied for permission to make use of that Church, announce their
"intention" of holding a Parade Service there, and I am to add that no such
Service can be held.'

The battalion adjutant was Major Edmund Roche-Kelly. Born in April 1881 in
the family home, Firgrove House, near Bunratty, Co. Clare, he was thirty-five in
1916 and also a regular soldier. He had attended Downside School in Somerset
before being commissioned in January 1901 into the Royal Irish Regiment. He
served with the 1st Battalion during the Anglo-Boer War and by 1909 had risen
to the rank of captain. Before the First World War he also served in India and was
promoted to major not long before the Rising, in January 1916.

As for the Irish soldiers in the battalion, they were a mixture of young and
inexperienced recruits, men who had signed up for home service only, soldiers

recovering from wounds received at the front, and veterans. One young soldier in the 3rd Battalion was 21-year-old Private Edward Goodchild from Waterford. A former messenger boy and then grocer's porter, he joined up in Waterford as a reserve soldier in April 1914, aged nineteen; his older brother, Patrick, was already a sergeant in one of the regiment's regular battalions. Edward Goodchild was mobilised for war on 7 August 1914.

Goodchild did not take well to the army. On 20 October 1914, while stationed in Richmond Barracks, Dublin, he went 'absent from 10 p.m. until 12.30 a.m.' the following morning, for which he was deprived of three days' pay. Then in November he was 'absent from tattoo [the signal to return to quarters, usually an hour before lights out] until apprehended by civil police at Waterford 5 p.m. 3-11-14.' For whatever reason, Goodchild – who was still stationed in Dublin at the time – had left his unit and returned to Waterford without permission. He was again deprived of three days' pay and this time was additionally given seventy-two hours' detention in barracks.

A month after Goodchild finished his period of detention he was posted to the 2nd Royal Irish Regiment, and he landed in France on 17 December 1914. Over the next few months he served in and out of the trenches, at some point being given fourteen days of 'field punishment no. 1', whereby a soldier was shackled to a heavy object, such as a carriage wheel, and also forced to do hard labour for hours while on a restricted diet, a punishment amounting to torture.

In March 1915 Private Goodchild was invalided home, suffering from mastoid disease (a serious infection of the middle ear), and was posted to the regimental depot at Clonmel; he had previously been admitted to hospital in Rouen from 24 January to 17 February, also with an ear complaint. But he appears to have been cured, as his medical records do not mention the condition any further.

Despite his previous misconduct, Private Goodchild was promoted to lance-corporal on 26 May, not long after returning to the 3rd Battalion. But the promotion did not last long: on 6 June 1915 he was demoted to private for being 'absent from tattoo until 9.20 p.m.' Soon after, on 25 June, he was again 'absent from tattoo until 10.30 p.m.' Because of this second breach of regulations he was given twenty-one days of field punishment no. 1 and deprived of twenty-one days' pay. After this he had obviously had enough, and on 24 September he deserted. It was not until 25 October that he rejoined his unit. On 5 November 1915 he was tried by court-martial and sentenced to six months' detention on the charge of 'when on active service, deserting H.M. Service' and 'losing by neglect his equipment etc.' He was sent to a detention barracks on 10 November 1915, forfeited all former service, and was forced to repay the cost (£1 15s) of his lost equipment, which included his entrenching tool, water-bottle and haversack.

Goodchild was due to be released from detention and to return to his battalion in June 1916, but – ironically – because of good behaviour he was released on 4 April, 'having earned a remission of two months,' and returned to the 3rd Battalion in Richmond Barracks. This meant that he rejoined his battalion less

Items belonging to Company Sergeant-Major Frederick William Banks from Athlone,
Co. Westmeath (Banks family)

than three weeks before it would become involved in the Easter Rising. Had he
remained in detention he would have missed it.

While Edward Goodchild was obviously an unwilling soldier, at the other
end of the spectrum was Company Sergeant-Major Frederick Banks. A native
of Athlone, Banks was thirty years old, the eldest child of a soldier in the Army
Service Corps from Aldershot, Hampshire, who was a veteran of the Zulu War of
1879 and the First Anglo-Boer War of 1880–81.

In 1901 Frederick Banks was working as a civilian clerk in the Royal Arsenal
at Woolwich, London. He later joined the army and, like his father, became an
orderly-room clerk. On 13 August 1914, now a sergeant in the 2nd Royal Irish
Regiment, he landed in France. During the Battle of La Bassée the battalion
was almost completely wiped out near Le Pilly, the majority being captured and
becoming prisoners of war. By 24 October 1914 the few survivors were transferred
to the lines of communication. Sergeant Banks, however, was sent home; by April
1916 he had been promoted to company sergeant-major and was now in Dublin
with the 3rd Battalion.

* * *

A first-hand account of the battalion's experiences during the Rising was recorded by Private Albert Desborough, an Englishman, aged forty in 1916, who later became a sergeant and a Lewis machine-gun instructor. In April 1957, then aged eighty-one, he recorded his experiences for the Bureau of Military History in Dublin. Between 1947 and 1957 the bureau collected 1,773 witness statements, 334 sets of contemporary documents, forty-two sets of photographs and thirteen voice recordings relating to the revolutionary period. They are now housed in Cathal Brugha Barracks, Dublin.

Desborough had enlisted in Cork not long before the Rising, for home service only because of varicose veins. Previously he had moved in artistic circles, working variously as a 'character-reader' (claiming to determine what kind of personality someone had from the shape of their head and facial features), a novelist, and a music teacher, but by the time of the Rising he was servant, valet and batman to several officers in the 3rd Royal Irish Regiment, and on 24 April 1916 he was a member of the battalion's 100-man piquet – a group of soldiers kept on stand-by, ready to move out at a moment's notice. He recorded:

> Early on Easter Morning, Monday, an officer brought in the report of the murder of a policeman on duty near the City Hall. His killers had been seen, and chased into and through the building of the Irish Independent Newspaper Offices, but had escaped, through the means of a rear exit. This was considered as an act of retaliation by some criminal, and at the time, little more was thought of it. Then came the news, someone had cut the overhead cables. This was considered a foolish excapade [sic] by some unresponsible fools.

The men of the Royal Irish Regiment apparently had no idea that these incidents were part of a larger rebellion.

Just after midday on Monday 24 April a military band was playing in Richmond Barracks when the 3rd Battalion was contacted by higher command. After phoning Marlborough Barracks in Blackhorse Avenue to have cavalry despatched to Sackville Street, in response to a report by the DMP of disturbances in the area, Colonel Henry Cowan, assistant adjutant-general and second-in-command to Colonel Kennard, the commanding officer of all forces in Dublin, contacted the Royal Barracks, Portobello Barracks and Richmond Barracks to follow up another police report. Dublin Castle was apparently under attack, and so he ordered the regiments stationed in each of the three barracks to send a column of troops to the castle immediately. According to the regimental history of the 3rd Royal Irish Regiment, Lieutenant-Colonel Owens requested more information from Colonel Cowan but was given none.

Not far away, between Richmond Barracks and Dublin Castle, stood the South Dublin Union in James's Street. Built as a poorhouse in 1667 and converted into a foundling hospital in 1727, it became a workhouse by the middle of the nineteenth century. By 1916 the complex contained an infirmary, a hospital and a morgue as well as living quarters, churches and a bakery. It was spread out over fifty acres and housed 3,282 poor, elderly or disabled men and women, along with the resident doctors, nurses and other staff.

The South Dublin Union had been occupied that morning by a force of Irish Volunteers under Commandant Éamonn Ceannt. Its strategic position in the south-west of the city meant that a garrison there could threaten any British advance from Kingsbridge Station (where any troops coming from the Curragh would arrive), the Royal Hospital in Kilmainham, Islandbridge Barracks, or Richmond Barracks. Ceannt had allowed any staff members who wished to do so to leave, but many had remained behind, preferring to stay with their patients and to move them to safer, more centralised positions, which were subsequently marked by hanging Red Cross flags out the windows.

A few minutes after midday Ceannt was listening out, expecting to hear the explosion of the Magazine Fort in the Phoenix Park. Instead, however, he heard the music from the military band in Richmond Barracks. He turned to his second-in-command, Cathal Brugha, and told him that if the band was still playing it meant the army must have no idea what was going on in Dublin. But as soon as he said this, the music stopped. Private Desborough remembered the piquet being called to arms.

> I left the officers quarters, my valeting completed at twelve o'clock, and started to cross the barrack square to my quarters – A Section – for my dinner. I had only got half-way across, when the Regimental bugler sounded the 'alarm!' and immediately following it with the 'Fall in.' From all quarters our troops rushed while Commissioned men and N.C.Os rushed to their positions to serve as 'markers' for the various companies and sections … We were handed out rifles and side-arms, with bandoliers and 250 rounds of ammunition, formed into column-of-route order, and under our respective supervisors left Richmond Barracks, turning towards the South Dublin Infirmary.

In command of the piquet that day was Major Philip Holmes. Thirty-nine years old and originally from Cork, he was one of thirty-two RIC district inspectors who were seconded to the army between the outbreak of the war and December 1916. He had joined the RIC in February 1898, at the age of twenty-one, and in November 1915 he applied for a commission in the army. Attached to his application was a recommendation from the inspector-general (commanding officer) of the RIC, Colonel Neville Chamberlain (no relation of the later British prime minister of the same name), which stated:

> Throughout his service District Inspector Holmes has performed his duties with marked zeal and efficiency. He served for 11 years in Corofin in Co. Clare, one of the most disturbed districts in Ireland, and was afterwards

stationed for 3 years at the Head Quarters of the County Roscommon.
For the past year he has been in charge of a Company at the Royal Irish
Constabulary Depot. He has been awarded no less than five favourable
records for good police duty, one of them being awarded for bravery and
determination against a hostile crowd, and he has also been twice highly
commended for his work. He has an excellent manner in dealing with his
men and is an officer in whom I have the greatest confidence.

While the rest of the battalion got ready to follow them, the advance column,
led by Major Holmes and including Company Sergeant-Major Banks, turned east
down Emmet Road, marching with fixed bayonets but rifles not loaded. Passing
through Old Kilmainham, they were heading for Mount Brown and James's Street
when they came into view of the insurgents, 300 yards away at the McCaffrey
Estate, an area of open ground to the north and west of the South Dublin Union
(now the site of the group of houses known as Ceannt Fort). The battalion would
have to march along the 500-yard length of this ground it if it wanted to continue
on its route to Dublin Castle. On the approach road, at the corner of Mount
Brown and Brookfield Road, behind a wall that was low on the Union side but
steep on the side of the road, Ceannt had posted five men, including Lieutenant
William O'Brien, Section-Commander John Joyce and Volunteer Seán Owens,
with a further nine to their rear behind some hedges.

The 3rd Battalion kept coming, marching forward for another 100 yards before
Major Holmes gave the order to halt, the piquet stopping at the crossroads.
He had spotted the rebels behind the low wall to his front, and for a while he
simply kept looking forward, towards the insurgents and Mount Brown beyond.
His advance guard, of one sergeant and five privates, who had been moving 150
yards ahead of the rest of the piquet, had been allowed to pass by the rebels and
continue on towards Dublin, so Holmes was not sure what exactly was going on.

Another officer, Lieutenant George Malone, then came up from the rear of
the column, wondering why they had stopped. The soldiers were still in the dark,
and Malone believed that this was just another one of the emergency drills the
battalion had gone through in the past year. At about the same time Holmes
asked for the senior lieutenant present. As it turned out, this was Malone, and
Holmes gave him his orders. Malone was to take twenty men and move forward.

When he saw the rebels behind the low wall Malone realised that this was not
just another drill. Holmes told him to advance past them if possible but that if
they fired he was to respond immediately. Meanwhile the remaining eighty men
of the piquet would stay behind and support Malone from their present position
if needed.

Lieutenant Malone and Company Sergeant-Major Banks had a quick
discussion about how to proceed, after which Malone and Sergeant Thomas
McDonald assembled twenty men. McDonald was a veteran soldier who had
fought in the Anglo-Boer War with the 1st Royal Irish Regiment; more recently

he had served in France with the 2nd battalion, arriving there in August 1914 and, like Company Sergeant-Major Banks, escaping capture by the Germans at Le Pilly.

Malone and McDonald led their men forward, marching them in the centre of the tramlines that ran along Old Kilmainham towards Mount Brown. The more experienced men among this group apparently began to complain – which was understandable, considering that they were marching in formation with rifles sloped on their shoulders towards a group of armed men. They advanced until they were only yards from the rebels' position, and when Malone turned to tell his men to stop talking, with the military and the insurgents only about five yards apart, the Volunteers opened fire.

Three soldiers were hit and went down in the first volley; the rest ran for cover towards the north side of the street and broke into whatever buildings were nearest to them. The remaining men of the piquet opened fire from further down the road, while Sergeant McDonald – unlike his terrified comrades – simply remained standing in the centre of the road and directed his men to cover, which meant he was looking away from the rebels, not at them. When Section-Commander Joyce of the Irish Volunteers then tried to hit him, Sergeant McDonald began moving, and Joyce could never get a clean shot. His shot hit a wall just above the sergeant's head, but the sergeant simply ignored it.

In the chaos of firing, McDonald broke down the door of a tan-yard with the butt of his rifle and then ordered the remaining soldiers to get inside. Another soldier was obviously hit trying to run into the relative safety of the yard, as when Lieutenant Malone rushed for the door he found a dead soldier lying face down in the doorway. He grabbed the dead man's collar, intending to drag him into the yard, when he was hit by rebel fire. Malone later recalled that he managed to make it into the yard – where he continued giving orders and began to reload his pistol – before passing out on top of a pile of sheepskins. Private Albert Desborough recorded the event slightly differently:

> A first Lieutenant, one of my officers, trying to force open a door in a side wall, got three or four rounds through his hip, from a machine gun [rebel fire was so great that the soldiers believed that they were on the receiving end of machine-gun fire; in fact the insurgents had no such guns]. We carried him across the road into a butcher's yard and laid him upon some sheep skins, there to await an ambulance ... We surrounded the building, as a Sergeant [McDonald] went to various houses nearby, breaking holes in the windows, behind which he placed a man, with instructions to shoot anybody who refused to stop when challenged.

Malone later woke up on a sofa in a nearby house, with two young women dressing his wound. Beside him was Private John Moulton, a native of Liverpool, who had been shot in the jaw, the bullet fracturing his jawbone. (Having enlisted only on 6 January, Moulton was discharged in September 1916 because of his wounds.) On the floor beside the two men was the dead soldier that Malone had tried to drag into the yard.

Lieutenant Malone would later rise to the rank of major, despite having his leg amputated, and he would be interviewed by Max Caulfield for his book *The Easter Rebellion* (1963). Sergeant Thomas McDonald was later awarded the Distinguished Conduct Medal, the second-highest British award for valour, after the Victoria Cross. The citation was published on 24 January 1917 in the *London Gazette* (the official journal of record of the British government – hence the term 'gazetted' for an official announcement). It read: 'For conspicuous gallantry and devotion to duty. He rescued a wounded officer under very heavy fire. Later, he led an attack with great gallantry and successfully drove back the enemy.' In later life McDonald is known to have settled in Whitkirk in Leeds, where he was living in the early 1940s.

The 3rd Royal Irish Regiment was facing a total of 120 men of Éamonn Ceannt's 4th Battalion. Approximately sixty insurgents were based in the South Dublin Union, while they had outposts at Jameson's distillery in Marrowbone Lane, Watkins' brewery in Ardee Street, and Roe's distillery in James's Street, these three outposts being manned by roughly twenty insurgents each.

When the last of Malone's men had made it off the street and into cover, both the Irish Volunteers and the rest of the Royal Irish Regiment's piquet had ceased firing. Major Holmes quickly sent word back to the remainder of the battalion, who were now on their way from Richmond Barracks.

Since the departure of the piquet Richmond Barracks had received another phone call, this time from the seven-man guard stationed in the GPO, also members of the 3rd Royal Irish Regiment. This building was also under attack, and the guard were requesting immediate help. Lieutenant-Colonel Owens now knew that something serious was going on.

The GPO guard was based on the first floor of the building, and although they had rifles they had no ammunition. Before the insurgents came rushing up the stairs twenty minutes after entering the ground floor, the guard managed to barricade the short corridor that led from the top of the stairs to the nearby instrument room, then stood behind the barricade with bayonets fixed. When the insurgents arrived they fired several volleys through the barricade and into the room, one shot wounding the sergeant of the guard. However, the resistance they were experiencing prompted them to circle around and enter the instrument room by another door, which only one soldier was guarding. They finally stormed the room after a fight that had lasted thirty minutes. The guard were subsequently taken prisoner by the rebels while a 43-year-old telegraphist, Katherine Gordon, a native of Scotland, tended to the sergeant's wounds. They received permission to go to Jervis Street Hospital to have the sergeant's wounds treated, after which they both returned to captivity in the GPO. Katherine Gordon was released later that day.

When the rest of the 3rd Battalion arrived to join the piquet, Lieutenant-Colonel Owens was outraged when he heard what had happened at the

McCaffrey Estate. Firstly, he arranged with Major Roche-Kelly for a company to go immediately to the Royal Hospital in Kilmainham and set up firing positions there. A former home for retired soldiers, in 1916 it was also the official residence of the commander-in-chief of British forces in Ireland. It is a large three-storey building on high ground to the north of the workhouse, and any soldiers who took up position there would have an excellent field of fire into the complex.

Next Owens ordered the battalion's second-in-command, Major Milner, to lead two more companies around the back of the workhouse. Among these reinforcements were two friends, Captain Alfred Warmington and Captain Alan Ramsay.

Warmington was the older of the two. Aged forty-two, he was born in Mountrath, Co. Laois, the son of a bank manager from England and a mother from Co. Cork. Like his commanding officer and the second-in-command, he was a veteran of the Anglo-Boer War. He had served as a trooper (equivalent of private) with Thorneycroft's Mounted Infantry, a unit of 500 men raised in Pietermaritzburg in October 1899 by Major A. W. Thorneycroft of the Royal Scots Fusiliers. With them he was involved in the Orange Free State and Transvaal campaigns as well as the Relief of Ladysmith and several other operations. He subsequently transferred to the Cape Mounted Riflemen – a multiracial police force in peacetime – in Heidelberg in August 1900. When the Great War broke out Warmington was promoted to captain and served with the 6th Royal Irish Regiment in France, landing there in December 1915. By March 1916 he had returned to Ireland and joined the 3rd Battalion in Dublin.

Captain Alan Ramsay, now twenty-five, was from Ballsbridge, Dublin, where his family ran a successful nursery (what would now be called a garden centre). His father, a native of Dublin, was also a justice of the peace; his mother was from Co. Galway. The Ramsays had been running the nursery at Ballsbridge since at least the 1840s and now also had a shop at 33 Nassau Street. Alan Ramsay had previously been a member of Dublin University OTC while studying at Trinity College. On 11 August 1914, only days after the start of the war, he applied for a commission and was successful, being appointed a second-lieutenant in the 2nd Royal Irish Regiment. He left Ireland on Christmas Eve 1914 to join his battalion in France on 31 December, but on 9 May 1915, during the Battle of Frezenberg – part of the Second Battle of Ypres – he was wounded by shrapnel from a high-explosive shell. Two days later he was on his way to England.

After he had recovered, Ramsay was sent to serve with the 3rd Battalion of the regiment in Richmond Barracks, Dublin, until a medical board could declare him fit to serve overseas again. On 24 April 1916, now a captain, he wrote to the adjutant of his battalion, Major Roche-Kelly, requesting a gratuity for his injuries received at Ypres the previous May.

I was wounded on the 9th May 1915 at Ypres, in the Rt. Hand, Rt. Leg, Rt. Foot and Back (while with the 2nd Battalion The Royal Irish Regiment). My right hand is still considerably wasted, and the strength impaired. I rejoined the 3rd Battalion The Royal Irish Regiment on 8th October 1915, and have since been doing duty. I was examined by a Medical Board on 18th March [1916], and was found fit for General Service.

This meant that it was only a matter of time before Ramsay was due to depart for overseas service again and rejoin the war. Little did he know, however, that earlier in the day, when he had been typing this letter, the Easter Rising had been starting not far from where he was sitting.

* * *

The two companies of reinforcements travelled down the South Circular Road towards the south side of the Union. Commandant Ceannt had already foreseen the possibility that the British army would try to attack his position from the rear and so had ordered Captain George Irvine and nine men to cover the Rialto gate, an entrance to the complex on the southern perimeter. Irvine's men had occupied a 300-foot-long, 26-foot-wide corrugated iron auxiliary ward nearby, and one Volunteer had even set himself up in a shallow trench directly facing the entrance. Further back these insurgents were supported by six men guarding the canal wall, along with eight men positioned in Hospital 2-3, a building 250 yards behind the Rialto gate. (In addition to these men, and their comrades in the McCaffrey Estate, Ceannt had men stationed in the offices overlooking the main entrance in James's Street, while his headquarters was positioned in the nurses' home, a large three-storey building in the north-east area of the complex.) As it turned out, the 3rd Royal Irish Regiment had decided to attack the Union through the Rialto gate.

As the soldiers approached the gate, several small groups were ordered to occupy the upper floors of houses directly opposite the entrance, while fifteen men were told to cross the canal – a branch of which ran past the South Dublin Union and into the nearby Grand Canal Harbour – and to set up in Rialto Buildings, a block of flats. (This section of canal has long since been filled in; the Luas tram runs along its site on the southern side of St James's Hospital.) While these covering parties were being set up, the men who would make the assault against the Rialto gate got into cover behind garden walls. Lieutenant-Colonel Owens had arranged for the various groups of soldiers – the piquet in Old Kilmainham, the men in the Royal Hospital and the newly arrived reinforcements at the Rialto gate – to launch a combined attack at 12:55 p.m.

The soldiers positioned in the Royal Hospital opened fire with rifle and Lewis machine-gun fire while the piquet down in Old Kilmainham – who had earlier doubled back into cover – also opened fire and subsequently began to advance. The insurgents at the McCaffrey Estate began to retreat towards the Union's buildings, but British army fire inflicted several casualties among them. At the Rialto gate they launched their infantry assault, the first wave being led by Captain Alan Ramsay.

British army bullets punched dozens of holes in the front and side of the corrugated iron auxiliary ward where Captain George Irvine was positioned. The ward was used to house mental patients, all male, and they were still inside with their ward-master (having moved to the sixth dormitory, furthest from the gate) when the fighting began. The insurgents began to suffer casualties, and then the Royal Irish Regiment pushed forward. While one group rushed to the canal and made their way along the high stone wall on the southern side towards a small back entrance, Ramsay led his men towards the Rialto gate. Warmington soon led a supporting wave behind him. The gate was locked, and the men had to break down a smaller wooden door to the side of the main entrance. As soon as they had managed to do this Ramsay led the way through.

However, the Volunteers knew exactly where to point their rifles, and – along with the single fighter in the shallow trench – the rest of George Irvine's men opened fire on Ramsay from the corrugated iron ward. He was hit in the head and fell.

Ramsay's men were ultimately forced to retreat – with only a narrow entrance to advance through, it was suicide to keep going against heavy and accurate fire – and they fell back to join their comrades outside the Rialto gate. The firing briefly died away, and both sides arranged for stretcher-bearers to remove the badly wounded Captain Ramsay. He was brought into one of the wards but was then taken back outside and examined by a medical officer. Captain Warmington then learnt that his friend had only minutes left to live. Distressed and enraged, he ordered a group of men to form up for another assault and then led them through the narrow doorway at the side of the main Rialto gate. He was shot and killed instantly by heavy rebel fire, his men retreating not long after he was hit. Another short truce was arranged. Ramsay had already died of his wounds, and Warmington's body was now brought back outside and laid beside Ramsay's.

Alan Ramsay is buried in Mount Jerome Cemetery. He was twenty-five years old when he was killed in action on 24 April 1916. His name is commemorated on the memorial cross in the grounds of St Mary's Church in Donnybrook (*Men of Donnybrook Parish who died for truth and freedom 1914–1918. Let those who come after see to it that their names be not forgotten*) and also on the memorial tablet in St Andrew's College, Booterstown.

Alfred Warmington, from Mountrath, Co. Laois, who had also served in the trenches, was forty-two when he was killed in action on 24 April 1916. He was first buried in the grounds of King George V Military Hospital but now lies in Grangegorman Military Cemetery in Blackhorse Avenue. Not long after his death Father Francis O'Loughlin, a chaplain based in Portobello Barracks, wrote to the army, asking, 'Would you kindly let me know what steps it will be necessary for Mrs. Warmington to take in order to secure the pension to which I believe she is entitled.'

As for the soldiers of the Royal Irish Regiment who advanced along the southern wall by the canal, before they had managed to break down the small back entrance there they came under heavy fire from the rebel outpost in Jameson's distillery under Captain Séamus Murphy. Some soldiers returned fire while a few actually tried to climb the ten-foot wall to get into the grounds. However, anyone who made it to the top of the wall was hit by rebel fire, almost certainly from the six men who Commandant Ceannt had positioned to guard this area. One private apparently managed to climb the wall and hide behind a telegraph pole. For a while the rebels could not hit him; however, when he tried to take aim he was finally wounded and fell, hitting the bank before falling into the canal.

Several sources mention that an officer also managed to reach the top of the wall, only to be shot in the head and to fall down onto the canal side of the wall. Volunteer Gerald Doyle incorrectly believed, as he said in a witness statement in October 1956, that the soldier who climbed the telegraph pole and the officer hit in the head were the same person, namely Captain Alan Ramsay. The only source that names the fourth officer casualty (the first three being Malone, Ramsay and Warmington) is the regimental history, which states that it was Second-Lieutenant Francis North. This officer certainly took part in the Rising and is known to have been wounded, though his service file does not suggest when or where. If he was the officer shot in the head as he attempted to climb over the wall of the South Dublin Union, the head wound – if that is where he was hit – must have been minor, as he did not die.

Frank North was twenty-four years old and a former medical student from Ballsbridge. The records do not specify how he was wounded, but it is known that he was mentioned in despatches (named in a report sent to headquarters because of meritorious conduct) for his actions during the Rising. Attempting to enter a rebel stronghold by climbing a wall under heavy fire might certainly have earned him this mention. He subsequently recovered from his wounds and later entered the war, serving in the trenches with the 6th Connaught Rangers. On 9 September 1916, the first day of the Battle of Ginchy on the Somme, he was listed as missing. His uncle in Dublin – also Frank North – was soon informed as his next of kin. The telegram, dated 16 September 1916, read: 'Regret to inform you that 2/Lt FW North Irish Regt was missing September 9th. This does not necessarily mean he is killed or wounded. Will report any further news.' Frank's uncle wrote back to the army at the end of the month, asking if they had any more information. The reply read:

> No further report has been received respecting him, since he was reported missing on the 9th September. Second Lieutenant North's name has been included in a list of missing Officers, sent to the United States Embassy for circulation in all Hospitals and Internment Camps in Germany. In the event, however, of Second Lieutenant North becoming a prisoner of war, [you] will probably receive the earliest intimation of the fact from Second Lieutenant North himself. In this event the Military Secretary hopes that [you] will be so good as to inform this department.

Soldiers who disappeared were often considered 'wounded and missing' or even 'missing, presumed dead' only to turn up in German prisoner-of-war camps. This was obviously what Frank North's uncle was hoping for. In an attempt to help, he offered a description of his nephew: 'Abt. 6 ft. Slight build. Fair. Clean-shaven. 24 years old.'

On 26 April 1917 the army wrote to him again, having now come to the conclusion that Second-Lieutenant North must have been killed seven months previously, on 9 September. His uncle held out hope; but that December a discovery was made on the Somme. On 16 January 1918 – a year and a half after he had been reported missing – the army wrote to his uncle at his address in Grafton Street, Dublin, stating: 'Recovery of body reported by General Officer Commanding, 3rd Army, dated 13th December 1917. A further report received from a Graves Registration Unit, states that his grave is located 1,000 yards east of Guillemont.' This was proof that he had 'died of Wounds on or shortly after 9th September, 1916.' Today his remains lie buried in Delville Wood Cemetery, Longueval.

* * *

The 3rd Royal Irish Regiment continued fighting along the southern wall of the South Dublin Union, all the while under fire from Jameson's distillery. They finally managed to break down the back entrance here and establish a foothold inside the grounds, pushing back the six insurgents who were stationed in this area. Rebel fire was still extremely heavy, and while the first soldiers through the door ran into the grounds their comrades behind were soon crawling through in an attempt to stay low and safe. The soldiers in their supporting positions in Rialto Buildings across the canal hit several of the fleeing insurgents, while back at the Rialto gate the rebels' fire began to slow as their rifles began to overheat.

Captain George Irvine managed to get a runner through to Commandant Ceannt, asking for further orders, and Ceannt decided to let Irvine and his men withdraw. However, not long after Irvine had received his instructions the soldiers began firing on the ground behind the corrugated iron building, over which Irvine would have to retreat, while those in front of the Rialto gate made another push. This time three soldiers grabbed a large lawnmower and used it as a battering ram to break down the door of the building. The insurgents inside immediately surrendered.

At 2:30 p.m. fifty more soldiers made their way into the grounds through the small entrance in the southern wall. Still the insurgents were putting up a heavy resistance, but the soldiers managed to advance from two directions to Hospital 2-3, where eight Volunteers were positioned. About 3:30 p.m., when the soldiers smashed their way inside under heavy fire, the two insurgents on the ground floor, Volunteer Dan McCarthy and Volunteer Jim Kenny, briefly fought back – waiting at one end of a corridor or dormitory for the soldiers to appear, firing on them, then racing to the end of another corridor or dormitory and repeating the process. These two men were soon heavily outnumbered and were forced to retreat. However, despite the fact that Commandant Ceannt was nearby (tending to a wounded comrade), the soldiers did not immediately press on from Hospital 2-3 but instead concentrated on securing the building and defeating the six Volunteers still upstairs (commanded by Captain Douglas Ffrench Mullen). For men trained for trench warfare – who always knew where their enemy was: to their front – this kind of claustrophobic urban combat was completely alien. It put even experienced soldiers on edge.

The soldiers held their fire while they prepared to assault the second storey of Hospital 2-3. During this time Nurse Margaret Kehoe, who thought the brief ceasefire meant that the fighting was over, ran downstairs, while a fellow-nurse tried to stop her. She was frightened about the safety of the patients on the ground floor; but as she raced to the bottom of the stairs and ran out into a long corridor she was shot and killed by two soldiers of the Royal Irish Regiment. When her friend ran after her and saw what had happened, an army officer simply asked aggressively if there were any 'Sinn Feiners' upstairs. The nurse, shocked, merely replied 'No' and then asked for help in putting Nurse Kehoe's body on a nearby table. The officer detailed two soldiers to do this but told them to hurry.

At the same time a patient came down the corridor carrying the wounded Volunteer Dan McCarthy, who had fought against the soldiers on the ground floor. He was badly wounded, having been hit in the stomach while retreating from Hospital 2-3. The officer was apparently happy to see the wounded rebel in such a poor state, then led his men upstairs.

Dan McCarthy was subsequently placed in a ward by other soldiers, and while they briefly left the ward McCarthy hid his pistol under the pillow. When Irish soldiers in the British army returned, however, some threatened to bayonet him, until an officer ordered them to stop. A patient in the ward then warned the soldiers that McCarthy had hidden his gun under his pillow. When the officer discovered this weapon he ordered McCarthy to be placed under guard and moved to another ward.

When the soldiers in Hospital 2-3 got upstairs the patients in the bullet-pockmarked wards became hysterical, terrified that the fighting would resume among them at any moment. The soldiers needed a key to gain access through a partition to the west wing of the hospital's second floor, where Captain Douglas Ffrench Mullen and the remaining insurgents had withdrawn, and while waiting for the key they called out for the rebels to surrender once the door was opened. When it was opened the Volunteers did not surrender, and the two sides fought bitterly – with bayonets, rifle butts and fists, as the area was too small to open fire in – before the remaining Volunteers were forced to accept that they could not win. The survivors became prisoners, and the Royal Irish Regiment now secured the building, allowing them to set up firing positions that prevented any rebel attempt to rescue wounded comrades who were lying out in the McCaffrey Estate.

By 5 p.m. the soldiers had pushed back the Volunteers in all areas of the South Dublin Union. They now launched a renewed assault against the Women's

Infirmary, where Section-Commander John Joyce of the Irish Volunteers (who had earlier fired on Lieutenant George Malone and the twenty men of the piquet in Old Kilmainham) was positioned with about six comrades. The soldiers tried to force their way through the narrow entrance to Ward 16, where Joyce was (with many terrified women patients also still in the ward), but Joyce opened fire on them before managing to close the door and keep them out. He then retreated, the soldiers broke down the door, and they pursued him through other buildings before he managed to make it into Ceannt's headquarters in the nurses' home.

Soon afterwards the main fighting around the South Dublin Union ended for the day. William Murphy, a storekeeper at the Union (who provided food supplies to both sides during the week, travelling around with a white flag tied to a broom handle), later recalled that during the evening of Monday 24 April

> Ceannt gave my wife a written message to take to the Commanding Officer of the British Forces within the Union asking for a cease fire for twenty minutes while they, the Volunteers, were collecting the dead and wounded. My wife delivered this note to the British Officer in command and his reply was 'No, they have shot our Major (Ramsay) and we will give them no quarter.' He tore up the note. My wife reported back to Ceannt and told him what the British Officer had said. The Volunteers cheered when they heard the news. By late on Monday night the British had occupied all buildings at the back of the institution while the Volunteers held all the buildings at the front overlooking James's St. until the surrender.

In addition to the deaths of Captain Alan Ramsay and Captain Alfred Warmington and the wounding of Lieutenant George Malone and Second-Lieutenant Frank North, the 3rd Royal Irish Regiment lost four other ranks killed that day. These included Private Michael Carr, a forty-year-old former farmer from Parslickstown, near Mulhuddart, Co. Dublin; Private James Duffy from Co. Kildare, who died of his wounds before being admitted to Dr Steevens' Hospital; and eighteen-year-old Private Thomas Treacy from Killenaule, Co. Tipperary, who also died of his wounds before being admitted to Dr Steevens' Hospital. (As Michael Carr is the only one of these three men known to have been killed outright he is more than likely to be the dead soldier who Lieutenant George Malone tried to drag into the tan-yard.) All three are now buried in a communal grave in the grounds of the Royal Hospital, Kilmainham, along with 28-year-old Private Oscar Bentley of the 5th Royal Irish Lancers, a native of Montgomeryshire, who died on 24 April; 23-year-old Private George Barnett of the 2nd/8th Battalion, Sherwood Foresters, from Loughborough in Leicestershire, who died on 27 April; 24-year-old Volunteer Seán Owens of the 4th Battalion, Dublin Brigade, Irish Volunteers, an artificial limb maker, who died on 24 April; and Volunteer Peter Wilson of the Fingal Brigade, who died on 26 April.

A Welshman, an Englishman, three Irish soldiers in the British army and two Irish Volunteers are thus buried in the same grave. Ironically, if Michael Carr was killed at the McCaffrey Estate he is possibly buried beside the man who shot him, as Seán Owens, one of the five insurgents there, was killed there as soon as the soldiers of the Royal Irish Regiment began to return fire.

As for the fourth man lost by the Royal Irish Regiment on 24 April, the account of Private Albert Desborough suggests that he did not die in the fighting around the South Dublin Union. As Desborough recalled, 'a little later it was noised round, that one of our full-corporals was missing. He had been sent on some duty and had failed to return, and could not be traced. He was never seen alive again, but, after the trouble was over, his grave was pointed out. He had been buried in the grounds of Portobello Barracks.' This was Corporal John Brennan, a native of Gowran, Co. Kilkenny. He had enlisted in Kilkenny and had obviously been sent to Portobello Barracks – where the 3rd Royal Irish Rifles was stationed – or to the surrounding area on 24 April. With telephone communications badly affected by the insurgency, it is more than likely that he was sent as a messenger to another unit, only to be killed by insurgents in the Portobello area. His body was later exhumed and reinterred, and today he lies in Grangegorman Military Cemetery.

The *Sinn Fein Rebellion Handbook* gives a list of all those in the 3rd Royal Irish Regiment who were wounded during the Rising but does not include specific dates for each man. Furthermore, as only 30 per cent of British army service records for the period survive (the remainder having been destroyed during the Blitz) it has not been possible to trace the exact date on which every soldier was wounded. All the non-officer ranks of the battalion who were wounded during the Rising are mentioned, therefore, as a group at the end of this chapter. In all probability, however, most of them were wounded on 24 April, as this was the day on which the battalion experienced its heaviest fighting.

During the night of 24/25 April rifle fire could be heard from time to time in the vicinity of the South Dublin Union. The next morning, as recorded later by Annie Mannion, assistant matron, 'to the best of my knowledge the British troops seemed to be wandering around the grounds at a loose end rather than taking up any definite position. The one building I do remember definitely that they occupied was what is now known as the Acute Hospital, that is the building opposite the Convent where Nurse Keogh [*sic*] was shot by the British military.'

The soldiers of the Royal Irish Regiment had pushed the Volunteers back to the north-eastern part of the grounds – back to Commandant Ceannt's headquarters in the nurses' home. They had also severed Ceannt's communications with his outposts at Jameson's distillery, Watkins' brewery and Roe's distillery. At about the same time these outposts became virtually useless anyway. In Roe's distillery the rebel commanding officer there, Captain Thomas McCarthy, finding that he had no provisions, and believing that he could not hold the building, instructed his men to go home and then abandoned the position. He made no attempt to join Ceannt's forces in the Union grounds.

The following day, Wednesday 26 April, at 6 p,m., Captain Con Colbert (instructed by Major John MacBride in Jacob's biscuit factory in Bishop Street) abandoned Watkins' brewery in Ardee Street and led his men to Jameson's distillery, where he joined forces with Captain Séamus Murphy. The combined garrison now numbered about 100, including 40 women of Cumann na mBan. However, while they continued to fire at any British army soldiers they saw – including the snipers who set up in surrounding houses and a group of soldiers who began firing on their position from behind some nearby tree stumps – the garrison never ventured outside. For the duration of the Rising, the British army decided to simply contain and bypass them.

* * *

At 5:30 a.m. on Tuesday 25 April the 3rd Royal Irish Regiment opened fire on rebel positions in the South Dublin Union for ten minutes. Later that day Commandant Ceannt's men raised a home-made flag – a green harp on a yellow window blind – out of one of the upstairs windows of the nurses' home. From outside, the men of the Royal Irish Regiment could hear them singing 'A Nation Once Again'. The soldiers in the grounds and the machine-gunners overlooking the area from the Royal Hospital immediately opened fire. However, while they caused no casualties, and did not even damage the flag, a woman who was reading in her home in the Crimea House tenement building in James's Street and a man from Belfast out walking on the South Circular Road were hit and killed by stray bullets.

At 3:45 a.m. the same day the 5th Royal Dublin Fusiliers and the 5th Leinster Regiment – both part of the 25th (Irish) Reserve Infantry Brigade – arrived at Kingsbridge Station from the Curragh Camp, along with Brigadier-General William Lowe, commanding officer of the 3rd Reserve Cavalry Brigade. Lowe was now the seniormost officer in Dublin, and so he took command of all British forces in the city. He now had 4,650 men under his command.

At some point during the morning Brigadier-General Lowe ordered the 3rd Royal Irish Regiment to withdraw from the South Dublin Union and to set up at Kingsbridge Station. Lieutenant-Colonel Owens had no idea why he was being ordered to vacate his hard-won positions, and he was not happy about the move. The regimental history records that 'the battalion, under orders from headquarters, remained in occupation of the Union for the night and on the following morning, for some extraordinary reason, it was directed to evacuate the Union, and concentrate at Kingsbridge Station. This was done under protest ... The next thirty-six hours were spent in comparative idleness in the vicinity of Kingsbridge, but after many requests the battalion was allowed to rejoin the fighting.'

However, while the bulk of the battalion had withdrawn from the South Dublin Union, snipers remained behind in the Royal Hospital, overlooking the buildings, and fired on targets whenever they presented themselves. Furthermore, as Annie Mannion recalled, the houses around the Union were also secured by the British army.

During Easter Week the Nurses' Home was a very bad spot, there was a lot of shooting from and to it. My sister lived on the South Circular Road and her back window looked straight over to the Nurses' Home. I think it was on the Thursday that all the houses overlooking the place were searched by the military. After searching the houses a soldier was left on guard at each house. There was a young soldier left at the front of my sister's house and my brother-in-law said to him, 'Look here, boy, that is a hospital. Be careful,' and the boy said, 'Don't I know it well. Didn't I often go there to visit my grandmother.' He was a Dublin boy we discovered.

By evening Brigadier-General Lowe decided to concentrate his efforts on surrounding the main insurgent positions in the GPO and the Four Courts. The lack of a large-scale response from the British army was becoming apparent, and to the people of Dublin it was beginning to look as though the mighty British army was afraid of a few hundred rebels. The truth was that the military still had no idea how many insurgents they were facing, and they did not want to commit their forces entirely, as they feared that the Rising would soon be supported by a German landing.

Lowe instructed his forces to create a cordon around the city centre. Colonel Bertram Portal of the mobile column of the 3rd Reserve Cavalry Brigade from the Curragh was ordered to set up an outpost line, running from Kingsbridge Station, past Dublin Castle and on to Trinity College; this would separate the rebels on the north and south sides of the Liffey. When the 4th Royal Dublin Fusiliers from Templemore, the Ulster Composite Battalion from the north and the battery of four 18-pounders from the 5th (A) Reserve Artillery Brigade in Victoria Barracks, Athlone, arrived that afternoon they were ordered to set up another line of outposts on the north side of the city, beginning about 3 p.m., to concentrate on harassing the rebels in the Four Courts and the GPO.

Brigadier-General Lowe also decided not to advance further against the South Dublin Union and its one remaining outpost at Jameson's distillery in Marrowbone Lane, or the insurgents in Jacob's factory, the Royal College of Surgeons in St Stephen's Green or Boland's bakery. These could all be left alone for now.

Lowe had other plans. As soon as his wider cordons were in place he ordered that two smaller, inner cordons be set up around the GPO and the Four Courts. To do this, however, he would need to secure both Liberty Hall and the Mendicity Institution at Usher's Island. The following day, the 26th, he drew up a plan for capturing these two outposts.

* * *

Late on 25 April the 3rd Royal Irish Regiment was finally sent back into action. The regimental history records that

An improvised armoured car – possibly the one used by the 3rd Royal Irish Regiment – made from the boiler of a railway engine, in a Dublin street during the Easter Rising, May 1916 (Irish Defence Forces Military Archives).

the battalion proceeded to Trinity College and from there seized Grafton and Kildare Streets and Merrion Square, but shortly afterwards it was recalled and ordered with other troops to surround the General Post Office, the headquarters of the rebels. This was done by way of Butt Bridge, Gardiner Street, Great Britain Street [now Parnell Street] and Moore Street, and the battalion captured the northern end of Sackville Street, where battalion headquarters was established.

The 3rd Royal Irish Regiment now formed part of the smaller, inner cordon around the GPO. Lieutenant-Colonel Owens set up his headquarters in an artist's studio in Great Britain Street, opposite the Parnell monument, while the battalion set up barricades in the surrounding area, including Upper Abbey Street, Liffey Street and Marlborough Street. The regimental history records that 'reconnaissances were made by means of an improvised "Tank" and by small parties taking up positions in buildings near the Post Office.'

The 'tank' was in fact a three-ton Daimler lorry owned by Guinness's brewery plated with steel and carrying a locomotive smokebox from the Inchicore railway works with firing loopholes cut into it. These improvised armoured cars were devised by Colonel Portal, and their construction had been organised by Colonel Henry Allatt of the 3rd Royal Irish Rifles. The man who telephoned the Guinness brewery and arranged for the use of its lorries was Major Henry Deasy, a 49-year-old Dubliner in the 16th (Queen's) Lancers, now serving in the 8th Reserve Cavalry Regiment. A writer and explorer as well as a soldier, he was one of the first outsiders to write about Tibet after his travels there between 1897 and 1899 and in 1900 was the recipient of the Royal Geographical Society's gold medal, having surveyed 40,000 square miles of the Himalayas. Also passionate about motor cars, he had completed a 1,000-mile motor trial around Ireland in 1905. In 1903 he established H. P. P. Deasy and Company, a car import business, and in 1906 the Deasy Motor Company, which designed and constructed its own vehicles. Henry Deasy died in 1947, aged eighty.

* * *

By now, throughout the centre of Dublin, the streets were mostly empty, though crowds still gathered daily to watch the fighting. Martial law had been declared, and suspected sympathisers had been rounded up and interned for the duration of the Rising. Abandoned trams stood here and there, while rebel barricades made of tables, chairs, beds, oil drums, wooden barrels and crates, horse-drawn carts, cabs, lorries and even motor cars had been constructed in several streets. In their headquarters and outposts the insurgents had smashed windows and stacked flour sacks or coal bags to create loopholes for their rifles.

Aside from the violence, confusion had also descended on the city. The military had no idea how many rebels they were facing, their communications were poor at best, thanks to the insurgents having cut so many telephone lines, and several buildings of strategic importance had been occupied. The military believed that this was only the first phase in a plan that would certainly see German involvement – they felt that the rebels would never have gone ahead with the Rising without a guarantee of German support – and so German troops must definitely be on their way to Ireland; the only question was where they would land. They were also afraid that other republicans around the country might rise up in support of those in Dublin.

Rumours were soon spreading – among the military, the people of Dublin, and even the insurgents themselves – that the Germans had already landed. Some people even believed that they were already in Dublin, side by side with the rebels – or indeed that the rebels were Germans. Others said that John Redmond, leader of the Irish Party, had been taken prisoner and executed by the Volunteers, that Dublin Castle had been stormed and was now burning to the ground, that tens of thousands of Irish-Americans had landed in Co. Sligo to join the rebellion, and that Turkish soldiers had arrived and had captured Waterford. Some even claimed

British army soldiers measuring out bread and provisions in the streets of Dublin (from *Dublin and the Great War, 1914–1918*)

British army soldiers escorting women bringing a supply of flour from the depot established by the military authorities for the relief of the civil population of Dublin (from *Dublin and the Great War, 1914–1918*)

that Pope Benedict XV and the Archbishop of Dublin, William Joseph Walsh, had committed suicide.

Commandant Éamon de Valera of the 3rd Battalion of the Irish Volunteers, who had occupied Boland's bakery and the vicinity, shut down the gas works during the evening of 24 April and stopped the supply of gas to the city. He did this because of a fear that gas mains might be hit during the fighting, leading to an explosion that might kill or injure many people. In addition, the water and electricity supply soon stopped, and sewage quickly became a problem. The army banned wakes and funeral processions, so that when people died only the hearse-driver and one close family member were allowed to accompany the coffin to the cemetery. Weddings, however, continued; one took place in Clontarf during the Rising while a British army machine-gun fired from just outside.

By Tuesday 25 April the postal service had shut down, newspapers were not being printed, the DMP were off the streets, and all city shops were closed. Business premises and factories were shut, no one was working, and so no one was being paid. The wives of men in the trenches were not receiving their separation allowance. Obtaining food was becoming a problem; bread and milk vans were not delivering, and grocers' and butchers' shops were all closed or had been emptied by looters. People living in the suburbs began travelling out into the countryside in search of food, while in the city profiteers began to sell what they had at greatly inflated prices – sometimes ten times the usual amount – which resulted in mobs of hungry Dubliners attacking two grain stores in Phibsborough and Drumcondra and a grocer's shop in Ringsend. This led to both the rebels and the British army distributing what food they had to the civilian population of their respective areas.

There had also been heavy looting around Sackville Street. Noblett's confectionery shop had been smashed and looted, as well as Dunn's hatters, the Saxone shoe shop, Clery's department store, a tobacconist's next door, McDowell's jewellers, Frewin's Emporium, Lawrence's toy shop, and most of the pubs in the area. On 24 April, Seán Mac Diarmada (who would later be shot on the same day as James Connolly) tried unsuccessfully to reason with the looters, after which Seán T. O'Kelly (later President of Ireland) led a detachment out of the GPO and fired over the heads of the looters. This frightened some of them away temporarily but did not stop the looting. Captain William Brennan-Whitmore of the Irish Volunteers later asked James Connolly for permission to arrest and shoot two looters as an example; the request was denied.

Soon every type of debris was scattered across the street, while penniless Dubliners ran around in fancy clothing and boots, covered in expensive jewellery and drunk from champagne. Many of the shops were later set on fire, and when the flames reached Lawrence's toy shop they set off the shop's stock of fireworks.

On the Tuesday of Easter Week, Patrick Pearse stepped outside the GPO and announced to a crowd that soon gathered around him that 'such looting as has already occurred has been done by hangers-on of the British army.' Given that the Dublin tenements were some of the worst slums in Europe, and given just how miserably poor these people were, Pearse's claim seems very unlikely. In all probability, everyone who could was looting.

This was the situation in central Dublin when the 3rd Royal Irish Regiment arrived in Sackville Street late on 25 April. There had been only limited British firing against rebel positions along Sackville Street during the day, mostly rifle and machine-gun fire coming from south of the Liffey; but all was not quiet as the British army now set up its barricades. Private Albert Desborough later recalled that

> several of us were piqueted at the Cathedral end of Marlborough Street, and given the task of closing the road with barbed wire slung across. We had but just completed the task, when an elderly man, clothed in heavy overcoat and a cap pulled down low over his forehead came along, jumping from side to side like a frog, carrying a rook rifle, which he kept discharging in our direction, taking no notice of our challenge, that we would shoot, if he didn't cease. But on he came, reloading and firing. Suddenly two or three of our men at a command, fired at him. He must have been killed instantly, for he came forward automatically dropping his weapon, and meeting the barbed wire, erected across the road, hung over it, legs on one side, head and shoulders on our side streaming blood. We took him down and laid him on the pavement. He had been shot through the centre of the forehead, once through the throat, while two of his fingers dangled by the wool of the glove he wore. We covered his body with two shutters taken from a shop. He was not moved until the end of the week, for whenever an ambulance showed up in the street on its errand of mercy, it was fired upon which I nor any of the others were able to understand. We never knew who he was. Whether his actions were those of a would be bravado, or whether he was drunk. It was never discovered. But when his body was laid out in the mortuary afterwards and carefully examined, a wad of Irish notes was found upon him, to a considerable amount. This was the first death I witnessed.

Private Desborough was not the only person who recorded such events. After the Rising, Henry Cruise, a barrister who was working in the Four Courts, wrote to his brother Richard, an RIC officer based in Bantry, Co. Cork, that 'the terror of it all was very real ... Cases actually happened where a Sinn Feiner not in any uniform simply walked up to a sentry & when being questioned ... just pulled out his automatic & let fly.'

The following day, Wednesday 26 April, with the 3rd Royal Irish Regiment now in position around the Sackville Street area, snipers and machine-gunners on the roof of Trinity College opened fire, along with another sniper in McBirney's department store at Aston Quay. They fired at rebel positions in Sackville Street, including those in Hopkins and Hopkins, the watchmakers and jewellers on the corner of Eden Quay and Sackville Street, Kelly's fishing tackle and gunsmiths on the opposite corner of Bachelor's Walk and Sackville Street, the Dublin Wireless School of Telegraphy further up the street, and rebel snipers in the Dublin Bread Company building. This firing scattered a crowd of onlookers who had gathered on the south side of the Liffey every day since the Rising began.

Meanwhile the patrol yacht *Helga*, having been summoned from its base in Kingstown, sailed up the Liffey just before 8 a.m. This was an armed auxiliary steam yacht that had been operating as an anti-submarine patrol vessel and also took part in escorts in the Irish Sea. Its main armament consisted of two 12-pounder guns, and as it sailed up through the docks and stopped opposite the Custom House it aimed these guns at Liberty Hall, on the corner of Eden Quay and Beresford Place.

Inside the Custom House a detachment of the 3rd Royal Irish Regiment, along with men from the Ulster Composite Battalion, waited with fixed bayonets for the preliminary bombardment of Liberty Hall to end. Once that happened they would assault and secure the position, under covering fire from machine-gunners on the roof of the Custom House, along with others in the tower of Tara Street Fire Station and on top of Trinity College. The Custom House had earlier been occupied by soldiers from the Army School of Musketry at Dollymount Camp, under the command of Major Harold Somerville. His force had also taken over the North Wall railway terminus and Amiens Street Station (now Connolly Station) by late on the 24th, meaning that the docks were now controlled by the British army.

At exactly 8 a.m. on Wednesday the 26th the *Helga* opened fire. The first shell did not even make it as far as Liberty Hall but instead hit the Liffey Viaduct (commonly called the Loop Line Bridge), which crosses the Liffey at that point and blocked the *Helga* from having a clear view of its target; there was also a ship belonging to Guinness's brewery in the way. The gunners aboard the *Helga* raised their trajectory and fired again. This time the shell hit Liberty Hall, crashing through the roof and exploding in the interior but leaving the exterior walls standing.

The British forces believed that Liberty Hall was an important rebel outpost; but the truth was that there was not a single insurgent inside the building. Only the caretaker, Peter Ennis, was inside when the shelling began. He fled outside, only to be fired on by British machine guns. Miraculously, they never managed to hit him and he was able to run to safety.

The *Helga* continued to shell Liberty Hall for the next hour, while soldiers opened up with rifle and machine-gun fire. Unfortunately, while the army fired on an empty building, some of the people who lived in the surrounding tenements and fled their homes for safety were hit by the fire. When the shelling ended the *Helga* sailed back towards the mouth of the Liffey, while twenty soldiers from the Custom House advanced cautiously towards the ruin of Liberty Hall. They finally discovered that the building had been empty all along.

Meanwhile, in order to bring artillery fire down on the actual rebel positions in Sackville Street, six volunteers from Dublin University OTC came out of Trinity College dressed as labourers and carrying tools and began digging up sections of road near where Great Brunswick Street (now Pearse Street) meets College Street. They pretended to be fixing the gas mains leading into the college but in fact were exposing patches of soft earth where two 9-pounder artillery guns could be set up. (When an artillery gun fired, a steel plate was driven into the ground beneath it, fixing the gun in position; if the stone of the road was not dug up, the guns' plates would not be able to break through the surface.)

The rifle and machine-gun fire against rebel positions in Sackville Street continued. It was heavy until midday, after which the firing began to slacken, easing off so much that a crowd of people even gathered around the O'Connell Monument, only to be scattered across O'Connell Bridge by fire from the British army sniper in McBirney's department store and from a machine gun (which appears to have been designed to scare them out of harm's way). Just before 2 p.m. Colonel Portal ordered that, whether the road surface had been dug up or not, the two 9-pounders should be put in position and fired. They were brought on horse-drawn limbers from Trinity College into a back street, from where they were dragged by hand – with citizens helping the OTC members – into position. As they prepared to fire, soldiers of the 5th Leinster Regiment occupied the buildings along the south quays facing Sackville Street as well as the roofs of the Lafayette Building on the corner of Westmorland Street and D'Olier Street, which housed Purcell's tobacco shop in 1916, and the Tivoli Theatre on Burgh Quay. Just after 2 p.m. the two 9-pounders opened fire.

The guns fired on the insurgents in Kelly's fishing tackle and gun shop on the corner of Bachelor's Walk and Sackville Street, the first two shells making a direct hit. Meanwhile the riflemen and machine-gunners opened fire from their positions on the south quays and also from the Custom House. The guns were firing shrapnel shells – anti-personnel weapons that did not do much structural damage – and the insurgents soon began to fall back from their positions in Lower Sackville Street towards the GPO; the soldiers could see them occasionally darting across the street, individually or in small groups. The guns began firing on other targets up the street and also hit the offices of the *Freeman's Journal* – Ireland's oldest nationalist newspaper, which supported the Irish Party and Home Rule – in Prince's Street, which brought cheers from the insurgents in the GPO and in the Imperial Hotel opposite.

By 5 p.m., after three hours of bombardment, the two guns ceased firing; but even before this the insurgents had begun to reoccupy some of the positions they had abandoned earlier, having recovered from the shock of being fired on by artillery. The British army had not made much progress in the Sackville Street area, but by this time the 10th Royal Dublin Fusiliers had captured the Mendicity Institution, the last of the rebel outposts that Brigadier-General Lowe needed to secure. His two inner cordons, around the Four Courts and the GPO, were now complete.

By 7 p.m. on Wednesday 26 April, Sackville Street was predominantly quiet, with only intermittent bursts of fire breaking the silence. The insurgents in the GPO expected waves of British infantry to come at them at any time, believing the three-hour shelling to have been a preliminary bombardment before an attack. However, the British army was not planning to swarm the GPO and risk losing many men in the process; instead, higher command intended to besiege the rebel positions until they came out with their hands up. To the west, the smoke from Linenhall Barracks in Coleraine Street – captured and set on fire by men from Commandant Ned Daly's 1st Battalion – could be seen rising into the air.

All this while the men of the 3rd Royal Irish Regiment were manning the barricades around the area. Others, including Private Albert Desborough, were away at Kingsbridge Station on the far side of the city, where a field kitchen was set up. Desborough later recalled an incident that happened to them that day:

> It was mid-day, and we had just finished dinner. Everyone was lolling about or resting in any and every position, our rifles laid down, and the Officers' Sam Browns [Sam Browne belts, leather belts with a cross-strap over the shoulder] and holstered revolvers carelessly dropped by their side as they reclined smoking, when suddenly from a house opposite, standing on a slight rise and overlooking our section of the platform, came a burst of machine-gun fire. [Again, Desborough mistakenly believed that the insurgents had machine guns.] Thank goodness none of us was hit. There was a regular melee as each rushed for weapons and a place of safety. I was standing a few feet away from a piece of artillery at the time, and as I stooped to pick up my rifle and bandolier of rounds, and amidst the din of rushing feet and anxious voices, the artillery piece was fired at that gun nest. We learned afterwards that all the [rebel] gunners had been killed. Simultaneous with the sound of the explosion, there was a tearing shattering cacophony. We were stunned and bemused by that thunderous sound, and away we all rushed like so many scared rabbits, officers and men, each seeking to find a place of safety, either in or under the trucks standing at the platform. Eventually all was quiet again. The stillness descended on the place as suddenly as had that awesome crash. It was then found, that every pane of glass in the whole station had become detached, and shivered into thousands of pieces. The whole was a devastating sight. Suddenly, another machine gun commenced to fire, this time men were firing from the end of the road leading into the station. They soon turned tail when we started to fire in return. They got away without a casualty and that was the end of that excitement

This account suggests that a party of insurgents fired on Kingsbridge Station but were ultimately killed or driven back. Later that day Private Desborough rejoined his comrades at the barricades around Sackville Street, travelling by way of Trinity College.

Irish Rebellion ~ May 1916.
Soldiers holding a Dublin Street.

British troops man a street barricade in Dublin (Imperial War Museum)

During this time, also according to Private Desborough, 'each morning a Sergeant and I were detailed to escort many of the housewives who desired to shop to the shops to get the essentials for their families, accompanied in many instances by their young children, clinging to them, some laughing, others crying, many extremely poorly clad, half starved, dragging themselves wearily along in small groups. They were always pleased to have our company, and after shopping were escorted home again.' This suggests that at least some shops were still open, though perhaps only in the suburbs.

On the morning of the fourth day of the Rising, Thursday 27 April, the soldiers of the Royal Irish Regiment would have looked out from behind their barricades at a shattered city. Albert Desborough later recorded what he saw that morning:

On the Thursday morning I wandered round the corner by Parnell's Monument, to get a glimpse of the Post Office from which at times spasmodic rifle fire emanated. Opposite the building one or two Lancers horses lay magnificent in death. I ventured to take a walk across the road to Henry Street, where I saw the damage done through wanton destruction and looting. Arnott's windows out, and the windows bare. Samuels the small jewellers combining a small waxworks and entertainment hall burnt out, and a dismal wreck, while the picture palace, standing on the site of which was once Jame's cheap article emporium and waxworks stood derelict, doors wide open, with no one in charge to prevent any casual human or animal from entering unchallenged. Frekes the oriental shop, and Goggins Oak shop in Grafton street were also looted. Months after the end of the rising, flower sellers and paper vendors round the pillar, sported fur coats and bejewelled fingers, which in the usual way, they could never have bought with the profits from their flower selling. Dublin was a deserted and battered city, as far as the streets were concerned. Every private citizen was behind closed door, and those to be seen in the streets were those in uniform, or snipers occasionally on the roof-tops. The only sounds, stamping, heavy feet, a command and an occasional crack of a rifle ... [The men of the Royal Irish Regiment were] sleeping in the streets in full kit, experiencing only two hours rest each night.

During that hot morning, as recorded in the regimental history, 'a party of picked shots, under Major J. D. Morrogh, succeeded in getting a good position on a roof top and thence inflicted casualties on the rebels in the Post Office ... Another party succeeded in getting a position quite close to the Post Office in the Sackville Street Club.'

Although born in Cape Town, South Africa, 33-year-old Major John 'Jack' Morrogh was the eldest child of two parents from Cork. His father, John Morrogh Snr, a former teacher, had been a director of De Beers, the diamond mining company, and it was this industry that made him his fortune. About 1887 he brought the family home to Cork, where he established Morrogh Brothers and Company, a woollen manufacturing company. For four years he was also member of Parliament for Cork South-East.

Educated in Castleknock College, Jack Morrogh Jnr joined the army in 1901 while living in Douglas, Co. Cork. Ten years later, having served in India and subsequently retired from the army, he was back at home, living in Crosshaven, and had recently married. On 11 April 1912, as the biggest ship ever constructed, the *Titanic,* was leaving Queenstown (Cóbh) for New York, he and his brother followed it along the coast. Jack Morrogh, an amateur photographer, set up his camera on a tripod and took the last photograph ever taken of the doomed ship. Known as the 'Morrogh Image', it was rediscovered in 2001 and was sold as part of an album of *Titanic* photographs previously owned by a passenger, Stanley May.

On the outbreak of the war in 1914 Jack Morrogh rejoined the army, and in October – now serving with the 2nd Royal Irish Regiment and soon to be promoted to captain – he landed in France. On 9 May 1915, while in command of C Company at Saint-Julien, he was shot through the cheek (the bullet lodged in his throat and remained there for the rest of his life) and he was subsequently evacuated home. (A month later he would have learnt that his brother, Second-Lieutenant Frank Morrogh of the Royal Munster Fusiliers, had been killed at Gallipoli.) In November, Jack Morrogh was promoted to major, and by April 1916 he was serving with the 3rd Royal Irish Regiment in Dublin.

On 27 April snipers from the battalion spotted some insurgents building a barricade in Prince's Street, beside the GPO. One seemed to be in command, directing the others, and a sniper opened fire on him. He may have been unsure whether or not he hit the rebel leader, as the man simply walked back into the GPO. He had been hit, however, in the upper right arm. This was none other than James Connolly, who behaved as though he had not been injured so as not to damage the morale of his men.

Back inside the GPO Connolly required medical attention, and he was treated by a British army doctor who was a prisoner of the insurgents and who was also an Irishman. George Mahony was the son of a pharmacist from Bandon. He studied medicine at University College, Cork, and in January 1914 obtained a commission in the Indian Medical Service. Later that year, while serving on the North-West Frontier with the 1st Battalion of King George V's Own Gurkha Rifles (the Malaun Regiment) a pony reared up on a narrow mountain track and pushed him over a precipice. He hit a rocky outcrop after a forty-foot fall but somehow managed to hang on. It took his comrades two hours to get a rope around him and pull him to safety, and after being treated for a time at Dharamshala he was finally sent home to Ireland to recover.

At 10:30 a.m. on Tuesday 25 April, Lieutenant George Mahony arrived at Harcourt Street Station from Wicklow, where he had been spending time with friends, on his way to his sister's house in Drumcondra. He began walking towards St Stephen's Green after he saw that there were no taxis waiting outside the station.

Mahony, who was in uniform, was soon warned by a local man that 'the Shinners are out.' He did not know what this meant and so continued on his way, but he decided to bypass St Stephen's Green. As he was crossing Dame Street he was again warned about 'Shinners'. A crowd gathered around him and explained what was going on, and while they urged him to report to any of the nearby British army strongholds, such as Dublin Castle or Portobello Barracks, a Church of Ireland clergyman cycled up and informed Mahony of just how much danger he was in.

This clergyman was Canon Samuel Hemphill, a native of Clonmel, Co. Tipperary. He offered to take Mahony home to his house in Aylesbury Road, and so they began making their way south by back streets. However, as the two men were walking along Upper Leeson Street a woman came to her door and warned Mahony to stop, that a British officer had just been shot up the street. She also urged him to get out of his uniform, and when Mahony replied that he had nothing else to put on the woman brought him into her house and gave him a pair of trousers, a raincoat and a cap. He changed into these but left on his tunic under the raincoat, then managed to make his way safely to Canon Hemphill's house in Aylesbury Road.

After lunch, unable to contact his sister in Drumcondra because the phone lines had been cut, Lieutenant Mahony insisted on trying again to cross the city. He declined the offer of sanctuary in the Hemphill house until the Rising had ended and also the offer of one of Canon Hemphill's jackets to replace his British army tunic, and then made his way to a garage in Ballsbridge to find a taxi. With no drivers available, Mahony offered the garage-owner a £1 note if he would take him personally. The two then set off for Drumcondra.

They crossed the Liffey by Butt Bridge, but after driving up Amiens Street and into North Strand Road the taxi encountered insurgents at Newcomen Bridge over the Royal Canal. A couple of men ordered the car to stop and then approached, informing Mahony and the driver that they were going to search the vehicle for ammunition. A nervous Lieutenant Mahony was then asked to open his coat. As soon as the insurgents spotted his tunic, the driver began insisting – no doubt truthfully – that he had no idea that Mahony was a British officer. Mahony was ordered out of the car at gunpoint, after which the driver turned and quickly sped away.

He was brought to the building of the Dublin and Wicklow Manure Company, between Ballybough Bridge and Annesley Bridge on the banks of the River Tolka, where he was questioned by an Irish Volunteer officer. This officer was a former British army soldier who had served in India, and when he saw the insignia on Mahony's tunic he knew immediately that he was attached to the Indian Medical Service.

Mahony was placed in a small toilet with a guard at the door. He was offered a cup of tea and was then asked if he would like to be placed in a nearby office with three other prisoners, all British army privates. He agreed and soon found that one of these men was an angry member of the Royal Irish Fusiliers who had been captured while drinking in a local pub – angry because the rebels had not allowed him to finish his drink before taking him away.

That evening Lieutenant Mahony and his fellow-prisoners were brought to the GPO, where Mahony's watch and money were taken from him, though they were later returned. He also obtained permission to write a letter to his sister in Drumcondra to let her know that he was alive. Here he met 27-year-old Second-Lieutenant Alexander Chalmers of the 14th Royal Fusiliers, from London, who had been taken prisoner the previous day. Chalmers was terrified that the rebels would shoot them at any moment, and that night the two officers slept under a table, concerned that their comrades outside might launch a surprise attack in the dark and possibly blow in the roof of the GPO.

The following morning Mahony and Chalmers played bridge with another officer, Second-Lieutenant Stanhope King of the 12th Royal Inniskilling Fusiliers, who had also been taken prisoner the previous day. He then read *The Hunchback of Notre Dame*, which had been given to him by the insurgents. The three officers were given a large breakfast, after which they were questioned by two Volunteer officers, Michael O'Rahilly (who called himself 'the O'Rahilly') and Desmond Fitzgerald. Mahony asked if the rebels were intending to execute him and his fellow-prisoners, but the question shocked O'Rahilly, who replied that Mahony and his comrades were prisoners of war and could expect to be treated as such.

Mahony then informed the insurgents that he was a doctor, and so he was brought to the aid post on the ground floor of the GPO. Here he was shown a range of medical instruments and equipment, including some items the insurgents had managed to find in local chemists' shops, many of them useless for treating gunshot wounds. Lieutenant Mahony discovered that he was the only doctor present in the building – the insurgents had no medical officer of their own in the GPO – and so from this point on he would be primarily responsible for treating all casualties inside the rebel headquarters. He was assisted by a medical student named McLoughlin, who had been trying and failing for ten years to qualify as a doctor. McLoughlin had been walking down Sackville Street when an insurgent had called out to him from the GPO to come inside and help. The rebel in command of the aid post was another medical student, James Ryan. Mahony's first patient was a man lying on a mattress who had been shot in the lung, and he began by giving the wounded man an injection of morphine.

The following day, Thursday 27 April, after James Connolly was shot in the arm in Prince's Street by a sniper he had made his way back inside the GPO and had his wound quietly dressed by Lieutenant Mahony, who then returned to caring for other wounded. Captain Liam Tannam of the 3rd Battalion of the Irish Volunteers later recalled that 'in the Post Office at several times I saw an Indian Army Officer, an Irishman I believe, assisting Dr. James Ryan. He had his tunic off.' One of the wounded men Mahony soon found himself treating was a member of the Royal Dublin Fusiliers, as recorded by Joseph Good of the Irish Volunteers' Kimmage garrison: 'In the same room as Connolly was a wounded British soldier, a Dublin Fusilier. He was wounded in the groin, was delirious and was calling on Connolly, that is to say, he said "Jim Connolly, Jim Connolly" several times. I thought it somewhat peculiar that a private soldier was borne with in the same room as the headquarters staff.'

Connolly was later shot in the ankle in Middle Abbey Street and dragged himself to Prince's Street, where he was spotted by his men and brought back inside the GPO. Lieutenant Mahony was again called on to help. He bandaged Connolly's shattered ankle – the bone above it was broken and was protruding from the skin in two places – and then supervised the application, by McLoughlin and Ryan, of a makeshift splint made of board that did little or nothing to help. Seeing how much pain Connolly was in, Mahony stepped in and asked for an anaesthetic. McLoughlin returned with a weak and useless mixture of chloroform but insisted that it would be sufficient, while Ryan sent for some chloroform of the proper strength and ether. This was used on Connolly, after which Mahony was able to remove the bone fragments from the wound and stop some of the bleeding. He then made a proper splint, and finished by giving Connolly an injection of morphine.

Mahony was now ordered to remain by Connolly's side, and the insurgents provided a mattress for him. He was lying on this later in the day when Connolly woke up, turned to him and said, 'You know, you're the best thing we've captured this week!' Mahony, together with his two assistants, later tried to prevent

Connolly being brought on a stretcher to the main hall of the GPO, but Connolly insisted on returning to his men.

At 10 a.m. on Thursday the 27th, British artillery opened fire and hit the *Irish Times* printing office in Lower Abbey Street. This was possibly one of the worst targets that the shell could have hit, as the building was full of large rolls of paper. They immediately caught fire, and the flames soon began spreading from building to building. As another shell hit Lower Sackville Street, Wynn's Hotel in Lower Abbey Street caught fire and the blaze continued to spread. The British army tried to use this to its advantage, and some soldiers advanced towards Sackville Street, but they had to withdraw after coming under fire from Lieutenant Oscar Traynor and twenty other insurgents in Mansfield's on the corner of Middle Abbey Street.

The flames spread slowly but steadily, and by 2:50 p.m. everything between Lower Abbey Street and Sackville Place was on fire, and the blaze was also travelling in the opposite direction, towards the Liffey. Enormous clouds of black smoke billowed into the air. The British army ceased fire while soldiers rushed along Eden Quay, knocking on doors and calling for people to come out. The English actor Sir Henry Lytton had friends in Eden Quay, and he later recorded in his book *Secrets of a Savoyard* (1922):

> Our anxieties were increased in the meanwhile by the systematic operations of the military around Eden Quay. One by one the houses were being demolished by shellfire, and in one of the threatened houses, as we knew, were many of the ladies of the company. To get to them was impossible. Luckily for them a sergeant on signalling duty heard their cries, and at once rushed to their help. 'Who are you?' he shouted. 'What are you doing here?' 'We're the D'Oyly Carte,' they answered. The D'Oyly Carte name worked like magic. Signalling to the gunners to cease fire, the sergeant hurried them out and through the streets, where sniping was going on at every corner, and took them to a police-station for safety.

As soon as the area was cleared and the civilians had been escorted down towards Liberty Hall and the Custom House, the artillery opened fire again.

The building of the Dublin Bread Company in Lower Sackville Street subsequently caught fire, and not long after the flames had appeared on the roof it collapsed in a wave of smoke and fire. Waverly's Hotel followed, burning and collapsing at 7:30 p.m., after which Hopkins and Hopkins, on the corner of Eden Quay and Sackville Street, fell at 9 p.m., burying thousands of pounds' worth of gold and silver, melted down by the intense heat. Every time a building collapsed, shattered and charred brick washed across the street, while bursts of fire, smoke and heat erupted into the air. Worst of all, at 10 p.m. Hoyte's oil works, directly opposite the GPO, caught fire. The building quickly exploded, sending burning oil-drums shooting into the sky, detonating in mid-air and rocking the surrounding buildings. To the insurgents in the GPO and the soldiers of the

Royal Irish Regiment nearby they may as well have been in the trenches during one of the fiercest battles of the war.

Clery's department store and the Imperial Hotel above it soon followed, being rapidly engulfed by the flames, their façades crashing down into the street. At some point in the middle of all this chaos some horses came running out of a burning building and into Sackville Street. The insurgents opened fire on them, believing it to be a British cavalry charge.

If the soldiers of the Royal Irish Regiment could have heard anything over the flames they might have heard the rebels inside the GPO singing 'The Soldier's Song', which was sung frequently – and exclusively in English – by insurgents during the Rising. However, the GPO was now cut off from all surrounding rebel headquarters. That night members of the 3rd Battalion in Upper Abbey Street and Liffey Street were relieved by a unit of the Sherwood Foresters. Private Albert Desborough later recalled:

> Never shall I forget that Thursday night, April 27th, when the sky was lurid with the fires from the G.P.O, The Imperial or Gresham Hotel with the Y.M.C.A and other establishments, and above the crackling of the flames, the shouts of frenzied and excited people arose the sounds of artillery bombardment as they sought out the hiding places of the rebels, the rapid crackling of combatant rifles and the splutter of machine-gun fire. It was a night to remember, and as I write this letter I feel thankful, when remembering the chances we ran of being sniped.

With the arrival of units of the 59th (2nd North Midland) Division, by Friday 28 April the 3rd Royal Irish Regiment found themselves positioned mainly along Great Britain Street, near Lieutenant-Colonel Owens's headquarters opposite the Parnell Monument. That morning, under heavy fire, they helped to set up an 18-pounder gun at their end of Sackville Street, which subsequently opened fire on Arnott's drapery shop in Henry Street, behind the GPO. (Like Liberty Hall earlier, it housed no rebels.) Meanwhile the British army began advancing across O'Connell Bridge, small groups taking up cover among the debris around the O'Connell Monument.

The artillery across the Liffey was still firing only shrapnel shells, and because of the angle of fire it had still not hit the GPO, most of the shells hitting the Metropole Hotel next door. However, just after 4 p.m. a shell did hit the GPO, and this one was not a shrapnel shell but an incendiary one. The order to fire it had come from Lieutenant-Colonel Owens of the Royal Irish Regiment. Private Albert Desborough was the soldier sent by Owens with the order to fire. He later recalled in his witness statement:

> I can well remember near the end of that week, of being sent to an officer in charge of a piece of artillery. I found him and the gun's crew [under the

railway bridge at Beresford Place] within a few steps of what was left of that famous meeting place, Liberty Hall. It was then nothing but a battered hulk of a house. It had been the pride and I believe the headquarters of the Sinn Fein enthusiasts. Now here, I must relate an action, which to my knowledge has never been made general knowledge, nor can it be contradicted. This relates to the first shelling of the G.P.O. It is on record, and I have seen it in print on more than one occasion, that, the first round which penetrated the Post Office, was fired from a boat on the Liffey. No such thing ...

To return to the officer and the artillery piece. I delivered my message. At his command, after loading the weapon the crew manning it raised its trajectory exceedingly high, swivelled the gun round, and at another command fired it. The round went over the railway bridge which crossed the road nearby, at least my memory retains that glimpse of that moment, soaring high, then turned downwards, plunged through the roof of the G.P.O crashed through the floors and setting fire to the material stored in the basement. How true this statement is can be ascertained from those who may be living today, who helped to man the building at that time. That shot was NOT fired from the Liffey, for I stood close by and saw the whole manoeuvre, from start to finish. This was the order sent by me from our Commander Colonel Owens.

The officer in command of the artillery that fired on the GPO was 22-year-old Lieutenant John D'Arcy, son of Bishop Charles D'Arcy, Church of Ireland Bishop of Down, Connor and Dromore at the time of the Rising, later Archbishop of Dublin and then Archbishop of Armagh and Primate of All Ireland. John D'Arcy was commissioned in September 1914 and entered the war immediately. In November 1914, during the First Battle of Ypres, he was severely wounded and evacuated. He was still recovering in Dublin when the Rising began, and he volunteered to serve and so was placed in command of two of the four guns that had been brought to Dublin from Athlone.

D'Arcy later returned to the war, where he was again wounded. By the end of the war he had risen to the rank of major and had been awarded the Military Cross. He remained in the British army and fought in the North-West Frontier campaign in India (1930–31), where he was wounded once more. He served with distinction during the Second World War, retiring with the rank of lieutenant-general. After living for several years in Kenya, he and his wife returned home to Ireland and settled in the family home, Hyde Park, near Killucan, Co. Westmeath, where he lived until 1960.

Second-Lieutenant Edward Gerrard, who was also involved in the Rising in Dublin, recorded that at least one of the shells went extremely off target. He recalled that Lieutenant Charles Dickens, a 43-year-old career soldier and veteran of the Anglo-Boer War who had previously served in France as a regimental sergeant-major, told him that 'he had a shot at the flag on top of the G.P.O. with one of these guns. He did not realise that the shell would not burst. The shell travelled on to the lawn of the Vice-Regal Lodge [now Áras an Uachtaráin]. He told me that the Lord Lieutenant was very annoyed at being shelled.'

The incendiary shell fired at the GPO set fire only to the roof, and the insurgents were soon engaged in fighting the fire. They extinguished it within ten minutes, but another incendiary shell hit the building and another blaze erupted. This time the fire was not put out, and it quickly spread to a dozen places. Meanwhile the British army kept up sustained rifle and machine-gun fire on the roof of the building, part of which soon collapsed.

Though it still had no intention of making an all-out infantry assault on the GPO, the British army advanced closer. Men of the 3rd Royal Irish Regiment began moving cautiously down the street from their positions around the Parnell Monument, but rebel fire held them back. Soldiers could regularly be seen darting about the area now.

The insurgents in the GPO ultimately decided to abandon their headquarters, and at 5:30 p.m. on Friday 28 April, with the building now on fire, the evacuation of the sixteen or so rebel wounded was ordered. They would be brought to Jervis Street Hospital, and Lieutenant Mahony was told to accompany them. He insisted that Connolly should come too, but Connolly refused to leave his men.

Thirty minutes later, at 6 p.m., the evacuation of the wounded began. Captain Martin O'Reilly of the Irish Volunteers led Mahony, a pro-rebel priest named Father John Flanagan, twelve women and the sixteen wounded – who were carried on blankets or mattresses by other insurgents, who later returned to the GPO – out through a hole in the GPO wall, through two shops, across an exposed rooftop, and then up a ladder to the Coliseum Theatre in Henry Street. They arrived there by 6:30 p.m.

Meanwhile in the GPO the fifteen prisoners were brought to the Henry Street entrance and set free. One of them, Private Peter Richardson of the Connaught Rangers, as recorded by Max Caulfield in *The Easter Rebellion,* later stated that 'we were placed near the door where we could rush for our liberty. Then, shaking hands with each one of us in turn, The O'Rahilly said, "Good bye ... I may never see you again. Good-bye and good luck to you." Then the door was pulled open.'

But when the British army saw these men rushing out of the GPO they mistook them for retreating rebels and opened fire. Second-Lieutenant Alexander Chalmers was hit in the thigh by a machine gun, while the man beside him, said to have been a Royal Dublin Fusilier, was shot in the head and killed. Chalmers and the others miraculously managed to make it over a low wall and into the safety of an alley; here Chalmers collapsed and a sergeant from the Royal Irish Regiment picked him up and carried him into a cellar.

Another one of the prisoners set free was Constable Edward Dunphy of the DMP, who had been standing at the telegram counter inside the GPO at midday on 24 April when the insurgents seized the building. An Irish Volunteer had pointed a rifle at the terrified Dunphy, who began pleading with a nearby officer: 'Please don't shoot me. I've done no harm.' The officer had replied, 'We don't shoot prisoners.' Dunphy was taken into a room upstairs, tied to a chair, and then locked in the room. The Volunteer officer he had encountered was Captain Michael Collins.

During the escape of the prisoners from the GPO Constable Dunphy was shot in the hand and also received injuries to his cheek and forehead. He managed to escape and was ultimately taken to Jervis Street Hospital, where the bullet was removed from his hand. But after he returned to duty his injuries flared up, and by 1917 he was forced to resign from the DMP. Two years later, in late 1919, he died as a result of complications from the wounds he received during the Easter Rising. He was forty-seven years old.

Lieutenant Mahony was only a short time in the Coliseum Theatre in Henry Street when he was summoned back to the GPO. An insurgent had fallen on top of Connolly and broken the splint Mahony had made, and he was was needed to fix it. At this stage the fires inside the GPO were raging, but Mahony later recalled how calmly the insurgents were behaving. Soon afterwards he returned to the Coliseum Theatre. That night, with the fire from the GPO moving steadily towards them, the insurgents in the theatre made the decision to press on towards Jervis Street Hospital. Making their exit through a door that led to Prince's Street, they got over a burning barricade to Middle Abbey Street, where – despite waving Red Cross flags – they were fired on by soldiers of the Sherwood Foresters. No one was injured, and then a British army officer called for one of the Red Cross flag-bearers and one other man to advance. Father John Flanagan, who had a flag, turned to Lieutenant Mahony, who opened his coat to show his army tunic, and together the two men began to walk forward. George Mahony's time in rebel captivity had ended.

He was later promoted to captain and survived the war, one of very few British army personnel who could claim to have been inside the rebel headquarters during the Easter Rising.

* * *

Not every former prisoner of the insurgents left the Coliseum Theatre on the night of Friday 28 April in order to press on towards Jervis Street Hospital. As recorded in the *Sinn Fein Rebellion Handbook*,

> on Wednesday, 3rd May, more was heard of the soldiers who had been hostages. Mr. F. R. Ridgeway, managing director of Bewley, Sons, and Co., Henry street, discovered that there were two soldiers alive in the ruins of the Coliseum Theatre. It was not long before they were released, when it was found that they were Sergeant Henry [captured by Harry Boland on Tuesday 25 April], of the School of Musketry, Dollymount Camp, and formerly of the Royal Irish Constabulary, and Private James Doyle, of the Royal Irish Regiment. Both were unwounded but weak from want of food,

having had nothing to eat since Friday. How did they come to be in the Coliseum? Being of the party imprisoned in the Post Office, when sent forth they had sought refuge in the theatre, and there they stayed unaware of the fact that the fighting about the place had ceased.

As for the main rebel body in the GPO, after deciding to evacuate they planned to withdraw down Henry Street, up Moore Street, and then re-establish themselves in the premises of Williams and Woods, soap and sweet manufacturers, in Great Britain Street. They had no idea that Moore Street was barricaded by the Sherwood Foresters, and that Great Britain Street had been occupied by the British army for days.

By 7 p.m. on the Friday the fire worsened and spread more rapidly, forcing the insurgents to finally retreat from the GPO. O'Rahilly's advance party then ran into the Sherwood Foresters' impassable barricade in Moore Street, ultimately preventing the rebels from making it to Great Britain Street. As the interior of the GPO collapsed behind them, and with Henry Street blanketed in black smoke, the rebel leaders took cover in Cogan's grocery shop on the corner of Henry Place and Moore Street.

The regimental history of the Royal Irish Regiment records that 'the battalion caused many casualties to the rebels as they were endeavouring to get away from the Post Office. During the night various parties of the enemy attempted by rushes, one of which was headed by several maddened horses which they drove in front of them, to break through the ring of troops, but the battalion foiled all these attempts.'

On Saturday the 29th, the morning after evacuating the GPO, the insurgents had managed to tunnel through the buildings in Moore Street from Cogan's grocery up to Hanlon's fish shop (number 16); they were still heading in the direction of Great Britain Street, despite the impossibility of breaking through to it. Here they thought about what to do next. One plan was to try to break through to the Four Courts, where Commandant Ned Daly and the 1st Battalion of the Irish Volunteers were still holding out, but the idea was soon scrapped; it would cost too many lives.

Meanwhile the 3rd Royal Irish Regiment – obviously having no idea that the insurgents in the area had already been effectually broken – were finally getting ready for an infantry assault against the GPO. A hundred men of the 2nd/6th Sherwood Foresters had also been despatched to make the attack with them. At 12:45 p.m. Nurse Elizabeth O'Farrell, a midwife in Holles Street Hospital and a rebel despatch messenger, went from Hanlon's shop to the nearby British army barricade. Carrying a Red Cross flag, she had been sent to make contact with the military in order to discuss terms for surrender. However, they would accept no terms, and so in the end the insurgents were forced to surrender unconditionally. They were ordered to proceed to the Parnell Monument and to deposit their weapons there. The Rising in the vicinity of Sackville Street was over.

Private Albert Desborough, in a letter written in late May or early June 1916, described the aftermath of the Rising. It was a feeling that was certainly shared by many of his Irish comrades at the time.

> Dublin the 'Fair City' – and she was a fair city – is now desolate and partially in ruins. Through the madness of a few men, who thought they could beat the disciplined army, its resistance and numbers, coerce the Government, and raise a Republic [of] Ireland, many promising, clever men, leaders in their sphere of life, have met premature deaths. Many civilians have been killed, as the hastily-made mounds in the cemeteries will testify.

However, before the rebels ultimately accepted this unconditional surrender Lieutenant-Colonel Owens of the Royal Irish Regiment had a personal encounter with one of their leaders. On Saturday 29 April, Private Desborough was sent to Merrion Square to retrieve the wages for one officer's company – the officer had left them with his wife for safekeeping – and after returning with the money and handing it over he later recalled:

> I hadn't returned very long, when suddenly round the corner from the G.P.O. direction, came a Red Cross nurse carrying a white flag, whilst marching behind her followed six stalwart Citizen Army men carrying on their shoulders a stretcher supporting a wounded Officer of theirs. He had been shot in the knee and was obviously in pain. I ran inside and informed the colonel, who immediately came out to meet them. 'Well?' Colonel Owen [*sic*] snorted in his most officious and stentorian voice. 'Well?' he spluttered a second time, 'What do you want?' The six bearers lowered their burden to arms length, and as they did so, I saw the wounded man wince with pain. Then he answered in a clear voice, 'I have come personally to know, that if I and my officers surrendered, you would allow the rank and file to return to their homes unconditionally?'
>
> For a moment there was a tense silence. I saw the colonel getting red in the face, then spluttering he ejaculated, getting redder in the face like some school boy caught in some misdemeanour, – 'What!!! ... you ... you bloody rebel ... you ... dare ... If I had my way, I'd shoot you. I am the one to make terms not you. Listen, if you and your men, everyone of them don't lay down their arms and surrender before nine to-night, and without any conditions attached, and I want an answer as quickly as possible, I'll order the bombardment of the entire city, and raze it to the ground. But see to it that all your women and children, and non-combatant people are got to a place of safety. You'll be responsible for any of their deaths. Take him away' he spluttered. 'You ... bah!'
>
> Without another word, the colonel turned on his heel and re-entered the orderly room. It was the most poignant scene I witnessed from the start of

the rising to the completion of the courtmartials at our barracks. The six men raised the stretcher to their shoulders again, and the nurse taking her place at their head again, they marched off. [Desborough later noted that this incident took place at about 4 p.m. on Saturday 29 April.] Many conflicting thoughts and feelings assailed me just then, what I had seen seemed callous, for every now and again the face of James Connolly winced with the pain he was evidently enduring. But I suppose these are the episodes which often occur between belligerents.

Immediately they had gone, I was summoned to give a very important message to the Vice-regal Lodge. It covered all that had transpired between our Colonel and James Connolly, and also enquired if there were any further commands or orders to be issued, and if all should be carried out as Colonel Owens had stated. I reached the Lodge without further incident, delivered my message, after being conducted along many carpeted passages to the person I desired to see, and returned to our head-quarters with a message, which as far as I can nor rightly remember. 'Carry on as you intend doing. Drive home a decisive assault in the shortest possible time, with the least possible losses on either side. I expect the rebels to capitulate to you before the day's out.'

The regimental history later recorded that during the Rising 'the young soldiers of the battalion behaved in a splendid manner despite the trying conditions, and although to many it was their first experience of warfare ... After the surrender Brig. General Lowe, C.B., complimented the battalion, through Colonel Owens, on their excellent behaviour throughout, and said it was due to the aggressive manner with which the battalion dealt with the rebels that the surrender was brought about.'

The surrendering insurgents were first sent to the grounds of the Rotunda Hospital, after which they were marched to the battalion's station at Richmond Barracks. The treatment they experienced at the hands of the 3rd Battalion differed from person to person, but Charles Saurin, a member of F Company, 2nd Battalion, Irish Volunteers, later recalled that at the Rotunda Hospital

it was almost dark now and a guard of members of the Royal Irish Regiment encircled us the width of the drive away from our grass island. Very soon we were joined by a party of prisoners about equal in strength to ourselves. This was the Four Courts Garrison and there was just barely accommodation for us on the grass patch. At this point a party of soldiers was led into the grounds by an officer who preceded them round the grass patch, he and they striking matches and peering closely at us as if we were some peculiar type of animal they had never seen before. He led them out again and they formed up on the roadway outside where he addressed them in this way: 'Men, who are the worst, the Germans or the Sinn Féiners?' They all chorused 'The Sinn Féiners!' 'What will we do to the Sinn Féiners?' They all shouted, 'Shoot them, shoot them,' while one, more original than the rest, suggested 'Hang them.'

We believed these to be belonging to the Shropshire Light Infantry (though I doubt if any of that regiment were in Dublin [they were not]) but that the officer was an Irishman. The men of the Royal Irish Regiment who were kneeling or crouching around guarding us started an altercation with the alleged Shropshires through the railings and told them to shut up and clear off and so forth. One of them leaned across to near where I was on the edge of the grass and said: 'Do you know what them so-and-sos would do if they saw a so-and-so German? They'd run like so-and-sos hell!' A little later tea was served out to the Royal Irish Regiment, but it is hardly necessary to add that none was given to us. One of these soldiers, however, and perhaps, more for all I know, very decently crossed the gravel drive and handed a dixie half full of hot tea to a couple of us. Arthur Shields, Seán Russell and myself and a couple of others on the edge of the grass were grateful to him for this.

Later, when Saurin arrived in Richmond Barracks, this treatment continued.

The Staffords [either the North Staffordshire or South Staffordshire Regiment] stood at ease on each side of us, but when Arthur Shields with a cigarette in his mouth, attempted to smoke, a sallow faced Corporal came up and rudely told him to stop, and asked him sarcastically did he know where he was. This Corporal was joined by a lanky foxy-haired young Sergeant who proceeded to cast aspersions on our morals by saying with an air of disgust that we had women with us in the Post Office. He then told the Corporal that he had been digging graves all day yesterday. 'I hope,' he added, 'I'll be on a firing party to-morrow.' In contrast to him a very fine white moustached old N.C.O. of the Royal Irish Regiment pushed his way through the escort with a dixie full of water and handed it to a man in our ranks some distance in front of where I was. As it was emptied he filled it and brought it back and so on down the line. It was a bold thing for him to do in the circumstances and we thanked him fervently each time he came back with a full dixie.

Vinnie Byrne, another Volunteer from the 2nd Battalion (later a member of Michael Collins's 'Squad' during the War of Independence and the Civil War) had a similar experience in Richmond Barracks.

We were going over to the lavatory under military escort, which was across the square and I met a sergeant of the Royal Irish Regiment there one evening. He remarked to me that he did not mind fighting with genuine rifles, but firing these Mauser guns [the rebels' main weapon, a German rifle] was not playing the game. He told me that his captain had been killed at the South Dublin Union, or wounded – I am not sure now – 'a very decent man.' He said: 'You know, I am a Dublin man, and it is hard luck to get shot down by your own.' He asked me did we get any bread and butter since we came in. I replied, no, that we were only getting war ration biscuits. He said: 'If you can manage to come over in the morning' – that is, to the lavatory – about 10 a.m. – he would see me there and would have some bread and butter. I got over there the following morning and received two quarter-loaves of bread with two big chunks of butter slapped on them. I duly hid them in my pocket as best I could, and brought them back to the billet where I shared them among the remainder of the boys that were in the room.

In contrast, Joseph Good, a Volunteer who fought with the Kimmage garrison during the Rising, later recorded:

From the Rotunda we marched along O'Connell Street. A solitary fireman was working near Kelly's corner and he said out loud: 'I'm with you boys.' That was the first word of approval I had heard from Dubliners that week. As we proceeded through High Street, near St. Audoen's Church, crowds of women were in the side streets and they shouted 'Bayonet them,' but they were kept back by the British soldiers.

When Good arrived at Richmond Barracks, as he later remembered, 'a party of British soldiers – Irishmen of an Irish Regiment – rushed towards us shouting, and would have attacked us only they were halted by our guards'.

Captain Seán Prendergast, commanding officer of C Company, 1st Battalion, Irish Volunteers, also had a negative experience of the 3rd Royal Irish Regiment. 'At last we halted outside the Richmond Barracks, Kilmainham. When eventually we were marched into and rested in the Barrack square, we were guarded, ironically enough, by the Royal Irish Regiment, the men of which were none too fraternising or considerate and adopted the domineering and threatening attitude of being bosses of the show and showered on us much abuse, insolence and ill will.'

Finally, Patrick Colgan, a member of the Irish Volunteers from Maynooth, Co. Kildare, who had been caught while trying to escape from the GPO towards the quays, encountered both aggression and kindness from men of the 3rd Battalion.

I had just got clear of the gate pier when a shout 'Halt, put them up' came from the barrier which was only about fifty yards away. I halted. I was again ordered to put them up. This was terribly hard to do. I was helped to make up my mind quickly when ten or twelve rifles were pointed at me. Before leaving the yard we had decided we were not going to surrender. We had discussed the question of surrender and we had convinced ourselves that it was better to be killed even making a dash than to be caught and then killed. We felt there would be no live prisoners. I reached the sandbags and over them, much to my surprise still alive, I was taken by a little brat of a 2nd Lieutenant of the Royal Irish Regiment who kept prodding me with his revolver and telling me what a pleasure he would have in killing me. Luckily for me his attention was attracted when the other boys came out. We were put up against the front of a house beside the barricade. The brat placed a soldier facing each of us. He ordered the soldiers to kneel on one knee; the soldiers had levelled their rifles on us. Then a voice above and behind us spoke and enquired what was happening. The brat said he was going to shoot us swine. The voice said he was an Irishman, he was against us, [but] we had fought a clean fight and if the officer gave the order to fire he would fire on him. We thought it was a joke to prolong our agony. The brat was in a rage. He ordered the soldiers to stand up; the voice and the brat kept on arguing. The voice reminded the brat that only for the Rebellion they would be in France and he wouldn't like if taken a prisoner to be shot out of hand. An escort shortly afterwards marched us to Mary's Abbey. On the way the soldier on my right said to me, 'That was a near thing, I was the fellow facing you.' I said he couldn't help it. He then asked me if I remembered him. I didn't. He told me he came from Edenderry, Offaly and that he had travelled in the same carriage from Broadstone Station to Maynooth one Sunday evening some time before when we were returning from seeing a football game between Louth and Kerry.

From these accounts it would appear that some men in the Royal Irish Regiment were sympathetic – if not to the rebel cause then at least to their situation after they had surrendered – while others were obviously enraged at what the Volunteers and their comrades had done.

Among those who were sympathetic was one of the officers serving with the 3rd Battalion on the morning of Monday 24 April. This was 22-year-old Lieutenant George McElroy from Donnybrook. The son of the Donnybrook schoolmaster, Samuel McElroy, he was a Trinity College graduate and former civil servant. He had joined the army as a private when he enlisted in the Royal Engineers in September 1914, not long after the outbreak of war, going on to serve as a despatch rider with the motorcyclist section of the Royal Engineers, attached to the General Headquarters Signal Company in France. He was promoted rapidly to corporal, his potential for leadership was recognised, and he was soon sent to the cadet school in Bailleul at about the same time as the Second Battle of Ypres. On 8 May 1915 he was commissioned into the 1st Royal Irish Regiment. However, in October 1915 he was badly wounded by gas and evacuated back to Ireland. After he had recovered he was posted to the 3rd Battalion in Dublin.

During this time McElroy applied to join the Royal Military Academy at Woolwich, where artillery and engineer officers were trained at the time. He had an idea for his future in mind but needed a commission in one of the more

Captain George McElroy from Donnybrook, Dublin, during his time as a fighter pilot with the Royal Flying Corps (McElroy family)

technical corps first. He was accepted and was due to start in Woolwich on 31 May 1916. When the Easter Rising began, McElroy refused to take up arms against the rebels. He did not agree with their principles but he refused to take up arms against fellow-Irishmen. Lieutenant-Colonel Owens was no doubt outraged by this opposition to orders, and he transferred McElroy to the 4th Battalion in Co. Cork as punishment.

At this point in the war McElroy's name was completely unknown. But after attending the Royal Military Academy at Woolwich and receiving a new commission in the Royal Garrison Artillery he immediately transferred to the Royal Flying Corps in March 1917. He served in two reconnaissance squadrons and then in two fighter squadrons before being posted to the 40th Squadron in August 1917. Here he met the famous Major Edward 'Mick' Mannock, Britain's highest-scoring air ace of the First World War, a native of Ballincollig, Co. Cork. Mannock became McElroy's mentor, and McElroy went on to become a pilot to be reckoned with. He was decorated twice after shooting down forty-seven German planes (five was enough to earn the title of 'ace'). By now he was a celebrity and a hero.

But the life of a fighter pilot was a dangerous and a short one. On 31 July 1918 Captain George McElroy was killed by ground fire, at the age of twenty-five, only five days after his mentor, Edward Mannock, had been killed in action. George

McElroy is today remembered as the third-highest scoring British air ace of the First World War. He is buried in the Laventie Military Cemetery.

* * *

Whereas George McElroy's refusal to fire on the insurgents does not really reflect how much Ireland changed following the Rising, the later actions of Private Patrick Keane of the 3rd Royal Irish Regiment certainly do. Born in 1898 in Cashel, Co. Tipperary, Keane was the son of poor farm labourers. He worked as a farm labourer before joining the 3rd Royal Irish Regiment in July 1915 – about the time of his seventeenth birthday, though he claimed to be nearly nineteen – and he was still seventeen when the battalion took part in defeating the Easter Rising. Keane later remembered that

> my battalion of the Royal Irish Regiment was stationed in Richmond Barracks, Dublin, where many of the prisoners were detained during the weeks that followed the Rising. Except Pierce McCann, who was a native of Dualla, near Cashel, I knew none of the men who were prisoners. The attitude of the men of our battalion towards the prisoners was, I might say, one of sympathy and respect. After the first few executions we found ourselves listening in the early hours of the morning for the sound of shots from Kilmainham Prison and wondering how many more of the prisoners had gone to their doom. There was little we could do to assist the prisoners in Richmond Barracks, but I do remember managing to get a loaf of bread and a tin of bully beef for one prisoner who asked me to try and get him some eatables.

In September 1916 the 3rd Battalion was moved from Richmond Barracks to Templemore. Patrick Keane felt that, following the executions, higher command moved the battalion on purpose, because of the sympathy the men of the battalion had apparently shown to the rebels. He later remembered that they were moved at very short notice, and were not even allowed to take their rifles with them.

In October 1916 Keane was posted to the 2nd Royal Irish Regiment – which had recently become part of the 16th (Irish) Division – and soon joined them in France. Then, after the German army launched its Spring Offensive on 21 March 1918, its last big push to force the Allies to the negotiating table, Keane was one of the many British army soldiers taken prisoner on the first day. He was certainly one of the lucky ones, as by the time the British finally stopped the German advance fifteen days later the 16th (Irish) Division had lost 7,149 killed, wounded and missing out of the approximately 9,000 it had started out with.

Keane was held as a prisoner of war in a camp in Lamur, Belgium. He later recalled:

> It was from a German soldier that I first heard of the Armistice, and that night five of us, all prisoners of war, broke out of the camp and made our

way to Brussels. Here we met a party of Canadian soldiers, who sent us on to Dunkirk, and from Dunkirk we got a ship to Dover. After a few weeks in the military barracks in Dover, we were given a month's leave and instructions as to what to do at the end of our leave. My instructions were to report to Clonmel military barracks when the month was up.

Keane, now twenty years old, returned home to Cashel to spend his month's leave, but while there 'I found that most of my school companions were members of Sinn Féin or of the Irish Volunteers.' He attended a meeting in a hall in Friar Street and soon decided to join the republican forces. Before his month's leave was even up he had taken part in a raid – armed with a pistol, masked and in civilian clothes – on the home of George Wallis, an insurance agent who lived in Lower Gate Street and who was known to serve tea and refreshments to British army soldiers.

The British army does not appear to have followed up on Keane's desertion, as he was discharged in March 1919. Having been trained as a signaller during his time with the British army, he soon began to teach his signalling skill to his new comrades in the 2nd Battalion, 3rd Tipperary Brigade, while also instructing them in musketry, grenade-throwing, and foot drill. He soon came under suspicion from the RIC, but a sympathetic constable named Cable informed him that he was being watched.

As part of the battalion's active service unit Patrick Keane was one of eight men who took part in an attack on Ballinure RIC Barracks, near Cashel, in January 1921. He and his comrades were later informed by the commanding officer of the 3rd Tipperary Brigade, Séamus Robinson, that the IRA in Co. Cork was 'under very heavy pressure and that it was up to us to relieve that pressure.' Robinson told them that one way would be to 'shoot a Black and Tan or an R.I.C. man in every town or village in our areas.' So, on 3 March 1921, Keane and three other IRA men took part in the shooting dead of an RIC constable in Cantwell's public house in Cashel.

Soon arrested after a raid by British forces against his safe house, Keane later escaped from Cahir Barracks after overpowering a guard. He rejoined his comrades and was subsequently involved in the burning of Newcastle House, near Grange. The owner, a Mr Perry, was told that 'there was nothing against him personally but that as the British were about to occupy the house it would have to be destroyed.' The IRA then helped him to remove his valuables from the house before setting it alight.

Patrick Keane's final action in the War of Independence came not long after. While serving as a member of Dinny Lacey's flying column,

> I remember one evening near the village of Cloheen three of us met a man cycling. We were suspicious of him as at the time it was necessary to have a permit from the British authorities to own and ride a bicycle. We took him a prisoner and brought him to Lacey. He was recognised as a British

agent named George Stone. He was held as a prisoner that night, and on the following evening some members of the column took him away and executed him on the road near Fethard.

After the truce in July 1921 Keane's active service unit took over all policing duties in Cashel, despite the fact that the British army and RIC were still stationed in the town. After the Treaty had been ratified and the Civil War had begun, Keane joined the new Free State army in 1922 and was commissioned as a lieutenant. He served for two years before returning to live in Cashel in 1924. By that time he had served through all four of the major conflicts in early twentieth-century Irish history: as a British army private during the Easter Rising, in the trenches of the First World War, as a member of an IRA flying column during the War of Independence, and as a Free State officer in the Civil War. His fascinating witness statement was given to the Bureau of Military History on 6 December 1955, when Patrick Keane was fifty-seven years old, still living in his native Cashel.

* * *

Back in Sackville Street, despite the surrender the 'Irish Republic' flag still flew over the GPO. Even while the building burned and collapsed on 28 April, with one witness watching as burning pieces of paper floated up past it on heated air, it neither fell nor caught fire. The flagstaff bent over, but the flag remained attached. This flag, together with the IRB's Tricolour, had been brought to the GPO by Captain Seán T. O'Kelly. With nothing much to do after the initial occupation of the GPO on 24 April, he had been requested by Connolly to go to Liberty Hall and bring back two flags to be flown over the building. The 'Irish Republic' flag was raised over the GPO by Éamon Bulfin.

It was men from the 3rd Royal Irish Regiment who ultimately took down the 'Irish Republic' flag: Major Jack Morrogh and Company Sergeant-Major Frederick Banks, who had earlier fought in the South Dublin Union as a member of Major Holmes's 100-man piquet. (Private Albert Desborough recorded that 'during the marshalling of the G.P.O garrison, one of our orderly room men ascended to the roof and hauled down the Defender's flag.') Morrogh – who had earlier commanded the party of 'picked shots' overlooking the GPO, one of whom had inflicted the first wound on James Connolly – later returned to the war, being taken prisoner by the German army on 21 March 1918, the first day of the German Spring Offensive, while serving in the 7th Battalion of the regiment. On 21 July he managed to escape from Holzminden prisoner-of war camp, tunnelling out with twenty-eight other officers, the first known use of an escape tunnel in Europe during the First World War. However, he was recaptured near the Dutch border on 4 August after two weeks on the run but was subsequently repatriated on 15 December 1918 after the end of the war.

Morrogh then began to receive death threats, partly because it was known that he had taken part in defeating the Easter Rising. Then one evening – as

Irish Rebellion, May, 1916.

A group of British army officers pictured with the captured rebel flag, May 1916. On the far right is Second-Lieutenant Richard Burke from Dingle, Co. Kerry, of the 3rd Royal Irish Regiment. After earning a Military Cross in April 1917, he was severely wounded at Cambrai in September. He recovered, and settled in Dún Laoghaire after the war. Burke died in 1977, aged eighty-three. (Imperial War Museum)

later recalled by his granddaughter – a group of republicans burst into his house, looking for weapons. Morrogh was away, but when his wife recognised one of the republicans as the son of a friend of hers she began giving out to him. Shortly afterwards they left the house. Not long afterwards, however, as Morrogh, his wife and their four children were driving along a road at night three men stepped out in front of the car. Morrogh turned to his wife and said, 'This is it, Aileen.' He was obviously expecting to be killed; but when the republicans saw his children in the back of the car they let him go.

Jack Morrogh subsequently sent his family away: they pretended to be going to Dublin for a while but in reality fled to England, leaving everything behind. When Morrogh heard that they were safely there he followed them, and then the whole family travelled on to Uruguay. After a time there managing a ranch, Morrogh's partner embezzled his money, forcing him to move again, this time to Argentina, and begin rebuilding his life once more.

Between February and March 1942, at the age of fifty-seven, Jack Morrogh sailed through the submarine-infested North Atlantic from Buenos Aires to Belfast, via Montevideo and Halifax, then travelled on to England (his family later followed him). He attempted to re-enlist but was rejected on the grounds of his age.

After the Second World War he met an old friend from Ireland. This friend apparently asked Morrogh if he remembered a day when the friend was supposed to call and see Morrogh, but he was not home at the time. When Morrogh replied that he remembered the day, the friend then said, 'What luck you weren't in! If you had been I was going to shoot you.'

Company Sergeant-Major Frederick Banks – the man who actually took down the flag – was later commissioned in the Royal Irish Regiment. He survived the war and stayed on in the army.

As for the flag itself, Albert Desborough remembered that 'this was handed to Colonel Owens who had it displayed always in the Officer's Mess until the 3rd Royal Irish Regiment was disbanded in 1922 on July 31st, when its colours and five silk Union flags of the service battalions were deposited at St. Patrick's. I have been told, the Sinn Fein [flag] which flew over the G.P.O was deposited with them.' Taken as a regimental trophy, the flag was hung (upside down) in the regimental mess until the regiment was disbanded. It was then placed in the Imperial War Museum in London until 1966, when the Taoiseach, Seán Lemass, wrote to the British prime minister, Harold Wilson, about the possible return of the flag. This was agreed to, and the flag was returned to Ireland for the fiftieth anniversary of the Easter Rising. Today it can be seen in the National Museum of Ireland in Collins Barracks – the station of the 10th Royal Dublin Fusiliers at the time of the Rising.

* * *

During the courts-martial of the leaders of the Rising soldiers from the 3rd Royal Irish Regiment were called on to give evidence. One witness was 33-year-old Second-Lieutenant Samuel Jackson. A native of Dublin, he had been commissioned in July 1915, having formerly been a national school teacher. On 4 May he was called as a witness during the court-martial of John MacBride. Five days later, on the 9th, he was called again, this time for the court-martial of James Connolly. He stated: 'On the 1st May 1916, I searched the rebel John MacBride and found the document I produce to the court. It purports to be signed by James Connolly and I consider the signature the same as that shown to me by the court.' The document that Jackson had been shown – listed as Exhibit X – had been signed by Patrick Pearse, James Connolly and Thomas MacDonagh.

In 1917 Jackson, now a lieutenant, landed in France and joined the 2nd Royal Irish Regiment. Then, on 20 March 1918 – one day before the German Spring Offensive – he was killed in action. He was thirty-five years old. His name is commemorated on the Thiepval Memorial on the Somme.

* * *

Before the events of April and May 1916 were over, the 3rd Royal Irish Regiment had one more part to play in their history. On 3 May 1916, as later recorded by Private Albert Desborough,

> there is one other incident which relates to a further duty of mine connected with the rising. Every morning, for quite a period, the prisoners at our Barracks, were arraigned before the court held in our orderly room, sentenced, and dispersed to other jails, while many were sentenced to be taken to Kilmainham Jail and there executed. One morning before the Court sat, I was summoned before the Colonel [Owens]. I was ordered to go immediately to Kilmainham Jail, there to ask for the Commandant, and to give a most important and extremely private message. It was, 'Yes. To-night. The lady in question may take her own priest, and he MUST be recognised by the Prison Chaplain, who must assist.' I fulfilled my duty, bringing back an answer which was I think this. 'Tell your colonel, all is understood.' It never dawned on me who this could be or why the mystery, until quite recently [in] 1956 when the papers reported the death of a certain lady, an actress once who had been married to one of the prisoners, the night before his execution.

Unknown to him at the time, Desborough had helped to arrange the marriage of Joseph Plunkett, one of the leaders of the Rising, to Grace Gifford, an artist and cartoonist. They were married at 1:30 a.m. on 4 May, seven hours before Plunkett was shot. There was a problem with the lighting in the prison chapel, so the priest performed the ceremony while a single soldier of the Royal Irish Regiment held a candle. Meanwhile twenty other soldiers from the 3rd Battalion – mostly, or perhaps even all, Irish – lined the walls of the prison chapel with bayonets fixed.

* * *

After the Rising the prisoners sent to Fron Goch camp in Wales and elsewhere were ultimately granted a general amnesty in December 1916 and began returning home. The men of the 3rd Royal Irish Regiment served on, even those who had been wounded during Easter Week 1916. The battalion had lost six men killed, all Irish, and fifteen wounded, twelve of whom were Irish.

One of the wounded was Private Edward Goodchild, the unwilling 21-year-old soldier from Waterford who had previously served in the trenches, had been evacuated home because of mastoid disease and was granted an early release from detention in early April 1916, just in time to end up in Dublin for the Rising.

While still recovering from his wounds in Dublin he was soon misbehaving again. On 17 May 1916 he broke out of the Royal Hospital at about 2 p.m. '& remain[ed] absent until 11 p.m. the same day.' For this he was given seven days of field punishment no. 2, which was similar to the cruel field punishment no. 1

but differed in that it did not involve being shackled to a heavy object while being forced to undergo hard labour.

And the misbehaviour continued. On 9 July he was again 'absent from tattoo until 11.20 p.m.', for which he was given eight days' confinement to barracks and also deprived of eight days' pay, while on 17 July he was 'absent from tattoo roll call when duly warned for a draft until found breaking out of barracks about 4.30 p.m. on 18-7-16.' He had been ordered to return to France – something he obviously did not want to do – and for this latest crime he was given a further two weeks of field punishment no. 2 and deprived of twenty-eight days' pay.

Private Edward Goodchild subsequently returned to the war and was posted to the 2nd Royal Irish Regiment. He served in the trenches until mid-September 1916, when he again returned to Ireland for some unspecified reason. He rejoined the 3rd Battalion, now in Templemore, but was not with it for long. Two days before Christmas 1916 Private Edward Goodchild arrived in Egypt, and by the following May he had been posted to the 5th Battalion in Salonika, part of the 10th (Irish) Division in the Mediterranean Expeditionary Force. In April 1918 the battalion joined the 52nd (Lowland) Division and moved to France. Goodchild served with it here until the war ended, finally returning home in March 1919. Unusually for a man who had gone absent when he had been told he was going overseas again, he did not commit one military crime from the time he arrived in Egypt in late 1916 to the end of the war. A month after returning home, in April 1919, he was demobilised. He was now twenty-four years old, and he returned to civilian life.

* * *

The other nine Irishmen who were wounded while serving in the 3rd Royal Irish Regiment during the Easter Rising were: thirty-year-old Private John Crotty, a former farm labourer from Newcastle, Co. Tipperary; Private P. Doyle, who enlisted in Dublin; twenty-year-old Private Edward Cullen, who enlisted in Cashel, Co. Tipperary, in November 1915, entering the trenches after the Rising, where he was again wounded, being discharged because of his wounds in March 1918, aged twenty-two; Private M. Grayson, who enlisted in Thurles; nineteen-year-old Corporal James Keating from Blanchardstown, Co. Dublin, who went on to serve in the war; Acting Corporal Michael McGrath, a pre-war soldier who enlisted in Waterford in July 1911 and had previously served in France before the Rising, returning to the war and later joining the Labour Corps before being discharged in May 1919; Private Michael Traynor, who enlisted in Dublin and later served in the trenches; Private Peter Walsh from Mooncoin, Co. Kilkenny, who also went overseas before transferring to the Royal Engineers; and Private W. Walsh, who enlisted in Kilkenny.

Several men of the battalion were also mentioned in despatches for their actions during the Rising, including Second-Lieutenant H. C. Burke, Sergeant John McKeown (who later served in the 20th Royal Irish Rifles and then with the 1st Battalion in the trenches), Private John Woods, and Private Edward Young (who later served in the Army Ordnance Corps).

Another soldier mentioned in despatches was 21-year-old Sergeant Francis Wheelock, born in Thomastown, Co. Kilkenny, who grew up in Iveagh Buildings in Bride Street, Dublin, and trained as a typesetter and compositor before the war. He survived the war and ultimately moved to England. When the Second World War began he again put on British army uniform and by 1941 was serving as regimental sergeant-major with the 61st (South Lancashire) Searchlight Regiment, a reserve unit responsible for the defence of the city of Crewe. He died on 21 November 1941, at the early age of forty-six.

Private George Glendon of the 3rd Royal Irish Regiment was also mentioned in despatches for actions during the Rising. A 45-year-old farmer from Callan, Co. Kilkenny, living at Brenormore, near Clonmel, he was married with five children when he enlisted.

Private Maurice Prendergast from Clogheen, Co. Tipperary, the son of a clerk of petty sessions, enlisted in Clonmel. He earned his mention in despatches during the Rising and was later promoted to lance-corporal. On 7 June 1917, during the Battle of Messines Ridge in Flanders, he was killed while serving with the 2nd Battalion of the Royal Irish Regiment. He was eighteen years old. He has no grave, but his name is commemorated on the Menin Gate Memorial at Ypres.

A man with a similar story, though from outside the Royal Irish Regiment's traditional recruiting grounds, was Corporal John McClenahan. Born in Dundalk, he was living in Newry, Co. Down, when the war began. He enlisted in Belfast and served first in a hussar (light cavalry) regiment but was transferred to the 3rd Royal Irish Regiment in time to serve with it during the Rising, during which he was mentioned in despatches. He was later sent overseas and joined the 8th Royal Irish Fusiliers in the trenches, and was killed on 8 July 1916, two months after the end of the Rising. He is buried in St Patrick's Cemetery, Loos.

* * *

Major Philip Holmes, the former RIC district inspector from Cork who led the piquet out of Richmond Barracks on 24 April, was called as a witness for the prosecution during the court-martial of Joseph Plunkett on 3 May 1916. He stated:

> I identify the prisoner as a man who was one of the leaders of a large company of Sinn Feiners who surrendered on the evening of 29 April 1916. They surrendered at the northern end of Sackville Street in the area to which the Sinn Feiners who had been in the Post Office for several days had retired when the Post Office was burnt. The Sinn Feiners in the Post Office had been firing on the troops for several days & killed & wounded a number of soldiers. He was dressed in the green uniform he is now wearing with a Captain's badge of rank on his sleeves when he surrendered. The party at the head of which he surrendered was armed.

After the Rising, like many of his comrades, Holmes went on to enter the trenches. On 1 September 1916, four months after the Rising, he was gassed at Messines while serving with the 11th Royal Irish Rifles. He was evacuated and was treated for several months in hospital in London but in January 1917 was still suffering from nausea, vertigo, bronchitis and palpitations, but by June he had recovered and was ordered to join the 20th Royal Irish Rifles at Newtownards, Co. Down.

Major Holmes had been lucky, and later in 1917 he would be lucky again. On 16 August, while serving with the 11th Royal Irish Rifles, he was wounded during the disastrous Battle of Frezenberg Ridge near Ypres. By the end of the day the 16th (Irish) Division and 36th (Ulster) Division had been forced back to the trenches from which they had started out, having between them lost 7,816 men either killed, wounded or missing. A medical board later recorded that Major Holmes 'was struck by a fragment of shell which entered outer side on his left thigh about middle & lodged on inner side, whence it was extracted 2 days later ... At the same time he was struck by lump of clay on left side of face & left eye, causing considerable contusion.' He was evacuated to England on 19 August, and in October, though he still had some pain in his eye and weakness in his leg, he joined the 18th Royal Irish Rifles at Clandeboye, near Bangor, Co. Down.

After the war Major Holmes returned to his job as a district inspector with the RIC at its depot in Dublin. The War of Independence had begun, and the RIC was now involved in the fight against the flying columns of the IRA. Its members were also boycotted (some constables resorted to buying food from shops at gunpoint), which led to an increase in the number of resignations and a decline in recruitment. By 1920, with the IRA beginning to attack rural barracks, the RIC was forced to station its constables in the safer barracks in larger towns. As the violence increased, the British government – unwilling to commit regular soldiers – set up two paramilitary forces to assist the RIC. The first, commonly known as the 'Black and Tans' (from the mixture of army and police uniforms they wore), began operating in March 1920. Contrary to popular opinion, they were not prisoners recruited from British jails but were mostly demobilised soldiers from English and Scottish cities, many of whom had been unemployed since the end of the war. New research shows that about a fifth of the Black and Tans, or more than 2,300, were in fact Irish, most of them recruited in Ireland.

Many of these men were mentally scarred after their experiences in the trenches, and when the British members of the force arrived in Ireland – a foreign country containing a hostile population that they cared nothing about – they soon became infamous for their undisciplined and violent behaviour.

In July 1920 the Black and Tans were joined by the newly established Auxiliary Division of the RIC – popularly called the 'Auxies' – comprising 2,215 former officers (a tenth of them Irish), who served as the RIC's counter-insurgency wing. Their brutal behaviour soon gained both groups a reputation for using torture as a method of interrogation as well as for destroying several towns in reprisals – actions that even earned them the hatred of many older RIC members.

By October 1920 a total of 117 RIC men had been killed and 185 wounded; and by December the bloodiest period of the War of Independence had begun. Between then and the truce of July 1921 about a thousand – combatants and civilians – were killed, approximately 70 per cent of the total number who died in the war.

During this dark period Philip Holmes was now a divisional commissioner of the RIC in Cos. Cork and Kerry, with the military rank of major-general. In late January 1921 he travelled from the RIC Barracks at Union Quay in Cork, passing through the village of Kishkeam and taking the Ballydesmond road into Co. Kerry. Here the convoy of two large touring cars was spotted, and the information was passed to Commandant Seán Moylan, commanding officer of the Newmarket Battalion of the 2nd Cork Brigade. Knowing that this type of car was used by senior British officers, he set up an ambush here in the hope that the cars would return later by the same route.

In Tooreengarriv Glen (also known as Daly's Glen), on the Kerry side of the border, Moylan deployed twenty men, armed with rifles, shotguns, pistols and a machine gun. They dug a trench across the road and were in place and ready by 27 January. There was no sign of the RIC cars that day, but about midday the following day the two cars were seen approaching from the west. In the cars were Divisional Commissioner Holmes and six other RIC men. Exactly as Moylan had planned, the first car drove straight into the trench, thus blocking the road.

Moylan immediately demanded that the RIC men surrender, but Holmes ordered them to get out of the cars, get behind cover and open fire. Both sides now began firing, and Constable Thomas Moyles, a native of Co. Mayo, was killed almost immediately. The battle raged until Moylan ordered his men to cease fire; he then demanded again that the RIC surrender. Holmes refused and ordered his men to keep firing. Half an hour later Moylan tried again, but once more Holmes and his RIC comrades refused to surrender.

Their ammunition, however, was soon running low, there was no chance of escaping to safety, and they were isolated in a rural area with no reinforcements on the way, and they were ultimately forced to give up. By now all the surviving RIC men were wounded, including Philip Holmes. He had been hit in the head, and two other bullets had also fractured his arm and his leg. He asked for the IRA commander to come over to his position, and when Moylan arrived Holmes told him that he could not have authorised a surrender until his men were out of ammunition.

Moylan tried to make Holmes comfortable, giving him a cigarette when Holmes asked him if he had one, while other members of the IRA began tending to the RIC wounded, which apparently surprised the RIC constables and led them to thank the IRA for their kindness.

About this time another car came down the road. Moylan stopped the car and placed Holmes and the other seriously wounded RIC men in it, and it set off for Tralee Hospital. The next day two doctors from Cork travelled to the hospital to treat Holmes. He was subsequently transferred to Victoria Military Hospital in Cork, but he never recovered from his wounds and died not long after returning to his native city. He is buried in Mount Jerome Cemetery, Dublin, where many of his comrades who did not survive the Easter Rising also lie.

Following Holmes's death the Black and Tans attacked the villages of Knocknagree and Ballydesmond in revenge. In Knocknagree they fired with a machine gun on three children playing in a field, killing a fourteen-year-old boy and wounding the two others, aged nine and eleven. In Ballydesmond they used grenades in their attack, during which they burned down several houses and business premises.

* * *

Major Edmund Roche-Kelly, adjutant of the 3rd Royal Irish Regiment, who had helped Lieutenant-Colonel Robert Owens to organise the chaos the battalion experienced during the Rising, was promoted to lieutenant-colonel on 31 October 1916 and given command of his own battalion. By July the following year he had been awarded the Croix de Guerre and the Légion d'Honneur by the French government. He was also awarded the Distinguished Service Order by the British government, the citation stating that this was

> for conspicuous gallantry and devotion to duty in commanding his battalion through an attack, in which he displayed great fearlessness and exceptional skill. He moved up through very heavy enemy barrage, personally reconnoitred two advanced positions, and supervised all details of consolidation, all the while exposed to very heavy shell fire. His splendid personal example and disregard of danger imbued all ranks with a spirit that swept away all opposition.

Finally, in May 1918, having also been twice mentioned in despatches, he took over command of a battalion of the Somerset Light Infantry.

After the war Edmund Roche-Kelly stayed in the army and returned to the Royal Irish Regiment. In 1920 he was commanding officer of the 2nd Battalion, then stationed in Delhi. While here he would have learnt that his family home, Firgrove House, near Bunratty, had been demolished. By August 1922 he had again changed regiment, joining the Border Regiment. After his retirement he settled in England, where he died in September 1958, aged seventy-seven.

The commanding officer of the 3rd Royal Irish Regiment, Lieutenant-Colonel Robert Owens – whom Private Albert Desborough had described as 'a shrewd man and a just one, but at times very bitter and uncouth' – sat as a member of the courts-martial of several leading republicans following the Rising, including that of Eoin MacNeill, chief of staff of the Irish Volunteers, who had tried to call off the Rising. Owens subsequently commanded troops in Cos. Clare, Cork, Mayo and Tipperary, all considered 'disturbed areas' following the Rising. He was made

Major Edmund Roche-Kelly from Bunratty, Co. Clare, adjutant of the
3rd Royal Irish Regiment during the Easter Rising (Oliver Beck)

a commander of the Order of the British Empire in 1919 in recognition of his
services in Ireland, and in March 1920 he was appointed resident magistrate at the
Chief Secretary's Office. By 1925 he was living in Winchester in Hampshire.

A native of Dublin who had first served as a private soldier, then obtained a
commission as an officer and served in India and in the Anglo-Boer War, who
command the 3rd Royal Irish Regiment during the Easter Rising, who ordered
the firing of the gun that landed the first shell on the GPO and who met James
Connolly during that week, Robert Owens died in Norwich in February 1937 at
the age of seventy-seven.

* * *

Ultimately, the experiences and feelings of most men who served in the 3rd Royal
Irish Regiment during the Easter Rising – whether they were for, against or
indifferent to any political cause – were summed up by Private Albert Desborough.
In a letter written in late May or early June 1916 he wrote that 'I can assure you it
has been a never-to-be-forgotten experience, and one that will live in the memory
of every combatant.'

4

10th Royal Dublin Fusiliers
From the Quays to the Castle

On Monday 24 April 1916 the 10th (Service) Battalion of the Royal Dublin Fusiliers was stationed in the Royal Barracks, Dublin. It comprised thirty-seven officers and 430 other ranks and mainly recruited from Cos. Dublin, Carlow, Kildare and Wicklow. The regimental depot was at Naas, Co. Kildare.

At the time of the Rising the battalion was waiting for orders to go overseas. During the fighting in Dublin it would oppose the insurgents on the quays of the River Liffey before going on to take part in the defence of Dublin Castle. It also secured the first surrender of the Rising after battling for the Mendicity Institution – a fight in which a Royal Dublin Fusiliers officer fought against a friend from before the war.

In total, the battalion suffered a confirmed four men killed in action (three of whom were Irish) and a further nine wounded (seven Irish). However, because no record was made of the specific battalion to which other killed and wounded Royal Dublin Fusiliers belonged, the unit may have suffered an additional one man killed (who was Irish), and a further sixteen wounded (thirteen of them Irish).

Known as the Commercial Pals' Battalion, because of the employment background of many of its recruits, the 10th Battalion was a young unit, having officially come into existence only on 11 February, though the process of creating it had begun a few months earlier. On 10 December 1915 a meeting had been held at the offices of the press censor at 85 and 86 Grafton Street, which was now also a recruiting office, to announce that a new company of the 5th Battalion – to be known as the Commercial Company – would soon be ready to depart from Dublin and join its battalion at the Curragh, and that a new battalion, the 10th, would also soon come into existence. However, the committee decided to ask the men of the Commercial Company if they wanted to join the 5th Battalion, as planned, or instead to form the nucleus of the new 10th Battalion and stay in Dublin. The vast majority of the soldiers in the company agreed that the latter would be the best option, and so the 'Commercial Company' stayed in Dublin and became a battalion by itself.

Its commanding officer was also the man responsible for raising the battalion: Lieutenant-Colonel Laurence Esmonde. Aged fifty-two in 1916, he was the younger brother of Sir Thomas Esmonde, Irish Party MP for North Wexford, who would later be an Irish Free State senator. The family home was Ballynastragh House, near Gorey.

Despite having raised a new wartime service battalion, Lieutenant-Colonel Esmonde was not new to soldiering. He was a long-serving reservist before the war, a captain by 1893, and had fought in the Anglo-Boer War as a captain and later a major with the Waterford militia of the Royal Garrison Artillery. He later served in the South African Constabulary and then returned to the army reserve, joining the Waterford Royal Field Reserve Artillery.

Commanding B Company of the new 10th Battalion on the day the Rising began was Captain Norman Palmer. He was born in 1878 in Durrow, Co. Laois, the son of a general practitioner from Manchester and a surgeon's daughter from Limerick. Between 1898 and 1903 – before, during and after the Anglo-Boer War – he served as a bombardier (equivalent of corporal) with A Battery, New South Wales Regiment, Royal Australian Artillery. He saw eleven months of active service in South Africa and was wounded during the conflict. Soon

Captain Lodge Stephen 'Norman' Palmer from Durrow, Co. Laois, commanding officer of B Company, 10th Royal Dublin Fusiliers during the Rising (David Grant)

afterwards he and his wife moved to Inchicore, Dublin, where Palmer was in business as a peat manufacturer.

On the outbreak of war Palmer, now aged thirty-five, applied for a commission, and this was granted a month later. He joined the 7th Royal Dublin Fusiliers – now part of the 10th (Irish) Division – as a newly appointed captain. He landed with his battalion at Suvla Bay in Gallipoli on 7 August 1915; nine days later he was wounded in the neck by a grenade and had to be evacuated to England. He was mentioned in despatches for his part in the event. After his recovery he was cleared fit for light duty and in January 1916 was posted to the 10th Royal Dublin Fusiliers in the Royal Barracks, Dublin.

As with the other battalions of Irish regiments that were created during the war, the ranks of the 10th Royal Dublin Fusiliers contained some older and experienced men along with the fresh citizen volunteers. One such old soldier was Company Sergeant-Major Christopher Lynch. From Blanchardstown, Co. Dublin, and previously employed as a servant, Lynch joined the Royal Inniskilling Fusiliers in November 1887, at the age of twenty-two. He was sent to the regiment's training depot in Omagh, Co. Tyrone, and after his basic training was posted to the 2nd Battalion.

In October the following year Lynch was appointed an unpaid lance-corporal, and then in January 1889 he travelled to India. When he returned to Europe nine years later, in March 1898, he had risen to the rank of sergeant, had attended a mounted infantry course at Secunderabad and a musketry course at Ballari, obtained the army third-class and second-class education certificates, had been admitted to hospital with influenza and dysentery, had extended his period of service twice to allow him to serve a full twenty-one years, and had married.

When he returned from India the 33-year-old Sergeant Lynch was posted to the 1st Royal Inniskilling Fusiliers. He served at home during the Anglo-Boer War, being promoted to colour-sergeant in December 1900, and by 1901 he was based at Finner Camp, Co. Donegal, while his family lived in nearby Ballyshannon. Lynch was awarded the Good Conduct Medal in October 1907, and the following year he left the regular army, having completed his twenty-one years' service. However, he opted to stay in the reserve, receiving permission to serve on past twenty-one years, and was soon a colour-sergeant with the 4th Royal Inniskilling Fusiliers, based in Enniskillen, Co. Fermanagh. Two years later, in May 1911, he was finally discharged, his character recorded as 'exemplary'. He was now forty-six. He settled in Bellanaleck, south of Enniskillen, and probably never imagined that in three years he would be back in uniform.

In September 1914, after the outbreak of the First World War, Christopher Lynch re-enlisted in the Royal Inniskilling Fusiliers in Omagh, despite having no obligation to do so. Now forty-nine, he was quickly promoted to Company Sergeant-Major and sent to join the 5th Battalion, and on 7 August 1915 he landed at Suvla Bay. Eight days later he performed an act of bravery that earned him the Distinguished Conduct Medal, the citation for which read: 'For conspicuous gallantry at Suvla Bay on 15th August 1915. Company Serjeant-Major Lynch and Private Mason brought back into safety a wounded officer under heavy fire after two other men had been wounded in the attempt.'

Lynch later returned to Ireland from Gallipoli – possibly because of illness or wounds – and was subsequently posted to the 10th Royal Dublin Fusiliers, but before he left Gallipoli he was mentioned in despatches. By April 1916 this very experienced NCO was fifty-one years old.

* * *

Some officers and men of B Company, 10th Royal Dublin Fusiliers, in Royal Barracks, Dublin, shortly after the Rising (David Grant)

The 10th Royal Dublin Fusiliers had also its fair share of raw recruits, some of whom were legally too young to be in uniform. In late January 1916 Denis Byrne, a typewriter mechanic from St Paul's Place, off North King Street, Dublin, enlisted in the Royal Dublin Fusiliers at the recruiting office in Grafton Street. He claimed to be eighteen years and three months old but the truth is that he was only sixteen years and eight months.

One of the reasons he may have been able to fool the recruiting sergeant into thinking he was older was that he arrived at the recruiting office with a reference, dated 7 October 1915, from a 'Mister Lobo', head mechanic with the Bar-Lock Typewriter Company Ltd of Dame Street, where Denis had previously worked as a typewriter mechanic. The reference stated:

> Denis Byrne, the bearer of this reference has been in the employ of the above Company for the past two years, during which time he has proved himself willing, industrious and reliable. During the greater portion of that time he has been learning to repair typewriters for which work he showed considerable aptitude; in fact being intelligent and taking an interest in his work, he should be a quick pupil at any business. The Company was sorry to part with him, but as his father ceased to reside in the city a short time ago (though since, I believe, returned) we were compelled to release him.

The reference was genuine but perhaps suggested that Byrne was older than sixteen. He was soon posted to the 10th Royal Dublin Fusiliers, specifically to Captain

Norman Palmer's B Company. His medical examination found that he had very bad teeth, and he first had to agree to undergo dental treatment.

By March 1916 it had become apparent that Denis Byrne had physical problems other than bad teeth. Between 6 and 10 March he was admitted to hospital suffering from bronchitis. Then the army discovered the truth about his age. On 14 March his mother wrote to Lieutenant-Colonel Esmonde:

> Sir, I respectfully beg to report that my son Pte D Byrne B Compy of your Regt enlisted about 5 weeks ago. I enclose herewith certificate of his birth which proves that he is only barely 17 years old. Furthermore he has always been a delicate lad & will never make an efficient soldier. I would therefore request that you would be so good as to cause him to be discharged as being underage. Or if that is impossible under the present circumstances, then you will see that he is not sent abroad until he reaches the age of 18. Hoping for a favourable reply. I am Sir yours respectfully, Kate Byrne.

The battalion adjutant wrote to Captain Palmer to ask him if Byrne was willing to be discharged. He could not request his own discharge, as he had stated that he was over eighteen when he enlisted, but if the army offered to discharge him he could choose to accept this. Captain Palmer put the question to him and soon recorded, on 23 March 1916, that 'this man is willing to be discharged from the service. His health is bad. I have explained to him as requested ...' For some inexplicable reason, however, Byrne's discharge suddenly stopped; the papers were never processed, and the whole thing was taken no further. He was therefore still a serving soldier.

When the Rising began on 24 April, Private Denis Byrne – still one month away from his seventeenth birthday – was still in uniform with the 10th Royal Dublin Fusiliers.

* * *

One man in the 10th Battalion wrote an account of his experiences in Dublin during the Rising. Lieutenant Charles Grant, son of a DMP inspector from Co. Tipperary, was born in 1881 in the family home in Townsend Street. The family soon moved to New Bridge Avenue in Sandymount, and Grant later recalled a childhood spent paddling and swimming on Sandymount Strand. He also recorded that

> on the [South] Wall, mid way between Irishtown and the Pigeon House, there stood a Coast Guard Station manned by men of the Coast Guard Service of the Royal Navy. To small boys like me it was a treat to spend many hours in the company of the sailors, whose main duty was to check on ships entering and leaving Dublin ... Further along the road there was the Pigeon House Fort which was occupied by a Royal Artillery Battery and a company of infantry for the protection of the harbour. There were also

Lieutentant Charles Grant with his wife, Eliza 'Elsie' (née Proctor) (David Grant)

attractions for small boys here. The troops allowed us to play around the guns. I remember no live shells being fired in my youth, but the noise of the explosions of blanks gave us pleasure. Occasionally the battery was used in exercises for purpose of attack by troops stationed in Dublin ... The closing down of Pigeon House Fort in 1897 was a great disappointment for us boys, as no longer would the troops from Beggars Bush and other barracks enliven our martial spirits with their various manoeuvres.

Grant attended Merchant Tailors' School and later the Diocesan School in Molesworth Street, which had a reputation for preparing its pupils for the civil service. In 1901 he obtained a post with the Local Government Board of Ireland, based in the Custom House. Determined to develop his career, he soon also qualified as an accountant.

In 1903 Charles Grant put on his first military uniform when the joined the recently created South of Ireland Imperial Yeomanry, a reserve cavalry regiment (renamed the South Irish Horse in 1908). Enlisting with three friends, he was among the earliest men to join the regiment. They received their training in the Phoenix Park from the 21st (Empress of India's) Lancers, based in nearby Marlborough Barracks and during annual training camps at the Curragh. In

January 1908 he left the Yeomanry after his four-year period of engagement had ended.

In 1912 he became a law student at the Honourable Society of King's Inns, Dublin, while also attending evening classes in accountancy three nights a week at Rathmines School of Commerce. After only two years of legal studies he was called to the bar (the process normally took three years), and Grant found himself appearing before judges in the High Court.

In 1914, shortly after the outbreak of the war, Charles Grant was persuaded by an old friend, Major George Harris from Killashee, Co. Longford, an officer with Dublin University OTC at Trinity College, to join the corps. He quickly rose to the rank of platoon-sergeant, and when the war came, like many of the OTC's cadets, he immediately applied for a commission, asking to be posted to a home service battalion of the Royal Irish Rifles. However, civil servants had to obtain permission to join up, and because of the increased responsibilities placed on the civil service by the war his application was rejected. He kept trying and in the meantime continued to serve with the OTC, becoming a sergeant-instructor and then cadet sergeant-major and cadet quartermaster. He was considered 'a splendid instructor', with 'good powers of organisation', and in November 1915 he also won the prize for the unit's most efficient member. He later recorded: 'All this time I was unsettled and discontented. My close friends had joined up. So I again applied for permission to join the army, which was given with a grudge. I applied for a commission through the OTC, and was gazetted to the Royal Dublin Fusiliers 10th Battalion, which had been newly formed. I was sent to an officers' school of instructors at Government House, Cork for some weeks.'

Now aged thirty-four, in January 1916 Grant joined B Company of the 10th Battalion as a second-lieutenant. He was sent on courses in bombing (grenade-throwing) and gas at Elm Park Bombing School, a musketry course with the Army School of Musketry at Dollymount Camp, and also a company commander's course in Richmond Barracks. 'I questioned the reasons why I was being sent on so many courses and the adjutant told me that I was the officer who could get distinctions on the courses and the CO [commanding officer] made it a boast concerning these distinctions with other battalions ... I was appointed Battalion Bombing Officer, and the instructing of officers and men on this subject fell to me.' As battalion bombing officer, Grant was in command of a specialist platoon trained in the use of grenades and would be expected to lead trench raids when overseas.

By March he had been promoted to lieutenant, but on the 27th one of his trainees died in a training accident. Private Martin Rowe attempted to throw a grenade, but it got caught on his thumb and rolled back into the trench. It exploded, ripping into the chest, stomach and legs of another soldier, nineteen-year-old Christopher Mitchell from Aughrim Street, Dublin. Mitchell died within ten minutes from loss of blood and shock and now lies in Grangegorman Military Cemetery. Lieutenant Grant had the sad duty of informing Mitchell's family.

Four weeks later the Rising began. Grant later recorded:

> On that Easter Sunday I had spent the day with my fiancé and at midnight walked back to the Royal Barracks through the Coombe Slums of the city. Beyond small gatherings of people apparently chattering at various points, I noticed nothing unusual. On Easter Monday I was detached to give a lecture to officers and men of my battalion on trench bombing and the use of explosives. At 11 a.m. we were assembled on the grass slopes of the barracks facing the River Liffey. Shortly after this rifle shots were heard from the city, and on hearing the bugle alarm call, I doubled the party into the barrack square. Here I found about 50 men of the regiment assembled with two staff officers and other senior officers of the regiment. Orders were given for troops to be equipped and armed. A party of men from A Company were marched out of the barracks ... I received orders to take B Company, about 50 men to the Castle. No further orders and there was no inkling that rebellion had broken out.

The bugle call that summoned Lieutenant Grant back inside the barracks had been ordered after Colonel Henry Cowan had phoned to alert the barracks that Dublin Castle was apparently under attack. The 3rd Royal Irish Regiment in Richmond Barracks and the 3rd Royal Irish Rifles in Portobello Barracks were contacted at the same time. The 100-man piquet of the 10th Royal Dublin Fusiliers – fifty men from A Company and fifty from B Company – was immediately assembled and, as in the other barracks around the city, ordered to march to Dublin Castle. Lieutenant Charles Grant was at the head of this column.

* * *

Immediately behind Lieutenant Grant in the column was another Irish officer, one with a strong nationalist background. This was 34-year-old Lieutenant Gerald Neilan from Ballygalda, Co. Roscommon. The son of a farmer and justice of the peace, he attended Clongowes Wood College between 1895 and 1898, after which he joined the 2nd Sherwood Foresters (Derbyshire Regiment) as a private, going on to serve in Malta and then in the Anglo-Boer War. He was later taken prisoner but was released on 12 February 1902 only to be severely wounded on 6 March. After the war he travelled to China and later Malaya and Singapore with his regiment, remaining there until he left the regular army in 1907, now a corporal. He subsequently became a police constable with the Birmingham City Police while also serving his compulsory four years in the army reserve, being discharged in 1911.

In December 1914, now living with his family at Mount Harold Terrace in Harold's Cross, Neilan applied for a commission. He was successful and was soon appointed a second-lieutenant with the 24th (1st Tyneside Irish) Battalion of the Northumberland Fusiliers, where he also became a musketry instructor. Three of his brothers were doctors, and two of them – Captain Alan Neilan and Lieutenant Charles Neilan – were serving with the Royal Army Medical Corps in France and Mesopotamia (Iraq). In February 1916 Lieutenant Gerald Neilan transferred to the 10th Royal Dublin Fusiliers.

The piquet of the 10th Royal Dublin Fusiliers marched out of the barracks into Benburb Street, marching four abreast with rifles sloped on their shoulders (but not loaded) and bayonets fixed. They turned down West Liffey Street onto Sarsfield Quay, then headed eastwards down the quays. Their plan was to cross the river at Queen's Bridge (commonly called Queen Street Bridge, now Mellows Bridge), move along the south quays, then turn into Parliament Street and break straight through to Dublin Castle. It was not to be.

Not far away, in the Mendicity Institution at Usher's Island, was Captain Seán Heuston and his detachment of D Company, 1st Battalion, Irish Volunteers (who were also members of Fianna Éireann). With only a dozen men under his command – all in their late teens or early twenties – Heuston had been ordered to slow any advance along the quays and into the city, in order to give the rebel headquarters at the GPO and the Four Courts time to occupy those buildings and establish themselves.

As the piquet advanced eastwards they passed crowds of people gathered at the junctions of Ellis Street, Blackhall Place, John Street and Queen Street, while a tram full of people ran along the tracks beside them. Across the Liffey, in the Mendicity Institution, more than a dozen rifles were now pointed at the men of the Royal Dublin Fusiliers.

One of the men in the piquet was nineteen-year-old Private Richard Walsh. Born in London in 1898 to an Irish father and English mother, he moved with his family to Dublin before 1901. By 1916 they lived on the South Circular Road at Rialto. Before enlisting in January 1916 he had been an engineering student, having previously worked for four months as a wireless operator for the Marconi Company in London. A few years older than Richard Walsh was 28-year-old Private Robert Wheatman, originally from Tramway Cottages, Terenure. After marrying in 1915 he was living in Old Camden Street. He had enlisted in Dublin in January 1916, having previously worked for two years as an oil blender in the Greenmount Oil Works in Harold's Cross.

* * *

Inside the Mendicity Institution the insurgents anxiously watched the piquet of Royal Dublin Fusiliers moving along Ellis Quay and across the Liffey. All of a sudden they opened fire. Lieutenant Grant reported that he was not far from turning off Ellis Quay and leading the piquet across Queen Street Bridge when he heard the firing begin. A member of the garrison in the Mendicity Institution, Volunteer Paddy Joe Stephenson, later recalled that, without waiting for Heuston's signal, someone on the ground floor of the institution fired the first shot, prompting the rest of the insurgents to blaze away.

Immediately, the piquet scattered in all directions. As the moving tram stopped and the people on board ran for safety, some soldiers took cover behind the quay wall, others dived for nearby doorways, while some rushed into the side streets. As with elsewhere in the city when the fighting began, most of the onlookers who were gathered on the street corners stayed put.

The first volley caused several casualties among the piquet. Lieutenant Grant later recorded that 'we received a volley of rifle shots which scattered our party. The officer following me, Lt. Neilan, was killed, as were five or six men, and several more were wounded.' The *Clongownian,* journal of Neilan's old school, Clongowes Wood, added that Neilan 'was shot through the head from the opposite side of the river. He lived for a few minutes afterwards ... His kindly, cheerful disposition made for him many friends who will all regret the tragic end of a very promising officer.'

The exact spot where Neilan was killed is known, as John Styles, a courier for Commandant Éamonn Ceannt during the Rising, later recorded that 'there is nothing I can say about Easter Week that has not been told already except this incident – the first of the enemy to be killed in Easter Week was an officer (young) of the Dublin Fusiliers. He was shot outside my [bicycle repair] shop, 23 Ellis's Quay, when the attack was opened by the men in the Mendicity Institution, under the command of the gallant young officer, Seán Heuston.' Gerald Neilan was thirty-four when he died. There is a memorial plaque dedicated to him in the Sacred Heart Church, Roscommon, while in St Mary Magdalene Church in Seaham Harbour, Durham – where Neilan's older brother John had a medical practice – the eleventh station of the cross is dedicated to his memory.

Ironically, Gerald Neilan's younger brother, 21-year-old Arthur, was serving in the 1st Battalion of the Irish Volunteers just down the quays, inside the Four Courts. He survived the Rising and was taken prisoner, being sent to Knutsford Detention Barracks in Cheshire. When he died, in 1944, he was laid to rest beside his brother Gerald in the family plot in Glasnevin Cemetery, Dublin.

Stephen Lucius Gwynn – Irish Party MP and also a Connaught Rangers officer – later wrote in *John Redmond's Last Years* (1919) about the ambush that killed Gerald Neilan on Ellis Quay. He recalled that Neilan 'was so strongly Nationalist in his sympathy as to be almost a Sinn Féiner', and that among the other Royal Dublin Fusiliers casualties 'Others had been active leaders in the Howth gun-running. It was not merely a case of Irishmen firing on their fellow-countrymen; it was one section of the original Volunteers firing on another.'

* * *

Gerald and Arthur Neilan were not the only brothers to serve on opposite sides in the Rising. Private Thomas Saurin, 22 years old, from Vernon Terrace, Clontarf, served with the Royal Army Medical Corps in Dublin. His younger brother, twenty-year-old Charles Saurin of F Company, 2nd Battalion, Dublin Brigade, fought with the Irish Volunteers in the GPO, while another brother, sixteen-year-old Frank, tried to join the insurgents but was turned away because of his age.

Seosamh de Brún of B Company, 2nd Battalion, recorded that after the Rising, Jacob's factory in Bishop Street 'was then taken over by a detachment of the Dublin Fusiliers and by a curious coincidence as one brother left the factory in the Republican ranks another marched into it in the uniform of the British army.'

And Joseph Sweeney of the 4th Battalion of the Irish Volunteers, a native of Burtonport, Co. Donegal (who later became a Sinn Féin TD, then a major-general and chief of staff of the Irish army) recorded that after surrendering at the end of the Rising

> we filed out onto Moore Street and were lined up into fours and were marched up O'Connell Street and formed into two lines on each side of the street. We marched up to the front and left all our arms and ammunition and then went back to our original places. Officers with notebooks then came along and took down our names. A funny incident happened there. One of the officers just looked at one of our fellows and without asking him anything wrote down his name and then walked on. After he had gone a certain distance, somebody asked this fellow, 'Does that officer know you?' 'That's my brother,' he said.

After recovering from the shock of being fired on, some of the men of the 10th Royal Dublin Fusiliers who had taken cover in Ellis Street attempted to get aboard the now stationary tram in order to return fire against the Mendicity Institution. However, the young Volunteers took aim at the gaps in the tram – between the base of the tram or its platforms and the ground beneath – and fired whenever they saw a soldier moving. One soldier was hit trying to crawl to the front of the tram along its length and was dragged away by a comrade, while others were hit after exposing their boots while moving.

Both sides were now firing ragged volleys across the Liffey. Lieutenant Grant knew that he had to press on towards Dublin Castle, but first he had to get his men off Ellis Quay. He ordered some men to stay behind the quay wall to provide covering fire while the rest of the piquet were instructed to withdraw into the side streets. On a single whistle blast, some men began firing furiously at the Mendicity Institution while others jumped up and rushed into cover. Suddenly, all was quiet again.

One of the wounded men was nineteen-year-old Private Richard Walsh, the former engineering student. He had been shot in the shoulder, left lung and groin. He managed to survive this collection of wounds and was soon undergoing treatment in King George V Military Hospital, but he was never again fit enough to serve. On 25 November, only ten months after enlisting and without ever seeing a trench or a German, he was discharged as 'no longer physically fit for war service.' His character was listed as 'very good' and he was granted a weekly pension of 18s 9d for the following six months. What became of him afterwards is not known.

Private Robert Wheatman was wounded in the left side of his jaw, for which, as his service file recorded, he was 'entitled to wear one gold braid wound distinction' on his uniform. He did not go overseas with the 10th Battalion in August but was instead transferred to the 11th Battalion. By March 1917 he had risen to the rank of acting sergeant and had qualified as a musketry instructor after a course at Dollymount Camp.

By the end of May 1917 Acting-Sergeant Wheatman had also completed a platoon commander's course and a Lewis gun course. The job of platoon commander was normally performed by a lieutenant, a commissioned officer, which suggests that Wheatman was a very capable NCO. But by February 1918, now aged thirty, Wheatman was still an acting-sergeant when he was discharged as 'no longer physically fit for war service' as a result of 'GSWs [gunshot wounds] Irish Rebellion.' It would appear that he never fully recovered from the wound to his jaw. On discharge he was hoping to return to working as an oil blender. The army wrote him a reference that refers to Wheatman as a 'good man' who had 'served his country [and] was wounded in its defence.' He later settled in Kimmage with his wife and family. A keen footballer, he was on the board of the Football Association of Ireland when it was formed in June 1921. He also became secretary of the Royal Dublin Fusiliers Old Comrades' Association.

During the Second World War, Robert Wheatman, now in his fifties, served as an air raid precautions (ARP) warden for the Kimmage area. This meant that he ended up wearing an Irish uniform, having been wounded while serving in British army uniform during the Easter Rising. His family recall that he took part in ARP competitions and won trophies for fire-extinguishing and defusing incendiary devices. He died in his native Dublin in 1971 at the age of eighty-three.

* * *

As Lieutenant Charles Grant and his men regrouped in the side streets off Ellis Quay, another Irish officer of the battalion, 22-year-old Captain John Esmonde, arrived at the scene, bringing Father Austin Murphy to the body of Lieutenant Gerald Neilan. Born in England, Esmonde was the son of Irish parents. His father, a doctor practising in Shropshire at the time, soon brought the family home to Ireland, settling in Drominagh, near Terryglass, Co. Tipperary. The family were strong supporters of Home Rule, and in 1910 Dr Esmonde was elected Irish Party MP for North Tipperary. Lieutenant John Esmonde's great-great-grandfather, also John Esmonde, had been executed for his part in the 1798 Rebellion, while his great-uncle Thomas Esmonde had been awarded the Victoria Cross in 1855 during the Crimean War.

Young John Esmonde attended Clongowes Wood College and then schools in Germany and Belgium before becoming an engineering apprentice with the Harland and Wolff shipyards in both Belfast and Liverpool. He did not join the British army as an officer but in November 1914 enlisted in Fermoy, at the age of twenty, in the 7th Leinster Regiment. Eight days later, however, he was sent away to be trained as an officer. One of the references with his application was provided by Brigadier-General William Hickie, also from Terryglass, who went on to command the 16th (Irish) Division during the war. After his period of officer training was completed Esmonde was commissioned as a second-lieutenant and posted first to the Royal Irish Regiment and then to the 27th (4th Tyneside Irish) Battalion of the Northumberland Fusiliers.

John Esmonde's younger brother Geoffrey also joined up during the war, as did his father, Dr John Joseph Esmonde. However, on 17 April 1915, while serving in France, Captain John Joseph Esmonde of the Royal Army Medical Corps died from 'pneumonia and heart failure consequent on the strain of overwork.' He was fifty-three years old. His body was brought home and buried in the family vault in Terryglass.

Lieutenant John Esmonde was later elected to replace his father as MP for North Tipperary, making him, at twenty-one, one of the youngest members ever elected to the House of Commons and also one of the six Irish Party MPs who served in Irish regiments of the British army during the First World War. He was promoted to captain in May 1915, after which he transferred to the Royal Dublin Fusiliers in November. About this time he came into contact with James Connolly, informing him of the opinion of the Irish Party leadership that the dock strikes then taking place in Dublin should be called off. (Connolly told Esmonde to 'go to Hell.')

When the 10th Royal Dublin Fusiliers was created early in 1916 Captain Esmonde joined this new unit, whose commanding officer, Lieutenant-Colonel Laurence Esmonde, was his late father's cousin.

Captain Esmonde survived the Rising unhurt, but on 7 October 1916 his younger brother, Second-Lieutenant Geoffrey Esmonde of the 26th (3rd Tyneside Irish) Battalion of the Northumberland Fusiliers, was killed in action on the Western Front, aged nineteen. Today he lies in Cité Bonjean Military Cemetery, Armentières.

Captain Esmonde served with the 10th Royal Dublin Fusiliers during the winter of 1916 but by February 1917 had left this unit to take up 'special duty in France', as his service file records. He had been appointed to the Intelligence Corps, attached to the headquarters of the 16th (Irish) Division. He served in this capacity until October, when he was recalled home – along with Captain William Archer Redmond, Irish Party MP for Tyrone East and son of the party leader, John Redmond – at the request of the prime minister. A War Office report dated 19 November 1917 stated that this 'was connected with the Irish question.' They had been requested to take part in the Irish Convention, an assembly that had been meeting since July 1917, formed to discuss how Irish self-government might be implemented in response to the increase in support for Sinn Féin and republicanism following the Easter Rising. The British government was clearly hoping that prominent members of the Home Rule movement might be able to make a difference.

The army wrote several letters to the prime minister's private secretary, requesting the return of Esmonde and Redmond to the British Expeditionary Force in France, but they were repeatedly informed that both men were otherwise employed on 'parliamentary duties'. Captain Esmonde relinquished his commission in October 1918. He went on to study at the King's Inns, Dublin, and was called to the bar in 1921.

In 1922 he emigrated to Canada, arriving in Quebec in May. On his travel documents he was listed as single, a barrister, and intending to settle in Canada. However, within a year he had married and returned to Ireland, living first with his sister in Lower Baggot Street, Dublin, before moving to Clarinda Park in Dún Laoghaire. In March 1923 he applied to join the Colonial Service. In 1937 he stood as a Fine Gael candidate for Dáil Éireann in the Wexford constituency, a seat previously held by his second cousin, Osmond Esmonde. He served as a Fine Gael TD, with a four-year absence, until 1951. Ironically, after the 1948 general election in Ireland – which ultimately saw five Irish political parties along with some independents come together to form the First Inter-Party Government – former IRA chief of staff and current Clann na Poblachta TD Seán MacBride suggested John Esmonde as a possible candidate for Taoiseach, on the basis that he had had no links to either side during the Civil War. He died in Dublin in 1958, aged sixty-four, and was buried in Dean's Grange Cemetery.

* * *

At Ellis Quay on 24 April 1916 Lieutenant Charles Grant began leading his men into Benburb Street, where they would be hidden from fire from the Mendicity Institution, before turning down Queen Street and moving directly towards Queen Street Bridge. According to Paddy Joe Stephenson, who was in the Mendicity Institution, some men of the Royal Dublin Fusiliers also advanced from Blackhall Place back onto Ellis Quay and directly towards Queen Street Bridge, now carrying only picks and shovels, but were forced to retreat, having suffered at least one man wounded.

Three of the men still with Lieutenant Grant were Private Michael Byrne, Private Francis Brennan and Private John Thompson. Byrne was a former postman from Lucan, Co. Dublin; he was about twenty-eight and had enlisted in January 1916. Nineteen-year-old Francis Brennan had previously lived at Essex Quay and then in Murtagh Road in Arbour Hill, but his parents were now living at Usher's Island, in the same street as the Mendicity Institution, and in fact he could now see their house across the Liffey. In contrast, John Thompson was far from home. Also nineteen, he was from Mackan, near Enniskillen. He enlisted in Dublin, which is probably why he was serving in the 10th Royal Dublin Fusiliers, but records suggest that he was officially with the 5th Battalion, then based at the Curragh. Why he was in the 10th Battalion on the morning of 24 April 1916 remains a mystery, but his family believe that he was at home on leave from the Western Front when he was called upon to help in the defeat of the Rising.

Lieutenant Charles Grant of B Company,
10th Royal Dublin Fusiliers, May 1916
(David Grant)

By this time reinforcements had begun to arrive from the Royal Barracks. Under covering fire, one group – sent to deal with some insurgents who were believed to be positioned in the bathing-house of Guinness's Brewery in Watling Street – advanced from the barracks to the quay wall at Albert Quay (now Wolfe Tone Quay), after which, with bayonets fixed, they rushed across Victoria and Albert Bridge (now Rory O'More Bridge) to the south quays. Some local citizens, afraid that the soldiers might mistake them for rebels, began cheering and, as the soldiers approached, began advising them how best to catch the rebels, as well as telling them to keep to the walls to stay safe. However, when the men of the Royal Dublin Fusiliers ran past without saying a word, these local people – clearly feeling annoyed by this lack of attention – began grumbling about how badly the army was running the war in France.

Back in Queen Street, Lieutenant Grant and the piquet were now directly opposite Queen Street Bridge and ready to run the gauntlet to reach the south quays. The reinforcements from the Royal Barracks had brought a machine gun with them, and this was set up at the corner of Queen Street and quickly opened fire on the Mendicity Institution. Immediately, Lieutenant Grant and the piquet began rushing across the bridge. As soon as they had all reached the far side they were at an angle where they were no longer in immediate danger from fire from the Mendicity Institution. Grant later recorded: 'I re-assembled the party, leaving the injured on the road, and sent out an advance party of six men.' However, instead of continuing east along the quays (a lucky decision, as they would soon have encountered the 1st Battalion of the Irish Volunteers at the Four Courts) the piquet moved west along Usher's Island towards the Mendicity Institution. As the dozen or so insurgents inside, expecting an assault against their position, hurriedly lit the fuses on home-made bombs, the piquet simply ran past the front gate of the institution, one by one, and continued on towards Watling Street.

Even taking into account the casualties they had already suffered, the piquet outnumbered the insurgents in the Mendicity Institution by perhaps five or six to one. Inside, the garrison, who held their fire and simply let the soldiers pass, were baffled by this behaviour, but Lieutenant Grant had orders to proceed to Dublin Castle: the Mendicity Institution was for someone else to deal with.

Grant led the piquet up Watling Street to James's Street, then down Thomas Street, Corn Market and High Street to Christ Church Place. He later recorded that 'the rifle firing in the adjoining neighbourhood had become intense from the South Dublin Union which was being subject to heavy attack. A few shots passed over us without any effect.' This was the battle being fought between the 3rd Royal Irish Regiment and Commandant Éamonn Ceannt's 4th Battalion of the Irish Volunteers. En route to Dublin Castle, Grant later recorded,

> I met Colonel Tighe of the Royal Irish Fusiliers [Lieutenant-Colonel Michael Tighe, actually an officer with the Royal Irish Regiment] making his way to the Royal barracks. He joined our party, and as senior officer took command. Passing Christchurch Cathedral a few revolver shots were fired. We entered a street running along the side walls of the approach to the entrance to the Lower Castle Yard [Palace Street]. Here we came under heavy fire from rebels in the City Hall, which resulted in a further 20 wounded.

At least three of these wounded were the two young soldiers Francis Brennan and John Thompson, together with 28-year-old Michael Byrne. However, by the time Brennan and Thompson had been brought to the nearby Adelaide Hospital in Peter Street both had died of their wounds. Private Francis Brennan, who had earlier almost certainly run past his parents' home at Usher's Island as the piquet moved towards Watling Street, was nineteen years old. He is buried in Grangegorman Military Cemetery. Private John Thompson from Mackan, Co. Fermanagh, was also nineteen. Today his body lies in Kinawley Churchyard, Co. Fermanagh.

The file on 28-year-old Private Michael Byrne, the former postman from Lucan, records that he received 'Bullet Wds [wounds] Chest, Abdomen & Arm, 24/4/16, Dublin Rebellion,' and specifically that the wounds were '6 puncture wounds ... from shrapnel.' First taken to the Meath Hospital in Heytesbury Street, by mid-May he was being treated in King George V Military Hospital.

Michael Byrne's British War medal (Damien Cawley)

Private Byrne subsequently landed in France on 18 August 1916 when the 10th Royal Dublin Fusiliers entered the war. On 13 November he was wounded in the back by shrapnel and was evacuated home. By July 1917 he had been posted to the Command Depot in Ballykinler, Co. Down, but that September he returned to Dublin to join the 11th Battalion. This battalion moved to Aldershot in January 1918 and in May was absorbed into the 3rd Battalion, which was soon based in Grimsby, Lincolnshire. When the war ended Michael Byrne was thirty years old and a lance-sergeant, and in January 1919 he was posted to a dispersal centre at Park Hall Camp in Oswestry, Shropshire. The following month he was discharged, with his character listed as 'very good'.

* * *

After the battalion had suffered these casualties, as Lieutenant Grant recorded, 'the colonel decided that we should divide the rest of the party. He proceeded with his group down the long steps to the Ship Street entrance to the Castle. I took my group of about 10 men round by Ship Street Barracks, where we entered the Castle, having got them to open the gate for us and re-joined the rest of our original party.'

By 2 p.m., less than two hours after leaving the Royal Barracks, Lieutenant Grant and the piquet of the 10th Royal Dublin Fusiliers – along with some other reinforcements from the battalion – had reached Dublin Castle. By this time 130 men from the 10th Battalion and fifty from the 3rd Royal Irish Rifles are recorded as having reached and entered the castle by the Ship Street gate. They found the castle not under attack but under siege.

Earlier in the day, a few minutes after midday, Captain Seán Connolly, an actor at the Abbey Theatre, had led a detachment of the Irish Citizen Army – ten of them women – against Dublin Castle. Constable James O'Brien, a 45-year-old policeman from Kilfergus, near Glin, Co. Limerick, who had served for twenty-one years in the DMP, was on duty at the Cork Hill gate. Seán Connolly marched towards him at the head of his detachment, drew a pistol, and shot the unarmed constable in the head at close range, killing him instantly. This probably made James O'Brien the first casualty of the Easter Rising.

Going off duty at the same time was Constable Peadar Mac Fualáin (also referred to as Peter Folan), a 37-year-old from An Spidéal, Co. Galway, who witnessed the event and later recorded what happened next.

> The second shot of the Rising was fired at me ... At the very beginning of the Rising when the Citizen Army marched up to the Upper Castle Gate, I happened to be standing at a ground floor window at the left-hand side of the Gate as you go in, preparing to go home, as Sir Matthew Nathan had informed me there was no more to be done for the day. I saw the first shot being fired and Constable O'Brien, who was standing at the left-hand side of the Gate as you go in, fall. When the Citizen Army approached, the

constable made a sign to them with his left hand, to pass on up Castle Street. [Believing the rebels were simply marching in parade, he was directing them away from the Cork Hill gate.] The Gate was open all the time, as usual. I think it was a man in the first or second line of marchers that raised his gun and shot the policeman. Another took aim and fired at me, but I threw myself on the ground. A pane of glass was shattered.

A priest who had been nearby tried to stop the insurgents from going any further, but they ignored him, prompting the priest to turn his attention to Constable O'Brien and begin administering the last rites. The Irish Citizen Army detachment opened fire on the castle while rushing through the gate into the castle grounds and launching an attack on the gate's guardroom. Two soldiers who had been on duty at the Cork Hill gate had already fled into this guardroom, joining several more inside who had been cooking a meal for lunch when they had heard the rebel gunfire. They were armed only with blank ammunition, as no one ever expected the fortress of Dublin Castle to be attacked; and when Seán Connolly's force fired shotguns through the guardroom windows and then threw in a home-made bomb (which failed to explode), the terrified soldiers quickly surrendered.

Unknown to Captain Connolly and his detachment, Dublin Castle – which contained its own barracks, Ship Street Barracks, which normally garrisoned hundreds of men – was guarded by only two officers and twenty-five soldiers that bank holiday morning. Only these, along with sixty-seven wounded men in the Dublin Castle Red Cross Hospital, stood in the rebels' way. However, instead of pressing on or attempting to take over the castle, Connolly ordered a withdrawal (which was possibly his plan all along). While some insurgents remained in the captured guardroom, the bulk of the Irish Citizen Army force subsequently occupied City Hall, just outside the Cork Hill gate, while the remainder took over the premises of Henry and James, men's outfitters, and the offices of the Dublin *Daily Express* on opposite corners of the junction of Parliament Street and Cork Hill. From these positions they commanded the streets in all directions, together with the main Cork Hill gate of Dublin Castle, thus forcing all British army reinforcements to enter the castle through the Ship Street gate.

The insurgents were still in these positions when Lieutenant Charles Grant and the piquet of the 10th Royal Dublin Fusiliers reached the castle by 2 p.m. Though the insurgents had not pressed home their attack, rebel snipers were still firing into the castle from their positions outside, and so orders were given to deal with them. While some men of the 10th Royal Dublin Fusiliers and the 3rd Royal Irish Rifles opened fire on rebel positions from within the castle, others were instructed to set up sniping positions at high points around the castle, in order to find and kill the rebel snipers.

Lieutenant Grant was one of those ordered to establish a sniping position, and he called a sergeant to go with him. This was 21-year-old Lance-Sergeant Frederick Burke. Born in India and of Irish descent (Tullynacross, Lisburn, Co.

Down), he was the son of a highly decorated English-born colour-sergeant in the 2nd Royal Dublin Fusiliers, who later went on to become an honorary major, and the daughter of a Scottish sergeant in the 45th (Nottinghamshire and Derbyshire) Regiment. He grew up in the British army, having lived in South Africa as a young boy while his father was stationed there, and at sixteen he was a student at a military school in Aldershot. In 1914 he enlisted in the army at Gravesend in Kent. His brother was also a soldier and was severely wounded at the Battle of Mons, and in 1915 his father was also wounded in the war.

Lieutenant Grant and Lance-Sergeant Burke began climbing a ladder to reach the roof of a building where they intended to set up a sniping position. As they were climbing, an Irish Citizen Army sniper spotted them and opened fire. Grant was unhurt, but Burke was hit. Grant later recorded:

> We decided on placing sniper posts at various vantage points in order to curtail the sniping that we were receiving from houses overlooking the Castle. Sergeant Burke, who was an army schoolmaster, was killed when he and I were climbing a ladder to get up on to the roof to establish a point to deal with snipers. Burke was the finest type of man. He and I were great friends. He was a good soldier and it was sad that he should pass out in the way that he did.

Records suggest that Lance-Sergeant Burke may not in fact have died that day but lingered on before dying four days later, on Friday 28 April. He was subsequently mentioned in despatches for 'distinguished services rendered' during the Rising. He was twenty-one. Today he lies in Grangegorman Military Cemetery. He had never entered the trenches and was stationed in what should have been a safe location but did not survive his first day of action. His father, on the other hand – who had fought during the Anglo-Boer War, had been 'dangerously wounded' and later served in Singapore, India and South Africa and was wounded again during the First World War – died in 1941, aged seventy-seven.

* * *

Éamon (Ned) Broy, a detective-sergeant in the DMP, was a clerk in the detective office in Dublin Castle and was on duty there when the Rising began. (He was later an IRA intelligence agent inside the castle during the War of Independence, going on to become a colonel in the Free State army and then commissioner of the Garda Síochána.) He later recorded what happened after the initial fighting around the castle had ended.

> Gradually Dublin members of the British army home on leave, some armed with rifles and some without any weapons, began to drift in to the Detective Office ... The soldiers who had rifles were placed at upstairs windows to defend the building in case of attack ... Many members of the public called at the Detective Office during the week, mostly seeking information about

relatives who had failed to return home from their outings on the Bank Holiday. All condemned the rising, which was, as a matter of fact, most unpopular during that week and for a couple of weeks afterwards.

The next task was to defeat and capture the rebel positions outside the castle gates, but for this task newly arrived reinforcements were called on. At 12:30 p.m. – just after the three main Dublin barracks had been phoned – the 1,600 men of the mobile column of the 3rd Reserve Cavalry Brigade, made up of the 8th, 9th and 10th Reserve Cavalry Regiments, were summoned from their base at the Curragh to Dublin.

Serving in this latter unit was shoeing smith Charles O'Gorman. Twenty-two years old and a native of Limerick, O'Gorman had previously worked as a locomotive brake fitter with the railway. Before the war he had emigrated to England and was living in London when he enlisted. As an Irishman he may have been serving with the Depot Squadron of the 8th (King's Royal Irish) Hussars, which formed part of the 10th Reserve Cavalry Regiment.

At 4:45 p.m. on 24 April the first train carrying the dismounted cavalrymen arrived at Kingsbridge Station; the last train arrived thirty-five minutes later. Once his men were all in Dublin the commanding officer of the column, Colonel Bertram Portal, began to deploy them. He sent one train, carrying 330 soldiers of the 9th Reserve Cavalry Regiment, on from Kingsbridge via the Loop Line to the North Wall in order to guard the docks (they soon joined forces with Major Harold Somerville and his men from the Army School of Musketry, who were already in the area) while the main body of cavalry advanced towards Dublin Castle at 5:30 p.m. They travelled past Guinness's brewery along the south quays, then marched up side streets to reach the Ship Street gate of Dublin Castle.

Meanwhile soldiers who were on leave in Dublin began also to make their way, either alone or in groups, to Dublin Castle to join the fight. Machine guns were set up and by late evening began firing on City Hall. In the middle of this scene a milkman brought a large drum of milk into the castle through the Cork Hill gate. The soldiers inside the castle cheered him: somehow the milkman had made it through the Cork Hill battleground to make his delivery as scheduled.

At some point after dusk on the 24th, 200 men of the 10th Reserve Cavalry Regiment prepared to assault City Hall. Orders were given throughout Dublin Castle for a black-out, to help hide the attacking troops as they advanced, and so blinds were pulled and lights were extinguished. One hundred men formed the first wave, and after receiving their orders, and under covering fire from machine guns, they began moving forward in small groups at about 9 p.m.

One group tried to enter the guardroom at the Cork Hill gate but were unsuccessful because of a rebel barricade. (They managed to break down the door two hours later, finding the guards who had been captured earlier still inside and tied up, but the rebels had escaped through a steel grating in the wall.) Meanwhile another group quickly pressed on towards City Hall. The soldiers making the assault attempted to storm the building by the front entrance, but as soon as they approached they came under fire from insurgents positioned in the Henry and James premises and the *Daily Express* offices. The commanding officer of the assaulting party, 21-year-old Second-Lieutenant Guy Pinfield of the 8th (King's Royal Irish) Hussars – just arrived in Dublin from the Curragh – was killed, while men were constantly being hit by rebel fire; the soldiers simply could not make it into City Hall. Orders were soon given to withdraw, and they fell back, having suffered approximately twenty killed and wounded, who had to be left behind in the street.

However, the attack was not halted completely. Another group of soldiers had moved through the cellars of Dublin Castle and come up into the street at the back of City Hall, right under the building's windows, and threw grenades into the building. Insurgents on the roof who tried to manoeuvre themselves into position to fire at this second wave of soldiers were fired on by the machine guns in Dublin Castle; and then the troops climbed into City Hall through the windows, with bayonets fixed.

The first men inside rushed towards the stairs but were met by a group of insurgents coming down. The Irish Citizen Army opened fire, killing or wounding most of this first wave. However, soldiers were now pouring into City Hall, and the insurgents were forced to retreat back up the stairs. The soldiers pursued them, but the insurgents fired a volley down on them, again killing or wounding several men.

What happened next was a tragedy from the viewpoint of the British army. In the darkness the men retreating from this latest volley were mistaken for Irish Citizen Army men by their comrades rushing into City Hall behind them – who were themselves mistaken for rebels by the retreating men. The two groups fired on one another and then began fighting hand to hand, while the real rebels continued shooting at them all.

After a few moments someone obviously realised that they were fighting their friends. Orders were given to withdraw, and everyone quickly rushed out of City Hall. They did not call off the attack, however, but regrouped and launched another assault against the building. This time, instead of piecemeal groups, the renewed assault came on in large waves. The soldiers quickly established a foothold on the second floor of City Hall, and as soon as firing had ceased on this floor, leaving only those on the roof to deal with, they began searching each room with torches while calling on the rebels to come out and surrender.

When they had finally rounded up all the Irish Citizen Army members from the second floor they were amazed at how few captives they had, and at how many of them were women. When one young member, Jennie Shanahan, was discovered by a British army officer he assumed she had been a captive of the rebels. She played along and, when asked how many rebels were still on the roof, took the opportunity to tell the officer that there were still hundreds up there, as a result of which the final assault was called off until morning.

When dawn came on Tuesday the 25th the British army troops, under covering fire from a machine gun in the Bermingham Tower of Dublin Castle, advanced up through a skylight from the second floor of City Hall and out onto the roof. They found the remaining rebel garrison there – less than a dozen strong – who soon surrendered.

City Hall had finally been secured, but at a cost of many killed and wounded on both sides. One of the dead – wounded either in the street outside or in the dark interior of City Hall on the night of the 24th – was Charles O'Gorman, a shoeing smith. He was twenty-two years old and had been mortally wounded only hours after arriving in Dublin. Today he lies in Grangegorman Military Cemetery. On the other side, one of the dead was George Geoghegan from Co. Kildare of the Irish Citizen Army. He had previously served with the 5th Royal Dublin Fusiliers during the Anglo-Boer War. Today he lies in the 1916 Plot in Glasnevin Cemetery.

* * *

About two hours before the battle for City Hall had taken place Lieutenant Charles Grant was ordered to take a group of men on a reconnaissance mission to the Grafton Street and St Stephen's Green area, to find out what rebel forces were there. He assembled his men and set off; but, as he later recorded,

> near Jacobs's factory [where the 2nd Battalion of the Irish Volunteers, under Commandant Thomas MacDonagh, was based] the party was recognised and the question arose as to how to get back to the Castle. In front of St Matthias Church [Hatch Street] I saw a number of men in military formation, and I went back down Harcourt Street, and in front of the Children's Hospital I noticed a number of rifles in the windows of the upstairs apartments. I was turning over in my mind as to a safe route to take, when suddenly a man walked the hall of a tenement house near Montague Street where we had halted. I covered him with my revolver, got all the information I could out of him, and realising he was of the neighbourhood, asked him if he could guide us back to Dublin Castle. He agreed to do this, and as I knew the streets round well, took him and told him if we were attacked we would shoot him immediately. I placed him in charge of Sergeant Robinson my platoon sergeant, whom I knew would not hesitate in acting should anything untoward arise. Our prisoner was shaking with fright and could as a result scarcely speak. As I knew in a general way how to get back to the

Sergeant Sidney Robinson, Lieutenant Charles Grant's platoon sergeant. Forty years old and from Bristol, Robinson was the son of a retired army officer from Foxford, Co. Mayo. He was later killed in action in France on 13 November 1916 and now lies buried in Ancre British Cemetery, Beaumont-Hamel. (David Grant)

Castle, and warned him with a revolver in my hand, that any move to give us away would be devastation for him. He brought us back through alleys which I was not aware of, and guided us to the back gate of the Castle. I had not much money on me, but I gave it all to him, and told him not to mention the guidance that he had given to anyone.

At 10 p.m. Grant was summoned to headquarters in Dublin Castle and given a new mission. As he was from Dublin and knew the city, he was instructed to take a group of twelve men and make his way to the Shelbourne Hotel on the north side of St Stephen's Green. His orders were to make sure that all civilians were out of the rooms at the front of the hotel, facing the park, and to find out if there were any rebels in or near the building.

Just after midday on Monday 24 April, Commandant Michael Mallin and Lieutenant Constance Markievicz (also known as Countess Markievicz) had occupied St Stephen's Green with their Irish Citizen Army forces, which numbered about a hundred. While St Stephen's Green was the main Irish Citizen Army centre, it had early outposts at Davy's pub (on the corner of South Richmond Street and Charlemont Mall, commanding Rathmines Road), Harcourt Street Station and Leeson Street.

The insurgents in the green began to dig trenches to fortify their positions, having first helped the park keeper to evacuate the women and children in the grounds, after which Mallin set up snipers in some surrounding buildings and sent a detachment to occupy the Royal College of Surgeons at the west side of the green.

The nearby Shelbourne Hotel contained many British army officers, drinking at the hotel bar. When one left the hotel he was shot at; others, realising what was happening, occasionally fired at the rebels with their pistols, but – concerned that they might try to take over the hotel – decided to save their ammunition. (Ultimately, Mallin made no attempt to occupy the building.)

St Stephen's Green had been approached during the day by Constable Michael Lahiff of the DMP from College Street Station, who walked up to the entrance to the park near the junction of Cuffe Street and Harcourt Street. The insurgents had already blocked access to St Stephen's Green, but Lahiff insisted on getting in. He was told to go away but refused. When Markievicz heard what was going on she moved to a position along the railings at the edge of the park, and when she could finally see Constable Lahiff she fired at him, as did two other Irish Citizen Army soldiers who were with her. Lahiff was hit three times and fell to the ground. He was taken to the Meath Hospital, where he shortly died of his wounds. Having joined the DMP in 1911, he was twenty-eight when he died. He had previously been a farmer, originally from Co. Clare. He is buried in Glasnevin Cemetery.

That night Lieutenant Grant led his men to the Shelbourne Hotel without coming under rebel fire. He later recalled:

With the aid of the manager I entered every bedroom facing the front, and had an embarrassing job, first to request the occupants to leave the rooms, and if they did not willingly comply with my request, to get them out by force if necessary. Being a Bank Holiday, and many visitors having returned from the Curragh Races, needless to say carrying out my job, I came across visitors who were keen on preserving their identity. In doing so there were many who thought it well to quietly comply with orders. At the same time I directed the members of my party to barricade the entrances to the hotel with heavy furniture. My orders having been carried out, I returned alone to the Castle, leaving the men to guard the hotel. I slipped out of the back door of the hotel into Kildare Street where I occupied the attention of snipers. I ran down Kildare Street like a hare and into [Schoolhouse] Lane and into Molesworth Street, as a number of rebels were marching along [Dawson] Street. I got into cover under the front outside wall of the Diocesan School [which Grant had attended as a boy] and lay on my tummy for about 20 minutes until the rebels had passed, after which I proceeded back to the Castle without interruption.

When Grant arrived at Dublin Castle he was brought before Major Ivor Price, whose orders had sent him to the Shelbourne Hotel in the first place. Price was fifty years old and originally from Lucan. One of his sons, Lieutenant Ernest Price, had already been killed in action on 19 March 1916, aged twenty-two, while serving with the 2nd Royal Irish Rifles on the Western Front; another son, Ivor Jnr, was serving as an officer with the Army Service Corps on the Western Front; while a third son, sixteen-year-old James Price, was a cadet with Dublin University OTC in Trinity College. Also serving with the OTC during the Rising was Major Price's brother, a 46-year-old barrister, Cadet Quartermaster-Sergeant Frederick Price.

Before the war Ivor Price had been an RIC district inspector, stationed in Athboy, Nenagh and various towns in Cos. Meath and Wicklow before being seconded to the army in 1914 and given the rank of major. (He was one of four RIC district inspectors to become involved in the Rising.) Because of his knowledge of Ireland, and because he had headed the RIC's Crimes Special Branch before the war, he was appointed director of military intelligence for Irish Command and given the task of setting up the Special Intelligence Section in Dublin Castle. In his book *Michael Collins and the Anglo-Irish War: Britain's Counterinsurgency Failure* (2011), J. B. E. Hittle wrote of Price that

it was his job to collect and analyse information on subversive activity in Ireland, including that collected by the RIC Crimes Special Branch and G Division [the detective division] of the DMP – and whatever information Admiralty NID [Naval Intelligence Division] listening stations could supply – and provide it to the army's Irish Command and the Castle. Price also co-operated with the Ministry of Munitions Intelligence Branch and the Irish

Post & Telegraph Department. With a staff of fewer than a dozen men, he concentrated his own collection efforts on mail censorship, through which his team gleaned substantial information on suspected subversives ... Price's collection network was good but his analysis and assessments left much to be desired ... When the indicators of an uprising grew stronger, Price passed these on at the theatre level through his military intelligence summaries, only to learn later that Castle officials had not bothered to read them.

On the morning of the 24th Major Price had actually arrived at Dublin Castle – minutes before Captain Seán Connolly and the Irish Citizen Army launched their attack against the Cork Hill gate – to attend a meeting with Sir Matthew Nathan, under-secretary for Ireland, and Arthur Hamilton Norway, secretary of the Post Office. Ironically, the meeting had been called to plan the arrest of prominent Sinn Féin members and republicans around the city – a response to Casement's failed attempt to land arms from Germany in Co. Kerry, which had been taken as a sign that republicans were preparing for an uprising. The office in which the meeting was being held was next to the Cork Hill gate, and Major Price and his companions heard the shot that killed Constable O'Brien and the rebel firing that followed.

Price had subsequently summoned the twenty-five men on duty in Ship Street Barracks to the Upper Castle Yard, then phoned the headquarters of Irish Command in Parkgate Street for help. It was this call that prompted Colonel Henry Cowan to telephone the main Dublin barracks and order them to send their piquets to Dublin Castle at once.

When Lieutenant Grant returned from the Shelbourne Hotel he reported to Major Price about the situation there. Though Grant had been sent out of the relative safety of Dublin Castle twice already, he was again ordered out. At midnight he received further orders to lead a detachment of 100 to 120 men from the 3rd Reserve Cavalry Brigade, including four machine-gun crews, back to the Shelbourne Hotel as soon as they were ready to depart so as to prevent the rebels from attempting to occupy the building, and also to help push them out of St Stephen's Green.

The cavalrymen began gathering their weapons, ammunition and equipment at 1:45 a.m. on Tuesday the 25th, and thirty minutes later they began to leave the castle. In the quiet darkness Lieutenant Grant led them slowly through back streets to Kildare Street. He later recorded that the party 'was under the command of a fat major, who was slow in his movements, and as speed was necessary the poor chap was almost exhausted. I am afraid I made the pace too fast for him. We managed to get through to the Shelbourne without any mishaps. We were lucky as Rebel patrols were all around.' This force also occupied the nearby United Services Club and the Alexandra Club.

Once he was back inside the Shelbourne Hotel – it was now 3:20 a.m. – Grant led the major through the now-empty front rooms. Guards were placed at all entrances to the hotel, and the ground floor windows were barricaded, while two soldiers were placed at every second window facing the green. The four machine guns were set up on the fourth floor, their crews instructed to stay hidden from view and to open fire only when they heard the signal: a whistle blast.

By now the insurgents in St Stephen's Green had another prisoner. The *Sinn Fein Rebellion Handbook* records that Station-Sergeant John Hughes of the DMP, 'while off duty in plain clothes returning to Green street Barracks, was stopped, searched, and arrested by rebels at Stephen's Green, West, between 12 midnight and 1 a.m., 25th April, and was kept in Stephen's Green Park.' Hughes was forty-eight, a native of Co. Armagh, and had served in the DMP for twenty-seven years. Towards morning, as also recorded in the *Sinn Fein Rebellion Handbook,* Hughes was released by Constance Markievicz; but

> when endeavouring to leave the park his right forearm was shattered by a gunshot fired by one of the rebels entrenched there. He remained lying in the park for about five hours, when he was discovered by Mr. Carney, Superintendent of Board of Works, who had him removed in the Corporation [city council] Ambulance to Mercer's Hospital. He had to undergo two operations for the wound, and remained a patient until 22nd July, but was unable to resume duty until 6th January, 1917.

Unarmed Persons Shot by Rebels adds that Hughes was 'taken prisoner into Stephens Green by S. Feiners. He was kept for the night and then told he could go. As he left the Green he was shot. He was left lying outside the Green where he fell for 5 hrs, till brought to Hospital by Students from Mercers Hospital. S Feiners made no attempt to dress his wounds.'

At 4 a.m. in the Shelbourne Hotel the whistle was sounded.

The machine guns overlooking the green opened fire and began raking the rebel positions below them. Soldiers in the United Services Club and the Alexandra Club also opened fire on the park. The insurgents had dug trenches, but these were next to useless when the British army had elevated firing positions and could fire straight down into them. One young insurgent, exposed and in the process of building a barricade, was hit and killed, while a comrade was wounded. Another was killed trying to escape from the park over the north-side railings, facing the hotel. Those who tried to fire back from the trenches could never get a clear shot. One machine gun ceased firing temporarily, however, after its crew came under accurate fire from Constance Markievicz, but the remainder of the British army soldiers continued to pour a heavy weight of fire on the insurgents, keeping them pinned down.

Staying low and crawling from cover to cover, the insurgents began to withdraw from their trenches. Mallin, Markievicz and the rest of the Irish Citizen Army soon withdrew to the south-west corner of the green, but still under fire from the hotel. Orders were quickly given to withdraw to the College of Surgeons, on the western side of the park, which had been occupied earlier by a rebel detachment. Realising what the insurgents were doing, the soldiers in the Shelbourne Hotel redirected some of their firing towards the College of Surgeons. The Irish Citizen Army were soon rushing out of the park and into the college, all the while under heavy machine-gun fire.

By 7 a.m. the green was empty: the Irish Citizen Army had fully withdrawn into the College of Surgeons, leaving most of their rations and medical supplies behind. They had also suffered five killed and others wounded. Mallin and his comrades would remain in the College of Surgeons for the rest of the Rising.

Lieutenant Charles Grant was still in the Shelbourne Hotel when the machine-gunners opened fire. He later wrote: 'The Green was occupied by many Rebels, there were women there, but no exception was made as women had already been found using rifles and taking part in the rebellion. Camp fires and trenches were in the Green ... The signal to fire was given. It was a cheerful but sad sight to see the campers scattering and running out of the far side of the Green.' At 6 a.m., while firing was still going on, Grant gathered the men from the 10th Royal Dublin Fusiliers and led them back to Dublin Castle, where he once again reported to Major Ivor Price.

Price would survive the Rising and on 25 May would give evidence to the Royal Commission set up to investigate the causes of the rebellion. He stated that 'the one unfortunate thing which hindered us a good deal was the attitude of the official Nationalist party [Irish Party] and their press. Whenever General Friend did anything strong in the way of suppressing or deporting the Sinn Fein leaders from Ireland, they at once deprecated it in the Nationalist press and said it was a monstrous thing to turn any man out of Ireland.' Price was awarded the Distinguished Service Order and mentioned in despatches for his services during the Rising, and was later promoted to lieutenant-colonel.

Price's office was only one of five independent intelligence offices operating in Ireland at the time, and this system was inefficient. There was a plan in 1918 to unify the various offices – perhaps with Major Price in overall command – but it never happened. When the war ended, the Special Intelligence Section was disbanded and in January 1919 Price returned to his job as a district inspector with the RIC, the same month the War of Independence began. Ivor Price later settled in England and died in November 1931, aged sixty-five.

Lieutenant Charles Grant appears to have remained in Dublin Castle for the duration of the Rising. He later recorded:

> During the rebellion, I found many opportunities of nosing into places in Dublin Castle that were normally off limits to all but a very few. I knew some of the history of the Castle to appreciate the opportunities. For example, on a couple of nights, with a few of my troops, we slept in the pews of the Royal Chapel, on the cushions on which some of the highest in the land had sat during divine service. In the chaos that arose during the rebellion, it was a case of seizing any opportunity which would give one a respite.

On Tuesday the 25th another assault was launched from Dublin Castle against the remaining rebel positions beyond the Cork Hill gate. This attack was made by the men of the 5th Royal Dublin Fusiliers, recently arrived from the Curragh, and they successfully pushed the insurgents back from their positions in the area.

However, Irish soldiers in the British army were still being killed and wounded at Dublin Castle. Sergeant-Major Patrick Brosnan was killed while in Dublin Castle – however, it was not a rebel that fired at him but a fellow-soldier. Brosnan, from Dunmanway, Co. Cork, was a former constable with the RIC. Having enlisted in Dublin after the start of the war he was now serving in the 3rd Royal Irish Fusiliers, a unit stationed on the far side of the country in Buncrana, Co. Donegal. He was in Dublin to visit his wife and children, who were living in family quarters inside Dublin Castle. When the castle was attacked, Brosnan had volunteered to help, though wearing civilian clothes, and at some point in the hours following the start of the Rising he was in the process of disarming an insurgent outside the Castle when a fellow-soldier, thinking he was a rebel, shot him. Patrick Brosnan was fifty when he died, and he is buried in Grangegorman Military Cemetery.

Meanwhile men of the 10th Royal Dublin Fusiliers were still coming under fire. Private Cecil Craddock of A Company was a native of Clonmel, a 22-year-old

Cecil Craddock from Clonmel, Co. Tipperary, in later life (Barry Dalby)

teacher and a student of divinity at Trinity College. His younger brother, Sydney, was also in the army, serving during the war as an officer with both the Royal Dublin Fusiliers and the Connaught Rangers. Cecil Craddock had enlisted in November 1915. When he was wounded his record shows that he received 'GSW [gunshot wounds] Hand Leg Jaw.' He was treated in King George V Military Hospital, and survived.

Private Craddock subsequently applied for an officer's commission. He was successful, and after a period of training in Fermoy he was commissioned in February 1917 as a second-lieutenant in the 3rd Royal Dublin Fusiliers, then based at Cóbh. At some point during the war he served in the trenches, on attachment to the 1st Royal Munster Fusiliers. In February 1919 he was demobilised, resigning his commission the following April. He is known to have suffered from health problems for the rest of his life. He later completed his divinity studies in Trinity College and was ordained a Church of Ireland minister in 1923. He served as a curate in Grangegorman Parish before moving to Manchester; his family recall that he considered the Church of Ireland 'too high-church' for his views, and so he decided to go to the Church of England. In 1952, now aged fifty-nine, he retired and returned to live in Ireland. He had developed tuberculosis, from which he never recovered, and he died in 1959 at the age of sixty-four.

On Tuesday 25 April, Lance-Corporal Thomas Cox was also wounded. A 21-year-old pattern-maker from London, he was the son of a bricklayer from Dublin. He had enlisted in December 1915, being posted to B Company, 10th Royal Dublin Fusiliers. On 25 April he was shot in the right thigh and left eyebrow. As a member of B Company he may have been part of Lieutenant Grant's piquet that had travelled from the Royal Barracks to Dublin Castle the previous day.

Cox survived his injuries and joined the war in August 1916, but on 6 February 1917 he was again injured, receiving a gunshot wound to the chest. On 25 March 1918 – four days after the German army launched its Spring Offensive, during which he was 'slightly gassed' – he was captured at Hadencourt and spent the rest of the war in a prisoner-of-war camp. He did not return home until January 1919 and was demobilised in April that year.

* * *

On Tuesday the area around the Mendicity Institution was generally quiet. The men of the 10th Royal Dublin Fusiliers had set up a barricade at the back of the building in Island Street, near the junction with Watling Street, and had also begun tunnelling through buildings from Watling Street. Inside the building the insurgents could hear them hammering away. The fact that they had mostly withdrawn from the quays allowed a dozen reinforcements to reach Seán Heuston and his men from across Queen Street Bridge, effectually doubling the size of the garrison. These reinforcements also brought a prisoner with them, a British army soldier they had captured en route.

That day and during the night nothing happened, but the following day, Wednesday the 26th, there was some early firing between the insurgents and the British army. As recorded by Stephen Gwynn, the writer and Irish Party politician, then serving as an officer with the Connaught Rangers, an 'inlying piquet' from the 10th Royal Dublin Fusiliers, positioned on the north quays, was fired on from across the river—most probably from the Mendicity Institution, though there were small groups of insurgents positioned in other buildings nearby. The fire ultimately forced this group of soldiers to withdraw.

Gwynn recorded that this group of Royal Dublin Fusiliers was commanded by Lieutenant Daniel O'Mahony-Leahy, a 38-year-old insurance broker from Shandon in Cork, who had served in South Africa with the Irish Yeomanry. He was a son-in-law of Lord Justice John Francis Moriarty, a native of Mallow, formerly solicitor-general and then attorney-general for Ireland, a man known for his fair dealing of cases connected with the 1913 Dublin Lockout. In January 1915 O'Mahony-Leahy enlisted in Dublin as a private. He was posted to the 7th Royal Dublin Fusiliers and soon joined it at the Curragh. His enlistment as a private soldier may have been intended to show how keen he was to serve, as three days after enlisting he applied for a commission; he also requested to be posted, if successful, to the 7th Royal

Second-Lieutenant Daniel O'Mahony-Leahy from Shandon, Cork (David Grant)

Dublin Fusiliers. However, General Bryan Mahon, commanding officer of the 10th (Irish) Division, requested that he be sent instead to the 6th Battalion.

O'Mahony-Leahy was commissioned in March 1915, but he was almost immediately incapacitated, as a medical report later stated, 'on account of acute rheumatism (rheumatic fever) followed by influenza and its sequelae.' When the battalion departed for Gallipoli, O'Mahony-Leahy did not go with it.

When he had recovered from his illness he was posted to the 10th Battalion in January 1916. He survived being fired at on 26 April 1916 and came through the Rising unhurt. He then entered the trenches with the 10th Royal Dublin Fusiliers in August 1916. However, in mid-November he was sent to a hospital in France, again suffering from illness. Before the end of the month his condition had worsened and he was evacuated home, to be treated in Leopardstown Hospital, Co. Dublin. By February 1917 he was well enough to carry out light duties, and he was subsequently posted to the 11th Battalion in Dublin. By June he was found fit for overseas service but in 'a tropical or sub-tropical command' only. The army considered sending him to Africa but ultimately decided to send him to India.

As a result, O'Mahony-Leahy – who also owned and raced horses, an interest he developed after returning from South Africa – began selling his horses in preparation for the move. As it turned out, however, his health deteriorated and he was again found unfit for service throughout 1917. It would seem that he was never sent overseas again, and in April 1919 he was demobilised, finishing the war with the 3rd Battalion in Grimsby, Lincolnshire. He had been recommended for promotion to captain but did not receive it, because of a lack of vacancies. He later settled in Stackallen House, near Slane, Co. Meath, where he became a well-known racehorse owner. He died in August 1937, aged fifty-nine.

* * *

On the same day that Lieutenant O'Mahony-Leahy's piquet was fired on, the men of the 10th Royal Dublin Fusiliers were finally preparing for an assault against the Mendicity Institution. Brigadier-General Lowe had earlier decided to create two inner cordons around the GPO and the Four Courts, but to do this he had identified two rebel outposts that needed to be secured first. Liberty Hall was one, which the 3rd Royal Irish Regiment and the Ulster Composite Battalion were ordered to capture (though, as it turned out, there was no one in the building), while the Mendicity Institution, which was protecting the Four Courts, was the second.

The battle for the Mendicity Institution did not begin, however, with a loud burst of firing but with the gentler sound of knocking. From about 6 a.m. the men of the 10th Royal Dublin Fusiliers began knocking on the doors of nearby houses, asking the people inside to leave for their own safety. Once the area was cleared of civilians – though crowds of onlookers still gathered nearby – the battalion took up firing positions in Bonham Street, Bridgefoot Street, Thomas Street and Watling Street and about midday launched their assault.

While one group advanced from the Royal Barracks and began crossing Queen Street Bridge under heavy rebel fire (with a crowd of onlookers watching them from Queen Street), exactly as Lieutenant Charles Grant and his piquet had done two days previously, the soldiers on the south side began moving along Usher's Island towards the front gate of the Mendicity Institution. Bombers were ordered to get as close as possible, and once in position they began furiously throwing grenades through the building's windows. Some detonated inside, while others were picked up by desperate rebels who were quick enough to throw the grenades back outside.

As more grenades were lobbed into the building the Volunteers and the Royal Dublin Fusiliers kept up a heavy fire on one another. However, the insurgents were simply outnumbered and outgunned, and fifteen minutes after the assault on the building had begun, and approximately an hour after the British army had begun moving in, Heuston was forced to surrender.

As with other battles of the Rising, when the survivors were assembled outside, the soldiers were amazed by how few they had been fighting against – and, at the Mendicity Institution, how young they were. Having been ordered to hold out for only a couple of hours, Heuston and his men had occupied their position for two days. Captain Richard Balfe of D Company, 1st Battalion, Irish Volunteers (also a member of Fianna Éireann), later recorded what happened.

> Heuston ordered the surrender and put out a white sheet as a flag but we were immediately attacked again. Eventually the British accepted the surrender but shot one of the men in the process, namely Peter Wilson of Swords. Being injured at this time I was left behind when the Company surrendered as I was thought to be dead. I am not familiar with what subsequently happened outside the Institute. Some time late in the evening I heard the British breaking in and then after an interval a British Officer appeared armed with two automatics; also a Dublin Fusilier arrived with fixed bayonet. I was at this time able to sit up but had no use of my legs. While they were deciding whether to use a bayonet or a bullet on me an Officer of the R.A.M.C. [Royal Army Medical Corps] came in and claimed me as his prisoner saying that there had been enough of this dirty work. I was removed to King George V Hospital (now St. Bricin's) where I received rough handling by Army Orderlies until rescued. Although not recovered I was removed in an armed ambulance to Richmond Barracks.

Two Irishmen in the British army who were present at the battle for the Mendicity Institution were Captain Alfred MacDermott and Lieutenant William Connolly. MacDermott, a wine merchant's clerk from Co. Wicklow, was living at Burgh Quay, Dublin, when he enlisted. In September 1914, at the age of thirty-one, he was commissioned as a lieutenant in the 7th Royal Dublin Fusiliers. He landed at Suvla Bay in Gallipoli on 7 August 1915 and the following day was promoted captain. Two weeks later, however, he received multiple small fragments of shrapnel to the face that destroyed most of his teeth while also suffering concussion from the shell burst, which resulted in partial deafness in his left ear as well as tinnitus. He was evacuated to England, and though the shrapnel fragments were removed he was soon complaining of headaches and intermittent heart palpitations. With no teeth left, he had to have dentures fitted to replace them. He was subsequently given a period of leave, which he spent at Blessington, Co. Wicklow.

By April 1916, MacDermott was serving with the 4th Royal Dublin Fusiliers. Based in Templemore, Co. Tipperary, the battalion arrived in Dublin during the afternoon of the 25th. Captain MacDermott travelled with it but appears to have ended up fighting alongside the 10th Battalion during the battle for the Mendicity

Institution. (There is evidence that at this point a large number of men from the 5th Battalion were also working alongside the 10th Battalion and may even have played a significant role in defeating the insurgents in the Mendicity Institution.) MacDermott did not know it at the time, but during the Rising embarkation orders to return to the war were on their way to him but were delayed until after the fighting in Dublin had ended. Had they arrived on time he might not have been in Ireland when the Rising began.

Captain MacDermott was called as a witness during the court-martial of Seán Heuston on 4 May. He stated:

> On 26 April I was present when the Mendicity Institution was taken by assault by a party of the 10th Royal Dublin Fusiliers. Twenty-three men surrendered on that occasion. I identify the four prisoners as having been in the body of men who surrendered. They left their arms except their revolvers in the Mendicity Institute when they surrendered. Some of them still wore revolvers. One officer of the 10th Royal Dublin Fusiliers [Lieutenant Gerald Neilan] was killed and 9 men wounded by fire from this Institute on the 24th April. I searched the building when they surrendered. I found several rifles, several thousand rounds of ammunition for both revolvers and rifles. I found 6 or 7 bombs charged and with fuses in them ready for use.
>
> I found the following papers: An order signed by James Connolly, one of the signatories to the Irish Republic Proclamation, directing 'Capt. Houston' to 'Seize the Mendicity at all costs.' Also papers detailing men for various duties in the Mendicity Institute. All these papers are headed 'Army of the Irish Republic.' Also two message books signed by Heuston 'Capt.' One contains copies of messages sent to 'Comdt. General Connolly' giving particulars of the situation in the Institute. The other message book contains copies of messages commencing on the 22nd April two days before the outbreak. One message contains a reference to MacDonagh who is stated to have just left Heuston. Another is a message to 'all members of D Coy. 1st Batn.' stating that the parade for the 23rd is cancelled and all rumours are to be ignored. Another message dated the 23rd states 'I hope we will be able to do better next time.'

Captain MacDermott then testified that Seán Heuston had commanded the rebels who surrendered on 26 April at the Mendicity Institution.

MacDermott later returned to the war, serving in Salonika, Egypt, Palestine and France; he was mentioned in despatches in July 1917 and briefly held the rank of acting major. He stayed in the army, going on to serve in the army of occupation in Germany, before relinquishing his commission in March 1920.

William Connolly was born in New York to Irish parents, who were temporarily living in America at the time. He attended Blackrock College before moving to Carterton, Oxfordshire. He had been working in the National Insurance Audit

Department of the civil service since September 1913 and in September 1914 was living in Manchester. He enlisted as a private in the 2nd/15th (County of London) Battalion of the London Regiment (also known as the Prince of Wales's Own Civil Service Rifles). This was part of the Territorial Force, an organisation intended only for home service, whose members had to volunteer to serve overseas. Eight days after enlisting, Private Connolly signed an agreement to be sent wherever he was needed. In November 1914 he was transferred to E Company, 1st/15th (County of London) Battalion, a front-line unit, at about the same time that this battalion moved to Watford in Hertfordshire.

On 18 March the battalion landed in France, but Connolly had left it seven days earlier to train as an officer. He specifically asked to be commissioned in an Irish infantry battalion. He ultimately became a lieutenant in the 10th Royal Dublin Fusiliers and took part in the fighting around the Mendicity Institution. Like Captain Alfred MacDermott, he was called as a witness at the court-martial of Seán Heuston and his three comrades.

> I was present when 23 men surrendered on the 26th April at the Mendicity Institute. I identify the four prisoners before the court as being amongst them. The leader was J. J. Heuston. I was present when the troops were fired on from the Mendicity Institute on the 24th April, when Lieutenant G. A. Neilan was killed and 6 men wounded to my knowledge. Heuston was without a coat when he surrendered and also had no hat on. He was not in the uniform of the Irish Volunteers. I was present when the building was searched and found arms and ammunition in it and also the documents now before the court. Among the arms there were some old German Mausers. Among the ammunition there were two cardboard boxes of 'Spange' German ammunition.

On 18 August, Lieutenant Connolly landed in France with the 10th Royal Dublin Fusiliers. By November he had been promoted to captain, but on 13 November he was severely wounded at Beaumont-Hamel, receiving a gunshot wound in the buttocks. A medical report stated that the wound was 'a large open wound 13" [inches] long, 6" wide, 3" deep … He has much deficiency in left buttock and the action and strength of his left leg is greatly impaired. This Officer states he has pain in the track of the sciatic nerve which is aggravated by cold. He appears to be slowly improving.'

By the end of March 1917 he was well enough to return to light duty and he joined the 11th Battalion in Dublin. By October, however, it had become apparent that his wounds would prevent him from ever serving in the infantry again, and so he transferred to the Labour Corps, joining it at Fort Charles, Kinsale. By February 1918 he was serving in Belfast. He relinquished his commission in March 1919, now aged twenty-five, and returned to live in Oxfordshire.

* * *

Second-Lieutenant William John 'Jack' Mount from Belturbet, Co. Cavan, a close friend of insurgent leader Seán Heuston from before the war (David Grant)

For at least one Irish soldier in the 10th Royal Dublin Fusiliers the fight for the Mendicity Institution had a very personal side to it. Before the war William John 'Jack' Mount from Belturbet, Co. Cavan, had worked as a clerk with the Great Southern and Western Railway in Kingsbridge Station. A supporter of Home Rule, he had worked under, and had become a friend of, Seán Heuston, who was employed by the GSWR as a clerk in the station (which would be renamed in his honour in 1966).

In August 1914 Jack Mount enlisted as a private in D Company, 7th Royal Dublin Fusiliers, a unit known as the Dublin Pals. He was promoted to lance-corporal in June 1915. His battalion landed at Gallipoli on 7 August 1915, and two days later Lance-Corporal Mount joined them at Suvla Bay. He obviously displayed the potential for leadership, as in mid-September, while still fighting in Gallipoli, he was commissioned as a second-lieutenant and posted to the 1st Battalion – a regular army battalion containing veterans of the Gallipoli landings – in April. He was soon invalided home to Ireland, however, probably because of sickness, and was transferred to the 10th Battalion in time to take part in the defeat of the Rising. Second-Lieutenant Mount was now twenty-three years old. His new battalion would find itself fighting against Jack Mount's old friend Seán Heuston and his garrison of Irish Volunteers in the Mendicity Institution.

Heuston's brother would later write that it was Second-Lieutenant Mount who accepted the surrender of the garrison in the Mendicity Institution. Mount denied this, but as a junior officer with personal ties to the leader of the garrison he may well have been sent to take Heuston's surrender, perhaps to ensure that there was no further trouble. It is also alleged that Mount, together with some other soldiers of the 10th Royal Dublin Fusiliers, wanted to release Heuston after the Rising, apparently even appealing to higher command on the grounds

Royal Dublin Fusiliers, Four Courts barricade (from *Dublin and the Great War, 1914–1918*)

that Heuston was no longer a threat. One thing that is certain is that, while imprisoned, Heuston wrote to the adjutant of Arbour Hill Prison asking him to thank Second-Lieutenant Mount for his kindness at the time of the surrender, thus confirming that, at the very least, Mount was present at the event.

Jack Mount was soon promoted to lieutenant and later entered the war with the 10th Royal Dublin Fusiliers. Then, on 13 October 1916, as recorded in the battalion war diary, at 6:10 p.m. 'Lt Mount and 4 Other Ranks left the head of 6th Avenue [a trench] to post LG [Lewis gun] in Redan Crater.' Fifteen minutes later 'Sgt Liddy returned from the LG party stating that party was bombed by enemy patrol.' Rescue and search parties were sent forward, but they failed to find Mount and his men. It was finally concluded that 'Enemy patrol seems to have worked under a pre-arranged plan beginning with smoke bombs. The LG post must have been under observation for some time.'

In fact Mount and his men had been taken prisoner. Having served in the trenches for only two months, Jack Mount spent the next twenty-six months in captivity, being repatriated only after the end of the war on 18 December 1918. After the war he lived on the North Circular Road but by 1920 he was living in Natal, South Africa. It appears that he returned to Ireland at some point and, after marrying, worked in the Provincial Bank of Ireland at St Stephen's Green before returning to Africa. During the 1950s it is known that, now in his sixties, he was retired and living in Southern Rhodesia (Zimbabwe).

* * *

After the fall of the Mendicity Institution the soldiers of the 10th Royal Dublin Fusiliers moved further along the quays and established positions at Usher's Quay and in buildings on the south side of Whitworth Bridge (commonly called Church Street Bridge, now Father Mathew Bridge). Here they would have seen other soldiers set up an artillery gun to the east in Lower Exchange Street, behind Essex Quay, and open fire – ineffectively – with shrapnel shells at the Irish Volunteers' main position in the Four Courts.

The artillery soon stopped firing, and the Royal Dublin Fusiliers took over by firing at the western end of the Four Courts and at the barricade in Church Street. This prompted two insurgents, Lieutenant Peadar Clancy and Volunteer Tom Smart, to rush out from under cover, carrying cans of petrol, cross the Liffey, break into the buildings the Royal Dublin Fusiliers were in, and set them alight. They managed to make it safely back to the Four Courts, while the soldiers were forced to evacuate their positions.

Other soldiers of the Royal Dublin Fusiliers had set up a machine gun near Smithfield, which continued to fire at the western end of the Four Courts. In addition, elements of the 2nd/6th Sherwood Foresters also began surrounding the Four Courts from Thursday the 27th. The 10th Royal Dublin Fusiliers continued fighting in this area until the Rising ended, and the battalion is known to have been present for the surrender of the Four Courts garrison. Joseph McDonough of C Company, 1st Battalion, Irish Volunteers – who had previously been based in the Church Street area during the Rising – recorded:

> When we got into the Four Courts we found that the 'Pals' Battalion [10th Battalion] of the Dublin Fusiliers (a British Regiment) was lined up in Charles St. and we were ordered to proceed to the railings separating the Four Courts from Charles St. and hand our arms through the railing to the British. While I was doing this I recognised a sergeant of the Dublin Fusiliers who had been a customer of mine in our hairdresser's shop in Dorset St. He recognised me, but beyond that took no further notice. I met him many times afterwards and he never referred to the incident.

The Royal Dublin Fusiliers were also involved in the surrender of Jacob's factory, as recorded by Lieutenant John MacDonagh (brother of Commandant Thomas MacDonagh). He noted that after the garrison had surrendered 'our arms were taken from us. Major McBride had a beautiful rifle that had been presented to him in commemoration of his Boer campaign. It was suitably inscribed and a Dublin Fusilier thinking no doubt he would get a stripe for his pains who read that inscription, told his officer that McBride had fought against the British in the Boer War. The officer looked at the rifle, but took no further notice of the matter.'

Finally, in the days that followed, the regiment was involved in escorting prisoners to the docks for deporting. As recorded by two members of the Irish Volunteers from Killarney, Michael Spillane and Michael O'Sullivan, 'the following evening a party for deportation were picked and marched to the North Wall under an escort of the Dublin Fusiliers, and thousands lined the streets and gave the prisoners a great send off.' The change in public opinion was already beginning to be seen.

By the time the fighting had stopped, the 10th Royal Dublin Fusiliers had suffered several more wounded, including Lance-Corporal Michael Nolan from Monasterevin, Co. Kildare, who later went on to serve in the Labour Corps. The battalion suffered a confirmed total of four men killed in action (three of whom were Irish) and a further nine wounded (seven Irish). However, because the battalion to which other killed and wounded belonged was not recorded, the unit may have suffered an additional one man killed. This was nineteen-year-old Private James Byrne from Dublin, who was officially attached to the regimental depot in Naas. He may have been on leave in Dublin at the time of the Rising (which seems likely, given that his unit was in Naas) and was either called on to help or travelled to a barracks to offer his services. A veteran of Gallipoli, he died on 1 May 1916 of wounds received during the Rising and is buried in Grangegorman Military Cemetery. On his headstone are the words *Not a day goes by, dear Jim, that I do not think of you. Aunt Sarah.*

The battalion may also have suffered a further sixteen wounded, thirteen of whom were Irish. These were Private William Baird from Dublin; Private Thomas Barnes from Dublin (probably injured while fighting with the 10th Battalion in the vicinity of the Mendicity Institution, as records show that he was admitted to the nearby Dr Steevens' Hospital); Private D. Byrne from Dublin; Private Henry Byrne from Lucan; Lance-Corporal Matthew Kerrigan (a former railway labourer from Kilmainham); Private J. E. Healy from Co. Clare; Private P. Healy from Co. Cork; Private J. Lawlor from Dublin; Private Bernard McAlister (a former RIC constable from Granard, Co. Longford, son of a local metal-moulder and tinsmith, known to have been wounded in Dublin Castle); Private M. McNally from Dublin; Lance-Corporal M. Mullins (shot in the leg and taken to the Voluntary Aid Detachment hospital in Trinity College); Lance-Corporal Michael Smullen (a former cab-driver from Seville Place, Dublin, who later died of wounds received on the Western Front on 6 May 1918 while serving with the 1st Battalion, and is buried in Nieppe-Bois (Rue-Du-Bois) British Cemetery, Vieux-Berquin); and Private Robert Smyth from Dromore, Co. Down (later killed in action on 8 October 1918 while serving with the 6th Battalion, who now lies buried in Serain Communal Cemetery Extension).

Another wounded man and confirmed member of the 10th Royal Dublin Fusiliers was Corporal Martin Dolan, a 25-year-old from Lower Bridge Street, Dublin. In September 1915 he enlisted in the 5th Battalion, which had only just returned to the Curragh, having previously been based in Sittingbourne, Kent. Dolan had earlier worked as a salesman, traveller and delivery clerk for an egg and butter merchant in Little Britain Street. He was one of the men who formed the new 'Commercial Company' of the 5th Royal Dublin Fusiliers but which in

8th (King's Royal Irish) Hussars cap badge
(Author's Collection)

fact became the nucleus of the 10th Battalion. He was soon a corporal and orderly-room clerk with A Company, 10th Battalion.

During the Rising, Corporal Dolan received a gunshot wound to his thigh. By the end of July he had recovered and was subsequently posted to C Company, 11th Battalion, in Dublin. By February 1917 it had become apparent that Corporal Dolan's injuries were preventing him from serving satisfactorily, and on 8 February he was 'sent to his home on warrant with orders to await instructions as to his final discharge; he has been given £1 advance and a suit of plain clothes.' He was ultimately discharged as 'no longer physically fit for war service,' because of the injuries he received during the Rising. On 1 March 1917 the discharge came into effect, and shortly afterwards he wrote to the army applying for his Silver War Badge (worn to forestall women who handed a white feather to men who appeared to be able-bodied so as to humiliate them into joining up). Because of his previous work as an orderly-room clerk he also requested help with finding 'light clerical work,' while acknowledging at the same time that he had 'not much clerical training.' He remained living in Dublin for the rest of his life and died in 1945, aged fifty-four.

* * *

Also wounded while serving in the 10th Royal Dublin Fusiliers during the Easter Rising was Private Joseph Coroner. Aged thirty-one and from St James's Parish in the south-west of the city, he had enlisted as far back as 1902, at the age of eighteen, having previously worked as a messenger and then as a printer while living in Abercorn Terrace in Inchicore. He was posted to the 8th (King's Royal Irish) Hussars at the Curragh for training. Over the next three years he served variously with the 13th, 11th (Prince Albert's Own) and 14th (King's) Hussars, while also being awarded a good-conduct badge in September 1904.

In September 1905 he left the regular army and returned to live in Dublin, first staying with his father in Airmount Cottage, Emmet Road, Inchicore. However, he remained a member of the reserve, and in the meantime he married and settled in Queen Street. When the war began he was called up. Now aged twenty-nine, he was mobilised at Scarborough, Yorkshire, on 5 August 1914 and posted to the 20th Hussars and on the 22nd landed in France. Four months later, on 22 December, he was found 'drunk in billets on active service' and also 'creating a disturbance in his billets,' for which he was given seventy-two hours of field punishment.

The trenches of the First World War may have been taking their toll on Joseph Coroner. He was in hospital in Rouen from 29 March to 2 May 1915; and two days after leaving hospital he was found drunk again in his billet at 10:45 a.m. He had never committed a military offence during his time with the army between 1902 and 1905 and had even been awarded a good-conduct badge, but now he had been found drunk twice in the space of six months.

And the lapses in discipline did not end there. After being given seven days' field punishment no. 1 for this latest breach of conduct he was given a further twenty-eight days of this cruel punishment for being absent from his duty as a stable guard between 9:15 a.m. and 3:30 p.m. on 29 June.

He returned to duty at the end of July, but by mid-September he had been posted home to the regimental depot, as he was now being discharged 'on termination of his 1st period of engagement,' in accordance with regulations, and on 21 September 1915 he left the army. It was noted that he wanted to find work as a groom or a porter. This obviously never happened, as two months later a Dublin recruiting office wired a cavalry centre in York to know what Joseph Coroner's character had been when he was discharged.

By April 1916, now aged thirty, Coroner was back in uniform and serving in the 10th Royal Dublin Fusiliers. (His older brother Charles was a soldier in the 4th Battalion of the same regiment.) He was wounded during the Rising, though the records do not state how or where, and – like Private Francis Brennan – he may have found himself fighting in the vicinity of his own home. His wife and children lived in Queen Street, just across the Liffey from the Mendicity Institution, a street in which the men of the 10th Royal Dublin Fusiliers found themselves at several points during the Rising.

Joseph Coroner was one of the many men who survived the Rising but did not survive the trenches. After serving in France with the 10th Royal Dublin Fusiliers he was killed in action on 20 November 1917. He was thirty-two years old, and he now lies in Croisilles British Cemetery. He left a widow and three children.

* * *

Private William O'Riordan had a similar fate after the Rising. From the Cork-Tipperary border near Ballyporeen, he grew up in Enniskean, Co. Cork. His father was a mason and his mother was an assistant teacher. By the time William enlisted, his father had died and his mother was living in Leinster Street, off North Strand Road. Though only seventeen, he fought with the 10th Royal Dublin Fusiliers during the Rising and was wounded by rebel fire. He recovered, but after being sent to the war he was killed on 13 November 1916 at Beaumont-Hamel on the Somme. His body was never recovered and his name is commemorated on the Thiepval Memorial.

Other men of the 10th Royal Dublin Fusiliers came through the Rising unhurt only to be killed in the trenches. Lance-Corporal William Butler, from Moy, Co. Tyrone, son of a Trinity College librarian, grew up in Kingstown (Dún

Lance-Corporal Evans Hadden
from Tinahely, Co. Wicklow
(Helen Masterson)

Laoghaire). In February 1916 he enlisted, at the age of nineteen. He came through
the Rising unhurt and was later sent overseas with his battalion. On 24 April 1917
– the first anniversary of the Rising – he died at No. 19 Casualty Clearing Station
of wounds received while commanding a machine-gun detachment during the
Battle of Gavrelle. Today his remains lie buried in Duisans British Cemetery at
Étrun, and his name is commemorated on the roll of honour in Christ Church,
Dún Laoghaire. (Butler's younger brother, Robert, also took part in the Rising as
a member of Dublin University OTC. He survived the war and remained in the
army but did not survive the Second World War. He died in 1941, and his name is
also commemorated in Christ Church, Dún Laoghaire.)

   Another man who suffered a strangely similar fate was Evans Hadden. A
native of Tinahely, Co. Wicklow, son of a farmer, he attended Methodist College
in Belfast between 1911 and 1914 before enlisting in October 1915 at the age of
eighteen. He was soon promoted to lance-corporal and then acting corporal
and fought with the 10th Royal Dublin Fusiliers during the Rising. When the
battalion was serving in France he commanded a Lewis machine-gun section in
the trenches, where, on either 29 or 30 April 1917, during the Battle of Gavrelle,
he was hit in the stomach by a fragment of a shell or a grenade. He did not die
instantly but lingered on for several days before dying on 2 May at Aubigny.

   A list of past pupils who died in the war was later published by Methodist
College. Its entry on Evans Hadden states: 'The death of this young soldier has

a sombre significance for the College. We recalled that he was a member of the winning cup-team of 1913–1914 with Fred Williamson, Cyril Cullen and Eric M. Wilson. All four had before them the wide vistas of ambition and with high-hearted courage chose what was to be the way of death.' The *Weekly Irish Times* of 8 September 1917 recorded that Hadden 'offered himself for active service shortly after the outbreak of war, but was rejected on account of age (17). On his third attempt he was accepted in October, 1915 ... He went to the front with his battalion in August, 1916, where, according to a letter from his sergeant, he went through much tough work cheerfully, and was beloved by his comrades.' He now lies in Duisans British Cemetery at Étrun – the same cemetery as Lance-Corporal William Butler.

* * *

One other uninjured veteran of the Rising who died in the trenches was Second-Lieutenant William Brereton-Barry. Born in Lower Mount Street, Dublin, in 1898, he was a son of Judge Ralph Brereton-Barry of the County Court and Claire Roche from Dublin, daughter of William Roche, a former crown solicitor for Co. Limerick. By the start of the First World War the family were living in Glenageary, Co. Dublin, and William was eighteen. While attending the Oratory School in Birmingham he had been an OTC cadet from March 1913 to December 1914. He then entered Trinity College, Dublin, and become a member of Dublin University OTC from February 1915, and in January 1916 he applied for an army commission. The City and County of Dublin Recruiting Committee, based at 102 Grafton Street, wrote him a letter of recommendation, stating that the committee

> desires to support very strongly the application of Mr. Barry (second son of Judge Brereton Barry) for a temporary commission in an infantry regiment. He is a gentleman who as by education and military training qualified himself for such an appointment. His father, Judge Brereton Barry, has been an indefatigable worker upon this Committee, has been a prominent speaker at its public meetings, and has contributed largely to the success of recruiting in both the City and County of Dublin.

William was subsequently commissioned as a second-lieutenant in the 10th Royal Dublin Fusiliers. He took part in the defeat of the Easter Rising, which he came through without being wounded, but he did not travel overseas when his battalion went to the war in August; instead he was transferred to the 11th Battalion, a new reserve battalion based in Dublin.

On 5 December 1916 Brereton-Barry was tried by general court-martial on the charge of being drunk on 20 November. He was found guilty and sentenced to be severely reprimanded. In March 1917 he finally entered the war when he landed in France. He was posted to the 9th Royal Dublin Fusiliers, part of the 16th (Irish) Division. He fought for five months with his new battalion and was awarded a parchment certificate for gallant conduct and devotion to duty on 16 April, signed by the commanding officer of the division, General William Hickie. Then, on 16 August, the day of the disastrous Battle of Frezenberg Ridge, Barry was reported wounded and missing.

On 23 August his father received the following telegram: 'Regret to inform you that 2/Lieut W.R. Brereton-Barry is reported wounded & missing sixteenth august. Further reports will be sent if received.' No word was received for some months. A maternal relative of William's, Sir George Roche, former president of the Law Society of Ireland, wrote to the War Office in November. It replied that it had no further information and that when it had, this would be sent directly to William's father. The family were no doubt hoping that William would turn up in either a hospital or a German prisoner-of-war camp.

On 16 March 1918 Judge Brereton-Barry received the following information:

> Further enquiries have been made at the base. All the available witnesses were closely interrogated by Major J.P. Hunt D.S.O., and Captain H. Hurst M.C., both in regard to any information they might have of this officer's fate and in regard to any previous statements made by them. 'In no case,' Major Hunt says, 'Could we get a witness to state with certainty the actual facts as they happened.' Captain Hurst states that he personally examined all available witnesses on their statements to Major Hunt but no further information was obtainable, that Serjeant Fagan stated that he helped to dress Lieutenant Barry's wounds (left arm) in the early morning of 16th August, that Private Hill stated that he was in a shell hole with the officer on the evening of the 16th, Lieutenant Barry's leg was then broken, and that in response to a letter from Lieutenant Barry, a stretcher party went out to look for him after dark on the evening of the 16th August, 1917, but without success. Captain Hurst adds, that in view of the statements made he is of opinion that Lieutenant Barry's death may be assumed. It is stated that no further information is available at the Base. As a result of the exhaustive investigation made, the Army Council fear that there can now be no possible hope that 2nd Lieutenant Brereton Barry is alive, and would be prepared to consider official acceptance of death on the ground of lapse of time and I am to ask you to inform this office whether you would wish this course to be taken.

Brereton-Barry's father was forced to accept finally that his son was dead. But the official investigation must not have been as detailed as was claimed, for two months earlier, in January 1918, the commanding officer of the 4th Royal Dublin Fusiliers had sent a report to the War Office based on witness statements from men under his command who had been on Frezenberg Ridge with Second-Lieutenant Brereton-Barry. The two men, Lance-Corporal Meckin and Sergeant McCullagh, jointly stated that

Zero [hour] was about 4.45.a.m., when the Battalion immediately rose from front lines to advance. 2nd Lieut. Barry was hit at once in the arm, and immediately went back to Battalion Headquarters in order to get it dressed by Stretcher Bearers. The Battalion advance was almost immediately held up, and started to consolidate in a line of shell holes. Meanwhile, 2nd Lieut. Barry had been dressed, and volunteered to return at once for duty with B. Company. He went forward, and Sergt. McCullagh met him in the shell hole where the Company was waiting to advance. Immediately our 2nd Barrage moved forward, and the Battalion attempted to push forward, both N.C.O's lost sight of 2nd Lieut. Barry.

Sergt. McCullagh states that at about 10.30.a.m., when moved round to see how the situation stood, [he] found 2nd Lieut. Barry and Lance. Corpl. Meckin lying together in a shell hole, both wounded. 2nd Lieut. Barry was conscious and told him that a shell had hit almost between his legs. Both N.C.O's did all they could for him, binding up the wounds with first field dressing, and giving him both rum and cocoa, but during the day he grew steadily weaker. During day light, it was impossible to move him, but when night came, Sergt. McCullagh volunteered to carry him on his back as far as Battalion Headquarters. This 2nd Lieut. Barry would not allow, saying he was a heavy man, and in addition to McCullagh not being able to do it, it would give him too much pain.

Both N.C.O's started at about 9.p.m., to make their way back to Battalion Headquarters, where they reported to 2nd Lieut. J.G. Greene, the Battalion Signalling Officer of the 9th Bn. R. Dub. Fus., Lce. Cpl. Meckin was sent back by the Medical Officer. Sergt. McCullagh told 2nd Lieut. Greene what the situation was, and where 2nd Lieut. Barry was lying badly wounded. Mr. Greene said he would do what he could, but almost immediately afterwards, the situation became extremely critical, as the enemy brought down a very heavy barrage on both what was our front line and also no man's land, and another attack was expected. Our Artillery also opened heavily. This would be about 9.30.p.m.

Next morning, at day light, 2nd Lt. Greene asked this time Sgt. McCullagh to point out exactly where he thought 2nd Lt. Barry was lying, and from outside Battalion Headquarters it was possible to do so, the exact shell hole being picked out by means of a shattered telegraph pole which was beside it. Immediately afterwards Sgt. McCullagh was hit by shellfire, but before going back, he saw 2nd Lt. Greene start off, wearing two waterbottles, to look for 2nd Lt. Barry.

Since then, Sgt. McCullagh has heard nothing more, except a letter from 2nd Lt. Greene saying that his search was entirely fruitless, and that he had been reluctantly driven to the conclusion that the enemy barrage and our own must have proved fatal to 2nd Lt. Barry.

There was one last witness statement that could have revealed exactly how William Brereton-Barry died but that had been discarded because of a simple error. Lieutenant Charles Kennedy of the Leinster Regiment sent a witness statement to the garrison adjutant in Dublin Castle on 2 January 1918. The letter was sent from Monkstown Auxiliary Hospital in Co. Dublin, where he was obviously recovering from injuries; but somewhere along the line 'Leinster Regiment' became 'Lincolnshire Regiment', and as no record of a Lieutenant Charles Michael Kennedy in the Lincolnshire Regiment could be found they chose not to accept his statement as valid. It stated that just after the Battle of Frezenberg Ridge

> I heard the Dublins were near us in the line so I went over to see Lieut. Barry. On arriving at the Battalion I was informed that there were two Barry's there and one was wounded. A Sergeant of the R.D.F. [Royal Dublin Fusiliers] said he would take me to the place where Lieut. Barry was and pointed out a stretcher on which he had been lying. While we were talking a shell burst near the stretcher and as far as we could see, stretcher and all were blown away. Shortly after I was told that I was wanted with my own Battalion, so I returned and heard no more of the Dublins as we were relieved soon after and I was invalided home. I do not know for certain if this was Judge Barry's son, but presume it was as I heard he was missing and heard of no other person of that name in the R.D.F.

No other Barry was killed with the Royal Dublin Fusiliers during August 1917, and so this has to mean that he was recovered from the battlefield by stretcher-bearers only to be vaporised by a shell soon after.

Second-Lieutenant William Brereton Barry was only nineteen when he died on 16 or 17 August 1917. A fellow-officer later wrote that 'he was a splendid fellow; whenever I mention his name, both officers and men speak of him as one who was respected by all, because he knew his job, and did it with pluck and cheerfulness. The Army could do with hundreds like him.' With no known grave, William Brereton-Barry is commemorated on the Tyne Cot Memorial.

* * *

As with the other regiments that fought during the Easter Rising, several men from the 10th Royal Dublin Fusiliers were decorated for their part in the fight. One such man was 27-year-old Second-Lieutenant Alphonsus Henchy, who was awarded the Military Cross after the Rising. From Freshford, Co. Kilkenny, he attended De La Salle College in Waterford before going on to become a teacher. He was not the first teacher in his family, as his father, John Henchy, was a national school teacher from Co. Clare. In September 1914 Alphonsus Henchy left his job and enlisted in Dublin. He soon found himself serving as a trooper with the South Irish Horse, based in Beggarsbush Barracks; by August 1915 he was in Wensley Camp at Leyburn, Yorkshire.

On 20 August he applied for an officer's commission, specifically requesting to be commissioned into the 10th Royal Dublin Fusiliers if successful. By December his application had been approved, and he travelled to Cork to begin officer training. In February 1916 he was commissioned, soon joining the 10th Battalion as a new second-lieutenant. (His brothers Albert and Dudley were officers in the 5th and 7th Battalion, respectively.) On his discharge from the South Irish Horse his conduct was considered 'very good,' and he was described as 'honest, sober and hardworking.'

After the Rising he was awarded the Military Cross, for reasons that are not stated, simply 'in connection with the Dublin Rising.' He subsequently entered the trenches when the 10th Royal Dublin Fusiliers joined the war in August. Then, on 12 October, the battalion war diary records: '6.35 p.m. Patrol left head of 1st Avenue [a trench] returning 11.15 p.m. with nothing unusual from the enemy to report. Casualties 1 wounded. Patrol worked along enemy wire and into sap [a tunnel under an enemy position]. A tunnel from Redan [a shell crater] to the enemy line suspected. 2 Lt A W Henchy complimented on his patrol report by the Brigadier.'

The following day, when Lieutenant Jack Mount went missing after leading a machine-gun patrol to Redan Crater, Second-Lieutenant Henchy was sent out with a rescue party of bombers to find him. He was unsuccessful – Mount and his men had already been taken prisoner – and Henchy was wounded by enemy fire while out in no man's land. His wounds necessitated him being evacuated to England.

It was not until March 1918, now aged twenty-nine and a lieutenant, that Alphonsus Henchy returned to the war. Records show, however, that by September he was back in an English hospital. When he was released, just as the war was ending, he was posted to the 3rd Royal Dublin Fusiliers in Grimsby, Lincolnshire. He relinquished his commission in September 1919.

However, he did not stay out of uniform for long. Shortly after his marriage, in June 1920 he was commissioned again as a lieutenant and sent to Saint-Pol-sur-Ternoise, north of Amiens, for duty as a surveyor with the Directorate-General of Resettlement and Employment. He served in France for five months until he returned to England in January 1921, and immediately relinquished his second commission 'on ceasing to be employed.'

Henchy later became a film director, working at Ealing Studios, near London. When the Second World War began, at the age of fifty Henchy applied to be put on the reserve list. He remained on this list for nine years, finally having his name withdrawn from it in October 1948. Eleven years later, in 1959, now aged seventy, Alphonsus Henchy died in St Mary's Abbot Hospital in London.

* * *

It is worth mentioning that not every man in the 10th Royal Dublin Fusiliers agreed with fighting against the insurgents in Dublin. Though he was certainly in a minority, there was at least one officer in the battalion who did not wish to take up arms against his fellow-Irishmen.

In April 1916 Second-Lieutenant Robert Barton was thirty-five years old. Born in Glendalough House at Annamoe, Co. Wicklow, he attended Rugby School in Warwickshire and later the University of Oxford, where he studied economics. In October 1915 he joined the Inns of Court OTC in London as a private. Two months later he applied for a commission.

In July 1954 Barton gave a witness statement to the Bureau of Military History, in which he stated:

> In 1914 I had been acting for a time as Secretary to Colonel Moore, Inspector General of the National Volunteers ... I was a member of the National Volunteers. I worked in the office only and did not drill or parade ... I was in the office when the split in the Volunteers took place. There was divergence of policy. Redmond wanted to support the war and, of course, Colonel Moore did too, but the Sinn Féin leaders wanted a more nationalistic programme. So great was the divergence of opinion that the two parties split ... That was up to the time when I left. Dermot Coffey took over from me in the National Volunteers offices. In June, 1914, John Redmond took control of the Volunteers. I was not present at any discussions, although I was there at the time he took over ... Immediately prior to the outbreak of the war – 4th August – Erskine Childers was acting as Colonel Moore's Secretary. Erskine Childers was a first cousin of mine. His mother was my aunt – a sister of my father. When Childers joined the navy, I took over from him. It was very shortly after the war broke out. I carried on until September, after the Sinn Féin Volunteers had broken off from the National Volunteers. I may have stayed on for about two months after the division. At that time it appeared to me that the National Volunteers were rather a futile body and that I was not doing anything of much use. So I went home to Annamoe after handing over to Coffey. It was in October, 1915, that I joined the British Army and went to train as an officer.

Barton was stationed with the Inns of Court OTC in Berkhamsted, Herefordshire, when he was commissioned into the 10th Royal Dublin Fusiliers on 21 April 1916. He was ordered to join the battalion by 24 April, the very day the Rising began in Dublin. Because of the outbreak of the Rising, Barton was late arriving in Dublin, and he later recorded that

> I reached Ireland on the Wednesday following Easter Monday, 1916, under orders to report to my Commanding Officer, Colonel Lawrence Esmonde of the 10th Dublins in the Royal Barracks ... I arrived in Kingstown. Dublin was more or less under siege and part of it in flames. Being unable to get

in to the city, I reported to the Provost-Marshal [officer in command of the military police] at Kingstown. He told me that, as I had no uniform, I had better go home – my officer's uniform was in Phillips's shop, the tailors in Dame Street. I went to my home in Annamoe, Co. Wicklow, and, as I received no further order, I stayed there as long as I thought proper.

Barton's sister, Dulcibella Barton, also gave a witness statement to the Bureau of Military History. She stated:

Next day I went out fishing in the brook beside the house. I was surprised to see my brother Bob walking up to me. I thought he was still in London where I knew he had joined the British Army. I asked him did he not know what was going on in Dublin. He said that he did but that being in the Army he had to do what he was told. He had been in training somewhere near London and had been sent to Ireland to join a certain unit. I said 'You can't go to join the Army without a uniform.' He said 'I'll go to Dublin and get one.' We both went and he also went to see the Commanding Officer of the unit he was to join. He turned out to be Larry Esmonde from Wexford, a great friend of ours. He asked Bob if he wanted to fight. Bob said 'No.' 'I have got a job for you,' said Colonel Larry Esmonde. He made him O/C. [officer commanding] Prisoners' effects.

Robert Barton continued his story:

After about a week, I reported to Colonel Esmonde in the Royal Barracks and, as he knew where my sympathies lay, my duties were confined to the Barracks. Some days later, he received an instruction from the Provost-Marshal in Dublin Castle to send two officers to Richmond Barracks to report to the officer in charge there for duty in connection with the prisoners in Richmond Barracks. I reported to Colonel Frazer. Another officer was sent with me, Lieutenant [Charles] Grant. He took charge of the post office, that is, of letters coming for the prisoners, and acted as censor and distributor.

Colonel Frazer instructed me to take over the duties of officer in charge of prisoners' effects. He made some statement to the effect that the War Office was greatly concerned because the troops in Dublin had been looting, an offence for which they would be shot if they were in France, and that the War Office wanted this situation cleared up. There were a great many charges of looting against the British troops, and the War Office had instructed the authorities in Dublin to stop the looting and to collect what had been looted and return it.

I was a 2nd Lieutenant when I took up duty as officer in charge of prisoners' effects, and my authority as a junior officer was very limited. I took over from

Lieutenant Healing, who was my predecessor, any documents and property which had been collected in [the] prisoners' effects office. That must have been about the 17th May, 1916. I found things in a chaotic state. Prisoners' effects were in buckets and bags littered around the office, and I first tried to put them into order and to find out to whom the properties belonged. The bundles had been systematically pillaged. I missed a packet of Republican stamps which a British officer told me he had at one time seen in the room. I thought they were stamps specially issued by the Volunteers. They had been there and somebody had taken them. A number of the parcels were labelled, but a number had been pillaged and the owners' names had disappeared. I could not tell to whom the properties belonged. I instituted an inquiry and went around to all the prisoners to ascertain what each had lost. I was unable to return a quantity of property because I could not find claimants amongst the prisoners in the barracks.

From information thus obtained I tried to identify the Officers, N.C.O's and Privates who had arrested or searched the prisoners in the various places to which they had been taken, and to recover missing property. I compiled a long list of lost property and had much difficulty in collecting it and in getting co-operation from senior officers. Accordingly, Colonel Frazer decided to appoint a more senior officer to deal with senior officers. Major Heathcote of the 6/7 [Battalion] Sherwood Foresters was appointed. He was told to take over my department and that I would work under him. It was much easier to get the information when he put 'Major' after his name than it had been for me.

Not long afterwards Barton would have learnt of the death of his brother, Second-Lieutenant Thomas Barton of the 4th Royal Irish Rifles, who was killed in action on 16 July 1916 on the Somme. He now lies in Ovillers Military Cemetery.

As to how long this work of collecting prisoners' effects occupied my time, I should say I remained in the army until June, 1918, and I was all the time on this work. When the 10th Dublins went to France, the Assistant Adjutant General in Headquarters, Parkgate Street, refused to permit me to go with them and I was transferred to the 11th Battalion in order that I could complete the task I had been set. I believe that Major Heathcote remained on this work until 1919. I left before he did, because I was taken out of the army at the request of T. P. Gill, Secretary, Department of Agriculture. There came a time when the provision of food was as important as fighting. The English decided to take out of the army the principal leaders of farming in all districts, and T. P. Gill was asked whether there were any persons in the army whom he would like to get back into agriculture. I was one of those he named and I was given my release.

Barton had previously applied to resign his commission in order to concentrate on farming in March 1917, but this was refused. He reapplied in August, while posted to the 11th Royal Dublin Fusiliers, stating that

> I occupy a farm of 2,560 acres ... 74% of the arable land of which is in tillage & I keep a large herd of dairy cows. When I joined the army my sister undertook the superintendence of my farm but the physical ... strain has proved too much for her strength. She has completely broken down & is unable to render me any further assistance. I have set up a wheat milling plant in my farmyard & the plans are completed for the erection of an oatmeal mill. I have the only mills within a 10 mile radius & much of the grain of the district will be sent to me for grinding.

He was on leave until 31 August 1917, having secured release for harvest time, and the Department of Agriculture for Ireland, which strongly supported his application to resign, also wrote to the War Office in London on his behalf. It argued that 'Mr. Barton's agricultural training [he was a graduate of the Royal Agricultural College in Cirencester, Gloucestershire], experience and public spirit, not to mention his great local influence, would be invaluable' to the farming community in Co. Wicklow in helping them to meet wartime production requirements.

The army took all this into account, along with the fact that Barton was still only a second-lieutenant though now thirty-six years old. His application was ultimately successful and he was soon discharged.

It has often been claimed that Barton's resignation from the British army was in protest against the events and the executions that took place in the aftermath of the Rising. However, as his service record and his own witness statement show, he did not voice any objection at the time. He was refused permission to travel to France with the 10th Royal Dublin Fusiliers in August 1916 – confirming that he tried to get into the trenches – and when he ultimately left the army, two years after the Rising, he did so in order to give his energies to farming.

Not long afterwards Barton lost a second brother in the war when 35-year-old Captain Charles Barton of the 4th Royal Irish Rifles, died of wounds on 23 August 1918. He now lies in Terlincthun British Cemetery at Wimille. He had also been involved in the Easter Rising, having served with the 3rd Royal Irish Rifles in Portobello Barracks.

It cannot be doubted, however, that Robert Barton had republican sympathies during the Rising, and he went on to become a republican himself. In 1918 he was elected as Sinn Féin candidate for West Wicklow, subsequently sitting as a member of the first Dáil Éireann. Arrested for sedition in February 1919, just after the start of the War of Independence, he was imprisoned in Mountjoy Prison, Dublin, until Michael Collins helped to organise his escape during the early hours of 17 March. Recaptured in January 1920, he spent the next fifteen months in Portland Prison in Dorsetshire (during which time he was the leader of a strike in protest against the conditions endured by political prisoners), after which he was moved to Portsmouth Prison. After two months there he was freed under the general amnesty following the truce of July 1921.

Having been re-elected in his absence as Sinn Féin candidate for Wicklow-Kildare in May 1921, Barton became minister for agriculture and then secretary for economic affairs. He was one of the Irish delegates who travelled to London to negotiate the Anglo-Irish Treaty, and though he did sign the Treaty he immediately rejected it, referring to it as 'the lesser of two outrages forced upon me and between which I had to choose.' He was elected for a third time in June 1922 as a candidate for anti-Treaty Sinn Féin. During the ensuing civil war, on 24 November, his first cousin Erskine Childers was shot by the Free State army in Beggarsbush Barracks.

In 1923 Barton was defeated in the general election and so turned to practising law as a barrister, later becoming a judge. When he died on 10 August 1975, at the age of ninety-four, he was the last surviving signatory of the Anglo-Irish Treaty.

* * *

Several men of the Royal Dublin Fusiliers appear to have gone further than Robert Barton in supporting the insurgents during the Rising, some even being allowed to join the republican forces, as shown in several statements to the Bureau of Military History.

Captain Liam Tannam of E Company, 3rd Battalion, Irish Volunteers, who fought in the GPO, recorded that 'in the Post Office ... I also saw a Dublin Fusilier and a Connacht Ranger assisting in washing and peeling potatoes. The Dublin Fusilier volunteered to go into action with us but this was the job allotted to him.'

Another insurgent, Patrick Rankin, having taken cover in a house in Moore Lane while retreating from the GPO, later claimed that one of his comrades there was a deserter from the Royal Dublin Fusiliers (possibly the same man mentioned by Liam Tannam). Other insurgents were former soldiers of the Royal Dublin Fusiliers who had deserted before the Rising; it was alleged that republicans often assisted in the desertion of soldiers who were on their way to the front and who had made it known that they did not want to go, sometimes plucking them out of marching columns as they moved down the quays towards the ship that would take them to the war. Captain Thomas Byrne of the Irish Volunteers later wrote that he served alongside more than one of these men during the Rising. 'There were a couple of young men with me who were deserters from the Dublin Fusiliers and they asked me, seeing that the fight was over, would I give them a chance to make their getaway as it would be very serious for them if they were caught fighting with us. This was on Friday. I saw the force of their necessity and let them go.'

At least one other Royal Dublin Fusilier is alleged to have handed his weapon over to the republican cause. Robert Holland of F Company, 4th Battalion, Irish Volunteers, who fought in the vicinity of the South Dublin Union, recorded that on Wednesday 26 April another insurgent, Con Butler, 'told us he had got 3 pints of stout in a pub in Cork Street and that whilst there he learned that a Dublin Fusilier home on leave from France had a rifle in a house somewhere near Cork Street. Con Butler had called on him and took his rifle.' This account (if true) does not make it clear whether the soldier handed over his rifle freely or under duress.

Finally, Patrick Pearse apparently had a more widespread plan to recruit volunteers from the Royal Dublin Fusiliers. Lieutenant Laurence Nugent, an officer of K Company, 3rd Battalion, Irish Volunteers, recorded that 'we met Rory O'Connor who told us to get in touch with the Dublin Fusiliers and offer them £2 per man if they would join up with the Irish Volunteers. These were Pearse's instructions. We had no chance of making the contact [as] the Dublins were in Kilmainham and that district was well held by the British.'

Other soldiers in the Royal Dublin Fusiliers are known to have treated the rebels decently after the Rising ended. Vice-Commandant Peter Paul Galligan of the Enniscorthy Battalion of the Irish Volunteers, who was imprisoned for a week in Mountjoy Prison after the Rising, later recalled being

> transferred to Dartmoor Prison. In our party were Eoin MacNeill, Seán McEntee and Teddy Brosnan from Kerry. We travelled by B. & I. boat from the North Wall to Liverpool and from there to London and on to Dartmoor. Our escort was a detachment of the Dublin Fusiliers. They were good fellows and treated us well … One of the men of the Dublin Fusiliers who was escorting us to Dartmoor told Brosnan and me that he was on fatigue duty in Arbour Hill Prison when the ambulance brought in Connolly's body. This man stated that when Connolly was buried he was grasping the 'rung' of the chair in his hand [Connolly had been shot by firing squad while strapped to a chair]. The escort were very decent and treated us well and bought refreshment for us, the officer in charge giving a £1 for this purpose. They sang songs mostly rebel ones throughout the journey.

Furthermore, Helena Molony, a member of the Irish Citizen Army who had fought during the battle for City Hall, later recorded that while she was imprisoned in Ship Street Barracks 'the soldiers were decent enough to us. The Dublin Fusiliers were there. They would bring us in a dish of fried bacon and bread. On Friday, we got nothing except hard biscuits and dry bread. We were glad when the sergeant said: "It is bad stuff, but that is what we are getting ourselves." We were delighted that they were cut off from supplies. They were only getting bully beef. That caused us more joy than anything else.'

Of course there were plenty of Royal Dublin Fusiliers who certainly had no sympathy for the insurgents, as Andrew McDonnell of E Company, 3rd Battalion, Irish Volunteers, discovered after the Rising. 'One night, in Richmond Barracks, we talked plenty and were shouted at every so often by the sentry outside on the landing, but the voice was different and we were quick to notice this. Gone was the Cockney accent and in its place a good Dublin one. This gave us a little cheer. Not that the shouts were by any means friendly; if anything, the threats were even more savage.'

Later, after being interrogated by British army officers, McDonnell and his comrades 'were taken out to a toilet, and on the way back our landing sentry not alone smiled but slipped a few cigarettes. Yes, he was a Dublin Fusilier home on leave and had been rounded up for duty. This Information was given in fits and starts through the closed door – we were bloody fools, but we had put the wind up the so-and-so British Regiments and that was to his liking.'

James O'Shea, a member of the Irish Citizen Army who served in the St Stephen's Green area, encountered aggression after being marched away from the College of Surgeons.

> We were all right until we got to Grafton Street when the guards got tough. Smoking or talking was forbidden. We were marched to the Castle and got a good idea of what we would have to go through from the Dublin Fusiliers, who cursed and jeered us in Dame Street. [He had earlier heard a rumour that the Royal Dublin Fusiliers had actually mutinied in support of the rebels.] We were marched into the Castle Yard and into a yard on the left, where we saw a big pit. We were told that in an hour's time we would be in it. They made a jeer and joke of Madame Markievicz. This, I am sorry to say, was done by the Dublin Fusiliers. After a time we were marched down to Kingsbridge, through Thomas Street, where there was a great display of soldiers' women shouting, 'Bayonet them,' etc., and then on to Richmond Barracks.

As the Irish Citizen Army men arrived at Richmond Barracks, as later recounted by Lieutenant Thomas O'Donoghue – a founder-member of Fianna Éireann, later a Catholic priest – they encountered some 'separation women' (soldiers' wives who were receiving separation allowance). 'Some of the women shouted: "Shoot them!" The soldier nearest to me seemed to be very bitter towards us and said we had destroyed everything on them, and, strange to say, he wore the badge of the Dublin Fusiliers.' Later on, in Kilmainham Jail, it appears that the violence towards the rebels only increased, as James Burke of the Irish Volunteers later claimed.

> We were brought over to Kilmainham jail, where some drunken soldiery of the Dublin Fusiliers immediately set upon us, kicking us, beating us and threatening us with bayonets. As a matter of fact my tunic was ripped off me with bayonets, and our shirts and other articles of clothing were saturated with blood. We looked at one another the next morning and we thought we were dead. The Dublin Fusiliers were the worst of the lot. The English soldiers were mostly decent. Most of them were young fellows who did not know one end of a rifle from the other as far as I could see.

Finally, even when the prisoners were deported to England, they were still not beyond the reach of angry Irish soldiers in the British army. Volunteer Gerald Doyle of B Company, 4th Battalion, Irish Volunteers, later recorded that

> when we arrived at Southampton station, we were taken from the train, to await another connection. While waiting on the platform, a troop train from France pulled in alongside us. They were the Dublin Fusiliers, and how they had got to know who we were, I do not know, but they started to call us all sorts of names. One soldier started to spit at us, and called us 'Casement's bastards,' and it certainly looked real ugly for us, as some of them started to climb out of the window of the train. At this stage, officers came running along the platform, with revolvers in their hands, shouting that they would shoot the first man who came through a window.

* * *

When the Rising ended, Private Denis Byrne from St Paul's Place – the former typewriter mechanic aged sixteen years and eleven months, who should have been discharged before the Rising – had luckily come through the event unhurt. By early August 1916 he was still in the army, and in that month he was transferred to the 11th Royal Dublin Fusiliers, a newly established reserve battalion. Having had no satisfaction with her earlier attempts to get her son discharged, Kate Byrne wrote to the military secretary of the War Office in London.

> I wish to apply that the above named soldier who is my son should get his discharge on the grounds that he was only 17 years of age on 30th May last. Six months ago I applied to his C/O and furnished his birth certificate. I never got an acknowledgement or even the return of the certificate. He was on duty during the Rebellion and shortly before that he was in the King George Hospital for bronchitis. According to military regulations I now claim that my son should get his discharge as he is under age and still in delicate health.
>
> Your obedient servant,
> Kate Byrne.
> P.S. I have another son ... at the front.

In late September 1916 Lieutenant-Colonel Laurence Esmonde, now commanding the 11th Battalion, wrote to the officer in charge of records in Dublin that 'the attached birth certificate and correspondence were found in this man's documents. I was not informed by the 10th Bn that this man's discharge had been applied for.' The response came a day later from Captain Mooney in the records office: 'His discharge should be carried out please as at the time the application was made the soldier was under 17 years of age.'

Within a few days Esmonde wrote to Kate Byrne, saying: 'Herewith birth certificate of your son. He will be discharged from the Service tomorrow.' The following day, 29 September 1916, Denis Byrne was discharged on the grounds of 'having made a misstatement as to age on enlistment.' He was finally out of the army, having come through the Easter Rising without a scratch.

* * *

Company Sergeant-Major Christopher Lynch – who had joined the Royal Inniskilling Fusiliers in 1887 and retired before the war, then re-enlisted – earned another mention in despatches while serving with the 10th Royal Dublin Fusiliers during the Rising. Posted to the 11th Battalion in Dublin when he recovered from his wounds, he never returned to the war. In April 1918 he was discharged from the army as being 'no longer physically fit for war service' because of his increasing age (he was now fifty-three). His discharge medical report stated that he had gunshot scars on his upper left arm, and that he had '27 years service including 3½ years in the present war, during which he has served in Gallipoli and France. Owing to increasing debility, the result of increasing age, he finds himself unequal to carrying on the duties of Sergeant Major.' His character was given as 'very good', and his army reference described him as a 'very good man; served his country well, awarded the Distinguished Conduct Medal for bravery at Suvla Bay. Attained the rank of W.O. [warrant officer] Class II.' Lynch was hoping to obtain employment in Manchester as a caretaker, and the army requested prospective employers to look upon him favourably 'in appreciation of his war services.'

* * *

Captain Norman Palmer, officer commanding B Company, 10th Royal Dublin Fusiliers during the Rising also went to war with his battalion in August 1916. Two months later, however, he left the trenches and was evacuated to England suffering from severe myalgia (muscle pain). By January 1917 he was well enough to serve again and was posted to the 4th Battalion, now based in Mullingar. He was soon found fit to serve overseas, though only in a tropical or sub-tropical climate, and some time after June 1917 he was posted to a battalion of the Essex Regiment and sent to join it in the Egypt-Palestine theatre of war.

On 16 May 1918, while stationed in Alexandria, Captain Palmer had two unpleasant experiences in one day. Firstly, he discovered that he had sores that were later identified as a sexually transmitted bacterial infection. Later in the day, when he was departing from Alexandria, the ship he was travelling on was torpedoed and sunk by a German submarine. He was badly scalded but survived, spending the next three weeks in a hospital in Marseille.

When the war ended, Palmer stayed in the army, being briefly promoted to acting major while serving between February and November 1919 as second-in-command of the 52nd (Graduated) Battalion of the Royal Northumberland Fusiliers. ('Graduated' battalions were created in the summer of 1917 to provide specialist training to infantrymen under the age of nineteen who had completed their basic training.) The following year his higher rank was made permanent when Major Palmer became an intelligence officer attached to the headquarters of Dublin District during the War of Independence. He served in this capacity for a further seven months before finally resigning his commission in February 1921. He was now forty-two years old.

In October 1922, now living in London, he applied to be placed on the list of reserve officers, either as an infantry or an intelligence officer. His request was granted, and he was placed on the list in December. However, he was never called up for active service, and in January 1925 he wrote to the army offering his services 'for Intelligence and S.S. [Secret Service] work. I have a knowledge of the East and I know Australia well ... I also served in Ireland from July 1920 to February 1921. I am Irish and know the South well and the people.' But the army replied that 'there is no opportunity of offering you any employment in a military capacity.' Over the following years he repeatedly wrote to the army, hoping to be reinstated as an intelligence officer, on one occasion even offering to gather intelligence while on a holiday on the Continent.

Finally, on Palmer's fiftieth birthday, 26 December 1928, he was taken off the reserve list, having reached the upper age limit for recall to active service. He died eleven years later in London, in September 1939, the month in which the Second World War broke out. He was sixty years old.

* * *

Lieutenant-Colonel Laurence Esmonde, commanding officer of the 10th Royal Dublin Fusiliers, did not go overseas when his battalion joined the war in August 1916 but instead was directed to establish and to command a new reserve battalion, the 11th. He was later mentioned in despatches for his services during the Rising. Then, in May 1917, Lieutenant-General Bryan Mahon, commander-in-chief of the forces in Ireland, wrote to the War Office to state that Lieutenant-Colonel Esmonde

> raised the 10th Battalion Royal Dublin Fusiliers in December, 1915, from the professional and commercial classes in Ireland who up to that time had not come forward to enlist, and when that Battalion was accepted for service overseas he raised the 11th Battalion to form a reserve. He has not however the knowledge and military experience necessary for the arduous duties of the Commander of a draft finding unit in war time; and I am of the opinion that greater efficiency would be obtained in the Battalion by the appointment of a Regular Officer, many of whom are now, I understand, available for Home Service.

Esmonde was now also fifty-three years old, the upper age limit for his rank. However, when it had been decided to remove him from command of the 11th

Royal Dublin Fusiliers, the military secretary at the War Office, Lieutenant-General Francis Davies, wrote on 23 May to Mahon that 'in communicating this decision to Lieutenant-Colonel Gratton Esmonde I am to ask that you will convey to him the thanks of the Army Council for the excellent services he has rendered during the present crisis, and he should also be informed that his name has been noted for consideration should a suitable opportunity arise for his re-employment.' Though actually a major and only an acting lieutenant-colonel, Esmonde was allowed to keep the honorary rank on his retirement.

Six years later, during the Civil War, the *Irish Times* of 12 March 1923 reported that

> Ballynastragh, the beautiful residence of Senator Sir Thomas Henry Grattan Esmonde, Bart., about three miles from Gorey, County Wexford, was set on fire on Friday night, and burned to the ground ... The only occupants of the house at the time of the outrage were Colonel Laurence Esmonde, his brother, together with five servants. The raiders, of whom there were about 50 in all, forced an entrance through one of the lower windows at about 9.30 p.m., and gave the occupants ten minutes to get ready. They were kept under armed guard in an out-building till the house was well alight, the rooms and furniture having been sprayed with petrol. With the permission of the man in charge, Colonel Esmonde removed the golden chalice and sets of vestments from the beautiful little chapel in the upper portion of the building before the raiders had commenced their work of destruction. These articles are all that was saved. With the aid of a fairly strong wind, gas bombs being also used, the flames made great headway, huge tongues of fire rising towards the sky. They were seen at least ten miles away. The garrison of National troops at Gorey, attracted by the fire, arrived shortly after 11 o'clock, about half an hour after the raiders had left, but they were too late to save the building. Only the bare walls of it remain.

The burning of Ballynastragh House by the anti-Treaty IRA, including the museum it housed and its collection of historical documents, was viewed as a loss almost equal to that suffered when the Four Courts was destroyed in the war a year earlier. Laurence Esmonde lived for another seven years and died in Dublin in February 1943 at the age of seventy-nine.

* * *

Lieutenant Charles Grant later recalled the arrival of James Connolly at Dublin Castle after the fighting in Dublin had ended. 'Connolly was wounded ... and was brought to the Castle Hospital. The rumour got around the Castle that an attempt was to be made to rescue him and the other leaders by attacking the Castle. The result was that guards were doubled and the troops were more or less at "stand to" all night.'

When the prisoners were transferred to Richmond Barracks, 'on the cessation of the fighting in the city, after about 6 days, I was posted to the Court Martial Court, which was held in Richmond Barracks. My job was censor to prisoners' correspondence, which in parts proved interesting and amusing. Some of it contained reference to extramarital family affairs, and affairs of the heart. I saw in the course of my duties all the leaders of the rebellion.'

Grant remained at this work for three weeks before rejoining the 10th Royal Dublin Fusiliers in the Royal Barracks. In August 1916 he joined the war and soon found himself leading trench raids in an attempt to gather intelligence on German positions and also to capture prisoners for interrogation. During one raid in October he and his men were attacked by German soldiers. 'Casualties ensued and many good companions failed to return. One of these unfortunately was Tom Boyd, a close friend of our family who was captured and taken back by the Germans to work in a Salt Mine. I was in command of the party at the time, and had to leave behind some seven men including Tom, some were killed fighting, some including Tom were captured. It was my painful duty to inform his mother, who I knew well in Ireland.'

The following month the 10th Battalion was involved in the Battle of the Ancre, which began on 13 November. Lieutenant Grant later wrote that on that day,

> between 4 and 5 a.m. ... the order was given to advance. I was in command of the bombing section on the right of the battalion. The enemy apparently anticipated the attack, as immediately we crossed into no man's land we came under heavy fire, which lost us time to get to the wire entanglements on the Bosch [*Boche,* i.e. German] line. Our army brought heavy fire to bear on the German line and its rear. After some hours of severe fighting the German trenches were taken and the enemy forced back for some fifteen miles. We took over the former German line, and around 6 p.m. I received orders to go to Headquarters and report the position. I found the General and his staff. He offered me a whisky, which I took. I also asked him for a drink for my runner, which he gave him. We had had neither food nor drink since early morning, so the whisky had some effect. I then left to rejoin the battalion. We were in such a good mood that we sat for a short time amid the shambles of the wounded, and watched the Jerries [Germans] giving a shell dump some miles away a terrible artillery pounding. They got their target and the explosion together with the blowing up of a tunnel created such a scene as to remind me of the old fashioned pictures depicting the 'last day on earth'.

When the Battle of the Ancre had ended, on 18 November, the 10th Royal Dublin Fusiliers had lost 41 men killed, 141 wounded, and 57 missing. This meant that the battalion had suffered 239 casualties in five days – 48 per cent of its previous strength of 493 officers and men.

After marrying his fiancée while on leave the following January, Lieutenant Grant was ordered to take command of B Company (formerly commanded by Captain Norman Palmer), but two weeks later 'I received a bullet wound and further injury from the explosion of a shell ... in the attack on part of Bapaume.' He was also temporarily buried alive after the explosion. He was admitted to hospital on 28 January 1917 for his wounds, and neurasthenia (or shell shock) was diagnosed, believed to have been caused by his recent injuries and experience of being buried alive but also 'contributed to by being under shell-fire in the course of his duties as bombing officer, & also by sepsis resulting from injuries received from barbed wire in Sept or Oct 1916 at Mailly-Maillet.'

After he had been a month in a French hospital the neurasthenia became more severe in late February 1917, and Grant was evacuated from France. After treatment in hospitals in England and in Dublin, and then a period spent in Lady Desart's Hospital in Co. Kilkenny, in November 1917 he was transferred to the Dublin Castle Red Cross Hospital. When he was examined by a medical board in Dublin it stated that 'he is still suffering from Neurasthenia ... Since last seen by the Board on 6/9/17 he has distinctly improved [but still] complains of tremors, nervousness, excitability, & mental confusion, hesitation of speech, pulse 100, though all these symptoms, except the last, are less severe.' The doctors subsequently decided that he should not be sent to a convalescent home but instead allowed to go home for a period of extended leave. 'His home surroundings are favourable, as [he] proposes to stay with his wife at the home of her father, a clergyman, which is situated in a quiet & healthy suburb of Dublin [Kenilworth Square] where he can see as much of his friends as is desirable & be free from all sources of worry.'

In February 1918 Grant was again examined in Dublin, the medical officer stating that 'he has very much improved. He is sleeping fairly well as a rule, & headache is not so frequent but when tired & worried insomnia and headaches return to some extent. Tremor, nervousness, & hesitation in speech are all much improved, as is also the mental confusion. He has, however, lost weight & still shows some of the symptoms named so that in the opinion of the Board he is not yet fit even for light duty, & they recommend further leave for a least a month.'

The following month there were no further medical reviews, and Lieutenant Grant was sent to join the 11th Royal Dublin Fusiliers, now based in Aldershot. Almost immediately he requested to resign his commission, writing that 'my health has been seriously impaired and I feel that I am unable to satisfactorily perform the duties of an Infantry Officer on service. On the outbreak of war I was a Barrister-at-Law and a Civil Servant of 15 years service, in the Department of the Local Government Board for Ireland, and having regard to my present state of health, I consider I would be more useful to the State in that capacity.'

His request was successful, and he soon left the army. He subsequently returned to study at Trinity College and was soon back working with the Local Government Board in the Custom House, now as a legal assistant to the department. On 25 May 1921 he was inside the building when it was attacked and subsequently burned by IRA forces during the War of Independence. Later that year he was offered the job of principal officer in the Local Government Division of the Ministry of Home Affairs in Northern Ireland, and in August he and his family settled in Holywood, Co. Down. He was made a member of the Order of the British Empire in 1924 and became senior auditor for the Ministry of Home Affairs in 1927. During the Second World War (in which his son, Alan, served as a medical officer in North Africa and Italy) he was chief air raid warden for the Holywood area. He died at his home in March 1970, aged eighty-eight.

* * *

The date 13 November 1916 has been mentioned more than once. This was the day on which the 10th Royal Dublin Fusiliers, and the great majority of the men in the battalion, experienced their first battle in the First World War. Many survivors of the Easter Rising were killed or wounded during the fighting that followed. The wounded included Private Michael Byrne, the former postman from Lucan, who had previously been wounded during the Rising, and Lieutenant William Connolly, the officer who testified at the court-martial of Seán Heuston. The dead included Sergeant Sidney Robinson, who was Lieutenant Charles Grant's platoon sergeant, the under-age Private William O'Riordan from Enniskean, Co. Cork, previously wounded in Dublin, and Lieutenant Frederick O'Neill, who served with the 5th Royal Dublin Fusiliers during the Rising. Others, including Lieutenant Charles Grant, were present at both events but were lucky enough to come through them physically unscathed.

There were certainly many more veterans of the Easter Rising in the 10th Royal Dublin Fusiliers who did not survive to see the end of 1916 – men whose names do not appear in connection with the Rising but who were there nonetheless.

And the war would continue for two more years.

5

3rd Royal Irish Rifles
The 'All-Ireland' Battalion

Just before midday on 24 April 1916 Second-Lieutenant Cecil McCammond was riding on horseback in the vicinity of St Stephen's Green, accompanied by his orderly. He was only seventeen years old, a native of Belfast and an officer in the 19th Royal Irish Rifles – a reserve battalion stationed in Newcastle, Co. Down. He had attended Rockport Preparatory School in Belfast, followed by St Bees School in Cumberland, where he had also served as a private in the school's OTC, before applying for a commission in April 1915.

He was then only sixteen but was honest about his age on his application; as a result the army rejected him outright. He then enlisted as a private in the 17th Battalion two months later, this time lying about his age, claiming to be eighteen. He was successfully enlisted, and after being quickly promoted to lance-corporal he applied for a commission in October 1915. This time it was granted, and Cecil McCammond was commissioned – though still only sixteen – in January 1916. In April he was on leave in Dublin and visiting his father, Lieutenant-Colonel Walter McCammond, officer commanding the 3rd Royal Irish Rifles, stationed in Portobello Barracks.

He was riding along when, from the direction of Grafton Street, a group of Irish Citizen Army soldiers, under the command of Captain Richard McCormack, approached St Stephen's Green, having been sent to capture temporary outposts surrounding the Irish Citizen Army centre in the green and prevent the British army advancing on it before the insurgents there had time to establish themselves properly. This group were on their way to take over Harcourt Street Station (at the southern end of the street, adjoining Adelaide Road) when they found themselves walking towards Second-Lieutenant McCammond and his orderly, who were riding towards them. Nervously, the rebels kept advancing, some taking off the safety catch on their weapons while Captain McCormack ordered them to stay calm. Just as the two groups were about to pass each other Captain McCormack saluted McCammond, who automatically returned the salute. The two groups then passed by one another, but McCammond and his orderly soon halted and stared – even more confused now – at the Irish Citizen Army men advancing towards Harcourt Street. They decided to follow them.

At Harcourt Street Station the insurgents stopped and Captain McCormack led a detachment inside. McCammond and his orderly rode past the remaining Irish Citizen Army men and stopped further up the road.

At this point accounts differ about what happened next. The more commonly repeated account is that when the remainder of the insurgents – about ten in number, under the command of Sergeant Joseph Doyle, who were intending to occupy Davy's pub on the corner of South Richmond Street and Charlemont

Royal Irish Rifles cap badge
(Author's Collection)

Mall – began moving, McCammond kept riding ahead of them. However, after turning into Harcourt Road he rode on to the next junction before turning left into South Richmond Street – the main road to Portobello Barracks. This allowed Sergeant Doyle to rush his detachment up a smaller street that acted as a short cut.

Now the Irish Citizen Army men were facing the two British army soldiers. Sergeant Doyle ordered his men to fix bayonets and to spread out across the road. When McCammond saw this happening right in front of him, and now aware that the Irish Citizen Army were not just carrying out manoeuvres but were engaged in the beginning of a military action – he was determined to get past them before they formed a roadblock and opened fire on him. He galloped forward with his orderly, and as he rode past them one insurgent lunged at him with his bayonet and then opened fire, allegedly missing him. McCammond and the orderly galloped on up the road, across the Grand Canal and into Portobello Barracks. Meanwhile, the insurgents seized Davy's pub.

The alternative account comes from Cyril Falls' book *The History of the First Seven Battalions: The Royal Irish Rifles in the Great War* (1925), which states that

> Lieutenant McCammond had been in Dublin, and about noon, when returning on horseback to barracks, was set upon by rebels at Portobello Bridge. These had established themselves in Davy's public-house, which overlooked the bridge and commanded the Rathmines Road and Richmond Street. A number came out of the house to attack him, while others fired at him from the windows. Fortunately they were incredibly bad marksmen.

Lieutenant McCammond got clear, only slightly wounded and rode on to barracks to give the alarm.

This account suggests that the insurgents were already in Davy's pub as McCammond and his orderly approached. Furthermore, McCammond's service file shows that he was wounded on 24 April, which tallies with Falls' account of him being hit, and differs from the other account, which claims that the rebel fire missed him.

Either way, just after midday on 24 April – thanks to the wounded son of its commanding officer – the 3rd Royal Irish Rifles was aware that the Rising had broken out on the streets of Dublin. The battalion, comprising 21 officers and 650 other ranks, was part of a regiment that recruited its men from Cos. Antrim, Down and Louth, with the regimental depot at Belfast; but after the war had broken out and the battalion had mobilised in August 1914 it had been moved to Dublin. As a result, this battalion of a northern Irish regiment had steadily gained recruits from southern Ireland, especially Dubliners who had simply enlisted into this locally stationed unit. Often referred to as an exclusively Protestant and unionist formation, by April 1916 it contained many southern Irish Catholics. Furthermore, out of the seven men killed and thirty-three wounded that the battalion suffered during the Rising, three of the dead were northern Irish Protestants while another two were southern Irish Catholics (the sixth man was English, while the seventh cannot be identified), while in terms of the wounded, fourteen were from the north of Ireland, fourteen from the south, and the remaining five were English. However, this unit would become infamous during the Rising for the murder of innocent civilians committed by one of its officers.

By the time of the Rising the 3rd Battalion was considered one of the best of the twenty-eight 'draft-finding' battalions in Ireland. It had already sent 128 officers and 4,569 other ranks to the regular or service battalions in the war, and this was credited to the work of its commanding officer and second-in-command.

Lieutenant-Colonel Walter McCammond was forty-one years old and a native of Belfast. He was a justice of the peace and a long-serving reserve officer who had taken over command of the 3rd Battalion in December 1912. When the war began he was appointed commanding officer of Kinnegar Training Camp in Holywood, Co. Down, and after a period spent commanding the 8th Lincolnshire Regiment he returned to Ireland and to the 3rd Royal Irish Rifles. He lived in Lissonfield House, adjoining Portobello Barracks (later the home of General Richard Mulcahy).

On 22 April 1916 – two days before the Rising began – Lieutenant-Colonel McCammond left the battalion suffering from pleurisy. He was admitted to hospital the following day; as a result, the battalion would be without its commanding officer when the Rising began. Many would see this as having disastrous consequences.

With Lieutenant-Colonel McCammond on sick leave, temporary command of the battalion fell to Major James Rosborough, the battalion's second-in-command

and training officer. Forty-six years old and a native of Derry, Rosborough now had a home at Marlborough Park in Belfast. He had attended Foyle College in Derry and then Trinity College in Dublin, where he completed the first year of the law course. Commissioned in June 1893, he was clearly a promising officer, having reached the rank of captain within two years.

For a reserve officer, Rosborough had a good deal of military experience. From 1899 to 1900 he served as a captain with the 2nd Battalion of the Central Africa Regiment in Zomba, British Central Africa (later Nyasaland, now Malawi). In 1901 he was involved in the Gambia Expedition against the slave-raiding chief Fodi Kabba. The following year his unit became part of the newly formed King's African Rifles, and in 1902–04, while serving in the 1st Battalion, Rosborough took part in the Somaliland Campaign, a British, Italian and Ethiopian war against the Dervishes – a Somali Sunni Islamic people – who were supported by the Ottoman and German empires. He then served during the Nandi Rebellion of 1905–06, an uprising of the Nandi people of east Africa against the construction of the Uganda Railway through their land, during which Rosborough was mentioned in despatches, before taking up the position of depot commander of British Central Africa until 1907, finally acting as officer in command of troops in Nyasaland from 1907 to 1910. Through all these campaigns Rosborough was on attachment from the 6th Royal Irish Rifles.

Captain Rosborough joined the 3rd Royal Irish Rifles in 1908, and just after the outbreak of the First World War, in September 1914, he was promoted to major.

Lieutenant-Colonel Walter McCammond from Belfast, commanding officer of the 3rd Royal Irish Rifles (Jimmy Taylor/ Bobby Rainey)

Lieutenant Samuel Morgan, adjutant of the 3rd Royal Irish Rifles during the Rising (Jimmy Taylor/Bobby Rainey)

In April 1916 he suddenly found himself in command of a battalion caught up in a rebellion.

Rosborough had some assistance in his temporary role as commanding officer. The battalion's adjutant – essentially an officer who assists the commanding officer – was Lieutenant Samuel Morgan. Contrary to the popular view of the 3rd Royal Irish Rifles, Morgan was actually a Catholic officer (one of several in the battalion). Thirty-six years old and originally from Newtownards, Morgan was the son of a former reserve sergeant; he was also one of four brothers to serve in the Royal Irish Rifles. He had not begun his army career as an officer: in January 1896, aged fifteen and only 5 feet 0½ inch tall, he had joined in Belfast as a 'boy'. He was posted to the 3rd Royal Irish Rifles as a bugler, but in June 1901, after receiving his first promotion – to lance-corporal – within two-and-a-half years Morgan had risen to orderly-room sergeant with the 6th Battalion. In 1908, when Lieutenant-Colonel A. R. Cole-Hamilton was leaving the battalion, he delivered a farewell message in which he mentioned 'Sgt S. V. Morgan, whose never-failing hard work, good temper, zeal, and tact have contributed so much to the excellent state of the battalion.'

By June 1908 Morgan had returned to the 3rd Battalion and was immediately promoted to colour-sergeant. Promotion to company quartermaster-sergeant followed three years later, in the same year that Morgan married. Now with more than eighteen years' service, when the First World War broke out Morgan was recommended for a commission by Lieutenant-Colonel McCammond, who wrote in September 1914: 'During the six years that this non-commissioned officer served in the Battalion he always carried out his duties in a satisfactory manner and I believe he is in every way qualified for the position of a commissioned officer. His father was a non-commissioned officer for twenty five years, in the Royal Irish Rifles, & was awarded the Long Service & Good Conduct, which medal QM [Quartermaster] S. V. Morgan was recommended for in June last.' The application was approved, and Morgan was commissioned in October 1914. The *Irish Times* of 11 February 1915 wrote:

> On parade yesterday of all officers, non-commissioned officers and men of the 3rd (Reserve) Battalion, Royal Irish Rifles ... Brigadier-General F. E. Hill ... Commanding 31st Infantry Brigade and Dublin Garrison, presented Lieutenant and Adjutant S. V. Morgan with the Long Service and Good Conduct Medal ... In making the presentation General Hill said it was unique for a combatant officer to receive this distinction which was usually awarded to NCOs and men after 18 years service whose character was irreproachable. He further said that any soldier might earn the VC for an act of bravery committed on the spur of the moment, but it took a soldier 18 years to earn the Good Conduct Medal. Lieutenant and Adjutant Morgan was awarded the medal on 1st October 1914 on which date he was also gazetted to commissioned rank from the rank of Quartermaster Sergeant.

General Hill quotes this officer to the rank and file as an example of how any soldier might rise from the ranks.

In May 1915 Morgan learnt of the death of his younger brother, Lieutenant John Morgan, formerly a law clerk, who was killed on 16 May 1915 while serving with the 2nd Royal Inniskilling Fusiliers at Festubert on the Western Front. He was thirty-one years old when he died and now lies in Bethune Town Cemetery.

Major Rosborough and Lieutenant Morgan were thus the two officers running the 3rd Royal Irish Rifles when the wounded Second-Lieutenant McCammond rode in the gate with his orderly. Before long a phone call from Colonel Henry Cowan of Irish Command would confirm what young McCammond had already told them. An order was issued for troops to assemble immediately. However, it seems that the Easter holiday weekend – and perhaps also the absence of Lieutenant-Colonel McCammond – had created a more relaxed environment in Portobello Barracks than in Richmond Barracks or the Royal Barracks. According to Cyril Falls, 'on Easter Monday morning the troops were off parade, prepared to enjoy themselves, and a holiday mood pervaded the barracks.' Unlike the situation in the other barracks, when the order to march on Dublin Castle was received, an advance piquet of 100 men was not speedily assembled. The garrison adjutant ordered all available soldiers to parade with fifty rounds of ammunition, and small groups began to organise themselves, but when the first group was ready to leave the barracks there were only fifty of them; and they did not leave the barracks until some time after 12:40 p.m., at least thirty minutes after receiving Colonel Cowan's phone call.

This group of fifty soldiers was commanded by Major William Leatham, a 37-year-old officer from Downpatrick, Co. Down. Formerly an RIC district inspector, Leatham had joined the RIC in September 1898, aged nineteen. Before joining the army he had spent three years as a musketry instructor at the RIC's depot in Dublin. After the war broke out he was seconded to the army in November 1915 – one of thirty-two such RIC officers and one of four who would serve through the Rising.

Leatham led his fifty men out of Portobello Barracks and past St Mary's College, turning north into Rathmines Road. They were now advancing towards Portobello Bridge over the Grand Canal, on the opposite side of which was Sergeant Joseph Doyle and his Irish Citizen Army detachment in Davy's pub. As the soldiers approached the bridge, the insurgents opened fire.

Knowing that the only direct way to reach Dublin Castle would be to fight across the bridge and assault the rebels, Leatham ordered his men to press forward. But the attack was beaten back and there were several casualties, one of whom was Major Leatham. He was shot in the back of his right hip or thigh, and the bullet lodged in his body. Unable to fight on, he was withdrawn from the battle. He survived his injuries but remained in hospital for two months, until the end of June. When he was released he was obliged to walk with a stick, and it was a year before he was well enough to serve again. He spent the last period of his recovery in Queen Alexandra's Home of Rest for Officers in Glengarriff, Co. Cork, and even when he finally returned to the army he was permitted only to do light duty. He then rejoined the 3rd Royal Irish Rifles, now in Belfast. However, he had to return to hospital in August 1916 for a few weeks.

Leatham subsequently served as an intelligence officer in the Lough Swilly Garrison, Co. Donegal, from November 1917 to February 1919, while living in Fahan on the shores of the lough. A report stated that Leatham was 'employed on work connected with disaffection in Ireland ... [He was] a Military Intelligence Officer who would be constantly moving about the Counties of Donegal and Londonderry, the former especially. The whole Coastal area of Donegal is important as being very extensive and giving natural facilities for secret landing of arms.' When he left this position, in February 1919, it was because his wound had still not improved, and he was asked to relinquish his commission because of ill-health.

By April 1920 William Leatham was living in Duleek, Co. Meath, when he wrote to the War Office stating that his wound pension of £100 a year had now expired, but 'my leg [shows] no signs whatever of improvement. I beg to apply to have the pension renewed and made permanent.' A medical report stated that his 'leg is still enlarged. His walking powers are consequently interfered with. His general health is good, but the disability is of such a nature that it handicaps him considerably in earning a livelihood in civil life as he is unable to follow any active employment, the leg tending to swell on any undue exertion.'

William Leatham died in November 1933, aged fifty-four, while living in Portrush, Co. Antrim.

* * *

Another man wounded on Portobello Bridge was nineteen-year-old Lieutenant John Battersby, the only other officer with the first group of fifty soldiers from Portobello Barracks. He was born and grew up in Donadea Rectory near Kilcock, Co. Kildare, son of the local Church of Ireland clergyman. Commissioned in March 1915 and promoted to lieutenant in February 1916, he was shot in the left hand on 24 April in the assault on Davy's pub. Two bullets hit the knuckles of his index and middle fingers and fractured several bones. A later medical report described his injury:

> Whilst on active service, against the Irish Rebels in Dublin, on 24.4.16, Lieutenant J.A. Battersby was twice struck on the left hand by bullets fired by the enemy ... The wounds were dressed at the time in Portobello. Great crippling of hand continued till March, 1917. Then Lieutenant Colonel Sir T. Miles operated in Dublin to relieve stiffness. Great good resulted. The hand shows scars. First and second fingers are stiff. Flexion is largely limited. Extension almost completed.

Another report added that the operation included the 'removal of some dead bone and pieces of lead.' Battersby was granted medical leave for several months, and when he recovered he joined the 7th Royal Dublin Fusiliers in Salonika. Then, in June 1917, he contracted malaria in the Struma Valley. He remained on duty for another two months until eventually he was unable to carry on. After being treated in hospital he returned to his unit in time to sail with it to Egypt in September. As soon as he arrived in Egypt, however, he was admitted to hospital again for six weeks. By the time he was discharged the 7th Battalion was in Palestine, but after travelling to join it Battersby was again sent to hospital. It seemed that every time he travelled or exerted himself the malaria would flare up.

The army ultimately decided to send Lieutenant Battersby back to Ireland, and by March 1918 he was being treated in King George V Military Hospital in Dublin. A medical report recorded that 'he states that since 2.7.18 he has had seven attacks of ague [fever], with a cold stage and rigors and a sweating stage. The M.O. [medical officer] of Unit reports that he has seen him in two of those attacks which are typically malarial – He is debilitated – Any physical strain or exposure causes an attack of malarial fever – X Ray shows spleen distinctly enlarged ... is performing Sedentary duty (Missing Officer) in his battalion.'

Because of his condition Battersby was recommended for a discharge on medical grounds in November 1918, and this was granted. Over the years that followed he appeared before several medical boards, the reports from which showed that he was debilitated and subject to repeated attacks of malaria. There were still pieces of bullet in his hand, causing pain and stiffness and loss of power in the hand. By 1927, now aged thirty, Battersby is finally known to have settled at Mount Merrion Avenue in Blackrock, Co. Dublin.

* * *

Having been pushed back at Portobello Bridge, and having suffered the severe wounding of their commanding officer, the piquet of the 3rd Royal Irish Rifles was joined by another detachment of fifty men coming from Portobello Barracks, the second half of the battalion's 100-man piquet, who left the barracks at about 1:10 p.m. – a full hour after receiving Colonel Cowan's call for help. They were under the command of Major William Rigg.

A native of Sevenoaks in Kent, 41-year-old William Rigg joined the RIC in 1899 and, like Major Leatham, had risen to the rank of district inspector before being seconded to the army in January 1916. He had been living in Ireland for seventeen years.

As soon as Major Rigg and his reinforcements reached their comrades at Portobello Bridge he took over command and began to organise a second assault against Davy's pub. This time the attack would have greater firepower, not just because of the increased number of soldiers but also because the second group had brought a machine gun with them.

William Rigg and his RIC troop (Robin Coningham)

At the same time Prof. Liam Ó Briain, a lecturer in romance languages at the National University and a member of the IRB and the Irish Volunteers, arrived at Portobello Bridge, on his way home to collect his weapons and equipment before joining the Rising. As recorded by Max Caulfield in *The Easter Rebellion*, he witnessed what happened next at the bridge.

> Ó Briain saw the soldiers pull a Maxim gun up to the bridge, on a wheeled bogey, and open fire on the pub. He saw riflemen, lining the whole southern bank of the Canal, firing with a careful parade-ground precision, the first line lying flat on their stomachs, the second kneeling, and behind them an officer [Rigg], his coat ripped to shreds by bullets but still scornful of the rebel marksmanship, directing their fire. To Ó Briain it had all looked an extraordinarily formal way of fighting.

Records show that Rigg was wounded in the fight; but this time the assault on the Irish Citizen Army position was successful, and they were forced to abandon the building, beginning to withdraw north into the city. Major Rigg survived his injuries and later fought at the Battle of the Somme. Having returned to the RIC after the war, on 22 August 1920 he was ambushed by the IRA at Lissarda, near Crookstown, Co. Cork, during the War of Independence, but he survived. (Some of the men who attacked him were responsible for ambushing and killing Michael Collins during the Civil War two years later at nearby Bealnablath, only five miles from the site of the Lissarda ambush.) William Rigg died in Tonbridge, Kent, in 1962, aged eighty-seven.

* * *

After pushing the insurgents out of Davy's pub, the piquet reorganised themselves and continued the advance. However, they were now moving straight towards the 150 men of Commandant Thomas MacDonagh's 2nd Battalion in Jacob's factory in Bishop Street. As the men of the Royal Irish Rifles advanced down Camden Street and then Wexford Street – with a small advance party pushed out to the front for security, with the Maxim gun to the rear, behind the main body – they were being watched by insurgents along the way. With Jacob's factory tucked in off the main road further ahead, Commandant MacDonagh was planning to let the main body of the piquet advance until they came into view of the factory right beside them, at which time MacDonagh intended to pour fire down on top of them. At such close range, firing into a large group of soldiers would have inflicted heavy casualties.

The advance party moved through the junction at the end of Wexford Street and into Redmond's Hill. Where the road here curves to the right, the advance members of the piquet came into view of Jacob's factory, and some of those inside suddenly opened fire. MacDonagh's plan had been to let them pass and wait for the main body to arrive before firing, but excitement obviously got the better of some of his men. Rebel reports state that about seven soldiers were killed or wounded in this opening volley.

The rest of the piquet now knew that they could not advance past Jacob's factory and that they would have to find another way to reach Dublin Castle. But before they could continue towards the castle they had first to rescue the wounded members of the advance party, who were lying in front of the factory. The British army is known to have suffered further casualties in the process of doing this. One of these was Captain John McCullagh, a doctor with the Royal Army Medical Corps. He may have travelled with the piquet from Portobello Barracks, or perhaps he was simply in the area or was based in one of the nearby hospitals – such as Mercer's or the Adelaide – and was either summoned to Aungier Street or made his way there after hearing gunfire. Whatever the case, it is known that he took part in the rescue of the wounded men.

Though only twenty years old, McCullagh was a veteran of Gallipoli. He was a native of Arklow, where his parents ran a grocery, bakery, tea, wine, and spirit merchants' shop. In *Unarmed Persons Shot by Rebels,* produced after the Rising, it is stated that Captain McCullagh was 'shot from Jacobs at 50 yards range while out bringing in wounded with 4 stretcher bearers. After being wounded he was being brought back in a stretcher when he was again fired on at very close range so that the Sinn Feiners must have seen it was a wounded man.' The information that went into the compiling of this section was received from Mercer's Hospital in Lower Stephen Street, where McCullagh was subsequently treated. He was not the only army doctor fired on at Jacob's factory: the same report recorded that a Major Balch of the Royal Army Medical Corps was also shot and injured while attempting to reach wounded soldiers.

Captain McCullagh ultimately survived his wounds, and by September 1920 he is known to have been residing in the Special Surgical Hospital in Blackrock, Co. Dublin. However, the records do not clarify whether he was there as a patient or as a member of the staff.

Having retrieved their wounded, the piquet withdrew from in front of Jacob's factory and turned down Lower Kevin Street and into Bride Street. From there they could reach the Ship Street gate into Dublin Castle, and it is known that by 2 p.m. at least fifty men had managed to reach the castle through this entrance. Here they joined the men of the 10th Royal Dublin Fusiliers who had also reached the castle and were later involved in the defence of the area.

* * *

Back in Portobello Barracks another group of 100 men was ready to depart for Dublin Castle. Under the command of Captain Reginald Rodwell (who would go on to serve as a brigadier in the Second World War in the Mediterranean and the Middle East), at 1:50 p.m. they left the barracks and began making their way down Camden Street and into Wexford Street. Once more they were heading right towards the insurgents in Jacob's factory.

With this new group was Second-Lieutenant James Calvert, a twenty-year-old native of Lurgan, Co. Armagh. He was from a strong unionist background; his father, James Calvert, was a signatory of the Ulster Covenant in 1912. His older brother, Edwin, was serving as a doctor with the Royal Army Medical Corps in France. James Calvert had attended Lurgan College, after which, having won a scholarship, he studied mathematics, science and English at Queen's University, Belfast, while also serving as a member of the OTC. He was commissioned in 1915 and was due to join the 6th Royal Irish Rifles (records show that he had already been transferred to this battalion in preparation for joining it in Salonika) but on 24 April 1916 he found himself advancing through the streets of Dublin.

Unlike the response to the earlier piquet, the rebel observers along Wexford Street did not simply watch these soldiers and let them pass by: this time, as the men of the Royal Irish Rifles neared the junction with Cuffe Street, they opened fire from houses on both sides of the road. The soldiers were caught in the crossfire. Second-Lieutenant Calvert – ten days away from his twenty-first birthday – was hit and killed instantly by an insurgent who fired from a window just above him. On Wednesday the 26th Calvert's father received a telegram stating that the War Office 'deeply regret to inform you a report from the Irish Command states that Lieut JH Calvert Irish Rifles died from gunshot wounds skull. Lord Kitchener expresses his sympathy.' The army later wrote to him, asking if he was 'aware of any amounts due to, or claims against the estate of,' his son. Calvert replied, stating that 'my dear boy had no property and left no will.' James Calvert is buried in Seagoe Cemetery, near Portadown.

The men under Captain Rodwell's command withdrew back up Camden Street, turned into Harrington Street and then travelled down Heytesbury Street, New Bride Street and then Bride Street to reach Dublin Castle. By now the unit had also suffered the death of two private soldiers. Mortally wounded by rebel fire outside Jacob's factory, or perhaps somewhere along Wexford Street, was Private David Wilson from Lurgan. He had been living and working in Glasgow when he enlisted in the British army. Comrades obviously managed to pull him back from where he was hit, as records show that he was taken to the nearby Adelaide Hospital before being pronounced dead. He now lies in Mount Jerome Cemetery.

Meanwhile, lying dead somewhere on the streets of Dublin, was Private John Mulhern, a native of Carrick-on-Shannon, Co. Leitrim. In his early thirties, he had lived in Dublin for at least fifteen years, where he worked as a hairdresser. It is not known whether he survived long enough to reach a hospital, but as he was first reported wounded and later reported killed he may have made it to a hospital alive, only to succumb to his injuries later. John Mulhern now lies in Deansgrange Cemetery.

* * *

The British army were aware of just how much of an impregnable fortress Jacob's factory was, and so they decided to simply contain it and bypass it for the time being. However, while the garrison at the factory made no attempt to get out, they continued to inflict casualties on the British army, even at great distances. From the factory roof they were able to fire into the grounds of Dublin Castle and reportedly as far as Portobello Bridge and even into Portobello Barracks itself. Several accounts suggest that a sentry on Portobello Bridge was wounded, perhaps even killed, by fire from Jacob's, apparently spotted because of the sun shining off the soldier's buckle and bayonet. Thomas Meldon, brigade musketry officer for the Dublin Brigade of the Irish Volunteers, who fought in Jacob's factory, later recorded:

On another occasion it was reported to me that it was possible to see Portobello Bridge from the tower overlooking Camden St. and that a soldier was on sentry on the bridge. I at once proceeded to the tower and, finding the information correct, sent for one of our first-class shots and a Thom's map of Dublin, and, with the assistance of it and a range-finder, which I carried, for the distance and picked off the sentry. Someone would never in this world hear that voice again – perhaps an Irish mother or wife. The following morning the bridge was sandbagged, but owing to the wind having shifted and a stack of chimneys coming in the line of fire, we were prevented from further action.

When the British army realised that fire was coming from above Jacob's factory they began firing a machine gun at the tower from the direction of Portobello.

One man who is definitely known to have been wounded on Portobello Bridge was 35-year-old Constable Patrick Myles of the DMP. The *Sinn Fein Rebellion Handbook* records that Constable Myles, 'while on duty at Portobello Bridge on 24th April had his left forearm shattered by a bullet. He was brought to City of Dublin [Baggot Street] Hospital, where he remained till 31st May. He was unable to resume duty till 20th September. He is 35 years of age, and has over 12 years' service.' Whether the bullet that hit him was fired from Jacob's factory or from somewhere closer is not known.

As well as the piquet and the second group of 100 men who fought their way to Dublin Castle, the 3rd Royal Irish Rifles despatched men to guard various sites around the city, including the Royal Hospital at Kilmainham, the Ordnance Depot at Islandbridge, the electric power station at the Pigeon House, the Bank of Ireland in College Green and the Central Telephone Exchange in Crown Alley. Regarding the telephone exchange, Cyril Falls recorded that

> information being received that the Telephone Exchange was in danger of falling into the hands of the insurgents, 2nd-Lieutenant J. Kearns left with 25 men at 1.45 p.m. to forestall them and take possession of the building. After an adventurous journey through the streets the party just managed to get there first, being fiercely attacked soon after their arrival. It was a remarkable and fortunate circumstance that the leaders of the revolt, at the time when they 'captured' the much less important General Post Office and other public buildings, neglected to possess and garrison the Telephone Exchange. The telephone afforded the principal means of military communication, and proved invaluable.

It certainly was a 'remarkable and fortunate circumstance' that the insurgents had not seized the Central Telephone Exchange, but the British army had a local Dublin woman to thank for that. Though the insurgents managed to cut the telephone lines from Dublin to Belfast and from Dublin to Britain, and Dublin Castle's own lines to the outside world, they failed to destroy the city's internal telephone lines. On 24 April, Connolly and Pearse decided to send men directly from the GPO to Crown Alley to finish the job. However, when they approached the exchange they were warned by an old woman that the building had already been occupied by the British army. Believing her, they turned back, though there was not a single soldier inside. The Royal Irish Rifles arrived only hours later and, finding the building free of insurgents, occupied it without difficulty. (According to Cyril Falls, the insurgents appeared to have realised their mistake and attacked the building, though unsuccessfully.)

Second-Lieutenant John Kearns – another of 3rd Royal Irish Rifles' Catholic officers – was thirty-eight years old. Born at the Curragh Camp in 1877, he was the son of Laurence Kearns from Blessington, Co. Wicklow, a soldier of the Royal Irish Rifles with twenty-one years' service. Laurence Kearns died when John was a child, and at about the age of nine John was sent to the Royal Hibernian Military School in the Phoenix Park, a school established to educate the orphaned children of the British forces in Ireland. Here he spent four-and-a-half years, earning three good-conduct badges and gaining the school rank of corporal. He enlisted in the British army in Dublin on 25 May 1891, his fourteenth birthday, as a bugler. The records show that he was only 4 feet 9 inches tall. His mother had remarried and was raising a second family in Fermoy, Co. Cork. One of John Kearns's half-brothers from this marriage, William Dillon, would go on to serve in the Royal Irish Rifles during the First World War.

Kearns enlisted in his father's old regiment, the Royal Irish Rifles, and was posted to the 1st Battalion as a bugler and musician-in-training. In April 1897 he set sail for South Africa, remaining there for two years before coming home in June 1899. However, after transferring to the 2nd Battalion he was soon on his way back to South Africa following the outbreak of the Anglo-Boer War, arriving in late October 1899 and going on to take part in the Cape Colony and Orange Free State campaigns. At the end of 1901 he was a sergeant-bugler. While stationed in Natal he was admitted to No. 8 General Hospital in Bloemfontein in July 1902 for dysentery and abscesses of the liver (his condition considered to be the result of 'climate and service'). This ultimately necessitated his evacuation from the country, where he had spent three years; and after three weeks aboard a hospital ship he arrived at Gosport, Hampshire, in November 1902.

First posted to Derry, Kearns was transferred to a garrison in Dublin in January 1903, where he remained for four years, having married in 1904, before going on to serve at various bases in England. By 1911 he was a colour-sergeant and musketry instructor and had obtained the first-class army education certificate while also having completed a course in the Maxim machine gun.

On the outbreak of the First World War, John Kearns was regimental sergeant-major of the 2nd Royal Irish Rifles. He landed in France with the battalion on 15 August 1914 (the same day as his younger brother, Michael Kearns, who had also joined the regiment on his fourteenth birthday and who was now a company sergeant-major in the same battalion) and was still with the battalion on 14 December when he developed myalgia (muscle pain) and was admitted to No. 7 Field Ambulance in Locre. Rheumatism was diagnosed the following day and he was sent on to No. 8 Casualty Clearing Station, from where he was evacuated to Britain on Christmas Eve 1914. By February 1915 Regimental Sergeant-Major Kearns was posted to the 3rd Royal Irish Rifles in Dublin. Commissioned as an officer that December (his brother Michael had been commissioned in October 1914), by this time he had spent more than twenty-two years in the ranks. He was considered an 'exemplary' soldier and had no breaches of conduct against his name in all those years.

After the Rising the standing orders of the 3rd Royal Irish Rifles recorded:

A party under 2nd Lt. Kearns held the Telephone Exchange against all assaults, thereby greatly facilitating the authorities in the work of communication ... It will be observed that only for a party sent from the unit under my [Major Rosborough's] command to hold the Telephone Exchange there would have been no means of communication between the different military stations during the actual fighting, as it was impossible to send any message or telegraph by orderly.

It is also known that Second-Lieutenant Kearns and his men were joined by at least one other Irish soldier from another regiment. On 2 May 1916 Kearns wrote:

I have the honour to report that no 7136 Sergeant C Leeson 3rd Connaught Rangers reported to me at 8-30am 25th April. I examined his [leave] pass which expired on the 27th April; on the authority of G.O.C. [general officer commanding] Dublin Garrison I detained him! He is an excellent NCO. On several occasions he exposed himself in the open street in order to reply to the fire of snipers, the latter causing a great deal of discomfort to the female operators of the District Telephone Exchange. He was also useful in obtaining food on requisition and escorting the operators to their homes, often under heavy fire from the rebels. He also gave me great assistance in the suppression of looting.

Sergeant Charles Leeson, a pre-war regular soldier from Dublin, now serving with the 3rd Connaught Rangers – a reserve battalion stationed at Kinsale at the time of the Rising – was home in Dublin on leave when the Rising began. Obviously having learnt that some fellow-soldiers had occupied the Central Telephone Exchange, he travelled there to lend a hand.

In January 1917 Second-Lieutenant John Kearns was promoted to lieutenant. It is not clear whether he returned to the war, but in July he was found unfit for further overseas service though fit for home service. However, after being admitted to hospital in May 1918 he was found permanently unfit in October for any further military service because of neurasthenia. As a result of his poor health he subsequently retired in January 1919.

Shortly afterwards Kearns was living in Joy Street, Belfast, from where he wrote to the army to complain about the five shillings a day that they were offering him. (In October 1918 he had been placed on half pay – essentially a retainer paid to officers who might be reactivated for full-time service in the future – and this was apparently the maximum rate an officer on half pay could receive.) Kearns argued that he did not want to stay on half pay as he had subsequently retired and was also no longer physically capable of serving in any capacity: he wanted to retire properly and receive the full 'retirement pay', along with a disablement pension and his war gratuity. He desperately needed the money, as he had no other income, his war wounds – as confirmed by the medical board – preventing him from ever working again. He was now also taking care of his invalid wife, who had been suffering from a mental illness for the previous twelve years and for whom he had been paying £1 10 shillings a week to an institution for her care. With his drop in income he had been forced to take her out of the institution and was now looking after her at home. After several heated letters to the army, Kearns finally wrote:

> As an old soldier of long service, I do not like to take any action that might be considered not in keeping with Army traditions but I have done my duty to the country, and I expect to be treated as the country believes its disabled old soldiers, especially men like myself who have gained their Commissions for service in the Field, are treated; on the contrary, a paltry payment of 5/– [five shillings] per day to an officer of my standing is a disgrace to the Army, and if I receive no satisfaction as a result of this letter, I shall be reluctantly compelled to make a public exposure of my case.

He had written earlier that 'if I am compelled to accept your ruling I will be obliged to degrade myself by appealing to charity or the workhouse' (indeed he had already applied for himself and his wife to be admitted to a workhouse); he also pointed out that he would have been better off remaining a regimental sergeant-major instead of accepting his commission in 1915. One officer wrote on his behalf that he believed Kearns to be 'practically starving'.

His service file does not record the outcome of his appeal, but it does show that in 1921 Kearns was living on Ormeau Road, Belfast, and by April 1927, as part of the National Scheme for Disabled Men, he had received work as a contract officer with the Post Office.

* * *

During the course of the Rising, Hanna Sheehy Skeffington got in touch with a despatch rider, Captain Thomas Wilson of the 10th Royal Dublin Fusiliers, in the hope of finding some information about her husband, the well-known pacifist Francis Sheehy Skeffington, after he was arrested and taken to Portobello Barracks.

Captain Wilson, from Baltinglass, Co. Wicklow, was a former clerk and shorthand typist with the Local Government Board. (He would later be wounded in the left arm and left leg on 27 March 1918 on the Somme, just after the start of the German army's Spring Offensive.) Hanna Sheehy Skeffington later recorded: 'I appealed to him after rumours had reached me that my husband was being held prisoner in Portobello Barracks to go there and make enquiries. He refused point blank, asking me if I wanted him to go to his death. When he realised I didn't understand the situation, he explained. He dared not go near the Royal Irish Rifles. He was a Catholic!' This was a belief about the 3rd Royal Irish Rifles that has persisted to the present day.

From Lower Tyrone Street (now Railway Street), Dublin, 24-year-old Private Edward 'Ned' Donnelly was one of the many Catholic soldiers in the 3rd Battalion during the Rising. Ned was the youngest of six children. His father was a labourer with the Dublin Glass Bottle Works and his mother reared pigs in their back yard and sold seconds of military equipment purchased from the Junior Army and Navy Store.

At fifteen, Ned had emigrated to the United States, but soon returned home because of homesickness. He subsequently became an electrician and married Mary Ellen Devereux from Govan, Glasgow, in the Pro-Cathedral, in June 1912. In October 1915, Ned – along with two friends – was sent on a job to Govan. One night in a local pub, the three men were handed white feathers by some women. Immediately, to prove the women wrong – and also because they did not particularly like their employer in Ireland – the three men enlisted in the British army. Ned joined the 3rd Royal Irish Rifles and was serving in Portobello Barracks when the Rising began.

Within weeks of the end of the rebellion, Ned found himself posted to No. 9 Platoon, C Company, 1st Royal Irish Rifles in the trenches. Then, on 1 July 1916 – the first day of the Battle of the Somme – Private Edward 'Ned' Donnelly was killed in action at Ovillers, aged twenty-four. A comrade later reported that Ned had been hit by shrapnel during the advance, losing part of his foot. In an effort to keep him safe, comrades moved Ned into a shell-hole, but he was subsequently buried alive by another shell blast. And so, with no known grave, today his name is commemorated on the Thiepval Memorial on the Somme.

* * *

Among the men of the 3rd Battalion in April 1916 was Lance-Corporal James Emerson. Aged nineteen, a native of Collon, Co. Louth, he was a son of the land agent of the Collon Estate (also known as the Foster-Massareene Estate). He had enlisted in September 1914. James was one of three brothers to serve in the war; his brother Herbert managed to fight with the Canadian army despite having accidentally sawn off the tops of the fingers of his left hand before enlisting, while his brother Egerton was a pre-war Connaught Ranger and veteran of Malta and India who was taken prisoner by the German army in late August 1914. (He and his fellow-prisoners were visited by Sir Roger Casement, who was attempting to recruit men for his Irish Brigade, which would return to Ireland and fight in the planned Rising. Casement is known to have secured only fifty-three recruits out of the 2,500 Irish prisoners he spoke to in German prisoner-of-war camps, prompting the Germans to abandon the idea of raising an Irish Brigade – and while protesting and refusing to accept concessions on offer, one prisoner delegation is also on record as having told Casement that: 'In addition to being Irish Catholics, we have the honour to be British soldiers'.)

The First World War had broken out the day after James Emerson's eighteenth birthday, and in April 1915 he was sent to France to join the 1st Battalion of his regiment. He served as a machine-gunner and was soon promoted to lance-corporal, but on 29 September he was shot in the right wrist and right foot at

The Bank of Ireland guard from the 3rd Royal Irish Rifles, after the Rising. The soldiers are: (*back row, l–r*) Private John Heatley, Lance-Corporal Denis Lehane, Sergeant W. Main and Private John Luby; (*front row, l–r*) Lance-Corporal James Emerson, Private J. Burton, Private P. Hughes and Private Thomas Barr.

Hooge, near Ypres. He was evacuated to Britain and after recovering from his wounds was posted to the 3rd Battalion in Dublin.

When the Rising began, Lance-Corporal Emerson was sent as part of a detachment of eight men to guard the Bank of Ireland in College Green, commanded by Sergeant William Morris (who had previously landed in France on 30 April 1915 to join the 2nd Royal Irish Rifles in the trenches). The other six men of the detachment were Lance-Corporal Denis Lehane, Private John Heatley (records suggest that he was from Belfast), Private J. Burton, Private P. Hughes, Private Thomas Barr, and Private John Luby. Luby was from Clarke's Court, off Boyne Street, in Dublin, and had previously served in France with D Company, 1st Royal Irish Rifles. Wounded in 1915, he was sent to Colne House Red Cross Hospital in Cromer, Norfolk.

After the Rising, Major James Rosborough of the 3rd Royal Irish Rifles, wrote that 'a detachment on guard at the Bank of Ireland resisted all attempts of the rebels to obtain possession of the Bank.' Cyril Falls noted that 'the Bank of Ireland, with the consent of Colonel McCammond, presented £5 to Sergeant Morris, £3 to Lance-Corporal Lehane, and £2 each to the six Riflemen of the Guard' in gratitude for defending the bank during the Rising. However, the bank may never have been in danger, as Thomas Slater of the Irish Volunteers, who served in Jacob's factory during the Rising, later said: 'I was definitely told on Easter Monday, however, by Thomas MacDonagh at Jacob's, that the bank of Ireland was not to be entered on account of its sentimental associations.'

Lance-Corporal Emerson was soon out of the frying pan and into the fire. Within two months of the end of the Rising he had been promoted to corporal, and on 1 July 1916 – the infamous first day of the Battle of the Somme – he was in the front line with the 9th Royal Irish Rifles as part of the 36th (Ulster) Division. That day – the bloodiest day in the history of the British army, during which 20,000 men were killed and a further 40,000 wounded – the 9th Battalion lost all fifteen of its officers, while 520 of its 615 men were killed, wounded or missing – a casualty rate of 85 per cent. Corporal James Emerson was one of the survivors.

Soon spotted as having the potential for leadership, Emerson on his return to Ireland in February 1917 began training to become an officer. He was commissioned as a second-lieutenant in August and posted to the 9th Royal Inniskilling Fusiliers. He joined the battalion in France but on 6 December – the day before the end of the Battle of Cambrai – he found himself caught up in a German counter-attack. The *London Gazette* of 12 February 1918 recorded what happened next:

> He led his company in an attack and cleared 400 yards of trench. Though wounded [Cyril Falls recorded that he had 'a hole in his steel helmet and blood running down his face from a bomb-splinter in his skull'], when the enemy attacked in superior numbers, he sprung out of the trench with eight men and met the attack in the open, killing many and taking six prisoners. For three hours after this, all other officers having become casualties, he remained with his company refusing to go to a dressing station and repeatedly repelling bombing attacks. Later, when the enemy attacked again in superior numbers he led his men to repel the attack and was mortally wounded. His heroism, when worn out and exhausted from loss of blood, inspired his men to hold out, though almost surrounded, till reinforcements arrived and dislodged the enemy.

This was the citation for Second-Lieutenant James Emerson's Victoria Cross. Emerson was twenty-one years old when he died, and his body was never recovered. His name is commemorated on the Cambrai Memorial at Louverval, on a memorial stone at the Ulster Memorial Tower at Thiepval on the Somme, on the war memorial in Mary Street, Drogheda, and on a memorial at the Church of Ireland church in his native Collon, Co. Louth. His mother, Ellen Emerson, had been invited to receive the medal from the king at a ceremony in Buckingham Palace but felt she was too old to make the trip; instead, on 3 April 1918 she received her son's Victoria Cross from Brigadier-General William Hacket Pain during a packed public ceremony in the Whitworth Hall in Drogheda. (A former commanding officer of the 108th Brigade, part of the 36th (Ulster) Division, Hacket Pain was a prominent unionist figure who played a leading part in the setting up of the Ulster Volunteers during the Home Rule crisis of 1912. He had been in Dublin during the Rising, had been mentioned in despatches for his actions there, and at the time he met Ellen Emerson he was serving as commanding officer of all British forces in the north of Ireland.)

At the present-day Army Foundation College in Harrogate, Yorkshire, where sixteen and seventeen-year-old school-leavers are trained for a career in the British army, one of the school's training companies contains a platoon named No. 8 (Emerson VC) Platoon, named in his honour. He is the only known Irish soldier to have served during the Easter Rising who went on to be awarded the Victoria Cross.

* * *

At Rathmines during the afternoon of 24 April 1916, as they began to learn what was happening, soldiers and officers on leave in the area began making their way to Portobello Barracks. Sometimes, however, they encountered the insurgents first.

Twenty-year-old James Nolan, a private in the 3rd Royal Irish Rifles, was on leave in Dublin. He was a native of the city, as was his mother; his father was a native of Co. Carlow. The family lived in Power's Court, off Lower Mount Street, but on 24 April James Nolan was staying at a different address. Father James Doyle of St Mary's Church, Haddington Road (who later became a British army chaplain), met Nolan and later recorded:

> I got another sick call to Turner's cottage [in Shelbourne Road]. I went down and when there I met a boy named Nolan who was in the Dublin Fusiliers [actually the Royal Irish Rifles] and home on leave. His father was a cabman who lived in Waterloo lane. There was a mark on his nose. He told [me] his father's horse bit him, I said to the women who were there, 'don't let this boy out of this; he will be shot at sight being in uniform.' I heard about 6 or 7 o'clock that evening that a boy named Nolan was shot, so I went down to the mortuary. A large number of bodies were there piled up on top of each other. I looked among them and then I saw the mark on the boy's nose.

All this happened on Wednesday 26 April. The Royal Dublin Fusiliers did not lose any man named Nolan during the Rising, whereas records show that James Nolan of the 3rd Royal Irish Rifles died on Easter Monday. He had obviously attempted to make his way to Portobello Barracks but was spotted and killed en route. He was twenty years old when he died, and he is buried in Grangegorman Military Cemetery.

* * *

One man who did make it safely to Portobello Barracks was Second-Lieutenant William Monk Gibbon. A nineteen-year-old officer from Dundrum, Co. Dublin, he had grown up in Taney Rectory, where his father, Rev. William Monk Gibbon, was the rector and dean and, from 1900, vicar of St Nahi's Church in Dundrum.

The family were strongly unionist, and they commemorated the memory of Captain Daniel Frederick Ryan, Gibbon's great-great-grandfather, who had been mortally wounded by the United Irishmen leader Edward Fitzgerald on 18 May 1798 during the arrest of Fitzgerald at his hiding-place in Thomas Street. (Another relative, named Boxwell, from Butlerstown, Co. Wexford, who had fought with the 1798 rebels during the Battle of Vinegar Hill, was dismissed as a wild fool.) Unlike the majority of his relatives, however, young William was less resistant to the idea of Home Rule for Ireland. He attended St Columba's College in Rathfarnham, Co. Dublin, where he was bullied so badly that he would have violent nightmares when he returned home on holidays.

While staying in Gorey with his sisters in 1914 Gibbon learnt that the First World War had begun. He attempted to join the Royal Naval Division – perhaps because he had an older half-brother who was a sailor – but he was rejected because he did not meet the required chest measurement. The following year, after hearing that the Germans had allegedly crucified a Canadian soldier on a barn door on the Western Front, Gibbon again tried to join up. This time his father talked him out of it.

In October 1915 he began studying at the University of Oxford, where he joined its OTC. Through this he applied for a commission in the Army Service Corps, which he tried to take up after only one term at the university. This request was at first rejected, but after the Gibbons' family doctor wrote a letter to his brother-in-law, a general with the Army Service Corps based at the War Office in London, Gibbon's commission suddenly came through and he was appointed a second-lieutenant in January 1916, at the age of nineteen.

In April 1916, having trained in England and due to depart for the war in several weeks' time, he was granted four days' leave in Dublin and so returned home. On the third day of his leave, 24 April, after hearing that the Rising had begun, he wanted to travel into Dublin to offer his services. His family tried to stop him, terrified that he would be shot because he was in uniform, but he insisted, and he soon made his way to Portobello Barracks, getting a lift from a Dublin University OTC cadet who was driving around on a motorbike.

Gibbon reported to Major Rosborough as soon as he arrived at the barracks and was put to work under the quartermaster of the 3rd Royal Irish Rifles, Captain Forster. He soon befriended the quartermaster's son, sixteen-year-old Lionel Forster, as well as another 3rd Battalion officer, Lieutenant Richard Hayward, the regiment's bandmaster (who would later be mentioned in despatches for his actions during the Rising).

By now Second-Lieutenant Gibbon was beginning to have his doubts about the war, and especially about his place in it. The events of that week would deeply affect him, and he would soon become known as a conscientious objector and an ardent pacifist. For now, however, he was a young – and still somewhat willing – British army officer caught up in a rebellion. Many years later he would write about his experiences during the week, and the result was his memoir *Inglorious Soldier,* published in 1968.

That evening after dark, with the men of the 3rd Battalion scattered around Dublin in their various positions, Lieutenant Michael Malone of C Company, 3rd Battalion, Irish Volunteers, left his position at number 25 Northumberland Road and climbed up a nearby telegraph pole. He tapped the phone line to Portobello Barracks and rang the barracks. He pretended to be phoning from the Curragh and tried to ask subtly about how many men were stationed in the barracks, but the soldier on the other end became suspicious and refused to give any information. Meanwhile, as recorded by Monk Gibbon,

> around 9.0 p.m., a sergeant called MacAdam returned safely to barracks disguised in women's clothing. He had been in a house in Cuffe Street, quite near to the Green, and it would have been fatal for him to emerge into the street in khaki. But some kind soul had provided him with a shawl and a skirt and, leaving the quartermaster's office, the Forsters and I listened to the account of his adventure, delivered in a voice that would speedily have given the lie to the shawl over his head if he had been compelled to use it.

Rumours were now circulating that groups of soldiers and police in the city had been massacred by the rebels, that columns of Germans and Irish-Americans were marching on Dublin, that the country was in complete revolt, that the Irish Volunteers wanted to seize weapons and free prisoners taken by the British army and that with these goals in mind they were going to launch an all-out assault against Portobello Barracks at any moment. With the firing that could be heard almost constantly outside the barrack walls, many of those inside began to feel that they were under siege.

The next morning, Tuesday the 25th, after a period spent as captain of the guard, Second-Lieutenant Gibbon was having breakfast in the officers' mess when he heard a story that after firing had broken out on O'Connell Bridge the horses of an ammunition wagon had run terrified all the way back to Portobello Barracks. He heard another story that two privates had managed to make it back to the barracks from the quays disguised as 'corner boys'. He was now beginning to notice the nervous atmosphere in the barracks and later recalled that when a rumour went around that there might be a sniper in a church spire across the Grand Canal from the barracks some men immediately began firing on this position.

* * *

That day men continued to arrive at the barracks to report for service, and other members of the 3rd Royal Irish Rifles now helped to form the cordon around Dublin. One Irishman who turned up was Gerald Keatinge. From Terenure in Dublin and only seventeen years old, he was a medical student in Trinity College, where he was also a cadet-sergeant with Dublin University OTC. On the first day of the Rising he had reported to Beggarsbush Barracks, somehow making it safely in and out despite the fact that it was surrounded by insurgents; but after

Gerald Keatinge from
Terenure, Dublin, *c.*1919
(Rachel Keatinge)

first being ordered to make his way to Trinity College – something that would be too dangerous to attempt because of rebel forces along the route – he was instead instructed to go home. The next day, determined to do something and not simply sit out the Rising at home, he made his way to Portobello Barracks.

Gerald Keatinge attended St Andrew's College in Dublin and the Moravian Boys' School in Ockbrook, Derbyshire, and Denstone College in Uttoxeter, Staffordshire. Then, on 26 July 1914, an event took place that almost saw him end up in a green uniform. At 6:30 p.m. that day, after a failed attempt to confiscate the weapons that the Irish Volunteers had landed at Howth earlier that morning, 180 men of the 2nd King's Own Scottish Borderers were marching back to the Royal Barracks from Clontarf when they were assaulted by an angry crowd, ultimately about a thousand strong. Stones, rotten food and bottles were thrown at the soldiers.

The soldiers had been followed for about three hours by the mob when they were joined in Sackville Street by their commanding officer, Major Alfred Haig. He did not know that his men were armed with live ammunition, and when he led them onto the quays at Bachelor's Walk some of the crowd attempted to drag a soldier out of the column. Haig ordered the mob to disperse but was hit three times in the face with stones. He then ordered twenty men to halt and form two lines before raising his hand to try to silence the crowd. Suddenly one of the men fired, prompting the two lines of soldiers to pour two volleys into the crowd. It is not clear whether Haig gave the order to fire, intending to scare off the mob with what he thought was blank ammunition, or whether the soldier who fired first misunderstood Haig's hand signal. Horrified, Haig now realised that his men had had live ammunition all along.

Three people were killed instantly, a fourth later died of bayonet wounds, while thirty-eight more were injured. The event resulted in an increase in support for the Volunteers, with many people interpreting it as yet another example of how the British cared little for the Irish people.

Following the Bachelor's Walk massacre Gerald Keatinge considered joining the Irish Volunteers. In the end he did not, and later in 1914, when he entered Trinity College to study medicine, he also joined the OTC. When the First World War broke out he tried to obtain a commission in the army and join the fight. He was only sixteen but pretended to be seventeen – the minimum age – but his father found out and reported his son's true age. Gerald later wrote that it was 'very likely I would not have been here to write this essay if I had indeed got myself into the Army and if I had I would almost certainly have joined the Dublin Fusiliers and been killed in Gallipoli.'

On the morning of 25 April 1916 Cadet-Sergeant Keatinge made his way to Portobello Barracks, accompanied by three friends who were also members of Dublin University OTC: Eugene Long, William Spence and Alfred Mathews.

Cadet Eugene Long was twenty years old, a native of Limerick. Later during the Rising he would be sent to the headquarters of Irish Command at Parkgate and from there to Dublin Castle. After the Rising he served in the trenches as a second-lieutenant with the South Irish Horse and as a lieutenant with the 7th Royal Irish Regiment. He survived the war and died in Dublin in 1956, aged sixty-one.

Cadet-Corporal William Spence was a 21-year-old from Oakley Road in Ranelagh, the son of a civil and mechanical engineer. (His grandfather, also William Spence, had founded the Cork Street Foundry and Engineering Works in Dublin, one of the most important industries in the area at the time.) A member of the Architectural Association of Ireland, Spence had won the Downes Medal for Excellence in Architectural Design and in 1914 had become a student in the office of the architectural firm Batchelor and Hicks; that year he also exhibited 'an excellent set of measured drawings of Trinity College chapel' at the exhibition of students' work at the Metropolitan School of Art. Later in the Rising he too was sent to the headquarters of Irish Command before being redirected to Dublin Castle. After the Rising he served in Mesopotamia (Iraq) as an officer with the Royal Engineers, where he was mentioned in despatches, and after the war worked for several architectural firms in London. He was working at the British Ministry of Supply in London when he died in 1956, aged sixty-one.

Eighteen-year-old Cadet-Corporal Alfred Mathews was born in Dundrum, Co. Dublin. His father was a manager with the Northern Bank, a native of

Ballymena, Co. Antrim, and his mother was from Clones, Co. Monaghan. He had been on duty as commander of the OTC guard in Trinity College on the morning of the 24th until he was relieved by another cadet at 8 a.m., four hours before the start of the Rising. He appears to have remained in Portobello Barracks for the duration of the Rising, after which he went on to serve as a second-lieutenant with the Royal Dublin Fusiliers before becoming a captain in the British Indian Army. He stayed in the Indian Army after the war and by the early 1920s was serving in the 112th Infantry Battalion, soon to be renamed the 3rd Battalion of the 4th Bombay Grenadiers. He died in his native Dublin in 1950, aged fifty-three.

Gerald Keatinge later wrote a detailed account of his experiences during the Easter Rising, After arriving at Portobello Barracks,

> Spence acted as our Spokesman and he laid our case before the Officer at the gate. The Officer was very decent and told us to change into uniform and report to him as soon as possible. This we did about an hour and a half afterwards, i.e. at 12.45. I took off my Red Cross brassard [armband] and stripes [sergeant's insignia] as I wanted to stop with the other chaps and anyhow I felt pretty sure the rebels would not respect the Red Cross, and in this I was right. On our arrival we were immediately handed over to the Sergeant Major who in turn handed us over to a Sergeant who provided us with fifty rounds of ammunition, rifle and bayonet. Dinner was the next consideration and I may state it required all the consideration possible. After this 'meal' the rest of the afternoon was occupied by numerous parades for selecting guards.
>
> Needless to say the OTC chaps stuck together like the proverbial ivy but we had no luck and had to remain in barracks all afternoon. Here I might conveniently mention that after a short time in the barracks we discovered that we were not the only pebbles on the beach – in other words that there were two other Trinity OTC men and several Inns of Court [OTC] chaps along with us.

One of these other members of Dublin University OTC is later named as 21-year-old Cadet Ronald Boyd, while one of the Inns of Court OTC was Ronald's nineteen-year-old brother, Private Lionel Boyd. The Boyds were Dubliners – sons of a justice of the peace and assistant land commissioner from Co. Roscommon and a mother from Co. Galway – and had previously lived in Morehampton Road and later in Terenure. Cadet Ronald Boyd later travelled to the headquarters of Irish Command at Parkgate and from there was sent on to Dublin Castle. After the Rising he was commissioned and served in France with the Royal Munster Fusiliers, entering the war in November 1917. By 1922 his address was given as the Irish Land Commission, 25 Upper Merrion Street, Dublin. Not long afterwards, however, his address changed to Cobb Hall,

Sharnbrook, Bedfordshire. This was part of a military base, showing that Boyd continued to serve in the military after the war.

On the outbreak of the Second World War, Ronald Boyd was a flight-lieutenant with the Royal Air Force Volunteer Reserve. On 19 March 1940 he died of wounds in the Royal Victoria Hospital, Netley, Hampshire, while serving in No. 920 Balloon Squadron. Given that he received his wounds in Britain and during a period long before any German aircraft appeared in British skies, it seems that he died as a result of an accident. He was forty-six years old and is buried in Bedford Cemetery, Bedfordshire.

Private Lionel Boyd of the Inns of Court OTC served alongside (and at one point under the command of) Cadet-Sergeant Gerald Keatinge during the Rising, in the later half of the week at Amiens Street Station, working alongside the Ulster Composite Battalion. He was later commissioned as a second-lieutenant, landing in France on 31 January 1917 to join the 1st Royal Munster Fusiliers in the trenches. He was wounded following the start of the German Spring Offensive and was subsequently evacuated. After the war he transferred to the Royal Corps of Signals and remained in the army.

By the time of the Second World War he had reached the rank of colonel. He served throughout the war – he is known to have served in Italy for a time – and in 1944 was made an officer of the Order of the British Empire; he was also mentioned in despatches during both world wars. He died in Australia in 1972, aged seventy-six, having been there to visit his daughter.

In his account of the OTC members present in Portobello Barracks, Gerald Keatinge continues:

> This gallant little band kept together as much as possible because we were all of the same corps and as all the world knows the [Royal Irish] Rifles are an Ulster Regiment, and it was next to impossible to understand them.
>
> There were of course exceptions as all the men who were on leave in the neighbourhood had reported like ourselves so that the men in the barracks were a very mixed lot from the RFC [Royal Flying Corps] to the ASC [Army Service Corps].
>
> About four o'clock we had tea – so called – which was drunk out of basins. The less said about this meal the better. About six o'clock we were paraded and provided with another fifty rounds of ammunition. These parades were very trying on the nerves as we did not know when we would be going out against the rebels, moreover continual sniping was going on at the barracks from the houses round.

* * *

That evening events began to happen that would ultimately make the battalion's role in the Rising infamous. These centred on one man: Captain John Bowen-Colthurst.

John Bowen-Colthurst from Cork,
of the Royal Irish Rifles
(Richard J. Hodges/W. T. Pike)

Born in Cork in 1880, Bowen-Colthurst was thirty-five when the Rising began. His family home was Oak Grove in Coolnagearagh, near Carrigadrohid, Co. Cork, but he also had links to Dripsey Castle at Coachford. Educated at Haileybury College in Hertfordshire, he later attended the Royal Military Academy at Sandhurst and on 12 August 1899 – his nineteenth birthday – was commissioned into the 2nd Royal Irish Rifles. He took part in the Anglo-Boer War, during which he was one of 600 members of the Royal Irish Rifles surrounded by Boer forces under General Christiaan de Wet on 4 April 1900. The next day 546 members of the battalion were forced to surrender, including Bowen-Colthurst, who had been wounded.

After being released from captivity and later serving in the Transvaal, in 1901 Bowen-Colthurst, now a lieutenant, transferred to the 1st Royal Irish Rifles and began serving with the battalion in India, where he became known for organising prayer meetings for his men. In 1904 he took part in the Tibet Expedition – a British attempt to stop Russian influence from expanding into the country – during which he commanded a machine-gun detachment. (At least one soldier under Bowen-Colthurst's command with this detachment, James Lyle from Belfast, would go on to serve during the Easter Rising with the 3rd Royal Irish Rifles, by then a company sergeant-major.)

Promoted to captain in 1907, Bowen-Colthurst left India the following year. He returned home to Ireland and in April 1910 was married. Three years later he qualified for admission to the Staff College for training as a senior officer, and after the start of the First World War, on 14 August 1914, he landed in France with the 2nd Battalion. In command of one of the battalion's companies, Bowen-Colthurst fought at the Battles of Mons and Le Cateau.

On 15 September he took part in an attack that ended his war in France. While the commanding officer of the battalion, Lieutenant-Colonel Wilkinson Bird, was temporarily commanding the 7th Brigade (to which the battalion belonged), Major Charles Spedding, the battalion's second-in-command, was in charge. At Vailly-sur-Aisne, Captain Bowen-Colthurst occupied a wood, as ordered – it was due to be used as the starting-point for a flanking attack against a nearby enemy position – but then spotted a German trench to his front manned by only a platoon (about fifty men), and he led his men in a successful assault against it. However, though he and his men captured the trench he was subsequently wounded in a strong enemy counter-attack that resulted in eighty casualties among his company.

Lieutenant-Colonel Bird was outraged, claiming that Bowen-Colthurst had been specifically ordered not to advance from beyond the wood. Bowen-Colthurst insisted that Major Spedding had instructed him to make the assault on the German trench. There followed a bitter row between Bird and Bowen-Colthurst over whether the attack on the trench had been authorised or not. Attempting to prove that Bird was wrong, and furthermore that he was a bad commanding officer, Bowen-Colthurst claimed that Bird had been appointed commanding officer of the battalion solely to qualify him for further promotion, and that as an Englishman he knew nothing about the sensitivities of his Irish troops. He wrote to the army to say that

> as a Colonel of an Irish Regiment Lt. Col. Bird proved himself by a thousand different follies an impossible individual and in April 1914 his crowning folly was volunteering the services of the Royal Irish Rifles he commanded for active service in Belfast and Ulster [during the Home Rule crisis]. Entirely also on his own responsibility he ordered me and the other Company Commanders to prepare our Companies immediately to fight in Belfast. As far as I was concerned this was the final breach. I immediately informed Lt. Col. Bird that his order was an impossibility, that the Regimental Depot was at Belfast, and that I as an Irishman declined to give my men orders to fire, on the peaceful citizens at Belfast. It was forthwith reported to the W.O. [War Office] by Lt. Col. Bird but the order was withdrawn ...
>
> The C.O. could have had me tried by court martial no doubt for insubordination, disobedience of orders, or any other charge he cared to have drawn up – for saying that I belonged to a Belfast regiment, and was not going to order my men to fire on their own brothers & sisters and fathers and mothers to please Messrs. Asquith, Lloyd George, Sir John Simon, Winston Churchill or other politicians.
>
> I was an Irishman first last and all the time and told Lt Col Bird that he did not understand the Irish and never would. Whoever appointed Bird to command an Irish Batt. was capable of appointing a Brahmin to command a regiment of Pathans.

Regarding Bird's conduct in the war, Bowen-Colthurst claimed that, after requesting unsuccessfully to be removed from under Bird's command before going to France, 'during the retreat from Mons ... Bird was on many occasions a gibbering, incoherent maniac, his highly strung nervous system gave way completely under the strain,' and 'after Mons he broke down – and wailed "I've got no orders – I don't know where to go – I'm going to take refuge in Maubeuge." The intention was fortunately prevented.'

The army had also received a report from Lieutenant-Colonel Bird, stating that

> during the first few weeks of the campaign of 1914 Capt. Bowen-Colthurst displayed military capacity and judgement of so low a standard, with lack of mental balance, as to induce the belief that he was not fitted to command a company in the field. He had broken down on the morning following the action at Mons with such dispiriting effects on the men that Colonel Bird [the writer] had been obliged to suspend him from command, though he reinstated him 3 or 4 days later when matters were more normal. This reinstatement Col. Bird had intended as a tentative measure only.

Bird went on to insist that Bowen-Colthurst had been under orders not to advance from beyond the wood on 15 September 1914, and that Major Spedding had known this.

Bowen-Colthurst denied that he had broken down after Mons, and claimed that he had been removed from command of his company only for one day, and not three or four days, as Bird stated. The man whose testimony could have settled the dispute, Major Charles Spedding, had been killed four days after the event during an enemy attack on 19 September.

John Lucy, a member of the 2nd Royal Irish Rifles, wrote an account of his experiences, entitled *There's a Devil in the Drum* (1938). He was present for Bowen-Colthurst's attack on 15 September 1914, referring to him as 'a tall gaunt captain with the light of battle in his eye ... A very religious man he was too, always talking about duty, and a great Bible reader.' However, Lucy does not clarify whether the attack was authorised or not, only that Bowen-Colthurst asked for volunteers from A Company – which was in position alongside Bowen-Colthurst's own company – to advance in support of his men during the attack. Lucy concludes that 'I suppose he knew very well that the native pride of Irish troops could be depended on. Anyway the whole of "A" Company immediately volunteered to assist.' (Lucy's older brother, Lance-Corporal Denis Lucy, was killed during Bowen-Colthurst's attack on the German trench.)

Bowen-Colthurst submitted accounts by several NCOs in support of his claim, along with the names of ten senior officers who could be contacted to testify to his character. He also stated that Lieutenant-Colonel Bird had made this 'extremely bitter and mendacious report' against him because of the strain he had been under, the loss of a leg after being wounded in the same enemy attack that killed Major Spedding, and the subsequent possibility of his being forced to retire from the army. Both men were able to call on the support of a major-general, one of whom stated that Bowen-Colthurst was a capable officer, the other that he was useless; and the army finally decided to let the matter drop, as without Major Spedding the exact truth could not be uncovered.

However, Bowen-Colthurst's alleged breakdown after Mons, and the fact that after he was wounded a medical board reported that he was suffering from 'nervous exhaustion' (possibly some form of shell shock) – something that was not made known to any of his future commanding officers – were ominous signs of what was to come.

The army ultimately decided that Bowen-Colthurst should not be promoted to major, a promotion he had been qualified for since 1909 and that he had been due to receive, and that he should not be returned to the British Expeditionary Force in France. After recovering from the wounds he received on 15 September 1914 (a bullet wound in his right upper arm, a broken forearm – which remained crooked for the rest of his life – and a bullet wound on his left side, near his heart), he briefly served in England as brigade major with the 111th Brigade, part of the 37th Division, before being sent home to Ireland. He soon joined the 3rd Royal Irish Rifles in Dublin and was put to work in recruiting.

During this period Bowen-Colthurst also learnt of the death of his brother, Captain Robert Bowen-Colthurst of the 1st Leinster Regiment, who was killed, aged thirty-one, on 15 March 1915. With no known grave, he is commemorated on the Menin Gate Memorial in Ypres. This news could not have helped Bowen-Colthurst's condition, and it seems that his mental state continued to degrade. In his article 'A short history of Portobello Barracks' P. D. O'Donnell wrote that

> the Great War veteran, Michael Slater, who ... visited the barracks in 1967, was a soldier of Captain Bowen-Colthurst's company. This was unusual luck. He filled in some hitherto unpublished background information about his company commander. Colthurst, it seems, was greatly feared, though respected by the men since he had returned from the fighting in Belgium the previous year. He became, however, more and more erratic, keeping aloof, stalking about, repeating phrases (Biblical or poetic) to himself, and venting his spleen openly against the rebels. Colthurst's orderly was well known to Slater as a soldier who was very often drunk, and it is related that the Captain had expressly asked for the services of this man, so it was said, that he might convert him. There were tales of Colthurst reading long passages of the Bible to his orderly, and to coin a Rocheism, the Captain stuffed the Bible down his throat by beating him on the head with the good book.

Bowen-Colthurst's behaviour would soon reach an insane and bloody conclusion. The event that triggered his final breakdown was the arrest on the second day of the Rising of the feminist and pacifist Francis Sheehy Skeffington, a well-known Dublin personality and journalist, editor of the weekly *Irish Citizen,* published by the Irish Women's Franchise League. As later recorded by Lieutenant Max Morris of the 11th East Surrey Regiment,

> at Dublin on 25th April, 1916, between 6 and 7 p.m. I was in command of a picquet of the 3rd Battalion, Royal Irish Rifles, one N.C.O. and fourteen

privates, guarding Davy's Public House and Portobello Bridge. My orders were to defend my post, but to avoid a conflict if possible. I observed several large and noisy crowds in the direction of Jacobs Factory, and shots were fired at my picquet from that direction. A civilian reported to me that Sheehy Skeffington was approaching my post from the direction of Jacobs Factory. Shortly afterwards I saw Sheehy Skeffington advancing towards me. I recognised him from a photograph and description I had been given of him. I was impressed by the fact that the crowd became quiet on his approach, and a large crowd which was on Portobello Bridge retired in the direction of Portobello Barracks. I was informed by several civilians that the Sinn Feiners were approaching my post and intended to attack Portobello Barracks that night. When Skeffington who appeared to be unarmed, but was followed by a large crowd, reached Davy's Public House, where I was, I and two of my men followed him, without stopping him. The two men, at my order, seized him by the arms and marched him across the bridge and into Portobello Barracks. I remained with my picquet. The crowd which had been following Skeffington then dispersed. I could not see whether the crowd following him was armed or not.

Sheehy Skeffington had been a member of a peace committee set up to try to bring an end to the Dublin Lockout in 1913, had served as vice-chairman of the Irish Citizen Army until it became a military body, when he resigned, and more recently had served six months in prison for anti-recruitment activities. Though he supported the aims of the Irish Volunteers, he did not agree with their use of force to achieve them.

When Second-Lieutenant Guy Pinfield of the 8th (King's Royal Irish) Hussars was mortally wounded in the first attempt by the British army to recapture City Hall on 24 April, Sheehy Skeffington had run towards him through the crossfire in an attempt to help. By the time he reached Pinfield his comrades had dragged him back inside the castle grounds. Sheehy Skeffington again ran out under fire to a nearby chemist's shop to get medical supplies.

During the first two days of the Rising, Sheehy Skeffington also tried to stop the looting in Sackville Street and elsewhere, successfully requesting that the insurgents in the GPO send out some men to deal with it. On Tuesday the 25th he travelled around Dublin putting up posters asking for volunteers to form a civilian police force that might be able to stop the looting and the violence that had broken out following the removal of the DMP from the streets. When he was arrested by Lieutenant Morris, Sheehy Skeffington was returning home to Rathmines from a meeting arranged to discuss the setting up of his citizen force. Given that martial law had been declared earlier that day, and that suspected rebel sympathisers and known accomplices of the leaders were being rounded up and interned, this was almost certainly the reason he was arrested. He knew several of the leading figures and so would certainly have been considered a 'known accomplice'. The fact that Morris had earlier been shown a picture of him and been given a description of him certainly suggests that this was the reason, and Morris seems to have been specifically looking out for him.

After being taken to Portobello Barracks, Sheehy Skeffington was searched, questioned and then placed in a cell in the guardroom. It was Bowen-Colthurst who performed the search of his person, but he found nothing incriminating. At about 8:30 p.m. Sheehy Skeffington came into contact with Sergeant John Maxwell, the regimental provost-sergeant (in charge of the regiment's military police). Maxwell was a pre-war regular soldier and veteran of France, the son of an RIC sergeant from Co. Antrim and a mother from Co. Kilkenny. (He was later commissioned as a second-lieutenant and returned to the war, where he was wounded on 15 October 1918 while serving in the 1st Royal Irish Rifles. He survived his wounds and retired from the army in December 1919. Settling in Leeds, he died there in 1970, aged eighty-three.) Maxwell recorded that

> at Portobello Barracks, Dublin, on 25th April, 1916, about 8-30 p.m. being Regimental Provost Sergt., I went to the Guard Room. The Officer in charge of the guard, whose name I do not remember as there were three officers of that duty who relieved one another [Second-Lieutenant William Dobbin, Second-Lieutenant Alexander Wilson and Second-Lieutenant Fred Tooley], told me to take a prisoner named Skeffington to the orderly room. I did so, and brought him in front of the Adjutant [Lieutenant Samuel Morgan], who interviewed him.

Lieutenant Morgan later stated that

> at Portobello Barracks, Dublin, on 25th April, 1916, about 8-15 p.m. Sergt. Maxwell brought Skeffington to the Orderly Room. I asked Skeffington if he was a Sinn Feiner. He replied that he was in sympathy with the Sinn Fein movement, but was not in favour of militarism. I ordered him to be taken back to the Guard Room. My impression as to what Skeffington meant by not being in favour of militarism was that he objected to the Sinn Feiners being out and shooting people.

After this meeting Sergeant Maxwell was ordered to return the prisoner to his cell, which he did. Lieutenant Morgan phoned the headquarters of Irish Command and, having been unable to form an exact charge against Sheehy Skeffington, had asked whether or not he should release the prisoner. He was told not to, and so Sheehy Skeffington remained in his cell, despite having no charge against him. (As with other suspected sympathisers interned during the Rising, higher command wanted them locked up and secure until the rebellion had ended.)

Cadet-Sergeant Gerald Keatinge also witnessed the arrest of Francis Sheehy Skeffington and later recorded that on 25 April,

> from 6 till about 11.30 we had no parade but Long and I acted as escort to a Sergeant bringing a message to the guard at Davy's 'pub'. It was here that I saw Sheehy Skeffington being marched up to the barracks under escort surrounded by a crowd who were very excited and making demonstrations against him. Later I saw Skeffington in the Guard Room. On returning we were paraded with others and definitely divided up into Sections and Platoons. The Major who was commanding them [Rosborough] addressed us saying that an enemy was advancing from the Wicklow Mountains, and that we should probably have to go out and meet them next morning at 3.30 a.m. but that whether we went or not, we should parade at that hour. He further said that he hoped we would behave well under fire and do our duty to our King and Ireland. During this speech I was trembling like a leaf from sheer fright – the ghastly inaction had told only too well on me.

So it was that as midnight approached, in the atmosphere of fear that existed in Portobello Barracks, a mentally unstable officer full of religious fervour and a hatred for Irish nationalism was ordered to take a group of soldiers on a mission outside barracks.

Knowing that Francis Sheehy Skeffington was being held in the guardroom, Bowen-Colthurst decided to make use of this prisoner. The captain of the guard that night was Second-Lieutenant William Dobbin, who had been on duty almost constantly since the Rising began. Dobbin was eighteen years old. Although born in Bendigo, a town in Victoria, Australia, he grew up in Ireland and was the son of Major William Dobbin from Co. Cork who was currently the governor of the Borstal Institution in Clonmel, Co. Tipperary and who had previously served as governor of Waterford Prison. William Dobbin had applied for a commission in June 1915, two months before his eighteenth birthday. He had been relieved for a few hours the previous night by Second-Lieutenant Gibbon, who recorded that, after going to the guardroom with orders to relieve the officer in charge there at about 3 a.m., he found a

> tall, slight, fresh-complexioned youth named Dobbyn [sic]. He was eighteen years old and had not long left school ... [He was] friendly, gentle, gracious, following what appeared to him to be the unchallengeable and imperative path of duty. He was dog-tired. His eyes were leaden, he stooped, and, as soon as I told him that I had come to relieve him, he went into the guardroom, lay down, placed a copy of the *Daily Sketch* under his head on the dirty floor, and fell asleep.

Gibbon was relieved by 8 a.m., and Dobbin appears to have gone back on guard duty, having had only five hours' poor sleep. He was still on guard duty close to midnight when Captain Bowen-Colthurst arrived. The captain demanded that Dobbin hand Sheehy Skeffington into his custody. Bowen-Colthurst had no authority to give this order – only the commanding officer, at this time Major

Rosborough, would have been able to give this order – but Rosborough had no idea what Bowen-Colthurst was up to, and the captain was not looking for permission. Dobbin was a junior officer, half Bowen-Colthurst's age and with none of the captain's combat experience, and was exhausted after being on almost constant guard duty since the start of the Rising. He obeyed the order given to him by a superior officer, and – not knowing what the captain intended to do with the prisoner – handed him over to Bowen-Colthurst. The captain then had Sheehy Skeffington's hands tied behind his back, and told him to say his prayers. When Sheehy Skeffington refused, Bowen-Colthurst instructed his men – about forty in all, mostly from the 3rd Royal Irish Rifles – to remove their caps before he recited the words 'O Lord God, if it should please Thee to take away the life of this man, forgive him for Our Lord Jesus Christ's sake.'

There was a reason for these words. Acting on an outstanding arrest warrant for Alderman James Kelly, a conservative member of Dublin City Council, issued on the introduction of martial law (in mistake for Alderman Tom Kelly, a member of Sinn Féin), he had been ordered to go on a raid to find Kelly but had decided to take Sheehy Skeffington with him as a hostage, and he intended to make sure that if he and his men came under fire Sheehy Skeffington would be shot in retribution. Having secured his prisoner, Bowen-Colthurst led his men out the main barrack gate and towards the Rathmines Road.

With Bowen-Colthurst was Second-Lieutenant Leslie Wilson, his second-in-command for this raid. Wilson had studied at Trinity College, where he had been a member of Dublin University OTC. He was not an officer with the Royal Irish Rifles but had been attached to the regiment in October 1915, having begun training in preparation for joining the 5th Royal Irish Fusiliers in Salonika but then having been commissioned as an officer with – as he later claimed – almost no training. On 31 January 1916 he developed pneumonia from exposure on a rifle range and was given sick leave, while also being transferred to the reserve 4th Royal Irish Fusiliers, which he spent at his home in Dublin, and he was still on sick leave when the Rising began. He had then made his way to Portobello Barracks.

Wilson had been studying to take holy orders in the Church of Ireland when he joined the army. Given Bowen-Colthurst's religious zeal, this may have something to do with why he chose Wilson to come with him on this raid – or, alternatively, why Wilson volunteered to go with him, if that is what happened.

Captain Bowen-Colthurst – now, as far as he was concerned, in the middle of enemy territory – turned north into Rathmines Road. He drew his pistol and began firing into the air while also giving orders that shots were to be fired in the direction of anyone who appeared at a window. As he came close to the Catholic church in Rathmines Road he saw two young men coming out. They were James Coade, a nineteen-year-old mechanic who lived in Mount Pleasant Avenue in Ranelagh and whose father worked in the weights and measures office of Dublin Corporation (as Dublin City Council was called at the time), and his friend Laurence Byrne, a twenty-year-old from Church Place. As it was past curfew, Bowen-Colthurst approached them, shouting, 'Don't you know martial law has been proclaimed, and I could shoot you like dogs?' Coade tried to walk away, prompting Bowen-Colthurst to order one of his men to 'bash him.' A soldier hit Coade in the face with the butt of his rifle, and he fell to the ground. Bowen-Colthurst then pointed his pistol at Coade and pulled the trigger, killing him instantly. (The next morning Second-Lieutenant Monk Gibbon spoke to a corporal who was part of this raid. From this meeting Gibbon learnt that Coade may have said, 'Down with the military!' as he turned to walk away, which could have been what prompted Bowen-Colthurst to kill him.)

After killing young Coade, Bowen-Colthurst simply moved on. The soldiers soon reached Portobello Bridge, where Bowen-Colthurst left Wilson in command of half the raiding party – about twenty men – ordering him to wait there while he went on. He also told him to take command and carry on if he was killed or wounded in the raid. But he also handed Francis Sheehy Skeffington over to Wilson with much darker instructions: if Wilson or his men were fired on while waiting at Portobello Bridge, or if Bowen-Colthurst or his men were attacked as they moved on, Wilson was to shoot the prisoner.

Crossing the Grand Canal, Bowen-Colthurst continued to fire, both randomly and in the direction of people who appeared at windows, as he and his men advanced. He was now heading towards his main target, the tobacco shop run by Alderman James Kelly at Kelly's Corner (named after the shop), the junction of Camden Street and Harcourt Road. When Bowen-Colthurst and his men reached Kelly's shop the soldiers were ordered to throw grenades in through the windows. They exploded, destroying the shop, and then Bowen-Colthurst sent his men inside. They found four people cowering in the rubble: two barmen from the pub next door, who had been taking shelter in the shop, and two newspaper editors. These were Thomas Dickson, a 31-year-old disabled Scotsman who lived in nearby Harrington Street, editor of the *Eye-Opener,* and Patrick McIntyre, aged thirty-eight, who lived in Fownes Street, editor of the *Searchlight* and the *Toiler.*

Ironically, the papers edited by these men were pro-British, and McIntyre was also a bitter opponent of James Larkin and the Irish Transport and General Workers' Union. McIntyre, a friend of Kelly's, had been in the shop for a time, while Dickson had rushed in to take shelter after hearing Bowen-Colthurst firing his pistol as he approached. Kelly himself was not found.

Bowen-Colthurst ordered that the men be arrested and taken prisoner. Along with Sheehy Skeffington, who was retrieved at Portobello Bridge on the return trip, they were brought back to the barracks, where they were locked up in the guardroom. Bowen-Colthurst then went back to the officers' mess. He did not sleep that night but stayed awake in the billiard room, praying throughout the night. At some point he turned to his Bible and ultimately came across the lines 'But those mine enemies, which would not that I should reign over them, bring hither, and slay them before me.' This verse would have a terrible influence on his mind. (Earlier he is also alleged to have said, 'In any other country except Ireland it would be recognised as right to kill rebels.')

In the meantime Captain William Murphy of the 1st Royal Irish Fusiliers was sent with a party of men to search Thomas Dickson's house in Harrington Street. Murphy, a native of Rathfriland, Co. Down, was a pre-war regular soldier who had been the regimental sergeant-major of the 1st Battalion and had landed in France as part of the original British Expeditionary Force on 22 August 1914. He was later commissioned and at the time of the Rising was attached to the School of Instruction at Portobello Barracks. After the war he lived in Killylea, Co. Armagh.

The next morning, Wednesday 26 April, Second-Lieutenant Gibbon saw Captain Bowen-Colthurst and later described him: 'Around his eyes were two huge black circles, almost as though they had been blacked in to allow him to take part in some circus turn. One flinched from the sight of that face. He looked as though he were carrying the whole weight of the insurrection upon his shoulders.' Gibbon then visited the prisoners in the guardroom, along with the quartermaster, Captain Forster, who was going there to inspect their breakfasts. The men were handcuffed. All asked if it was possible to get word to their relatives, who would certainly be worrying about them by now. Gibbon was particularly moved by Sheehy Skeffington; he believed him to be a quiet and dignified man caught up in a terrible situation.

Bowen-Colthurst now left the officers' mess and made his way towards the guardroom. The exhausted captain of the guard, Second-Lieutenant Dobbin, was back on duty, but this time Bowen-Colthurst was not even going to ask him for the keys to the prisoners' cells. As Dobbin later recalled, 'about 10-20 a.m. Captain Bowen Colthurst entered the guardroom. He shortly afterwards came out and said to me "I am taking these prisoners out of the guardroom and I am going to shoot them as I think it is the right thing to do" or words to that effect.'

On duty in the guardroom that morning was 47-year-old Sergeant John Aldridge of the 10th Royal Dublin Fusiliers. Though he was born and raised in England, Aldridge had been living for many years in Newcastle, Co. Wicklow; his wife was Irish, and all but one of his nine children had been born in Ireland. Aldridge was also a veteran of the Anglo-Boer War, having served throughout the conflict in the Gloucestershire Regiment. He had been on leave in Dublin when the Rising began and had reported to the nearest barracks. Sergeant Aldridge later recorded that

> at Portobello Barracks, Dublin, on 26th April, 16, about 9 a.m. I mounted guard on the main gate. I relieved Sergt. Kelly 3rd R. Irish Rifles … To the best of my recollection there were 10 civilian prisoners in the Detention Room and the prisoner Skeffington was in a cell. There were no military prisoners in the main guard room. About 10-20 a.m. [Captain Bowen-Colthurst] told me that he wanted to see the prisoners, Dickson, McIntyre and Skeffington

in the yard at the back of the Detention Room at the same time ordering
seven of the guard to go out with them.

Captain Bowen-Colthurst had simply bypassed the authority of the captain of the
guard, walking right by Dobbin, who had been standing outside the guardroom,
and ordered Sergeant Aldridge to have the prisoners taken outside. Aldridge did
not know Bowen-Colthurst and did not know what appointment or position he
held in the barracks – for all he knew, Bowen-Colthurst was fully entitled to have
the prisoners removed from the guardroom – and so he complied with the order.
Bowen-Colthurst had afterwards come back outside and spoken to Dobbin and
only then informed the young second-lieutenant of what he intended to do.

As Sheehy Skeffington, Dickson and McIntyre were taken from their cells
and led outside, Dobbin sent another officer attached to the guard to the orderly
room to let the adjutant know what was going on. This was Second-Lieutenant
Alexander Wilson of the 7th Royal Dublin Fusiliers, a Scotsman who had been
living in Dublin since he was a child and who had previously served as a private
in the 6th Black Watch (Royal Highlanders). (Wilson would later be killed in
action on 20 April 1917, aged twenty, while serving with the 10th Royal Dublin
Fusiliers. With no known grave, his name is now commemorated on the Arras
Memorial.)

Wilson quickly made his way on a bicycle to the orderly room, where he met
the adjutant, Lieutenant Morgan. This officer later recalled that 'on Wednesday
26th April, 1916, about 10-20 a.m. 2nd Lieut. A.S. Wilson, 7th Royal Dublin
Fusiliers, reported to me at the Orderly Room and said that Captain Bowen-
Colthurst wanted to remove three civilian prisoners, Skeffington, Dickson and
McIntyre out of the Guard Room.' Crucially, while Wilson informed Morgan that
the prisoners were being removed from their cells, he did not mention why they
were being removed – perhaps because Dobbin, who was obviously concerned
that Bowen-Colthurst was going to have them shot, did not express this fear to
Wilson before sending him to Morgan.

With no apparently urgent reason to interfere, Lieutenant Morgan simply told
Wilson 'that Major Rossborough, the Commanding Officer, was out, attending
to various duties in barracks, and that I could not give permission for the removal
of the prisoners. I directed Mr. Wilson to warn Capt. Bowen-Colthurst that if he
took them out, he would do so on his own responsibility.'

Second-Lieutenant Wilson made his way back towards the guardroom; but
whatever orders he might have been able to return with, it was already too late.
He was in the process of passing on Lieutenant Morgan's instructions to Dobbin
when the two young officers heard a volley of shots.

In the yard behind the guardroom Sergeant Aldridge watched as 'Capt. Bowen
Colthurst told the three prisoners to go and stand against the far wall. He told the
guard to load, present arms and fire. The prisoners were shot dead. Capt. Bowen
Colthurst then walked away.'

It all happened so shockingly quickly that other civilian prisoners in the guardroom later stated that the three men could not have known that they were going to be killed. As they had begun walking to the far end of the yard there had been no soldiers in the yard with them. As they were walking to the far wall – a distance of only a few yards – Bowen-Colthurst called in the seven men of the firing party, gave them the order to fire, and the three prisoners were shot just as they reached the far wall and turned back to face him. The seven soldiers of the firing party – at least some of them, in all likelihood, Irishmen – were then marched back out of the yard as quickly as they had come in. Second-Lieutenant Dobbin later stated:

> I heard shots fired, apparently at the back of the guard room. Capt. Bowen Colthurst then left the guard room. I went into the yard attached to the guard room and found the three prisoners Thomas Dickson, Patrick McIntyre and Sheehy Skeffington had been shot. The two first named were quite dead, I noticed a movement in one of Skeffington's leggs [sic]. I sent an officer [Second-Lieutenant Fred Tooley] to the Orderly Room to ask what I was to do. He returned [having met Bowen-Colthurst en route] and told me that Capt. Bowen Colthurst gave authority that I could have the prisoner shot again. I did so.

Sergeant Aldridge was a witness to this second volley. He reported: 'Mr. Dobbin then came into the yard, said something about seeing a movement, left the yard and came back in about two minutes. Mr. Dobbin then ordered 4 men of the guard to load and fire another volley at the prisoner Skeffington. It was my impression that Skeffington was dead after the first volley.' Aldridge was probably correct: Dobbin had probably been witnessing involuntary muscle contractions in Sheehy Skeffington's body.

At this point Captain Bowen-Colthurst ran into Major Rosborough, acting commanding officer of the 3rd Royal Irish Rifles. Rosborough later stated: 'On 26th April, 1916, about 10-30 a.m. I was crossing the Barrack Square when Captain Bowen Colthurst came to me and informed me that he had just shot on his own responsibility the three prisoners who were confined in the guardroom. He appeared to think he might get into trouble over it.' Shocked by the news, Rosborough took a moment and then told Bowen-Colthurst to make a written report, stating exactly what had happened. (In this report, written later that day, Bowen-Colthurst stated that he had taken the prisoners out of their cells in order to examine them, not shoot them, but after discovering that they could potentially escape from the yard into which he had taken them he ordered them to be shot to prevent this. According to the statements from all the other witnesses to the event, none of this could be true.)

After talking to Rosborough, Bowen-Colthurst made his way to the orderly room to report the shootings and also to explain himself. Here he met Lieutenant Morgan, the battalion adjutant. Morgan later stated that 'Captain Bowen-Colthurst came to the Orderly Room and reported to me that he had caused the three above mentioned prisoners to be shot, to prevent any possibility of their escaping or being rescued by armed force. At that time there was heavy firing going on round barracks.' Bowen-Colthurst claimed he had shot the men to prevent them being rescued by rebel forces – something the insurgents would never have attempted, given their limited strength and the fact that Dickson and McIntyre were pro-British and that Sheehy Skeffington did not support the Rising. He also told Lieutenant Morgan that he had 'lost a brother in this way' – suggesting a revenge element in what he had just done – and that 'I'm as good an Irishman as they are.'

After making this report, Bowen-Colthurst left the orderly room and made his way back towards the officers' mess. Lieutenant Morgan reported what had just happened to Major Rosborough – who obviously already knew – and word was quickly passed to the garrison adjutant and to the headquarters of Irish Command.

Elsewhere in Portobello Barracks, Second-Lieutenant Gibbon had heard a rumour that Captain Bowen-Colthurst was intending to shoot some prisoners. With his friend Lieutenant Hayward he was heading towards the ammunition store near the guardroom to inform Captain Forster, who was there, when he heard the sound of rifle volleys. After meeting Forster, Gibbon came back outside and saw three stretchers being removed from the nearby guardroom. There were blankets over two of the bodies and a bowler hat over the face of the third. This body was Sheehy Skeffington's; Gibbon recorded that his arms hung limp from the stretcher and were dripping blood onto the ground. Gibbon had been talking to Sheehy Skeffington in the guardroom about an hour previously; he would later write that 'my whole subsequent military career was to be influenced by the event.'

Major Rosborough's various reports to higher command fell on deaf ears. Captain Bowen-Colthurst had previously served as aide-de-camp to Lord Aberdeen during his time as Lord Lieutenant of Ireland. Furthermore, the various generals involved in the Rising did not necessarily know Bowen-Colthurst, or the circumstances surrounding the shootings, and so they decided to ignore what he had done and continue the fight against the rebels instead of starting a new fight against one of their own, which might weaken the perception of the British army's moral superiority. And so no arrest order or removal from duty instruction was issued against Bowen-Colthurst. He was not even reprimanded: Major Rosborough was simply told to do nothing.

The reality was that, even in the barracks, the killings had not been met with unanimous disgust. Republicans had started a rebellion that had already resulted in the deaths of many fellow-soldiers and innocent civilians, Portobello Barracks was apparently under siege, and many soldiers believed the three executed men to be rebel leaders who, if rescued, would help the rebel cause and put them and their comrades in danger. Many even saw the killings as a form of striking back against the rebels; and when Bowen-Colthurst decided to go on a second raid outside barracks on the morning of the 26th there were – according to Gibbon – some younger officers of the 3rd Royal Irish Rifles enthusiastically volunteering to go with him.

Cadet-Sergeant Gerald Keatinge would end up in the middle of this second raid, but the events of that morning would be something of an anti-climax.

> On 3.30 a.m. on this awful day I was awakened from a fitful slumber by a stentorian voice billowing [*sic*] from the doorway. 'Fall In.' We fell in at our appointed places as we had been ordered and after about 5 minutes on parade were dismissed. The enemy apparently did not come from the Wicklow Mountains as they had intended. I had no soap, towel, shaving materials or toilet requisites of any kind, but I managed to borrow soap and towel, and so got a wash, but had to do without a shave, morbidly thinking that I might as well die clean. At about 5 o'clock a civilian came into the barrack room, and I got into conversation with him. I discovered that he was a Scoutmaster in charge of the troop in connection with Portobello Barracks. He had volunteered at the outbreak of the Rebellion and had been ordered to remain in mufti [civilian clothes] and act as Secret Service Agent. I afterwards found out that he had obtained most valuable information, one item of which was the fact that Byrne's shop in Camden Street was occupied by Sinn Feiners. His was most dangerous work and he did it all without turning a hair.

While Bowen-Colthurst was carrying out his executions, Keatinge – who had been assigned to a section of new recruits and been appointed a sniper, because he had completed a rifle course – was out of barracks, taking part in house searches in Grove Park, between the barracks and the Grand Canal, where nothing except 'some rusty bayonets' were found. He later went to the Camden Street area, where he took part in setting up cordons in the surrounding streets, both to push the curious crowds of citizens back and to contain any rebels that might be in the area.

The British army was preparing for a raid against Byrne's grocery shop, at the corner of Grantham Street and Camden Street, which the Rathmines scoutmaster had said was occupied by Volunteers. Captain Bowen-Colthurst now arrived on the scene, again accompanied by his second-in-command, Second-Lieutenant Leslie Wilson.

Bowen-Colthurst told Keatinge and the other men present, as Keatinge later recorded, that they were going to take Byrne's house.

> After these few remarks we marched down the street and past the shop, all the windows of which were open, leaving a small detachment up Grantham Street. About six men went as far as Pleasant [Pleasants] Street and kept the crowd up there. The Captain then ordered a Second Lieutenant [Wilson], Long [Cadet Eugene Long] and me to search Delahunt's shop which lies opposite Byrne's. Mr. Delahunt at first professed to know nothing of the Sinn Feiners but when we were on the first floor, and the rebels opened fire on us from across the Street, he soon showed that he did know something. It was my first time under fire and strange to say now that I was really in it

I didn't feel at all nervous. Delahunt was however, and told [us] that the insurgents were on the top of a house which he owned two doors away on the same side, and also on the house opposite. We quickly searched the rest of the house and hurried down stairs where our chaps were blazing away. This lasted about 5 minutes with bullets whizzing all over the place ...

At this moment Bowen-Colthurst who, to do him justice, seemed completely fearless, strode down the street and ordered one of the sergeants to throw a hand grenade through the plate-glass window of the shop where the Volunteers had established themselves. This naturally blew out most of the inside of the place and as we were directly opposite to the shop, Wilson called on me and a rifleman to go with him and search it. We climbed through the shattered window and into the shop which was empty; at its further end was a circular, metal staircase leading to the upper floors and led by Wilson we went up it. Obviously we were sitting targets for anyone on the upper floors but nothing happened and when we got to the top each of us chose a room to search. As it turned out all were empty except the one that I had chosen and there propped up against the back wall of one of the rooms from which the firing had come was a young Volunteer with his rifle and ammunition by his side. Pale and drawn he was, I think a very frightened fellow and perhaps was well aware that his companions had deserted him. Certainly we found no trace of them although we made thorough search of the roof-tops and the cellars. Of course they could have got away by discarding their uniforms, if they were wearing them, or perhaps they were in ordinary civilian clothes as many of the Volunteers did not have uniforms ...

I immediately covered him while the Officer [Wilson] took his ammunition and rifle from him and searched him. The other soldier took the rebel downstairs whilst the officer and I continued the search, but all the others had fled. We secured 750 rounds ammunition, a lot of which was Mauser, and dum-dum to boot. In addition we got 16 rifles and a large number of bandoliers of which I have one ...

The captured Volunteer was Richard O'Carroll. Forty years old, he was secretary of the Dublin Bricklayers' Trade Union and a member of Dublin City Council. After completing his search upstairs, Keatinge went down and reported to Bowen-Colthurst and sought his instructions regarding the prisoner.

They were short and terrible. 'Shoot him,' he said, 'Shoot him.' So this poor, terrified wretch was made to kneel down on the pavement and make his peace with God while fellow Irishmen in the British Army, including myself and, of course, hundreds of local people from the nearby streets looked on. At first Bowen-Colthurst directed himself to me, but suddenly changing his mind, thank God, he turned to one of the sergeants and ordered him to do the shooting which he did at point-blank range through the chest but did not kill him. I think that even Bowen-Colthurst was shaken by this incident and he made no attempt to give the man a coup de grace. Instead he commandeered a bread van which was delivering bread in the neighbourhood and, having disposed of the contents, this poor wounded man was put into the van and taken to Portobello Barracks Military Hospital. I am ashamed to say that I did not follow up this incident so cannot say whether he lived or died [he died ten days later] ...

Meanwhile, the shop on the other side of the street was captured and another rebel wounded. A bread-cart was commandeered and the second wounded man put in it with all the captured equipment. We then returned to barracks.

Most accounts of the shooting of Richard O'Carroll state that Bowen-Colthurst shot him, but Keatinge's account makes it clear that someone else pulled the trigger. Bowen-Colthurst is also believed to have asked O'Carroll if he was a 'Sinn Féiner', to which O'Carroll is believed to have replied, 'From the backbone out,' which may have prompted Bowen-Colthurst to shoot him. Keatinge, however, does not record this detail (though this exchange may have taken place before Keatinge had finished his search upstairs).

On his way back to Portobello Barracks it is generally believed that Bowen-Colthurst also shot a teenage boy. The account is that he stopped the teenager and asked for information, the boy would not speak, and Bowen-Colthurst ordered him to his knees and shot him in the back of the head as he went to make the sign of the cross. Keatinge makes no mention of this but does mention a second wounded Volunteer – who does not appear in other accounts surrounding the raid on Byrne's shop – placed on the bread cart along with Richard O'Carroll.

By 1 p.m. Bowen-Colthurst and his men had returned to barracks with their cartload of wounded Volunteers and captured weapons, ammunition and equipment. Not long afterwards Captain Philip Kelly of the 1st Royal Irish Fusiliers – a pre-war regular officer from Co. Mayo – walked into the officers' mess. Also in the mess was Captain James McTurk of the Royal Army Medical Corps. Bowen-Colthurst was sitting, his torso lying across a table in front of him with his head resting on an arm. Captain Kelly took a seat and began watching the captain, who every so often would look up and gaze around the room, then lie back down across the table. He was behaving so strangely that Kelly turned to McTurk and said, 'For goodness' sake, keep an eye on Colthurst. I think he's off his head.'

McTurk decided to go over to Bowen-Colthurst and began talking to him. He listened as Bowen-Colthurst repeatedly mulled over what he had done that morning. He was completely preoccupied by his earlier actions and finally said to the doctor: 'It's a terrible thing to shoot one's own countrymen, isn't it?'

* * *

Another officer stationed in Portobello Barracks learnt about what Captain Bowen-Colthurst had done. This one, however, was determined to do something

Francis Fletcher-Vane (Prof. Davis Coakley)

about it. His name was Major Sir Francis Fletcher-Vane.

A 54-year-old officer, born in Dublin in 1861 to an English father and an Irish mother, Fletcher-Vane had grown up in Sidmouth, Devon. After attending Oxford Military College he was commissioned as a regular officer with the Scots Guards, having previously served with the reserve 3rd Worcestershire Regiment; but because 'the experience of the Regiment was extremely unfortunate' Fletcher-Vane soon resigned his commission. In fact he had been the victim of 'ragging', an aggressive and humiliating initiation activity that was particular to the Guards regiments at the time.

Fletcher-Vane seems to have returned to 'militia' or reserve service, as he was soon a reserve lieutenant with the Submarine Mining Service of the Royal Engineers. During this time he also became involved in Toynbee Hall, a charity in the East End of London, as well as founding the Working Boys' Cadet Corps. In 1888, now serving with the 26th Middlesex (Cyclist) Battalion of the Rifle Volunteer Corps, he was promoted to captain, and the same year he married.

During the Anglo-Boer War, in which he also acted as a correspondent for several English newspapers, Fletcher-Vane volunteered for full-time service. Posted to the 3rd Lancaster Regiment, he arrived in South Africa in February 1900 and served on the transport staff from March to June and later as brigade transport officer for the 1st Motor Transport Brigade, and was involved in several skirmishes. In 1901 he was appointed district commandant of Glen and then Karree.

During this period the Boer commandos were still fighting a guerrilla campaign, and Fletcher-Vane raised a police force of local burghers. This was so effective that his district only ever received one attack. He also served as an intelligence officer and then in 1902 as district commandant of Bloemfontein, where he was commended for winning over the confidence of the local Boers. The Boer general Louis Botha, in a speech at Cape Town in December 1902, said: 'If all officers had behaved with the sense of justice and fairness as did Captain Fletcher-Vane much less bitterness would have existed and the settlement would have been earlier.' Fletcher-Vane also sat as a military judge during the trial of the Cape Colony Boer rebels.

Fletcher-Vane returned to Britain and left the army in 1903, having been awarded an honorary captaincy for his services in South Africa. Unhappy with the peace settlement, however, he became critical of the government and returned to South Africa for a time. He toured the country, made contact with several campaigners who were trying to bring the unsatisfactory post-war situation in South Africa to the attention of the British public, and then wrote *The War and One Year After* (1903), which was heavily critical of how the British had fought the conflict, followed by *Pax Britannica in South Africa* (1904), an extended version of his earlier pamphlet.

In the years that followed, Fletcher-Vane became deeply involved in the emerging boy scout movement. After falling out with the association's founder, Lord Robert Baden-Powell – disagreeing that scouting should be so militaristic, and also having made policy decisions instead of simply being an inspector, in line with his position as commissioner – he became the second president of the breakaway British Boy Scouts in 1909. In 1910 he founded the scout movement in Italy, and the same year helped to form a French scouting movement. In 1911, with the worldwide spread of scouting, he formed the Order of World Scouts and became its grand scoutmaster. He personally financed this organisation, but this soon proved too much. As an underwriter for Lloyds banking he suffered serious financial losses after the sinking of the *Oceana* in March 1912 and the *Titanic* the following month, which, coupled with the costs of financing the Order of World Scouts, forced him to declare bankruptcy.

Before the First World War, Fletcher-Vane also stood unsuccessfully as a Liberal candidate for the constituency of Burton upon Trent in Staffordshire in the 1906 general election, while publishing several books on a wide variety of subjects, including Italian tour guides and often eccentric political and philosophical works. He inherited a baronetcy in 1908 and by this time had also become a prominent defender of socialism and women's rights as well as an anti-war campaigner.

When the First World War began Fletcher-Vane was living in Italy. He immediately began travelling back to Britain, and he later claimed that while en route through France he presented himself at the front to the French general Paul Pau at Belfort on 14 August 1914. Why he did this and what he was hoping to achieve is not clear, but he claimed that this made him the first British army officer to join with the French. (As he held no commission at the time, this is not technically true.)

Fletcher-Vane was soon back in London, where – strangely, given his recent political views – he apparently began making unofficial recruitment speeches. He later claimed that between 25 August and 5 September 1914 he personally recruited five hundred men in London at his 'own expense and own initiative.' He also applied to rejoin the army. His application was accepted, and on 8 September he was appointed a major and sent to Leicester as a staff officer with responsibility for recruiting.

In October, Major Sir Francis Fletcher-Vane returned to Ireland, joining the recently raised 9th Royal Munster Fusiliers in Kilworth Camp, near Fermoy,

Co. Cork. He got to work recruiting locally while training the men under his command, but in December – long before his battalion was due to depart for the war – he applied to be sent overseas on active service. Curiously, General Lawrence Parsons, commanding officer of the 16th (Irish) Division, of which the 9th Royal Munster Fusiliers were a part, supported Fletcher-Vane's request but, clarifying why he was agreeing to the loss of one of the officers under his command, he wrote that Fletcher-Vane 'will probably be a very useful officer on active service with a regular unit. He is an active and energetic man but too sketchy & erratic with too loose ideas of discipline and too strong political ideas to be a suitable officer to command & train a company in a new Irish Battalion.'

Various senior officers then discussed what to do with Fletcher-Vane, whose personality was beginning to bring him into conflict with higher command. One officer, in response to a suggestion that Fletcher-Vane might be useful as a regimental transport officer, stated that 'without something more in his favour I do not care to promise this officer employment. Officers who are sketchy & erratic are no use in RTO [regimental transport officer] work where method endurance & precision are essential.' So, with no other position offered to him, Fletcher-Vane stayed put with the 9th Royal Munster Fusiliers.

While obviously not viewed as an ideal officer, Fletcher-Vane was for the most part tolerated until March 1915. Then, towards the end of that month, he made a recruiting speech in Cork in which, he later claimed, he declared himself to be a nationalist and a supporter of Home Rule. This gained him fifty recruits from the ranks of the Irish National Volunteers (he had already recruited 350 other men from Co. Cork since 20 November 1914), but General Parsons was apparently not happy about this and severely reprimanded him, soon claiming that he was now unfit to command troops. Fletcher-Vane protested against this and even demanded a court-martial to settle the issue, but this was refused.

As Home Rule for Ireland was officially supported by the British government, and was being used as an incentive in recruitment campaigns being run by the Irish Party, and as many of the men in the 16th (Irish) Division would have been known to be nationalist in opinion, it is high unlikely that Parsons had a problem with Fletcher-Vane referring to himself as a nationalist or a supporter of Home Rule. It seems possible that Fletcher-Vane began speaking on some of the other topics that he supported – such as women's rights and perhaps socialism – and that this was what actually angered the general.

Before the end of March, Fletcher-Vane applied to transfer to the 13th Royal Warwickshire Regiment at Golden Hill on the Isle of Wight as the battalion second-in-command. However, he stopped the transfer process when he learnt that the battalion was to remain in England as a reserve unit. In May he applied for a second transfer, this time to the Italian army as a liaison officer (he had lived in Italy for many years and spoke the language), but he was informed that it was unlikely that a request for such a liaison officer would be made by the Italians. Fletcher-Vane insisted in reply that he had already been in touch with the Italian ambassador in London, along with 'the highest people in Italy to have my name sent in,' and that, as he had left his home in Italy 'to lend a hand' during the war, he hoped that the War Office might make an exception and put him forward without waiting for the Italians to request him first. In the end the Italians did not ask for him, and the War Office did not suggest him to them.

Fletcher-Vane's relationship with his commanding officers only worsened, and in September 1915 General Parsons wrote a second negative report on him. He claimed that Fletcher-Vane was 'a source of worry and annoyance to his Commanding Officer and Brigadier ... He has no sense of discipline, affected a sort of contempt for all the ordinary rules, regulations and customs of the service, and wasted everyone's time with long reports on trifles and imaginary personal grievances.' He was also felt to be undermining the authority of the commanding officer of his battalion, Lieutenant-Colonel Williams, by continually sending him 'insubordinate' letters, and it was noted that Williams 'had had trouble with him over money matters and that a cheque he had given in payment of his Mess bill had been returned dishonoured.'

That same month the general officer commanding the Aldershot Training Centre in Hampshire had also written that Fletcher-Vane was 'devoid of any military knowledge, discipline or procedure, and was either incapable of learning them or unwilling to do so,' and that he cavilled at the orders and instructions issued to him. 'It was said that he was fond of public speaking and of airing his extreme political views and the G.O.C. [general officer commanding] 16th Division had to issue a stringent order to him not to attend or speak at any public meeting. It was also stated that Major Sir Fletcher Vane writes long and very flippant or insubordinate official letters on every possible occasion.' He was considered 'active [and] energetic and apparently took an interest in his Company but that he was such a "crank" that his good qualities only made him more dangerous ... He was so inordinately conceited that it was hopeless to improve him at his age.'

This was certainly not the kind of officer that the army wanted, prompting one general to maintain that Fletcher-Vane was 'eaten up with personal vanity.'

As a result of all these reports against him, the War Office requested Fletcher-Vane to resign his commission. He refused, and demanded that a court of inquiry be held. This was not done, and Fletcher-Vane was 'involuntarily gazetted' (dismissed from the army) on 15 January 1916.

It looked as though his military career had ended; but by the time this happened General Parsons, together with Lieutenant-Colonel Williams and another critic, Brigadier-General Buchanan, had all been removed from their commands (for reasons 'other than physical incapacity,' as a report later noted).

Then, according to Fletcher-Vane, on 21 March 1916, four months after the 9th Royal Munster Fusiliers had entered the trenches, the officer commanding the men Fletcher-Vane had trained wrote to him to say that 'the men are absolutely indifferent to shell fire, there is no crime or grumbling. I know that I am right in saying that this is entirely due to the early training and the spirit of discipline and esprit de corps which you always were at such pains in inspiriting into them.' Fletcher-Vane now began pushing hard to be reinstated, and with the help of the under-secretary of state for war, Harold John (Jack) Tennant, he was reinstated as a recruiting officer in Ireland on 31 March 1916, less than four weeks before the outbreak of the Easter Rising.

Shortly afterwards, according to a report, Major Fletcher-Vane was 'sent by the Department [of Recruiting] to Longford where a meeting was to be held, but his conduct was so extraordinary that he was recalled to Dublin. On the 12th April he was granted a week's leave and left for England. It was afterwards extended by the Department of Recruiting as they no longer desired to employ him.' With regard to his 'extraordinary' conduct in Longford, Captain R. C. Kelly, chief organiser of the department, wrote that

> on the evening of the day on which this Officer commenced duty in Longford I received a telephone message from the Chairman of the Longford Committee, T. W. Delany ... informing me that a deputation was coming up on the following morning on urgent business. The Deputation arrived ... Mr. Delany informed me that unless the above Officer was recalled from Longford, it was felt that the local recruiting helpers could not proceed with the work, and that they would therefore feel bound to resign. They informed me in confidence of certain peculiarities of conduct on the part of the above Officer which had forced them to this conclusion.

Fletcher-Vane was recalled, and the Department of Recruiting placed him on indefinite leave until it could decide what to do with him; and he was still on leave when the Rising began.

On Monday 24 April, Major Fletcher-Vane was having lunch in Bray when he learnt what was happening in Dublin. He immediately made his way back to the city and offered his services at Portobello Barracks, which he found in a state of confusion and with rumours spreading like wildfire. He was officially attached by garrison order to the 3rd Royal Irish Rifles and was soon appointed second-in-command and later commander of the barracks' defences. In carrying out these duties, he later wrote, 'I consolidated the Defences – ordered a special Map of these to be drawn up, and instituted General and Special Orders for the perimeter and for the various positions.' It is not clear when he first met Captain Bowen-Colthurst, but the next day, as recorded by Max Caulfield in *The Easter Rebellion,*

> shortly before noon, Major Sir Francis Fletcher Vane ... sauntered into the mess looking for something to eat. He found the place empty, save for a single officer who sat slumped over a table, his head cupped between his hands. Vane recognised him as Captain J. Bowen-Colthurst ... When

Vane approached Bowen-Colthurst raised his head. Then he said, 'Isn't it dreadful, Sir Francis, to have to shoot Irishmen?' 'Indeed,' replied Sir Francis, perceiving no special significance in the words. Indeed, he forgot all about the remark until next day events rather forcibly reminded him of it.

Clearly the two men knew of one another, but Bowen-Colthurst allegedly had a dislike of Fletcher-Vane. This is not hard to believe, given how different their political opinions were; and in the officers' mess Bowen-Colthurst was later heard denouncing Fletcher-Vane as a supporter of the Boers and of Irish nationalists.

Fletcher-Vane had been out of barracks at the time the prisoners were shot on the morning of the 26th – setting up an observation post with snipers in the tower of Rathmines Town Hall – but on his way back to barracks he encountered a crowd of people shouting 'Murderer! Murderer!' at him as he passed by, which suggests that word of the killings had quickly spread outside the barracks. Not knowing the reason for this, Fletcher-Vane asked if anything had happened while he was away. A soldier explained; and Fletcher-Vane was horrified.

Reporting to Major Rosborough, Fletcher-Vane felt that Bowen-Colthurst should be arrested immediately and publicly denounced, in order to protect the reputation of the British army, both in Ireland and abroad. Rosborough, under instructions from higher command, would not give this order, but Fletcher-Vane continued to argue, insisting, as commander of the barracks' defences, that Bowen-Colthurst was now a threat to the barracks. A compromise was reached: Bowen-Colthurst would be confined to barracks, and he would not be allowed to leave to conduct any more raids, capture prisoners, or potentially shoot anyone.

This was mere damage-limitation, but Fletcher-Vane accepted the terms. Rosborough then ordered Fletcher-Vane to give a lecture on martial law to all the officers in the barracks, so that they would clearly understand what they were and were not allowed to do.

Fletcher-Vane gave this lecture in the billiard room of the officers' mess at 4 p.m. He made it clear that if any innocent civilians were killed the killers would be considered murderers and would be prosecuted under common law when the period of martial law had ended. Second-Lieutenant Monk Gibbon was at this lecture – he had briefly met Major Fletcher-Vane the previous morning while serving as captain of the guard – and it was during this talk that he developed a lasting respect for Fletcher-Vane. The two would later become friends, and supporters of the cause of peace.

Two hours after the lecture, at about 6 p.m., Fletcher-Vane was ordered to find and arrest Alderman James Kelly. (The authorities had obviously not yet worked out their mistake about the identity of the two aldermen.) Gibbon volunteered to go with him, and the two officers, with some soldiers from the barracks, made their way to the tobacco shop at Kelly's Corner.

Kelly had not been found in his shop when Bowen-Colthurst raided it the night before, and when Fletcher-Vane and Gibbon arrived they began to search the building. Upstairs was empty, but then they discovered Kelly in the cellar. His wife and sister were with him. When Fletcher-Vane announced that he and his men were there to arrest him, the two women burst into tears. Word had spread of what had happened to Sheehy Skeffington, Dickson and McIntyre, and Kelly's wife and sister must have been terrified that Kelly would end up in front of a firing party. Fletcher-Vane gave his word that Kelly would not be hurt.

Alderman Kelly left the cellar and caused no trouble as he was brought to Portobello Barracks under escort. As the soldiers moved off, some firing could be heard from the direction of Jacob's factory, and so Gibbon took command of the rearguard for the return trip to barracks. When they arrived, Kelly was taken to the orderly room, where he was questioned by Lieutenant Samuel Morgan before being placed in the cells in the guardroom. Fletcher-Vane later recalled that 'shortly after arresting Alderman J. J. Kelly at his shop in Upper Camden Street Dublin, owing to certain papers shown to me by my prisoner, I became convinced that he was innocent of any offence in connection with the Rebellion. I then applied to Major Rossborough for his release, but this officer informed me that he was acting under direct instructions from the Garrison Commander.'

Later that night the bodies of Francis Sheehy Skeffington, Thomas Dickson and Patrick McIntyre were buried in the grounds of Portobello Barracks. Lieutenant Morgan had earlier been instructed by the garrison adjutant, Captain Burton, to have them buried in the barrack square. Second-Lieutenant Alfred Toppin of the 3rd Royal Irish Rifles was present and wrote a report about it for Lieutenant Morgan the following day:

> Sir, I have the honour to report that I was last night detailed by Captain Kelly (Royal Irish Fusiliers) to superintend the interment of three prisoners who were shot within the walls of these Barracks yesterday forenoon, viz: F. Sheehy Skeffington, Thomas Dickson, Patrick McIntyre. The bodies were identified by Dr. McWalter, R.A.M.C. in the presence of Captain Kelly and myself, as those of the above-named prisoners. I was present at the graveside with the Reverend Father F. E. O'Loughlin who conducted the burial service and can personally state that everything necessary was duly and properly carried out. The time of interment was 11.15 p.m.

Captain Philip Kelly was the officer who had earlier seen Captain Bowen-Colthurst in the officers' mess after his raid on Byrne's grocery shop and who had asked an army doctor who was present to 'keep an eye on Colthurst. I think he's off his head.' (Kelly later rose to the rank of lieutenant-colonel and commanding officer of the 9th Royal Irish Fusiliers. On 10 October 1918, aged only twenty-nine, he was killed in action on the Western Front. He now lies in Dadizeele New British Cemetery.)

The priest who officiated at the burial of Sheehy Skeffington, Dickson and McIntyre, Father Francis O'Loughlin, a native of Australia, was parish priest in

Rathmines and at the time of the Rising was also a British army chaplain, based in Portobello Barracks.

* * *

Forty-seven-year-old Dr James McWalter, a native of Dublin who identified the three executed men, was educated at the Catholic University of Ireland (which would later become UCD) and qualified at the Royal College of Surgeons in 1897. He later received an MA from the Royal University of Ireland (precursor of the NUI) and an MA and MD from the University of Dublin (Trinity College). In 1907 he was also called to the bar and would later receive doctorates of law from both the NUI and the University of Ottawa. He was also a member of Dublin City Council.

McWalter was a prominent figure during the Dublin Lockout of 1913. Following one confrontation, during which the police baton-charged the crowd, Seán Prendergast (who would later serve as commanding officer of C Company, 1st Battalion of the Irish Volunteers during the Rising) recorded that 'the doctors and chemists were busy that day. The next day Alderman Dr. McWalter at the Corporation raised his voice in protestation against the savage conduct of the police on the occasion in question.' After the clash McWalter's surgery 'was crowded with absolutely harmless, inoffensive citizens returning from devotions, who had all been batoned.' McWalter called for the DMP and the RIC to be removed from Dublin; but there was not enough political support for this action.

When the First World War broke out Dr McWalter became the only city councillor to join the army in response to Redmond's call. After the war, as the political situation continued to change, Sinn Féin candidates replaced the great majority of the older generation in elections to the Senate of the National University. Dr McWalter wrote in the *Evening Herald* on 7 October 1919: 'Isn't it a bleeding shame to boot out Dr. Douglas Hyde, Professor Sigerson and Fr. Finlay from the Senate of the National University? As in Jerusalem of old, we stone our prophets. If any man strives to be sane, reasonable, practical, level headed, really serviceable to his country, he is contemptuously cast aside in favour of some Bolshevik bosthoon!'

After the events of 21 November 1920, known as Bloody Sunday, James O'Connor, an RIC constable at the time and later a solicitor, recorded:

> After the Sunday when a number of British Intelligence Officers were shot in Dublin and a number of civilians were shot in Croke Park by the British military, a young man named Potter [Edward Potter] was arrested, charged before a British Courtmartial with being concerned in the shooting of the British Officers, found guilty and condemned to death. His defence was an alibi. There was considerable doubt as to his guilt. A deputation from the Dublin Corporation went to see General Sir Neville Macready, who was

then G.O.C. of the British Forces in Ireland, to intercede on this young man's behalf and to ask that he be reprieved. Alderman McWalter, who was a member of the deputation, dropped dead that day.

Dr McWalter's obituary in the *British Medical Journal* of 19 February 1921 recorded:

Dr. J.C. McWalter, of Dublin, died suddenly at his residence in North Circular Road in the early morning of February 5th, at the age of 53 [actually 52]. On the previous evening he had attended a meeting in Merrion Square which lasted until after 9 o'clock, and when the members dispersed Dr. McWalter's last tramcar had gone. He made a great effort to reach the other side of the city on foot before curfew, and entered his house in a state of exhaustion. The news of his death caused a painful sensation among all classes of citizens in Dublin ...

Dr. McWalter took a prominent part in public life. He was a member of the Senate of the National University of Ireland, a member of the Royal Irish Academy, and had been a governor of the Apothecaries' Hall. He was an alderman of the Dublin Corporation and he was appointed High Sheriff of Dublin in 1920. In politics he was a Constitutional Nationalist, who did not conceal his dislike of Sinn Fein ...

Dr. McWalter's interests were as varied as his character was many-sided; he was known in every circle in Dublin, but more especially among the poor of the city, who have lost in him a generous champion and helper. Modest and unassuming, ever moving about, though without fuss or apparent anxiety; gentle and kindly towards patients or callers as towards opponents in controversy, he was for years one of Dublin's outstanding citizens. In politics, as in everything else, he was outspoken and straightforward, and those who differed from him always acknowledged his transparent sincerity. The writer of a character sketch in the *Irish Independent* describes McWalter as belonging to a type that is fast becoming extinct in Ireland – a type prevalent a quarter of a century ago, but rare to-day – original, elusive, many-sided; of sound common sense one moment, annoying the next, amusing now, bitter then; but taking him all round, whether in or out of one of his moods, a sincere and delightful personality. As a controversialist he was better on paper than in debate. National life was barren in his young days, so he turned to words and allowed his passion for them overmaster him. 'He wrote hard and he spoke hard, yet on the day of his death he had not a personal enemy in all Ireland.'

Dr James McWalter was married and had two young daughters when he died in 1920. He is buried in Glasnevin Cemetery.

* * *

In the early hours of the following morning, Thursday 27 April, at about 2:30 a.m. – having had about four-and-a-half hours' sleep after returning from the arrest of Alderman Kelly – Second-Lieutenant Monk Gibbon was woken up by a corporal who was passing on new orders to him. He was to take command of three transport wagons and bring them to Portobello Bridge; the British army did not want the alcohol in Davy's pub falling into the hands of looters. It took a few hours to complete the job.

After another couple of hours' sleep – during which time soldiers from the 3rd Royal Irish Rifles, positioned in the University Church and surrounding buildings at St Stephen's Green, had begun firing on insurgent positions with rifle and machine-gun fire – Gibbon was given another mission at 9 a.m. He was sent to Kingsbridge Station as part of a convoy of eight wagons, escorted by two officers and fifty men, to collect supplies and return with them to Portobello Barracks. Advised not to ride there on horseback, as this would make him an obvious target for snipers, Gibbon travelled with his convoy along the South Circular Road in the intense heat of the day, listening to almost constant firing in the distance, passing the rebel-held South Dublin Union en route to Kingsbridge Station. (No assaults had been made against the Union since the 3rd Royal Irish Regiment had been ordered to withdraw from the grounds two days earlier.) They had no idea that there were rebels still inside the grounds, and the Volunteers – assuming that they saw the convoy – did not open fire on it.

Second-Lieutenant Gibbon and his party arrived safely at Kingsbridge, and the men began to load the wagons. Gibbon took a walk on the crowded platform, with soldiers sleeping or sitting around everywhere, and by chance he ran into his first cousin, Captain Arthur O'Morchoe of the Deputy Assistant Provost-Marshal's District and formerly of the Leinster Regiment. 23-year-old Arthur Donel MacMurrough O'Morchoe claimed descent from the ancient kings of Leinster, including both the twelfth-century Diarmaid mac Murchadha and the first High King of Ireland, Brian Bórú. His father was Church of Ireland rector at Kiltiernan, Co. Dublin, and the family lived in nearby Glencullen. During Arthur's childhood there the O'Morchoes were neighbours and friends of Joseph Plunkett, a future leader of the Easter Rising. Arthur had been educated at Trinity College and was one of three brothers who served as officers in the British army during the First World War. One of them, 22-year-old Captain Kenneth O'Morchoe of the Royal Dublin Fusiliers (also formerly of the Leinster Regiment), was also in Dublin during the Rising and in fact was ordered to take charge of the firing party that executed his childhood friend Joseph Plunkett on 4 May; but when he made known his connection to Plunkett and asked to be removed from the detail, another officer was given the task. He later transferred to the Gordon Highlanders, served during the Second World War, and ultimately retired as a colonel. He died in 1962, aged sixty-eight.

In 1915, during the Battle of Loos, Arthur O'Morchoe had served as aide-de-camp to Major-General Edward Montagu-Stuart-Wortley (who was later dismissed following his division's failed diversionary attack at Gommecourt on the first day of the Battle of the Somme). He continued to serve in the Deputy Assistant Provost-Marshal's District during the War of Independence, and in 1924 he joined the Colonial Service. Between 1930 and 1931 he was aide-de-camp and private secretary to the British resident (governor) of Zanzibar (Tanzania). After a period spent as Commissioner of Police in the Gold Coast (Ghana), during the Second World War he served on the general staff at the War Office. He died in 1966, aged seventy-four. Today his name is commemorated on a memorial plaque in the Anglican Church at Inch, Co. Wexford.

By 1:30 p.m. on Thursday the 27th Gibbon and his party had loaded their wagons at Kingsbridge Station and were ready to make the return trip. By now they could hear firing much closer than before. As they approached the South Dublin Union they were stopped by a British army officer. The insurgents in the South Dublin Union were now firing on another British army convoy attempting to cross Rialto Bridge from the far side, and it was not safe to pass. (The bridge, part of the South Circular Road, was over a branch of the Grand Canal that has since been filled in.)

After Gibbon and his convoy had passed by the South Dublin Union earlier that morning the 2nd/7th and 2nd/8th Sherwood Foresters had taken the same route along the South Circular Road on their way towards the Royal Hospital. These two battalions, which had been summoned to Ireland on the outbreak of the Rising, had suffered serious losses the previous day during the Battle of Mount Street Bridge. (Facing only seventeen insurgents, they had lost more than 150 men killed and wounded, the highest number of casualties incurred during any action of the Rising.) Ordered to move from the Mount Street area to the Royal Hospital, the two battalions, as they approached the South Dublin Union, were fired on by some of Commandant Ceannt's forty-one remaining Volunteers. The battalions were now prevented from crossing Rialto Bridge and from continuing safely on their way, and the commanding officer sent a message to Portobello Barracks requesting help.

Forced to stay put for the moment, Second-Lieutenant Gibbon posted some men in nearby houses to defend his position (having first asked permission of the people who lived in them) and then went upstairs in one house with a sergeant to survey the area. He spotted a man crouching behind a low wall and ordered his sergeant to fire in the man's direction to move him on, and then opened fire with his own rifle when he saw shots coming from the window of a house on the other side of the canal. Going back outside, he instructed some of the soldiers to continue firing at the house. A local man came out of his house to offer Gibbon a pair of binoculars, apparently concerned that the soldiers might be firing on his father's house across the canal. Gibbon was soon approached by more local people, this time a father and daughter who offered him tea and cake.

Before long – showing how nervous the soldiers were – Gibbon's men had fired on some men of the Sherwood Foresters who were moving through a nearby field;

and while scouting along the canal Gibbon himself was fired on by other soldiers of the regiment. No one was injured in either incident.

Meanwhile in Portobello Barracks, Major Fletcher-Vane received the request for help from the Sherwood Foresters and quickly assembled a group of fifty soldiers not already on duty, along with six officers; the men were mostly from the 3rd Royal Irish Rifles, while Fletcher-Vane later stated that the six officers came from five different regiments. One of the soldiers in the relief force was 23-year-old Private Cornelius 'Condy' Duggan of the 3rd Royal Irish Rifles, a farmer's son from near Anagaire, Co. Donegal. He had previously been employed as a farm labourer in Co. Tyrone and was probably living in Letterkenny when he enlisted.

This relief force was joined by two RIC constables, 29-year-old Christopher Miller and 26-year-old Martin Meany. who had both been attending the Dublin School of Instruction for Non-Commissioned Officers. Christopher Miller was a native of Ballycahane, near Pallaskenry, Co. Limerick. He had eight years' service and was based in Belfast. Martin Meany, who had four years' service, was normally stationed in Co. Galway.

As soon as Fletcher-Vane arrived at the South Dublin Union he was given command of the assaulting troops and was ordered to attack the Union. Seeing the improvised rebel flag flying from an upstairs window of the nurses' home, as well as the fire coming from this building, he assumed that this was the rebels' headquarters and ordered his men to advance towards it. Second-Lieutenant Gibbon volunteered to take part in the assault.

Advancing by groups in short dashes across open ground, the soldiers then moved through a convent chapel containing praying nuns, followed by wards of screaming mental patients. Steadily they closed in on the nurses' home. Both sides were firing frantically, while snipers and machine-gunners in the Royal Hospital were also firing on the rebel positions inside the Union.

A group of soldiers finally managed to establish themselves in a ward directly opposite the nurses' home and began firing at it in preparation for an assault on the building. Another group prepared to make the dash into the nurses' home, but when they ran out from cover towards the large three-storey building they were beaten back by heavy fire. This assault group lost several men killed and wounded, one of whom was Constable Meany.

The soldiers attacked again and again and each time were driven back, but they finally managed to reach the barricaded front door of the nurses' home. Realising that British forces were about to break into his headquarters, Commandant Ceannt, along with Volunteer Peadar Doyle, rushed to the front door. Together the two men began pushing on the door to keep it closed, while on the far side someone else was pushing back in an attempt to open it. The man on the other side of the door was also an Irishman: Constable Christopher Miller. A tall, strong man, he was slowly but surely forcing the door open, even with two men trying to stop him on the other side; but then Ceannt drew his pistol, shoved it through the gap in the door, and pulled the trigger. Miller stumbled backwards and collapsed. The officer leading this attack called for water, and Gibbon heard the call. He took a water-bottle from one of his men and ran forward, but when he reached Miller he found the constable lying on his side and grey-faced. He was dead.

Christopher Miller was twenty-nine years old. He now lies in the cemetery of the Royal Hospital at Kilmainham.

Major Fletcher-Vane now instructed the assaulting force to call off the frontal attacks and instead tunnel into the nurses' home through an adjoining ward, which turned out to be full of terrified elderly people. They began hacking at the wall and soon knocked their way into a small room off the ground-floor lobby of the nurses' home. The insurgents saw the soldiers breaking into their headquarters and began firing at them and hurling grenades. Fletcher-Vane, who was present, called out, 'Who is there? I am Major Vane.' A rebel inside the nurses' home shouted back, 'Go to hell!'

The soldiers fought their way into the nurses' home through the hole in the wall but then found that the lobby was cut in half by a tall barricade; they could not get through it or go around it. However, other soldiers were beginning to surround the rear of the nurses' home, and so Ceannt withdrew from the building in an attempt to make contact with reinforcements elsewhere. Many of the Volunteers believed that an order to retreat had been given, and they began to pull back from the nurses' home.

It looked as though the British army was about to capture the building. The insurgents had retreated, the building was nearly surrounded, and heavy fire was still being directed towards it from the grounds and from the Royal Hospital. However, when the soldiers in the lobby threw a grenade they managed to badly wound Vice-Commandant Cathal Brugha, second-in-command of the 4th Battalion. Bleeding heavily, he chose to remain behind and positioned himself on the far side of the barricade. Intending to fight for as long as he could, he fired occasional shots at the barricade to let the British army soldiers know he was still there.

Even though they had fought all the way into the Volunteers' headquarters, the British army officers in the lobby of the nurses' home – unaware that they were facing only one man – decided to withdraw their men back into the small room off the lobby. Brugha began to sing 'God Save Ireland' in defiance, and this prompted Ceannt to lead his surviving volunteers back into the nurses' home. The battle had now raged for four hours. While a soldier of the Sherwood Foresters now regularly threw grenades into the lobby to keep the insurgents back, the Volunteers continued firing on the small adjoining room with rifles and pistols to prevent the soldiers from advancing again.

At about 7 p.m. another unsuccessful attempt was made to assault the nurses' home by frontal attack. The soldiers making this attack were not beaten back by the rebels but were fired on by some comrades who mistook them in the dusk for Volunteers.

Orders would later be given to withdraw entirely from the grounds of the South Dublin Union, after the convoy of the Sherwood Foresters had rushed across Rialto

Bridge and made its way safely to the Royal Hospital. When the last assault was being made against the nurses' home Second-Lieutenant Gibbon also rejoined his own convoy and continued on his way back to Portobello Barracks. He later recalled that 'as we get near the canal and Portobello the men begin singing Tipperary. A girl rushes out from the side of the road and flings her arms round one of the soldiers' necks. It is her brother or sweetheart who is with the column.'

Gibbon, filthy and deafened from the battle, reported to Lieutenant Morgan in the orderly room. Morgan, perhaps understandably, berated the young second-lieutenant – who was not a combatant officer – for risking his life.

Major Fletcher-Vane and his relief force from the 3rd Royal Irish Rifles also returned to the barracks; but not everyone who had marched out towards the South Dublin Union had survived to march back. Major Rosborough later recorded that the battalion lost three men killed and four wounded during the fighting. While one of the dead cannot be positively identified, the other two were Company Quartermaster-Sergeant John Coyle and Private Cornelius Duggan. Neither man was killed outright but succumbed to their wounds days after the battle, Duggan in the Meath Hospital on the 29th and Coyle at an unknown place the following day. They both now lie in the same grave in the cemetery of the Royal Hospital, together with Private Patrick Leen of the 5th Royal Irish Lancers, killed in Sackville Street at the start of the Rising.

* * *

The following day, Friday 28 April, two women called to Portobello Barracks at 1 p.m. looking for information about Francis Sheehy Skeffington. They were Margaret Culhane and Mary Kettle, wife of the former Irish Party MP Tom Kettle (who would die later that year with the Royal Dublin Fusiliers during the Battle of Ginchy). Both were sisters of Hanna Sheehy Skeffington, who did not yet know that she was a widow, and were hoping to learn what had happened to their brother-in-law. After mentioning his name the two women were arrested as 'Sinn Feiners' and were taken before Captain Bowen-Colthurst. He refused to give any information about Sheehy Skeffington, then ordered that the women be separated and removed from the barracks.

The event clearly had an effect on Bowen-Colthurst. At 7 p.m. that evening – in defiance of his confinement order – he went with a party of soldiers to the home of the Sheehy Skeffingtons at 11 Grosvenor Place in Rathmines to search for anything that might incriminate Francis and link him to the rebels. The raid was sanctioned and led by Colonel Henry Allatt, the draft-conducting officer for the 3rd Royal Irish Rifles, who had only recently returned to Portobello Barracks. (Allatt would die only days after the Rising, on 8 May, after being shot by a sniper in the vicinity of the South Dublin Union.) For three hours Bowen-Colthurst ransacked the house in front of Sheehy Skeffington's distraught widow – who had learnt by now, or was soon to discover, that her husband was dead – and their six-year-old son. When the soldiers left, Bowen-Colthurst took away all the written material he could find belonging to Sheehy Skeffington, including correspondence, rejected manuscripts, scribbles, and even love letters to his wife. (Monk Gibbon obtained a key to the storeroom in which this material was subsequently placed and kept a few pieces of Sheehy Skeffington's writing as souvenirs for several years before returning them to Sheehy Skeffington's son when they began to weigh on his conscience.)

Bowen-Colthurst was obviously now concerned that his activities might result in disciplinary action. Gibbon heard him talking to a sergeant outside the orderly room who was about to be interviewed by Lieutenant Morgan concerning the raid on Byrne's shop on Wednesday the 26th. He overheard Bowen-Colthurst telling the sergeant that 'the prisoner was trying to escape.' This was obviously the sergeant Bowen-Colthurst had ordered to shoot Richard O'Carroll. When he spotted Gibbon listening to him, he moved out of earshot.

The Easter Rising, for the 3rd Royal Irish Rifles, was now coming to an end. On Saturday the 29th the rebel forces in Dublin began to surrender. From the witness statement of Private Albert Desborough given to the Bureau of Military History it is known that at least some members of the battalion took part in the surrender of the rebel garrison in the College of Surgeons.

> We were carrying on slowly one morning, when we heard a sound of tramping feet, and the singing by a crowd, men and women, of the Sinn Fein marching song, 'Soldiers are we' ['The Soldier's Song']. We were immediately alerted, and made preparations for some kind of attack. Suddenly, rounding a corner we saw a procession of uniformed men, looking very smart in their uniforms, marching proudly along, as if on some ceremonial parade, and at their head, a slim jaunty, tall woman dressed in a tailor made costume entirely of green coloured cloth ... This was the contingent under the command of Countess Markievicz, whose head-quarters had been at the College of Surgeons somewhere on St. Stephen's Green, and the first contingent to capitulate. They were being marched up to Richmond Barracks, between files of Irish Rifles and our men [3rd Royal Irish Regiment]. There they were kept until their trial and sentence, when they were dispersed to other places. The Countess, she at their heads was taken immediately to Kilmainham Jail, as we had no accommodation for women.

When the prisoners were transferred to Richmond Barracks, Captain Frank Henderson, who had fought in the GPO, later recalled:

> We continued via Kilmainham to Richmond Barracks. There were a few civilians knocking around in the vicinity of the barracks. During the whole march we had not been allowed any food or water. There was a very heavy escort of military, almost two to every prisoner. The soldiers were mainly of the Royal Irish Rifles. A great many of them were from Belfast and were very

unfriendly. Amongst them, however, were some men from other Counties in Ireland who were inclined to be sympathetic and who handed their water bottles around. The soldiers who did this were abused by the other soldiers ...

Some of the insurgents found at least one officer of the Royal Irish Rifles to be compassionate in victory. Séamus Grace, of C Company, 3rd Battalion, Irish Volunteers, was taken to the RDS grounds in Ballsbridge after he surrendered. While there,

> at about 12.30 on Sunday an officer of the Royal Irish Rifles named either Hutchinson or Henderson came to me and said, 'the rest of your men have surrendered, would you like to be taken to them?' I said, 'yes.' He brought me a tumbler of hot black tea and some Army biscuits and said, 'I am sorry I have no milk or sugar for the tea.' I was then brought over to some stables where I found Captain Donnelly and the rest of the garrison of Boland's Mills were prisoners, I had been four days and four nights without food or drink.

This same officer is referred to in a witness statement provided by Séamus Kavanagh, who had also served in Boland's bakery. 'We were marched off to the R.D.S. Grounds, Ballsbridge. We were placed in horse stalls, 10 men in each stall, which normally housed one horse. We remained there until 3rd May. During our stay in Ballsbridge we were given bully beef, hard biscuits and water, three times daily. On one occasion an officer of the Royal Irish Rifles purchased tea for us at his own expense.'

However, while most of the 3rd Royal Irish Rifles had worked to defeat the insurgents, at least one Irish private did not take part in the fight. There was a very significant reason for this: he was also a Volunteer with A Company, 3rd Battalion, Irish Volunteers. This was Joseph Byrne, who later recorded:

> I joined the Youth Organisation known as Fianna Éireann at Camden Street in 1911 ... I graduated from the Fianna to the Volunteers in 1913 in Camden Row. I was associated with 'A' Company of the 3rd Battalion. At that time the Volunteers were in their infancy and our activities were mainly confined to training, drilling and marches. I was with the Volunteers until the latter end of 1915 when I enlisted in the British Army and in 1916 I was stationed in Portobello Barracks. A few days before the Rebellion I was home on compassionate leave. On Easter Monday morning a knock came to my door. When I answered it there was a D.M.P. man outside who informed me I was to report back to my regiment immediately as there was trouble in the city. I said I would report at once. I then left my home and made my way to my mother's house where I knew I would find my brothers, this already having been arranged between us. At this time the streets were lined with soldiers and I was allowed to pass through, being in possession of a military

pass. I contacted my brothers at home who were living with my mother, on the Easter Monday. My two brothers and myself left my mother's house in Camden Street and proceeded down Kevin Street where we met Tom Hunter in charge of a party in Kevin Street. He told us to get whatever arms we had, that he was moving off immediately and that he was trying to get into Jacob's factory. We, therefore, returned to my mother's house for whatever arms we had, but by the time we got back Hunter had left. We did not contact him subsequently.

I stayed at home until late on the Monday night when I went back to my own home, having meanwhile made an appointment with my brothers to contact or meet them first thing next morning. In the meantime they had contacted 'A' Company of the 3rd Battalion in Boland's Mills and had gone off without acquainting me of their destination. At this time I was living at Usher's Island. When I left the house that Monday morning the streets were lined with soldiers. Being in British uniform I was allowed through the ranks. I got to my mother's house in Camden Street. My mother put her arms around me, and when she saw me she said, 'God bless you, I knew, you, would do it,' and she burned my British uniform. I tried to make contact with some of the Companies and approached Peadar Clancy at a barricade on the Church Street bridge and he regretted that I could not get through to him. The barricade was between us at that time. He suggested I should try to get across some of the other bridges and join him. I got as far as Watling Street bridge when I was arrested by a Sergeant of my regiment (Royal Irish Rifles) and I was lodged in the Royal Barracks, as it was known at that time. It is now Collins Barracks. I escaped a couple of days later with another soldier named Ryan.

When the Rebellion was over I returned to Portobello Barracks to the British Army minus my uniform, my mother having burned it. I was again placed in arrest but owing to the hurried departure of my regiment to Belfast the charge was not proceeded with. Remaining in Belfast for about a week I was drafted to France and served there until the end of the War in 1918.

Byrne's is a particularly interesting account, since he was a member of both the British army and the Irish Volunteers during the Easter Rising. Furthermore, after unsuccessfully attempting to fight on the rebel side during the rebellion, he simply returned to the British army and served with them for two more years in the trenches. During the War of Independence he became a lieutenant in the IRA and took part in ambushes against British forces in the Camden Street and Wexford Street area. Then, in 1920, he became a member of Michael Collins's 'Squad' and was later involved in several assassinations, the capture of an armoured car, and the burning of the Custom House.

* * *

By the end of the Rising the 3rd Royal Irish Rifles had suffered the loss of seven men killed and thirty-three wounded. Five of the dead were Irish, a sixth man was English, while the seventh cannot be positively identified. Twenty-eight of the wounded were Irish and the remaining five were English.

One of the wounded was thirty-year-old Captain John McClughan, a former civil engineer from Lisburn, then living in Strandtown, near Belfast, with his wife of seven years. He had already served in France, having landed there in October 1915 with the 8th Royal Irish Rifles. This battalion was mainly composed of men from the UVF's East Belfast Battalion, suggesting that McClughan may also have been involved in that organisation. However, after neurasthenia (shell shock) was diagnosed in March 1916 he was sent home and posted to the 3rd Royal Irish Rifles in Dublin.

It is not known where or when Captain McClughan was wounded during the Rising, but Major Rosborough's report shows that it did not take place during the initial advance to Dublin Castle on 24 April, or during the fighting around the South Dublin Union on the 27th. He survived his wounds and stayed in the army, but in January 1918 he was asked to relinquish his commission because of 'inefficiency', being considered physically unfit to serve. He resisted, writing to the army that 'I beg to make an application that some use be made of my services either in the Infantry or Engineers or Labour Corps. I am a Civil Engineer and have been in the employment of the Belfast Corporation for 17 years practically all of this time being spent in the supervision of Road Construction.' But the army declined to employ McClughan in any capacity, and he was forced to resign.

Later in the year he chose to fight his forced resignation, feeling that the army had been unfair to him, as he was 'still suffering from injuries received on Service, [and] should not have been ordered to apply to resign.' Now working as a civil engineer in the surveyor's department in Belfast City Hall, he wrote to the army in August 1918 to explain his position, saying that 'in consideration of the following facts I beg to ask for a review of my case with a view to my either being granted the Honorary Rank of Captain or being re-instated in my old rank.' He went on to explain that after serving in France from October 1915 to March 1916 with the 8th Royal Irish Rifles he was evacuated, suffering from neurasthenia. While home he was 'wounded during the Dublin Rebellion and was recommended for Distinguished Conduct by Col. W.E.C. McCammond, Comdg 3rd Bn R Ir Rif with which Battn I served during the Rebellion.'

McClughan had rejoined the 8th battalion in France, just in time to be in the front line with it for the first day of the Battle of the Somme, 1 July 1916. That day, as he later wrote, 'at Thiepval, Somme, a trench was blown in on me and as a result I was evacuated to England suffering from shell shock.' After being discharged from hospital McClughan was posted to the 17th Battalion at Dundalk. He remained with it until May 1917, when he returned to France. However, as a result of heart trouble that developed only two weeks after his return to France, while he was still at the 36th Infantry Base Depot at Le Havre, he was admitted to hospital.

A doctor of the Royal Army Medical Corps stated that he should never have been allowed back overseas in the first place. McClughan pleaded not to be sent home and so was allowed to perform 'light duty' at the depot until September 1917, when he was suddenly found 'inefficient' and forced to return to his battalion in Dundalk, with the request for his resignation soon following.

Regarding the unexpected verdict of 'inefficiency', McClughan wrote in his letter of protest that

> an attempt was made to show that my physical condition rendered me unsuitable to be retained as an officer ... This apparently was dropped and later on although I was still at the Base on Light Duty I was pronounced 'inefficient' by Major JD McCallum D.S.O. 8th Bn R. Ir. Rif. who I had not served with or seen for 12 months. This inefficiency report was corroborated later by the C.O. 36th I.B.D. [Infantry Base Depot] with whom I was serving. My contention is that I should not have been asked to resign (3 Feby 1918) while I was still suffering from injuries received on Service and still unfit, also the very irregular way in which the reports were brought against me ... [I am] Hoping that my case will receive the consideration that I hold it deserves as I am still in the doctor's hands.

He added that at the time when he was found to be inefficient he had not been serving with Major John McCallum (a former solicitor from Belfast), or the 8th Royal Irish Rifles, for over a year. How then, he asked, could they have known whether he was efficient or not.

The truth was that Major McCallum was not the only man to blame for McClughan being considered inefficient. Unknown to McClughan, the commanding officer of the 107th Brigade (to which the 8th Royal Irish Rifles were attached), Brigadier-General William Withycombe, had written on 8 July 1917 that 'in view of the fact that [McClughan has] been twice evacuated suffering from "neurasthenia" with no special circumstances to account for this condition and after very short period of service in the field I am of the opinion that [his] physical condition renders [him] unsuitable to be retained as [an officer] in the army.'

McClughan was a victim of bad luck. Having arrived in France for the first time on 3 October 1915, he left his battalion on 9 November after only seven days in the trenches – possibly the battalion's first tour. He stayed in France, out of the line, until March 1916, when he was evacuated to Ireland, suffering from neurasthenia. This was a recognised condition at the time, the symptoms including fatigue, anxiety, headaches, nerve pain and depression; today it is called 'combat stress reaction' or 'combat fatigue'. One month later he was wounded during the Easter Rising, only to be sent back to France and spending eight to ten days in the trenches before being buried alive on the first day of the Battle of the Somme, the result this time being full-blown shell shock with accompanying headaches, insomnia and nightmares. Although he was never classified as completely unfit to serve by any military doctor – in August 1918 a medical board saw no reason why he should not return to some form of duty, and another in September stated that his condition was improving – the commander-in-chief of British armies in France ultimately approved his rating as inefficient. Despite his plea to be reinstated, or be at least granted the honorary rank of captain, the army refused both requests.

As it turned out, John McClughan did regain his rank, after a fashion. In January 1949, now aged sixty-three, he was made a member of the Order of the British Empire as Captain John Charles McClughan. However, as the *London Gazette* made clear, he was serving as a district commandant with the Ulster Special Constabulary. This paramilitary reserve police force, attached to the Royal Ulster Constabulary, had been mobilised as part of the Home Guard during the Second World War.

* * *

Another of the wounded Irishmen was Private William Smyth. Born in Kiltubbrid, Co. Leitrim, he was twenty-two when the Rising took place. He was working as a gas stoker and living in Morrison Street, Edinburgh, when he enlisted in February 1916; the following month he joined the 3rd Royal Irish Rifles in Dublin. Having been wounded during the Rising, on 8 July 1916 – one week after the start of the Battle of the Somme – he joined the 14th (Young Citizen Volunteers) Battalion of the Royal Irish Rifles, part of the 36th (Ulster) Division. In November he was again wounded; and on 16 August the following year, during the Battle of Frezenberg Ridge, he was wounded for a third time when he was hit by enemy fire in the arm and hand. When he recovered he was posted to A Company of the 15th Battalion in April 1918; but with this new unit he was again wounded, in August 1918, this time receiving a gunshot wound to his left leg.

When the war ended the now 25-year-old William Smyth found himself serving in his original battalion, the 3rd Royal Irish Rifles, then based in Larkhill, Wiltshire. When he was discharged, in March 1919, he returned to live in his native Co. Leitrim with his parents at Prughlish, near Keshcarrigan.

* * *

Also wounded was 24-year-old Company Sergeant-Major William Taylor. Born in Fermoy, Co. Cork, the son of a soldier from Co. Down and a mother from Co. Westmeath, he grew up in army barracks in Ireland and Britain. By 1911 the Taylor family seemed to have settled at Newtown Terrace in Athlone, where Taylor's father was working as the local barrack warden, but by this time William had enlisted and was serving as a lance-corporal with the 2nd Royal Irish Rifles in Dover Castle, Kent.

Promoted to sergeant before the outbreak of the First World War, in January 1915 William Taylor landed in France with his battalion, and he was still there early the following year when he was awarded the Distinguished Conduct Medal for 'conspicuous gallantry and coolness in assisting an officer, under heavy artillery and machine gun fire, to organize men of other units'. According to the *London Gazette* of 11 March 1916, 'when the Company Serjeant-Major was wounded, Serjeant Taylor at once took his place, and by his courage and example assisted to keep the men steady under very trying conditions.'

Wounded during the Rising, Taylor later returned to the war, where he was again wounded on 21 March 1918 – the first day of the German Spring Offensive. He was sent to Oaklands Red Cross Hospital in Cranleigh, Surrey; here he met a woman named Evelyn Hunt, who wrote in a letter to Captain John Bowen-Colthurst:

> I think you will be interested to hear that only this afternoon I was talking to one of the soldiers, at the hospital here where I work, an Irishman and a Company Sergeant Major, and talking about Ireland I mentioned your name. 'Oh,' he said, 'he was my officer and I was with him in Dublin at the time.' He is CSM Taylor, and you must know him quite well. He spoke so warmly of you and Mrs. Bowen-Colthurst, and it seemed to me so curious to hear all this just after I had got your letter, as he has been here some time. He says he was with you where you were wounded. I also hear that he was recommended for the VC when he was wounded on March 21 last ... He said how much he would like to see you again.

Taylor survived the war and settled in his new home in Athlone. By 1949, now aged fifty-seven, he was honorary treasurer of the Southern Irish Branch of the Royal Ulster Rifles Association.

* * *

The other wounded members of the 3rd Royal Irish Rifles were: Private Michael Atkins, who enlisted in Kilkenny in October 1915 and was discharged because of sickness in August 1916; Private John Cunningham, who enlisted in Youghal and continued to serve after the war in the Leinster Regiment; Private Lawrence Doyle, who enlisted in Dublin and later served in the Royal Irish Fusiliers; Private J. T. Duffy, who enlisted in Kilteel, Co. Kildare; Private J. Gilmore, who enlisted in Toomebridge, Co. Antrim; Private Thomas Holohan, who enlisted in Waterford in October 1915 and was discharged on 24 April 1917, a year after the start of the Rising, because of 'Wounds GSW [gunshot wound] Rt Thigh Sinn Fein Rebellion Dublin' (he had first been reported dead in the *Belfast Telegraph* of 15 May 1916); Private Samuel Hutchinson, who enlisted in Belfast; Private George Irvine, who enlisted in Newry; Private D. Johnston, who enlisted in Belfast; Corporal Henry Maher, who enlisted in Dublin and who had previously served in France, landing there in November 1914; Lance-Corporal R. McCord, who enlisted in Belfast; Sergeant Arthur McMaster, who enlisted in Belfast in September 1914, was awarded the Military Medal for his actions during the Easter Rising and later served with the 9th Royal Irish Rifles in the trenches before he was discharged because of wounds in February 1917; Private R. Mitchell, who enlisted in Belfast; Sergeant H. Mulholland, who enlisted in Belfast; Sergeant J. Mulholland, who enlisted in Belfast; Private P. Murray, who enlisted in Dublin; Private Samuel Patton, who enlisted in Ballymoney, Co. Antrim; Corporal Donald Swan, who enlisted in Belfast in November 1914 and was discharged in October 1916 because of wounds received during the Easter Rising; Private A. Taylor, who enlisted in Dublin; Private C. Wilson, who enlisted in Waterford; and Private Sidney Wilson, who enlisted in Mossley, Co. Antrim.

* * *

While the Rising was now over for the 3rd Royal Irish Rifles, the events connected with Captain John Bowen-Colthurst were far from finished. In fact with the return of Lieutenant-Colonel Walter McCammond, commanding officer of the battalion, on 29 April 1916, the situation became even more serious.

McCammond had been admitted to hospital suffering from pleurisy two days before the Rising began, leaving Major James Rosborough to take command in his absence. When he learnt of Bowen-Colthurst's activities he not only made no attempt to reprimand him but instead summoned Major Francis Fletcher-Vane to his office and informed him that he was no longer required to act as commandant of the barracks' defences. The job, in fact, would be given to Captain Bowen-Colthurst. At the same time, in what was perceived as the action of a man attempting a cover-up, Lieutenant-Colonel McCammond ordered soldiers of the Royal Engineers to replace the bullet-damaged bricks in the back wall of the yard beside the guardroom, where Bowen-Colthurst had ordered the shooting of the three prisoners.

Fletcher-Vane was shocked, and felt that he now had to take determined steps to deal with Bowen-Colthurst. He travelled to Dublin Castle and met the under-secretary for Ireland, Sir Mathew Nathan. When Nathan refused to do anything, Fletcher-Vane made his way to the headquarters of Irish Command to report the matter there. (Colonel Henry Cowan, the assistant adjutant-general, later stated that he had no recollection of this second report made at Irish Command.)

Having received no support from the authorities in Dublin, Fletcher-Vane decided to travel further afield. On 2 May he went to London, where he reported what had happened to the under-secretary of state for war, Jack Tennant (who had earlier helped Fletcher-Vane get his commission back), and the following day to the secretary of state for war, Lord Kitchener, as well as the principal private secretary to the prime minister, Maurice Bonham Carter. Kitchener, as Fletcher-Vane later wrote, 'stated that I had acted quite rightly.' He was apparently outraged, and angry that this was the first he was hearing of Bowen-Colthurst's actions. He immediately issued a telegram ordering the captain's arrest. (Kitchener allegedly then said, 'This officer must be shot,' to which Fletcher-Vane replied, 'Sir, you would not shoot a madman – for he must be mad.')

General John Maxwell, in command of British forces in Dublin since his arrival there on Friday 28 April – and the man responsible for the swift courts-martial and executions of the Rising's leaders – did not carry out the arrest until 6 May. Bowen-Colthurst had been preparing to lead a party of fifty-five men of the 3rd Royal Irish Rifles to Newry Barracks. He was placed under 'open arrest' and then from 11 May under 'close arrest'.

Before Bowen-Colthurst's court-martial Major Fletcher-Vane was ordered by General Maxwell to return to London and report to the War Office, which he did on 26 May. Because 'recruiting had practically ceased' in Ireland during the weeks immediately following the Rising (it would later recover, with 35,990 Irishmen joining the British forces between August 1916 and the end of the war), and because Fletcher-Vane was a recruiting officer, it had apparently been decided that he should be 'relegated to unemployment', as there was no longer any work for him in Ireland. On 30 May the War Office informed Fletcher-Vane of the decision, and it came into effect a month later. Once again, Francis Fletcher-Vane was out of the army.

He subsequently called for an inquiry into this decision; his request was refused. He was also reduced to the rank of captain for retirement purposes, as his rank of major had only been temporary. He reminded the army that he had been commended for his leadership during the assault on the South Dublin Union, which proved that he was not a useless soldier, and insisted that they review the report on this action with a view to his reinstatement. On 14 August he wrote: 'In these circumstances I ask you to support my claim for an enquiry, so that I may again take my place in defence of the Country, which I am now prevented from doing.' On 6 September in a letter to the secretary of state for war, David Lloyd George, he stated, regarding his reporting of the shootings in Portobello Barracks: 'I think that you will admit that it required some moral courage to do what I did and I can assume that moral is quite as necessary as physical courage in the Army at war.'

Major Rosborough had written favourably about Fletcher-Vane's activities under his command during the Rising, and Fletcher-Vane also claimed that, because of 'my action in reporting the illegal shootings of Messrs. Skeffington, Dickson and McIntyre, and to certain precautions which were taken by me to prevent further crimes ... I have acquired considerable popularity among the Irish people. They declare every day through innumerable letters and in the Irish Press that their gratitude to me is sincere.'

Fletcher-Vane believed that Maxwell, and the War Office in general, were angry with him for bringing the activities of Captain Bowen-Colthurst to light. Though he was ostensibly redundant as a recruiting officer because of the change in political opinion in Ireland following the Rising, he saw the timing as suspicious. There is no doubt that he was an annoyance to many senior officers, and there were almost certainly many who were glad to see him gone (though 'relegated to unemployment' was not a 'dishonourable discharge', as some who have written on the subject have stated). Furthermore, his actions in bringing the Bowen-Colthurst affair to light were supported by Lord Kitchener, suggesting that higher authorities in London had no problem with his actions; and when Fletcher-Vane had been gazetted out of the army in January 1916 as a result of negative reports about him, the army had not used the term 'relegated to unemployment' or any other term to disguise a supposed 'real reason' why they were taking his commission from him: they had simply stated that it was because he had been negatively reported on. There is no reason, therefore, to think there was a hidden 'real reason' why he was being involuntarily gazetted out of the army this time either.

Fletcher-Vane tried to be reinstated as a recruitment officer, but a report noted that 'the military opinion here is that no one could be less suitable for this or any other position connected with the Army.' He also tried once again to be attached to the Italian army as a liaison officer, but this request was again denied. He continued to write letters to various authorities, giving his story and asking for reinstatement, but his concerns were not addressed to his satisfaction and he was simply told that 'if you should wish to appeal to the Houses of Parliament, you should take whatever course is open to you as a civilian. You are no longer an officer.' (He did in fact manage to get the issue raised by means of a question in the House of Commons, but again it came to nothing.)

By now other information was coming to light about Francis Fletcher-Vane. In a report written after the Easter Rising, Colonel Cowan commented that 'on several occasions, when he had previously come to my Office, I had found his statements unreliable, and had doubts as to whether his eccentricities were natural, or due to being under the influence of drink.' It is true that Fletcher-Vane had earlier been accused of not paying a mess bill while serving with the 9th Royal Munster Fusiliers, and in late August 1916 it was noted that he also owed a sum to the officers' mess in Portobello Barracks. Monk Gibbon had alluded to a possible drinking habit and recorded that 'Vane was not prepossessing to look at. His flushed red face – Fletcher [Second-Lieutenant Donald Fletcher] had assured me that he [Fletcher-Vane] liked to linger over his whiskey and soda in the evening and had hinted vaguely at rumours of other suspected flaws in his character ...'

By November 1916 all appeals by Fletcher-Vane had failed. The same month he and Major James Rosborough were charged by Alderman James Kelly with 'illegal arrest and imprisonment.' (Kelly was paid an initial £1,400 by the losses compensation committee and a further £3,250 in May 1917, when the case was settled out of court).

In July 1917 Fletcher-Vane was still trying to clear his name, and in a letter to the former prime minister Herbert Henry Asquith he maintained that he was suffering 'libellous persecution' and repetitive 'abominable allegations' and that 'my enemies in Dublin and elsewhere spread reports of the most villainous kind affecting my personal character. I have no doubt that these were invented to weaken me as a witness or possibly to injure my career as a soldier. At any rate they did and I can show that these were secretly put into motion by responsible officials, possibly those who were directly or indirectly implicated in the shootings.' He felt that his character had been publicly damaged and once again called for an inquiry.

Two months earlier, in May 1917, Fletcher-Vane, obviously having accepted that the British army would not take him back, had applied for a passport in order to join the French Foreign Legion. The Army Council noted that they had no objection to this, so long as he could prove that the French Foreign Legion had already accepted his services. Fletcher-Vane could not prove this, and so no passport was issued. It would appear that he had been hoping to travel to France first and then join the Foreign Legion once he got there.

Fletcher-Vane's correspondence was now being intercepted by MI5 (section 5 of Military Intelligence), and this revealed an apparently sudden change in his political opinion. Three months after his failed attempt to join the French Foreign Legion he seems to have suddenly and wholeheartedly changed his allegiance to the cause of pacifism. In August 1917 he wrote to Edmund Morel, a prominent British politician, journalist and pacifist, to say that he was

> anxious to form among soldiers a propagandist body. In fact for the three months before the War broke out I had been engaged with the late Baroness v. Suttner [Bertha von Suttner, an Austrian novelist and pacifist], in trying to get together officers of various nations – who had seen war – with the object of making its futility, brutality and stupidity known. Indeed when she died I was under a pledge to go to Vienna to pay her a visit and to arrange this with her.
>
> But do not misunderstand my position. As a retired officer I came into this war completely voluntarily ... I did this deliberately ... because it was a fight for a small nation – and being so it was pledging the predatory Powers in a course of moral action – and because I saw a chance through this war of making it thoroughly hateful to the peoples, while it had the effect of training the proletariat in arms, and thereby transferring the physical force from the exploiters to the exploited ... I am opposed to racial and capitalist wars – and prefer to reserve our strength to fight the powers of evil. I am against this war now because its aims have been changed from idealistic ones to realistic – from defence to conquest.

He went on to state that he could call on the support of a fellow-veteran of the Easter Rising, Lieutenant William Monk Gibbon, who had now become a conscientious objector while serving at the front. 'He wishes to be in danger but absolutely refuses now to kill.' Along with Captain Craig Jennings of the 5th Royal Irish Lancers (who had earlier refused to take part in the Curragh Mutiny), Fletcher-Vane suggested that a Colonel Whyte would help to form the beginnings of his soldiers' propagandist body. 'They are men who know all about the atrocious tyranny – as brutal as stupid – of the Army Council, and if anywhere Democratic Control is necessary it certainly is at the War Office.' He then expressed his outrage at the War Office for having relegated him to unemployment.

Fletcher-Vane also claimed that he was in contact with a German princess who was sending him letters that were pro-English. He felt that 'it is of the utmost importance for our people to understand, whether they agree or not, the opinions of unprejudiced Germans. That she is unprejudiced is shown by the fact that she has corresponded with me throughout the war.' He was looking for a publisher for these letters. He named his German contact as Princess Marie zur Lippe (Marie Adelheid of Lippe-Biesterfeld). In fact this 'unprejudiced German' would later become a strong supporter of the Nazis. Part of the 'Nordic Ring', a Nazi movement concerned with race and eugenics, she became an assistant to the Nazi minister of food and agriculture, Richard Walther Darré. After the Second World War she retained her extreme right-wing views and was responsible for publishing several books that denied that the Holocaust happened, as well as providing funds for neo-Nazi publications.

Fletcher-Vane wrote that 'I have been for long in correspondence with the leading Sinn Feiners, with a view to causing them (which they have now done) to adopt our attitude in respect to affecting a permanent Peace,' while in another letter written in July 1917 to the prominent communist Tom Quelch he claimed to have founded the 'World Order of Socialism'.

Before the end of 1917 Fletcher-Vane had applied for a passport to travel back to his home in Italy (which was also refused) and had written two books, *The Easter Rising* and *War Stories* (about the Anglo-Boer War, the First World War and the Easter Rising), but both were prevented from being published by the army censor.

In 1918, after chairing meetings between Labour and Liberal candidates in the campaign for the general election that year, he finally returned to live in Italy, where he remained active in the Italian scout movement until the Italian fascists replaced it with a fascist youth organisation. Then, in 1927, he moved to England, now aged sixty-five, and settled at Hutton Forest, Cumberland. Two years later he published his autobiography, *Agin the Governments*. In 1933 he was taken into hospital, where he remained, and he died on 10 June 1934 in St Thomas's Hospital, London, at the age of seventy-two.

* * *

Second-Lieutenant Leslie Wilson of the Royal Irish Fusiliers, the pre-war student of holy orders who had accompanied Captain Bowen-Colthurst during his raids on Alderman Kelly's tobacco shop and Byrne's grocery – returned to sick leave after the Rising, having previously contracted pneumonia after exposure on a rifle range and been on sick leave when the Rising began. By early August 1916 he was still considered 'delicate ... with a weak constitution' and unfit except for light duty. A medical board recommended that he be allowed to resign his commission, which he agreed to do.

By July 1917, however, Wilson had recovered and wanted to return to the army. He wrote to the War Office, and they agreed to commission him again if he passed a medical examination. In August he was passed by a medical board and was subsequently reappointed as a second-lieutenant in the Royal Irish Fusiliers and posted to the 3rd Battalion in Clonmany, Co. Donegal.

After seven months with his new battalion – during which time he studied platoon drill and map-reading but never gained any practical knowledge of his job as an officer – he was sent to the British Expeditionary Force in France, joining C Company of the 1st Battalion in April 1918. His commanding officer soon noticed that Wilson had no real understanding of trench warfare and was an inefficient platoon commander, and he sent him away on a course of instruction to the II Corps Infantry School. Wilson later recorded that the course was excellent but that he found it difficult to keep up with the rest of the class, as he had no fundamental understanding of what was being taught. The commandant of the school wrote that 'this officer lacks power of command. Is very poor [at] drill & is weak in most subjects. He tried hard to improve himself & took an interest in the course.' When Wilson returned to his battalion the commanding officer saw no improvement in him, and this led Wilson to apply for a transfer to the Machine Gun Corps, hoping that – if he was accepted into the 'Suicide Squad', as it was known – at least he could learn the job properly from the beginning, as full training would be given to new members. The transfer was not approved.

On 12 July 1918 Brigadier-General E. Vaughan, commanding officer of the 108th Brigade, part of the 36th (Ulster) Division, wrote that 'I have seen this officer, and from my conversation with him and from his own letter, I consider he is quite unsuitable as an officer, and unfit to lead men in the field. He is lacking in military spirit & I do not consider he should ever have been given a commission, and I recommend that his services be dispensed with.' A week later the commanding officer of the 36th (Ulster) Division, Major-General Clifford Coffin, mirrored these comments. 'I have seen 2nd Lt. Wilson. There is nothing against this officer except his inability to command men. He has had a Public School & University education & his services may be of use in some capacity where he does not have to exercise command, but I recommend that he no longer be kept with a unit in the field, or where he shall be in command of men.' Finally, on 23 July 1918, the commanding officer of X Corps, Lieutenant-General R. B. Stephens, wrote: 'It is evident that 2nd Lieut. Wilson is of no use as a combatant Officer, but he appears to be well intentioned. I recommend that, if possible, he be transferred to a non-combatant Service either at home or abroad.'

In the end Wilson was not offered a position elsewhere in the army, and in August 1918 it was decided that his services should be dispensed with. He had previously pleaded by letter to be allowed to remain serving in some capacity, as he felt he would be publicly disgraced if he was simply let go from the army. He was also afraid that no bishop would ordain him in the future as a result, and that his career after the war would therefore be ruined.

Wilson returned to Dublin, living at his old address on the South Circular Road. As it turned out, the war ended by the time the process of relinquishing his commission was completed, and so he does not appear to have been publicly disgraced, as he had feared. Nothing more is known about his later life, but in one of his final letters to the army he stated that he was due shortly to be ordained.

* * *

Second-Lieutenant William Dobbin, the eighteen-year-old captain of the guard at Portobello Barracks who had been forced to hand over Francis Sheehy Skeffington to Captain Bowen-Colthurst for the raid on Alderman Kelly's shop and had later been ordered to fire a second volley into his body, entered the war some time later in 1916. He served with the 2nd Royal Irish Rifles in the trenches of the Western Front and in early 1917 successfully applied for his temporary wartime commission to be made permanent. That year he was also awarded the Military Cross.

In November 1917 Dobbin's battalion became part of the 36th (Ulster) Division. Early the following year, on 21 March, Lieutenant Dobbin was in the trenches when the German army launched its Spring Offensive. He was never seen or heard from again. It was not until 27 April that his father, Major William Wood Dobbin, governor of the Borstal Institution in Clonmel, received word that his son had been killed in action by shell fire. He then wrote to the War Office, stating that 'I am informed he fell in a counter attack at Contescourt ... In the circumstances I should greatly appreciate being allowed a map to note the spot where my Son is reported to have fallen ... If you are aware of any other Officer or Man who could give us the least information concerning how my Son met his death I need hardly say how much this would comfort us.'

William Dobbin was twenty when he died at Contescourt in March 1918. With no known grave, today his name is commemorated on both the Pozières Memorial and on a memorial plaque in Christ Church Cathedral, Waterford.

* * *

Lieutenant-Colonel Walter McCammond, commanding officer of the 3rd Royal Irish Rifles, who was absent suffering from pleurisy during the period of the Easter Rising, travelled with his battalion to Belfast when it was transferred there from Portobello Barracks in May 1916, just after the end of the Rising. In May 1917 a report referred to McCammond as 'an efficient and reliable officer.' Out of six colonels of Irish regiments named in the report, which dealt with the implementation of new orders, McCammond was the only one not cautioned or warned about his lack of attention to the new rules.

In August 1917, however, Lieutenant-Colonel McCammond was found unfit for general service, but fit for home service, for twelve months as a result of *E. coli* poisoning and was granted three weeks' leave. However, when this leave was up he was found unfit even for light duty at home for a further month.

In April 1918 the battalion moved again, this time to Larkhill in Wiltshire, but that month arthritis was diagnosed in McCammond's shoulder joints and his hands. He was given three months' leave from mid-July 1918 to mid-October in order to undergo 'hydropathic treatment' (a form of physiotherapy using water). The need for this leave was apparently urgent, suggesting that his condition had worsened very quickly. After the treatment McCammond's condition was still a problem, as he was regularly given periods of leave to go home. By December 1918 he was 'still unable to raise his arms without pain, the right shoulder giving him most pain.' On 6 December 1918 he finally relinquished his commission. He returned home to his native Belfast and died only five years after the end of the First World War in 1923. He was forty-nine years old.

Walter McCammond's son, seventeen-year-old Second-Lieutenant Cecil McCammond of the 19th Royal Irish Rifles – who had been wounded by rebel fire on the first day of the Rising and subsequently rode into Portobello Barracks to inform the garrison that a rebellion was breaking out – entered the war in September 1916. He joined the 14th (Young Citizen Volunteers) Battalion of the Royal Irish Rifles, part of the 36th (Ulster) Division, in the trenches but was evacuated home after five weeks suffering from shell shock. He was posted to his father's 3rd Battalion in Belfast and remained with it until July 1917, when – now aged eighteen and a lieutenant – he joined the 2nd Battalion in France. Four months later his new battalion became part of the 36th (Ulster) Division.

In December 1917 Lieutenant McCammond was wounded. The *Irish Times* of 19 December 1917 recorded that he 'has been admitted to hospital overseas. His condition is favourable and he is in no danger. He was blown up by a shell last week.' Back with his unit by January 1918, on 21 March he was serving in the same battalion as Lieutenant William Dobbin when the German army launched its Spring Offensive. He was wounded and gassed at Saint-Quentin, but he survived the battle. A medical report later stated that 'he was hit by a fragment of shrapnel on Rt. Ear, causing an abrasion, which has not caused any untoward symptoms. It was suspected in France that the F.B. [foreign body] had penetrated skull.' McCammond was evacuated to England and arrived at a hospital in Bristol on 26 March. By early April the wound had completely healed and he was given three weeks' leave.

Back in France by May 1918, McCammond was again wounded on 10 July at Méteren, just west of Bailleul in France, a report stating that 'when in action he was struck on the right side of the chest by a shell fragment which inflicted a contour wound about 8" in length, and slightly scored the lower ribs.' He was again evacuated from France and was on medical leave when the war ended. He was demobilised in April 1919.

The following year, however, Cecil McCammond was back in uniform. In 1920, during the War of Independence, he joined the notorious Auxiliary Division of the RIC and served with it at Killaloe, Co. Clare, finally being discharged after the end of the conflict in January 1922. During this time he also married.

After his second war Cecil McCammond returned briefly to live in Belfast before emigrating to Canada in May 1924. Now aged twenty-five and with £10 10s on his person, he listed his occupation as 'ex-army officer' and his intended occupation as 'anything'. He seems to have settled in Montreal; but seven years later – possibly because of the start of the Great Depression – he returned to live in Belfast. He was now thirty-two, had four young children and was working as a salesman, suggesting that his return home was for economic reasons. It was noted that he and his family sailed home in 'steerage' or third class.

By 1934 McCammond and his family were living in Glasgow, where he appears again to have been working as a salesman but also as a caretaker. On the outbreak of the Second World War he joined the Officers Emergency Reserve list in November 1939, aged forty, and he would remain on this list until February 1959, when he would be sixty. After this, Cecil McCammond disappears from official records.

* * *

After the Rising, Lieutenant Samuel Morgan, adjutant of the 3rd Royal Irish Rifles, was cleared of any blame for the actions of Captain Bowen-Colthurst. General John Maxwell had written on 2 July 1916 that, 'as regards the Adjutant, Lieutenant S.V. Morgan, he appears to have been constantly with Major Rosborough when these reports were made or to have at once reported events to him, so that he cannot be held responsible for the inaction in this matter.'

The battalion moved to Victoria Barracks in Belfast after the Rising. In December 1916 Lieutenant Morgan reported to the barracks hospital. He had been suffering from tonsillitis and chronic pharyngitis (inflammation of the back of the throat) for the previous four weeks and had now decided that his condition needed treatment. He was found unfit for general service and given light duty for two months; he had been due to depart for the war but because of his illness this was postponed.

In May 1917 he joined the 2nd Battalion of the regiment in the trenches, and on 1 August he was promoted to acting captain. Nine days later the battalion took part in an attack against the enemy at Westhoek in Belgium. The position was captured, but the 74th Brigade, which contained the 2nd Royal Irish Rifles, lost 1,291 men killed, wounded or missing during the battle. On the 15th Morgan's wife in Belfast received a telegram stating: 'Regret to inform you that Lieut S.V. Morgan Irish Rifles was wounded august tenth. Particulars will be sent when received.' However, on the 18th a second telegram arrived: 'Deeply regret to inform you that Lieut S.V. Morgan Irish Rifles previously reported wounded is now reported killed in action august tenth. The army council express their sympathy.'

Hanna Sheehy Skeffington had described Samuel Morgan as 'the only man at Portobello Barracks who treated my husband kindly. Very shortly after my husband's murder he was removed from the regiment, deprived of his adjutancy, and sent to the front "under a cloud". There he was killed in 1917.' This, however, was not true: Morgan was not the only man to show kindness to Sheehy Skeffington; he was not removed from his position as adjutant after the Rising; and he was not sent to the war 'under a cloud'.

Samuel Morgan was thirty-seven years old when he was killed in August 1917. With no known grave, today his name is commemorated on the Menin Gate memorial in Ypres.

* * *

Major James Rosborough, acting commanding officer of the 3rd Royal Irish Rifles, was heavily criticised afterwards for allowing Bowen-Colthurst's actions. For the most part it was accepted that he had not always known what Bowen-Colthurst was up to but that as acting battalion commander it was his job to know. Arguably, higher command chose not to reprimand Bowen-Colthurst in the immediate aftermath of his shooting of the three prisoners, and so in this instance Rosborough was simply following command policy. The claim that he simply deferred to Bowen-Colthurst and allowed him to 'roam free' because of the captain's alleged greater military experience also does not hold: Rosborough had eleven years' active service in Africa to his name, where he had served in at least three separate campaigns; in contrast, Bowen-Colthurst had only nine years' overseas service before the First World War and had seen only two months in the trenches in 1914.

It is more likely that Rosborough, however inexcusable it may be, did not know what Bowen-Colthurst was up to, rather than that he simply deferred to him. However, during the court-martial the battalion adjutant, Lieutenant Samuel Morgan, swore that he had told Rosborough at 10:40 p.m. on 25 April that Bowen-Colthurst had taken Sheehy Skeffington out of his cell in the guardroom and had left the barracks with him, along with a party of twenty-five NCOs and men. Rosborough insisted that he had no recollection of being told. He was criticised for this: for if Morgan's account was true he should have arrested Bowen-Colthurst at this point for removing a prisoner from the guardroom without authority. (It was also noted that Bowen-Colthurst himself claimed that he had reported to Rosborough after the raid, but again Rosborough could not recall this.)

Interestingly, Morgan's and Rosborough's statements, no matter how apparently conflicting, may both be true. Rosborough suffered from deafness in one ear, a result of malaria that he had contracted years previously while serving in Africa, and at the time of the Rising he was still being treated for it. He also claimed, as recorded in his service file, to suffer from a recognised condition called 'African memory', the symptoms of which included poor memory; so it is quite possible that he was not lying when he said he did not remember Morgan coming to him and telling him about Bowen-Colthurst's removal of Sheehy Skeffington from the guardroom, or about Bowen-Colthurst visiting him after the raid to inform him. Lieutenant-Colonel McCammond wrote something just after the Rising that might support this hypothesis, stating that 'under prolonged stress and strain when suddenly confronted with unexpected and unusual circumstances [Major Rosborough] may require some time to fully grasp the situation.'

This possible explanation was not taken into consideration at the time; and after the Rising Major Rosborough was suspended from duty and it was recommended that he be placed on retired pay. It was claimed that he was 'inert, wanting in quick and sound judgement and unfitted to command troops,' that 'he did not effectively exercise his authority,' and 'that he is slow to appreciate events and take action.' He was further reprimanded for not arresting Bowen-Colthurst after the captain had reported the shooting of the three prisoners to him, and for not confining him to barracks immediately.

The War Office ultimately insisted that Major Rosborough should resign his commission because of 'inefficiency' as a commanding officer, and so in July 1916 he was forced to leave the army. Two future prime ministers then discussed his case. In August, Andrew Bonar Law wrote to David Lloyd George, looking for information on Rosborough. It was decided to postpone any further action until the Simon Commission had finished its work, but a report about Major Rosborough written about this time outlined his case, stating that,

> handicapped therefore through the shortage of Senior Officers, through the kind of Senior Officers he had, through want of sleep for days and nights together, through having to answer numerous calls on the telephone (the only available means of communication) in regard to missing relatives, etc., and through the miscellaneous character of the multitude that had now assembled in the Barracks – Major Roxborough [sic] was placed in a position of exceptional, if not wholly unparalleled difficulty.

The report found that the officer in charge of prisoners, Second-Lieutenant Dobbin, had unlawfully allowed Francis Sheehy Skeffington to be taken from his cell by Captain Bowen-Colthurst, and that there was doubt over whether word of this event had been passed on to Major Rosborough. Subsequently, when Rosborough was replaced in his position of command by Lieutenant-Colonel McCammond, this officer made no attempt to arrest Bowen-Colthurst either. The report on Rosborough concluded that

> the only person dealt with by the military authorities is Major Roxborough [sic] who is asked to resign his Commission. All the others are left as they were. Even Colthurst, who committed the murders, is allowed to retain his pay as a retired Officer, whilst Major Roxborough, who has behind him 23 years of honourable military service, who has been mentioned in despatches, and who has never hitherto had a charge of any kind preferred against him, is threatened with the loss of everything.

After the Rising, Colonel Cowan of Irish Command recorded that two officers of higher rank than Rosborough were present in Portobello Barracks during the Rising but 'did not assume command.' One was Colonel Henry Allatt, who led Bowen-Colthurst and a group of men on a raid against Hanna Sheehy Skeffington's house on 28 April, though he appears to have only recently arrived in Portobello

Major Albert Clerke from Castlemartyr, Co. Cork, later a lieutenant-colonel (Mr & Mrs Robert William Boyles)

Barracks. The other was Lieutenant-Colonel Albert Clerke, commanding officer of the 3rd Royal Munster Fusiliers, a reserve battalion based in Aghada, Co. Cork, at the time of the Rising. Clerke, who was forty-eight at the time of the Rising, was a veteran of the Anglo-Boer War, having served with the 9th King's Royal Rifle Corps through the conflict before joining the Royal Munster Fusiliers in 1908. Colonel Cowan does not record when Lieutenant-Colonel Clerke arrived in Portobello Barracks, but if it was during the early days of the Rising he should have taken command.

Albert Clerke, a native of Castlemartyr, Co. Cork, survived both the Easter Rising and the First World War. After living in Blackrock, Co. Dublin, and later in Dún Laoghaire, he died in the Mellifont Nursing Home, Dún Laoghaire, in 1934, aged sixty-six.

On 26 July 1916, the day after Rosborough was asked to resign, his wife, Erdie Rosborough, wrote to Queen Mary explaining the situation and begging that the queen consider the 'sad case of one of Your Majesty's loyal Irish subjects.' In September and again in October, after the Simon Commission had completed its work, Rosborough's father-in-law, Rev. Joseph McKinistry of Randalstown, Co. Antrim, who had personally recruited about a hundred men for the 36th (Ulster) Division from his congregation, wrote to various politicians and to the War Office, petitioning them to reinstate his son-in-law and quoting from the findings of the Simon Commission, which completely cleared Rosborough's name and his involvement with the shootings. The Ulster Unionist leader Sir Edward Carson also took an interest in the case; but after petitioning the King not to become involved, the War Office ultimately decided to cancel Rosborough's resignation, and four months after being forced to leave the army he was restored to the rank of major in November 1916 and returned to duty.

That same month Major Rosborough and Major Fletcher-Vane were charged with the 'illegal arrest and imprisonment' of Alderman James Kelly. The case was later settled out of court.

Major Rosborough landed in France on 20 December 1916. Captain Arthur Weir wrote in a letter to Captain Bowen-Colthurst that 'Major Rosborough went out to the front last week. We went to see him off at the station. He was quite cheery but Mrs. R. says she does not think he will be able to remain long as he is not strong.' She was right. After serving with the 2nd Royal Irish Rifles for four months, Major Rosborough was re-designated a permanent base officer, removed from his battalion and the trenches, and appointed town major at Bully-Grenay. He remained there until November 1917, when he was evacuated home, now physically unfit for further overseas service, and returned to his old position as second-in-command of the 3rd Royal Irish Rifles in Belfast.

After the war Major Rosborough served with the 30th Battalion of the King's (Liverpool) Regiment, a battalion raised in France in May 1919 and disbanded in April 1920, after which (arranged by Sir Edward Carson) he served as an education officer and unit instructor in the 10th (Prince of Wales's Own) Royal Hussars, firstly in Canterbury, Kent, and then in Ennis, Co. Clare, when the regiment moved there in May 1920 during the War of Independence. Finally, in 1921 he performed the same role with the 1st Northamptonshire Regiment.

Rosborough was then informed that he was soon to be demobilised. He wrote to the army in December 1920 in the hope of finding a new role that would allow him to remain serving. 'I understand that officers with some legal knowledge may be required for Courts Martial duty. I have passed the first year's course at Law School, Trinity College Dublin, also being a graduate of that University. I have had more than average experience in Courts Martial work, especially in Dublin 1915–16, and when there acted for the officer who reviewed Courts Martial during his absence.' The army replied that only qualified barristers or solicitors could be employed as court-martial officers.

When Major Rosborough was finally demobilised in April 1921, having served for twenty-three years, including eleven years overseas, his former commanding officer, Lieutenant-Colonel Walter McCammond, referred to him as 'a very capable, hardworking and energetic officer. He has great tact and exercises a very good influence over all his juniors.' But Rosborough refused to accept retirement, and in May 1921 he applied for a commission in the Army Educational Corps, which was soon to be formed. However, his last commanding officer, Lieutenant-Colonel Seymour of the 10th (Prince of Wales's Own) Royal Hussars, wrote at about this time that 'I am unable to express an opinion on this Officer's qualifications as an Education Officer ... I do not think this Officer is competent to teach candidates for 1st Class Certificates. I am informed that N.C.O's left his class and went to an Army Schoolmaster.' It was noted that great progress had recently been made in Ireland with soldiers' education, and that more than a fifth had obtained second-class education certificates. However, in the last unit Rosborough had been working with – the 10th (Prince of Wales's Own) Royal Hussars – no positive educational results had been achieved recently, and it was doubted that Rosborough had 'any real ability and drive' as an educator. He was ultimately rejected for a commission. But he kept trying, and in November 1921, now aged fifty-one, he applied to become a senior cadet – an Auxiliary – with the RIC. This application also was rejected.

Two-and-a-half years later, in July 1924, Rosborough applied for compensation, stating that he could not find work in Ireland because his reputation was ruined. He argued that Irish Command had

> committed an error of judgement in suspending me and that before the Public Inquiry had been held. This was prejudicial to my position in public opinion, and, as a witness at the Public Inquiry, caused me to appear in the ignominious position of one under the bane of suspension. This fact being generally known, intensified my unenviable notoriety in a country inhabited by a people hostile to the military with long memories and distorted vision. Counsel also publicly stated at the Inquiry that attempts had been made to throw mud at me, while the public press of the period and subsequent literature testify to the notoriety ... I find myself after 3 years unsuccessful effort (since reverting to civil life) discredited and unable to obtain any form of permanent employment in Ireland, therefore, I respectfully request that the question of compensation in the form of employment or remuneration be considered in the light of British justice for the wrongs for which I am still suffering ... It is only financial necessity which has compelled me and my family to be in a country which has been made extremely unpleasant and almost impossible for us.

A report on the matter stated that Rosborough 'is now living in Ireland and states that he finds it impossible to procure employment. He maintains that people in Ireland have not forgotten the Skeffington affair and the part he played in it and he attributes his inability to find work to the [stigma] that attaches to his name as a result of that affair.'

It was ultimately decided that there were no grounds for compensation: 'This retired officer is like many other retired officers who found it impossible to get employment in Ireland or indeed to live there.' In 1950, now aged eighty, Rosborough emigrated to Australia. Seven years later he died in the War Veterans' Home in Narrabeen, New South Wales.

* * *

On Sunday 30 April 1916 Second-Lieutenant Monk Gibbon was involved in operations to enforce the curfew that had been operating since martial law had been declared five days earlier. For this he drove one of the improvised armoured vehicles, and he later recalled that he was fired on several times during this duty.

After the Rising, Gibbon gave a lift home to Shankill, Co. Dublin, to two friends of his, brothers originally from Derby in England who had lived in Dublin since at least 1905 and both of whom had served through the Rising. They were 27-year-old Lieutenant Arnold Fletcher and nineteen-year-old Second-Lieutenant Donald Fletcher, both serving in the 4th Leinster Regiment, who had also been in Portobello Barracks along with Gibbon. Their father was an assistant secretary in the Department of Agriculture and Technical Instruction for Ireland. Donald Fletcher had been mentioned in despatches after fighting in the South Dublin Union, where he had seen a fellow-soldier's head blown off by a grenade.

Neither brother would survive the war. The *Waterford News* reported on 11 May 1917:

> Mr. George Fletcher, assistant secretary to the Department – well known in Waterford, where he periodically inspects the Technical Institute classes – has lost a second son, Sec.-Lieut. D. L. Fletcher, in the war. The poignancy of the loss is intensified by the fact that the announcement of it has followed almost immediately on the intimation of [the death of] Lieut. Arnold Fletcher. Sec.-Lieut. Donald Lockhart Fletcher, of the Leinster Regt., died of wounds on April 28th at Salonika at the age of 20. He was educated at Dublin High School, entered Dublin University on April 27th, 1914, and joined the army on May 22nd, 1915. His gallant conduct won him mention in despatches.

The younger brother, Donald Fletcher, was killed at the age of twenty on 28 April 1917. Gibbon records that he died in an accident after pulling the pin out of a grenade during an instruction class. He now lies in Struma British Military Cemetery in Greece. His older brother and fellow-veteran, Arnold Fletcher, had graduated from the University of Dublin in both arts and civil engineering, after which he had become an assistant in the university's Department of Geology. He had written several papers on the distribution of radioactive elements in rocks and minerals and was considered a young academic with a bright future. He was twenty-eight when he was killed on 30 April 1917, two days after the death of his brother, while attached to the 193rd Company of the Machine Gun Corps, and he now lies in the cemetery of Saint-Sever, Rouen. (In his book Gibbon says that he gave a lift to Donald and Gilbert Fletcher, before going on to say that both died in the war. Gilbert Fletcher – a third brother, also an officer in the Leinster Regiment – did not die in the war, and so Gibbon must have been referring to Arnold.)

When Gibbon returned home he soon earned himself the nickname 'the Sinn Féiner' among his family for offering possible explanations why the Irish Volunteers had taken the action they did. His family, apparently, would

Leinster Regiment cap badge
(Author's Collection)

accept nothing other than complete condemnation.

When he returned to his unit in England, Gibbon encountered another officer and fellow-Irishman in the Army Service Corps who had been involved in the Rising. This was thirty-year-old Second-Lieutenant John Dunbar, a native of Ferns, Co. Wexford, where his father ran a pub. He had been on leave, staying at his home in Charleston Avenue in Rathmines, when the Rising began. Before the war he had worked as a clerk in the GPO, and from what he told Gibbon it seems that he too was in Portobello Barracks and was also involved in operations with the improvised armoured cars.

Gibbon was subsequently sent to the war, but he was deeply affected by Easter Week, 1916. He became a pacifist, and after the war – having relinquished his commission in September 1918 on the grounds of ill-health caused by his overseas service – he left Ireland to teach English in Switzerland. He later taught in England, and in 1928 he married. He subsequently returned home to live in Ireland, settling with his family in Sandycove, Co. Dublin. He was soon a well-known and respected author and poet, moving in literary circles that included Austin Clarke, Pádraic Colum, George Moore, Katherine Tynan and his cousin W. B. Yeats (whom he famously did not get on with). In the 1970s and 80s, now over eighty, he was still teaching and could be seen cycling around Sandycove as well as gathering driftwood on the beach near his house in his pyjamas. He died in October 1987 at the age of ninety.

* * *

During his court-martial Captain Bowen-Colthurst declined to cross-examine any of the witnesses called against him. He made no attempt at defence but stated that 'I was very much exhausted and unstrung after practically a sleepless night, and I took the gloomiest view of the situation and felt that only desperate measures would save the situation.' He was found guilty but insane and was committed to Broadmoor Criminal Lunatic Asylum in Berkshire. The court-martial was followed by a Royal Commission of Inquiry (the Simon Commission), held in the Four Courts in Dublin on 23 August, which upheld the verdict.

Bowen-Colthurst's service was terminated on 10 June 1916. Though enquiries were made as to whether he should be paid the full amount of retirement pay to which he was officially entitled (one argument being that his mental condition seriously affected his future earning power), it was decided that it would be inappropriate, especially as he was being kept in Broadmoor at public expense. It was decided instead to deduct £1 a week from his retirement pay in order to help pay for his upkeep in Broadmoor and to pay the remaining £2 9s a week to his wife, who was living in Wokingham, Berkshire. She had earlier stated that she was in 'poor financial circumstances' and that she badly needed the money.

Bowen-Colthurst remained in Broadmoor for only nineteen months and was discharged on 26 January 1918 after a medical report stated that there had been a change in his condition. His retirement pay was reinstated, and he received it for the remainder of his life. However, he was not simply released and allowed to go directly to his family but was kept in another medical institution, Dr Crouch's private nursing home in Chobham, Surrey, until 19 October, after which he went to live with his family in Ascot, Berkshire. While in this nursing home and undergoing psychological and physical evaluations he complained that his retirement pay was not enough to pay for the costs of his stay there, and also complained about the £1 a week deducted during his time in Broadmoor. He cited the act of indemnity under martial law, which he believed should have resulted in the state paying the total amount for his upkeep in Broadmoor.

He soon had some assistance in improving his financial situation. During his time at Chobham a Conservative politician, Sir Arthur Griffith-Boscawen, who had recently received information from a doctor that Bowen-Colthurst should be considered disabled, wrote to the Ulster Unionist leader James Craig, with whom he had clearly been working on Bowen-Colthurst's behalf. 'This will enable us to make some addition to his service retired pay and also to assist him with the expenses of his treatment with Dr. Crouch.' If nothing else, this gives an insight into Bowen-Colthurst's political allegiances.

When Bowen-Colthurst learnt that Alderman James Kelly, whose shop he had destroyed in 1916, had been awarded £1,400 and then a further £3,250 after a case against him (and another against Major Rosborough and Major Fletcher-Vane) had been settled out of court, he was outraged. The settlement had noted that Alderman Kelly was 'the perfectly innocent victim of a lamentable occurrence.' Bowen-Colthurst wrote an angry letter to the Treasury solicitor in October 1918, wondering exactly what this 'lamentable occurrence' was. He also demanded to know why his mother, who had been acting as his representative following the diagnosis of insanity, had not been informed of the Kelly settlement, why the settlement was made in the first place and the case not brought to court and tried before a judge and jury, and who had assessed the amount to be granted to Kelly. In reply he was informed that, as the Crown had taken over financial responsibility for the case brought against him by Kelly, the Crown's legal representatives had been within their rights in settling the case however they saw fit. No one else need have been informed or consulted, especially not Bowen-Colthurst himself – who, because of the act of indemnity that protected him, would not have stood to lose money anyway, even if the case had gone to court and the Crown had lost.

Bowen-Colthurst wrote back claiming that he had had no idea that he was indemnified against financial loss, and was grateful to have this confirmed.

However, he reminded the Treasury solicitor that he had not answered all his earlier questions, and also that 'in entering Mr. Kelly's house, I was acting under the orders of the Officer Commanding the Dublin Garrison. I was specifically ordered to arrest the occupant.' He added that he had friends who, in the press and in Parliament, would demand answers to his earlier questions.

In 1919 Bowen-Colthurst, now living in Christchurch, Hampshire, attempted to claim expenses from the army, including an unspecified amount for postage, relating to his court-martial. His mother also claimed expenses for enquiries and interviews she conducted in Dublin and Belfast in an attempt to gather information that could help her son's case. However, while Bowen-Colthurst's own claims were not considered strictly speaking legal expenses and were therefore rejected, his mother was found to have been operating under the instructions of Bowen-Colthurst's legal representatives, and so she was paid £14 14s.

At some point after the end of the war Bowen-Colthurst and his family emigrated to Canada and settled in British Columbia. In June 1920, during the War of Independence, his family home, Oak Grove, in Coolnagearagh, Co. Cork, was burned by republican forces. His sister Peggy was living there at the time. (The following year the IRA allowed eight men arrested following the recent Dripsey Ambush to be represented at their courts-martial in Victoria Barracks, Cork. One of the witnesses who appeared for their defence was Peggy Bowen-Colthurst.)

In 1940 Bowen-Colthurst wrote to the military secretary, once more repeating his complaints from 1914 and 1915 against Lieutenant-Colonel (now Major-General) Wilkinson Bird, who had been the officer commanding the 2nd Royal Irish Rifles. He felt the matter had never been resolved and that 'in the strenuous life of a settler in an undeveloped portion of British Columbia I have not hitherto had the leisure to give the matter the attention it deserved, but the outbreak of another war with Germany makes it imperative that I should bring this matter to your notice and request that such an occurrence should get full examination by the War Office, London, England, and if necessary by Parliament, with a view to its non-repetition during the present war.' He was apparently concerned that a junior officer might be abused by his commanding officer in the way that he felt he had been years previously.

In their deliberations over this letter the army wrote in one internal message that 'we do not consider that we are really concerned with this matter.' The writer of this note added that in Bowen-Colthurst's letter 'no mention is made of the charges on which this former officer was convicted in 1916.' They were surprised that Bowen-Colthurst was complaining about an old report by a former commanding officer, and that he apparently did not see his having shot three innocent men as something that could do similar damage to his reputation.

In the same year John Bowen-Colthurst remarried, his first wife having died some time previously, and had a son, who was born in 1946 but died at the age of fourteen in 1960. Bowen-Colthurst was then living in Naramata, near Penticton, British Columbia. Here he came to know Jim Hume, editor of a local newspaper, the *Penticton Herald*. He informed Hume that he had left England after the First World War because the IRA had become a threat to him. Having moved to Terrace, British Columbia, he had later been tracked down, and he moved again, this time to Sooke. Again, he claimed, the IRA found him, which was what had prompted him to move to Naramata. (Hume allegedly met an IRA man in Dublin in the 1970s who confirmed that they had been after Bowen-Colthurst and would have killed him had they found him.)

On 11 December 1965, nearly fifty years after the events of the Easter Rising, John Bowen-Colthurst died, at the age of eighty-five, while still living in Naramata. Described by Hanna Sheehy Skeffington as 'simply the Englishman with the veneer removed,' he was in fact an Irishman, as he referred to himself many times during his military career. His remains are buried in Lakeview Cemetery, Penticton, British Columbia.

When all the evidence surrounding John Bowen-Colthurst is put together, it should have been taken as a sign that he was a mentally unstable man: his alleged breakdown after Mons, the wounds he received on 15 September 1914 and the subsequent medical report that stated he was suffering from 'nervous exhaustion', the dual blow of receiving a negative report from Lieutenant-Colonel Bird and learning of the death of his brother on the Western Front, and the subsequent erratic change in his behaviour, especially his new religious passion. The army do appear to have attempted to counter this possibility, by refusing to promote him and by preventing him from returning to active service overseas; and had he served out the remainder of the war in a quiet home garrison he might never perhaps have gone 'over the edge'. Arguably, given the volatile situation in Ireland and Bowen-Colthurst's unionist views, he should never have been stationed in the country, or at the very least not in a district where the majority of the people were nationalists. But he was, and the outbreak of the Easter Rising appears to have been what finally broke him, with horrific results.

Several witnesses at his court-martial stated that Bowen-Colthurst 'was more unbalanced [after his return from France in 1914] than before ... was not capable of exercising any sound judgement or discriminating between right and wrong ... He was probably unequal to any strain which would probably have brought about a nervous breakdown, probably affecting him mentally ... His history for over a year was one of mental weakness.' One witness had even made a report against him in April 1914, before the First World War, suggesting that his mental instability may have extended back to that time.

It is sometimes said that Bowen-Colthurst escaped the proper punishment for murder by being declared criminally insane, but all the evidence suggests that this was an accurate verdict.

The story of the 3rd Royal Irish Rifles during the Easter Rising is a complicated and often bloody one. However, as has been shown, the significant personalities of the story – even those in British army uniform – were nearly all Irishmen.

6

Irish Units Summoned to Dublin

Thirty miles west of Dublin lies the Curragh Camp in Co. Kildare. The area was used as a military mustering site since the sixteenth century, its first permanent structures being built in 1855 during the Crimean War. Today it is home to the Defence Forces Training Centre, its seven barracks named after the seven signatories of the Proclamation of the Irish Republic.

In April 1916 the Curragh was home to the 3rd Reserve Cavalry Brigade (comprising the 8th, 9th and 10th Reserve Cavalry Regiments) and elements of the 25th (Irish) Reserve Infantry Brigade, namely the 5th Royal Dublin Fusiliers and 5th Leinster Regiment. The former had been stationed at the Curragh since September 1915, while the 5th Leinster Regiment had arrived at the camp from Wellington Barracks (later Columb Barracks), Mullingar, on 20 April 1916 – four days before the start of the Rising.

The Curragh, as the nearest source of help beyond Dublin, was the first place outside the capital to be contacted by Irish Command. Reinforcements were ordered to make their way to the city. Special trains were sent from Kingsbridge Station, and when they arrived in the vicinity of the camp they were boarded by the 1,600 men of the 3rd Reserve Cavalry Brigade. This brigade – a mixture of fifteen cavalry, lancer, hussar and yeomanry units (only one of them Irish) – began arriving in Dublin at 4:45 p.m. on Monday 24 April and ultimately helped to secure the North Wall and docks area as well as Dublin Castle.

After the seriousness of the situation in Dublin had begun to make itself clear a second wave of reinforcements was called for at 11:15 p.m. The 5th Royal Dublin Fusiliers and 5th Leinster Regiment, with a combined total of approximately 1,000 men, were ordered to prepare to move. At 1:15 a.m. an initial group of several hundred men of the 5th Royal Dublin Fusiliers, along with the 262 men of the service detachment of the 5th Leinster Regiment, marched out of the camp towards the nearby railway station.

British army cavalry, Dublin quays, 1916 (from *Dublin and the Great War, 1914–1918*)

Like the other Irish regiments already in the capital, these battalions contained a mixture of veterans, men recovering from wounds or illness, and new recruits in training.

The trains arrived in Dublin at 3:45 on Tuesday morning. As soon as they stepped off the trains the men of the Leinster Regiment went straight to Dublin Castle. They remained there until 2 p.m. that day, when an order was received to clear the vicinity of Tara Street and Westmorland Street of rebel forces. The regimental history states:

> On passing the Lower Castle yard gate, the leading platoon was met by a sharp fire from the neighbouring houses, but the platoon commander coolly steadied his men, dealt with the snipers and proceeded to occupy Dame Lane. The Battalion later passed through to Trinity College and occupied the south side of Dame Street with a picquet line, a support of one officer and 20 other ranks being located at Jammet's Restaurant in St. Andrew's Street.

The men of the Leinster Regiment, bringing with them two machine guns, were the first reinforcements to arrive at Trinity College. Up to that point its garrison had consisted of OTC cadets together with some individual British army and Commonwealth officers and soldiers who had been on leave in Dublin when the Rising began.

The following day, with Tara Street now controlled by the British army, the 5th Leinster Regiment was ordered to press on with its mission to clear the area between Tara Street and Westmorland Street. They had completed this job by 1 p.m. but had been under heavy sniper fire the whole time. An hour later, with the south side of the Liffey now secure and with the 5th Leinster Regiment positioned in College Street, D'Olier Street and Westmorland Street, as well as having a machine gun on the roof of the Tivoli Theatre at Burgh Quay and another on top of Trinity College, British artillery positioned south of O'Connell Bridge opened fire on Kelly's fishing tackle and gun shop on the corner of Bachelor's Walk and Sackville Street, which was held by insurgents. Several hours later, after the artillery fire had died down, the 8th Reserve Cavalry Regiment relieved the Leinster Regiment from these positions. However, the battalion retained its piquet in Dame Street.

At some point on Wednesday 26 April 28-year-old Private Christopher Moore was hit by rebel fire in the vicinity of Trinity College. He was not killed outright but later died of his wounds and was buried in the Provost's Garden of Trinity College. Christopher Moore had enlisted in Dublin, received his initial training in Mosney Camp, Co. Meath, and landed in France in May 1915 only to be wounded at Hooge not long afterwards and evacuated home. After the Rising his body was exhumed, and he now lies in Grangegorman Military Cemetery. Christopher Moore was the only member of the Leinster Regiment to die during the Rising.

Wednesday the 27th saw the 5th Leinster Regiment return to Dublin Castle. That morning at nine o'clock, now reinforced by a company of the 3rd Royal Irish Rifles and another from the 2nd/6th Sherwood Foresters, it was ordered to barricade the area between the GPO and the Four Courts to prevent the insurgents in one stronghold from reaching or communicating with the other. Travelling by armoured car down Parliament Street, across the Liffey and into Capel Street, the battalion established positions in Little Britain Street, Little Mary Street, Mary's Abbey, Little Strand Street, Lower Ormond Quay, Great Strand Street and Upper Abbey Street. Two days later it had also occupied Liffey Street.

When the insurgents eventually began to surrender, the 5th Leinster Regiment was involved in rounding up the prisoners. Patrick Colgan, a member of the Irish Volunteers from Maynooth, later recalled: 'At Mary's Abbey we were searched and our particulars were taken ... We were then taken to Capel Street where there were a great many men who had been collected from the Church Street area. We were kept separate from the Church Street men by a couple of sentries from the Leinster Regiment.'

* * *

Corporal Herbert Brogan of the 5th Leinster Regiment, a pre-war regular soldier who had enlisted in November 1911 and had landed in France in February 1915, would later be awarded the Military Medal for bravery during the Rising. He would survive the war and be discharged as an acting sergeant in January 1919.

Other Irishmen of the 5th Leinster Regiment had been mentioned in despatches for their actions during the Rising. One of these was 41-year-old Major Robert Metge. A native of Dublin, he was a descendent of a Huguenot, Peter Metge, who fled from religious persecution in France in the seventeenth century and ultimately settled in Ireland, building Athlumney House at Navan, Co. Meath. Robert Metge's father, Robert Henry Metge, was a barrister, Irish Party MP and magistrate for Co. Meath, while his mother was from Dublin.

Robert Metge had served in the regular army during the Anglo-Boer War as a lieutenant with the 1st Welsh Regiment and was wounded and taken prisoner at Paardeberg on 19 February 1900, after which he was transferred to the 2nd Battalion for a time before leaving the regular army and joining the 5th Leinster Regiment as a reserve officer. Just before the First World War he was living in Whitchurch, Herefordshire. After the Rising he landed in France on 18 April 1917 to join the Leinster Regiment in the trenches. He survived the war and returned to Ireland, first living in his wife's home town of Mallow, Co. Cork. His younger brother, Captain Rudolph Metge, also of the 5th Leinster Regiment, a former land agent, was killed on 4 October 1919, aged thirty-three, and now lies in Bective (St Mary) Church of Ireland Churchyard outside Navan. Robert Metge later returned to live in his home town of Dublin, where he died in 1953, aged seventy-eight.

* * *

Lance-Corporal James O'Connor of the 5th Leinster Regiment, who later served in the Labour Corps, was also mentioned in despatches during the Rising. So too was twenty-year-old Private Peter Nugent of the same battalion. Nugent was a native of Abbeyshrule, Co. Longford; his father was from Co. Westmeath and his mother from Dublin. Along with his father and brothers Nugent worked as a carpenter, painter and plasterer before the war. After the Rising he was promoted to acting corporal. He survived the war and in March 1925 emigrated to the United States, and the following year, while living in New York and working as a plasterer, applied for and was granted US citizenship. When the Second World War began he was required to fill in a draft (selective conscription) registration card, and on it he noted that he was now living in New York and working as a painter. When he retired he moved to Florida, where he died in September 1982, aged eighty-seven.

Private Edward Lambe, thirty-two years old, from the Chancery Street area of Dublin was a former labourer. He had landed in France in December 1914, and after the Rising he served in the Royal Defence Corps before being discharged in February 1919. He died in 1937 in Dublin, aged fifty-three.

Three other men of the 5th Leinster Regiment were wounded during the Rising. They were Private J. Callaghan who enlisted in Trim, Co. Meath; Private Henry Dardas, who enlisted in Navan; and 33-year-old Corporal Robert Fitzgerald, a former cotton piecer from Glossop, Derbyshire. Fitzgerald's father was from Kilmanagh, Co. Kilkenny, and his service file records that he received a gunshot wound to his wrist. The records do not clarify exactly, but the injury either amputated his hand – essentially blew it off – or necessitated amputation later on. Having enlisted in April 1915, Robert Fitzgerald was discharged because of his wounds two months after the Rising, on 28 June 1916.

One officer was wounded while serving with the 5th Leinster Regiment during the Rising. This was 21-year-old Second-Lieutenant Herbert Norman. Born in Co. Kilkenny, he grew up in Newtown, near Tramore, Co. Waterford. His father was an RIC pensioner and farmer from Co. Kildare, while his mother was from Co. Dublin. Before enlisting he had worked as a clerk. It is not known how, where or when he was wounded, but he survived and by 1919 was living in Southsea, Hampshire, and was now a lieutenant.

* * *

The men of the 5th Royal Dublin Fusiliers who arrived in Dublin on 25 April were also marched straight to Dublin Castle on arrival. However, they were soon ordered to take part in a battle just outside the castle gates.

By daylight on 25 April, though the British army had already recaptured City Hall from the insurgents, the Henry and James shop and the *Daily Express* offices on opposite corners of the junction of Parliament Street and Cork Hill were still occupied by the Irish Citizen Army. The men of the 5th Royal Dublin Fusiliers were ordered to assault the *Daily Express* offices. Taking part in this attack was 29-year-old Corporal John Humphreys of A Company. Originally from Clonmel, Co. Tipperary, he appears to have lived in Canada for a time, arriving there in 1909, before returning to Ireland and enlisting in Dublin on the outbreak of the war.

Also preparing to take part in the assault was Sergeant Peter Brophy, a native of Donnybrook, Co. Dublin. His enlistment fourteen years earlier suggests that there was something mysterious about him. In May 1902, while working as a builder's labourer with G. and T. Crampton of Dublin, he had joined the 5th Royal Dublin Fusiliers but under an alias: Peter Byers. It is not known why he did this: he was twenty years old and was therefore not too young to enlist and in need of a false name for that reason. He signed on for an initial six years with the reserve. However, when he renewed his engagement for a further four years in 1908 he requested that he be re-enlisted under the 'alias' Peter Brophy. For whatever reason, he was returning to using his proper name; presumably something had happened between 1902 and 1908 that made him feel it was safe to use his real name again. The army granted his request, and Byers became Brophy once more.

Private Brophy was present for three weeks of annual training in Maryborough (now Port Laoise) in June and July 1909 and again in July 1910. In January 1911 he was called up for a period of continuous active duty, during which he qualified as a stretcher-bearer after a course in Dublin in March. This period of active duty was supposed to end on 11 May, but six days before this Brophy deserted, remaining absent for more than three months. In late August he rejoined the battalion. In

May the following year he re-engaged for another term of reserve service and immediately served two months of active service, during which he was promoted to lance-corporal. The day after completing his two months of active service he went on to annual training camp in Maryborough for another three weeks. In January 1913 he started another five-month period of active duty – reverting to private during this time – and again, like the year before, immediately went on annual training camp. Before the outbreak of the First World War he served another two periods of active duty, for two months in late 1913 and two months in early 1914. For a reserve soldier, he spent a lot of time in uniform before the war.

Brophy was again promoted to lance-corporal in May 1914 at the beginning of a period of nearly two months of active service. This time he held on to the rank. In July and August he attended annual training camp in Youghal, being promoted to corporal at the start of the camp.

When war came, Brophy was mobilised on 6 August 1914. The 5th Royal Dublin Fusiliers was immediately sent to Cóbh, before being moved to Sittingbourne, Kent, in October. It stayed there for eleven months, during which time he received leave in early 1915 to return to Dublin and marry his fiancée. He was also promoted to sergeant in February. The battalion returned to Ireland in September 1915 when it was posted to the Curragh. While Sergeant Brophy and his family were living at Turner's Cottages in Ballsbridge, he was still stationed at the Curragh Camp when the Rising began.

* * *

The officer who would lead the assault against the *Daily Express* offices was Second-Lieutenant Frederick O'Neill. A 36-year-old from Liverpool, O'Neill was the son of an Irish mother and an English father of Irish parentage. He attended Stonyhurst College in Lancashire and in the late 1890s, while in his late teens, accompanied his father, a merchant and estate-owner, on several business trips to New York.

O'Neill enlisted in the Inns of Court OTC at Berkhamsted, Hertfordshire, in July 1915 while studying law. He served with the OTC as a private until November 1915, when he was commissioned into the 9th Oxfordshire and Buckinghamshire Light Infantry. First stationed in Portsmouth, he soon transferred to the 5th Royal Dublin Fusiliers, joining it in March 1916 at the Curragh.

* * *

Some time around 2 p.m. on 25 April 1916 British army riflemen and machine-gunners given the task of supporting the attacking troops began laying down covering fire against the *Daily Express* offices and other buildings held by the insurgents in the area. This firing scattered a nearby crowd of onlookers, but because some people inadvertently fled into the line of fire – with both Irish Citizen Army men and British army soldiers roaring at them to get out of the way – a ceasefire had to be called until the streets were empty. At 2:10 p.m. the machine-gun and rifle fire burst into life again.

Fifteen minutes later Second-Lieutenant O'Neill blew his whistle, and the assault against the *Daily Express* offices began. With bayonets fixed, the first wave of twenty soldiers of the Royal Dublin Fusiliers rushed out from the grounds of Dublin Castle towards their target. They were quickly being pounded by rebel fire coming from the upper storeys of the offices, while other insurgents manning a nearby barricade – along with recently arrived Irish Citizen Army reinforcements positioned in houses and hotels behind the *Daily Express* offices – also began to inflict casualties among the advancing soldiers. The first wave was beaten back.

A second wave of twenty soldiers swiftly formed up and was launched towards the *Daily Express* offices. Some of them managed to make it from Cork Hill across Dame Street and into the building, establishing a foothold on the ground floor, while onlookers cheered them on. However, if they were not quickly reinforced they would not be able to maintain this position for long. A third wave, this one of forty men, began fighting their way across Dame Street, using 'fire and manoeuvre' tactics: instead of running headlong across the road they moved in short hops, with some firing at the insurgents while others moved. This was a more defensive way of advancing, and the third wave soon reached the outside of the offices, having suffered very few casualties. However, they could not get inside the building, as their comrades inside had not advanced far enough to make room for them.

The ground floor was now full of wounded soldiers, and attempts to rush upstairs were being met with heavy volleys of fire. Slowly but surely, however, the soldiers began to make progress.

Fifteen minutes after the third wave Second-Lieutenant Frederick O'Neill entered the fight when he and another officer led a fourth wave of thirty men across the street. As they rushed across, stretcher-bearers were carrying the wounded in the opposite direction, back towards Dublin Castle, while at least one wounded Royal Dublin Fusilier was limping back with the help of a friend. Ten minutes later a fifth and final wave of twenty soldiers entered the *Daily Express* offices.

Max Caulfield, in *The Easter Rebellion*, records what happened to one soldier at this point in the battle: 'A shock awaited one Dublin Fusilier. As he worked his way round to the rear [of the *Daily Express* offices], he came face to face with his younger brother. Lowering his bayonet, he hissed, "Run, you young fool, run!"'

The fight had now moved to the upper floors of the building, and in confined and smoke-filled offices the men of the Royal Dublin Fusiliers and the Irish Citizen Army fought with bullet, grenade, bayonet, rifle butt and bare hands until the building had finally been secured by the British army. The battle for the *Daily Express* offices ended at 2:59 p.m., prompting the insurgents in the Henry and James premises to retreat.

* * *

At the far end of Dame Street the fighting had been watched by 58-year-old John Joly. A native of Bracknagh, Co. Offaly, he was professor of geology and mineralogy in the University of Dublin at Trinity College. He was also an honorary member of the university's OTC and was now taking part in the defence of the college. In his book *Reminiscences and Anticipations* (1920) he wrote about his experiences during the Easter Rising.

> The great event of Tuesday was the recapture of the *Daily Express* offices by the military. We were at the time in ignorance of what was actually happening; for we were possessed with the idea that the Sinn Feiners held the Castle. When, therefore, we saw at the head of Dame Street men in successive waves rush across the street from the City Hall towards the *Express* offices, we thought they represented the enemy in process of expulsion from the Castle. As a matter of fact the waves of men were composed of the troops. From our position in front of the College we could see that a terrific fire was being directed against the *Daily Express* building: plaster and powdered brick were flying in showers from its façade. This fire was to cover the advance of our soldiers. But in spite of this we saw, more than once, one of the running figures pitch forward and fall. It was expensive tactics; and later a better method of dealing with the Rebel strongholds was found when the artillery came into the City. The fight seemed to last a considerable time, about an hour at its greatest intensity before the firing began to wane. Not till later did we learn that the final phase of the struggle took place, under deadly conditions for the soldiers, in the narrow passages of the newspaper office. But they were not to be withheld, and the Rebels were ultimately bombed out or captured.

Apart from a number of wounded, whose identities are unknown, the 5th Royal Dublin Fusiliers lost one man killed during the battle for the *Daily Express* offices on 25 April. This was 29-year-old Corporal John Humphreys of A Company, a native of Clonmel, who was first taken to Mercer's Hospital. He is buried in Grangegorman Military Cemetery; on his headstone are inscribed the words *Peace, perfect peace.*

During the fight Sergeant Peter Brophy performed an act for which he would later be awarded the Distinguished Conduct Medal. The citation in the *London Gazette* of 24 January 1917 stated that he had received this award 'for conspicuous gallantry and devotion to duty. He assisted to establish a permanent footing in the upper stories of a building under heavy fire. He set a splendid example to his men.'

Brophy later entered the war when he landed in France in April 1917 to join the 1st Royal Dublin Fusiliers in the trenches. It was not long before he suffered his first injury, though it was a minor one. On 4 July 1917, as a report later stated, 'when getting out of the train when returning from a Court Martial, a box of bully beef fell on his hand and bruised it. He was in no way to blame.' He did not serve with this battalion for the rest of the war: he left it in August 1917 but not before he earned himself another medal for bravery. In the regimental orders issued by the commanding officer of the 1st Royal Dublin Fusiliers for 28 August 1917 it was announced that Sergeant Peter Brophy had been awarded the Military Medal.

About the same time Brophy attended a field ambulance suffering from gastritis. This soon developed into stomach inflammation and he was sent on to a casualty clearing station. He had been complaining of pain on the left side of his chest, and he had noticed that he had been losing weight for the previous three months as well as developing a cough in the mornings. By late August he was in the 7th Canadian General Hospital, where his condition was now diagnosed as chronic bronchitis. He had told the doctors that he had suffered from pneumonia in 1914. He had a strong pain in his chest, his heartbeat was rapid, and his voice was hoarse. He was treated and subsequently spent some time in two convalescent depots before he was fit to return to duty. When that time came, in October 1917, he was sent to the Base Depot at Étaples. Here, instead of being posted back to the Royal Dublin Fusiliers, he was sent to join the Labour Corps, possibly because of his recent illness.

However, the Labour Corps was not the last unit that Sergeant Peter Brophy served with during the war. In June 1918 he transferred again, this time to the 17th Royal Sussex Regiment, part of the 59th (2nd North Midland) Division. By June 1918 he was an acting company sergeant-major, and by August he had been officially promoted to the rank.

The war was nearly over, and even though he had fought during the Rising and had been in France for nearly a year and a half Brophy had never been wounded by enemy fire. This all changed on 6 October 1918 when he received a gunshot wound to his left forearm. His file records that it was a bullet from a machine gun that hit him, that his radius (one of the bones of the forearm) was fractured, and that a fragment of bone had to be removed. He survived and was soon on his way to the Northumberland War Hospital in Gosforth in Newcastle-upon-Tyne, where a metal plate was attached to the broken bone in his arm. In time he was transferred to the Red Cross Hospital in Dublin Castle to recover – the very place he had helped to defend and from where the assault against the *Daily Express* offices was launched in April 1916.

Peter Brophy was finally discharged in May 1919 – now aged thirty-seven – and returned to live with his family in his native Donnybrook.

* * *

Second-Lieutenant Frederick O'Neill, who led the attack against the *Daily Express* offices, was later mentioned in despatches for his actions. However, on 13 May 1916, barely two weeks after the end of the Rising, he was admitted to King George V Military Hospital in Dublin suffering from shell shock. As he had never served overseas, this could only have been a psychological response to his experiences during the Rising, and suggests how intense the battle had been. It is the only known case of shell shock to arise from the Easter Rising.

He recovered and was later posted to the 10th Royal Dublin Fusiliers. He joined it on the Western Front in time to take part in the Battle of the Ancre, but on the first day of the battle, 13 November 1916, he was killed in action at Beaumont-Hamel. He was thirty-seven years old. He now lies in Knightsbridge Cemetery, Mesnil-Martinsart; his name is also commemorated on a memorial in St Teresa's Church in Clarendon Street, Dublin.

The day after the capture of the *Daily Express* offices the 5th Royal Dublin Fusiliers lost four men killed in action. No records are explicit about the place where these deaths took place; it may have been in the battle for the Mendicity Institution, in which the 10th Battalion is known to have been involved, and there is also evidence that the 5th and 10th Battalions were working alongside each other at this point in the Rising.

The 5th Battalion is known to have established its headquarters in St Catherine's Church in Thomas Street. From here it set up a number of cordons, centred on Thomas Street. This area is very close to the Mendicity Institution at Usher's Island.

On 3 May, just after the end of the Rising, thirty-year-old Second-Lieutenant Wilfred Clarke of the 5th Royal Dublin Fusiliers (who would be killed in action on 9 September 1916 while serving in the 8th Battalion and who, with no known grave, is now commemorated on the Thiepval Memorial) wrote a letter to the commanding officer of the 3rd Connaught Rangers in Kinsale, stating that 'Sergeant Barror [3rd Connaught Rangers] has been associated with me throughout the operations against the Sein Feiners. He brought me much valuable information from time to time, and on one occasion we were able to bag two snipers, who had been worrying us for some time. He is an excellent shot and I only wish I could be associated with him at the front.'

Sergeant John Barror, a 33-year-old veteran of Gallipoli, was a Dubliner whose family ran a catering business. He had been home on leave, visiting his wife and children, and had managed to make it to a barracks on 25 April, ending up serving alongside the Royal Dublin Fusiliers for the remainder of the Rising. (He was later wounded when he returned to the war and was discharged as a result on 9 November 1918 – two days before the end of the conflict.) However, the commanding officer of the 10th Battalion, Lieutenant-Colonel Laurence Esmonde, wrote on 8 May to the commanding officer of the 3rd Connaught Rangers 'to certify that Sergeant J Barror 3rd Battalion The Connaught Rangers has been doing duty with the 10th Battalion Royal Dublin Fusiliers, from 25th April 1916 to 8th May inclusive, and has done good service.'

As Sergeant Barror could not have been in two places at once, or served with both the 5th and the 10th Battalions of the Royal Dublin Fusiliers simultaneously, it seems probable that the two battalions were intermixed and working together, and that this is how officers from both units commended him after the Rising. Therefore, the fatalities suffered by the 5th Battalion on 26 April may have taken place during the battle for the Mendicity Institution. Furthermore, the fact that the 10th Battalion did not lose any men killed during this action suggests that the 5th Battalion may have made up the bulk of the assaulting troops.

Either way, the men of the 5th Royal Dublin Fusiliers who died on 26 April 1916 were Private Richard Coxon, Private Francis Lucas, Private Abraham Watchorn and Sergeant Henry Hare.

Richard Coxon and Francis Lucas were both Englishmen. Coxon was a native of Murton in Durham. The son of a coalminer, he enlisted in Sunderland, having previously served in the Royal Field Artillery, and was already a veteran of Gallipoli by the time he arrived in Dublin. He was twenty-six years old when he died, and he is buried in Grangegorman Military Cemetery. Francis Lucas was from Leeds in Yorkshire. He enlisted in Maryhill and also now lies in Grangegorman Military Cemetery.

Private Abraham Watchorn was from Rathdrum, Co. Wicklow, and grew up on a farm at Williamstown, Co. Carlow. In February 1914 he enlisted in Carlow, aged nineteen at the time, in the Royal Regiment of Artillery. However, because of certain regulations he was immediately transferred to the infantry, specifically to the Royal Dublin Fusiliers. He joined this regiment at its depot in Naas for his initial training, after which he was posted to the 2nd Battalion in Gravesend, Kent, on 9 May. Twelve days later he left the army, having purchased his own discharge for £10. (Before the war new soldiers could buy themselves out within three months of enlistment if they so wished.) He clearly had not taken to army life.

However, in November 1915 Watchorn re-enlisted in Naas, again joining the Royal Dublin Fusiliers. Posted to the 5th Battalion at the Curragh, he travelled to Dublin after the start of the Rising and was killed in action on 26 April. His body was taken to Dublin Castle Red Cross Hospital, and he is buried in Grangegorman Military Cemetery.

John Henry Hare was born in 1876 in James's Street, Dublin. His father was from Co. Wicklow and his mother from Dublin. He enlisted in the 2nd Royal Irish Rifles in Newry in May 1894, aged seventeen at the time. Shortly afterwards he was tried by field general court-martial for an unknown offence. He served in India from December 1895 to February 1899. Having returned to Ireland after three years overseas he was home for only eight months before he set sail again, this time to fight in the Anglo-Boer War. He survived the conflict, and upon returning home he left the regular army.

The following year Hare was imprisoned in Mountjoy Prison for a time, though the records do not specify the offence. He remained in the reserve until May 1906, when he was finally discharged. Two years later, in June 1908, now working as a labourer and living in Meath Street, Dublin, Hare re-enlisted in the reserve. Now thirty-two years old, he joined the 5th Royal Dublin Fusiliers. By 1911 he was working as a packer in Jacob's factory while living in Meath Place; and the same year he was back in Mountjoy Prison for using 'profane and obscene language'.

On the outbreak of the war Hare was called up for active service and was soon promoted to sergeant. He was killed in Dublin on 26 April 1916 during the Rising and is buried in Grangegorman Military Cemetery. Inscribed on his headstone are the words *Ever remembered by his loving wife and family*. They had been living in Cupar Street, Belfast, at the time of the Rising.

It is possible that most of these four men died during the battle to secure the Mendicity Institution on 26 April 1916. However, at least one of them may have died in Sackville Street, and furthermore may have been killed by 'friendly fire'. Michael Knightly, who served with F Company, 1st Battalion, Irish Volunteers in the GPO, later recorded that

> on the Wednesday – when O'Connell St. was a 'No Man's Land' ... I think it was about this time that a man appeared in front of the G.P.O. – he had come apparently from a side street – threw up his cap and shouted: 'I am a Dublin Fusilier and want to die like a Dublin Fusilier.' Rifle fire rang out from the Tommies [British army soldiers] down about O'Connell Bridge and this time the fire was immediately effective. The poor fellow crumpled up.

Lieutenant Éamon Bulfin of the Irish Volunteers' Rathfarnham Company, who was also in the GPO at the time, recorded the event in greater detail.

> An incident occurred on Wednesday morning that I would like to mention. There was a tram upturned at Earl Street and in the middle of all this shooting, scurrying and general tumult, we heard a voice shout: 'I'm a bloody Dublin Fusilier. I don't give a damn about anyone.' He staggered out to the middle of O'Connell Street where he was riddled with machine gun fire. One of our men, with a white flag, went over to where he lay, knelt down, said a prayer over his body, and dragged him in to the side. I don't know who that Volunteer was. I have never heard that incident referred to.

Neither of these accounts clarifies whether or not the man was in uniform, so it is not known whether he was a serving soldier or an ex-soldier. If he was a serving soldier, the fact that Private Richard Coxon, Private Francis Lucas, Private Abraham Watchorn and Sergeant Henry Hare were the only Royal Dublin Fusiliers killed that day suggests that it must be one of these four men. Perhaps the man had been psychologically broken by the fighting. This lone figure crossing Sackville Street was spotted by British army machine-gunners near O'Connell Bridge, who at that distance obviously mistook him for a rebel. And if he was a serving soldier, there is a 50 per cent chance that he was an Irishman.

* * *

The 5th Royal Dublin Fusiliers, operating from its headquarters in St Catherine's Church in Thomas Street, subsequently took part in manning the cordons, checkpoints and barricades in the Thomas Street area, and soldiers from this unit are also known to have been involved in establishing positions around the GPO.

However, during the night of Friday 28 April some men of the battalion were involved in a much darker event.

That evening it was decided that the malt-house in Roberts Street, in the south-western corner of the 65-acre Guinness brewery complex, needed to be defended in case the insurgents in the nearby distillery in Marrowbone Lane attempted to attack the brewery. While further reinforcements would be assembled as soon as possible, one officer and nine men of the 5th Royal Dublin Fusiliers were despatched immediately from the main Guinness brewery to the malt-house.

The officer in command of this section was 22-year-old Captain Charles Rawdon MacNamara. Though born in England, he was descended from an Irish family that had once been lords of Bunratty Castle in Co. Clare. A more recent ancestor was Dr Tadhg MacNamara (born 1721), who was personal physician and close friend of Colonel Sir John Rawdon, Earl of Moira (who owned Moira House in Dublin, which by 1916 had become the Mendicity Institution). Because of his friendship with Lord Moira, Tadhg MacNamara named his son Rawdon. Born in Ayle, Co. Clare, he also became a doctor and by 1831 had become president of the Royal College of Surgeons in Ireland; and the name remained in the family ever since. Rawdon MacNamara's son, also Rawdon, born in Dublin in 1822, was a doctor who became president of the College of Surgeons, like his father before him.

Unlike his ancestors, Charles Rawdon MacNamara had become a soldier and not a doctor, and he was commissioned in December 1910 at the age of seventeen. In June 1912 he was promoted to lieutenant and in March 1915 to captain. He does not seem to have enjoyed good health, and he was easily susceptible to illness.

When he arrived at the Guinness malt-house Captain MacNamara posted his men and ordered them not to reveal their positions by opening fire on snipers: they were to begin shooting only if there was a rebel attack against the building. They were also not to open any windows, as this would also give away their position. MacNamara had been informed that three brewery 'night clerks' (night watchmen), who would all be carrying lamps, were on duty that night.

The senior NCO present with Captain MacNamara in the malt-house was Company Quartermaster-Sergeant Robert Flood. A 32-year-old native of London, Flood was an orphan who had grown up in a foundling home. He joined the 1st Royal Dublin Fusiliers in 1899, at the age of fifteen, and after serving in Egypt and India he joined the 5th Battalion as a colour-sergeant in 1913. In December 1914 he was promoted to company quartermaster-sergeant.

Another of the soldiers in the section guarding the malt-house was 21-year-old Private Maurice McCarthy. Born in Sheffield, McCarthy was the son of a valet from Co. Cork and a mother from Co. Kildare. The family moved to Ireland when Maurice was a few years old, and after living in Co. Kildare for a time they settled in Dublin, living firstly in the Summer Hill area of the city and later in Mount Pleasant Buildings, a well-known slum in Ranelagh.

McCarthy enlisted in the 5th Royal Dublin Fusiliers in October 1912, at the age of eighteen and while working as a messenger. He had previously served two days in another regiment at some point in the past (having been under age, he was quickly discovered and discharged). His enlistment medical examination revealed a 'slight functional murmur' in his heart, but it was considered 'not sufficient to cause rejection.'

After obtaining an army third-class education certificate in Dublin in November 1912, on the outbreak of war McCarthy was promoted to lance-corporal and in February 1915 to corporal. From 6 April he spent forty-five days in hospital in Sittingbourne, Kent, suffering from synovitis (painful inflammation and swelling of a joint) in his knee; it appears that he had received a kick while playing football. He reverted to the rank of private in June 1915, the same month that he landed in France to join the 2nd Battalion of the regiment in the trenches. By November he had been posted back to the regimental depot in Naas, possibly because of injury or illness, and by February 1916 he had joined the 5th Battalion at the Curragh. By now his family were living in the equally poor Hollyfield Buildings in Rathmines.

After a short while Captain MacNamara was due to be relieved, and Captain Auston Rotheram of the 4th (Queen's Own) Hussars, attached to the 10th Reserve Cavalry Regiment, prepared to lead reinforcements to the malt-house.

Auston Rotheram was born in Sallymount House, near Fore, Co. Westmeath. His father was a justice of the peace from Co. Meath and his mother's family owned Killenure Castle at Knockavilla, Co. Tipperary. He later lived in the family home, Crossdrum House, near Oldcastle, Co. Meath, after his father inherited it. After attending Cheltenham College and then the Royal Military Academy at Sandhurst, Rotheram was commissioned in the 4th (Queen's Own) Hussars in 1896. He spent the next three years in India (where he played polo with Winston Churchill). He left the regular army in 1903 but went on to serve in the North Irish Horse, a special reserve cavalry regiment, during which time he was promoted to major. In civilian life he returned to farm at Castlecor, near Oldcastle.

When the First World War began Rotheram seems to have reverted to the rank of captain and also returned to his old regiment, the 4th (Queen's Own) Hussars, landing in France to join it there in October 1915. He later returned home and by the time of the Easter Rising he was serving in the 10th Reserve Cavalry Regiment at the Curragh.

Among the reinforcements with Captain Rotheram was Second-Lieutenant Algernon Lucas of the 2nd Battalion of King Edward's Horse (the King's Overseas Dominions Regiment), which contained separate squadrons of Asians, Canadians, Australians, South Africans and Rhodesians, and New Zealanders. A farmer's son from Wiltshire, he was thirty-seven years old and a graduate of the University of Cambridge. He had previously worked as a teacher in Montreal, where he enlisted when the war began.

At 11 p.m. on 28 April the reinforcement party set off towards Guinness's brewery. When they arrived there they were led to the malt-house by one of the night clerks, William Rice, a 35-year-old Dubliner who had worked for Guinness's for sixteen years. Here Captain MacNamara passed on his orders to Second-Lieutenant Lucas, in the presence of Company Quartermaster-Sergeant Flood; he added that if the soldiers did need to open fire it would be better to fire through the closed windows than to open them first. Rotheram and MacNamara then left the small garrison at the malt-house, which now numbered fifteen men, and left the brewery. Rotheram is known to have arrived at Kingsbridge Station.

In the pitch-dark and silent malt-house the men of this isolated party could regularly hear firing in the distance. Tensions were high, partly because of earlier experiences. The previous day Flood had found a box of German dum-dum ammunition (bullets that expanded on impact) in a clerk's office in the main brewery; a civilian was standing near the ammunition, and when asked about it he had said nothing. Someone in the brewery had earlier asked one of the privates if he was Irish; the man replied that he was and was then told: 'Then fire high; sure you won't shoot your own countrymen.' Another private had been warned by a civilian that the brewery was 'a nest of Sinn Feiners.'

Now, in the gloomy malt-house, these men were under the command of an officer they did not know, with some of the guard also apparently confused about what he was doing there, unaware that he had relieved their own captain, MacNamara. As he inspected the area, Lucas was alleged to have had brief conversations with some of the guard that made them view him with suspicion. For example, he told Private Joseph Murphy not to open fire under any circumstance unless he gave the order first – contradicting the earlier order allowing the men to fire if attacked.

Just after midnight Second-Lieutenant Lucas approached Private Murphy at his position beside a third-floor window. Lucas opened the window, and this drew the attention of Company Quartermaster-Sergeant Flood. Flood came over and reminded Lucas of the order concerning the windows, but Lucas simply replied that 'I am in charge here, and you are to do as I tell you.' Flood now began to believe that Lucas might be a rebel sympathiser, and that he might be trying to signal to the Volunteers in the nearby distillery in Marrowbone Lane. Lucas increased this suspicion by mentioning that he had once been in America, where he had twice been taken for an Irish republican.

After opening the window, Lucas moved away towards the other end of the room. Flood then assembled five men of the guard, one of whom was Private Maurice McCarthy. In the meantime he heard footsteps approaching his position in the dark. He shone a torch in the direction of the footsteps, whereupon he saw William Rice, the watchman who had earlier led Lucas to the malt-house.

There seems to be some confusion about whether Rice was permitted to be in the malt-house or not. On the one hand, Captain MacNamara's orders concerning the night clerks, who had keys to the malt-house, were that they were the only persons (other than soldiers) who were allowed access to the building. On the other hand, in a statement given later Flood said that, as a civilian, Rice should not have been in the malt-house.

Flood ordered his men to cover Rice with their rifles; he then called on Lucas, who emerged from the darkness. Both Lucas and Rice were now illuminated by the torch. The *Sinn Fein Rebellion Handbook* records a statement from Flood about what happened next.

> He [Lucas] made a remark [to Rice] which I did not catch, and then the two of them moved over towards my position at the window, and he ordered the civilian to sit down close just behind him. About that time one of my men shouted that there were lights outside, right, left and front, and I myself saw lights like signals, but not military signals. I thought it peculiar that the officer who was close to me did not take any notice of the lights. I turned round to call his attention to them, and then I saw him bending down as if in conversation with the civilian, who had been placed under arrest ... Then my suspicion was aroused. I was sure there was treachery.

Flood ordered that both men be covered by rifles, after which both Lucas and Rice were searched, and Lucas's pistol was taken. According to his own statement given later, Flood found that Lucas was wearing a civilian shirt under his overcoat, and he began to wonder whether Lucas was not a civilian impersonating an officer. He ordered Private Patrick Short to telephone for Captain MacNamara; Short tried to do this but failed, but he passed a message to a brewery employee that they had two men under arrest.

Flood now decided to try to bring his two prisoners to a British army picket (guard) in James's Street; but while they were being moved, Rice attempted to escape and ran towards a nearby canal bridge, only to be stopped and returned by Private William Fox, who was on guard there. Another soldier, Private Byrne, was now claiming that he could see shadowy figures moving outside the malt-house. Flood sent Private Short to investigate – both to see if there was anyone outside and also to try to find an exit by which they might be able to report to Dublin Castle – but he could not get out of the building because of locked doors.

Flood now believed that an attack against the malt-house was imminent, and so he made an extreme decision: he told Lucas and Rice that he was going to have them shot. According to his own testimony, Flood said, 'I am sorry that there is treachery going on. My men's lives are at stake, and I will have to give an order to fire.'

Lucas begged Flood not to shoot him, saying: 'Don't fire, sergeant. I am only a poor farmer's son.' But when Flood ordered his men to make ready, the officer realised that the sergeant was going to go through with it. The terrified Lucas first apologised, saying that 'the boys led him into it,' then asked permission to say his prayers, which Flood granted. He knelt down briefly, and when he stood up he was crying; when asked why he replied that he was thinking of his wife and child.

Flood had the distraught officer placed against a wall. William Rice said nothing. The order was given to load, present arms and fire, and Second-Lieutenant Lucas was killed by a volley of five shots. Flood then directed the firing party to turn in the direction of William Rice, and the order to fire was repeated. Rice apparently did not die immediately and appeared to be still alive when he fell to the floor, though perhaps this was a case of involuntary muscle contractions, similar to what had happened with Francis Sheehy Skeffington. Private Maurice McCarthy stepped forward and fired another round into William Rice.

Not far away, at number 101 James's Street, which appears to have been a house used for Guinness employees while on duty, Cecil Dockeray, another Guinness night clerk, became concerned for his friend William Rice after he failed to turn up when he should. Dockeray received a phone call from the brewery to say that Rice was under arrest; he immediately contacted the British army and ended up being put in touch with an officer from the 2nd Battalion of King Edward's Horse – Lucas's regiment. This was Second-Lieutenant Basil Worsley-Worswick, a native of Weobley in Herefordshire. He had emigrated to Canada in 1913 to become a farmer, enlisted there when the war began, and was serving in the Canadian Squadron of the 2nd Battalion of King Edward's Horse.

Worsley-Worswick phoned Captain Rotheram in Kingsbridge Station to report what Dockeray had told him, but Rotheram instructed him to do nothing until the next morning. He ignored this order, however, and he and Dockeray set off for the malt-house.

Having shot Lucas and Rice less than half an hour earlier, the men of the 5th Royal Dublin Fusiliers who were guarding the building heard more footsteps approaching. Flood was summoned, and he demanded that whoever was nearing his position should halt. The order was ignored, and he repeated it. Again the approaching footsteps did not stop. Flood shone his torch in the direction of the approaching persons and saw Second-Lieutenant Worsley-Worswick and Cecil Dockeray coming towards him. He pointed his rifle at the two men, and summoned more of the guard to his position.

When the two newcomers arrived, Flood ordered his soldiers to search them. Worsley-Worswick handed over his belongings without resisting; Flood later noted that the officer had no pistol or other arms in his possession and was not wearing his Sam Browne belt. While the search was going on, Worsley-Worswick and Dockeray were asked what they were doing at the malt-house. The officer simply answered: 'I refuse to say who I am ... I don't know who you are. You may be Sinn Feiners for all I know.'

That was all Flood managed to hear. Worsley-Worswick dived at Flood and knocked him to the ground; but with several rifles pointed at him, the inevitable happened: the soldiers who were covering both men immediately opened fire, and Second-Lieutenant Worsley-Worswick and Cecil Dockeray were killed instantly. Four men had now been shot in the Guinness malt-house within the space of half an hour.

Both officers who were shot were later buried in the grounds of Dublin Castle. The site of their graves was lost until they were rediscovered by accident in May 1962, when the remains of both men were exhumed and reinterred in

Grangegorman Military Cemetery. The two Guinness watchmen are buried in Mount Jerome Cemetery.

At 3:30 a.m. the following day Captain Auston Rotheram was informed that there was an NCO outside looking for him. He came out of his room and found Company Quartermaster-Sergeant Robert Flood and the men of the 5th Royal Dublin Fusiliers who had been guarding the malt-house. They wished to report to him what had happened.

When Rotheram heard their report he was shocked. Flood was disarmed and arrested, and on 12 June 1916 he was court-martialled in Richmond Barracks for the murder of Lucas and Rice (but not for that of Worsley-Worswick or Dockeray). He was defended by Henry Hanna, who had previously defended the British army following the Bachelor's Walk massacre of 26 July 1914 (and later defended the insurgents who were court-martialled following the Rising).

Flood was found not guilty of murder and acquitted, a verdict that was greeted with applause in the courtroom. Though he had not been tried (or charged) for the deaths of Worsley-Worswick and Dockeray, the verdict was allowed to encompass those deaths as well. The managing director of Guinness, Henry Renny-Tailyour – an Englishman and former colonel in the Royal Engineers – issued a statement (mirroring an earlier one by the court-martial board) that neither William Rice nor Cecil Dockeray were rebel sympathisers or in any way connected with Irish republicans, while Lucas and Worsley-Worswick were defended by fellow-officers of King Edward's Horse, who insisted that neither man had supported the rebel cause.

Algernon Lucas's behaviour is certainly difficult to explain or understand, as there was a standing order not to open any of the malt-house windows; when Flood reminded Lucas of the order Lucas simply told him that he was in command. Nevertheless Flood had no authority to summarily shoot anyone, any more than Captain Bowen-Colthurst had earlier in the week in Portobello Barracks.

While Flood was not punished for his actions the army soon showed that they were aware of how sensitive the issue was. Flood was transferred away from his regiment into the Royal Berkshire Regiment before the end of July 1916; then in September he was posted to the 7th Royal Berkshire Regiment in Salonika. The following year, on 9 May 1917, having been promoted to company sergeant-major, he was killed in action during the advance on Jumeaux Ravine. With no known grave, today Robert Flood's name is commemorated on the Doiran Memorial.

Private Maurice McCarthy, who had been one of the party who shot Lucas and Rice (and who finished off Rice after he apparently survived the first volley), was also transferred out of the 5th Royal Dublin Fusiliers after the Rising. He was posted to the 9th Battalion and joined it in France before the end of June 1916. Within a month he had been moved to the 8th North Staffordshire Regiment. Later promoted to lance-corporal, on 19 November 1916 he was killed in action on the Somme, aged twenty-two. With no known grave, Maurice McCarthy is now commemorated on the Thiepval Memorial.

Captain Charles Rawdon MacNamara survived the Rising and was later sent to France to join the 2nd Royal Dublin Fusiliers in the trenches. However, following a bout of sickness he was admitted to hospital before he managed to reach his new battalion. Operated on for an unspecified condition, he was evacuated home in early August 1916. Two months later he applied for a transfer to the Army Service Corps, stating that he was no longer fit to serve in the infantry. It was instead decided to demobilise him, and this was done in January 1917. However, his treatment continued in a military hospital, while a fellow-officer, a Captain Chalmers, attempted to find him some employment. He was unsuccessful, and finally MacNamara is known to have resigned his commission in March 1918, aged twenty-four, while living in Worcester.

Captain Auston Rotheram later accepted the surrender of the 4th Battalion of the Irish Volunteers, the unit that had fought in the South Dublin Union. Lieutenant William T. Cosgrave of the 4th Battalion, who had fought in the South Dublin Union and who would later become the first president of the Executive Council (head of government) of the Irish Free State, recorded:

> Eventually there was a general acquiescence to surrender, Captain Rotheram accepted our surrender ... Captain Rotheram, one of the best known sportsmen of the Co. Westmeath, the best polo-player at No. 1 in Ireland, took the surrender of the Volunteers at South Dublin Union and Marrowbone Lane, and marched with the prisoners to Bride Road. He was called upon the following day to give evidence of the surrender in both places. His reply was that he had seen these men yesterday, that he did not know them, not having seen them before, that he would not know them again; that he would not feel justified in giving testimony. It is but fair to say that his sight had become impaired, which was the reason assigned for his relinquishing polo. It was further added that he had been reprimanded and that he received no promotion subsequently.

However, it would appear that Captain Rotheram was promoted later, as when the reserve cavalry regiments were reorganised in early 1917 he is listed as serving as a major with the newly restructured 2nd Reserve Cavalry Regiment at the Curragh. He survived the war, left Ireland in 1929 to live in England, and went on to have a daughter and seven sons, one of whom, Sisson Rotheram, was killed in action on 15 June 1944 while serving as a flying officer with the Royal Air Force. Auston Rotheram died in 1946 at the age of seventy while living in Cheltenham, Gloucestershire.

* * *

Apart from those already mentioned, two other members of the 5th Royal Dublin Fusiliers were awarded medals for their actions during the Easter Rising. One of these was Corporal George Parsons, who enlisted in December 1912. He was awarded the Military Medal for bravery during the Rising; he was later discharged with the rank of acting sergeant in March 1918.

Private Dominick Dunne, who was nineteen in 1916, was a native of Derrymullen, Co. Kildare, but was living at nearby Allenwood. He enlisted in Dublin in November 1915, having previously been working as a labourer, and was posted to the 5th Royal Dublin Fusiliers at the Curragh. In February 1916 he was given two days of confinement to barracks for not complying with an order. Nevertheless during the Rising he was awarded the Distinguished Conduct Medal 'for conspicuous gallantry and devotion to duty. He displayed great courage and initiative in engaging a portion of the enemy at a critical time.' Given the actions that the 5th Battalion is known or believed to have been involved in during the Rising, Dunne was probably awarded the medal for his actions during either the battle for the *Daily Express* offices or the battle for the Mendicity Institution.

Dominick Dunne later landed in France in July 1916, joining the 8th Battalion in the trenches. In September he was given ten days of field punishment no. 2 for not complying with orders, and the following year, on 22 December 1917, while serving in the newly formed 8th/9th Battalion of the Royal Dublin Fusiliers, he was awarded twenty-eight days of field punishment no. 1 for hesitating to obey an order.

By February 1918 Private Dunne was serving in the 1st Battalion, but following the start of the German Spring Offensive he was shot in the right forearm during one enemy attack. He survived, and is known to have been admitted to hospital in Rouen on 1 April 1918. A month later he was evacuated home and was admitted to the Military Hospital at the Curragh to recover from his wound. He was still a patient there six months later, in late November 1918 – the war having now ended – when the senior medical officer sent a telegram to the RIC station in Robertstown, Co. Kildare, informing them that 'Pte Dunne 1st R.D.F. absent from Curragh hospital. Believed to be at Robertstown. Take action please.' Dunne had apparently gone absent at about 8 p.m. on 18 November, and he was believed to be at home.

Two days later a telegram was sent by an RIC sergeant at the station saying that Dunne was in his custody and requesting that the army send someone to retrieve him; he had been apprehended in Derrymullen at about 6 p.m. on 20 November after two days of absence. When he finally returned to the hospital he forfeited five days' pay. (This was not the first time that Dunne had broken out of hospital: he had forfeited two days' pay in September for being absent for a day. It was also noted that Dunne regularly returned late when on a leave pass.)

Dunne was obviously well enough to be discharged from hospital now, and three days after being caught during this latest escape he was posted to the 3rd Royal Dublin Fusiliers and sent to join it in Grimsby, Lincolnshire. The following year, in April 1919, Private Dominick Dunne was finally discharged from the British army. He now had three cases of absence against his name and two of misconduct, but his military character was still considered 'very good'. A month after being discharged he wrote to the army to 'remind you of my DCM medal which I did not receive yet, also of the bounty which is due along with it.' The medal was posted to him two days later, and he was told to contact the regimental paymaster in Dublin regarding his bounty or gratuity of £20, which he did.

The following year, 1920, Dominick Dunne died while living in his native Co. Kildare. He was twenty-three years old.

* * *

Two Irishmen in the 5th Royal Dublin Fusiliers who were mentioned in despatches during the Rising were Captain Francis Popham and Private Edward Nolan.

Francis Popham was a 33-year-old officer from Kinsale, where his father was a bank manager. After attending Trinity College he was commissioned in the reserve 3rd Royal Munster Fusiliers in 1898. He served on attachment to the 1st Sherwood Foresters (Derbyshire Regiment) during the Anglo-Boer War, and in September 1908, now a lieutenant, he was transferred to the 5th Royal Dublin Fusiliers after three weeks with the 4th Royal Munster Fusiliers.

In 1911 Popham was still living in Kinsale but was now a captain in the 5th Royal Dublin Fusiliers. During the Rising he is known to have been based at Kingsbridge Station for a time, and he is mentioned in the Easter Rising diary of Phyllis Fry and Elizabeth Freeman. At 9:30 a.m. on Tuesday 25 April, as the diary records, 'Captain Popham telephoned from Kingsbridge and reported that Mrs. Webb and Co. spent the night feeding soldiers at the Buffet [a subsidised refreshment room for soldiers at the station], but their supplies were run out so they would like to get home.'

After being mentioned in despatches during the Rising, Captain Popham survived the First World War. He later settled in Manchester, where he died in August 1945, aged sixty-three.

Private Edward Nolan of the 5th Royal Dublin Fusiliers was a 34-year-old Dubliner and former butcher's porter and labourer who lived in Nicholas Street with his sister and her husband. He enlisted in the 5th Royal Dublin Fusiliers in November 1915, and not long after serving during the Rising, on 28 May 1916 he landed in France to join the 8th Battalion in the trenches. On 9 September he received the first of several wounds, a gunshot wound to his head and finger, during the Battle of Ginchy on the Somme. He was evacuated back to Ireland, but clearly the head wound was not very serious, as he was soon discharged from hospital and by November had been posted to the 5th Battalion. A month later he returned to France, this time joining the 9th Battalion; the following October he was transferred to the 10th Battalion. In late November or early December he was again wounded, this time receiving a gunshot wound to his left thigh, and was evacuated.

He returned to France for a third time when he joined the 1st Battalion in April 1918, but after being wounded for a third time in late May and evacuated once more he never entered the trenches again, and he was discharged in February 1919, aged thirty-seven. In March 1942, now aged sixty and living in Cork Street, Dublin, he wrote to the British army with a enquiry relating to his medals.

The 5th Royal Dublin Fusiliers also suffered a number of confirmed wounded, two of whom were Lance-Corporal Edward Cope and Captain Arthur Delany.

Albert Edward Cope, who was twenty-four in 1916, was born in St Paul's Parish in the north-west of the city. His father was a coal porter from Queenstown (Cóbh), and his mother was from Kimmage in Dublin. Cope grew up in Manor Street and later in Benburb Street, but by the time of the First World War the family were living in Hendrick Place, beside the Royal Barracks.

Cope enlisted in August 1914 in the Irish Guards, aged twenty-three, having previously worked as a messenger, a labourer and a porter. He joined the regiment at Caterham, Surrey, for his initial training, but on 5 September 1914 he was discharged as 'not being likely to become an efficient soldier'; his service file does not record the reason for this decision. But the following year he tried again. In February 1915 he re-enlisted, this time in the 6th Royal Dublin Fusiliers. In his medical report his teeth were described as 'very low grade' but his body as 'well nourished'. Two months after enlisting he learnt that his younger brother, Private John Cope of the 2nd Royal Dublin Fusiliers, had been killed in action in Belgium during the Second Battle of Ypres, aged nineteen, on 25 April 1915.

Edward Cope subsequently landed at Suvla Bay in Gallipoli in August 1915. Three weeks later he was admitted to hospital in Gallipoli suffering from dysentery. This necessitated his evacuation to Malta, and from there he was invalided home. By November his condition had improved and he was posted to the 5th Royal Dublin Fusiliers at the Curragh. Before the Rising began he had also been promoted to lance-corporal. He was wounded during the fighting, receiving a 'superficial' gunshot wound to his right wrist. In August he returned to the 6th Royal Dublin Fusiliers, now in Salonika. There he contracted malaria, but he was well enough to qualify as a Lewis machine-gunner by early November. Not long after obtaining this qualification, Cope reverted to the rank of private.

He left Salonika when the 10th (Irish) Division, of which the 6th Royal Dublin Fusiliers formed part, was withdrawn from the country in August 1917, landing in Egypt in preparation for being sent to Palestine. However, between January and April 1918 Cope was admitted to hospital in Alexandria for intermittent periods – the longest being one month – for malaria. He rejoined his battalion only in June, less than a month before it set sail from Alexandria, and five days later landed in Taranto in Italy. The same day Cope was given seven days of field punishment no. 2 for 'disregarding ship's orders.' The battalion then travelled by train to France, where it joined the 66th (2nd East Lancashire) Division.

In August 1918 Cope was back in Britain on two weeks' leave, but he did not report back until four days' after his leave was up. As a result he forfeited three days' pay.

On his return to the trenches, on 8 October Cope received a gunshot wound to his left thigh, though the medical report noted that he had 'no bone injury.' He was taken first to a casualty clearing station and later evacuated and admitted to the Red Cross Hospital in Netley, Hampshire, a month before the end of the

war, before being transferred to the Dublin Castle Red Cross Hospital. By the
end of October he had been discharged from hospital, and in April 1919 he was
demobilised.

A medical report from this time states that Cope was 'pale and anaemic, much
debilitated. Suffers from pain in his head and pain in his legs [and] shoulders.
Complains of relapses of malaria from time to time. Suffers from breathlessness
on exertion. Complains of pain in left knee after walking any distance. Complains
of attacks of diarrhoea since he had dysentery.' Now aged twenty-seven, he was
again living in his native Dublin, where he is known to have married in 1922.

* * *

Captain Arthur Delany was thirty-two in 1916. Born and raised in London, he was
the son of an Irish father, who worked as a fur warehouseman, and a mother from
London. He considered himself an Irishman, and at the immigrant inspection
station at New York, where he landed on 20 August 1913 from the *Olympic* (sister-
ship of the *Titanic*), he gave his nationality as Irish. He was working as an auditor
in the banking industry and had travelled to New York from Khartoum with
his older brother William, who was a bank sub-manager working in Cairo. The
brothers were in America on business, and intended to return to Africa once they
had finished their trip.

When the war began, Arthur Delany travelled to Ireland and joined the British
army, obtaining a commission in the 5th Royal Dublin Fusiliers. On 27 November
1915 the *Kildare Observer* records: 'On Saturday night last a recruiting meeting
was held outside the Town Hall, Naas, the speeches being delivered from the
balcony of the hall. There were numerous interruptions during the proceedings,
most of them being from "Sinn Fein" sympathisers.' After James Butterfield, a
local justice of the peace, had spoken,

> Lieut. Delaney, 5th Battn. R.D.F., was next introduced. He said he came
> there that night to address them as an Irishman speaking to Irishmen, and
> as an Irishman who had done a great deal of service for his country. So that
> they would not doubt his sincerity, he told them that he had come 6,000
> miles to join the Dublin Fusiliers (applause). He left Ireland years ago as
> many another man did, to seek his fortune in a far distant land, and after
> years of hard work and study he attained a certain position in life which he
> was very loath to leave. But on the day the first German crossed the borders
> of Belgium he had no hesitation as an Irishman, and the son of another small
> nationality, in starting on a 21 days voyage back to Ireland to offer his services
> to the Dublin Fusiliers (applause).

He went on to speak about the Irish concern for 'liberty and freedom and justice,'
and how the Germans had destroyed those things for Belgium. He insisted that
there was only one course for Irishmen to take – to enlist to fight back against the

German menace – and that the Irish revolutionaries 'Emmett, Fitzgerald and Tone if they arose from their tombs would tell Irishmen that in this war their duty lay in the direction of upholding the cause of the liberty and justice of Belgium.' At this point, the newspaper reports, 'there was some disorder in the crowd, a woman's loud laugh being audible above the commotion.

> 'A couple of months ago,' said Lieut. Delaney in reprimand, 'when we passed through Marseilles there was not a smile on the face of a woman or a girl or a child. The only time their features relaxed at all was when they heard we were coming to fight for the cause of freedom' (applause), and a voice: 'What are we fighting for?' Lieut. Delaney – 'You are not fighting at all yet; come and fight' (laughter and applause). Continuing, the speaker said he had the privilege of talking to a Belgian priest, and he told him some of the things which had happened in his own province. These things he [Delany] could not tell them, because they were awful beyond words. They were deeds committed not by the German soldiers, but by the German officers as well. God help Ireland the day the Germans set foot in it. (A voice: 'They never will') 'We are going to take jolly good care they never will,' retorted the speaker. 'What is more, I may tell you Germany is done, but we intend to absolutely crush her and prevent her ever again attempting to do what she is endeavouring to do now, and what she has miserably failed to do' (applause). (A soldier's voice: 'You were playing football at the Curragh when we were retreating from Mons'). Naas, continued Lieut. Delaney, had done very well, and Ireland had done very well. He was speaking to a soldier the other day who had come back from the front. A German officer had been brought in a prisoner and the man asked him whom the Germans were most afraid of – the English or the French – 'neither,' said the officer, 'we fear the Irish soldier most' (applause). The paper did not, continued the speaker, tell much about what the Irish regiments had done. The 'Dublin' motto was: 'Judge us by our deeds.' That was how they wanted to be judged – they wanted no advertisement (applause). It was unnecessary for him to tell them what the Irish regiment had done in Gallipoli Peninsula and in France (applause). Were they going to allow their Irish regiments to be filled up with Englishmen and Scotsmen? (No). That was the right answer, but that was likely to be done if they did not come in and join. No one attempted to deny the fighting traditions of the Irish or the immortal glory of their achievements on the battlefield.

There were several more speakers, including a Lieutenant Armstrong of the Connaught Rangers, and at the end of the recruitment meeting two men presented themselves for enlistment.

By the time of the Easter Rising, Arthur Delany had been promoted to captain, and he was wounded during the fighting in Dublin. After recovering he landed in

France in August 1916 to join the 10th Royal Dublin Fusiliers, where he was soon appointed to command D Company.

He survived the war and returned to live in Africa. Based in Cairo during the 1920s, he worked as an assessor trustee in the banking industry, but by the 1930s he was director-general of Egyptian State Radio. During the Second World War he was reactivated as a captain in the British army and attached to the Intelligence Corps in Cairo. In 1943, now aged fifty-nine, he was made a member of the Order of the British Empire for his services in the war. After 1945 he became chairman of the Marconi Radio Telegraph Company of Egypt, before retiring in 1955 to live in Ireland. He became involved in running the Ashford Castle Hotel in Cong, Co. Mayo, before dying in Dublin in July 1957 at the age of seventy-four.

* * *

Of course there were those in the 5th Royal Dublin Fusiliers who also came through the Rising unhurt. One such man was 39-year-old Major Robert Robinson of Dublin. Born four days before Christmas in 1876, he lived with his family at Sandford Road in Ranelagh. His father was a British army surgeon.

Having earlier served during the Anglo-Boer War and then married in Dublin in 1905, by 1916 Robert Robinson was a major in the 5th Royal Dublin Fusiliers. He took part in defeating the insurrection and then sat as a waiting member of the general court-martial of Eoin MacNeill, chief of staff of the Irish Volunteers, and other republicans . He was subsequently promoted to lieutenant-colonel and was made a member of the Order of the British Empire in 1919.

Company Sergeant-Major Patrick Cullen from Co. Carlow was a forty-year-old former grocer's assistant who enlisted in the Royal Dublin Fusiliers in 1894. A veteran of the Anglo-Boer War, he had also served in India. He had probably been a musketry instructor, as after the Rising the acting commandant of the School of Musketry at Dollymount, Second-Lieutenant H. M. Lee, wrote to the commandant of the Army School of Musketry at the Curragh to say that Company Sergeant-Major Cullen had been commended for supplying 'good information regarding the movement of rebels by day and night,' suggesting that Cullen was temporarily attached to the Dollymount school at the time of the Rising, or at least ended up serving alongside them.

Later promoted to regimental sergeant-major, Cullen was then commissioned as a second-lieutenant in the 8th Royal Dublin Fusiliers and found himself with it in the trenches from at least June 1917. However, after developing trench fever at Bullencourt on 27 October 1917 he was admitted to No. 22 Casualty Clearing Station and subsequently to No. 2 Red Cross Hospital. Ultimately evacuated back to the 2nd Western General Hospital in Manchester, Cullen arrived there 'debilitated and anaemic'. He was discharged from hospital in December and then in April 1918 was posted to the 1st Royal Irish Rifles as part of the 36th (Ulster) Division. By June he was an acting captain and a company commander. Before the end of the year Captain Cullen had been awarded the Military Cross for an action in September 1918.

He was on leave in Britain when the war ended. Then, in February 1919, he was appointed commanding officer of No. 855 Area Employment Company of the Labour Corps at Calais and later appointed claims officer for the Calais area. In September he resigned his commission while requesting that his war gratuity of £1,000 should be paid to him as soon as possible, as he was intending to move to South Africa. He never did (or did so only for a brief time), as by 1921 he was living in Wellington Road in Ballsbridge, having earlier lived in Vernon Road in Clontarf.

Three years later, Patrick Cullen's life took a turn for the worse. Now aged forty-eight, he was charged with embezzlement and falsification of accounts. It was alleged that he had taken two sums of £9 and £19 4s 5d from his employer, Sydney Robson of the Associated Supply Company at Thanet in Kent. He pleaded guilty at Maidstone Assizes and was sentenced to twelve months' imprisonment. He made no attempt to appeal. His Long Service Medal, Good Service Medal and First World War medals were forfeited and taken from him (though they were restored in February 1925), and he was deprived permanently of his discharge rank.

* * *

After the arrival of the 5th Leinster Regiment and the 5th Royal Dublin Fusiliers in Dublin on Tuesday 25 April 1916, the next group of reinforcements to arrive came from the far end of the country. Not generally believed to have been involved in the Rising, soldiers of the 3rd Royal Dublin Fusiliers from Victoria Barracks (now Collins Barracks), Cork, arrived at Kingsbridge Station at about daybreak on Tuesday the 25th.

The involvement of this battalion is proved by the first-hand account of one of its soldiers, Private Edward Casey, which was published in 1999 as *The Misfit Soldier: Edward Casey's War Story, 1914–1918*. Casey was an eighteen-year-old Londoner, the son of Irish parents. Having already served in France and Salonika, he was serving with the 3rd Royal Dublin Fusiliers in Cork in 1916 when the barracks received word that the Rising had begun in Dublin. As he later recorded,

we were talking and the bugle blew the Assembly. Rushing to the Barrack Square, it took a while for them to be assembled in fours, and numbered, and the Batt SM [battalion sergeant-major] (the same old Bastard which delighted to see me in trouble) calling us to attention. Our Commander addressed us, telling us our Easter was cancelled, and that trouble had broken out in Dublin, and a special [train] was being prepared, and we would leave in full marching order, and Live ammo will be issued. Dismiss. The order was calmly received. There was no panic. The packing for the full marching did not take long (it was always ready for night operations training). Later, marching down the hill to the Station, we saw little or no folks on the streets.

The special train was waiting. We detrained at Dublin in a few hours, [when] it was just getting daylight.

The battalion reached Dublin at dawn on Tuesday 25 April, not long after the 5th Leinster Regiment and the 5th Royal Dublin Fusiliers had also arrived there from the Curragh.

> Marching in columns of fours, we were told by our Officers, 'This is not war; it's rebellion.' Our Company were detailed to cover the Four Courts ... It was not long before every post was manned by troops. My post was lying down behind an iron Urinal on the banks of the Liffy, and right opposite Guinness Brewery. Streets were deserted, although on the way from the Station the crowds of men and women greeted us with raised fists and curses. I noticed a dead horse and a tram car pushed over on its side. [We] were visited by our Officers and no word was spoken. The day dragged on. We were relieved every two hours and marched to Victoria Barracks for meals. [Casey is confusing the nearby Royal Barracks with the name of his own barracks in Cork]. It was two [hours] on, two off.
>
> I was standing behind my iron box when I noticed an old Lady walking slowly along the street. When she was in hearing distance, I yelled, 'Halt! who goes there!' 'Oh Jesus, Mary and Joseph!' came the reply. It was amusing, but to me very sad. That old lady with her Irish accent reminded me so much of my Mother. Leading her by the arm to the shelter of [the] urinal, I told her she may have to stay a while. Shots were being fired now and again from the big concrete building across the road [probably the Mendicity Institution].

When the fighting in Dublin had ended, Private Casey saw both Constance Markievicz and Éamon de Valera after they had surrendered. Finally, he recorded that, after 'a few days on duty patrolling the streets, we were marched out, entrained for Cork and [sent] back to duty.'

The 5th Leinster Regiment and the 3rd and 5th Royal Dublin Fusiliers would soon be joined by more reinforcements. By the afternoon it was reported that the 4th Royal Dublin Fusiliers from Templemore, a battery of four 18-pounder artillery guns from the 5th (A) Reserve Artillery Brigade in Victoria Barracks, Athlone, and the Ulster Composite Battalion – a speedily assembled unit drawn from the various reserve infantry battalions in Ulster – had arrived in Dublin. The great majority of the soldiers in these units were Irish.

* * *

The 4th Royal Dublin Fusiliers, stationed in Templemore since the end of 1915 but in the process of moving to Wellington Barracks, Mullingar, is known to have been deployed on the north side of Dublin during the Rising, though a detachment was also sent to Dublin Castle. It was instructed to take part in establishing the outer north-side cordon that ran from Parkgate, along the North Circular Road and on to the North Wall. After arriving at Kingsbridge during the afternoon of the 25th the battalion proceeded up Infirmary Road and on to the Cabra Road before turning east towards Phibsborough.

There had been some concerns about how the men would react to having to fight other Irishmen, as recorded by eighteen-year-old Lieutenant Arthur Killingley of A Company. Killingley was born in Co. Wexford and grew up in Co. Dublin, and he had been commissioned in March 1915. His father, a Church of Ireland clergyman from Queenstown (Cóbh), was vicar of the parish of Whitechurch, near Rathfarnham, Co. Dublin.

Lieutenant Killingley kept a diary during the Rising, and on Monday 24 April 1916 he wrote: 'We [the officers] had a general discussion as to how men will behave if ordered to fire on their fellow countrymen.' The following day, however, when the battalion reached the capital it came across some rebel prisoners at Kingsbridge Station who had been captured earlier. The officers' concerns proved to be unfounded when, as Killingley noted, the men of the Royal Dublin Fusiliers 'booted the prisoners with great gusto.'

Killingley later entered the war when he joined the 1st Battalion in the trenches on 12 July 1916, though he later served on attachment to the 86th Trench Mortar Battery. (On 23 October his older brother, Lieutenant Hastings Killingley of the 2nd Battalion, was killed in action on the Somme, aged twenty-one.) Arthur Killingley survived the war and died in 1979 in Greystones, Co. Wicklow, aged eighty-two.

The commanding officer of the 4th Battalion was 47-year-old Lieutenant-Colonel James Meldon. Born in Westland Row, Dublin, he was educated in Brussels, Clongowes Wood College, and Trinity College. His grandfather was James Dillon Meldon, a well-known Dublin solicitor who had changed his surname from Muldoon to Meldon. Meldon's father, Austin Meldon, born in Roebuck, Co. Dublin, was a doctor and also deputy lieutenant for Co. Dublin. James Meldon was originally commissioned in the 16th (Queen's) Lancers in 1889, aged twenty-one, but in 1897 he left the regular army and transferred to the reserve 4th Royal Dublin Fusiliers. That year and the following year he served on attachment to the Uganda Rifles and was involved in defeating the 'Uganda Mutiny', an uprising of the Sudanese troops under the British colonial government's control. Meldon raised and commanded his own unit during the campaign, known as 'Captain Meldon's Swahilis', and he was mentioned in despatches after the end of the campaign.

Not long after the Uganda Mutiny, Meldon travelled to South Africa to take part in the Anglo-Boer War, after which he was promoted to major. In 1913 he was serving as chief of police and commandant of local forces in the British colony of Saint Vincent in the Caribbean.

Lieutenant-Colonel Meldon was again mentioned in despatches for his actions in Dublin after the Rising. In June 1918 he finally entered the war when he took

command of the 1st Royal Dublin Fusiliers in the trenches. He survived the war
and retired from the army, and by 1920 he was living in his native Dublin when
he was called to the bar. By 1921 he had been appointed resident magistrate for
Co. Mayo and had moved to Rossymailley, near Westport. He also wrote several
books on topographical subjects. Between 1924 and 1926 he lived in Co. Armagh
and later lived in the United States for a time before settling in Camberley, Surrey.
He died in December 1931, aged sixty-three.

Another officer in the 4th Royal Dublin Fusiliers during the Rising was 33-year-
old Second-Lieutenant Eugene Sheehy. Born in Loughmore, near Templemore,
Co. Tipperary, he was the son of David Sheehy, Irish Party MP for South Meath
who was also a former member of the IRB and Land League activist who had been
imprisoned six times during the Land War. This made Eugene Sheehy the younger
brother of Hanna Sheehy and brother-in-law of Francis Sheehy Skeffington;
another brother-in-law was the writer and politician Thomas Kettle, who was
married to Sheehy's younger sister Mary. The Sheehys moved to Dublin when
Eugene was four, and he grew up in the new family home in Belvedere Place.

Both Sheehy and his father were firm supporters of John Redmond and Home
Rule, though Eugene also had an ardently republican uncle, a priest, also named
Eugene Sheehy. This Eugene Sheehy had been imprisoned in 1881 for a speech in
favour of the Land League. He was also a member of the IRB, had been present
at the founding of the GAA in 1884, and had later taught Éamon de Valera when
he was a boy. During Easter Week 1916, while Second-Lieutenant Sheehy was
in British army uniform his uncle was in the GPO in support of the republican
insurgents.

Before joining the army Eugene Sheehy had worked as an attorney at the High
Court in Dublin. He had applied for his commission in April 1915, and by 1916 he
was living in Dartmouth Square in Ranelagh.

After the Rising, Second-Lieutenant Sheehy entered the war when in July 1916
he joined the 1st Royal Dublin Fusiliers in the trenches. He was later transferred
to the Intelligence Corps and attached to IV Corps' heavy artillery as part of its
'counter-battery' unit, suggesting that he was responsible for identifying enemy
artillery positions. Promoted to lieutenant in July 1917 and to captain in June
1918, he survived the war and was demobilised in March 1919, returning to live
in Dublin. He subsequently became a legal staff officer in the Free State army and
later a judge in the Circuit Court. In 1951, now aged sixty-eight, he wrote:

> The Rising in Easter Week was a source of heartbreak to me and to the many
> tens of thousands of Irish nationalists who joined the British army. We had
> done so at the request of our leaders who were the elected representatives of
> the people, and the vast majority of the nation applauded our action. The
> Rising was not even approved by the leaders of Sinn Féin ... As the tide of Irish
> public opinion gradually changed and hostility to England grew we did not
> quite know where we stood, or where our duty lay. The threat of conscription

in 1918, and the ultimate betrayal of Redmond by the British Parliament, made those of us who survived feel that the thousands of Irishmen who died in Flanders, France and Gallipoli had made their sacrifice in vain.

Eugene Sheehy died in 1958, aged seventy-five.

* * *

As the 4th Royal Dublin Fusiliers continued its advance eastwards along the Cabra Road during the afternoon of 25 April 1916 it was raining heavily – the only time during the Rising when the sun was not shining brightly.

The battalion was now entering the area defended by Commandant Ned Daly's 130-strong 1st Battalion, whose position was centred on the Four Courts. These insurgents had already achieved some successes against the British army. Not long after midday on Monday the 24th at Church Street they had ambushed a detachment of the 6th Reserve Cavalry Regiment that had been travelling along the north quays from the North Wall railway depot to the Magazine Fort in the Phoenix Park, escorting an ammunition convoy comprising five carts of weapons and explosives. The cavalrymen had suffered several killed and wounded in the ambush, but the survivors managed to barricade themselves in the nearby Collier Dispensary and Medical Mission in Charles Street, along with the weapons and ammunition from the convoy. Here they would remain for three days, holding out under frequent attacks from the Volunteers.

During the early hours of Tuesday the 25th other British army cavalrymen were escorting six transport wagons along the south quays on their way to Dublin Castle when they came under fire near Church Street Bridge from men of the 1st Battalion of the Irish Volunteers. The soldiers soon retreated the way they had come, having suffered at least five casualties. (After dawn Daly's men found five rifles at the site of this latest ambush.)

As the battalion continued its advance up the Cabra Road during the wet Tuesday afternoon it was approaching the most northerly outposts of the 1st Battalion of the Irish Volunteers, a barricade set up near the junction of Charleville Road and Cabra Road, supported by another at the junction of Charleville Road and the North Circular Road, both of which were overlooked by rebel snipers positioned in nearby houses. (There was another barricade further east at the junction of the North Circular Road and Phibsborough Road.)

However, before the battalion managed to reach these positions the Irish Volunteers in the area had come under fire from one of the 18-pounder artillery guns recently arrived from Athlone. The artillerymen had travelled by train to Blanchardstown, after which they had advanced to the Richmond Lunatic Asylum (later St Brendan's Hospital) at Grangegorman, just to the west of Broadstone Station, having almost certainly come by way of the Navan Road, along the northern perimeter of the Phoenix Park, and then down the Old Cabra Road to the asylum. Here they set up their gun at the gate of the residence of the asylum medical officer and opened fire with shrapnel shells against the rebel position at the junction of the North Circular Road and Phibsborough Road. One shell blasted away the barricade, and the fifteen Volunteers defending the position were forced to retreat westwards towards their comrades at the Charleville Road barricade. From here they sent six scouts westwards down the Cabra Road, but these soon encountered the Royal Dublin Fusiliers coming right towards them.

The insurgents took cover in nearby doorways and opened fire, but the soldiers responded aggressively, charging the Volunteers and forcing them to retreat. The scouts withdrew to their comrades at the Charleville Road barricade; but while the Royal Dublin Fusiliers began laying down heavy rifle and machine-gun fire against the barricade, they did not attempt to charge it. In the pouring rain the two sides fired at one another until suddenly, just before 3:45 p.m., the Royal Dublin Fusiliers stopped shooting. The insurgents should have recognised this as an ominous sign. At 3:45 p.m. the artillery opened fire once more, and shrapnel shells began exploding over the barricade. The insurgents defended their position for forty-five minutes, but when the barricade was finally blown apart the thirty Irish Volunteers scattered in all directions, having unsuccessfully attempted to blow up both the Midland Great Western Railway bridge over the Cabra Road and another railway bridge over the North Circular Road.

With the way forward now clear, the Royal Dublin Fusiliers continued their advance eastwards. Reaching the junction of the North Circular Road and Phibsborough Road, they turned south and advanced towards Broadstone Station. The day before, Commandant Daly had ordered Captain Nicholas Laffan, acting commanding officer of G Company, 1st Battalion, to occupy the railway station; but without enough men they had finally decided to establish a fortified line of sniper-occupied houses and barricades along North Brunswick Street, slightly to the south of Broadstone Station. The 4th Royal Dublin Fusiliers was therefore able to occupy the station without any serious resistance. The commanding officer, Lieutenant-Colonel Meldon, set up his headquarters in the building.

However, the 4th Battalion was now facing the main rebel defences in the area. Aside from the rebel positions in North Brunswick Street there were barricades – along with supporting snipers in houses and business premises in the vicinity – in nearby Red Cow Lane, Church Street, North King Street, Lisburn Street and Coleraine Street. The men of the 1st Battalion of the Irish Volunteers were strategically scattered over the area, stretching south to the Four Courts and the Liffey, and they also had snipers in elevated positions in Jameson's malt granary tower, Clarke's dairy and Moore's coach factory.

It was while attempting to press further south towards the Liffey from Broadstone Station that the 4th Royal Dublin Fusiliers lost its only man killed during the Rising. As later recorded by Captain Nicholas Laffan of the Irish Volunteers, 'on Tuesday ... the upper portion of Clarke's Dairy and of Moore's Factory were used for sniping positions and a constant fire was directed on the Broadstone Station which prevented the enemy from coming down the side streets to Constitution Hill. A lieutenant of the Royal Dublin Fusiliers was shot while attempting to get down Prebend St. to Constitution Hill.' This was 22-year-old George Gray, a dental student from Newcastle upon Tyne. He did not die that day, however, but succumbed to his injuries on Friday 28 April. He is buried in Grangegorman Military Cemetery.

It would appear that the 4th Royal Dublin Fusiliers was ultimately prevented from advancing further south than Broadstone Station. Similarly, the insurgents could not advance further north than North Brunswick Street; and after dusk on 25 April a dozen men were sent out to try to recapture the railway station from the British army. They managed to get within fifty yards of the main entrance, but the Royal Dublin Fusiliers spotted them and fired on them, driving them back.

Soldiers of the 4th Royal Dublin Fusiliers subsequently continued eastwards and finally completed the battalion's task in helping to establish the northern cordon around Dublin, which by Wednesday the 26th had stopped all traffic from entering or leaving the north inner city unchecked. Since the plan for the Easter Rising had called for snipers and barricades to defend the north of the city – rather than any main occupied positions, like those in the city centre or on the south side – the 4th Royal Dublin Fusiliers had a large number of dispersed rebel snipers to deal with in the Phibsborough and Drumcondra areas, which made any movement extremely dangerous. However, this is where it was ordered to establish its positions. As later recorded by Father Michael Joseph Curran, secretary to the Catholic Archbishop of Dublin, on Tuesday the 25th 'the Dublin Fusiliers from Tipperary occupied Phibsborough, the fork of the road at Glasnevin Orphanage [where Finglas Road and Botanic Road diverge] and the top of Iona Road. At 5 p.m. several machine guns and ambulances were assembled in Dorset Street and Mountjoy Street.'

They are also known to have occupied Aldborough House in Portland Row on Wednesday the 26th – along with some members of the Royal Irish Rifles from the Ulster Composite Battalion – in order to establish firing positions against rebel snipers in the area.

By the end of the Rising the 4th Royal Dublin Fusiliers had suffered a number of confirmed wounded. Eighteen-year-old Lieutenant Thomas Addis from Nottingham was one of them. His father was a clergyman from Edinburgh; his mother was born in London to Irish parents. His Irish grandfather had been a carpenter, and his grandmother was from Co. Tipperary. After recovering from his wounds Lieutenant Addis landed in France on 12 July 1916, joining the 2nd Royal Dublin Fusiliers in the trenches. On 21 March 1918, during the German Spring Offensive, he was killed in action. He was twenty years old when he died, and he now lies in Unicorn Cemetery, Vendhuile.

* * *

Another wounded officer was nineteen-year-old Second-Lieutenant James Dunn, a native of New Zealand. Dunn's father was an English watercolour artist of

Irish descent; his mother, also an artist, was the daughter of John Acland, a long-serving member of the New Zealand Legislative Council. After attending Wanganui Collegiate School, Dunn applied for a commission in May 1915 while living in Bath, Somerset. He was commissioned a month later in the 4th Royal Dublin Fusiliers.

After being wounded in the Rising, Dunn was again wounded, this time severely, on 7 September 1916, between Guillemont and Leuze Wood, while serving in the 8th Royal Dublin Fusiliers. He received a gunshot wound to his right shoulder that also fractured his shoulder blade. Evacuated to England, by the following year he was serving on attachment with the headquarters of the 25th (Irish) Reserve Infantry Brigade in Cork.

On 22 November 1917 – showing how much the political situation in Ireland had changed since the Rising – Lieutenant Dunn was again severely wounded, but this time in Ireland. He received an injury to his left eye, and he later wrote a statement describing what happened. 'While walking through Bridge Street, Cork immediately after a Sinn Fein procession had been dispersed by the police I was suddenly attacked by five or six unknown men, one of whom threw a stone or heavy instrument which struck me in the left eye, resulting in the loss of sight in that eye.' A later medical report added that 'vision in left eye may improve ... but will be permanently impaired.'

Shortly afterwards promoted to captain, Dunn applied for compensation for his injury, but a report dated 11 March 1918 stated: 'It is quite possible the officer was set upon because he was in uniform but I do not think that these Sinn Feiners could technically be called "the enemy" because it is not stated that the military were called out. Nor is it stated that he was at the time on duty.' On the other hand, another report claimed that 'in this case the injury should certainly be considered to have been received through the performance of military duty ... It may not have occurred to the writer [of the previous report] ... that many of these Sinn Feiners were and probably are in active association with the enemy and the recollection of the execution of Roger Casement is an illuminating example.' It was later accepted that Captain Dunn had been wounded on duty, and he received his compensation.

After the war Dunn was demobilised in September 1919, now aged twenty-two, and he stated that he was intending to return to live in New Zealand. However, in September 1923 he is known to have crossed the border from Mexico into the United States at El Paso, Texas. He may have been on his way to visit his parents, who had been living in San Diego since 1921. His border crossing documents note that he had a large scar on his left ear, more than likely the result of the same assault in 1917 that left the sight in his left eye permanently impaired.

* * *

One Dubliner who was wounded while serving in the 4th Royal Dublin Fusiliers during the Rising was nineteen-year-old Second-Lieutenant John Hawe, who was born and raised in Marlborough Road, off the southern end of the North Circular

Road, near the Phoenix Park (meaning that, as the 4th Royal Dublin Fusiliers moved up Infirmary Road and on towards the Cabra Road, he would have marched past his old front door). Hawe was the son of a customs and civil service official from Dublin and an English mother. He attended Stonyhurst College in Lancashire, where he was a cadet in the school's OTC, and in September 1914 he applied for a commission, at the age of seventeen, requesting to be commissioned in the Royal Dublin Fusiliers or the Royal Munster Fusiliers. His commission was approved and he became an officer in the 4th Royal Dublin Fusiliers on 26 March 1915, three days after his eighteenth birthday.

After recovering from the wounds he received during the Rising, Hawe landed in France on 23 October 1916, joining the 9th Battalion in the 16th (Irish) Division. On 9 January 1917 he was severely wounded. At Wytschaete (now Wijtschate) in the Ypres sector, as a medical report later stated, 'a piece of shell penetrated the left frontal lobe of the brain – entering at junction of left forehead and temporal region. This was removed by trephining [trepanning] the same evening and [the piece of shell] is reported as being found 1¾ inches deep in the cerebrum ... He has a 2 × 2 [inch] hole in the skull with visible brain pulsation. The little finger of left hand was damaged at the same time ...'

This severe wound obviously necessitated Hawe's evacuation from France, and after first being treated at Bailleul Hospital, then at Boulogne, he was sent to the 2nd Western General Hospital in Manchester. He survived his injuries but soon began suffering from poor health and extreme symptoms. A medical report noted that he 'complains of increasing attacks of giddiness. Cannot read or study. States he is losing weight. Cannot stoop on account of giddiness.' He also had headaches any time he engaged in mental or physical work, could not sleep because of the pain, and sometimes lost his balance and fell down. The area where his skull was missing still visibly pulsated when he coughed. He later had a metal plate installed to protect the area of exposed brain, which apparently helped with his fits of giddiness.

He was granted leave as soon as he was well enough to be discharged from hospital, which was extended because of his poor condition. In June 1917 what was left of the little finger on his left hand was amputated; in his own words it had been 'reduced to pulp' by the shell. By August 1917 his health had begun to improve and he rejoined the 4th Royal Dublin Fusiliers, now stationed in Wellington Barracks, Mullingar, becoming its railway transport officer. However, the effects of his wound never went away completely, and in January 1918 he was found permanently unfit for any further military service. He left the army in March that year and was soon living at Taumerary Lodge, Carrick-on-Suir, Co. Tipperary.

In August 1917 John Hawe had written to the army asking about the 'disabilities under which I shall in future have to live and through which I am permanently compelled to relinquish all hope of a professional or other reasonably lucrative career.' As it turns out he became a fruit farmer, and in September 1923, now aged twenty-six and having married, he set sail for Costa Rica. He was working for Fyffe's fruit company and appears to have taken up a position at one of its plantations. Only three years later, however, possibly as a result of his head wound, John Hawe died in July 1926, aged twenty-nine, while living in Puerto Limón, Costa Rica.

* * *

One other member of the 4th Royal Dublin Fusiliers wounded during the Easter Rising was 38-year-old Lance-Corporal Martin Merry. A native of Dublin, he had lived with his family for many years in Golden Lane but by the time of the Rising was living in Hackett's Court, off Upper Kevin Street. Merry had enlisted in Dublin in November 1915. He was illiterate but was qualified as a hammerman or blacksmith's striker and as a scaffolder. He had previously worked as a labourer for two months for Vickers Ltd of Barrow-in-Furness and also for eighteen months as a hand driller for Dublin United Tramways Company. Working in the building trade had obviously resulted in a few injuries for Martin Merry, and his enlistment medical report noted that he had a scar on the bridge of his nose, another on his front left forearm, and a large scar on his right kidney.

Posted to the 4th Royal Dublin Fusiliers, Merry was promoted to lance-corporal in early April 1916. During the Rising he is known to have received a gunshot wound to his leg and right forearm, and he was soon undergoing treatment in King George V Military Hospital, where he was listed as 'seriously ill'. It was not until November 1916 that he was well enough to return to duty, though he also had to revert to the rank of private.

Soon transferred to the 5th Battalion at the Curragh, Private Merry appeared before a medical board on 24 April 1917 – the first anniversary of the Rising – and was 'sent to his home on warrant with orders to await instructions as to his final discharge; he has been given £1 (one pound) advance and a suit of plain clothes.' His Rising wounds were obviously preventing him serving efficiently as a soldier, and by the middle of May 1917 he was discharged as 'no longer physically fit for war service.' His character was recorded as 'very good', and when he was asked what employment he would like to obtain upon discharge he wrote 'Labourer or Door Porter, Dublin.' His previous appointment within the army had been 'dutyman'.

* * *

Meanwhile 29-year-old Captain James 'Bob' Carroll of the 4th Royal Dublin Fusiliers had managed to come through the Rising unhurt. Born in 1887 at number 3 Northumberland Road, Dublin, he grew up living in Lower Fitzwilliam Street. One brother, Joseph, was an RIC district inspector, while another, Stanislaus, was a British army officer who served during the war with both the 10th Royal Dublin Fusiliers and the 3rd Tank Battalion. Carroll's parents were both from Dublin; his father was a barrister and his paternal grandfather, Redmond Carroll, had been Lord Mayor of Dublin in 1860.

Having attended Belvedere College in Dublin, Bob Carroll joined the RIC, and after qualifying as an officer he was posted to Callan, Co. Kilkenny. In 1913 he applied for a commission in the British army's special reserve of officers and was soon commissioned into the 4th Royal Dublin Fusiliers as a second-lieutenant.

Before the end of 1913 Carroll applied for leave of absence from the RIC for one year 'to take up a job in Siam [Thailand] as Conservator of Forests.' He is known to have landed in Bangkok on 16 January 1914 and subsequently travelled four hundred miles overland to the Lakhon Forest Station with three elephants, fifteen pack ponies and a dozen local helpers.

When the First World War began, as recorded in the Belvedere school magazine, the *Belvederian,* 'without his knowledge his friends at home got him an extension of that leave and cabled the fact to him to his station in the forests of northern Siam. But he refused to avail of it, believing it to be his paramount duty to rejoin his regiment, which he actually did at Sittingbourne in Kent, early in January 1915.' Having returned to the 4th Royal Dublin Fusiliers, which soon moved to Templemore, Lieutenant Carroll was appointed the battalion's signalling officer and in December 1915 was promoted to captain.

He travelled to Dublin with the battalion in April 1916 and came through the Rising unhurt. In June he landed in France, joining the 8th Battalion in the trenches. Two months later, as the *Belvederian* records, on 18 August 1916 'the parapet of the trench in which he was posted was overthrown by a shell, with the result that he was buried under the debris, but was dug out by his men. He was found unconscious, and was pronounced to be suffering from concussion.' He was unconscious for more than ten hours after being dug out.

Carroll later wrote his own account of what happened that day. 'On [18 August 1916] I was rendered unconscious in the support line at Hullock [Hulluch], France, I believe by a shell bursting close beside me and burying me. I was conveyed to hospital suffering from "head concussion".' He was sent to England, and after several months spent recuperating he rejoined the 4th Battalion, now in Wellington Barracks, Mullingar, in November 1916. In March 1917 he wrote:

I have since [November 1916] been before medical boards monthly and am still only fit for home service. Since being discharged from hospital I have (& still do) continually suffered from severe neuralgia headaches. As a result of which I have been compelled on six occasions since November 1916 to proceed ... to Dublin on sick leave to consult medical specialists. I have in all consulted five medical men (civilians) about these headaches. This has entailed a considerable expenditure of money on my part and has caused me considerable financial embarrassment. Under above circumstances I would be very grateful if I would be granted a gratuity.

Three days after making this request, on 6 March 1917, Captain Carroll was sent to the 7th Officer Cadet Battalion at Kilworth, Co. Cork, as a training officer. He was still suffering from the headaches when he attended several medical boards in late March, May, July and October that year. It was not until May 1918 that he returned to his battalion, which was now in Brocklesby, Lincolnshire. Not long afterwards he returned to the war when he was posted to the 1st Battalion in France.

Before the war had ended Captain Carroll was again injured when, on 28 September 1918, he suffered a sprained ankle at Ypres, having fallen into a shell hole while advancing during an attack at dawn. He was sent to England and subsequently granted one month's convalescence at home, after which he joined the 3rd Battalion at Grimsby, Lincolnshire, in late November 1918, the war now having ended.

Captain Carroll later came back to Ireland and was appointed demobilisation officer at the Royal Dublin Fusiliers' depot in Naas. However, he soon became ill and was admitted to hospital. His condition worsened, and on 24 March 1919 he suddenly died of heart failure following influenza, a victim of the 'Spanish flu' epidemic. He was thirty-one years old and left a young widow. He was buried in the New Chapel area of Glasnevin Cemetery, Dublin.

* * *

Another officer of the 4th Royal Dublin Fusiliers who survived the Rising uninjured was Captain Ulick de Burgh Daly. He was not the only member of his family in British army uniform to serve in Dublin during the Rising: his father, Captain Charles de Burgh Daly, a doctor with the Royal Army Medical Corps, was also serving in the city. Charles de Burgh Daly was born in 1861 in London to an Irish father and an English mother and was raised in Ireland. After qualifying as a doctor and marrying he travelled to China, where he and his wife were prominent in Red Cross work during the Sino-Japanese War of 1894–95. A few years later he was awarded a silver China War Medal for his part in the 'Boxer Rebellion' of 1900, where he served as a medical officer, and later in the Russo-Japanese War of 1904–05. By the time he finally came home to Ireland, having been in Manchuria for more than twenty years, he and his wife had three children, all born in China, the eldest of whom was Ulick, born in Ningbo in 1892.

When the First World War broke out, Charles de Burgh Daly obtained a commission in the Royal Army Medical Corps in April 1915 and was promoted to captain some time before the Rising. On 24 April 1916, when Constance Markievicz drove up to St Stephen's Green to join her Irish Citizen Army comrades, she spotted a British army officer behind one of the windows of the Dublin University Club and fired at him. This was Captain Charles de Burgh Daly. He avoided being hit thanks to a man standing beside him having exclaimed, 'Look out! There's a woman on the Green pointing a gun at us!' The two men moved, and the bullet passed between them.

After the Rising Captain de Burgh Daly was given a particularly gruesome task. A Red Cross ambulance-driver, Albert Mitchell, was instructed to collect bodies from the streets of Dublin and bring them to Deansgrange Cemetery. He later recorded that 'we [de Burgh Daly and Mitchell] buried over 200 bodies of civilians and Irish soldiers, also some English soldiers in Deans Grange.' (Because of the number of people killed, some bodies were buried without coffins, many in common graves. After the Rising many of the families of the dead began making requests to have the bodies exhumed for reburial, but because of the risk to public health these requests were denied.)

Dr Charles de Burgh Daly ended the war as an acting major and in 1919 was made an officer (military) of the Order of the British Empire 'for services in connection with the war'. He was living in Priory Lodge in Grove Avenue, Blackrock, Co. Dublin, in the 1930s and on Knocksinna Road in Stillorgan when he died in 1947 at the age of eighty-six.

Dr de Burgh Daly's son Ulick was educated in Tonbridge, Kent. On 30 December 1914, at the age of twenty-two, he landed in France to join the British Expeditionary Force. By April 1916, now a captain, he was serving with the 4th Royal Dublin Fusiliers in Templemore. He arrived in Dublin during the afternoon of 25 April and went on to be mentioned in despatches during the Rising. (Not long afterwards he would have learnt of the death on the Western Front of his brother Second-Lieutenant Arthur de Burgh Daly, who was serving in the 9th Royal Dublin Fusiliers. He was killed in action, aged eighteen, on 9 September 1916 during the Battle of Ginchy. He now lies in Delville Wood Cemetery, Longueval.)

Ulick de Burgh Daly was subsequently promoted to major, and after the war, in January 1919, he was serving as commandant of the bombing school in Templemore. He later joined the 1st Leinster Regiment and travelled to India, serving in the Malabar campaign of 1920–21 on attachment to an Indian auxiliary unit. He retired from the army before the mid-1920s and returned to live at the family home in Grove Avenue, Blackrock. He went into business as a petroleum merchant, and in 1927, after making several business trips to Canada and Japan for the Shell Oil Company and Asiatic Petroleum, he emigrated to the United States. After becoming an American citizen in October 1940 he began working for the British Purchasing Commission in Washington. He registered for the Second World War draft on 26 April 1942. He subsequently retired to live in Jamaica, possibly because of health problems, and he was living there when he died in Saint Ann's Bay Hospital on 23 December 1960 from heart failure and multiple sclerosis at the age of sixty-eight.

* * *

At least one soldier in the 4th Royal Dublin Fusiliers played no part in fighting against the insurgents, despite being in Dublin at the time. 29-year-old Corporal Edward Handley, born in St Nicholas's Parish in the south-west of the city and having subsequently lived in Ardee Row and Brown Street, had enlisted in October 1904 at the age of seventeen while working as a labourer. He served his six years with the reserve, attending periods of annual training each year, and completed his first term of service in October 1910. At the time his character was listed as 'very good'. He re-enlisted for another term of service, and when the First World War began Handley, now a corporal, was called up for active service.

He landed in France on 9 October 1914, and on 14 December he was wounded in action at Ives, receiving a gunshot wound to his right thigh. After having his wounds treated at a dressing station he was transferred to a hospital at Wimereux, near Boulogne, where he remained for a month before being evacuated to England. After treatment at a hospital there he was sent to King George V Military Hospital in Dublin; by now he had had two operations to remove fragments of shell. For at least the next two years he would complain that his wound gave him great pain and that he could not walk for long distances; doctors soon noticed the leg beginning to waste.

By April 1916 Corporal Handley was on leave in his native Dublin, though officially re-attached to the 4th Royal Dublin Fusiliers. In 1951 he gave a witness statement to the Bureau of Military History, in which he stated:

> At the outbreak of the 1914–18 War I was serving with the 4th Battalion, Dublin Fusiliers. Prior to that, I had worked in White's Public House, 79, The Coombe, where Andy Redmond, who was later a member of the Volunteers, was manager. I knew a number of men in the area who were, or later became members of the Citizen Army. In 1916 I was on sick leave, having been wounded in France. As a matter of fact I was in Liberty Hall on Easter Sunday night with a comrade who was in British Army Uniform. I did not know that there was anything unusual going on.

He made no attempt to join up with British army forces during the Rising, no doubt because of his republican sympathies. Afterwards, as he later recalled, 'when my leave was up, I went absent but was apprehended, courtmartialled and reduced from the rank of Sergeant [actually Corporal] to Private. After spells in Hospitals in Naas; Shoreham, Surrey and Dublin, I was on account of my wound sent to [Wellington] Barracks, Dublin, as a storeman.' He was now serving in the 11th Royal Dublin Fusiliers.

Here, after being approached by republicans, Handley helped them obtain pistols and rifles from the barrack stores. Before the war had ended he was transferred to the 653rd Area Employment Company (later the 542nd Home Service Employment Company) of the Labour Corps, which was also stationed in Wellington Barracks, and he continued to supply weapons to republicans, often with the help of a sympathetic military policeman.

When the war ended Private Handley was discharged in March 1919. He was intending to live in Clane's Lane, off the Coombe, and when the army asked him what employment he was hoping to obtain he simply wrote 'Job. Dublin'. However, it appears that he did not find the job he was looking for, as he soon re-enlisted in the British army.

During the War of Independence, Private Handley found himself stationed in Dublin and again working as a storeman. After two rifle collection huts were set up at the North Wall and in Kingstown (Dún Laoghaire) for storing weapons belonging to men heading to Britain on leave, he resumed his supplying of weapons to republicans. He would claim that certain rifles were defective and take them from these huts, pretending to be bringing them to an armourer at Islandbridge for repair. As he later recorded,

> when I had sufficient time I would arrange for some Citizen Army man to meet me down the line a little distance from Westland Row ... It was extraordinary that I should be asked to take rifles unescorted to Islandbridge when soldiers weren't allowed to take them home and that I wasn't held up once by the I.R.A. which led me to think that they were aware of what was happening. We had an officer in charge of the post but he did not take any interest in the collection or return of the rifles ... I was never suspected at Kingstown as far as I know. This may be due to the fact that although I had permission to sleep at home, I was never seen taking anything out when going on pass.

Private Handley was discharged for a second time in 1922, now aged thirty-five, and is known to have settled at Kildare Road in Crumlin.

* * *

At the other end of the political spectrum was Sergeant Thomas Davis, though it is not clear whether he was a soldier in the 4th or the 5th Battalion of the Royal Dublin Fusiliers. What is known is that Davis, a 39-year-old man from Lisburn, was in Dublin during the Rising. He was a veteran of the Anglo-Boer War who, after retiring from the army some time between then and the First World War, had married and settled in Lisburn and had obtained work as a thread-finisher. He then re-enlisted when the war began.

Following the Rising, Sergeant Davis is known to have secured the second flag, the Tricolour, that had flown over the GPO (the 'Irish Republic' flag having been secured by Major Jack Morrogh and Company Sergeant-Major Frederick Banks of the 3rd Royal Irish Regiment). Sergeant Davis went on to serve in the 16th Royal Irish Rifles in the 36th (Ulster) Division and then with the Royal Irish Regiment before being wounded at the Somme and invalided home, ultimately being discharged because of his injuries.

He later gave the flag to his doctor in Lisburn in gratitude for treating his war wounds. This was Dr George St George, a native of Co. Down with close links to the UVF. Dr St George died in 1922, and the flag passed into the possession of his daughter, Ethel. She lived in Kells, Co. Meath, and was married to Captain Samuel Waring of the British army. When she died, in 1951, Captain Waring gave the flag to the Sweetman family in Kells, who were neighbours and friends of his. This family were the children of John Sweetman, a founder-member of Sinn Féin and its president from 1908 to 1911. When he gave the flag to the Sweetmans, Captain Waring is reputed to have said, 'You may have more use for this than I have.'

Ultimately the flag came into the possession of a Dublin family who decided to auction it in America. On 23 March 2010 it was auctioned by Bloomsbury in New York. It was expected to reach a sale price of between $500,000 and $700,000; however, after the bids failed to pass the $400,000 mark it was withdrawn from auction. It was believed that the Irish Government would make a bid in an attempt to return the flag to Ireland, but it declined to do so. At the time of writing the flag is on loan to the American-Irish Historical Society in New York.

* * *

Research into another member of the 4th Royal Dublin Fusiliers has resulted in the rewriting of a little piece of Easter Rising history.

Fred Watson enlisted in the 9th Battalion of the regiment in Dublin in March 1915, claiming to be a nineteen-year-old clerk. In reality he was only fifteen. (He was also only 5 feet 4 inches tall, but in early twentieth-century Ireland this would not have been considered particularly small.) He was a native of Rathdrum, Co. Wicklow; his father was a groom and a Wicklow man, while his mother was from Dublin.

Frederick Watson at the Bath Royal Hotel, Bournemouth, September 1918 (Doreen Watson)

After completing his initial training (during which he forfeited a day's pay for overstaying a leave pass by several hours in June while stationed in Buttevant, Co. Cork), Private Fred Watson was sent overseas when the 9th Royal Dublin Fusiliers entered the trenches in December 1915. He served in France for four months before returning to Ireland on 13 April 1916, now sixteen years old, when he was posted to the 4th Battalion in Templemore, just in time to join it before it was summoned to Dublin during the Rising.

He served throughout the Rising, being mentioned in despatches for his actions. Then, on 19 May, the army discovered that he had been under age when he enlisted, and he was discharged immediately.

However, Fred Watson was out of uniform only temporarily. He enlisted again, this time in the Tank Corps. He underwent his initial training with this new unit at Bovington Camp in Dorset.

The notification of Frederick Watson's mention in despatches, received for service during the Rising (Doreen Watson)

He survived the war and returned to live in his native Rathdrum and was still living there in 1921. Ten years later, having married, he was living in Lymington, Hampshire. The couple settled in Poole, where Watson worked as a driver for a petrol company, and he died there on 31 March 1997, aged ninety-seven. This makes Fred Watson the last surviving combatant of the Easter Rising. Currently, the last surviving combatant is believed to be Lily Kempson – who served as a courier for Patrick Pearse and the GPO garrison, aged nineteen at the time, during the Rising – when she died in Seattle, Washington on 22 January 1996, aged ninety-nine. Fred Watson passed away on 31 March 1997, over a year after Lily Kempson died, making him the new last known surviving combatant of the Easter Rising.

* * *

On Wednesday 26 April 1916 – the day after the 4th Royal Dublin Fusiliers fought the members of the 1st Battalion of the Irish Volunteers in the Phibsborough area – a group of RIC men, together with another group of British army soldiers, found themselves under attack from Commandant Ned Daly's men.

The Irish Volunteers had launched a snap assault against the Bridewell DMP Station and took twenty-four RIC men prisoner who they found hiding in the cells. The Volunteers then attacked Linenhall Barracks – just south of Broadstone Station and the King's Inns – where fewer than forty soldiers of the Army Pay Corps were stationed. The insurgents first demanded that the garrison surrender, but they refused – though they were not combat soldiers and were unarmed, and some were not fully trained – so the insurgents blew a hole in the barrack wall, forcing them to give up. Taken to Father Mathew Hall in Church Street, the Pay Corps men were made to bake bread and fill sandbags for the insurgents.

Meanwhile Linenhall Barracks – one of the oldest barracks in Dublin, formerly the eighteenth-century Dublin Linen Hall – was set on fire. By that night it was blazing, lighting up the night sky and threatening to burn down nearby houses and business premises. As the Dublin Fire Brigade was unwilling to tackle the fire, for fear of having its men shot in the process, Commandant Daly ordered the Volunteers to fight the fire they had started. The barracks was reportedly still alight the next morning.

* * *

The last of the reinforcements to reach Dublin during the afternoon of Tuesday the 25th was the speedily assembled Ulster Composite Battalion, raised on the orders of Brigadier-General William Hacket Pain after he received a phone call from Colonel Cowan at Irish Command in Dublin. Hacket Pain accompanied the battalion to Dublin and would later be mentioned in despatches for his actions there.

The Ulster Composite Battalion was composed of 1,000 men drawn from the various reserve battalions of the Royal Inniskilling Fusiliers, Royal Irish Fusiliers and Royal Irish Rifles that made up the 15th (Ulster) Reserve Infantry Brigade. The reserve battalions of the Royal Inniskilling Fusiliers that supplied men were the 3rd (based in Derry), 4th (in Buncrana) and 12th (in either Enniskillen or Finner Camp); those of the Royal Irish Fusiliers were the 3rd (Buncrana), 4th (Carrickfergus) and 10th (Newtownards). The reserve battalions of the Royal Irish Rifles that supplied troops were the 4th (Carrickfergus), 5th (Holywood, Co. Down), 17th (Ballykinler, Co. Down), 18th (Clandeboye), 19th (Newcastle, Co. Down), and 20th (Newtownards).

Only one reserve battalion of the 15th (Ulster) Reserve Infantry Brigade was not stationed in Ulster at the time, but it was already heavily involved in the Rising: this was the 3rd Royal Irish Rifles, based in Portobello Barracks, Dublin. While this battalion may have had its northern unionist heritage diluted by nearly two years of local recruiting in Dublin, the opposite was the case with the Ulster Composite Battalion, with many of its soldiers being also members of the UVF, mainly recruited in Ulster as reserves for the 36th (Ulster) Division.

The man who would lead the Ulster Composite Battalion to Dublin was also the commanding officer of the 20th Royal Irish Rifles and of the 15th (Ulster) Reserve Infantry Brigade, Lieutenant-Colonel Thomas McCammon. The records show that he had been appointed officer commanding the 15th (Ulster) Reserve Infantry Brigade in addition to his other command in December 1915 because of his excellent work in recruiting, and by the time of the Easter Rising he still held this dual command.

Ironically, McCammon was a Dubliner by birth, born there to Thomas McCammon Snr, a native of Co. Antrim, a barrister and colonel of the 5th Royal Irish Rifles. When Thomas McCammon Jnr joined the army he was commissioned into his father's old battalion. By 1901 he had served in the Anglo-Boer War and had risen to the rank of captain.

When the First World War began McCammon was a lieutenant-colonel and commanding officer of the 5th Royal Irish Rifles, as his father had been before him. The battalion was based in Belfast until it moved to Holywood, Co. Down, in May 1915. Then, on the formation of the 20th Battalion in Holywood in November that year, Lieutenant-Colonel McCammon was appointed commanding officer of this new unit. The command of the 15th (Ulster) Reserve Infantry Brigade was added to his responsibilities the following month. The 20th Battalion later spent a period in Dublin before returning north in February 1916, and by the time of the Rising it was based in Newtownards. (Lieutenant-Colonel Thomas McCammon has often been confused with the commanding officer of the 3rd Royal Irish Rifles, based in Portobello Barracks, Lieutenant-Colonel Walter McCammond, because of the similarity of their surnames.)

Another Dubliner who found himself on the train to the city on 25 April was 25-year-old Captain William Howard. Born to a solicitor father from Dungannon, Co. Tyrone, and a mother from Co. Offaly, Howard had been living in his father's home town. The family appear to have later returned to live in Dublin for a while and then spent several years in Belfast before ending up again in Dungannon. However, by 1911 William Howard and his family were living in Rathgar Road in Dublin.

While living in Dublin during this period William Howard attended Trinity College and was a member of its OTC. In May 1913 he was commissioned as a second-lieutenant in the reserve 4th Royal Irish Rifles. Promoted to lieutenant in June 1914, he was sent to France on 14 October after the start of the First World War. In early June 1915 he joined the 2nd Battalion, and on 16 June he was badly wounded in action. The Irish Times of 25 June reported the contents of a letter received by his father in Ireland: 'In a letter from his son in hospital in France, dictated to his nurse, he states that he had lost his left eye in the fight on the 16th inst. The bullet entered his head low down at the back, coming out through the eye. Lieutenant Howard writes cheerily and characteristically, and says "Sure one is tons".'

Howard survived this wound and, after recovering and being promoted to captain in September 1915, rejoined his old unit, the 4th Royal Irish Rifles, then stationed at Carrickfergus, Co. Antrim. When the Rising began and orders were issued for the formation of the Ulster Composite Battalion, Captain William Howard returned to his home town once more, this time leading a company of reinforcements from the 4th Battalion to help defeat a republican uprising. Howard survived the Rising and the war and settled in Reigate, Surrey, where he died in 1945, aged fifty-four.

Another man on the Ulster Composite Battalion's train to Dublin had previously been thought to have been killed in action. 21-year-old Private John Byers from Belfast, who had enlisted in August 1914 and was now serving in one of the reserve battalions of the Royal Irish Rifles, had landed at Gallipoli in July 1915 while serving in the 6th Battalion. There, as his son later recorded, Private Byers was 'wounded at Gallipoli by sniper fire. He was left for dead on the beach and a Padre [chaplain] removed one of his identification discs to be returned to his family in Belfast. An Australian soldier covered him with his overcoat and my father was put onto a hospital ship.' Here it was discovered that Private Byers was still alive. 'After surgery and hospitalization in several army hospitals he was sent home to recover, but was called out for the Easter Rising or, as he called it, the Dublin Revolt, where he witnessed the atrocities [at] first hand.'

Private Byers stayed in the army after the war, serving in the 3rd (Reserve) Battalion of the newly renamed Royal Ulster Rifles. He was discharged in April 1922, at which time he was considered 'a willing and hard working soldier.' He died in 1963, aged sixty-eight.

The Ulster Composite Battalion was predominantly Ulster unionist in composition, but there were some notable exceptions. One such was Corporal Patrick Doherty from Buncrana, Co. Donegal, who had enlisted in the 5th Royal Irish Fusiliers in 1915 in the belief that this would promote Home Rule. He had a tattoo on his forearm showing clasped hands with the words 'Erin-go-bragh' (i.e. Éirinn go brách, 'Ireland for ever'). At the time of the Rising he was serving in one of the reserve battalions of the Royal Irish Fusiliers and so was sent to Dublin as part of the Ulster Composite Battalion to help defeat it. His attitude towards the insurgents was recorded in a letter written to him later by a friend: 'I remember you in the Dublin Rising ever anxious to be in the thick of the fight.' Like most of the Irishmen in the British army at the time, Doherty saw the Rising as a betrayal of his and his comrades' sacrifices in the trenches.

Corporal Doherty later fought at the Somme with the 7th/8th Battalion of the Royal Irish Fusiliers, where he was badly wounded during the Battle of Ginchy in September 1916. He was in and out of hospitals for the rest of his life, suffering from psychological as well as physical problems, but, as his granddaughter Yvonne McEwen recently wrote, he 'was left with a profound belief that he and his Irish brothers in arms would eventually be acknowledged and that years of abuse, humiliation and poverty would not go unrecognised.'

* * *

While the train carrying the Ulster Composite Battalion sped towards Dublin, some Ulster reservists were already in the city. A detachment of the 12th Royal Inniskilling Fusiliers was undergoing a course of instruction at the Army School of Musketry at

Dollymount. The commanding officer of this detachment was Second-Lieutenant Thomas Boston, a 23-year-old Belfast man. The son of a publican and auctioneer, he had worked in the linen trade before joining the army. He was also a member of the UVF, having been adjutant of the South Derry Volunteers before the war.

Second-Lieutenant Boston would be mentioned in despatches for his actions during the Rising. He later entered the war, subsequently transferring to the Machine Gun Corps and being promoted to lieutenant. After the war, on 12 December 1918, he developed symptoms of influenza while serving in Egypt. He was admitted to hospital in Cairo, but the influenza developed into pneumonia, and he died on Christmas Day 1918, aged twenty-five. He now lies in the Cairo War Memorial Cemetery, while his name is also commemorated on a plaque in the Masonic Lodge in Maghera, Co. Derry.

The Ulster Composite Battalion arrived in Dublin at about 2 p.m. on Tuesday. However, because of concerns that the insurgents might have destroyed the railway lines along the final approach to Amiens Street Station, the train was halted in the vicinity of Clontarf and the troops were ordered to disembark there. (As it turned out, the insurgents had attempted to blow up the railway bridge over the Tolka River, and had then ripped up the lines further north, in the Fairview area. An armoured train containing soldiers already at Amiens Street Station had been sent out to repair the damage, but these soldiers were fired on from Annesley Bridge, further up the Tolka. The British troops attempted to surround the insurgents here but were forced to withdraw because of superior rebel numbers.)

Having disembarked at Clontarf, the battalion advanced through Fairview and appears to have forced its way across Ballybough Bridge and Annesley Bridge across the Tolka. They then spread out west until they reached the junction of Clonliffe Road and Drumcondra Road before resuming the advance towards the city centre, pushing back the insurgents in the Ballybough, Dorset Street, Fairview, Mountjoy, North Strand and Summer Hill areas as they went. The 4th Royal Dublin Fusiliers and the artillery from the 5th (A) Reserve Artillery Brigade had already secured everything west of Phibsborough, and with the soldiers from the Army School of Musketry having taken Amiens Street Station and the North Wall area the previous day, the northern cordon around Dublin was now complete. The insurgents were soon encountering the men of the Ulster Composite Battalion who manned the cordon around the north of the city.

Francis Daly, commanding the engineers of the 1st Battalion of the Irish Volunteers, was ordered to retrieve some explosives from the GPO and use them to blow up railway lines outside the city. He later recorded:

> I went down to the G.P.O. and got a very small supply of gelignite there from Michael Staines. We set out and tried to get out from the city. The Royal Irish Rifles had come down through Frederick St. and were then at the corner of Frederick St. For some time we could not get through. We noticed that they were allowing some women, with loaves of bread and other provisions under their arms, to pass through, we decided we would buy a loaf, but failed to do

so. We only got a few apple-cakes. With these held very conspicuously in our hands, we were let across over at the Parnell Monument.

On 25 April, Commandant John Joseph Scollan of the Hibernian Rifles was sent from the GPO with some of his men, together with thirteen recently arrived Irish Volunteers from Maynooth, to reinforce the rebel force in the Cork Hill area by occupying the Exchange Hotel in Parliament Street. (This was about the same time that the 5th Royal Dublin Fusiliers recaptured the *Daily Express* offices from the Irish Citizen Army.) Scollan later recorded:

> We got into the Exchange Hotel and on to the roof. At this time some of the Volunteers were supposed to be trapped in the Evening Mail Office and in the City Hall. We found that the City Hall was occupied by British soldiers and we engaged them by fire. In the afternoon units of the Irish Fusiliers and Enniskilling Fusiliers advanced to storm our position and were met by a fusillade from our shot-gun men and Rifles. They were actually slaughtered by our fire. Twenty-three or four of them were killed or seriously wounded. [This is a wildly inflated figure: the Ulster Composite Battalion lost no-one killed that day.] I was on the roof near a chimney when a bullet caught Edward Walsh, one of our men, and literally tore his stomach out. He died that evening ... At about 4.30 p.m. that evening we received orders to retire to the G.P.O.

By the evening of the 25th the Ulster Composite Battalion had occupied Amiens Street Station, where Lieutenant-Colonel McCammon established his headquarters. The battalion is also known to have sent a detachment to occupy the Custom House, where a detachment from the 3rd Royal Irish Regiment was also present.

The following day, Wednesday the 26th, when the *Helga* opened fire on Liberty Hall at 8 a.m. in preparation for an infantry assault against the building the soldiers of the Ulster Composite Battalion in the Custom House waited with fixed bayonets for the order to advance. As mentioned earlier, the building was empty except for its terrified caretaker. Soldiers from the Ulster Composite Battalion, along with men from the 3rd Royal Irish Regiment, entered the building after the shelling had ended, where one of the battalion's officers found a personal possession belonging to one of the Rising's leaders.

The ITGWU and the Irish Citizen Army regularly arranged plays and concerts on Sunday evenings in Liberty Hall. Sergeant Frank Robbins – who served with the Irish Citizen Army in the St Stephen's Green area throughout the Rising – later recalled that

> one of the plays produced was one of James Connolly's entitled 'Under Which Flag?' Michael Mallin organised a small orchestra from members of St. James Band and these players took part in the insurrection, James

Geoghegan paying the supreme sacrifice. In 1948 the instrument played by Michael Mallin [a flute] was presented to the National Museum having turned up after 32 years with the following inscription:– 'By Capt. G. Hewson, Presented to Band, 18th R.I.Rifles, Taken at Liberty Hall, Dublin Rebellion 1916.'

Captain George Hewson was a justice of the peace and land agent from Dunganstown, Co. Wicklow, where his father was the Church of Ireland rector. George Hewson married in 1890 and settled with his family in Drumahaire, Co. Leitrim. At the time of the Rising he was presumably serving in the Ulster Composite Battalion; and after he found Michael Mallin's instrument he presented it to the band of the 18th Royal Irish Rifles, then stationed at Clandeboye Estate, Co. Down.

Captain Hewson later served in the Royal Irish Regiment and then in the Essex Regiment before the end of the war. He subsequently returned to live in Drumahaire, and he died in 1941 while living in Manorhamilton, Co. Leitrim, at the age of eighty-two.

* * *

On the day that Liberty Hall was shelled and occupied the cordon around the north of the city was now firmly in place. Patrick Rankin, a member of the Irish Volunteers from Newry, was staying with his sister, who lived on the North Circular Road. He was determined to make it to the GPO but, as he later recorded, he knew he

> would have great difficulty getting away from the house without raising the suspicions of those in the house. I put my cap in my pocket and told my friends I was going into the yard to clean my bicycle. As soon as I got into the yard I cleared over a little wall into Innisfallen Parade, thence to Dorset St. I was stopped by soldiers of the Royal Irish Rifles. This being a Northern Regiment I had to be careful. The troops were clearing all people from southwards to northwards of Dorset St. I asked someone to direct me to Parnell St. and they guided me down to Kennedy's Bakery in that street as there were no troops about I decided to procure some bread in the Bakery.

On 26 April seventeen-year-old Cadet-Sergeant Gerald Keatinge (who had taken part in Captain Bowen-Colthurst's raid on Byrne's shop and witnessed the murder of Richard O'Carroll) was sent to join the Ulster Composite Battalion at Amiens Street Station. With some other OTC cadets he had been sent from Portobello Barracks to the headquarters of Irish Command at Parkgate for further instructions (during which journey he was fired on and nearly hit by a sniper in Infirmary Road). The cadets were soon called on and given a new mission. Keatinge later recorded: 'We were just making arrangements for bedding when a yell of "Cyclist Orderlies" went up, so we doubled for the yard outside. Here, Cpl Spence, Cadet

Long and Cadet Boyd were separated from the rest of us. They were sent to the Castle while I was put in charge of the second party.' This party included Private Lionel Boyd and Private Douglas Davies, both from the Inns of Court OTC.

Douglas Davies was twenty-two years old, the youngest son of an RIC district inspector from Co. Sligo and a Dublin mother. He was born in 1893 in New Ross, Co. Wexford, while his father was stationed there. After his father's death Davies' mother moved with her children to Kenilworth Park in Harold's Cross, Dublin. Davies (whose older brother, Second-Lieutenant Noel Davies of the 8th Royal Dublin Fusiliers, was serving in the war) was commissioned in February 1917, and in May he joined the 10th Royal Dublin Fusiliers in the trenches. Having been appointed to command this three-man team of cyclist orderlies, Keatinge

was given a dispatch to take to Colonel McCammon at Amiens Street Station and to remain under his orders. I was not given any instructions as to what route to follow simply that I was to get there. I knew of course that the Rebels had the Four Courts and that it was therefore impossible to follow the ordinary route via the Quays. The only alternative was to proceed by way of the North Circular Road but as I knew that it had only piquets on it for a certain distance as far as Phibsborough, and moreover as I was not very sure of how to get to Amiens Street after passing down to the left of the Mater Hospital, I thought it extremely unlikely that we should ever get there. Outside Irish Command Headquarters we all shook hands because we were all convinced that we should never reach the Station alive – and then we set out. It was quite dark by this time and there were no lights so that to find one's way was by no means easy. However, we got to Phibsborough without accident and I was getting (from the Officer in charge of the piquet on the Bridge) information about the way when a cyclist who had run the gauntlet from Amiens Street volunteered to pilot us. The Officer advised us not to go on but again we had our orders and we had no option but to obey. The cyclist we discovered was a private in the Dublins [Royal Dublin Fusiliers] and a very decent chap. Unfortunately, he was only able to accompany us a short distance as the detachment to which he belonged appeared just beyond Phibsborough engaged in some expedition with the help of the armoured car.

We managed to find our way to Amiens Street with some difficultly but arrived without any further adventure other than a few badly aimed shots from snipers which whistled harmlessly overhead. The main entrance of the Station we found sandbagged, so we had to go on to the car entrance [a sloped road leading south from the station, now the site of the tram terminus]. Here we were admitted through a little wicket gate which was extremely difficult to get a bicycle through and at last were at our destination. I need hardly say I was relieved – that barely expresses my state of mind because it was not so much I that mattered but there were the other two fellows who I was in charge of, that was what made the difference. As soon as we got inside the Station I started to look for Colonel McCammon. Of course, nobody knew where he was to be found but finally I got hold of his adjutant, and he took the message. Yes, he knew all about us and we were to go to the Headquarters of the Ulster Composite Battalion which was in one of the offices of the railway up the platform and await further orders outside. Yes, we could get some food provided one man remained on duty. We tossed for it and the lot fell on one of the others. I and the other chap went out and got our rations – bully-beef and biscuits, and also 3 blankets – and having eaten as much as we could of our 'supper' we asked permission to be allowed to sleep. This was granted, provided we slept somewhere close by ready for duty. That meant sleeping on the platform with everything except our equipment on and the platform of Amiens Street is not a comfortable place as I know to my cost. We put one blanket on the ground and covered ourselves with the other two, huddling together for warmth. I was so tired that I soon fell asleep but wakened about three which as anybody knows who has ever slept in the open is the coldest time of the morning. From then on till about 5 I dozed fitfully but was glad when at last I had the energy to get up and walk about and instil some warmth into my body.

That morning – Thursday 27 April – the Ulster Composite Battalion was detailed to assault a new rebel position near its headquarters at Amiens Street Station. After a bad breakfast of bully beef and 'biscuits which were a great deal harder than the platform we slept on and tea which had the one redeeming feature of being hot,' the men of the Ulster Composite Battalion were paraded at 9 a.m. and given their latest mission. Nearby Lower Gardiner Street was occupied by the insurgents, and the order was to push them back from this area.

I suppose it must have been 10 before we moved off, though not having a watch and the unusual circumstances combined made it very difficult to judge time all through the week. The Adjutant gave us (the cyclist orderlies) instructions to follow them (the staff) wherever they went, and then the battalion marched out of the Station. Again though I knew I was going into action, I didn't feel nervous or anything – on the contrary I was filled with an odd sensation of elation. We passed out through the carriage entrance of the Station which we had come up the previous night and then on into Store Street to Beresford Place. In Beresford Place the battalion halted and we (the cyclists) followed the Colonel to the Custom House just outside which apparently was our Headquarters for the time being. In the meantime, the battalion had formed into two single ranks and lined each side of Store Street. After another delay the order to advance was given and our men entered Lower Gardiner Street. Up till this only stray shots had whizzed by but fusillade burst out from the Sinn Feiners who were in possession of practically all the houses in this street and needless to say our men replied to it.

The Rebels had the advantage over us every time because they were hidden in the houses, and our fellows were in the open. Thanks to the rotten marksmanship of the rebels we had very few casualties and thanks to the bravery and dash of the Royal Irish Rifles we succeeded in taking Lower Gardiner Street in a very short time. The casualties consisted of one man killed and 3 severely wounded.

This fatality was the first suffered by the Ulster Composite Battalion during the Easter Rising. The soldier was Private Alexander McClelland, a member of the Machine-Gun Section of the 4th Royal Irish Rifles. Then eighteen years old, McClelland was a native of Balliggan, Co. Down, where his father and older brother both worked as stonemasons. His body was recovered from Lower Gardiner Street by members of the St John Ambulance Brigade, and he is buried in Grey Abbey Cemetery, Co. Down.

Not long afterwards, as also recorded by Gerald Keatinge, two 18-pounder field guns of the 5th (A) Reserve Artillery Brigade arrived from Athlone and set up under the railway bridge at Beresford Place. They began firing at rebel positions in Lower Abbey Street, famously hitting the *Irish Times* printing office and setting alight the giant rolls of paper inside, which would ultimately cause the burning of a large number of buildings in the area.

> Shortly after this it was observed that one of the houses at the Sackville Street end of Abbey Street had taken fire and shortly after this again a crowd of people came marching down the street headed by an old man carrying a pole with a white sheet attached to it as a flag of truce. We were taking no risks, however, and they were halted half way and made to put their hands above their heads. They were then questioned and taken to the Custom House. Two separate bodies of people came down in this way, bringing several wounded with them.

During the remainder of his time with the Ulster Composite Battalion, Keatinge was mainly based at the Custom House after Lieutenant-Colonel McCammon moved his headquarters there from Amiens Street Station. He subsequently took despatches to the fire station in Tara Street, to Irish Command headquarters at Parkgate, and once to Dublin Castle. He was fired on by snipers on several occasions during his travels – sometimes narrowly escaping – and by the evening of Friday the 28th he had moved to the new battalion headquarters in Harvey's 'Great Remedies for the Horse' shop in Gardiner Street. When the Rising ended he was carrying despatches to various British army barricades throughout the city.

The next two fatalities suffered by the Ulster Composite Battalion were incurred on 27 April; but both these men were killed accidentally. The first was 37-year-old Private Francis Knox, a former clerk from Delgany, Co. Wicklow, whose father was from Co. Armagh and mother from Dublin. He enlisted in Bray when the war began and was serving in the 12th Royal Inniskilling Fusiliers at the time of the Rising. He died of wounds received that day, according to one source, when 'a shell he was firing exploded.' As it is unlikely that he would have been manning an artillery gun, this probably refers to a grenade or rifle-grenade. Private Knox is buried in Breandrum Cemetery, Co. Fermanagh.

The second accidental death was a result of 'friendly fire'. Second-Lieutenant Charles Crockett – a native of Derry and a signatory of the Ulster Covenant – was two days away from his twentieth birthday. The son of a hardware merchant from Co. Tyrone, he had attended Foyle College and was a member of the Derry Boys' Brigade and Queen's University OTC. Having previously worked as a labourer, he enlisted in September 1914 and was posted to B Company, 10th Royal Inniskilling Fusiliers, then based at Finner Camp. He applied for a commission less than two weeks after enlisting. This request was denied, but Crockett was determined to become an officer. After seven months' service as a private, in April 1915 he applied again. This time he was successful, possibly because of the recent formation of the reserve 12th Battalion, which would need new officers to run it. Having been promoted to lance-corporal, Crockett left the 10th Battalion to begin training as an officer. He was subsequently commissioned into the 12th Battalion.

The commanding officer of the 12th Battalion, Colonel Sir John Leslie (former commander of the UVF in Co. Monaghan and an uncle of Winston Churchill) later wrote: 'On Thursday 27th ... he [Crockett] went out at 10-15 p.m., and was posted at Aldborough House, near Fitzwilliam Street, with the Lewis Gun Section. He was instructed to get in touch with the Officers of the Dublin Fusiliers, whose headquarters were about 100 yards up the Street, and about 10-15 p.m. he left his post to do so. On running across the Street he was fired at and hit by a Sentry, death being instantaneous.' (Aldborough House is in Portland Row, not Fitzwilliam Street, which is on the other side of the city; this mistake shows that the officers of the Ulster Composite Battalion were not familiar with Dublin.) On the morning of Wednesday 26 April Aldborough House was being used as a British army headquarters, occupied by 100 soldiers of the 4th Royal Dublin Fusiliers and by members of the Royal Irish Rifles in the Ulster Composite Battalion.

Crockett was two days from his twentieth birthday when he was shot. His body was taken to King George V Military Hospital. For some reason it proved impossible to obtain a coffin in Dublin, and one had to be driven down from Derry, his home town. His parents requested that no military honours be rendered and no military symbols be displayed at his funeral on 3 May. They did, however, permit four of their son's fellow-officers from the 12th Royal Inniskilling Fusiliers to walk behind the hearse, which was saluted by soldiers along its route to Derry City Cemetery.

* * *

At this point in the Rising some members of the Ulster Composite Battalion were performing actions for which they would be mentioned in despatches.

Royal Inniskilling Fusiliers cap badge
(Author's Collection)

One such man was Sergeant George Dixon of the Royal Inniskilling Fusiliers; another was Sergeant John Beattie of the same regiment, a native of Hillsborough, Co. Down. A pork cutter by trade, in 1912 Beattie had signed the Ulster Covenant. After the Rising he joined the 11th Battalion in the trenches. Then, on 16 August 1917, during the Battle of Frezenberg Ridge, he was killed in action, aged thirty-two. With no known grave, today he is commemorated on the Tyne Cot Memorial.

Also commemorated on the Tyne Cot Memorial is nineteen-year-old Second-Lieutenant John Carrothers, who died the same day while serving in the 8th Royal Inniskilling Fusiliers at Frezenberg Ridge. A former member of the Inns of Court OTC from Tamlaght, Co. Fermanagh, he had also been in Dublin during the Rising. While positioned in Ship Street Barracks, attached to Dublin Castle, he recorded that 'the Sinn Feiners are rotten shots ... A chap was standing in the open street and they fired a volley at him but never hit him ... It is wonderful how soon one gets used to fighting. We lounge about here reading and yawning while volleys are being fired over our heads. It is very boring listening to crack of rifles all day.' Clearly his experience of the Rising was far less active than Sergeant Beattie's.

Another officer of the Ulster Composite Battalion mentioned in despatches was Lieutenant William McKee of the Royal Irish Rifles. Aged thirty-six at the time of the Rising, he was born at Castle Espie, near Comber, Co. Down, but raised in Belfast. McKee's father was a linen merchant; William McKee had also been an apprentice in the Belfast linen industry. In March 1917 Lieutenant McKee landed in France, joining the 12th Royal Irish Rifles in the trenches. Five days before the Battle of Frezenberg Ridge, on 11 August 1917, he was killed in action on the Western Front. With no known grave, today he is commemorated on the Menin Gate Memorial in Ypres.

Thirty-one-year-old Lieutenant Thomas Kennedy of the 12th Royal Inniskilling Fusiliers, a native of Cookstown, had attended Dundalk Educational Institution (now Dundalk Grammar School) and then Trinity College, Dublin. While studying in Trinity, from 1903 to 1906 he served in the South of Ireland Imperial Yeomanry (later renamed the South Irish Horse) and reached the rank of troop-sergeant. After finishing his studies he became a newspaper reporter and journalist, serving his apprenticeship in the offices of the *Mid-Ulster Mail* in Cookstown and later becoming editor of the *Northern Standard* in Monaghan for a time.

When the war began Kennedy was living in Dawson Street, Monaghan. He applied for a commission in December 1914 but by February 1915 had still not received a response, so he wrote to the army, informing them that he was now in a position to give up his civilian job. He was keen to hear whether a decision had been made and was planning to 'join the cadet corps at Brownlow House, Lurgan, until I am gazetted. I can obtain immediate entrance to this corps in view of my services as Asst. Bttln. [Assistant Battalion] Instructor, 1st Battln. Monaghan Regiment U.V.F.'

In March he joined the cadet corps at Brownlow House, as planned. Attached to the 16th Royal Irish Rifles as a private, he trained there for a month before his application for a commission was approved and he was gazetted as a second-lieutenant in the 12th Royal Inniskilling Fusiliers. By November 1915 he had been promoted to lieutenant, and when the Rising began he was sent to Dublin along with the Ulster Composite Battalion. Here, as later recorded in an account of Kennedy's actions in Dublin during the Rising,

> while attached to the 12th Inniskillings he was deployed to the Pro-Cathedral [in Marlborough Street] in Dublin, where he signalled to have the iron gates and doors open, and arranged to have his men cross under heavy fire without loss. It was through his courtesy afterwards that arrangements were made for a fifteen minute ceasefire so as to enable Mr. Richard Bowden, Administrator at the Pro-Cathedral, to procure provisions for a large number of refugees who were compelled to take refuge with the men in the building.

Perhaps unusually for a Presbyterian and unionist, and member of the UVF, Kennedy ended up working alongside Father Bowden at the Pro-Cathedral. He is also known to have been complimented by the clergy of the Pro-Cathedral both on his own conduct and on that of the soldiers under his command. For this action he was later mentioned in despatches.

After the Rising, Kennedy was posted overseas to the 8th Royal Inniskilling Fusiliers in the predominantly Catholic and nationalist 16th (Irish) Division. On 4 August 1916 he was wounded in the trenches. It seems that the wounds were not very severe, as by September he was back with the 8th Battalion. However, on 9 September 1916, during the Battle of Ginchy on the Somme, he was killed in action.

Major Arthur Walkey, a Dubliner and a former accountant, wrote to Kennedy's father in Cookstown, saying: 'I regret to inform you that your son was killed while leading his men during an attack on the 9th September. I have gathered that he was going down a trench with his bombers, when they met a party of Germans, who put up a fight, one of them throwing a bomb [grenade] which killed your son. I am glad to say that afterwards some of his men got him away and buried him in decency.'

Father Patrick McCaul, professor of Greek at St Eunan's College, Letterkenny, also wrote to Kennedy's father to say:

During the week of the Dublin rebellion I met with Lieutenant Kennedy a good deal, and I must say that he was a general favourite with all the people staying in the Hammam Hotel [in Upper O'Connell Street]. He was more than kind to myself, personally. He was affable, gentlemanly, fearless, and good humoured. I am deeply touched by his death. The loss of such a noble son is a crushing blow. His parents and other members of the family have my deepest sympathy. May God comfort you in your sorrow is the earnest prayer of one who greatly admired your darling son.

A letter of condolence was also sent by Major-General William Hickie, commanding officer of the 16th (Irish) Division, to Kennedy's brother David.

I must offer you my very sincere sympathy at the death of your most gallant brother. Since he joined us in May last he has served most devotedly, and I cannot speak too highly of his work and of his courage. He was slightly wounded at the beginning of August, but rejoined his battalion only a few days later. The 8th Inniskilling Fusiliers, under their brave Colonel Dalzell-Walton, had distinguished themselves on 6th September, when they held a difficult and dangerous part of the line between Leuze Wood and Guillemont. It was there that Colonel Dalzell-Walton was killed. On the 9th September the Division, which had helped to take Guillemont on 3rd September, was ordered to attack Ginchy. This was carried out with the greatest dash and determination. The enemy were holding a trench to the N.E. of the village and the 8th Inniskillings found themselves opposite it. Your brother led his platoon to the attack with the greatest gallantry. He was struck by a bomb and killed instantaneously. He is buried near where he fell to the N.E. of Ginchy. I enclose a little sketch of the place. Will you please convey to the lady who was to have become his wife and to his relatives my appreciation of his service and our sorrow at his loss.

Thomas Kennedy was thirty-one at the time of his death. The site of his grave was later lost, and so his name is now commemorated on the Thiepval Memorial, on the Cookstown Cenotaph, and on the Molesworth Presbyterian Roll of Honour in Cookstown.

A higher award earned by a member of the Ulster Composite Battalion in Dublin was the Military Cross awarded to Second-Lieutenant Charles Weir of the 18th Royal Irish Rifles. Twenty-three years old in 1916, he was a native of Ballindrait, near Gaoth Dobhair, Co. Donegal. He was the son of farming parents, also a signatory of the Ulster Covenant, and had applied for a commission while a member of the OTC of St Andrew's College, Dublin. He had worked as a draper's assistant in Derry before the war. Commissioned in the 18th Royal Irish Rifles in October 1915, he travelled to Dublin with the Ulster Composite Battalion.

Less than a month later, on 27 May 1916, he landed in France and was shortly afterwards posted to the 2nd Battalion in the trenches. Six days after the start of the Battle of the Somme, on 7 July 1916, he was wounded in the left hand, and his wounds ultimately necessitated his evacuation to Britain. Shortly after recovering he was transferred to the 5th Royal Irish Lancers, part of the 6th Reserve Cavalry Regiment, in Dublin. In February 1917 he returned to France to serve with the training squadron at the British Cavalry Training School, during which time he was promoted to lieutenant. In February 1918 he fell from his horse and fractured his scapula (shoulder blade), which again saw him evacuated to Britain. In May he travelled to France for a third time but was evacuated in August suffering from dysentery.

When the war ended, Lieutenant Weir was back serving with the 1st Reserve Cavalry Regiment in Dublin. After a brief period of illness he was given duty under the Ministry of Labour, and in September 1919 he relinquished his commission. His occupation was shortly afterwards listed as farmer. After a brief period living in Belfast he moved to live permanently in Barnet, Middlesex. In a letter to the War Office dated 14 April 1921 he clarified why he had moved to England, stating that he 'had to live in London for some considerable time owing to being threatened by the IRA' after it had learnt about Weir's involvement in the Easter Rising. Some time in the 1930s he died from complications arising from routine tonsil surgery.

* * *

Another exception to the predominantly unionist make-up of the Ulster Composite Battalion was 29-year-old Private John Hanna of B Company, 4th Royal Irish Rifles, a former labourer who was born in Downpatrick and later lived in Belfast. 'John Hanna' was in reality Edward Hanna. The real John Hanna and Edward Hanna were brothers, but John Hanna had enlisted in the 17th Royal Scots Regiment in May 1915, only to be discharged a month later because of epilepsy.

The grandchildren of Edward Hanna have a story about how their grandfather 'joined the army on the call of John Redmond, the Home Rule activist, served in Europe, and was home on leave in Belfast when the Easter Rising started, was recalled by the army and

Edward (a.k.a. John) Hanna (Walter Millar)

taken by lorry to Dublin.' No Private Edward Hanna served in the Royal Irish Rifles, but a Private John Hanna did, with the same service number that the real John Hanna attributed to his brother; and this man also enlisted in Newtownards in August 1914 and subsequently landed in France in November 1914, returning home by at least November 1915.

On Friday 28 April 1916 Edward Hanna, who for some reason had enlisted under his brother's name, was killed in action on the streets of Dublin, aged twenty-nine. He is buried in Grangegorman Military Cemetery, where his headstone still lists his name incorrectly as John Hanna.

* * *

The Ulster Composite Battalion suffered its next fatality the following day, Saturday 29 April 1916, when Lance-Corporal Nathaniel Morton of the 18th Royal Irish Rifles died of wounds. Born in the Shankill Road area of Belfast, Morton was the son of a Belfast man, who worked as a tenter in a weaving factory, and an English mother. A signatory of the Ulster Covenant in 1912, Morton had worked as a labourer before enlisting in Belfast in September 1914, joining the 9th Royal Inniskilling Fusiliers in Omagh. The battalion later moved to Randalstown, Co. Antrim, where Morton was transferred to the 18th Royal Irish Rifles in June 1915. He was soon promoted to lance-corporal but then demoted in February 1916 for misconduct. By March he had regained his lance-corporal's rank, and when he died of wounds on 29 April 1916 in Dublin he was nineteen years old. Nathaniel Morton is now buried in Grangegorman Military Cemetery.

The last man to die in Dublin while serving in the Ulster Composite Battalion was 38-year-old Private James McCullough of the 17th Royal Irish Rifles. A native of Donaghadee, Co. Down, who had previously served in France, he died on 2 May 1916 from wounds received earlier in the week. He is buried in Grangegorman Military Cemetery.

* * *

Quite a few members of the Ulster Composite Battalion were wounded during the Rising. One of them was hit by a sniper on 2 May, three days after the surrender of the insurgents. (It is known that some snipers refused to give up until they were individually defeated, and some firing is known to have continued until that date.)

Another member of the battalion wounded the same day was twenty-year-old Corporal Joseph Clarke of the 10th Royal Irish Fusiliers. A native of Newbliss, Co. Monaghan, and a farmer by occupation, Clarke was a committed unionist and a signatory of the Ulster Covenant. He enlisted in February 1915 in Monaghan, and on 2 May 1916 he received a gunshot wound to his left leg in Dublin, from which he recovered. He later joined the 9th Battalion of the regiment (in which his younger brother, William, had been killed on 1 July 1916) and fought with it during the Battle of Cambrai in late 1917, during which he was hit by shrapnel in the abdomen on 5 December. After evacuation to Britain he was posted to the depot of North of Ireland Command at Randalstown and ended the war serving in the 3rd Royal Irish Fusiliers at Bawdsey, Suffolk. He was discharged on 15 November 1918 as being 'no longer physically fit for war service' because of his wounds and later emigrated to Canada, where he became president of the 36th (Ulster) Division Old Comrades' Association in Toronto. He died at Timiskaming, Ontario, in 1968, aged seventy-two.

The other wounded Irish soldiers in the Ulster Composite Battalion were Private Robert Beattie of the Royal Irish Fusiliers, who is linked to Killygar, Co. Leitrim; sixteen-year-old Private Joseph Burnison of the 4th Royal Irish Rifles, a native of Lurgan and a tenter by trade who enlisted in Portadown in January 1916, claiming to be nineteen; Private William Cleland of the 4th Royal Irish Rifles, who is linked to Belfast (he had previously landed in France in September 1915 and later served in the Scottish Rifles); 36-year-old Private Henry Ferguson of the Royal Inniskilling Fusiliers, a farm labourer from Duneane, Toomebridge, Co. Antrim, who enlisted in Cookstown in November 1914 and after recovering from his Easter Rising injuries was transferred to the Labour Corps, being discharged in January 1918 because of his wounds; thirty-year-old Private

Royal Irish Fusiliers cap badge
(Author's Collection)

James Foley of the Royal Inniskilling Fusiliers, a pre-war regular soldier from Cork who enlisted in March 1910, landed at Gallipoli on 25 April 1915 with the 1st Battalion and later served in the Labour Corps after recovering from his Easter Rising wounds before being discharged in August 1919; 22-year-old Private Francis Gerrard of the Royal Inniskilling Fusiliers, a native of Ardbraccan, Co. Meath, son of a stonecutter from Co. Meath and a schoolteacher from Co. Cavan, who had previously worked as a grocer's apprentice and then as a shop assistant in Turner's of Navan; Private J. A. Henderson of the 18th Royal Irish Rifles, who is linked to Belfast; 21-year-old Sergeant John McAlonen from Belfast, a member of the Royal Inniskilling Fusiliers, a signatory of the Ulster Covenant and former riveter's labourer in the Belfast shipyards; Lance-Corporal P. Maguire, of an unknown background; and Private George Somerville of the Royal Irish Fusiliers, linked to Lurgan, who enlisted in November 1915 and was discharged because of his Easter Rising wounds in September 1916.

* * *

The insurgents' experiences after the Rising at the hands of Irishmen in Ulster regiments were as varied as with the other Irish regiments that were present.

Having been marched to Richmond Barracks after surrendering, Patrick Kelly of G Company, 1st Battalion, Dublin Brigade, later recalled that

> we halted in the centre of the square, where we remained standing for a couple of hours. The sun was strong and beamed down on us. We were both hungry and thirsty, and to make our lot worse a number of soldiers came to curse and jeer at us. They demanded our watches and anything of value we

had. I had a watch which was a present from my father. A soldier armed with
rifle and fixed bayonet ordered me to hand it over. I refused to comply and
he threatened me with the rifle. An officer passed near me and I called him
and asked if we were to give our watches etc. to the soldiers.

He ordered the soldier away and told us to retain our watches and
jewellery. We next had a visit from a soldier who wore the badge of the Royal
Irish Fusiliers. He was very friendly and said he was an Irishman and proud
of it and that he admired the way we fought. (He was somewhat under
the influence of drink.) He asked if he could do anything for us. We asked
if he could get us water to drink. He hurried across the square and soon
reappeared carrying two new buckets filled with water and some tin mugs.
One of our lads suggested that we pool any small change we had and give
it to him for his kindness. On being offered the money he flatly refused to
take it. When we insisted that he take it he seemed to have a brain wave. He
took the money and again made off across the square. When he returned
he carried a large quantity of biscuits and cigarettes which he distributed
amongst us.

After being arrested in Cashelnagor, Co. Donegal, on Saturday 29 April 1916
following a raid on the house he was staying in, Volunteer Daniel Kelly was
brought to Dublin by train. His guards on the journey were soldiers of the Royal
Inniskilling Fusiliers' reserve battalions. When Kelly arrived at Amiens Street
Station

we were marched to Trinity College. I remember the buildings were all
smouldering after the week's conflict. We were kept in Trinity College for
about an hour and then the soldiers got orders to bring us to Richmond
Barracks. When we arrived at Richmond Barracks we were put into the gym
room. We were kept there for a couple of hours and still nothing to eat. We
had the same escort with us, the Inniskilling Fusiliers. A British soldier of
the Sherwood Foresters came over to one of the Inniskilling Fusiliers, a lad
named Doherty, who was a Protestant, and said to him: 'All these characters
should be shot!' Doherty said to him: 'If you touch a hair on one of their
heads, you will be sorry for it. These men have a country to fight for. You men
have never been to a war. Our battalion is only after coming from France,
and now we are stuck on to this dirty job.'

Frank Thornton, who had fought with the Volunteers in the GPO, encountered
the Ulster Composite Battalion after the Rising. He later recorded:

After surrendering, we were marched down to the Custom House with quite
a number of others who were brought from different places. Before reaching
the Custom House, one officer of the Royal Irish Rifles did everything he

possibly could to have me shot. Why particularly myself, I don't know, but, however, through the intervention of a young Lieutenant, I was saved and eventually brought to the Custom House. When we arrived at the Custom House, quite a number of other prisoners were there already and the only place they had available to put us was in the yard. We were all ordered to lie down on the stone flags in a yard and we remained in this spot until some time on Monday. During all that period we were never allowed even a drink of water, or given any food, nor were our wounds attended to, and by this time, some of our men were in a very bad condition—with exhaustion, loss of blood, and with no attention they were really in a dangerous condition. This situation existed until the Royal Irish Rifles from Belfast were relieved by an Australian Unit on Sunday. The Australians, on taking over on Sunday evening, realising the position, divided their own rations with us and acted in quite a decent fashion.

Later, when Thornton was being marched to Richmond Barracks, he and his fellow-prisoners were guarded by men of the Sherwood Foresters. Thornton recalled: 'If it weren't for the fact that we were so strongly guarded by British troops, we would have been torn asunder by the ex-soldiers' wives in that area.'

Two particularly senior Irish officers of the Royal Inniskilling Fusiliers were present in Dublin during the Rising. These were Lieutenant-Colonel John McClintock and Brigadier-General Joseph Byrne.

Lieutenant-Colonel McClintock was the commanding officer of the 3rd Royal Inniskilling Fusiliers, which was based in Derry when the Rising began. A native of Seskinore, Co. Tyrone, he was a justice of the peace and high sheriff and deputy lieutenant of Co. Tyrone. His father, Colonel George McClintock, had once been the commanding officer of the 4th Battalion, while his grandfather Samuel McClintock had served as a lieutenant in the 18th (Royal Irish) Regiment of Foot during the first half of the nineteenth century.

After attending Cheltenham College in Gloucestershire and then Oxford Military College in Cowley, McClintock joined the reserve of the Royal Inniskilling Fusiliers and was commissioned as a

Lieutenant-Colonel John McClintock, from Co. Tyrone, commanding officer of the 3rd Royal Inniskilling Fusiliers (Sylvia Wright)

second-lieutenant while still in his teens. In 1909 he was promoted to lieutenant-colonel and took over command of the 3rd Battalion. When the First World War broke out he was too old to apply for active service overseas and remained in command of his reserve battalion in Derry.

He served in Dublin throughout the Rising, being mentioned in despatches. Promoted to colonel in 1917, he retired from the army after the end of the First World War. However, following the start of the War of Independence in 1919 Ulster unionists decided to reorganise the Ulster Volunteer Force, which they felt had been allowed to lapse in standards during the war years, and McClintock was appointed commander of the UVF in Co. Tyrone. In late 1920, when the Government of Ireland Act split the country into Northern Ireland and what would later become the Irish Free State, the paramilitary Ulster Special Constabulary was established, and many members of the UVF joined it. John McClintock was appointed commandant of the Co. Tyrone force and held this position until his death. An obituary noted:

> In those stirring years the Special Constabulary Force came frequently into conflict with bodies of organised Sinn Feiners. Colonel McClintock personally led many attacks and on two notable occasions routed massed formations of rebels. The first of these was a battalion review of Sinn Feiners near Dromore, and the second was during the truce period, when a training camp to which many Roman Catholic young men had forcibly been carried off, was broken up and all the leaders arrested, near Omagh.

Brigadier-General Joseph Byrne, Royal Inniskilling Fusiliers (*Weekly Irish Times*)

McClintock was made a commander of the Order of the British Empire in 1921 and was also appointed honorary senior aide-de-camp to the Duke of Abercorn when he became the first governor-general of Northern Ireland in 1922. He died in 1936, at the age of seventy-two.

Brigadier-General Joseph Byrne had in fact three ranks, thanks to the complicated British army system of official, brevet and honorary ranks: he was officially a major, a brevet lieutenant-colonel and an honorary brigadier-general. Byrne was born in Derry in 1874, though both his parents were from Dublin. His father was a doctor and also deputy lieutenant for Co. Derry. After attending St George's College in Weybridge, Surrey, and then Maison de Melle, a Jesuit school in Melle, near Ghent,

Joseph Byrne became a regular army officer when he was commissioned in the Royal Inniskilling Fusiliers in 1893 at the age of nineteen. He served in the 1st Battalion during the Anglo-Boer War, during which he was wounded at the Battle of Colenso on 15 December 1899, and by the end of the war he had risen to the rank of captain.

By April 1916 Byrne was an honorary brigadier-general and serving as assistant adjutant-general at the War Office in London, and on the 27th he was appointed deputy adjutant-general of Irish Command. For his actions while performing this role he was later made a companion of the Order of the Bath and mentioned in despatches after the Rising had ended.

In August, Joseph Byrne was appointed the last inspector-general of the RIC, a post he held until March 1920. After leaving the RIC he was called to the bar in London in 1921 and subsequently served as governor of a number of British colonies. He died in 1942 while living in England, at the age of sixty-eight.

* * *

Lieutenant-Colonel Thomas McCammon, commanding officer of the Ulster Composite Battalion, was mentioned in despatches for his actions during the Rising, after which he returned to recruiting and commanding troops in the north of Ireland. In February 1917 he was sent to the Third Army Infantry School in France for a course of instruction, apparently to prepare him for the command of a battalion in the field. Once he had completed this course he was appointed commanding officer of the 2nd Hampshire Regiment, and he joined his new battalion in the trenches on 22 April 1917.

The same day the battalion was involved in an attack at Monchy-le-Preux that resulted in more than two hundred men killed and wounded. McCammon was one of those wounded, receiving a gunshot wound to his right thigh. Four days later his wife received a telegram telling her that her husband had been wounded and was now 'dangerously ill'. She quickly obtained permission to travel to the French hospital where he was being treated, but it is not clear whether she arrived in time. Thomas McCammon died of his wounds on 28 April 1917, aged forty-two, at No. 20 General Hospital in Camiers. He now lies in Étaples Military Cemetery. His name is also commemorated on a memorial plaque in the Church of St Philip and St James in Holywood, Co. Down.

* * *

By the time all the reinforcements arrived in Dublin – the 5th Leinster Regiment, the 3rd, 4th and 5th Royal Dublin Fusiliers, the battery from the 5th (A) Reserve Artillery Brigade and the Ulster Composite Battalion – and joined with the 3rd Royal Irish Regiment, the 10th Royal Dublin Fusiliers and the 3rd Royal Irish Rifles, the number of Irishmen in British army uniform in Dublin numbered at least three thousand. The Irish men and women on the rebel side never outnumbered the Irishmen in British army uniform during Easter Week.

7

The Forgotten Siege of Beggarsbush Barracks

When the First World War broke out, numerous home defence units, raised and stationed locally, were set up throughout Britain and Ireland. As with the 'Pals' Battalions' of the British army, they were often formed from groups of men from the same area or who worked at the same job or shared a common interest. These units had no centralised command and were known by several different names, some referring to themselves as Local Defence Corps while others called themselves a Citizens' Defence Force or Citizens' Training League. Similar to the more well-known Home Guard of the Second World War, they generally consisted of men who were too old to join the British army, along with men who were medically unfit and some who simply preferred to serve in a home defence unit.

However, from January 1915 the Central Association of Volunteer Training Corps (covering England and Wales), the Scottish Association of Volunteer Training Corps and the Irish Association of Volunteer Training Corps (IAVTC) were set up to co-ordinate these disparate units, and all home defence groups were invited to join them. Those that did so were restructured into companies and battalions and issued with a grey-green uniform (purposely to make them look different from the army's khaki) and were required to drop their diverse names.

The 1st (Dublin) Battalion of the IAVTC contained four companies. These were A Company, the former Irish Rugby Football Union (IRFU) Volunteer Training Corps; B Company, previously the Dublin Veterans' VTC, comprising older ex-soldiers of the British army; C Company, an amalgamation of St Andrew's VTC and Glasnevin VTC, whose members came from the same parts of Dublin (its headquarters was the gymnasium in the Claremont Institution for the Deaf and Dumb at Glasnevin, and it is known to have had a rifle range in Finglas Quarry); and D Company, an amalgamation of the Great Northern Railway VTC, containing men who worked at Amiens Street Station, and the North City Veterans' VTC.

Despite the variety of units, the battalion totalled only about 120 men. But it did not include every VTC in the Dublin area: there were also the Great Southern and Western Railway VTC, the South City VTC, the Builders' VTC, the Howth and Sutton VTC, the Royal College of Science Platoon, and the Dublin Motor Cyclists' VTC. It is also possible that a Clontarf VTC existed, while it is known that there was an unsuccessful attempt to raise a Rathmines VTC. Several other VTC units existed around the country.

In addition to their distinctive uniform the members of the IAVTC wore an armband bearing the letters GR in red (and a man with no uniform at least wore the armband). These letters stood for *Georgius Rex* (Latin for 'King George'), but Dublin wits soon turned this into 'Gorgeous Wrecks', a nickname that stuck and became the common appellation.

In July 1915 the 1st (Dublin) Battalion of the IAVTC was reviewed by the commander-in-chief of British forces in Ireland, Major-General Sir Lovick Friend, at Lansdowne Road rugby ground, after which the force became closely associated with the South Irish Horse, a special reserve cavalry regiment, which assisted it with recruitment.

By August 1915 another home defence unit opted to join the IAVTC, one whose very existence shows that the political situation during the early years of the twentieth century was far from black and white. Though the formation of unionist volunteer units was believed to have taken place only in Ulster, a sister-unit of the UVF was formed in Dublin in 1912. Known as the Loyal Dublin Volunteers (also Dublin Volunteer Corps or Dublin Volunteer Force), it was formed in the first place because the UVF required members to have signed the Ulster Covenant in 1912. An article in the *Irish Times* in 1913 explained the new organisation's motivation:

> While Ulster is preparing to resist Home Rule by force if necessary, and is busy building up a great citizen army, the spirit of militarism that has gripped that province and fired the enthusiasm of its young manhood is also at work in Dublin ... Should a Home Rule Parliament be established in Dublin, this volunteer force is intended to be used in the preservation of the civil and religious liberties of Protestants in Dublin and the south ... Should civil war break out in Ulster as a consequence of Home Rule, the leaders of the Dublin Volunteers have undertaken to hold in readiness a force of at least 2,000 men for service wherever required by the Commander-In-Chief of the Ulster Army.

Membership at first was open only to members of the Orange Order, but after a large number of other unionists applied to join it was decided in 1914 to divide the Loyal Dublin Volunteers into two battalions: the 1st Battalion for members of the Orange Order and the 2nd Battalion for others. The organisation soon had more than 2,000 members, with a recruitment office at Dixon and Hempenstall's

Loyal Dublin Volunteers cap badge (Liam Boyne)

opticians' practice at number 12 Suffolk Street. (One of the partners, Thomas Hempenstall, an optician from Arklow, was a captain and adjutant in the new force.) The Loyal Dublin Volunteers were not the only such organisation outside Ulster: at least two others, the Loyal Cork Volunteers and the Loyal Wicklow Volunteers, are known to have existed, though the latter became part of the Wicklow Battalion of the IAVTC at some point during the First World War.

When the First World War began, eighty men of the Loyal Dublin Volunteers enlisted in one of the battalions of the Royal Dublin Fusiliers, probably the 'Dublin Pals' (D Company of the 7th Battalion), while a large number joined the 9th Royal Inniskilling Fusiliers, part of the 36th (Ulster) Division, a battalion that was soon known to contain an entire platoon made up of Dublin unionists. In total, 600 of the organisation's 2,000 men enlisted in the British army during the war. In August 1915 the remainder made the decision to become a part of the IAVTC.

By now it was becoming apparent to southern unionists that their Ulster counterparts were concentrating on keeping Ulster out of Home Rule, not on preventing Home Rule from being implemented in Ireland altogether. With the southern unionist cause slowly but surely becoming a lost one, the Loyal Dublin Volunteers joined the IAVTC, with 200 members transferring immediately. Some of these men would also become involved in the Easter Rising in Dublin.

* * *

In either 1927 or 1935 (according to conflicting sources) a 'time capsule' relating to the Loyal Dublin Volunteers was discovered in Dublin. While workers were removing presses from the cellar of the Post Office Customs Parcels Section at number 10 Parnell Square they discovered an arms cache hidden behind a wall, containing more than ninety rifles and 2,000 rounds of ammunition. As the building had been used as a post office linked to the GPO, and as the anti-Treaty IRA had also occupied it during the Civil War, it was believed at first that this was a republican arms dump from either 1916 or 1922. However, the rifles were British Lee-Enfields and Martini-Henrys, not the German weapons that the 1916 insurgents had mainly used, and one was engraved with the slogan *For God and Ulster*. When packets of Bible passages and cap badges bearing the words *Loyal Dublin Volunteers* were also found it became apparent that this cache had a different origin.

In 1914 number 10 Rutland Square (now Parnell Square) was known as Fowler Hall and was home to eleven Orange lodges. It was during the Civil War that the Dublin unionists were forced out of the building, with the anti-Treaty IRA destroying many of the documents inside relating to the history of the Orange Order in Dublin and of the Loyal Dublin Volunteers. Following the departure of many southern Protestants and unionists from Dublin in the early years of independence their history was largely erased.

* * *

By September 1915 the 1st (Dublin) Battalion of the IAVTC began to work closely with Dublin University OTC in Trinity College. The unit now began training in earnest, and regular route marches and lectures on military subjects were also organised. On Monday 24 April 1916 the battalion took part in another route march, leaving its headquarters at Beggarsbush Barracks early in the morning and setting off via Dundrum for Ticknock in south Co. Dublin, where it was due to take part in a joint exercise with the Kingstown and District VTC and Greystones VTC. While it was away, a rebellion broke out on the streets of Dublin.

At Ticknock at about 2:30 p.m. a despatch rider arrived from Beggarsbush Barracks and informed the IAVTC battalion that the Rising had begun, and it was ordered to return to headquarters immediately. The commanding officer quickly began forming the men into column for the march back.

This man was 36-year-old Major George Harris, a native of Killashee, Co. Longford, who now lived in Oaklands Park in Sandymount. A civil servant by profession, Harris was a graduate of the University of Dublin and was also serving there as both second-in-command and adjutant of Dublin University OTC and commanding officer of the OTC's Infantry Unit. He had previously served in both the 12th Middlesex Regiment and the 15th London Regiment (Prince of Wales's Own Civil Service Rifles) and had taken over command of the 1st (Dublin) Battalion of the IAVTC in August 1915.

The approximately 105 men of the battalion at Ticknock that day formed up into a column and began marching back to Dublin, with Major Harris

Major George Harris (Bryan Alton)

leading on horseback. They had no idea that they were heading straight into an ambush.

Not far from Beggarsbush Barracks the 3rd Battalion of the Irish Volunteers, under Commandant Éamon de Valera, had established its headquarters in Boland's bakery in Lower Grand Canal Street. C Company, under Lieutenant Michael Malone (whose brother had died eleven months earlier on the Western Front while serving in the 2nd Royal Dublin Fusiliers), was despatched to set up a line of outposts running along Northumberland Road to prevent British forces advancing into the city from the south along this route.

The most southerly outpost was Carrisbrooke House, at the junction of Northumberland Road and Pembroke Road. Next was Malone's own position in number 25 Northumberland Road, at the junction with Haddington Road. Further back towards the city centre were the rebel positions of St Stephen's Parochial Hall and St Stephen's School, and then on the far side of the Grand Canal was the rebel-occupied Clanwilliam House. The Volunteers in this area also later occupied Roberts's yard. These outposts would mean that any British forces coming from the south along Northumberland Road would have to run the gauntlet.

By 4 p.m., after an hour and twenty minutes of marching, the IAVTC column had reached Merrion Road and was about to cross the River Dodder. While history remembers the men of the 'Gorgeous Wrecks' as exclusively elderly middle-class Dublin Protestants, there were some notable exceptions.

In the column were three father-and-son pairs: the Barneses, the Fords, and the Sibthorpes. Private John Sibthorpe certainly fits the bill for an IAVTC member. Sixty-four years old and a native of Dublin, a merchant who sold decorating supplies and a member of the Church of Ireland, he lived with his family in Lesson Park. Much younger than the stereotypical IAVTC member was one of Sibthorpe's sons, 33-year-old Lance-Sergeant Arthur Sibthorpe, who worked in his father's business. Both Sibthorpes would survive the Rising: John Sibthorpe died in 1940, aged eighty-eight, while Arthur Sibthorpe went on to work as part of a building trades advisory committee based at the College of Technology in Bolton Street. He died in 1965, aged eighty-two, and was buried in the same plot as his father in Mount Jerome Cemetery.

Joseph Barnes, father and son, lived in St Joseph's Crescent, Glasnevin (making it probable that they were members of C Company). Private Joseph Barnes was a 43-year-old Londoner and the manager of a confectionery business. His son, Bugler Joseph Albert Barnes, had been born in Belfast and was now fifteen years old.

Private George Ford was a 42-year-old Dubliner who worked as a stationery salesman and lived in Sackville Gardens, off Ballybough Road. His parents were English, and his father had been a lithographic printer. George Ford is known to have survived the Rising and died in Dublin in 1947, aged seventy-three. His son, Bugler John Ford, was fourteen years old.

Even younger was Private John McLindon. A native of Dublin, he lived in Palmerston Park, son of a gardener and a domestic servant, both from Co.

Wicklow. He was thirteen years old; he is later known to have been gazetted as a temporary boy clerk in August 1918, then aged fifteen. He died in Barnet, Middlesex, in 1972, aged sixty-nine.

But thirteen-year-old John McLindon was not the youngest member of the IAVTC battalion that day. Ironically for a force that has been remembered as being made up of old men, ten-year-old Bugler Harold Green was marching with the column. He lived in the workers' houses at the Great Northern Railway terminus at Amiens Street Station, where his father, George Green, was the stationmaster. (Cadet-Sergeant Gerald Keatinge of Dublin University OTC, while serving as a cyclist orderly for the Ulster Composite Battalion, encountered George Green on Friday 28 April. He later wrote: 'As I had nothing to do all afternoon I became very friendly with the Station Master or something. He had a son in Beggar's Bush Barracks who was a bugler in the VTC and he was very anxious about him. He wanted me to make all sort of enquiries which of course I said I would do if I got a chance, but I couldn't help thinking that the chance was very remote.')

There was also a pair of brothers in the battalion. 36-year-old Platoon-Sergeant Arthur Shea was a Dublin man and an official with the Bank of Ireland who lived in Tritonville Road in Sandymount. His younger brother, 33-year-old Private Herbert Shea, lived in Lower Beechwood Avenue in Ranelagh and was an auctioneer. The Sheas' father had been a factory manager and commission agent. Herbert Shea is known to have died in Dublin in 1953, aged seventy.

* * *

As the battalion crossed the Dodder, Major Harris decided to split his force in two. Now approaching Beggarsbush Barracks, and aware that there was a rebellion on the streets of Dublin, he was taking every precaution. Instead of approaching the barracks by one route, which might be occupied by the rebels, resulting in a high number of casualties if his force was attacked, he approached it from two directions, minimising the chance of everyone being fired on. It was to prove a good idea.

Major Harris himself took command of the larger group, about sixty men, while the remaining forty were placed under the control of the second-in-command, Sub-Commandant Francis 'Frank' Browning. Browning – a former Irish international rugby player and cricketer – was forty-seven years old and a barrister. Originally from Rathmines, he now lived in Herbert Park Road in Donnybrook (so that when the battalion crossed the Dodder he would be at the bottom of his own street). In 1912 Browning had become president of the Irish Rugby Football Union, and after the outbreak of the First World War he founded the IRFU VTC and began actively recruiting. He issued a circular to rugby clubs in Dublin, encouraging their members to join up, and several hundred soon enlisted. Many became members of D Company, 7th Royal Dublin Fusiliers, a unit known as the 'Dublin Pals'; a photograph of this company taken in Lansdowne Road Rugby Ground shows Browning standing

Frank Browning and D Company, 7th Royal Dublin Fusiliers (the 'Dublin Pals'), Lansdowne Road rugby ground, September 1914. Browning had recruited many of this unit from the membership of the IRFU, and they would go on to fight at Suvla Bay in Gallipoli as part of the 10th (Irish) Division. Browning stands at the front of the group, to the right of the uniformed sergeant-major. (Author's Collection)

IRFU Volunteer Training Corps cap badge
(Author's Collection)

City of Cork Volunteer Training Corps
cap badge (Author's Collection)

in front of them. Meanwhile, the IRFU VTC became A Company of the 1st (Dublin) Battalion of the IAVTC.

Two of the platoon commanders in this company were 34-year-old George Allen, who was born in Trinidad, worked as a clerk for Dublin Corporation and lived with his family in Drumcondra Park, and 37-year-old Ewen MacNair, a native of Bray and a brewer's clerk who lived in Dartmouth Square in Ranelagh. He is known to have survived the Rising and died in 1965 in the Moyle Hospital, Larne, Co. Antrim, aged eighty-six.

Major Harris decided to lead his group up Shelbourne Road, which would bring it to the Beggarsbush Barracks end of Haddington Road. Sub-Commandant Browning was instructed to continue straight into Northumberland Road, which runs parallel to Shelbourne Road, then turn right into Haddington Road and approach the barracks from the other side.

This dividing of the IAVTC battalion must have been witnessed by the insurgents in Carrisbrooke House, at the junction of Northumberland Road and Pembroke Road. Browning's group of forty men would then have marched right past Carrisbrooke House as they continued on their way. However, the insurgents here did not open fire: they simply let the IAVTC men advance past them.

As Major Harris and his group moved on, they were soon marching parallel to the nearby railway line, which runs close to Shelbourne Road. Here some men from the 3rd Battalion of the Irish Volunteers, positioned on the railway bridge over South Lotts Road, were in the process of ripping up the railway lines and entrenching themselves between the sleepers – again in order to prevent the advance of British forces into the city from the south – when they encountered Major Harris and his men nearing their position. They let the IAVTC men turn into nearby Haddington Road and march towards the main gate of Beggarsbush Barracks, now open; then they took aim and opened fire.

Despite the fact that the IAVTC men were carrying rifles, they had not a single bullet or bayonet between them. Their weapons were also outdated (though this hardly mattered, as none of them had any ammunition); some of the rifles had not had ammunition produced for them in forty years. The IAVTC were in effect a group of uniformed but unarmed men.

Unable to fire back, Major Harris pressed forward and with a small party managed to make it through the gate into the barracks. The rest of his group, however, were forced to retreat before moving up Lansdowne Lane (now Lansdowne Park) in single file to the rear of the barracks and climbing, one by one, over the back wall.

This group of sixty men had now managed to make it to relative safety, but one man had been seriously wounded in the process. As he rushed through the front gate of the barracks Major Harris and his men had dragged in a member of A Company who had been hit by rebel fire. This mortally wounded man was another exception to the general belief that all IAVTC men were elderly Protestants: he was 22-year-old Catholic Lance-Corporal Reginald Clery, a

Reginald Clery, A Company, 1st (Dublin) Battalion of the IAVTC (Belvedere College, Dublin)

motorcyclist with the battalion. Clery's father was a retired lieutenant-colonel in the Leinster Regiment from Co. Limerick; but he was not the only British army soldier in Reginald Clery's family: one uncle had served as a major in the Royal Munster Fusiliers and another in the 4th (King's Own) Regiment of Foot, while a third was a surgeon-general with the Royal Army Medical Corps. Clery also had two cousins who fought in the First World War: Lieutenant-Colonel Vivian Clery of the Royal Engineers and Captain Noel Clery of the Royal Field Artillery, who outlived Reginald by only three months, being killed in action on 24 July 1916, aged twenty-three; he now lies in Quarry Cemetery, Montauban.

Reginald Clery lived in Harcourt Terrace and was working as a solicitor's apprentice, having attended Belvedere College in Dublin (where Éamon de Valera had taught mathematics). The *Belvederian* later recorded that

the death of Reggie Clery and the circumstances under which it occurred made it particularly painful for his family and friends. He and a group of volunteers were on their weekly practice 'route' around the vicinity of Ballsbridge. They were returning to Beggars' Bush barracks when Republican rebels shot at them ... Academically Reggie did extremely well through his school life. During his first year in the senior school, he won two prizes at Christmas 1905: one for Religious Knowledge and the other for getting 50 merit cards during the term. He did especially well in the Intermediate Exam (1907), getting more honours than any other student at the college.

After attending Belvedere, Reginald Clery studied law in Trinity College and was then apprenticed to the well-known firm of O'Keefe and Lynch of Molesworth Street, having obtained first-class honours in the solicitors' apprentices' examination in 1913. He was only weeks away from his final apprenticeship examination when he was killed.

The shot that killed Clery was witnessed by fifteen-year-old James Rowan, a telegraph messenger who worked in the GPO and a former member of Fianna

Éireann. He was watching the sixty or so IAVTC men turning into Haddington Road from Shelbourne Road under the command of Major Harris when he spotted some Volunteers on the railway bridge over South Lotts Road. He recorded that 'one of the [IAVTC] company must have had the same curiosity as myself, for I saw him down on bended knee and in a position ready to fire, but the Volunteer on the bridge fired first and I saw the "G.R." topple over. Some of his comrades doubled back and dragged him into the barracks. His name was Sergeant Cleary.'

Reginald Clery, who died on either 24 or 25 April 1916, is buried in Grangegorman Military Cemetery. In Belvedere College today there is a plaque commemorating past pupils who have died in various wars, from the Anglo-Boer War to the Cypriot War of Independence. There are only two names in the 1916 Rising section: Reginald Clery of the IAVTC and the executed Volunteer leader Joseph Plunkett – one man on each side of the conflict.

Lance-Corporal Reginald Clery was far from being the only Catholic in the IAVTC. Others who have been positively identified include 51-year-old Private John Dudley, a land agent originally from Doneraile, Co. Cork, who lived in Wellington Road; 42-year-old Sergeant Laurence Moriarty, a native of Durrow, Co. Laois, and a clerk with the Irish Land Commission who was living in Glasnevin (making him probably a member of C Company), who is known to have died in 1958, aged eighty-four; and 33-year-old Charles Reilly from Dublin who worked as a government office assistant while living in Sackville Street.

There were also at least two Jews in the 1st (Dublin) Battalion of the IAVTC. One of these was Private Lewis Humphreys, a 47-year-old master stamp and letter-maker who lived in Belgrave Road. He was born in Dublin, as was his wife; his father was from London and his paternal grandfather was from the Netherlands, though both settled and died in Ireland. Lewis Humphreys is known to have died in Dublin in 1946, aged seventy-seven. The other known Jewish member of the battalion is listed as Private Hy. W. Zeland (Hy. no doubt an abbreviation of Hyman). It has not been possible to discover any more information about him, but a Captain H. W. V. Zeland served with the Royal Army Veterinary Corps during the First World War; it cannot be confirmed whether this was a relative or possibly the same man.

* * *

Meanwhile in Northumberland Road the smaller group of IAVTC men was quickly approaching the second Volunteer outpost. Sub-Commandant Frank Browning and his forty men arrived at the junction of Northumberland Road and Haddington Road and began to wheel to the right. On the far side of this junction was number 25 Northumberland Road, where Lieutenant Michael Malone and his comrades were positioned. They had a perfectly clear view of the IAVTC men as they approached and moved through the junction, and then they took aim and opened fire. An eye-witness account by a local woman, reproduced by Max Caulfield in *The Easter Rebellion,* recorded what happened next.

As I stand at the drawing-room window, I see a small detachment of G.R. veterans. The afternoon has been warm, they look hot and tired. A sharp report rings out, and the man in the foremost rank falls forward, apparently dead, a ghastly stream of blood flowing from his head. His comrades make for cover – the shelter of the trees, the side of a flight of steps. Bullet follows bullet with lightning rapidity. The road is unusually deserted until one of the veterans dashes across the road, falls at the feet of a woman who sets up a wail of terror. I cannot bear to look and yet I feel impelled to do so. Of six men by the tree one is now standing – they must have lain down – but no, they have fallen on their backs, one over another – they are all wounded! Oh, the horror of it all – what does it mean? A wounded man is being borne in the direction of our house – we rush to open the door and offer assistance but they take him next door. I cannot watch any longer – I must go back to my mother, who is sitting quietly by the fire. She is very old and frail and must not know of what is passing so I try to appear as usual. After chatting to her for a short time, I return again to the window just in time to see a bare-headed white-coated doctor drive up in a motor-car. He disappears into one of the houses where he tends the wounded, some of whom are carried off to the hospital; the crowd which had gathered at the cross-roads gradually melts away.

Some IAVTC men were reportedly unable to climb over garden walls and railings in order to make it to cover because of their age, and several were hit by rebel fire while still out in the open. The survivors ultimately managed to take cover in nearby houses and called for medical aid while also changing out of their uniforms into civilian clothes, having decided that their uniforms were now too dangerous to wear; but by now they had lost three more killed or fatally wounded, as well as several others injured.

One of the dead or fatally wounded men was Private Thomas Harborne of C Company; he was also a motorcyclist with the battalion. A native of the Finglas-Glasnevin area, he was an organ-builder by trade, as his father had been before him, but in September 1914 he had begun work in the cooperage department of Guinness's brewery in James's Street as a temporary employee. (Given the date on which he began work it would seem he was hired as a wartime replacement for someone who had enlisted.) He either died in the ambush on 24 April or succumbed to his wounds later that day or the following day. He was forty-eight years old.

Another fatality was Private John Gibbs. A civil servant with the Commissioners of Inland Revenue who lived in Belgrave Square in Rathmines, he had been born in the Royal Barracks about 1860 or 1861, where his father, also John Gibbs, was serving as a corporal in the 1st (Royal) Regiment of Dragoons. Private John Gibbs was fifty-five years old at the time of his death on either 24 or 25 April 1916, and he is buried in Mount Jerome Cemetery.

The last IAVTC man to die as a result of the Northumberland Road ambush was the battalion second-in-command, Sub-Commandant Frank Browning, who had led the smaller group up Northumberland Road. He is almost certainly the man referred to in the eyewitness statement, 'the man in the foremost rank' who fell forward, apparently dead, as Browning is known to have received a single gunshot wound to the head on 24 April. He succumbed to this wound two days later. He was forty-seven years old at the time of his death, and he is buried in Deansgrange Cemetery. Members of the IRFU VTC subsequently erected a memorial to his memory, the inscription on which reads:

> This stone was erected by the members of the Irish Rugby Football Union Volunteer Training Corps, in affectionate remembrance of Francis Henry Browning B.A. Barrister-at-Law, its founder and commanding officer, and second in command of the 1st Dublin Battalion of the Irish Association of Volunteer Training Corps. He died from wounds received at Northumberland Road Dublin during the Sinn Féin Rising of Easter Week 1916 while returning with his men to Beggars Bush Barracks. He will live in the memory of all as an honourable comrade, and true distinguished sportsman, who by his untiring efforts and splendid patriotism obtained from his corps over 300 recruits for His Majesty's Forces during the Great European War. Born 22nd June 1868. Died 26th April 1916.

The men who were wounded by rebel fire included 54-year-old Sergeant Laurence Ford, a grocer's porter, who lived with his family in Limerick Alley, off Patrick Street. Listed as 'severely wounded', he survived the Rising and died in Dublin in 1936, aged seventy-four.

Another wounded man was Platoon-Commander William Horne, who lived on Howth Hill with his wife and two children. Born in Dublin to a father from Sussex and a mother from Kent, Horne was forty-one years old and worked as a railway official (making him possibly a member of D Company). Though wounded 'severely' he survived his injuries and died in Dublin in 1930, aged fifty-five.

Also wounded was 58-year-old Corporal George May, a barrister from Dublin who lived in Fitzwilliam Square with his wife and children. He was a son of George Augustus Chichester May, former Chief Justice of Ireland, while his brother, Sir Francis May, was the serving governor of Hong Kong. His wife, Margaret Egerton from London, was the daughter of Algernon Fulke Egerton MP. George May survived his wounds and ultimately died in 1924, aged sixty-six, while living in Shawford, Hampshire.

Three other men of the 1st (Dublin) Battalion of the IAVTC were wounded on 24 April 1916: Private H. Green, who was wounded severely; Company Sergeant-Major J. Redding; and Private W. Scott.

It was not possible to discover whether these six men were wounded in Major Harris's first group or while under the command of Sub-Commandant Frank

Browning. In all likelihood, however, the majority – if not all – were wounded in Northumberland Road.

Had Major Harris brought all his battalion up Northumberland Road there might have been even more casualties. Those who managed to escape the insurgents' fire were fortunate, however, in that they found cover in nearby houses. The *Sinn Fein Rebellion Handbook* records that

> the occupiers of Nos. 29, 31, and 53 took in several till they were able to proceed home. All the wounded 'G.R.'s' except two were dressed at No. 31 [and later taken to the Royal City of Dublin Hospital in Baggot Street], and here also all the others, with one exception, were supplied with change of clothing ... Two N.C.O.'s of B company managed to get down the lane behind Northumberland road and over the wall into the barracks. Mr. Edward Webb, Commandant of C Company (Glasnevin), ran for the front gate of the barracks, keeping close to the wall, and got in unhurt.

Considering the ambush from the viewpoint of the Irish Volunteers, Vice-Commandant Joseph O'Connor of the 3rd Battalion (Éamon de Valera's second-in-command at Boland's bakery) recorded that 'we had scarcely occupied our positions when 12 o'clock struck and we found ourselves in action. A volunteer force known as the "George's Rex" were returning to Barracks from some outdoor work. They were fully armed and before they entered the Barracks we opened fire on them. They replied as effectively as they could and some of them succeeded in gaining entrance to the Barracks. The fight was on.'

O'Connor was mistaken in his recollection of the time of the encounter; and the IAVTC were not 'fully armed', having weapons but no ammunition. As for replying 'as effectively as they could', the only option open to them was to flee into the relative safety of Beggarsbush Barracks nearby or into the houses in Northumberland Road. They did not – because they could not – fire a shot during their retreat.

It would appear that Lieutenant Malone and his comrades in number 25 Northumberland Road ceased firing once they realised that the IAVTC men could not shoot back, though by then they had already killed and wounded several of them. Later that evening, following outrage when citizens learnt what had happened, Pearse issued an order that from now on no insurgent was to fire at an unarmed man, whether he was in uniform or not.

There is some evidence, however, that the insurgents should have known that the IAVTC men were poorly equipped and had no ammunition or modern weapons. Sergeant Frank Robbins of the Irish Citizen Army, who served throughout the Rising in the St Stephen's Green area, later recalled:

> The Baldoyle section of the Citizen Army, with others, took part in the actual raid on the drill hall of the George Rex, the British Auxiliary Home Defence

Force at Sutton cross-roads, on the opposite side of the road from where the Sutton cinema now stands. The raiding party, to their consternation, found that all their work had been in vain because of the fact that the arms which were believed to be there were none other than wooden guns.

The IAVTC men who had managed to make it into Beggarsbush Barracks – a total of nine officers and eighty-one other ranks – were now under siege. However, they were not alone: also stationed in the barracks on Monday 24 April was the 2nd Garrison Battalion of the Royal Irish Regiment. Raised only a month earlier, this was one of two garrison battalions based in Dublin at the time of the Rising. (The other was the 2nd Garrison Battalion of the Royal Irish Fusiliers, raised only a couple of weeks before the Rising; it has not been possible to establish its station in Dublin at the time.) The garrison battalions were similar to the Volunteer Training Corps in that they were generally home service units, made up of men who for the most part were either too old or medically unfit to join a regular or 'service' battalion. Nevertheless, garrison battalions were a part of the British army.

Because the 2nd Garrison Battalion of the Royal Irish Regiment had only recently been established, its numbers were still low, and it too was poorly equipped. Furthermore, when the IAVTC men retreated into Beggarsbush Barracks they found only seventeen Lee-Enfield rifles in the weapons stores. The IAVTC men had six more Lee-Enfields, but the rest of their old Italian and Russian rifles did not take the Lee-Enfield's .303 calibre ammunition, and so the IAVTC men without a .303 rifle were told to turn their weapons upside down and use them as clubs if the insurgents attempted to capture the barracks – a tactic taken from old musket warfare.

While the insurgents never attempted to capture Beggarsbush Barracks, they did place it under siege. Snipers continually fired into the grounds, making it dangerous to cross the barrack square, especially during the evening. By that time on the first day the troops in Beggarsbush Barracks were also coming under fire from insurgents in a shop directly opposite the main gate. They had no idea how the rebels had managed to get so close and set themselves up there; in fact it was a result of Lieutenant John Guilfoyle having spent six hours tunnelling into the shop from some cottages behind it.

However, the IAVTC men and the garrison soldiers soon set up several of their own sniping positions on the barrack roof and fired back at the insurgents whenever a target presented itself. One soldier is also recorded as having left the barracks, made his way stealthily to Northumberland Road and established himself in the house directly across the street from number 25 before opening fire on Lieutenant Malone and his comrades. However, this unidentified soldier was soon killed or wounded by rebel fire.

Meanwhile, during the first hours of darkness on the Monday night a party from Beggarsbush Barracks appeared on the nearby railway line. The insurgents were still ripping up tracks, and some were sleeping in trenches dug between them. They appear to have spotted the approaching British army forces first and fired on them; the soldiers returned fire, then quickly retreated back to barracks.

A few hours before this encounter seventeen-year-old Cadet-Sergeant Gerald Keatinge arrived at Beggarsbush Barracks. He later recorded how he had responded when he heard that the Rising had begun.

> I realised at once ... that no time was to be lost, and after a short discussion with Father I decided to ring up Headquarters, and ask for instructions. This I was unable to do as I could not get any reply from the Exchange. I therefore decided that the next best thing to be done was to go and see Major Harris at his private address in Sandymount.
>
> Father drove me over there in his side-car only to find that he was in Beggar's Bush Barracks. We accordingly hurried off there and after much parleying at the gate, I was allowed inside, but Father had to remain outside. It was while I was inside that Father was fired at by a 'Sinn Feiner' but the shot was luckily wide. Inside the barracks I reported to Major Harris, and he enquired as to whether I was willing to take the risk of running some ammunition and rifles from the North Circular Road to the barracks as they had a large number of Veterans (who were unable to get home after their Field Day on account of rebels who had shot two or three of their Battalion some hours previously) and also about fifty soldiers with only twenty rifles and a few hundred round of ammunition. I immediately replied in the affirmative but I was not needed as it was finally decided to bring them in a taxi. Major Harris then ordered me to go to Trinity, but I pointed out that that was impossible as the insurgents held the road. (As a matter of fact, they were all around Beggar's Bush, and how Father and I got there and back safely is nothing short of a miracle.) The Major then said that I had better go home and sleep there which I did much against my will, as I felt that I ought to be up and doing. The Veterans in the barracks gave me messages to take to their relations which kept Father and me busy till about ten o'clock, so that I felt I was at least doing something to help.

The next morning, determined to do something more active, Keatinge reported to Portobello Barracks.

Some soldiers on leave in Dublin now began to make their way to Beggarsbush Barracks. One of these was Second-Lieutenant Edward Gerrard, a 23-year-old officer in the Royal Field Artillery. Gerrard was from the Donnybrook area and had attended Clongowes Wood College, after which he obtained a commission. He landed in Gallipoli on 19 July 1915, but by April 1916 he had returned to Ireland and was serving with the 5th (A) Reserve Artillery Brigade in Victoria Barracks, Athlone. On 24 April 1916 he was on leave in Dublin. In 1950 he give a witness statement to the Bureau of Military History, in which he recorded that

I was home on leave at Easter, 1916. I heard that there were disturbances in Dublin. I went to see what was happening. I was in civilian attire. I was in Harcourt Street when I heard a shout: 'Stop the man with the pipe.' I hastily removed my pipe and managed to escape. I did not know what was going on. I saw the insurrection troops assembling at the top of Grafton Street and going into Stephen's Green. I was specially struck with their magnificent physique. They were huge men. I realised there was something serious on, and I went home and got my uniform in a bag. When going home I met Sir Frederick Shaw, Bushy Park [Terenure], and he told me to go into Beggars Bush Barracks. I arrived there at about eight o'clock on Monday evening. There were no arms in Beggars Bush Barracks. Thinking over it now, the G.Rs. were there – but their rifles were not service type – and they had no ammunition.

Gerrard also recalled that the 2nd Garrison Battalion of the Royal Irish Regiment consisted of 'one or two ranker officers [who had been promoted from the ranks], four non-commissioned officers, and about ten men, three of whom were invalids [a figure much smaller than Keatinge's recollection of fifty] ... We had nothing to eat. There was not a scrap of food. That went on for two days.'

* * *

Sir Frederick Shaw of Bushy Park House in Terenure, Dublin, was the commanding officer of the 2nd Garrison Battalion of the Royal Irish Regiment. He also made his way to Beggarsbush Barracks during the evening of 24 April, arriving by horse and trap, which his coachman rushed in through the main gate. (Second-Lieutenant Edward Gerrard later recorded that Shaw's coachman drove in and out of the barracks on several occasions over the following days, managing to return with small amounts of food for the officers.) Born in Dublin in 1858, Lieutenant-Colonel Shaw was a descendent of an army officer named William Shaw who fought alongside William of Orange at the Battle of the Boyne in 1690 and had been awarded lands in Ireland for his services. Sir Frederick Shaw attended the University of Oxford and then the Royal Military Academy at Sandhurst, after which he was commissioned into the 1st (Royal) Regiment of Dragoons in 1879, at the age of twenty-one. He resigned from the regular army in 1885, the same year in which he married. He served on in the reserve, however, and by 1887 he had joined the 5th Royal Dublin Fusiliers as a captain. During the Anglo-Boer War he served with his battalion in South Africa; promoted to major, he commanded the battalion for two months in May and June 1901. After the Anglo-Boer War he was awarded the Distinguished Service Order 'in recognition of services during operations in South Africa.'

He remained with the 5th Royal Dublin Fusiliers and then took command of the battalion when he was promoted to lieutenant-colonel in 1907. In 1912 he also became commanding officer of the 2nd Battalion of the Loyal Dublin Volunteers, the battalion specifically raised for Dublin unionists who were not members of the Orange Order (an act that confirms his political views). The following year he relinquished command of the 5th Royal Dublin Fusiliers, but in 1914, after the outbreak of the war, he personally raised the 8th Battalion and became its commanding officer.

Despite being fifty-seven in 1915, on 20 December that year Lieutenant-Colonel Shaw landed in France with the 8th Battalion. (His two sons were also serving as officers in the war: Robert de Vere Shaw in the Royal Field Artillery and Frederick Charleton Shaw in the 5th Battalion of the King's African Rifles.) However, the trenches proved too much for him and he was sent back to Ireland, being appointed commanding officer of the newly raised 2nd Garrison Battalion of the Royal Irish Regiment in Beggarsbush Barracks.

When he arrived at Beggarsbush Barracks in his horse and trap on 24 April 1916 Lieutenant-Colonel Shaw was now the senior officer present, and so he took command in the barracks. He would survive the Rising and would appear as a character witness at the court-martial of Captain Bowen-Colthurst. In 1927 Shaw died while living at the family home, Bushy Park House. He was sixty-nine years old and is buried in Rathfarnham Cemetery.

* * *

On Tuesday 25 April, as recorded in the *Sinn Fein Rebellion Handbook*, several members of the 1st (Dublin) Battalion of the IAVTC made their way into the barracks, including Charles Dickinson, commandant of B Company. He was a 46-year-old land agent and justice of the peace from Kimmage in Dublin. After the Rising he would become commanding officer of the battalion.

During that day the garrison battalions based in Dublin suffered their first fatality of the Rising when Private Joseph Cullen of the 2nd Garrison Battalion, Royal Irish Fusiliers, was killed in action. From the Shankill area of Belfast, he had previously served in the 2nd Royal Irish Fusiliers of the regiment, landing in France to join it in October 1914, before being transferred to the 2nd Garrison Battalion. Joseph Cullen is buried in Grangegorman Military Cemetery.

Cullen's death probably took place away from Beggarsbush Barracks, depending on where the 2nd Garrison Battalion of the Royal Irish Fusiliers was stationed in Dublin. However, two deaths that took place just outside the barrack gate were later recorded by Second-Lieutenant Edward Gerrard. He wrote later: 'One of my sentries in Beggars Bush Barracks, about Tuesday evening, said to me, "I beg your pardon, Sir, I have just shot two girls." I said, "What on earth did you do that for." He said, "I thought they were rebels. I was told they were dressed in all classes of attire." At a range of about two hundred yards I saw two girls – about twenty – lying dead.'

One of the IAVTC men in Beggarsbush Barracks was Section-Commander Thomas St John Bagnall, a 43-year-old manufacturer who lived in Maxwell Road, Rathmines. His father was from Rahugh, Co. Westmeath, and his mother was

Thomas St John Bagnall with his
wife, Mary, in Ilfracombe, June 1939
(Betty-Jane & Bob Smith)

from Athy, Co. Kildare. The family business was Bagnall Brothers, boot and shoe makers, of number 14 Suffolk Street, Dublin. He survived the Rising and died in 1946, aged seventy-three, while living in Rathgar. An obituary stated that Thomas St John Bagnall

> was educated at Wesley College, and, after spending some time in the counting house [office] of Messrs. Pim Bros., he joined the firm of Messrs. Dunlop. After some years in Coventry he was appointed to take charge of the depot in Sweden, where he lived for a number of years. Resigning from Messrs. Dunlop he took over the business of Messrs. Thomas Pearson and Co., Ship Street, Dublin. A member of the congregation of the Methodist Centenary Church, St. Stephen's Green, he was greatly interested in the work of the Home Mission. He was married to Miss Mary A. Whiteside, eldest daughter of the late Mr. William Whiteside, Dublin. He was a member of the Rotary Club and held a high office in the Masonic Order.

Thomas St John Bagnall is buried in Mount Jerome Cemetery.

Another IAVTC member besieged inside Beggarsbush Barracks was 52-year-old Section-Commander Robert Davidson, who worked as a solicitor's managing clerk and lived in Montpellier Parade, Blackrock. He was a former British army soldier who had enlisted in Dublin in October 1882 in the Commissariat and

Transport Corps (which later became part of the Army Service Corps) at the age of nineteen. He had previously worked as a clerk. He served in Egypt from April to July 1885 during the Suakin Expedition, an unsuccessful campaign led by Major-General Sir Gerald Graham against the Mahdist leader Osman Digna. He then left the regular army in December 1888, and after six years in the reserve he was discharged in October 1894, aged thirty-one. Twenty-two years later he was back in uniform and fighting in Dublin.

There were also two scientists in the IAVTC: Corporal Joseph de Witt Hinch and Private Arthur Lyster.

John de Witt Hinch was a 41-year-old Dubliner who lived in Cambridge Road, Rathmines. His father had been a bookseller in the city. Hinch was a geologist, who had begun working at the National Library of Ireland as a boy attendant in 1890. He was subsequently one of the non-publishing participants in the Royal Irish Academy's survey of Clare Island, Co. Mayo, in 1909–1911, where he was employed in the survey as an expert on glacial geology.

Three years after the Rising, in 1919, having now published several papers on glacial deposits, he was appointed to the staff of the Geological Survey, first as superintendent of maps and collections and then from 1921 as a geologist, with his work soon published in the Survey Memoirs and in the *Irish Naturalist*. He was elected a member of the Royal Irish Academy in 1924. By now he was living in the Donnybrook area. He died a few years later, in 1931, aged fifty-six.

Arthur Lyster was fifty-five years old and a teacher of mathematics at Trinity College. Originally from Goresbridge, Co. Kilkenny, he lived in Charlemont Place in Ranelagh. Between 1892 and 1896 he was an assistant astronomer at the Astronomical Observatory of the University of Dublin (now part of Dublin Institute for Advanced Studies) at Dunsink, Co. Dublin, where his duties included conducting the observing schedule and the mathematical reduction of observations. He later taught mathematics at the King's Hospital, the private school in Palmerstown, Co. Dublin (where he passed on his interest in astronomy to Eric Mervyn Lindsay from Portadown, who would go on to become director of the Armagh Observatory). The University of Dublin's Arthur Lyster Prize for mathematics is named after him, having been established under the will of his daughter, Alice Lyster, in 1951.

* * *

On Wednesday 26 April the supply situation inside Beggarsbush Barracks appears to have improved for a while. At about six that morning James Rowan, the fifteen-year-old telegraph messenger who witnessed many of the events at the barracks during that week, observed that three motor vehicles belonging to Jacob's biscuit factory that had been commandeered by the British army succeeded in getting in and out of the barracks, apparently carrying rations and other supplies and equipment, while under rebel fire. Later that morning Rowan witnessed another case of mistaken identity when at about 10 o'clock on Wednesday morning the driver of the delivery van belonging to Horan's grocery shop at the corner of Grand Canal St. and South Lotts Road got permission from the Volunteers who were in occupation of the premises to go to the stable at the rear to feed the horse. As he was leaving he dashed across South Lotts Road and was riddled with bullets from Beggars Bush. He must have been mistaken for one of the Volunteer garrison.

Meanwhile the British army were also firing on genuine Volunteers, while the insurgents were sniping back at them. Second-Lieutenant Edward Gerrard recorded that

> while we were sniping in Beggars Bush Barracks I saw a Sinn Féiner. By some accident, he put his head up over the railway line wall and I saw him. I said, 'There's one fellow going to have it anyway.' I loaded the rifle and at a range of about 200 yards I fired. I saw the bullet hitting a stone within two inches of his head. I think this was on Wednesday morning. I was very glad afterwards that I had not hit him. I had never fired that particular rifle before. Of course, if he had seen me, he would have done the same.

Gerrard later recalled also that 'I saw R. A. Anderson shot. He was Fr. Finley's second-in-command, in the Irish Agricultural Organisation Society. He was hit by shotgun cartridge slugs through a loophole in Beggars Bush Barracks. He was in the G.Rs.' The *Sinn Fein Rebellion Handbook* also mentions this incident. 'Mr. R. A. Anderson was wounded by a charge of buckshot while in the "detention" post, commanding the corner of Northumberland road and Haddington road. He was taken to Portobello [Barracks] Hospital. Happily, the wounds were not serious, and he reappeared with his arm in a sling before the force left barracks on Tuesday, 2nd May.'

Platoon-Commander Robert Anderson of B Company, aged fifty-five, was born in Buttevant, Co. Cork, the son of a Scottish father and a Canadian mother. As a younger man he had been working as a clerk of petty sessions (court clerk) in Doneraile when he was approached by Sir Horace Plunkett with a view to helping with the founding of the agricultural co-operative movement. Anderson agreed. An article about him in the *Corkman* of 9 July 2009 states that his task

> was no easy one, it entailed traversing the length and breadth of the country, travelling by bicycle, horseback and by train to hold meetings explaining the ideals of the new movement to the farming community. Over 50 meetings were addressed before they had their first success. Farmers were suspicious of a venture spearheaded by a landlord and Protestant, and co-operation was seen as a threat by traders and shopkeepers. Anderson, whose life was threatened on at least one occasion in Co. Clare, graphically described it

as hard and thankless work, facing the apathy of the people and the active opposition of the press and politicians.

In 1889 the co-operative movement gained ground when the first co-operative creamery was opened in Drumcolliher, Co. Limerick. From then on the movement went from strength to strength. Anderson became known as an excellent organiser and administrator, and by 1914 he had become the secretary of the Irish Agricultural Organisation Society, the national co-ordinating body.

On 20 October 1914 one of Anderson's sons, 21-year-old Second-Lieutenant Alan Anderson of the 2nd Royal Irish Regiment, was killed in action on the Western Front. With no known grave, today his name is commemorated on the Le Touret Memorial. This was followed by the death of another son the following year, Second-Lieutenant Philip Anderson of the same regiment, aged twenty-six, killed in action on 24 February 1915. He had previously been mentioned in despatches, and he now lies in Bailleul Communal Cemetery, Nord.

Robert Anderson travelled to Canada in 1920 as a delegate to the Imperial Conference. Two years later he became managing director of the Irish Agricultural Wholesale Society. He continued working in the agricultural industry, and in 1932 – now aged seventy-two – he became president of the Irish Agricultural Organisation Society. In 1942 Robert Anderson died in Dublin, aged eighty-two. He is buried in Mount Jerome Cemetery.

In 2009 a commemorative plaque in his honour was unveiled at the house where he was born, Mount Corbett, at Churchtown, Buttevant, Co. Cork. Mairéad Nagle, widow of Billy Nagle, a former president of the Irish Co-operative Organisation Society, unveiled the plaque, and John Tyrell, director-general of the society, also spoke. The event was covered in the *Corkman,* and Anderson was hailed as a hero of Irish agriculture. His involvement in the Easter Rising was not mentioned.

While Platoon-Commander Robert Anderson was only slightly wounded in Beggarsbush Barracks in April 1916, 51-year-old Private Joseph Hosford of C Company was less fortunate. A native of Bandon, Co. Cork, he was now living in Belgrave Square, Rathmines. He had been employed by Brooks, Thomas and Company Ltd, the well-known building trade suppliers, for thirty-six years, and at the time was working in the paint department. On 26 April, as recorded in the *Sinn Fein Rebellion Handbook,* 'Mr. Joseph Hosford, of C Company, was killed in the barrack room. He had gone up to get his overcoat, and stood for a moment opposite a window. A bullet came through the glass and went through his body.' He was killed instantly, and he is buried in Grangegorman Military Cemetery. His name is also commemorated on the war memorial in Holy Trinity Church, Rathmines.

* * *

Not long after midday on Wednesday the 26th the 2nd/7th Battalion and 2nd/8th Battalion of the Sherwood Foresters, recently arrived at Kingstown (Dún

Laoghaire) after being summoned from England, advanced up Northumberland Road on their march into Dublin. These battalions constituted part of the 59th (2nd North Midland) Division, a Territorial (second-line reserve) division. As a result it suffered from a lack of equipment and poor training and had regularly lost drafts of trained soldiers to first-line units that were fighting in France. The average length of service for a soldier in the division was only three months. When it was called to Ireland to help defeat the Rising most of its soldiers were very inexperienced; some had never fired a rifle before.

These soldiers were soon marching straight into Lieutenant Michael Malone's position in Northumberland Road. The insurgents in their various positions along the street and on the other side of Mount Street Bridge opened fire on the ranks of poorly trained soldiers, who began rushing forward in waves in an attempt to storm the buildings – a tactic more suited to trench warfare than to urban combat – and were shot down. This fight would become famous as the Battle of Mount Street Bridge, in which seventeen insurgents inflicted more than one hundred and fifty casualties on the English battalions before they were finally defeated.

Though only English battalions were involved in the heavy fighting here, one Irishman played an integral part in the battle. During its disorganised and hurried move to Ireland the 59th Division had left all its machine-guns and grenades behind in England. With its men being killed and wounded in large numbers along Northumberland Road and on Mount Street Bridge, the Sherwood Foresters contacted the nearby Elm Park Bombing School for help.

The man they managed to contact was 25-year-old Captain Richard Jeffares of the 4th Royal Irish Rifles. A native of Leighlinbridge, Co. Carlow, he had been living in Scarke House, near New Ross, Co. Wexford (the home of his uncle, with whom Jeffares had lived for many years, being estranged from his father). He attended New Ross Endowed School and then Kilkenny College, after which he obtained a reserve commission in 1911. He had served in the British South African Police before the war, and would later fight for a time in the German East African campaign.

On 30 December 1914 Captain Jeffares had landed in France on attachment to the 2nd Royal Munster Fusiliers. He served with this battalion for several months before developing a bad case of measles as a result of 'exposure while on active service' and was ultimately evacuated to Britain. After recovering he was posted to his old battalion, now based in Carrickfergus, Co. Antrim, and then at some point before the Rising was attached to Elm Park Bombing School.

Captain Jeffares informed the Sherwood Foresters that he could supply them with plenty of grenades, and that he would bring them to Northumberland Road personally. He arrived there not long after 5 p.m., several hours into the battle, also bringing a machine-gun detachment with him. Having distributed his grenades, he watched as the Sherwood Foresters immediately launched three grenade assaults against number 25 Northumberland Road. The third attack managed to blow open the front door, and the soldiers poured inside. Slowly but surely, thanks to the arrival of these new weapons, the tide of battle began to turn.

Richard Jeffares survived the Rising and in October 1916 returned to the Western Front, this time serving in the 2nd Royal Irish Rifles. In 1917 he wrote to his Uncle John in New Ross that 'if I come out of this all right I may get married and settle down. How damned funny to think of me married.' He mentioned a woman he was thinking of proposing to but instructed his uncle not to say a word of this, 'as I don't intend taking the plunge while the war is on and I hate people talking.'

On 19 July 1917 he wrote another letter to his uncle in which he referred to the new scheme of pensions and gratuities that had been introduced in April.

> It all means that in addition to the £150/£200 I get alive or dead my nearest relative gets another £100 or £150 if I get killed ... Now you are down as my next of kin and it will all come to you if I go West. I would like you to hold on to it and spend it mostly on Mick [his younger brother, a lieutenant in the Royal Irish Rifles] if he gets safely through it all. Do as you like with it but give Mick a first call and preference ... I want to get things square as tho I don't at all imagine I am going to be bowled over by any ruddy Hun still we are in a hot place at present, there is a hell of a fight coming off soon. Now you know my wishes and after all I look on you as my father and Boss. My other and real father I have no feeling for.

Jeffares was right about being in a 'hot place'. In early August 1917 he was admitted to the 30th General Hospital in Calais with a severe gunshot wound to his left forearm. He survived this injury and, having also been mentioned in despatches, was soon back with his battalion, but on 6 October he received another wound. This time he was hit in the head, and whatever hit him – bullet, shrapnel or shell fragment – penetrated his skull. Later that day he succumbed to his wounds and died in No. 33 Casualty Clearing Station. He now lies in Bethune Town Cemetery, and his name is also commemorated on the Great War Memorial in his native Leighlinbridge.

* * *

The Battle of Mount Street Bridge also saw the awarding of the Military Medal to an Irish person but, unusually, the recipient was neither a soldier nor a man. Under the heading 'Girl wins Military Medal', the *Sinn Fein Rebellion Handbook* records:

> Sir John Maxwell in his despatch, specially referred to the severity of the fighting at Mount Street Bridge, 'where,' he said, 'our heaviest casualties occurred.' He further said he should 'like to mention the gallant assistance given by a number of medical men, ladies, nurses and women servants, who at great risk brought in and tended to the wounded.' Early in 1917, in a list of military honours issued by the War Office there appeared the name of Miss

Louisa Nolan who was awarded the Military Medal. Miss Nolan tended quite a number of wounded officers and men during the fighting at Mount Street Bridge, on the Wednesday of Easter week, and brought water and other comforts to the soldiers while bullets were flying thick through the air. Miss Nolan's conduct was highly spoken of at the time of the occurrence ... On Saturday, 24th February, 1917, Miss Nolan was decorated with the medal by His Majesty at Buckingham Palace.

Louisa Nolan, a native of Co. Cork, was the daughter of a former head constable of the RIC, Robert Nolan. She had lived in Dublin since at least the age of three and at the time of the Rising was nineteen years old. She was living with her father and stepmother in Somerset Street, Ringsend, and was working as a chorus girl with the Gaiety Theatre. The *Sinn Fein Rebellion Handbook* adds that 'two of her sisters are nursing in England, one brother is in the Army, and another in the Navy, and a third was killed in August last on the Western front.' One of the brothers, 23-year-old Lance-Corporal James Nolan of the 2nd Leinster Regiment, was alive at the time of the Rising but was killed in action on 24 August 1916 and now lies in Guillemont Road Cemetery, Guillemont.

Louisa Nolan wearing her Military Medal (Nolan family)

On 26 April 1916 Louisa Nolan and sixteen-year-old Kathleen Pierce, a master tailor's daughter, originally from Galway, had run out from the crowd that had gathered to watch the fighting at Mount Street Bridge. Both were carrying large water jugs, and after a shout from the crowd the rebel and military firing died away as the two young women gave water to the wounded and dying soldiers. At the same time a group of medical staff from nearby Sir Patrick Dun's Hospital advanced onto Mount Street Bridge under a Red Cross flag to remove the wounded. Again, both sides held their fire. In the *Freeman's Journal* of 26 February 1917 Louisa Nolan gave a first-hand account of what happened next.

During the firing of the military and rebels, I made my way to where soldiers were stationed. I saw a soldier fall on the bridge and I asked for volunteers to come with me to lift him. No one seemed anxious. I did not think of danger at the time, but I pitied that soldier, for I thought of my brothers at the front. I ran along on to the bridge and dragged the soldier out of danger.

Bullets were spitting all around me, but I escaped unharmed. I found the man was an officer ... After I brought the officer under cover, I was joined by several others and we were able to place the wounded man under cover of a hoarding. One poor fellow died with his hand in mine. His last words were God bless you. I shall never forget the grateful look in that man's eyes. Little I had done to comfort his last minutes.

The mother of the officer who Louisa Nolan had saved presented her later with a silver purse and the badge of the Sherwood Foresters. After the Rising, Louisa Nolan travelled to London to appear as one of the 'Ladies of the Chorus' in the revue *Three Cheers* at the Shaftesbury Theatre. She later left the Gaiety and moved permanently to London, where she died in 1982, aged eighty-five. Her Military Medal is now in the Ulster Museum in Belfast.

* * *

Louisa Nolan was not the only Irishwoman to be awarded the Military Medal for bravery during the Rising. Under the heading 'A heroic girl' the *Sinn Fein Rebellion Handbook* records that

> this district [Dublin Castle] was the scene of a series of gallant actions on the part of a young lady, Miss Florence Williams, 8 Bristol Buildings, Castle Street, who was afterwards awarded the Military Medal by the War Office for her conspicuous bravery. She was outside the Castle gates when the policeman [Constable James O'Brien] was shot, and some time later dragged two soldiers who were severely wounded from the street, where bullets were rattling, to her mother's house; here they were given all possible assistance. She went through the fire to the Castle in search of a stretcher to carry the wounded men to hospital, and after that rescued more wounded soldiers, and went out and brought a priest to minister to them. Frequently during the week she went out in the firing line, and secured bread and medicine and bandages for the wounded men in her house from the Adelaide Hospital. She was specially thanked and made the recipient of a presentation from the Commander and officers of the Dublin Fusiliers.

This account adds that Florence Williams's father was a sergeant in the Border Regiment, then on active service in the Balkans. Years later her medal was lost to the family when it was destroyed during an air raid in London during the Second World War.

* * *

During the afternoon of Wednesday 26 April 1916 some soldiers of the Sherwood Foresters scouted down Haddington Road as far as Beggarsbush Barracks while the Battle of Mount Street Bridge was raging. They were spotted by Lieutenant-

Colonel Sir Frederick Shaw, who commandeered a platoon of them to bolster the barracks' defences. Second-Lieutenant Edward Gerrard later recalled that 'at about four o'clock on Wednesday afternoon some of the Sherwood Foresters arrived in Beggars Bush Barracks – twenty-five – as far as I remember, untrained, undersized products of the English slums.' With more firepower present in the barracks, as again recorded by Edward Gerrard,

> Major Harris organised a continuous barrage of rifle fire against the windows of the houses in Northumberland Road. About three rifles were laid on each window and at a signal by whistle at least ten rounds from each rifle were directed at each window. Our men were in the windows of Beggars Bush Barracks. They had sandbags. I often thought there must have been a terrible lot of people killed, but what could they do. They were being sniped at the time.

Major George Harris was later involved in another incident while under siege in Beggarsbush Barracks. During the Rising, as recorded in *Unarmed Persons Shot by Rebels,* 'an old man [actually fifty-eight] named Synnott left his house in Haddington Rd to buy some tobacco. No sooner had he left his door than he was struck by 3 shots and subsequently died of his wounds. That these shots were fired by rebels is proved by the fact that [he was hit] by a charge of buck-shot ... Major Harris helped to carry Synnott into Beggars Bush Bks. He was attended by Capt. Hackett RAMC.' The report adds that 'Synnott was shot on leaving his house by rebels who were firing at the Military.' The dead man was George Synnot, a clerk, a native of Co. Westmeath. He is now buried in Deansgrange Cemetery.

The doctor named in the report was Captain Bartholomew Hackett, a native of Castlecomer, Co. Kilkenny. He had worked as a surgeon's assistant in Norfolk before returning to Ireland, where he married and was attached to Mountjoy Prison. He was gazetted as a lieutenant in the Royal Army Medical Corps in September 1914 and before the Rising had served in France, having landed there on 31 May 1915. Like many other Irishmen in British army uniform at the time, Bartholomew Hackett's family stood on both sides of the political divide. A brother also joined the British army, while his father, Dr John Hackett, had been a strong supporter of the Irish Party leader Charles Stewart Parnell; even after Parnell had been condemned by the Catholic hierarchy over his love affair with Katharine O'Shea, and her subsequent divorce and marriage to Parnell, he continued to support him, suffering financial loss and even physical attacks as a result.

On the other hand, four of Bartholomew Hackett's brothers supported the Irish Volunteers. One of them, a Jesuit priest, Father William Hackett, became a prominent figure in republican circles, helping to form an Irish Volunteers cadet corps while teaching at Crescent College, Limerick, and in February 1916 stood alongside Patrick Pearse on a platform in Limerick. He later took an anti-Treaty stance during the Civil War, though he was a friend of both Michael Collins and

Éamon de Valera and in fact tried on several occasions to bring the opposing leaders together; but Collins's death in August 1922 prevented this from ever happening. The last letter Collins wrote was to Father Hackett.

After the First World War, Dr Bartholomew Hackett returned to his former job in Mountjoy Prison. On 1 November 1920, during the War of Independence, he was the prison medical officer when Kevin Barry, the eighteen-year-old IRA member (and medical student) was hanged – the first republican to be executed by the British since the Rising. Hackett's brother, Father William Hackett, had visited Kevin Barry in the prison a few days earlier.

Dr Bartholomew Hackett died in Dublin in 1947, aged seventy-two. Major George Harris also survived the Rising and was mentioned in despatches as well as being awarded the Distinguished Service Order for his actions during the event, as well as another mention in despatches and membership of the Order of the British Empire before the end of the war.

* * *

Lieutenant-Colonel Sir Frederick Shaw also had plans for the newly arrived English soldiers. He summoned Second-Lieutenant Edward Gerrard, who later recorded:

> Sir Frederick Shaw said to me – we were being very badly sniped from the railway bridge, South Lotts Road – 'You take Q.M. [Quartermaster-Sergeant] Gamble and those men, climb up on the railway line and put them off.' I said, 'Very good, Sir.' We got over the side of the Barracks and through the houses on Shelbourne Road and up on to the railway by a ladder. I was over the wall first, followed by Sergeant Gamble.

Company Quartermaster-Sergeant Robert Gamble of the 2nd Garrison Battalion, Royal Irish Regiment, was a 26-year-old Dubliner, born in Stafford Street (now Wolfe Tone Street) in 1889. His father was a porter and his mother was a boot machinist. He attended school in the Coombe Boys' Home; then, in November 1907, while working as a draper's porter and messenger and living in Lower Dominick Street, he enlisted in the Royal Irish Rifles at the age of eighteen, having previously been in the reserve 5th Royal Dublin Fusiliers.

After undergoing his initial training in the regimental depot in Belfast, Gamble was posted to the 2nd Royal Irish Rifles and sent to join it in Aldershot. By the summer of 1911 the battalion had moved to Dover and Gamble had obtained an army third-class education award and promotion to lance-corporal. After being wounded in an accident at Dover on 12 July 1911 (when a local publican drove his car into a company of marching soldiers to avoid an oncoming motorcycle, hitting Gamble in the hip and dragging him along before finally stopping), by October 1913 Gamble was a corporal. He was considered 'sober, trustworthy ... a good disciplinarian.' He obtained an army second-class education certificate in April

1914, and when the war broke out he was promoted to sergeant and sent overseas with his battalion, landing in France on 15 August 1914. (His older brother William also served in the Royal Irish Rifles during the war.) Two months later he received a 'slight' gunshot wound to the toes of his left foot. Sent to hospital and then evacuated to Britain, he returned to the war on 16 February 1915, rejoining the 2nd Royal Irish Rifles in the trenches.

On 8 May he was wounded in action for a second time, receiving shrapnel wounds to the right arm, right hand, groin, scrotum and left leg. Evacuated to Britain once more, he was not discharged from hospital for nearly three months and even then still had shrapnel in his body that could not be removed. With these wounds he was soon reassigned to a reserve battalion, at first the 3rd Royal Irish Rifles in Portobello Barracks. Then, on the formation of the 2nd Garrison Battalion of the Royal Irish Regiment in March 1916, Gamble was promoted to company quartermaster-sergeant and posted to this new unit. He could expect to be safe here for the rest of the war.

Second-Lieutenant Gerrard later recorded that after climbing up onto the railway line,

> as soon as I got over the wall, at a range of about 200 yards, about eight Sinn Féiners advanced from the direction of the city to meet us. I saw them coming towards us, firing. There was what they call a fairly sharp fire fight. These men were standing up, not lying down. They came out of their trenches to meet us. They were very brave, I remember. They did not know how many of us there might be. The first casualty was Q.M. Gamble. He was shot dead, under the right eye. I was the next casualty. I don't know how many Sherwoods [men of the Sherwood Foresters] were killed. One of them was wounded on the approach to the railway. The young Sherwoods that I had with me had never fired a service rifle before. They were not even able to load them. We had to show them how to load them.

Company Quartermaster-Sergeant Robert Gamble was twenty-six years old when he died. He is buried in Bungay Cemetery, Suffolk.

On the same day that Gamble died, and possibly in the same action, another member of the 2nd Garrison Battalion of the Royal Irish Regiment was killed in action: Private James Cavanagh, a native of Co. Monaghan, also formerly of the Royal Irish Rifles, who had enlisted in Glasgow. He is buried in Grangegorman Military Cemetery.

Second-Lieutenant Edward Gerrard was badly wounded in the right arm during the attempt to defeat the snipers along the railway line. He was taken to Portobello Barracks Hospital,

> where I used see Captain Bowen-Colthurst raging along the perimeter of the walls. Even then I was told he was quite mad. He was heavily armed. He was

shouting and yelling and patrolling the place. That was why the troops were frightened of him. He was the boss of that place and was letting everyone know it. When I was in hospital, the soldiers used come in and say how many they had shot. These were Irish troops – Irishmen. They were not like the Sherwood Foresters.

This was virtually the end of Edward Gerrard's involvement in the Rising. He survived the First World War and in 1921, during the War of Independence, served as aide-de-camp to Sir Hugh Jeudwine, commanding officer of the 5th Division. He recorded that

> I rode through Carlow and Kilkenny with the Cavalry Brigade, 10th Hussars, and 12th Lancers, in June and July, 1921. I was actually in Carlow when the Armistice [Truce] came. Every field we got into was made into enclosures by trees cut down. I remember saying to the Major, 'If it is like this within twenty miles of the Curragh, what is it going to be like in Cork?' The Hussars could not see anyone. There was no one to attack. It was all so elusive.

Gerrard stayed in the British army after the formation of the Irish Free State and by 1922 was serving in India with the 95th Battery, 18th Brigade, Royal Field Artillery. He later served in British Somaliland (part of Somalia) and in the mid-1930s, having reached the rank of captain, retired to live in Rathfarnham, Co. Dublin. He died in 1969, aged seventy-seven, and is buried in Cruagh Cemetery, Rockbrook, Co. Dublin.

* * *

Later on during Easter Week the supply situation in Beggarsbush Barracks began to deteriorate again, and everyone inside the barracks was put on half rations. The soldiers of the garrison battalions, the IAVTC men and the recently arrived Sherwood Foresters mounted rotating guard parties around the clock. As recorded in the *Sinn Fein Rebellion Handbook,* 'Sunday [30 April] was not a day of rest. Sniping went on on both sides. Two Services were held in the church. Sergeant Robinson, of A Company [IAVTC], acted as chaplain, and preached a stirring sermon in the morning, taking as his text, "Keep your heads down and your hearts up".'

Sergeant John Lubbock Robinson, the IAVTC's musketry instructor, was a Church of Ireland clergyman. A native of Dublin, he lived with his family in Upper Leeson Street. His mother was English (a daughter of Sir John Lubbock and a sister of the banker and scientist John Lubbock, Lord Avebury); his father, Rev. John Joseph Robinson, was rector of Delgany, Co. Wicklow, and later dean of St Anne's Cathedral, Belfast. His grandfather John Robinson had been the owner of the Dublin *Daily Express.* John Lubbock Robinson's younger brother, David Robinson, who lost an eye while serving with the Canadian army during the First World War, later fought with the IRA during the War of Independence and with the anti-Treaty IRA in the Civil War and was later the first secretary of the Irish Red Cross Society and a Fianna Fáil senator. John Lubbock Robinson was also a cousin of Robert Barton, the Royal Dublin Fusiliers officer who later became a Sinn Féin TD; another cousin was Erskine Childers, who would later be shot in the same barracks by the Free State army.

Before the year ended Rev. John Lubbock Robinson was serving as a chaplain with the Royal Navy. At some point in his later life he was succentor of St Patrick's Cathedral and between 1935 and 1942 was vicar of Holy Trinity Church in Castlemacadam, Co. Wicklow. He was the author of *Handbook to the Cathedral Church of the Holy Trinity, Commonly Called Christ Church, Dublin* (1914) and joint author of 'On the ancient deeds of the Parish of St. John, Dublin, preserved in the Library of Trinity College' (*Proceedings of the Royal Irish Academy,* July 1916). He died in 1957 while living in Co. Wicklow at the age of seventy-seven.

Sergeant John Lubbock Robinson of A Company, 1st (Dublin) Battalion of the IAVTC (Chris Tangoniner)

* * *

The remaining members of the IAVTC who served in Beggarsbush Barracks that have been positively identified ranged in age from twenty-nine to sixty. They included a hardware shopman (shop assistant), a tailor's cutter, a grocer and provision merchant, a broker and commission agent, a bank manager with the Belfast Bank, a brewer's cashier, two brewer's clerks, an insurance clerk, a 'moneyed gentleman', a barrister, a solicitor, a printer (29-year-old Private Robert Harrison from Granard, Co. Longford, who lived in Upper Grand Canal Street, just around the corner from Beggarsbush Barracks), a sanitary engineer, an estate agent, a printing clerk with the Great Northern Railway, a dentist, a grocer's assistant, and a bookseller.

There were two GPO employees in the IAVTC battalion during the Rising: 47-year-old Corporal William Hawkins, originally from Cork, who lived in

Churchill Terrace, a GPO superintendent, and 48-year-old Private Robert Russell, a widower from Ravensdale, Co. Louth, who lived in Appian Way, an overseer at the GPO.

Not all members of the battalion were from Dublin, or indeed from Ireland; these included men from Co. Cork, Athy (Co. Kildare), Passage East (Co. Waterford), Clonmel (Co. Tipperary), Shinrone (Co. Offaly), and Limavady (Co. Derry).

There were also at least nine Englishmen and three Scotsmen. The identified Englishmen were 49-year-old Private Herbert Callear from Barrow, Lancashire, a head brewer; 44-year-old Private James Millard from Birmingham, a stockbroker; 47-year-old Private Walter Neale from Oxford, a bookseller; 54-year-old Private George Newnham from Southsea, Hampshire, a staff officer at the General Register Office; and, from unknown places in England, 39-year-old Platoon-Sergeant George Day, an accountant; 41-year-old Private Samuel Guy, manager of a cycle trade depot; 52-year-old Corporal William Mundy, a carpenter; 48-year-old Section-Commander Thomas Rae, a civil servant; and forty-year-old Private Francis West, a tailor's cutter.

The three identified Scotsmen were 52-year-old Private Robert Cosser from Edinburgh, a tailor's cutter; 52-year-old Platoon-Sergeant William McRae, a painting supplies clerk and former plumber; and 41-year-old Lance-Corporal George Tulloch, a chartered accountant.

By the time the Rising ended the 2nd Garrison Battalion of the Royal Irish Regiment had suffered an additional one man mortally wounded and two more injured. The two injured men were Lance-Corporal James Mangan, a thirty-year-old Dubliner who had been a regular soldier in the Royal Irish Rifles when the war began, had fought in France before the Rising and stayed in the British army after the war, joining the Royal Irish Fusiliers and being awarded the General Service Medal (with Iraq and Northwest Persia clasps) during the early 1920s, and Lance-Sergeant Francis Murphy, who had enlisted in Waterford before the war in the Royal Irish Rifles, served in France before the Rising and became a warrant officer, class 2, before the end of the war.

The last man of the 2nd Garrison Battalion of the Royal Irish Regiment to die as a result of the Rising was Private John Flynn. He was born in Carrick-on-Suir. Co. Tipperary, where he enlisted, and died on 2 June 1916 from wounds received during the Rising. He is buried in Owning Churchyard, Co. Kilkenny.

* * *

While the Battle of Mount Street Bridge was being fought and the siege of Beggarsbush Barracks was in progress, one Irish soldier in the British army was inside the headquarters of the 3rd Battalion of the Irish Volunteers the whole time.

Early on during the Rising eighteen-year-old Cadet George Mackay of the Inns of Court OTC was taken prisoner by the 3rd Battalion of the Irish Volunteers and brought inside Boland's bakery. He was from Mitchelstown, Co. Cork, a solicitor's apprentice and the son of a solicitor. Having attended Ampleforth College in Yorkshire, he joined the Inns of Court OTC in October 1915. Seven months later, on 6 April 1916, he began training with the 7th Officer Cadet Battalion at the Curragh in preparation for receiving a commission. During the Easter period he was on leave in Dublin, when he was captured by the insurgents.

Boland's bakery was coming under heavy fire from British army snipers in Sir Patrick Dun's Hospital; and Commandant Éamon de Valera informed the British army that if the firing continued he would have Mackay shot. This threat seems to have worked.

When the Rising ended and de Valera was forced to capitulate he decided that it would be a good idea to take Cadet Mackay along with him to Sir Patrick Dun's Hospital, where he had decided to surrender; he obviously felt that having an apparent hostage with him would guarantee his safety. The surrender is recorded in the *Sinn Fein Rebellion Handbook*:

> Dr. Myles Keogh, who, in company with Mr. L. G. Redmond-Howard [nephew of John Redmond MP] and others, acted so bravely in rescuing the wounded [during the Battle of Mount Street Bridge], tells of the actual incident of the surrender of De Valera near Ringsend. Dr. Keogh had just returned at half-past twelve from Glasnevin Cemetery, where he conveyed under the Red Cross flag the remains of a civilian who had been fatally wounded at Mount Street Bridge. Dr. Keogh had dismounted from the hearse and entered the hall of Sir Patrick Dun's Hospital, when two men came out of the Poor Law Dispensary opposite, in which the Sinn Feiners were installed. One was a military cadet who had been captured by the Sinn Feiners, the other was the Sinn Fein leader De Valera. 'Hullo!' cried De Valera. 'Who are you?' replied Dr. Myles Keogh. The response was, 'I am De Valera,' from one, and from the other it was: 'I am a prisoner for the last five days. They want to surrender.' De Valera asked permission to use the hospital telephone, in order to communicate with the military authorities. Dr. Keogh sent for Sir Arthur Ball, M.D., who informed De Valera that the telephone communication had been cut off, and suggested that he should proceed to the nearest military position, at the head of Grattan Street, off Lower Mount Street.

Myles Keogh was a dental surgeon and justice of the peace who later witnessed Kevin Barry's statement in Mountjoy Prison before Barry's execution on 1 November 1920. (He made appeals on Barry's behalf, but they came to nothing.) He was later elected to Dáil Éireann, first as an independent and then for Cumann na nGaedheal (later Fine Gael).

George Mackay was arrested along with the Volunteers of the 3rd Battalion who had surrendered and was brought to the RDS grounds at Ballsbridge, where he was kept until his identity could be established. (On his release he could claim to have been held prisoner by both sides during the Rising.) He returned to complete his training at the Curragh and was commissioned as a second-lieutenant in the Royal Flying Corps in early July 1916. By September he had been appointed a flying officer, and he soon travelled overseas to the Western Front. On 18 July 1917, while serving as an observer in No. 55 Squadron, he was injured. In his own words, as recorded in the *Ampleforth Journal* (1918), 'I was crossing the line when I was caught by machine gun fire from the ground. I was hit in the arm, back and chest. I got back safely and landed behind our artillery. I was in two hospitals in France before coming here, and whilst there both hospitals were hit by bombs during air raids, but I escaped further mishap on both occasions.'

After spending five months in hospital Mackay returned to flying duty. Then, on 30 March 1918, he was tried by general court-martial at Aldershot for 'neglecting to obey Training Division Orders [and] ... Conduct to the prejudice of good order and Military discipline, in that he, at Aldershot on the 21st day of February 1918, took a lady passenger in a Government Car [and] ... improperly took a lady passenger for a flight in a Government Aeroplane.' He pleaded not guilty to all charges; he was found guilty of neglecting to obey orders but not guilty of conduct to the prejudice of good order and military discipline. His punishment was light: he was simply reprimanded.

Mackay remained in the Royal Air Force after the war and rose to the rank of major. In 1930 he applied to join the Gold Coast [Ghana] Defence Force. When his application was being considered, letters exchanged between various high-ranking officers mentioned Mackay's court-martial, referring to it as an 'act of impropriety', but they felt this should be forgiven 'on account of his youth' at the time. Mackay's application was approved and he settled in Accra. When the Second World War began he returned to Britain and joined the army, soon being promoted to lieutenant-colonel.

When Éamon de Valera was elected president of Ireland in 1959, George Mackay wrote a letter of congratulation to the man who had held him prisoner in 1916 and at one point had threatened to have him shot. Nine years later George Mackay died in Brighton, Sussex, aged seventy-one.

* * *

With the Rising now over, rebel prisoners were being brought to Beggarsbush Barracks. Pádraig O'Connor, a member of the Irish Volunteers in Celbridge, Co. Kildare, later recalled the situation there.

> 4 o'clock on Saturday we were picked up by a British picket and taken to Beggars Bush Barracks and confined to the guardroom. There was a very heavy guard and the first to be brought to us was the Orderly Officer. I told the Orderly Officer that my address was Inchicore and that we had got lost, and he produced a railway veteran from Inchicore to identify us. The decent man did, although he did not know us – his name was Behan. [This was Private Timothy Behan of the 1st (Dublin) Battalion of the IAVTC,

probably a member of D Company.] We were put in the big cell. Resident there were two prisoners, elderly men of about 35, one with a red moustache, who had fifty rounds of ammunition on him when he was caught, which he said he picked up. The other was a religious maniac. We were later separated and the two other prisoners were put in the small cell and we were left in the big one with two military defaulters.

There was a parade of the garrison about 10 o'clock. There was not more than 150 in the garrison already and they were composed of a very mixed lot of all regiments and Battalions, but the kernel of the garrison seemed to be a small party of the Royal Irish Rifles. They were on quarter rations and they seemed to anticipate an assault on the Barracks and they expected it to last quite a long time. The two defaulters were working in the cook house, so they provided us with food.

On Sunday morning they investigated the cases of all the prisoners. The two men were taken away before us up to 'D' block and later on we were brought up. There were three officers there and they went through the interrogation of the whole story of all our doings. From 'D' block we could see the Clock Tower. The flagstaff had been cut by rifle fire from either Boland's or the Distillery. As a British soldier was repairing the flagstaff with a side of a stretcher he was hit and he fell to the ground. We were released at 6 o'clock that evening. I had considerable difficulty in getting home because they had run a line of sentries all along Baggot Street or the road was manned by British military.

The men of the IAVTC in Beggarsbush Barracks were soon employed as special constables. Twelve officers and 345 other ranks in Dublin were subsequently attached to the DMP, while around the country other IAVTC units performed similar duties, issued with RIC carbines and armbands. They were finally stood down from their police duties on 12 May, the 1st (Dublin) Battalion of the IAVTC having been reviewed by General Sir John Maxwell six days earlier in the grounds of Trinity College.

It would appear that members of the IAVTC were active in places other than Beggarsbush Barracks during the Rising. Father Michael Joseph Curran, secretary to Archbishop Walsh, met a Dr Cox who, while attempting to cross the city, had encountered a Trinity student who was working as a British army intelligence officer. He subsequently noted: 'Later on, I heard of several such intelligence officers, all organised by the military in T.C.D. They included many of those who were members of the organisation nicknamed "Gorgeous Wrecks".' Similarly, Lieutenant Laurence Nugent of K Company, 3rd Battalion, Irish Volunteers recorded that during the Rising 'they occupied Beggars Bush Barracks and Trinity College.'

After surrendering, Captain Frank Henderson and his comrades were marched to the top of Upper Sackville Street, beside the Parnell Monument, and there ordered to pile their weapons. Henderson later recalled:

About this time it was getting dark, and I noticed on the far side of the street a small number of men in a strange uniform which appeared to be of very light green colour. Tom Clarke, who was near me, said that he wondered if these were the men of Casement's Brigade. We had heard rumours during the week that the Germans had landed some troops, and Clarke's remarks left me under the impression that he believed the Germans had succeeded in landing some troops which included the men of Casement's Brigade. At a later period I formed the impression that these men were members of the Local Reserve of old time soldiers whom the British had got together in Dublin, popularly known as the 'Gorgeous Wrecks'.

It is possible also that some IAVTC men were involved in an attempt to press south from Broadstone Railway Station against the Volunteers there early in the Rising. Captain Nicholas Laffan of the 1st Battalion of the Irish Volunteers recorded that 'on Monday evening an armed party of G.Rs. – a British organisation – came down Constitution Hill in single file, but retired quickly when fired on by our men.'

The VTC organisations in Britain began raising funds for the families of the IAVTC men killed or wounded in Dublin, which were gratefully received, as members of the IAVTC were not considered soldiers of the British army but rather civilian members of a volunteer force and so were not at that time entitled to compensation or any financial assistance. However, by June 1916 there was an official move to issue some form of pension, and in late August compensation was finally approved.

The IAVTC itself did not last for much longer, and in November 1916 it was disbanded, never having received the level of recognition or support given to the Central Association of Volunteer Training Corps in England and Wales. At least one new organisation was born out of the disbanded IAVTC when in January 1917 the Kingstown and District VTC became the Soldiers' and Sailors' Guide Corps, formed with the goal of providing support to soldiers and sailors returning to Ireland, especially wounded men, as they arrived at Kingstown (Dún Laoghaire).

The disbanding of the IAVTC meant that two years later, when the war finally ended, they had been all but forgotten. Soon enough the siege of Beggarsbush Barracks disappeared under the shadow of the Battle of Mount Street Bridge, and the ambushing of pro-British volunteers became a footnote in the story of how seventeen insurgents had held off hundreds of English soldiers for several bloody hours. The 'Gorgeous Wrecks' became remembered as an exclusively elderly force, when this was far from true, and the individual character of their companies – IRFU members, railway workers, army veterans and Dublin unionists – was forgotten. But their story is a part of the Rising too, and deserves to be remembered.

8

Dublin University Officer Training Corps
The Defence of Trinity College, Dublin

Q ueen Elizabeth's College of the Holy and Undivided Trinity near Dublin
was established in 1592 by Queen Elizabeth I of England, who granted the
charter and licence for the college. It was constructed where the twelfth-century
Priory of All Hallows had previously stood, on land that had been known as
Hoggen Green or Hogges Green. The institution to which the college belongs is
known as the University of Dublin, or Dublin University; but as it has only one
college – Trinity College – the names of the university and the college are used
almost synonymously.

In 1916 the college was regarded as a unionist institution and was associated in
most people's minds with wealthy Protestants, as the great majority of its students
came from that background. Catholic students had been permitted to attend the
college since 1793, but this was forbidden by the Catholic hierarchy, and until as
late as 1970 Catholic students ran the risk of excommunication if they studied
there. Despite this, in April 1916 there were several Catholic members of Dublin
University Officers' Training Corps (OTC) who would become involved in
defending the college against rebel forces.

Spread over approximately thirty-five acres of central Dublin in 1916 (since
extended to about forty-seven acres), the college is roughly rectangular, 2,000
feet long from west to east and 900 feet from north to south. It is constructed
around a series of quadrangles or squares, with the bulk of the buildings gathered
at the western end, close to College Green. The college contains some of the most
impressive architecture in Dublin, including its oldest building, the Rubrics,
dating from about 1700, and the Old Library, with its world-famous Long Room,
completed in 1732. Most of the other buildings date from the nineteenth century,
including the Bell Tower, the palazzo-style Museum Building, and the neo-
Gothic Graduates' Memorial Building. Occupying the south-east of the grounds
is College Park, a large playing-field.

The famous graduates (and teachers) of the University of Dublin are too numerous to name but include Jonathan Swift (dean of St Patrick's Cathedral as well as the author of *Gulliver's Travels*), the philosophers George Berkeley and Edmund Burke, the writers Oliver Goldsmith and Oscar Wilde, the revolutionary leaders Robert Emmet and Theobald Wolfe Tone, the politician Henry Grattan, the author of *Dracula*, Bram Stoker, the playwrights John Millington Synge and Samuel Beckett, the Ulster unionist leader Edward Carson, and the first president of Ireland, Douglas Hyde.

Despite its situation in the centre of Dublin between several important insurgent headquarters, the Irish Volunteers and their comrades made no attempt during the Easter Rising to occupy Trinity College. As a result their lines of communication – especially those between the GPO and St Stephen's Green – were never secured, while the college gave the British army a perfect base for troops, essentially in the middle of rebel territory, once reinforcements began arriving in the city. Apart from securing the streets and areas immediately surrounding the college, the men (and women) who served inside Trinity College during the Rising kept a vital strategic position open for use by the British army.

The majority of those who made up the garrison of the college during the early period of the Rising were not British army soldiers, however, but members of Dublin University OTC. Officers' Training Corps had been formed in 1908, with close links to the Territorial Force, an army reserve that had also been created that year. In the years immediately preceding the First World War fewer and fewer young men had been joining the regular army seeking to make a career as army officers. The OTCs could give military training to university students in order to prepare them, if they wished to pursue this, for commissioning as army officers. The main purpose of the OTCs, however, was to produce men who could take up a commission at short notice. OTC officers would have Territorial Force commissions, and it was hoped that these arrangements would solve the recent problem of the shortage of officers in the army.

OTC cadets (as members were known) did not take the oath of allegiance, and could not be called up for service in the British army proper. Although OTCs were military organisations, therefore, and controlled by the War Office, individuals would have to enlist in the same way as anyone else for full-time or overseas service. There were various conditions that had to be met, including signing up for at least three years' service, agreeing to attend a certain amount of annual training, and meeting various training standards; but there were advantages also to being a cadet. Various training certificates could be earned, and anyone with these certificates was given preference for appointments in the civil service or colonial service that they might apply for; and service in the OTC was obviously of great benefit to anyone planning for a career in the army.

Dublin University OTC was established in the summer of 1910, with 259 men enlisted by November that year, the membership stabilising at about 400. It consisted of a Fortress Company or engineers' unit, an Infantry Unit of three companies, a Transport and Supply Section that constituted the Army Service Corps unit, and a Field Ambulance Section that made up the OTC's medical unit.

The OTC's headquarters was in the north-eastern corner of the college, consisting of a two-storey building with an adjoining parade ground. Cadets bought their own uniforms; they could also buy a swagger stick (a short cane carried under the arm) and cigarette cases, all with the Dublin University OTC badge on them. Some cadets went so far as to buy specially branded 'Officers' Training Corps' cigarettes and tobacco from Lawlor's of Nassau Street.

Dublin University Officer Training Corps cap badge (Author's Collection)

On 8 July 1911, during King George V's coronation tour of Ireland, the King and Queen visited Trinity College, where 350 members of the OTC formed a guard of honour. Three days later, cadets from Trinity College were also present at the royal review in the Phoenix Park, which involved 12,000 soldiers and 4,000 naval personnel.

When the First World War began, many Trinity students (and some who would soon have become students) began enlisting in large numbers. As a result, while the college had 1,074 students enrolled in 1914, it had only 535 students by November 1918. During this time the OTC also underwent several changes; and while membership had never been restricted to Trinity students – it had always been open to outside 'gentlemen' whom unit commanders and the college authorities were willing to admit – very few non-Trinity students had joined before the war; but from August 1914 onwards the number of non-Trinity students with the OTC increased dramatically.

A Graduate Corps was also formed for graduates of the university or of other universities; but because of the desperate need for new officers for the war effort the OTC began admitting suitable candidates from any and all backgrounds into the main OTC units, resulting in separate formations such as the Graduate Corps being quickly disbanded and its members incorporated in the OTC proper. Furthermore, during wartime many men were admitted to the OTC who were much older than their student counterparts. These cadets, many of them members of the legal profession, were often in their mid to late forties; in 1916 at least two cadets were over the age of sixty.

With the outbreak of war some of the regular British army soldiers who were attached to Dublin University OTC as instructors were also recalled to their units for overseas service, while many OTC members enlisted in order to serve in the war. This left some of the OTC units understaffed and under-equipped, with some of them, in particular the engineer unit and Army Service Corps unit, having their training suspended for a time. For the remaining Infantry Unit and Medical Unit, however, the pace and frequency of training was stepped up, with the Infantry Unit soon training in the digging of trenches as well as holding regular tactical exercises and route marches.

Ultimately, six regular army instructors attached to the OTC, ten OTC officers, three honorary OTC members and 148 cadets were active in helping to defeat the Rising in April 1916, either at Trinity College or in other places in Dublin. In addition, two civilian OTC employees, one a woman, assisted with the defence of the college, along with twenty-one college employees and six more civilian women. Finally, several individual British army and Commonwealth officers and soldiers who were on leave or on sick leave in Dublin made their way to Trinity College, and it is known that seventeen army officers ended up serving alongside the OTC, together with forty-nine other ranks (fourteen of them colonial soldiers, including members of the Australian and New Zealand Army Corps, South Africans and Canadians). At the start of the Rising, however, the entire complex was defended by a total of eight members of the OTC.

On the morning of Monday 24 April one man who would soon become involved in the defence of the college was out walking with a friend. This was Lieutenant Arthur Luce of the 12th Royal Irish Rifles. Thirty-three years old and originally from Gloucester, he had studied divinity at Trinity College between 1901 and 1911 and since 1908 was an ordained Church of Ireland clergyman as well as a former member of Dublin University OTC. He had been granted a commission in 1915 and had landed in France in October that year. However, he was admitted to hospital the following year suffering from measles. He was later evacuated to Ireland, and as soon as he was found fit for home service he was attached to Dublin University OTC.

In October 1965, nearly fifty years after the Rising, Arthur Luce wrote a short account of his experiences. He recalled that

> on Easter Monday morning with my venerable friend and former teacher, Dr. John Gwynn, Regius Professor of Divinity, I attended divine service at Christ Church cathedral. About midday I walked with him from College to Nelson's Pillar, the then terminus for the Clontarf tram. People were looking at my uniform, and over the bridge a man stopped me and said, 'I wouldn't go down there, Sir, if I were you.' It was the first we had heard of any trouble. When I had seen Dr. Gwynn into his tram, I turned to look at the General Post Office, as it then was. The windows were sand-bagged, and rifles looked out. At that moment a small troop of horse cantered up on the far side of the road; rifles rang out, and one or two of the horses and riders fell. I walked back to the College, and there heard the news of the rising.

The commander of the OTC guard that morning was eighteen-year-old Cadet-Sergeant Charles Mein. A native of Scotland, when he was about four years old he had moved with his family to Dublin, where they lived in Upper Leeson Street. Mein also wrote an account of the morning the Rising began. 'At 8a.m. on Easter Monday, April 24th, I took over the guard at Headquarters from Cpl. Matthews with the following cadets: T. [sic] Bridge, W.J. Ferguson, and W. Purcell.' Cadet-Corporal Alfred Mathews ended up, as recorded by Cadet-Sergeant Gerald Keatinge, serving in Portobello Barracks alongside the soldiers of the 3rd Royal Irish Rifles.

Cadet Allman Bridge was a twenty-year-old student, a native of Co. Offaly, who had been attending Trinity College since 1913; his father was a land agent and farmer near Roscrea. Bridge later served in France as a second-lieutenant with the 6th Royal Irish Regiment, landing there in December 1916. After being promoted to captain he was wounded three times before the end of the war and was awarded the Military Cross and bar. He died while living in Bristol in 1939, aged forty-three.

It has not been possible to positively identify Cadet W. J. Ferguson. Cadet William Purcell was a 32-year-old from Ennis, Co. Clare, who worked in banking. He is known to have been commissioned into the South Irish Horse as a second-lieutenant in December 1916.

After taking over the guard with his fellow-cadets, Cadet-Sergeant Mein recorded that 'Miss Webb arrived at about 9a.m. and worked in the office until the late afternoon.' G. V. Webb was a clerk employed by the OTC; she later became a deputy administrator with Queen Mary's Army Auxiliary Corps from March 1919.

The other women involved in the defence of Trinity College were a Mrs Molesworth; Mrs Annie Elizabeth Payne; Mrs Dorothy Hignett (née Rogers), a 43-year-old woman from Rainhill, Lancashire, who lived in Shrewsbury Road with her husband, a civil engineer from England, and their two daughters; Elizabeth 'Elsie' Mahaffy, aged forty-seven, who lived in North Great George's Street, daughter of the provost, John Mahaffy, and died in 1926, aged fifty-seven; Elise Mahaffy's younger sister, Rachel Mahaffy, forty-two at the time of the Rising, who died in 1944, aged seventy; and a Miss Renny-Tailyour. This could be any of the five daughters of Henry Renny-Tailyour, an Englishman who was managing director of the Guinness brewery at the time, also a former colonel of the Royal Engineers. His daughters, all born in England, were 39-year-old Florence, 35-year-old Eleanor, 29-year-old Eileen, 20-year-old Magdalene, and 19-year-old Stella. They all lived with their father in Shrewsbury Road.

Cadet-Sergeant Mein recorded that 'at 9.15 Major Harris arrived and despatched Cadet Ferguson to Pesterres's, Park Gate [Pesterre's riding school in Benburb Street], to bring down his horse. Major Harris left Headquarters at 9.50a.m. Nothing further happened until midday.' Major George Harris was second-in-command and adjutant of Dublin University OTC, as well as commanding officer of the OTC's Infantry Unit. He was also commanding officer of the 1st (Dublin) Battalion of the IAVTC, and in that capacity was about to set off to join the 'Gorgeous Wrecks' for their training exercise at Ticknock.

Word first reached the college that a rebellion had begun when a porter on duty at the front gate, George Crawford, met a friend who was passing, who told him what was happening. It was just after midday. Working near Crawford that morning was Patrick Dowling, a 46-year-old Dubliner who lived with his family in Holles Street and was directly employed by Dublin University OTC as a storeman. Crawford called him over and explained that a rebellion had broken out on the streets of Dublin, and that he had better inform someone in the OTC immediately. Dowling set off towards the OTC headquarters at the eastern end of the college.

Crawford went looking for his superior, the chief steward. This was 69-year-old Joseph Marshall, a native of Co. Laois, a widower who lived in the college with his three adult daughters. Crawford soon found Marshall, and then the two men came into contact with 22-year-old Second-Lieutenant Charles Mullan of the Royal Garrison Artillery. A former Trinity student and member of the OTC, Mullan was from Monkstown, Co. Cork. He was the son of a merchant seaman, Francis Mullan, who was the author of *Brown's Seaman's Wages Calculator* (1908) and who also served throughout the First World War, despite being fifty-seven years old when it began.

Second-Lieutenant Mullan instructed Marshall to order the front gate to be locked. Marshall passed on this order, also instructing the staff to close all the other gates, and then told the porters to call any passing soldiers they might see and bring them into the college for safety. Marshall then decided to arm his staff. However, his choice of weapons would turn out to be particularly ironic.

Many years earlier Joseph Marshall had been a constable in the DMP. At the age of twenty he had served during the Fenian Rising of 1867, after which he had confiscated several pikes that the rebels had been using. These had subsequently been stored in Trinity College; and now, forty-nine years later, Marshall retrieved these weapons and handed them out to his staff. As Marshall put it, they would now be used against the 'Fenians' ideological descendants.' Joseph Marshall survived the Rising and would die in Dublin in 1925, aged seventy-nine.

Later in 1916 Second-Lieutenant Mullan landed in France to join the 140th Siege Battery of the Royal Garrison Artillery on the Western Front. Though severely wounded in 1917, he survived the war and served for a time afterwards in India, where he joined the Indian Civil Service in 1919 and later worked for the civil service in Entebbe, Uganda. After a year as commissioner of income tax in Madras, from 1939 to 1942 he was commissioner of income tax for Bengal, at the end of which time he was made a companion of the Order of the Indian Empire. After a period spent working in Guernsey between 1948 and 1951 he retired, and in 1969 he died in Aldeburgh, Suffolk, aged seventy-six.

* * *

After arriving at the eastern end of the college, Patrick Dowling went inside the OTC headquarters and reported to Cadet-Sergeant Mein. Mein later recorded that 'Patrick Dowling brought in word that the Sinn Feiners had broken out in revolt in the city and were taking possession of public buildings. Patrick Dowling then went away again for further information. On receiving this news I ordered the Lincoln Place Gate to be locked and also the inner gate leading to the parade ground.' The order to close the Lincoln Place gate was received by a porter, William Willmot, a 51-year-old Dubliner who lived in Lincoln Place with his wife and their two sons. Mein continued:

> I then served out to each member of the guard a service rifle and fifty rounds of ball cartridge [live ammunition]. Sentries were posted at the door leading to the College Park, and at the inner Lincoln Place Gate, and at the side door leading to Westland Row. Instructions were issued to each sentry that should an attack in force occur, he was to retire to Headquarters and take up a defensive position already arranged on the balcony. Cpl. Malcolmson, who had arrived about 11a.m. then helped me to remove the service rifles and ammunition to the guard room. Cadet Welland reported himself at 12.20.

Charles Welland was a 61-year-old Church of Ireland clergyman from Co. Cork. Having previously ministered in Killiney and then Stillorgan, he died while living in Devon in 1929, aged seventy-four.

Mein also recorded that 'from midday we distinctly heard heavy firing in the city. About 1.10p.m. Lieut. Waterhouse arrived and inquired what measures had already been taken. Lieut. Waterhouse then went away and returned in about half an hour with a small party and took over the command.'

After the Rising, Cadet-Sergeant Charles Mein was commissioned into the Royal Scots (Lothian Regiment) and landed in France on 25 April 1917, a year after the start of the Easter Rising. By 1922 he was living in Edinburgh, and in 1930 he married in Knaresborough, Yorkshire. He died while living in York in 1967, aged sixty-nine.

Lieutenant Gilbert Waterhouse was twenty-seven, a native of Hipperholme, Yorkshire. A graduate of the Universities of Cambridge and Berlin, he had been an assistant lecturer in English at the University of Leipzig from 1911 to 1914. After a period spent as assistant master of Manchester Grammar School he came to Ireland, where he took up the position of professor of German at Trinity College in 1915. After the Rising he recorded that

> during the morning [of 24 April], while working in my rooms at 34 Trinity College, I heard fairly heavy firing from a southerly direction. Although the sound was remarkably close, I attributed it to the Volunteer Defence Corps, as I knew they were going to manoeuvre in the neighbourhood on that day. When I left my rooms at one o'clock for lunch I met Mr. Johnston, F.T.C.D.

and 2nd Lieut. Glen, R.F.A. [Royal Field Artillery], by the Printing Office
and they asked me if I knew that the Sinn Fein Volunteers were out.

Second-Lieutenant James Glen, a native of Newtown Cunningham, Co. Donegal,
a former Trinity student and OTC member, was a 22-year-old officer with the
Royal Garrison Artillery. He landed in France in May 1918 and after the war stayed
in the army and retired as a captain in 1923.

After discovering that the Rising had begun, Lieutenant Waterhouse

> at once hurried down to the O.T.C. Headquarters and found Cpl. Mein in
> charge with a small guard. I ordered him to close and secure the iron gates
> leading on to the parade ground from the Lincoln Place Gate and to keep a
> sharp look-out in all directions. He reported that the gates had already been
> closed and locked by his orders. I then told him I would return as soon as I
> had changed my clothes. After taking a little lunch in the Common Room
> Club, where I remained about ten minutes, I changed into uniform in my
> room. As I opened my door I found Lieut. Luce, 12th Bn. R. I. [Royal Irish]
> Rifles, who was home on sick leave, knocking at Major Tate's door.

Major Robert Tate, a 44-year-old fellow of Trinity College and commanding
officer of Dublin University OTC since its formation, was the son of a Church of
Ireland clergyman from Co. Leitrim, rector of Rossinver, and a mother from Co.
Monaghan. He was not in Dublin at the time of the Rising.

Arthur Luce had only arrived at Trinity College and was not aware that Major
Tate was away. Lieutenant Waterhouse spoke to Luce and told him that the major
was out of the city, after which, as Waterhouse recorded, 'he asked me whether
we ought to do anything and I said I was going down to Headquarters at once.
On the way we were joined by another officer, whose name I cannot recall, and
by Mr. Canning, F.T.C.D., who offered his services and did good work.' Hugh
Canning, forty-six years old, a lecturer in classics and mental and moral science,
was a native of Castlederg, Co. Tyrone. A former lieutenant in Dublin University
OTC attached to the Infantry Unit, at the time of the Rising he was an honorary
member of the OTC. Waterhouse continued:

> By this time there were about ten men available, including an officer in
> naval uniform. This was about 1.30p.m. After consulting Mr. Luce, I took
> command, armed the men present and others as they arrived, and posted
> additional sentries at the points I considered most vulnerable. I imagined
> that the immediate object of any attack by the rebels would be to seize the
> rifles and bayonets of the Officers' Training Corps and I therefore proceeded
> to put the Headquarters and Parade Ground into a state of defence. I
> ordered all gates opening onto the premises, including those which were
> never used, to be barricaded, and used for this purpose all available waggons

and a large quantity of barrels and railway sleepers. The open doorway by the Gymnasium was likewise barricaded against a possible attack from the direction of the College Park. I then caused all rifles and equipment to be removed from the Armoury, which is on the ground floor, and carried upstairs into the Officers' Room and the Orderly Room, as it was conceivable that the garrison might be forced to evacuate the ground floor in the last resort. I then proceeded to examine my barricades and was thus engaged when Captain Alton arrived about 3 p.m. and took over the command. The garrison numbered by this time about 25 men.

Gilbert Waterhouse would remain in Trinity as professor of German until 1932, after which he took up the same post at Queen's University, Belfast, until 1953. He died in 1977, shortly after his eighty-ninth birthday.

Command of the defences of Trinity College had now passed from Cadet-Sergeant Charles Mein through Lieutenant Gilbert Waterhouse into the hands of an Irishman, Captain Ernest Alton. He was one of the many OTC members who had by now been summoned to Trinity College by despatch riders sent out by Waterhouse to find OTC members at their homes and get them to report to the college immediately.

A native of Marlinstown, near Mullingar, son of a bank official from Co. Limerick and an architect's daughter from Co. Tipperary, 42-year-old Captain Ernest Alton was attached to the OTC's Infantry Unit. He had attended the High School in Dublin before going on to study classics and philosophy in Trinity College; he graduated with honours in 1896 and was made a fellow of the college in 1905. One of the longest-serving members of Dublin University OTC, he was

Captain Ernest Alton, Dublin University OTC
(Bryan Alton)

commissioned as a Territorial Force officer in June 1914 and the following year promoted to captain, at about the same time that he married.

Arthur Luce later recorded that by the time Captain Alton took over command, at about 3 p.m. on 24 April, after the gates were locked,

from this point the College authorities faded out, and soldiers were in command. Gradually a small defence force was built up, and in the early afternoon Captain E.H. Alton arrived, and took command. We were a motley crowd. There were soldiers on leave or holiday, like myself; there were several soldiers who came into College to take refuge from firing in the streets. I remember one or two Australians among them. There were a few Trinity students, a few members of the teaching staff, and several porters and skips [servants], including some veterans of the South African War. They were enrolled *ad hoc,* issued with rifles and ammunition, and, I think, with some sort of badge or armlet. With the O.T.C. detachment our numbers may have reached fifty. We evolved a rough plan of defence and communication. Sentries were posted at the Regent House windows, and outside on the roof, and at other key points. There were snipers in the Nassau Street windows, and crossing the Park was not safe; but we managed to keep up communications with the O.T.C.

In a report about the Rising, Captain Alton wrote:

As it was expected that the enemy would attack us at once, it was decided to concentrate for the present on the O.T.C. Headquarters; a small guard of six men was detailed for the Front Gate. Our numbers about this time (3.30 p.m.) were between twenty and thirty, but in the course of the afternoon we were reinforced by odd numbers of the O.T.C. and Regulars who were unable to rejoin their units. Commissariat was a serious difficulty; but we obtained provisions for the present from the College Co-operative. We could not get in touch with the Irish Command, and it seemed impossible to obtain correct knowledge of the situation.

To some extent we were enlightened by the reports of some students who went out in plain clothes through the city. We found that there was almost no military in Dublin, and that the police had been confined to barracks. The police in Brunswick Street [Pearse Street] sent over some Regulars, three of whom we armed and placed in charge of [i.e. under the charge of] a corporal with instructions to do their best for the Brunswick Street Police Station. By this measure it was hoped to protect in some way the north gate of the College, which was commanded from the barracks.

We succeeded in communicating by means of a despatch rider with Beggars Bush, where we had learned that Major Harris was confined with the G.R.'s. We could not do anything to relieve them, but we were satisfied that they could hold out. Our messenger later on in that evening was able to take a revolver to Major Harris. In the meantime the Headquarters was placed in some sort of security. The position was anything but a desirable one from the point of view of defence. We removed windows, which we filled with sandbags. Firing platforms were constructed along the walls. We organised our guards, firing parties, ambulance units, cooking, fatigue, etc.

There were obvious pros and cons regarding the defence of Trinity College. In the OTC's favour was the fact that, despite the college being encircled by main streets, there were very few entrances. However, the less built-up eastern end of the college, and College Park in particular, were overlooked by buildings in Great Brunswick Street to the north, in Westland Row to the east and in Nassau Street to the south and by the overhead railway line in the north-east corner of the college that ran from the nearby Westland Row Station – already occupied by insurgents – towards Amiens Street Station. If any of these buildings or the railway line were occupied by the insurgents it would make movement in College Park extremely dangerous. The OTC headquarters was at this end of the college. It had no telephone connection with the rest of the college, meaning that runners would be needed to get messages back and forth. Furthermore, the college was not surrounded by walls on all sides; along the southern boundary in Nassau Street the only barrier was a railing that could be easily climbed.

This was the tense situation facing Captain Alton when he took over command of the college's defences. The OTC was concerned that, if the insurgents made a determined effort to occupy the college, they might not be able to resist them for long.

Slowly but surely, however, OTC members, along with British army personnel, made their way into the college. Among the other OTC officers who soon made their way in was Lieutenant Arthur Baker, a 63-year-old dentist who lived in Merrion Square. A fellow of the Royal College of Surgeons and an officer with the OTC's Medical Unit, he had been born around the corner from the college in Dawson Street. He had joined Dublin University OTC in 1914 and was commissioned in January 1916. He was mentioned in despatches for his actions during the Rising and was later promoted to captain, after which he travelled overseas in 1917 and served at the General Hospital at Boulogne before the end of the war. A well-known academic who had a large number of publications to his name, Baker was also an accomplished yachtsman and a skilled cellist, composing tunes for several hymns. He died in 1924, aged seventy-one, from gangrene, having been dean of Dublin Dental Hospital for ten years. He is buried in Mount Jerome Cemetery.

One of the regular British army personnel attached to the OTC as an instructor was forty-year-old Company Sergeant-Major Julius Bosonnet of the West Yorkshire Regiment, a pre-war regular soldier who served in Dublin throughout the Rising. Bosonnet was born in Dublin in 1875. His father, also Julius Bosonnet, was a civil servant, also from Dublin, and his mother, Mary Anne Carter, was born in Kasauli, India; her father was a soldier in the Royal Irish Fusiliers, born in Barbados, who later became superintendent of Dublin Zoo. Julius Bosonnet's paternal grandfather, Jean Bosonnet, was a professor of languages from Taninges in the Haute-Savoie department of France who had come to Ireland in the mid-1830s. Having earlier served in India, Company Sergeant-Major Bosonnet was attached to Dublin University OTC from 1915 or early 1916. He would survive the Rising and the First World War and died in Dublin in 1949, aged seventy-three.

Outside the college the great majority of those who would ultimately become involved in its defence were going about their business on Easter Monday when the Rising began at midday. One of these was Cadet-Sergeant Gerald Fitzgibbon, a 49-year-old barrister from Clondalkin, Co. Dublin, who now lived in Merrion Street. He was a former student of Trinity College and had been called to the bar in 1887. After practising on the Munster Circuit he became a King's counsel (senior counsel) in 1908 and a bencher (senior member) of King's Inns in 1912. Fitzgibbon was descended from a distinguished line of legal professionals: his grandfather, Gerald Fitzgibbon, had been a Queen's counsel and master of the Court of Chancery, while his father, also Gerald Fitzgibbon, had been a Lord Justice of the Court of Appeal. Fitzgibbon's maternal grandfather was John Fitzgerald, Baron Fitzgerald, also a noted judge.

Letters written by Fitzgibbon to a Canadian law professor, William Hume Blake, in the immediate aftermath of the Rising are today held in Trinity College Archives. In one of these letters, dated 10 May 1916, Fitzgibbon explains that his role with the OTC as a cadet-sergeant was instructing recruits in exercises and squad drill. From 1915 there had apparently been a growing concern within the OTC about the Irish Volunteers, and from Christmas that year the OTC had begun mounting a night guard at its headquarters. The reason for this was that the headquarters contained 300 Lee-Enfield rifles and 5,000 rounds of ammunition, and it was thought that such a large cache would be high on any list of rebel priorities if a rebellion did break out. According to Fitzgibbon, the OTC believed that if a rising came it would begin as a night raid on Trinity College, with the objective of taking these weapons and ammunition. As a result the OTC was apparently surprised when the Easter Rising began the way it did, without any attempt to first steal their rifles.

Cadet-Sergeant Fitzgibbon was in his study at home when he heard the news that the Rising had begun; almost certainly, one of the despatch riders sent out of the college had called to his home in Merrion Street. He immediately changed into uniform and headed to the college, as he knew that every man would be needed. On his way, however, he began thinking that he was a fool to go, and every so often he contemplated turning back.

Ultimately, he did not turn back, and when he reached the college, some time during the afternoon, he found that the defenders now included a corporal of the Irish Guards who was home on sick leave and a member of the 5th Royal Irish Lancers who earlier that day had his horse shot from under him in Sackville Street. Fitzgibbon also noted in his letter that many of the soldiers on leave who ended up at the college had been fired on at some point during their journey there, despite all being unarmed.

* * *

Perhaps the most interesting character to become involved in the defence of Trinity College was the professor of geology and mineralogy, John Joly. Now fifty-eight years old, he was born in Hollywood House, the Church of Ireland rectory at Bracknagh, Co. Offaly. His father, who was of French descent, his ancestors having come to Ireland in the late 1700s, was rector of nearby Clonbulloge; his mother was a German countess with Greek, Italian and English ancestors.

Joly did not live in Co. Offaly for very long. His father died shortly after his birth and his mother took the family to Dublin, where he grew up. He attended Rathmines School, where even at that early age he acquire the nickname of 'the Professor' because of his intelligence and his inquisitive mind. In his youth he was known as a keen Alpine climber and cyclist, a photographer, and a capable yachtsman. He recalled in later life that he was one of the first boys to buy a bicycle in Kingstown (Dún Laoghaire), on which he cycled back to his house in Rathmines in great pain, while other

Prof. John Joly (Joly family)

boys threw stones at him along the way, apparently baffled by the sight of the bike.

He entered Trinity College in 1878 and studied physics, chemistry and mineralogy as well as English literature. After graduation he was appointed as assistant to Prof. Crawford, who taught civil engineering, and after Crawford's death in 1887 as assistant to his successor, Prof. Fitzgerald. In 1897, now forty, he became professor of geology, a position he would hold until his death. Joly was a prolific scholar, publishing papers on mineralogy, pure physics, geology (including pioneering work on the age of the Earth), astrophysics (he investigated the 'canals' on Mars), marine navigation (he calculated the age of the oceans from their salt content), and photography, among other things. He also invented the steam calorimeter, the meldometer (for establishing the melting-point of minerals) and other instruments, developed one of the first colour photography systems, and worked with X-rays; he is believed to have taken the first X-ray picture in Ireland, and helped to develop radiotherapy as a treatment for cancer.

In 1920 Joly published *Reminiscences and Anticipations,* one chapter of which is devoted to his experiences during the Rising. He wrote this chapter, he says, when the rebellion was 'not yet one fortnight old.'

At the time of the Rising he was living in Temple Road, Rathmines. Monday 24 April began for Joly with a visit to a sick friend in the city at about midday. During the afternoon he was out enjoying a cycle in the foothills of the Dublin Mountains when, all of a sudden,

> down the Dundrum road a band of the Veteran Volunteers the "G.R.'s" came swinging along at a steady pace, their faces towards the City. An officer on

horseback led them. As he passed us, we recognised in him Major Harris, of the Officers' Training Corps of the University of Dublin. He stopped us. 'Have you heard that the Sinn Feiners have risen in Dublin, and seized the General Post Office and Stephen's Green, and shot several of the police?' The Veterans passed on their way to the City, leaving us bewildered. Some of them were to meet death within an hour of that instant!

After hearing about the Rising from men of the 1st (Dublin) Battalion of the IAVTC – who were unknowingly heading into an ambush in Northumberland Road – Joly cycled directly into Trinity College, arriving there at about 4 p.m. On his way he found that the city was mostly quiet; however, there were groups of people rushing around, 'partly in terror, partly in curiosity,' and occasional firing could be heard.

Joly managed to get inside the college but almost immediately went back out again to scout rebel positions. He thought it would be a good idea to know where the rebels were, and how many of them were in each position, and so he made his way to the GPO and then to St Stephen's Green. While there he came across a crowd of onlookers. One of the men in the crowd pointed out a young-looking rebel in the park. What, the man asked, could this youth possibly know about right and wrong? Finished with his scouting mission, Joly returned to Trinity College and reported to the OTC headquarters.

Like most of those inside the college by this time, Joly was confused by the fact that the insurgents had made no attempt to capture the college, or at the very least the OTC's supply of weapons and ammunition. However, at this early point in the Rising there were fears that they might still attempt a raid against the college, and one of Joly's biggest concerns was that, if they did manage to occupy part of the college, the ensuing fight might result in the destruction of the university's library and archives as well as its historic buildings.

After visiting the provost, 77-year-old John Mahaffy, Joly again left the college. He cycled out the Lincoln Place gate, first making sure there would be a rifle ready for him by the time he got back, and then travelled home to Temple Road to let his housekeeper and gardener know that he was going to join the college garrison for however long the rebellion might last. With that he returned to the college; but, as he later recorded,

the ride in proved an anxious one. I had rather thoughtlessly put on a Swedish leather jacket which bore somewhat the appearance of a uniform. I had a pistol in my pocket [but with only one round]. Several groups of the enemy seemed on the point of challenging me. It was evident I had made myself an object of suspicion, and capture was the best I could hope [for] if I was stopped and searched. But at length I got back to the Lincoln Place gate and was admitted. A message had been got through to Beggar's Bush Barracks, and we knew that help from that quarter was no longer possible. By great good luck eight Anzacs [members of the Australian and New Zealand

Army Corps], who had been on leave in the city, had taken harbourage in the College. The total number of defenders amounted to forty-four.

Prof. Joly arrived back in Trinity College at about 6 p.m. By now sentries had been placed on the college's gates and on various rooftops. Joly soon made his way onto the roof of the physical laboratory to see if it would make a good daytime observation post. While there he received orders to help sandbag the back windows of the OTC headquarters; he found this to be hard work but recorded that the younger OTC members made light work of it.

Finally, towards evening, he had time to practise with his new weapon: a Lee-Enfield rifle. After thirty minutes of instruction under one of the OTC cadets he felt confident enough to fire and reload the rifle if need be. He was not worried too much about accuracy, as he believed that if the insurgents did attack the college most of the fighting would be at close quarters. With this in mind he was glad to get some more ammunition for his pistol – about a dozen rounds. Finally, despite his age, he was placed on sentry duty near the OTC's parade ground, a duty he was happy to perform.

* * *

Captain Ernest Alton later recorded that

> a considerable amount of desultory firing was proceeding, especially from the Nassau Street side, but evidently no serious attack was meditated for the present. When detailing posts for the night – our numbers now were forty-four – it was decided to remain at Headquarters for the present, but to strengthen the guard at the front. We succeeded in placing scouts in one of the Westland Row houses, who kept us informed of the enemy's movements in the Railway Station. His patrols passed frequently along the railway in our rear and an attack from the railway bridge would place us at a serious disadvantage.
>
> In the course of our patrols that evening we became convinced of the grave danger which was incurred in leaving the streets to the enemy without challenge. Dame Street especially seemed to demand protection as large bodies of the enemy were seen marching from Stephen's Green to the north side of the city ... About 7.30 our cooks provided us with a miscellaneous meal of tea, chocolates, and sandwiches. A few obtained bread, but bread was a scarce commodity with us that week. Parties had to remain at the posts all night for we had not enough men to provide relief. The circuit of the College was continually patrolled and a watch was kept on several danger points, such as the lanes in Brunswick Street.

Many years later Rev. Arthur Luce, also writing about the afternoon and evening of 24 April 1916 in Trinity College, recorded that

Soldiers guarding the entrance to Trinity College (Imperial War Museum)

I can see John Joly, F.R.S., who wrote about it in *Blackwood's Magazine* and Hugh Canning, F.T.C.D., marching up and down their respective beats with rifle on shoulder. Dr. L.C. Purser, S.F.T.C.D. [senior fellow of TCD], distinguished classical scholar, braved the dangers of the streets, and repeatedly went in and out of the Nassau Street gate, foraging for provisions. Provost Mahaffy, unruffled though bullets were cracking unpleasantly near, walked up and down the Front Square with me, discussing the situation. It was 'College business as usual' for Dr. Roberts, the Senior Lecturer; he sent to ask me to conduct a viva voce [oral examination] in logic; but I was obliged to decline. It was anti-cyclone weather which, I think, lasted for most of the week. Monday afternoon was hot and cloudless, and dragged slowly by, and still the expected attack did not come. It never came. There were one or two small affairs near the Front Gate. A few wounded men were brought in; and a first aid post was improvised.

The garrison was constantly growing with the arrival of OTC cadets and soldiers on leave. Among those who arrived on the Monday were two first cousins, Cadet-Corporal Charles Freeman, a twenty-year-old student from Dublin who lived in Aylesbury Road, and Cadet Godfrey Goodbody, an eighteen-year-old Dubliner who lived in Talbot Lodge, Blackrock. They were descended from the famous Goodbody Quaker family who had established themselves in Mountmellick, Co. Laois, starting with textile production during the eighteenth century before coming to Clara, Co. Offaly, in 1825, where they ran flour mills and a factory for making jute sacks and cloth that were exported around the world.

Other arrivals that day included Second-Lieutenant Louis Smyth, a 32-year-old OTC member who lived in Tyrconnell Road, Inchicore, who worked as an assistant to Prof. Joly; Second-Lieutenant Lancelot Lloyd-Blood of the 5th Royal Dublin Fusiliers, a twenty-year-old Dubliner who lived in Winton Road, Ranelagh; eighteen-year-old Second-Lieutenant Lawrence Elliott of the same battalion, a native of Belfast; 29-year-old Second-Lieutenant Arnold Earls of the 5th Royal Irish Regiment, from Kilrush, Co. Clare; Captain George Wood of the Royal Army Medical Corps, a 24-year-old from Ballina, Co. Mayo; seventeen-year-old Private Denis Grennell of the 5th Royal Irish Lancers, from North Anne Street; and Gunner Michael Kelledy, a 21-year-old from Dunleer, Co. Louth.

Towards evening Prof. Joly found himself on sentry duty near the OTC's parade ground at the eastern end of Trinity College. The only barrier protecting the eastern boundary of this area was a high wall topped with barbed wire, beyond which was a laneway that ran parallel to Westland Row. However, Joly knew that if any insurgents came down the laneway with the intention of getting into the college grounds, the wall and its barbed wire would not stop them for long. He later recalled:

> My beat extended from the small side door leading into the Chemical Laboratory (and so into the College Park) to the large gate opening near the main Lincoln Place entrance of the College Park. The inner gate, which limited my beat, had for better security been barricaded with a military waggon. Without, the couple of sentries watching the Lincoln Place gate could be observed and were within hail. It was part of my duties to keep in touch with these sentries, and to convey to Headquarters any alarm they might transmit to me. I had also to keep under observation the wall separating this part of the grounds from the lane, and to observe the rear of the houses overlooking the grounds.

By the time the sun set, Joly could hear occasional firing or shouting in the distance. In the eerie darkness he began to wonder if the fighting would soon spread into Trinity College, and whether his relatives and friends were safe out there in the city. He finally decided that 'a sentry must not indulge in imaginings. I endeavoured to banish gloomy forebodings from my mind and to school my attention entirely into the immediate present.'

As people entered and left the college through a side door near Joly's beat – members of the OTC, staff, students, or others who were helping in the defence of the college – Joly had to challenge each one of them to make sure they were not insurgents attempting to slip in or out. Meanwhile he scanned the buildings surrounding the college, trying to spot any possible rebel movement. All of a sudden he noticed something that unnerved him. Near where he was patrolling, two windows of a house in Westland Row – just above him in the darkness – had just been opened. There were no lights on behind the windows, and Joly's immediate fear was that a rebel sniper had spotted him and was preparing to open fire. He had orders not to use his rifle unless he was attacked first; and he also did not want to shoot at an innocent civilian. Slowly, as his eyes began to adjust to the shadows, he realised that there was a man in the window. As soon as the man noticed that Prof. Joly was staring at him, he moved back inside. Joly had no idea who the man was or what he was doing; and so he cautiously continued on his beat.

Just after midnight, as Captain Alton later recorded, the college finally managed to get in touch with the military authorities: 'About 12.30 a.m. on Tuesday it was discovered that our telephone in College was working, and we got in touch with Irish Command. We learned that there was not much prospect of relief for the present, but that the authorities were fully alive to the gravity of the situation.'

After four hours on patrol, during the last two of which he was accompanied by another sentry, Prof. Joly was relieved and went looking for something to eat and drink at the OTC headquarters; he had only had a sandwich to eat all day. In the headquarters' kitchen he found a group of anxious OTC cadets talking in low voices, some asking about what was going on, others giving their opinion on what was happening. Rumours were flying, and most of them were pessimistic. The cadets believed that the rebels had occupied more sites or achieved greater military successes than they had, and they felt that the only hope was to hold on until reinforcements arrived in Dublin from elsewhere. Joly later described the scene:

> On the fire a huge pot holds water for making cocoa and for washing plates. There is bully beef and bread, and there is a sack full of apples. You dip your cup someone else has just been drinking out of into the hot water; you shake a little cocoa powder into it, and you drink when the beverage is cool enough. Nearly everyone smokes, and few smoke anything but cigarettes. I am offered so many that I feel as if we were back in those apostolic days when men had all things in common.

Just as Joly had managed to get himself a cup of cocoa and some bully beef a man appeared at the door and whispered the word 'Alarm!' before rushing off. Everyone in the kitchen quickly made their way outside. While firing could be heard to the west, near College Green, what had brought Joly and his comrades out into the night was a signal from an OTC cadet posted on the roof of a house in Westland Row. This cadet had obviously believed that an attack was coming and had signalled back to someone near the OTC headquarters. Joly felt that this was it: the beginning of the assault against Trinity College; but after fifteen minutes standing outside with rifle in hand, and with patrols having been sent forward to make contact with any possible advancing rebels, the order was given to stand down.

It was decided to relieve the sentries immediately, and so Joly was put back on duty, this time overlooking the laneway that separated the OTC parade ground from Westland Row. At 3:30 a.m. on Tuesday the 25th he was finally relieved and allowed to get some sleep. He returned to the OTC headquarters, where he found that

> those off duty are lying down on the floor of a large store-room almost in darkness, for the light of dawn is as yet but feeble. Alongside forms lying prone, with rolled-up coats for pillows and one blanket serving as mattress and covering, sleep comes soon. But before yielding to oblivion I could not help brief thoughts on matters psychological. I had lately been worrying a good deal about various things, and often dreaded, rather than courted, a comfortable bed. I was now a more contented individual than I had been for weeks.

By this time the garrison had grown to about sixty men. Lieutenant Arthur Luce later wrote that 'it was an anxious night, and there was little sleep. Word of the defence had got round outside, and friends trickled in, and our force grew to a respectable size. All parts of College were patrolled, and sentry posts were visited and relieved. Hot meals were organised, and the kitchen played its part well.'

Unfortunately for Prof. Joly, Tuesday the 25th began for him almost as soon as the previous night had ended. After he had been lying on the storeroom floor for only fifteen minutes, orders were given to evacuate the building and move all supplies and equipment to the western end of the college. Warned that shots were occasionally being fired into College Park from the direction of Nassau Street, the cadets and soldiers piled rifles onto stretchers, took sandbags from the building's windows, and began stacking an Army Service Corps wagon with ammunition, rations, clothing, blankets, cooking equipment, eating

Prof. John Joly in November 1918
(Joly family)

utensils and anything else from the OTC headquarters they thought might be useful. Then, having placed caps on props in some of the windows, to give the impression that the OTC headquarters was still garrisoned, and having locked the building, the men began dragging the wagon past College Park towards the College Green end of the grounds, while others moved alongside carrying stretchers loaded with Lee-Enfield rifles.

By full daylight the men had evacuated their position and had made it safely to the college's main buildings and quadrangles. Here the cadets and soldiers were given new positions to defend, including rooftop positions overlooking College Green and Dame Street. Prof. Joly later recorded that 'one of the great windows on the stairs ascending to the Regent House is assigned to me, in company with Sergeant-Major B [Bosonnet]. These front windows of the College command a view which extends the whole length of Dame Street.' Immediately in front of the college he noted that College Green was completely quiet: no one dared to move across this area.

That morning OTC cadets continued to arrive at the college for duty. One of these was Cadet-Sergeant Robert Tweedy, a 41-year-old electrical engineer who lived in Killiney. Tweedy was born in Redruth in Cornwall and as a young man moved with his family to Dublin; his wife was a native of Co. Louth. On 7 May 1916, a few days after the end of the Rising, Tweedy wrote a letter to his mother, in which he described his experiences during the rebellion.

The whole thing came on us like a thunderbolt on Monday, and out here [Killiney] we could not gauge the seriousness of the rising. As I could not get in on Monday night, I went down to the Dalkey Police Station to see if they wanted special constables, but all the police were in barracks and seemed to be taking matters with a light heart. They assured me that everything would be quiet in the morning, so I went home to bed, and cycled in early on Tuesday morning in mufti, riding quite unconscious of danger down one side of Stephens' Green, which was in the hands of the rebels. I was the only living thing in the street at the time, and I went along slowly to get a good view of the barricades. Rifle firing from the Shelbourne Hotel into the Green, the sight of a dead horse at the corner, and a crowd more or less sheltered in Merrion Row, (which runs into Stephens' Green) gave me the first impression of danger.

There were no police or military to warn people from straying into side places, and I was to see later how idiotically contemptuous of rifle firing the crowd is until someone gets hit, and even then how quickly the effect is overpowered by morbid curiosity. I went straight to Trinity College, and found a dozen others arguing with the porter, who would not budge from his orders to admit no one. Nor would he send a message to head-quarters at the front gate facing College Green, so we gave it up for the time and wandered about for a bit to see how things were looking. There were crowds of foot passengers [pedestrians] quite orderly, and not in the least understanding the situation. Shots were being fired here and there, especially between Dublin Castle and the rebels in the Daily Express building just across the road, but the entire absence of any armed person in the streets produced a feeling of unreality, almost of deliberate drama, in the beholder. For instance, the huge breadth of Sackville Street at the G.P.O. was spanned by a strand or two of barbed wire, and one callow youth in the uniform of the Sinn Fein (pronounced 'Shin Fane') army was leaning on his rifle chatting to a knot of people while keeping the wire inviolate. The windows of the G.P.O. were smashed, mail-bags, office-furniture and miscellanea formed cover for the defenders, and some of these could be seen more or less at their ease looking down upon us, just as if they were awaiting the arrival of some royal procession. In Sackville Street there was no shooting, and the crowd laughed and talked gaily. A few shops had been looted to the last article, but it seems only those into which the rebels had forced an entrance for the purposes of defence. At that time the mob had not taken the initiative.

My friend and I returned to the College gates and obtained admission at about 11 a.m.

OTC cadets and soldiers on leave continued to arrive at the college on Tuesday the 25th. The new arrivals included Captain Algernon Crowe of the 4th Leinster Regiment, a native of Reaskaun, near Ennis, Co. Clare; Second-Lieutenant Joseph O'Dowda-Wade of the 3rd Royal Dublin Fusiliers, from Sandycove, Co. Dublin; Corporal Michael Mulhall of the 4th Royal Dublin Fusiliers, a thirty-year-old Dubliner who lived in Charlemont Street with his wife and three sons; Lance-Corporal William Bickerstaffe from Dunmurry, Co. Antrim, of the 17th Royal Irish Rifles (who was later taken prisoner by the Germans, died in captivity on 1 July 1918, and now lies in Berlin South-Western Cemetery); Private Francis Collins from Dublin of the 2nd Manchester Regiment (killed in action on the Western Front on 23 April 1917 and, with no known grave, now commemorated on the Arras Memorial); Private John Dillon from Great Clarence Street (now Macken Street), who was serving with the 3rd Royal Irish Rifles and later served for a year with the 36th (Ulster) Division; and Private Alfred Reynolds of the 2nd Royal Inniskilling Fusiliers, a native of Dublin.

By mid-morning on Tuesday the defenders were concentrated at the western end of the college and, from their elevated positions, dominated the surrounding streets. The previous order to hold fire unless attacked first was subsequently lifted – possibly because of the number of insurgents now seen moving around in front of the college – and the snipers on the roof now had permission to fire on any rebel targets that presented themselves.

Then, as recorded by Cadet-Sergeant Gerald Fitzgibbon in his letter to William Hume Blake, there was an encounter in front of the college

early on Tuesday morning, just after dawn. Three of their dispatch riders came pelting down on bicycles from Stephen's Green, bringing dispatches to the Post Office, and we had twelve or fifteen men posted in windows and on the roof in front of College. They fired on the cyclists, killed one, wounded another, and the third left his bicycle ... & bolted down a side street. No doubt he went back to his headquarters and told them the College was stuffed with armed men. The booty collected was three bicycles, four rifles, 400 rounds of ammunition, & some dispatches, and of course the corp [corpse].

John Joly also witnessed this event and noted that the marksman was a member of the Australian and New Zealand Army Corps.

> Already before daylight a despatch-rider of the enemy had been brought down by the fire of the Anzacs. It was wonderful shooting. He was one of three who were riding past on bicycles. Four shots were fired. Three found their mark in the head of the unfortunate victim [Fitzgibbon said it was two in the head and one in the lung]. Another of the riders was wounded and escaped on foot. The third abandoned his bicycle and also escaped. This shooting was done by the uncertain light of the electric lamps, and at a high angle downwards from a lofty building. The body was brought in.

The dead man was 22-year-old Gerald Keogh from Ranelagh, a member of the Irish Volunteers. An older brother, J. Augustus Keogh, was an actor and director and then general manager of the Abbey Theatre during 1916, while another older brother, John Keogh, had been killed in action on 25 October 1914 as a private in the 2nd Royal Irish Rifles. (With no known grave, Private John Keogh is commemoration on the Le Touret Memorial.)

After being taken into Trinity College, the body of Gerald Keogh was placed in an empty room for three days. Prof. Joly subsequently wrote:

> Later I saw him. In no irreverent spirit I lifted the face-cloth. He looked quite young; one might almost call him a boy. The handsome waxen face was on one side concealed in blood. Poor boy! What crime was his? That of listening to the insane wickedness and folly preached by those older and who ought to be wiser than he. And was not he, after all, but one of those who carry to its logical conclusion the long crusade against English rule which for generations has kept peace from Irish hearts? More honest than many of his teachers, he has been led into crime and now pays the penalty. It is true, if truth exists at all, that this life cut short and the rancour and bitterness with which it was filled are as much the handiwork of the 'constitutional' agitator as of many who are doomed to summary execution for this night's work. When will England appreciate the Irish temperament? When will our rulers learn that these rash and foolish sons of the Empire require quiet and resolute government, sane education, and protection from the fanatic and the agitator, to whose poison they are at present exposed from their earliest years?

Gerald Keogh was subsequently buried in the college grounds. Showing just how bitter the opinions of some Irishmen were towards the insurgents at the time of the Rising, Cadet-Sergeant Gerald Fitzgibbon wrote: 'We planted him out later on to fertilise the Provost's daffodils.' Volunteer Gerald Keogh was later reburied in Glasnevin Cemetery.

Robert Tweedy
(Tweedy family)

As the day continued, Prof. Joly spent some time on the rooftops with the Australian and New Zealand soldiers and then saw the men of the 5th Royal Dublin Fusiliers rushing out of Dublin Castle in waves to recapture the *Daily Express* offices in Dame Street. Meanwhile the garrison in Trinity College continued to grow, while elsewhere around Dublin other OTC cadets were helping to defeat the Rising.

By late afternoon on Tuesday reinforcements finally arrived at Trinity College when soldiers from the 5th Leinster Regiment, who had recently travelled from the Curragh before advancing to Dublin Castle, arrived at the front gate. The garrison, which had now grown to about 150 cadets and individual soldiers, was extremely relieved to see them. As Robert Tweedy recorded, 'during the afternoon of Tuesday, the first regiment of soldiers arrived from the Curragh and you may imagine that we cheered them as they entered the gates. From that time the College was the scene of the greatest military activity.'

The detachment from the Leinster Regiment brought two machine guns with them, and these were soon set up on the parapet of the college roof. Along with the snipers already on the roof, the machine-gunners now dominated Dame Street, College Green and Westmorland Street and could even fire on rebel positions in Sackville Street. Furthermore, the rebel lines of communication between the GPO and St Stephen's Green were now effectually severed.

The OTC garrison remained on guard duty within the college while the civilians who had been assisting them were redirected to humanitarian work. By the following day, however, Wednesday the 26th, as well as remaining as guards the OTC cadets were being used as local guides, escorts and despatch-riders for the ever-growing number of British army reinforcements arriving at the college, and during their various duties they often came under fire. As Robert Tweedy also recorded, 'the actual defence of the College was left in our hands and we had a strenuous ten days of manning windows and roofs and mounting guards.'

That same day two 9-pounder field guns arrived at Trinity College, and Brigadier-General William Lowe, who had now established his headquarters in the college, soon decided to set them up near the junction of Great Brunswick Street and College Street in order to fire on rebel positions on the other side of the Liffey in and around Sackville Street. However, there was a problem that would first have to be dealt with. The spade-shaped steel plate that fixed a gun in place when it was first fired would not be able to break through the stone sets of the Dublin streets, and these would have to be dug up first at any gun position.

To do this, six OTC cadets volunteered to go outside, dressed as labourers and carrying shovels, picks and crowbars, telling passers-by that they were fixing a faulty gas main that ran into the college. But they found the sets too difficult to dig up: one cadet broke his crowbar, and the team had to request more tools from the college.

Just before 2 p.m. Colonel Portal ordered that, whether the sets had been dug up or not, the two 9-pounders should be put in position and fired. The guns were brought out on horse-drawn limbers from the college into a back street, from where they were dragged into position by OTC cadets, with some Dubliners who offered to help. As they prepared to fire, other men from the 5th Leinster Regiment occupied the buildings along the south quays facing Sackville Street, as well as the roofs of the Lafayette building on the corner of Westmorland Street and D'Olier Street (which housed John Purcell's tobacco shop in 1916) and the Tivoli Theatre at Burgh Quay. Just after 2 p.m. the two 9-pounders opened fire. The force of the first shot broke a large number of the surrounding windows, while men in Trinity College could physically feel the blast.

The two guns began firing shrapnel shells at the insurgents in Kelly's fishing tackle and gun shop on the corner of Bachelor's Walk and Sackville Street before shifting their aim onto other rebel positions along Sackville Street. During the estimated three hours in which the guns were fired, the OTC cadets involved in setting up the guns acted as ammunition-carriers.

By now the OTC garrison in Trinity College had become about as big as it was going to get, though a trickle of individual newcomers was still arriving. One such man was Private James Rogers of the 12th Labour Battalion, Royal Engineers, a native of Trim, Co. Meath. (After transferring to the 711th Company of the Labour Corps and being promoted to lance-corporal, he was killed in action on 19 September 1917 while serving in Salonika. He now lies in Kirechkoi-Hortakoi Military Cemetery.)

That night the first elements of the 59th (2nd North Midland) Division, which had earlier suffered such horrendous casualties in the Battle of Mount Street Bridge, began arriving at Trinity College. The college would soon contain 4,000 troops, together with horses and artillery; it became in effect an island of the British army in the centre of Dublin.

By Thursday the 27th the only rations available in the college were hard biscuit. Meanwhile soldiers could be seen playing football on the college's tennis courts, men were encamped in the quadrangles, and cavalry horses were grazing on the lawns and playing-fields. Prof. Joly recorded: 'Horses tied to the chains which enclosed the grass plots gave the place the appearance of a vast open-air stable or horse fair. Men stood in ranks or sprawled on the pavements or on the doorsteps anywhere sometimes closely packed and fast asleep in every conceivable attitude. Many of them had put in a hard night's work.' Cadet-Sergeant Robert Tweedy later wrote that

> it was not a pleasant experience to do guard duty in the various quads, while rifle and machine gun fire was going on briskly overhead, but I got used to it in a short time. I know now what a diet of bully beef and biscuits means, for we had them three times a day almost the whole time, very rarely seeing bread or butter, and meat of the uncanned variety only once. Even jam was scarce, and after the first two days there were no potatoes. That was nothing, but we all felt that want of sleep, as the garrison was not strong enough to permit a proper system of reliefs. For five nights I slept something less than ten hours, and that of course with all clothes and equipment on. But what is that compared with one spell of duty in the driest trench at the front.

That day one young Irish officer and former OTC cadet was detailed for a mission that would change his life. This was Lieutenant Harold Mooney from Sandymount, a nineteen-year-old officer with the Royal Army Medical Corps. He had attended St Andrew's College in Booterstown and Clonmel Grammar School. His father was a clerk in the Registry of Deeds, and his mother was from Co. Laois. Mooney had applied for a commission in August 1914, aged eighteen at the time, expressing a preference for the Royal Army Medical Corps. He was was a third-year medical student in the Royal College of Surgeons and a cadet in the College of Surgeons OTC, and he noted on his application form that he had recently won a medal and prize for analytical chemistry.

Mooney's application was quickly accepted, and he was speedily commissioned into the Royal Army Medical Corps Special Reserve, where, though he was not yet a doctor, his medical skill would be of great use. He first served on attachment to the Royal Naval Volunteer Reserve as a surgeon sub-lieutenant from August 1915 until April 1916, when he returned to the Royal Army Medical Corps.

On 12 December 1916 Lieutenant Mooney wrote an account of his experiences during the Rising, in which he stated:

> While preparing for my Final Medical Examination which was to have been held in June last, the Rebellion broke out in Dublin on Easter Monday the

24th April. As I live at 51 Sandymount Road, Co. Dublin, which is somewhat convenient to Trinity College, I gained admission in uniform to the College on that day and took an active part in its defence till the following Thursday when two battalions of the South Staffordshire Regiment under Colonel Taylor entered and took up Quarters there. As no Medical Officer was attached to the South Staffords the Colonel requested me to act in that capacity and also to guide them to North King Street where the Sinn Feiners were in strong force, which I accordingly did.

And so it was Dublin-born Harold Mooney who led the men of the 2nd/6th South Staffordshire Regiment to North King Street, where some of them would soon commit one of the most notorious actions of the Rising.

By now the fight against the insurgents was beginning to mentally affect many of the inexperienced Territorial Force soldiers. Fighting an enemy that might wear no uniform and would be able to meld into the civilian population in seconds was beginning to take its toll on the men's psychological state. As John Joly recorded,

> many of these men were very young, and most of them had but recently joined the Colours. Looking now at their sleeping forms and tired faces, one must remember that the work of rounding up and hunting down the Rebels is not only arduous, it is in the highest degree dangerous. Not a few of the officers and men who had been through these nocturnal and diurnal operations told me that they would prefer being at the Front. At the Front, they said, you know the direction from which you may expect a bullet. Here the enemy is all round you. He lurks in dark passages and among chimney-stacks, and when at last you think you have hunted him down, you find yourself in possession of a peaceful citizen who gives some plausible reason for his presence. That these young fellows should be wearied after their night of peril and strenuous exertion was not to be wondered at.

When they reached North King Street the soldiers found themselves facing heavy and determined resistance. Strong barricades and hidden snipers in elevated positions halted their advance and caused many casualties among them. Men were forced to stay indoors and tunnel through walls in order to press forward, while an armoured car was also brought into the fight. But days passed and the insurgents held out; at one point they could even be heard singing defiantly.

At dawn on Saturday the 29th, Lieutenant-Colonel Taylor tried to take a barricade by a foolish frontal assault, which resulted in the men of the attacking force being either killed, wounded or scattered for cover into surrounding buildings.

The soldiers of the South Staffordshire Regiment ultimately pushed the insurgents back in the vicinity of North King Street, but at great cost. And by now they had committed the atrocity that would become known as the North King Street Massacre.

After the Rising the bodies of thirty-year-old Patrick Bealen, a pub foreman, and 44-year-old James Healy, a labourer in Jameson's Distillery, were found buried in the basement of number 177 North King Street; both had been missing since the fighting, and both had died from shock and haemorrhage resulting from bullet wounds. A witness, Mary O'Rourke, later stated that during the fighting in North King Street

they [the soldiers] brought Paddy down into the cellar again and when they brought him into the cellar they were told to shoot him. [She asked the soldier] 'Why couldn't you let him off?' and he said, 'No because the officers have seen him.' The soldier said that the man said his prayers and though he was not of his creed the soldier helped him say his prayers, because he pitied him and then they said they could not shoot him fair-faced. They told him to go down to the foot of the stairs and they let bang at him.

Several more victims soon became apparent. 21-year-old Patrick Lawless, 25-year-old Patrick Hoey, 36-year-old James McCarthy and forty-year-old James Finnigan were all killed at the Louth Dairy, number 27 North King Street; sixteen-year-old Christopher Hickey, 38-year-old Thomas Hickey and 39-year-old Peter Connolly were killed with bayonets in number 170; fifty-year-old Michael Hughes and 56-year-old John Walsh were shot in number 172; 34-year-old Michael Noonan and 51-year-old George Ennis were killed in number 174. (After the soldiers had left, Ennis, who had only been wounded, begged his wife to find them again so that they could put him out of his misery. He died later.) Meanwhile fifty-year-old John Beirnes had been shot and killed in nearby Coleraine Street by fire from a building that was believed to have been occupied by men of the South Staffordshire Regiment.

Altogether, fifteen civilians are believed to have been killed by the men of the 2nd/6th South Staffordshire Regiment on either Friday the 28th or Saturday the 29th. After the Rising there was an official investigation into the killings, but it essentially concluded that in the chaos and madness of the fighting some soldiers *may* have killed innocent civilians. No blame was ever placed on anyone, and no punishments were handed out.

* * *

The fighting in North King Street was certainly vicious and brutal. Lieutenant Harold Mooney of the Royal Army Medical Corps later recorded: 'Between Thursday and Saturday afternoon I medically tended and sent to Hospital from 35 to 40 cases mostly soldiers but also some Sinn Feiners.' Then he himself became one of the casualties.

Unfortunately on the Saturday afternoon, the 29th April, I was myself shot in North King Street by the Sinn Feiners when in the act of crossing a rebel barricade in order to bring in a wounded soldier lying at the other side of it. I was removed to the Dublin Castle Red Cross Hospital where I have since been detained as a patient, and am still [12 December] unable to get off my back, so severely have I been wounded – two bullets having passed through my buttocks, one of which fractured the pelvis and also the left femur in two places.

A medical report of January 1917 recorded the extent of his wounds: 'He suffered from a very severe G.S.W. [gunshot wound]. The bullet entered the head of the left Femur near the left Trochanter [which connects the femur to the hip bone], fracturing the bone and destroying the Trochanter, it passed through the Ischium [lower back part of the hip bone] ... then through the Rectum making two exit wounds near the Right [side of the hip bone] and close to the Anus.' This necessitated an operation to repair the area three weeks later, in which an artificial anus had to be made for him. His bladder had also been damaged.

> There had been severe secondary haemorrhage which was most difficult to control the day after admission. Later extensive bed sores requiring operation supervened. Various sinuses [cavities] formed requiring scraping operation which took place last November and also a large abscess containing 6 oz of puss found in the region of the sinus of which as well as two others is still discharging. His present condition is extremely low ... His condition during the past eight months has been very precarious and at times very critical. His present condition is one of exhaustion and anaemia and debility, he has only just lately been able to leave his bed and sit in a chair for a few minutes. There are still two or three sinuses open, including the operation for Colotomy [cutting through the colon]. His recovery is even now questionable.

At this time Harold Mooney was nineteen years old. Over the following years he was examined by a series of medical boards; by mid-1919 his injuries were still severe. While his bladder and urinary trouble had cleared up, he had frequent attacks of diarrhoea. Sinuses still regularly formed in his abdomen and groin, and each time he had to have a surgical operation to drain them. His left hip had fused, his thigh muscles and left leg (which was now two-and-a-half inches shorter) had wasted away, and he could barely flex his left knee. Cold weather gave him pain, and he had to wear a permanent knee splint as well as a special boot and use crutches or a walking-stick to help him walk. He could not dress himself, or reach his left foot, and he was still undergoing massage treatment and electric therapy in an attempt to repair his muscles.

His wounds ultimately stopped him from qualifying as a doctor, and in June 1917 he was sent to convalesce in Queen Alexandra's Home of Rest for Officers in Glengarriff, Co. Cork, followed by Monkstown House Hospital in Co. Dublin in December that year. He relinquished his commission on 7 April 1918. By July he was living in Dublin Castle Red Cross Hospital, though it was more than two years since he had been wounded, and it would appear that he left this hospital only towards the end of the war, returning to live in Sandymount Road.

Despite his extensive injuries, Harold Mooney still had to earn a living. He managed to find work as a ship's surgeon (though he was not a qualified doctor) aboard the Portuguese steamer *Porto,* having apparently chosen work aboard ship in the hope of improving his health by travelling to warmer climates. After a journey to Russia he took part in a three-month voyage to the Mediterranean. However, he was caught in a vicious circle: he had to earn money, which had led him to get the job aboard the *Porto,* but at the same time had to attend medical boards to have his wound pension renewed. Throughout 1919 he frequently missed these medical boards because of being away at sea, and both he and his parents wrote to the army in an attempt to explain the situation and ask for the medical board to be rearranged for a date when Mooney would be home.

At some point in 1920 Harold Mooney appears to have returned to dry land for a time. In December that year his address was given as Warwick County Asylum in Hatton, Warwickshire; the records do not clarify whether this was as a staff member or a patient. The following year he applied to join the colonial service but was not allowed to do so because he was not a qualified doctor.

In March 1923 Mooney was registered as a patient at Ham Green Hospital in Pill, Somerset. Then, in September 1925, aged twenty-nine, he died in Colombo in Ceylon (Sri Lanka). This may have been during a voyage with the Transportes Marítimos do Estado, the Portuguese shipping company that Mooney is known to have worked for since 1921. The rest of Harold Mooney's short and difficult life had been destroyed by his attempt to save a wounded comrade during the 1916 Rising.

* * *

On the same day that Lieutenant Mooney received his horrific wounds members of the OTC garrison carried another wounded man into the college. This was a British army soldier who had been mortally wounded, and he died shortly afterwards. Private Arthur Smith of the 4th (Queen's Own) Hussars, part of the 10th Reserve Cavalry Regiment, was from Malden, Essex. He had received his injuries in College Green and was brought into Trinity College by four OTC cadets: Cadet-Sergeant Denis McCarthy Mahony, Cadet-Corporal Eric Murray, Cadet Mervyn McBrien and Cadet Frederick Robertson. It was noted that the four OTC cadets brought Private Smith's body into the college grounds while being shot at and while 'under circumstances of special difficulty.'

Cadet-Sergeant Denis McCarthy Mahony was a 61-year-old barrister from Cork who was employed by the Irish Land Commission and lived in Howard Place, Kingstown. Called to the bar in 1878, by 1891 he had been practising at an address in St Stephen's Green, North.

Cadet-Corporal Eric Murray was an eighteen-year-old medical student from Dublin then living in Dundrum. His father was English, the owner of a chemical works, and his mother was from Co. Kildare. Murray later served as a surgeon sub-lieutenant aboard the British sloop *Poppy* from August 1917 until the end of the war. Made a member of the Order of the British Empire in 1953, he died in Clitheroe, Lancashire, in 1958, aged fifty-nine.

Cadet Mervyn McBrien was an eighteen-year-old student from Derrygonnelly, Co. Fermanagh, where his father was a farmer, shopkeeper and merchant.

Cadet Frederick Robertson was a nineteen-year-old medical student from Co. Mayo; he later served as a surgeon sub-lieutenant with the Royal Naval Volunteer Reserve aboard the British destroyer *Medea*.

Private Smith died on the Trinity College cricket pitch, where he was subsequently buried, the burial service presided over by Lieutenant Arthur Luce. He was later reinterred in Grangegorman Military Cemetery, where he now lies, and a memorial plaque was erected in the grounds of Trinity College by the OTC in his honour. (The plaque later degraded, but in November 2009 a service was held to mark the unveiling of a new plaque to Private Smith.)

On Saturday 29 April rebel forces around Dublin began surrendering. The Rising was now coming to an end; and Trinity College, despite the early fears of its OTC and staff, had survived unscathed. The OTC had suffered no casualties, and no precious buildings or manuscripts had been destroyed. The defenders of the college were praised for preventing Grafton Street, Nassau Street, College Green, Dame Street, Westmorland Street and D'Olier Street being taken over or freely used by the insurgents.

It was also noted that Dublin University OTC was the only OTC unit to have defended its own college. Writing eight weeks after the end of the Rising, the editor of the college magazine *TCD* wrote that 'to be called on to defend our University against the attack of Irishmen, to be forced in self-defence to shoot down our countrymen, these are things which even the knowledge of duty well fulfilled cannot render anything but sad and distasteful.'

* * *

One OTC officer at least would be for ever remembered for his activities after the Rising rather than during it. Second-Lieutenant William Wylie, a 34-year-old barrister, was born in Dublin and grew up in Coleraine, Co. Derry, the son of Rev. Robert Wylie from Co. Antrim and a mother from Dublin. William Wylie was made a King's counsel in 1914, only nine years after being called to the bar. During the war he joined Dublin University OTC and was commissioned as an OTC officer in June 1915. During the Rising he was active in Dublin and is known to have guided the 178th Brigade, and specifically the 2nd/7th Battalion and 2nd/8th Battalion of the Sherwood Foresters, to Trinity College after they had been ambushed by the Irish Volunteers during the Battle of Mount Street Bridge. He later took part in the defeat of the Volunteers in Jacob's factory, and was mentioned in despatches for his actions.

After the Rising, Wylie was appointed to prosecute the insurgents at the courts-martial that followed. Despite having fought against them only days before, he insisted that the trials should be carried out fairly. He attempted also to have the insurgents provided with defence counsel, and to have the trials held in public, but he was unsuccessful. He later stated that he was determined to 'bring out every damn thing I could in their favour.'

One way in which Wylie tried to assist the insurgent leaders was by interviewing each one before they appeared in court. This way he could incorporate each man's side of the story in his prosecution. For example, he mentioned that William T. Cosgrave had simply believed he was on a route march before finding himself in the middle of a revolution – which succeeded in gaining Cosgrave a reprieve. However, he had a lasting dislike of Constance Markievicz, and later recalled that during her court-martial

> she curled up completely. 'I am only a woman,' she cried, 'and you cannot shoot a woman. You must not shoot a woman.' She never stopped moaning, the whole time she was in the courtroom ... I think we all felt slightly disgusted ... She had been preaching to a lot of silly boys, death and glory, die for your country, etc., and yet she was literally crawling. I won't say any more, it revolts me still.

Wylie stated privately that he believed that one of the insurgent leaders was an unimportant figure who was not likely to be a problem in the future. This was Éamon de Valera, who would go on to lead republican forces during the War of Independence and the anti-Treaty IRA forces during the Civil War and later become Taoiseach and ultimately president of Ireland.

One Volunteer, William Corrigan, later recorded meeting Wylie during the courts-martial. It was an unusual meeting for both men, as Corrigan – a solicitor – had been a friend and colleague of Wylie before the Rising.

> In the year 1916 I took part in the Insurrection being in the South Dublin Union where I was taken prisoner and after some days was brought before Court Martial. Before going into the room in which the Court Martial took place I was seen by Mr. W.E. Wylie K.C. (afterwards Judge Wylie) who was acting as Prosecutor, he having a Commission and being attached to Dublin University O.T.C. We were both surprised to see each other in our respective capacities. He said to me 'Remember if you do not consider you are being fairly treated you can call on me.' Nothing occurred during my trial excepting a Sergeant who had given evidence in my case wished to amend his evidence. Before he was allowed to do so Mr. Wylie stated to him 'You have finished your evidence and you cannot add to or take from unless it is in favour of the prisoner' and the sergeant was not allowed to give any further evidence. I understand from some of the other prisoners that Mr. Wylie adopted a strict course with all the witnesses of the crown.

By chance one day during the War of Independence, Corrigan met Wylie on Capel Street Bridge in Dublin. The two men spoke, and when Wylie confirmed that he was still working as King's counsel in Dublin, Corrigan replied, 'Well, if Mrs Wylie is anxious, tell her not to worry, for if orders are issued to do you in, I'll probably hear of it and I'll give you a ring.' About this incident Wylie commented in his memoirs, 'What a country!'

Towards the end of the War of Independence, Corrigan and Wylie encountered one another yet again. Wylie was now law adviser to the Lord Lieutenant, Lord French, which made him the senior legal adviser to the British administration in Ireland, while the firm of Corrigan and Corrigan, comprising William Corrigan and his older brother, Michael Corrigan, were advisers to Sinn Féin and Dáil Éireann. The two men ended up working together to arrange for Arthur Griffith to meet the under-secretary for Ireland, Sir John Anderson, to discuss how the war might be ended. This meeting took place in the offices of Corrigan and Corrigan in St Andrew's Street on 26 September 1920 and, though not altogether successful, was one of the first steps leading to the Anglo-Irish Truce of 1921.

During the War of Independence, William Wylie attended a meeting of the British Cabinet in London together with other officials from Dublin Castle. When asked his opinion he stated that he disagreed with Britain's aggressive and repressive policy in Ireland (he had earlier opposed Lloyd George's introduction of martial law in Ireland) and also that once the IRA had been defeated an immediate settlement of the 'Irish question' should be brought about. This prompted Andrew Bonar Law, the future prime minister, to ask if Wylie was a Papist, to which Wylie replied that he was the son of a Presbyterian clergyman.

In March 1921 Wylie withdrew from prosecuting a case against an IRA man, John Joe Madden, who was charged with the murder of Sergeant Philip Brady of the RIC in Lorrha, Co. Tipperary. Though a member of the IRA, Madden had nothing to do with this particular incident, and after it became obvious that witnesses were giving false evidence against him Wylie – disgusted by the attempt at perjury by these witnesses – refused to continue prosecuting and withdrew from the case.

It is known that William Wylie had written an account of his experiences during the Rising but would show it to nobody during his lifetime. He bequeathed it to his daughter, allowing her to use it at her discretion. In 1953 he was interviewed by Colonel John Joyce of the Bureau of Military History, and from this interview Colonel Joyce was later able to write:

> Mr. Wylie stated that he was attached to the Dublin University O.T.C. prior to and during Easter Week. He stated that early in Easter Week he was detailed to guide two British Battalions across Dublin to a British Barracks, and when he was so doing he passed the gates of Dublin Castle where he saw the then Attorney-General and the then Solicitor-General standing. They smiled and waved to him as he was passing and he thinks that it must have

been as a result of this that he was noted and selected for court-martial work immediately afterwards.

Immediately following the Rising he was sent for by General Sir Joseph Byrne (afterwards Commissioner of the D.M.P.) and told that he was to prosecute at the forthcoming trials of the leaders of the insurrection. He asked General Byrne what they were to be charged with and was told that the charges were a matter for him to prepare; that that was his business.

Wylie insisted that the contents of this interview were not to be made public until after his death. Colonel Joyce concluded:

He emphasised that his reason for keeping his statement completely to himself was that he did not want any living person to see it while he was still alive, because, he added, no matter however well disposed he might be, there was always the danger that he might allude to it in some way or another. Even giving it to us under seal, which I had mentioned previously to him, did not seem to satisfy him.

After the War of Independence, William Wylie became a legal adviser to the Provisional Government of Southern Ireland (precursor of the Irish Free State) on the financial clauses of the Anglo-Irish Treaty. Soon afterwards he became a judge of the High Court, and he remained in this position until 1936. He died in 1964, aged eighty-three.

* * *

The Dublin University OTC cadets who were active during the Rising, at Trinity College or elsewhere in Dublin, included some particularly interesting individuals from varied backgrounds, and many would go on to lead fascinating lives after the Rising.

One of these was Cadet Abgar Aidinyantz, a nineteen-year-old medical student, born in Dublin in 1897. His mother, Isabella Read, had been the first woman missionary sent to Iran by the Church Missionary Society, with the support of the Society for Female Education in the East. While teaching there she married Joseph Aidinyantz, an Armenian, headmaster of the School for Persian Boys. The couple later settled in Blackrock, Co. Dublin, where Abgar was born and grew up. His two sisters, Nouhie and Nevarth, would also become well-known missionaries. After the Rising, Aidinyantz completed his medical studies and went on to work as a doctor in England. He died in 1971 in Worthing, Sussex, aged seventy-four.

Cadet Vivian Smythe, twenty-seven years old, from Dublin was an architect who lived in Kenilworth Square. His father, Alfred Smythe, a Dubliner, was an official with the Bank of Ireland and a justice of the peace for the city of Dublin; his mother was from Enniskillen. He had designed a new belfry for Harold's Cross

Second-Lieutenant Ernest Molyneux from
Dunlavin, Co. Wicklow, Royal Flying Corps
(Tom Molyneux)

Church in 1915. He was living in Carlisle in 1917 when he was elected a member of the Architectural Association of Ireland and by the following year had returned to Dublin. Commissioned in the British army in August 1918, just before the end of the war, in 1922 he moved to Southampton and was still living there when he resigned from the Royal Institute of the Architects of Ireland in 1930. In 1948 he founded the Wessex Numismatic Society in Bournemouth, Hampshire, where he died in 1954, aged sixty-five.

Another active cadet was twenty-year-old Henry Maginess from Lisburn. The son of a solicitor, he became a solicitor also. He was the older brother of William Brian Maginess, a future member of the Parliament of Northern Ireland for the Ulster Unionist Party, who also attended Trinity College, Dublin.

Cadet Ernest Molyneux, who was twenty-one in 1916, was a native of Dunlavin, Co. Wicklow, who served during the Rising despite being partially blind. When he was four years old he had eaten the sulphur heads of some matches, which permanently damaged his optic nerves and therefore his eyesight for the rest of his life. As a result he was schooled at home by a governess and only attended the High School, then in Harcourt Street, when he was a teenager. He served in Trinity College during the Rising, where he remembered having 'camped out' on the college's playing fields.

Later in 1916, despite his poor eyesight (or perhaps having been able to hide it), he was commissioned into the Royal Flying Corps as a second-lieutenant and soon began flying combat missions in France. He was wounded twice. The first time he was hit by enemy fire in the left wrist, forcing him to land his plane using only his right hand. His second wounding was more severe. While he was flying a reconnaissance mission over German trench lines his plane was attacked from behind by a German fighter. His observer was mortally wounded, while Molyneux was hit four times in the back. He miraculously managed to land his plane, but the four bullets remained lodged in his back for the rest of his life. He became a lieutenant in the Royal Air Force when that service was formed in April 1918, and after the war he returned to live in his native Dunlavin.

In 1933, on the death of his father, Ernest Molyneux inherited the family home, together with two other farms. All these properties were in debt, however, and

Molyneux was never able to fully clear them. He died in 1956, aged sixty-two, and is buried in St Nicholas' Churchyard, Dunlavin. An oak plate in the nearby church reads: *To the glory of God and in loving memory of Ernest T. Molyneux, the gift of his wife and family, 1957.*

Cadet Theodore Conyngham Kingsmill Moore was a 23-year-old student in Trinity College at the time of the Rising, a native of Dundrum, Co. Dublin. Moore's father, Henry Moore, was a clergyman and principal of the Church of Ireland Training College in Kildare Place, Dublin, while his mother was from Co. Cork. In July 1917, after Theodore Moore obtained his BA, he was commissioned into the Royal Flying Corps. After only a short time on operations, however, he was invalided out in February 1918. He subsequently returned home to Dublin and qualified as a barrister, being called to the bar in 1918, becoming a senior counsel in 1934 and subsequently a bencher of King's Inns in 1941. From 1943 he was a member of Seanad Éireann, representing the University of Dublin, but resigned in 1947 in order to take up the position of a judge of the High Court. In 1951 he became a judge of the Supreme Court, and he held this position until 1966, by which time he was seventy-three years old.

Curiously, Mr Justice Kingsmill Moore was one of two Trinity College veterans of the Rising to write a book about fishing. In 1960 he published *A Man May Fish,* one year after Arthur Luce's *Fishing and Thinking.* He died in Dublin in 1979, aged eighty-five. That year the T. C. Kingsmill Moore Prize was established by the Trinity College (Dublin) Trust to commemorate the long service of Mr Justice Kingsmill Moore as chairman and trustee. The prize is awarded to law students who obtain the highest marks in the junior sophister (third-year) examination in law.

Cadet Louis Witz was linked to one of Dublin's most famous employers, Arthur Guinness, Son and Company (Dublin) Ltd. A 24-year-old Dubliner and former medical student, Witz lived in Kenilworth Square in Harold's Cross, son of the manager of the brewery's cooperage department, Louis Alex Witz, who had been born in the West Indies. Louis Jnr had also worked for Guinness's brewery and before the war was employed in the company's Liverpool trade store. When the war came he enlisted as a private in the 23rd (2nd Football) Battalion of the Middlesex Regiment before becoming an OTC cadet in Trinity College, Dublin.

During the 1920s Louis Witz appears to have lived in Canada for several years at a time, often working in farming, before settling in England. He died in 1976, aged eighty-four, while living in the Chiltern and Beaconsfield District of Buckinghamshire. Today his name is commemorated on the memorial in Rathfarnham War Memorial Hall.

* * *

Several sets of relatives served in Dublin University OTC during the Rising. 44-year-old Company Sergeant-Major George Howell of the Royal Army Medical Corps was one of the regular army instructors attached to the OTC. Born in Hong

Kong, he was based in the Curragh Camp not long after the end of the Anglo-Boer War. By the time of the Rising he lived in St Clare's Terrace in Harold's Cross. Company Sergeant-Major Howell's son was Cadet-Sergeant Reuben Howell of Dublin University OTC. Though born in Aldershot, Hampshire, Reuben had lived in Ireland since at least the age of six, and by 1916 he was seventeen years old. He served throughout the Easter Rising, and in August 1917 he was commissioned into the reserve 11th Royal Dublin Fusiliers. He was subsequently attached to the 2nd Battalion and sent to join it on the Western Front. Days after the start of the German Spring Offensive he was mortally wounded and on 29 March 1918 succumbed to his wounds. He was nineteen years old and now lies in St Sever Cemetery, Rouen.

After the war Company Sergeant-Major George Howell worked as a secretary for a time before emigrating to Canada with his wife and remaining family in 1921. He intended to become a farmer, already having at least one son working and farming in Canada, and soon settled near Assiniboia, Saskatchewan. He died while living in Carievale, Saskatchewan.

Cadet-Sergeant Arthur Sharley was an Englishman who lived in Albert Villas, Drumcondra. His step-son (his wife's son from a previous marriage) was sixteen-year-old Cadet Louis Fenelon, born in Newry (his father had been an RIC constable from Co. Carlow). Both men were active during the Rising. The young Louis had attended Pearse's school, St Enda's; his name appears on the school roll for the year 1908/09, with Louis in third class at the time. He had later attended the Patrician College in Mountrath, Co. Laois, before entering Trinity College.

After the Rising, Louis Fenelon was commissioned as a second-lieutenant in the Royal Flying Corps. When the war ended he became a chiropodist, living in London for many years, and then in 1954 he emigrated with his wife to New Zealand, living in Wellington, where he died in 1963, aged sixty-three. His step-father, Arthur Sharley, is known to have had a dentistry practice in Upper Mount Street, Dublin, during the 1930s and 40s. He died in Dublin in 1949, aged seventy-three.

Cadet Quartermaster-Sergeant Frederick Price, a 46-year-old barrister who lived in Upper Fitzwilliam Street, was active in Dublin during the Rising, as was his nephew Cadet James Price, who was not quite seventeen at the time. (Frederick Price was a brother of Major Ivor Price, head of the RIC's Crimes Special Branch before the war and now director of military intelligence for Irish Command, while Cadet James Price was Major Price's son.)

After the Rising, Frederick Price was treasurer of King's Inns from 1932 to 1934, while James Price – who was born in Athboy, Co. Meath, while his father was stationed there as a district inspector – became joint owner of a poultry farm, Hills Place Farm, at Blackboys, Sussex; in 1924 his partner left the business and James Price continued trading under his own name. He died in 1971, aged seventy-one, while living in Eastbourne, Sussex.

James Price was certainly not the only teenage cadet active in Dublin during the Rising. Cadet Gerald Bowesman was a seventeen-year-old student from Dublin, living in Edenvale Road in Ranelagh. (He died in Worthing, Sussex, in 1961, aged sixty-two.) Another seventeen-year-old student, Cadet Charles Lynn-Grant from Dublin, who lived in Belgrave Road, Rathmines, also served during the Rising. He was commissioned into the Royal Irish Fusiliers in September 1917, served on attachment with the Northumberland Fusiliers in the trenches, and after the war emigrated to Canada, living in Saskatchewan. He joined the Canadian army and by 1951, now aged fifty-two, was a lieutenant-colonel in the Royal Canadian Armoured Corps.

Cadet Kenneth Switzer was another teenage OTC cadet active in Dublin during the Rising. Seventeen years old at the time, he had grown up in Moyvalley House on the banks of the Royal Canal near Moyvalley, Co. Kildare. His mother was from Dublin, and his father was a farmer and director of a mercantile company who was born in India, where Kenneth's grandfather had been serving as a surgeon-major with the Bengal Army. Moyvalley House had come into the possession of the Switzer family in 1848 when Kenneth's great-grandfather, John Wright Switzer from Newpark, Co. Tipperary, bought it and turned it into a hydropathic establishment, with spas, steam rooms, and bath houses. When this establishment closed the family retained Moyvalley House as their home until it was sold in 1912. In 1974 it was demolished to make way for the realigning of the nearby main road.

Cadet Kenneth Switzer attended Baymount Castle Boarding School in Dollymount before becoming a student in Trinity College. After the war he worked with Glyn, Mills and Company's bank in London. He made several trips to Africa in the decades that followed, often living in Nyasaland (Malawi) for long periods. He died in Okehampton, Devon, in 1992, aged ninety-three.

Perhaps the youngest of Trinity College's OTC cadets to be active in Dublin during the Rising was sixteen-year-old Cadet-Piper Arthur Hendy. Born near Listowel, Co. Kerry, he was the son of a bank messenger and former RIC sergeant from Co. Wicklow and a mother from Tarbert, Co. Kerry. At the time of the Rising the Hendys lived in Trinity Street, Dublin. In April 1919 Arthur was commissioned into the Indian army and posted to the 57th Regiment (Wilde's Rifles) of the Frontier Force. Promoted to lieutenant in 1920, from 1922 he served in the newly created 13th Frontier Force Rifles but by 1923 was serving with the South Waziristan Scouts. He retired from the army in November 1923 and died in Hitchin, Hertfordshire, in 1959, aged fifty-nine.

* * *

Though several members of Dublin University OTC were still teenagers when the Rising began, others who helped to defeat the rebellion, either inside the college or elsewhere in Dublin, were much older than the typical student.

Cadet-Sergeant Charles Kough was a 36-year-old barrister and former Trinity student who lived in Morehampton Terrace in Donnybrook. Though he was born in India, his father (who worked for the Indian Civil Service) was from Co. Wexford; his mother was from Co. Down.

His fellow-barrister Cadet-Sergeant Cyril Dickenson, also a former Trinity student, was a Dubliner who lived in Kimmage; he is known to have been with the motor service during the First World War. He died in Okehampton, Devon, in 1955, aged seventy-eight.

Cadet Walter Leslie was the same age as Cyril Dickenson: thirty-nine. He was a creamery manager from Tarbert, Co. Kerry, and his family lived in Tarbert House. Walter's father was deputy lieutenant for Co. Kerry. Walter Leslie had previously served as a private in the Army Service Corps, having enlisted in June 1915, and in August 1916 he was commissioned as a second-lieutenant. He landed in France in September 1916 and in 1918 was promoted to lieutenant. By 1920 he is known to have been living at Oak Park, Tralee.

Cadet John Moore, a Dubliner, was forty years old and lived with his wife in Dartmouth Square in Ranelagh. A member of the Dublin Stock Exchange, he was the son of a drapery merchant and justice of the peace from Bailieborough, Co. Cavan, who also owned a 'fancy goods' warehouse in South Anne Street, Dublin, and was a partner in Switzer's of Grafton Street (owned by the family of Cadet Kenneth Switzer, mentioned earlier). John Moore survived the Rising and ultimately died in Dublin in 1956, aged eighty.

Cadet William Boxwell, a doctor who lived in Harcourt Street, was a year older than John Moore, at forty-one. He was born in India; his mother was from Dublin, and his father's family were linked to Butlerstown, Co. Wexford. After the war, now professor of pathology at the College of Surgeons, he found himself struggling to cope with the 'Spanish flu' epidemic.

Cadet Albert Bolton, a 42-year-old barrister, was born in Rathmines and was now living in Esplanade Road, Bray, with his brother and three sisters. (This brother, Richard Denne Bolton, was the man who had attempted to raise a Rathmines VTC after the outbreak of the war.) The Boltons' father, Samuel Bolton, had been one of the leading builders in Dublin. He had started his business in the 1850s in South Richmond Street and had later purchased a timber and stone yard on the South Circular Road and an iron works at Portobello Harbour. As well as becoming a justice of the peace for Co. Dublin, a member of Rathmines and Rathgar Township Commission and chairman of its waterworks committee (which involved him in the Glenasmole water supply scheme), by 1883 Samuel Bolton had been described as a 'builder and contractor, proprietor of sawing, planing and moulding mills, joinery, and iron works, slate, brick, tile, and cement merchant, manufacturing locksmith, fire-proof safe maker, gas fitter, painter, plumber, and hot water apparatus fitter.'

In addition to his work as a barrister Albert Bolton went on to write *The Housing of the Working Classes (Ireland) Acts, 1890 to 1908* (1914), *The Courts*

(Emergency Powers) Acts, 1914 to 1917 (1918) and *Criminal Injuries (Ireland) Acts, 1919 and 1920* (1921). He died in 1947, aged seventy-three, while living in Co. Wicklow.

Cadet-Corporal Charles Ball, forty-four years old, was born in Harrogate, Yorkshire, to a father from Delgany, Co. Wicklow, and a mother from Bath, Somerset. His parents had married in India; Ball's father – a disabled man who had originally been a teacher of shorthand writing – had later become a clergyman and teacher of languages. By 1901 Charles Ball had qualified as a doctor and was working in the Royal City of Dublin Hospital (Baggot Street Hospital) and by 1911 was living in Merrion Road with his wife and son.

After being active in OTC uniform during the Rising, Ball became best known for a notorious event that took place twenty years later. In May 1936 Ball's son Edward, an actor, who had been born on 9 May 1916, a few days after the end of the Rising, was convicted of murdering his mother in their home at St Helen's Road in Booterstown. Lavinia 'Vera' Ball had been suffering from dementia for many years, and it was suggested that Edward had no longer been able to cope with his mother's condition. The fact that she had recently rejected his proposal that she would finance his tour with the Gate Theatre to Egypt was also mentioned.

Edward Ball was accused of killing his mother with an axe, then driving her body to Shankill, Co. Dublin, and dumping it in the sea. The body was never recovered. His father, Charles Ball, was called as a witness for the defence. Edward Ball was found guilty but insane and was committed to the Central Criminal Lunatic Asylum (now the Central Mental Hospital) in Dundrum, Co. Dublin, where he remained for the next fourteen years before being released in 1950. Charles Ball died in the Burlington Clinic, Dublin, in 1957, aged eighty-five.

* * *

Some of the oldest of Trinity College's OTC cadets at the time of the Rising were three men aged forty-nine. Cadet Charles Chute was a barrister and journalist from Dingle, Co. Kerry, who lived in Belleville Avenue, Rathgar. He died in 1939, aged seventy-two, while living in Tynemouth, Northumberland.

Another 49-year-old cadet was John Russell, a native of Dublin and a barrister who lived in Mountjoy Square. He also died in 1939, aged seventy-two.

Then there was 49-year-old Cadet John Johnston, a businessman whose family were the Johnstons of Johnston, Mooney and O'Brien, the well-known bakery company established in 1835 and that still exists today. Born in the Dundrum-Glencullen area of Co. Dublin in 1866, John Johnston had designed and patented a new type of flour and grain chute in 1893 while working with his family company. By the time of the Rising, however, he was concentrating on dealing in corn and coal. He lived with his family in Percy Place, which placed them in the middle of the Battle of Mount Street Bridge.

On Monday 24 April, Johnston had been cycling in the city with his seventeen-year-old daughter when they heard word that the rebellion had begun. Johnston soon joined the garrison inside Trinity College, while his daughter travelled on to Percy Place. Here, with her sisters and mother, she found herself having to take cover in an outbuilding at the end of the garden when the battle at Mount Street Bridge began. When the Johnstons later returned to their house they found that all the windows had been shattered and the front of the house was pockmarked by bullets. None of the family were hurt during the Rising, and John Johnston ultimately died in Dublin in 1936, aged seventy.

* * *

Another category of OTC cadets worth mentioning is those who were Catholics. Trinity College was an almost exclusively Protestant institution in the early twentieth century, and the Catholic hierarchy did not permit Catholics to attend it until 1970 (though many did so nevertheless).

Eighteen-year-old Cadet Robert Corbett, a native of Dublin, lived in Upper George's Street in Kingstown. The son of a surgeon from Co. Laois and a mother from Co. Kerry, he had entered Trinity College in 1915 to study medicine. After the Rising he served with the Royal Naval Volunteer Reserve as a surgeon-probationer (a position that allowed medical students to practise during wartime), and in September 1917 he was wounded while serving aboard the destroyer *Raider*. He later completed his studies and qualified as a doctor in 1921.

Seventeen-year-old Cadet Frederick Hoey, also from Dublin, served in OTC uniform during the Rising. Both his parents were from Dublin, and his father was a solicitor. Frederick Hoey had entered Trinity College in 1914 and in November 1916 was commissioned into the Royal Flying Corps as a second-lieutenant. Shortly afterwards, in June 1917, he was killed in a training accident in England, aged eighteen at the time. He is buried in Yatesbury (All Saints') Churchyard, Wiltshire, and his name is also commemorated on the Great War Memorial in St Mary's Church, Haddington Road, Dublin.

Cadet Norbert Murphy, twenty-nine years old, was linked to another famous commercial institution, the Murphy brewing and distilling family of Co. Cork. James Murphy and Company and the Midleton Distillery had been founded by his great-uncles James, Jeremiah and Daniel Murphy. The site of the distillery was an old army barracks, previously a woollen mill. Norbert's second cousin James Jeremiah Murphy later branched off and built the Lady's Well Brewery in Cork (in a district named from a former well). When the brewery opened, in 1856, James J. Murphy and Company was founded, and it began producing the now-famous Murphy's stout. The company is now owned by Heineken.

Norbert's strand of the Murphy family had stayed with the distillery business. His father, Nicholas Murphy, was director of James Murphy and Company and the Midleton Distillery during the second half of the nineteenth century. In 1912 the whiskey produced in the Midleton Distillery was renamed Paddy, in honour of one of the company's famous salesmen, Paddy Flaherty. In 1867 the company merged with four Cork distilleries – Watercourse, John Street, North Mall and the

Green – to form Cork Distilleries Company. Like Guinness in Dublin, after the outbreak of the First World War the company, along with other members of the Cork Employers' Federation, promised employees who enlisted that they would have their jobs back at the end of the war. It is known that eighteen immediately took up the offer (one of whom was only sixteen); ten of the eighteen did not survive the war.

By 1916 Norbert Murphy, who had previously attended the Oratory School in London and then Trinity College, was working as a distiller. He was active as a cadet with the OTC in Dublin during the Rising and by December 1916 had been commissioned into the South Irish Horse. He served in this unit, and later in the 7th Royal Irish Regiment, until the end of the war, after which he returned to his work as a distiller. He later had two sons and went on to become director of Cork Distilleries Company. In 1966 one of his sons, Ronald Philip Murphy, took over this position. That year Cork Distilleries Company merged with John Power and Son and John Jameson and Son to form Irish Distillers, with Ronald Philip Murphy becoming the first director of the new company. In 1972 the last independent Irish whiskey producer, Bushmills, joined the Irish Distillers group, giving the company control of all whiskey production in Ireland. The group is now owned by Pernod Ricard.

Norbert Murphy, who died in 1973, aged eighty-six, was also linked to a well-known republican. His sister Muriel was married to Terence MacSwiney, a member of Sinn Féin and Lord Mayor of Cork who was arrested by British forces for sedition during the War of Independence and died after seventy-four days on hunger strike in London on 25 October 1920.

Another Catholic cadet, who went on to have a distinguished military career, was nineteen-year-old Cadet-Corporal William Craig-McFeely from Bundoran, Co. Donegal. Craig-McFeely's father was a surgeon from Derry, while his mother (who would later die in Liverpool in 1918 of 'Spanish flu') was a Church of Ireland woman from Belfast. William, who was known as a devout Catholic, was educated at Ushaw College in Durham and St Francis' College in Liverpool before entering Trinity College, Dublin, to study medicine, and he was still a student there when the Rising began.

In September that year he was commissioned into the Royal Munster Fusiliers. He served with the 2nd Battalion on the Western Front from 20 January 1917 until he was wounded by enemy fire on 10 November and evacuated home. He stayed in the army until April 1920, when, now a lieutenant, he relinquished his commission. He returned to Trinity, this time to study law, and graduated in 1922.

He then decided to return to the army and in October 1922 was commissioned again as a lieutenant in the Royal Army Service Corps. Two years later he travelled to India, and he went on to serve on the Northwest Frontier from 1924 to 1928, during which time he was promoted to captain. He served in China until 1932 before returning to Britain. He was promoted to major in 1934 and served in Aldershot before being posted to Jersey between 1937 and 1939. While there he was promoted to lieutenant-colonel and also became commandant of Jersey Boys' School.

During the Second World War, Lieutenant-Colonel Craig-McFeely served in France in 1939 and 1940. He was promoted to colonel in 1943 and in April 1944 was appointed assistant director in the Department of the Quartermaster-General and assistant adjutant-general. From 1946 to 1950 Craig-McFeely was aide-de-camp to King George VI, after which time he retired from the army.

A bachelor, William Craig-McFeely raised his nephew Gerald Craig-McFeely after the death of Gerald's father, Cecil, in 1948. Gerald's daughter Julia later recalled: 'My mother is a physio [physiotherapist], and the most spectacular thing I remember about him was seeing my mother giving him a treatment for arthritis and seeing his back, which had numerous bullet-hole scars on it. I think he took something like sixteen bullets at Passchendaele, and it is incredible to think that he survived so many body shots.'

Following his distinguished career, Craig-McFeely returned to his native Ireland. He lived at Ballybrack, Co. Dublin, near Killiney beach, and went swimming there every morning, regardless of the season. In the late 1970s he went to England to live with another nephew, Michael, at his home in Tisbury, Wiltshire, where he died in 1988. He was ninety-two years old.

Cadet-Corporal Bernard Peirce of Dublin University OTC was born in Cape Town, South Africa, son of a commercial traveller from Co. Offaly and a mother from Dublin. He grew up in Tullamore, and at the time of the Rising he lived in Upper Pembroke Street, Dublin. In November 1916 he was commissioned into the 5th Royal Dublin Fusiliers. He survived the war, and in 1925 he travelled to India with his wife and son to become a tea planter with the Jokai Tea Company. He died in India in 1949, aged fifty-one, while working on the Kattialli Tea Estate in Assam.

Twenty-four-year-old Cadet-Corporal Richard Scallan from Dublin survived the Rising but did not survive the war. The son of a solicitor from Dublin and a mother from Co. Westmeath, Scallan lived in Dundrum at the time of the Rising. He was commissioned into the Royal Garrison Artillery and in March 1917 landed in France. On 31 May 1918, while serving on attachment to the Labour Corps as a prisoner escort officer with the 10th Prisoner of War Company, he was accidentally killed, aged twenty-seven; the details of his death are unknown. He now lies in Talence Communal Cemetery Extension.

Another OTC cadet at the time of the Rising was later believed to be a member of the IRB. 23-year-old Paul Guéret from Sandymount, Dublin, was the son of a mother from Dublin and a father from Paris. Paul Guéret Snr, formerly a commercial traveller, had emigrated to Ireland with his own parents in 1870, when he was fourteen. The family had a picture frame and print business in Paris, and the Dublin branch was doing so well that they decided to move to Ireland. Here they ran Maison Français, which also sold French religious artefacts. Paul Guéret Snr became a founder of the Sandymount Opera Company and was also a member of the Irish Party who tried on several occasions to get elected for South Dublin. In 1898 Paul Guéret was living at 145 Tritonville Road, and he would not be the house's only Easter Rising veteran: in 1911 Arthur Shea, a Bank of Ireland official who served during the Rising in the 1st (Dublin) Battalion of the IAVTC, also lived there.

Paul Guéret Jnr was educated at Castleknock College and then at Skerry's Civil Service and Commercial College in St Stephen's Green. By 1911 he was working as a clerk in a warehouse. In December 1914, now working in the income tax department at the Custom House, he attempted to obtain a commission in the British army. He was unsuccessful, because of a lack of vacancies, and he applied again in October 1915, with the same result. In February 1916, now working in the GPO Engineering Department in Aldborough House and serving as a cadet with Dublin University OTC, he applied for a third time. This time he was accepted, and he was due to begin his training to become an officer in early July.

In the meantime the Easter Rising had begun in Dublin, and Cadet Paul Guéret is named as one of the cadets who was active in Dublin, either at Trinity College or elsewhere in the city. In November 1916 he was commissioned, and in January 1917 he joined the 8th Royal Dublin Fusiliers in the trenches, having left for the front following an argument with his girl-friend. By mid-April phlebitis (inflammation of the veins) was diagnosed in his right leg (it had been noted in his enlistment medical examination that he suffered from varicose veins), and he was evacuated home.

During this period of leave, as recorded by Guéret's grandson, also Paul Guéret,

> he went to stay with his parents in Sandymount. His brother Joseph was away. On his third day back in the early morning the house was visited by [British army soldiers] and Paul was taken into custody by them and brought to Beggars Bush Barracks under suspicion of being an active member of the IRB. This despite the shouts and screams of his mother at the soldiers, that they'd be sorry as he was just back from the front. Two days later he was released and driven back to his home by Rolls Royce! That night he was disturbed and woken from his sleep by his sister, who brought him to the back garden, where later that night he met his brother Joseph. Joseph at the time was a 'runner' for the IRB and was himself on the run trying to avoid captivity.

The soldiers had clearly mistaken Second-Lieutenant Paul Guéret for his brother. When Guéret finally returned to the trenches in August 1917 he was posted to the 11th Royal Welsh Fusiliers. A month later he was found to have difficulty walking, or even staying on his feet, because of his varicose veins, and he was ultimately forced to transfer to a prisoner-of-war company in the Labour Corps.

Shortly afterwards he became engaged to Julia Fitzharris during a period of leave; and when the German prisoners of war under his charge found out they began making 'trench art' wedding presents for him, including vases, ornaments, cigarette boxes and carvings made from wood and brass shell and bullet casings. In March 1918 he was declared fit to rejoin the infantry and so returned to the Royal Dublin Fusiliers, soon joining the 1st Battalion in the trenches as a lieutenant. It was a bad time for his old regiment, as only two days later, on 1 May, the 1st Battalion was involved in a battle at Vieux-Berquin, where it was heavily shelled and gassed. The following month it was involved in another engagement at Petit Bois. But Paul Guéret survived the war, after which he returned to serving in the Labour Corps. He married his fiancée in Dublin during a period of leave on 23 April 1919 (one of the wedding presents was a brass casket made at Ypres by fellow-officers of his battalion), and was then demobilised in November that year. Guéret and his wife settled in Sandymount and went on to have four children, while Paul became a clerk in the High Court. He died of tuberculosis in 1940, aged forty-seven, and is buried in Deansgrange Cemetery.

Another Catholic cadet in Dublin University OTC during the Rising was Cadet Demetrio Sarsfield Salazar. Thirty-two years old, he was born in Naples, a son of Lorenzo Salazar, count consul of the King of Italy in Ireland (essentially the Italian ambassador). His Irish connection came from his grandmother, Dora Hannah Macnamara Calcutt, a painter who had come from a large landowning family in the Doolin-Ennistimon region of Co. Clare. She had married Demetrio's grandfather, also Demetrio, an archaeologist from Reggio Calabria who fled from Italy following the failure of the 1838 Italian revolutions. The couple had met in Luxembourg and had later returned to live in Naples.

Cadet Demetrio Sarsfield Salazar lived in Kingstown at the time of the Rising, after which he was commissioned as a lieutenant into a regiment of lancers and landed in France on 1 August 1917. He married in 1918 and after the war went on to become Italian vice-consul in Ireland.

In the 1930s he frequently travelled to Paris and Italy on business. Manuela Williams, in *Mussolini's Propaganda Abroad* (2006), states that, 'although his activities and personal contacts in Paris appeared perfectly legitimate, Salazar-Sarsfield was nevertheless believed to be in the service of the Italian [fascist] authorities.' This seems highly unlikely, as during the Second World War he was interned by the Mussolini regime. In June 1942 his son Count Tristan Salazar, a flight-lieutenant with the Royal Air Force Volunteer Reserve, was killed in action, aged twenty-one; today he lies in Sage War Cemetery, Germany.

Furthermore, when Italy surrendered to the Allies in 1943 Count Demetrio Sarsfield Salazar spent huge sums to finance an escape for hundreds of American and British prisoners of war still held by the Germans. The plan was successful and led to Salazar being nicknamed the 'Scarlet Pimpernel'. The rest of his once-large fortune was soon gone, and in later life he found himself being cared for by his two daughters, his only income a British pension of £30 a month. He died in his native Naples in 1968 after a long illness at the age of eighty-four.

* * *

There were at least two Jewish cadets with Dublin University OTC during the Rising. Cadet-Sergeant Lionel Wigoder was a nineteen-year-old medical student in Trinity College. Born in Dublin, he lived with his family in Harrington Street, next door to Lionel's maternal grandfather, Robert Bradlaw. Born Robert Brudno in Smargon in Belarus, Bradlaw was a prominent member of the local Jewish community and helped to establish the synagogue in St Kevin's Parade and the Jewish cemetery at Aughavannagh Road in Dolphin's Barn. Lionel's father, Dr George Selig Wigoder, originally from Russia, was president of the Dublin United Hebrew Congregation. It seems likely that Lionel was also related to the family that owned the well-known paint and wallpaper shops.

After the Rising, Lionel Wigoder completed his studies and went on to join the Royal Air Force Medical Service. He subsequently became a dentist before moving to live in England some time in the early 1930s. In 1935 he adopted the name Lionel Wigoder Bradlaw. He married in 1948 in London and he died in 1984, aged eighty-eight, in Newcastle-upon-Tyne.

The other Jewish OTC member, Cadet Edwin Solomons, was thirty-six when the Rising began. Born in Dublin, he was the son of Maurice Solomons, an optician from London, who was also manager of Adelaide Road National and Hebrew Schools. Edwin Solomons was a stockbroker, a founder and partner of Solomons, Abrahamson and Company and a member of Dublin Stock Exchange. He was also a former president of the Dublin United Hebrew Congregation and a former president of the Jewish Representative Council. He married in London in 1905 and later lived with his family in Elgin Road in Ballsbridge. He died on 22 April 1964, at the age of eighty-four, making him the oldest member of Dublin Stock Exchange.

Edwin's younger brother, Dr Bethel Solomons, was a friend of Arthur Griffith, the founder of Sinn Féin, and a supporter of the Easter Rising, while his younger sister Estella Solomons, an artist, served with Cumann na mBan.

* * *

One of the private soldiers of the Commonwealth forces who arrived at the gates of Trinity College on Tuesday 25 April 1916 was an Irishman in Canadian army uniform. It is known that several Commonwealth soldiers took part in the defence of the college, but it was previously believed that these were exclusively Australians, New Zealanders, South Africans or Canadians. Bugler George Webb, however, was a Dubliner. He was twenty-eight years old and a former clerk, whose late father had been a bank official from Co. Kerry.

When Webb enlisted in the 56th (Calgary) Battalion of the Canadian Expeditionary Force in October 1915 he had been living in Canada for some time, having previously served for four months in the reserve Canadian Army Service Corps. His battalion sailed from Nova Scotia for England in March 1916 aboard the *Baltic*, arriving on 11 April. Webb was given leave from 22 to 30 April, which he used to visit his mother in Dublin. Two days into his leave the Rising began, and so Webb made his way to Trinity College.

In July 1916 Webb's battalion was absorbed into the 9th Reserve Battalion of the Canadian Expeditionary Force, based at Tidworth Barracks on Salisbury Plain, and when he finally went to the war, in September 1917, he served in the 10th Battalion. A famous Canadian battalion in the history of the First World War, this unit took part in every major Canadian battle of the war, was awarded more decorations than any other Canadian battalion for a single battle (the battle for Hill 70 in August 1917) and won itself the nickname of the 'Fighting Tenth'. Bugler George Webb was still serving in the trenches with this battalion when the war ended. He sailed back to Canada in April 1919 and was discharged the same month at Calgary.

* * *

Other OTC members would later record their experiences during the Rising. Cadet-Sergeant Robert Tweedy wrote in a letter to his mother:

> There is still an O.T.C. garrison in T.C.D., but the business men are being relieved, and I gave up my rifle on Friday, after 9 days continuous duty. It is said that T.C.D. saved the city, and I am proud to have been one of the garrison ... If it were not for the wanton burning of Sackville Street, the city and country would have suffered no more than trifling inconvenience, and a few hundred casualties, but that immense act of arson has ruined Dublin for the time. I saw the fire, and it will never fade from my memory. No photographs can reproduce the awful devastation which it wrought, nor any writing the misery which it leaves behind. Nevertheless, this rebellion has done one good thing in that the reality of war has been brought to our doors, and I shall have more hope for Ireland from now on. Perhaps if the rebellion had flared up in the provinces before it was suppressed, the ultimate result would be happier, but in the Dublin area at least the people will turn from the pleasure of making profits out of the war to the sterner task of fighting adversity ... We call them madmen now because they did not succeed, but we shall not know for a long time how mad they really were.

In truth, the rebels who Tweedy called 'madmen' had paved the way for the formation of an Irish republic. Robert Tweedy died in 1956, aged eighty-one. His daughter-in-law was Hilda Tweedy (née Anderson), the well-known teacher, editor and women's rights and human rights campaigner. She founded the Irish Housewives' Association in 1942 along with Andrée Sheehy Skeffington (née Denis), daughter-in-law of Francis Sheehy Skeffington, who was murdered during the Rising in Portobello Barracks.

Lieutenant Arthur Luce, the Church of Ireland clergyman who served in the 12th Royal Irish Rifles, later wrote of the Rising that it was a bolt from the blue to most of us. Historians may say that Trinity backed the wrong horse; but at the time there was only one course of action open to law-abiding citizens in College, especially to those wearing British uniform. Trinity was a natural fortress in the heart of the city, containing a unit of the Officers' Training Corps with service rifles and a store of ammunition. Trinity must be defended. It was a spontaneous decision by a few of us on the spot, without any instructions from outside, or any communications with civil or military authorities.

In late July 1916 Luce rejoined his battalion in the trenches. Promoted to captain in December, he was awarded the Military Cross in October 1917 and then served with the headquarters of the 59th (2nd North Midland) Division – the Territorial Force division that had been summoned to Ireland during the Rising – before returning to the 12th Royal Irish Rifles in late March 1918. On 12 April he was buried by shellfire during an attack but luckily was dug out by comrades and removed to a hospital. He was subsequently evacuated to Ireland and, after a period spent serving again with Dublin University OTC, in December 1918 he resigned his commission because of poor health.

Luce settled with his wife and family in Bushy Park Road, Terenure. From 1934 to 1949 he was professor of moral philosophy at Trinity College (he was a noted authority on George Berkeley). During this time he suffered a personal tragedy when, in 1940, both his wife and his twelve-year-old daughter died in a drowning accident in Celbridge.

In 1955 Arthur Luce wrote about emigration and other population problems, saying that 'the hard core of the problem is the sad stark fact that one Irish child (more than one, statistically) in every three is born to emigrate, and grows up in the knowledge that he or she must emigrate. The moral and psychological effect of that fact is immense. It paralyses certain areas. It is a dead weight upon the spirit of the whole country, a dead hand upon her economy.' Luce was later vice-provost of Trinity College, from 1946 to 1952, and then life holder of the Berkeley Chair of Metaphysics. Meanwhile as a clergyman he had served as canon of St Patrick's Cathedral, Dublin, from 1930 to 1936, chancellor at the cathedral from 1936 to 1952, and then precentor at the cathedral until 1973.

Arthur Luce's death in 1977 at the age of ninety-four was not a peaceful one: he was attacked and beaten by a mentally unstable man and died in hospital two days later from his injuries. At the time of his death he had been a fellow of Trinity College from 1912, a total of sixty-five years – a record that still stands today. His philosophical library was subsequently acquired by Notre Dame University in Indiana. Luce's son John Victor Luce later became a prominent fellow of Trinity College and vice-provost of the university.

Cadet-Sergeant Gerald Fitzgibbon later recorded his experiences in a letter to William Hume Blake. He wrote that between Monday the 24th, when he turned up at the college, and Friday the 28th he did not go home or get out of his clothes or boots even once. He was also on guard for twenty-four hours on several occasions. 'The rebels were bluffed by the confident face we put on ... I haven't the satisfaction of knowing that I hit any of these Home Rule rebels. I only got shots at windows with snipers in them, and at a couple of looters. I didn't want to fire at looters, it was rebels I wanted, and the only time I ever was on a really good pitch for them, they weren't rising.' As a committed unionist, Fitzgibbon felt that 'if that accursed Home Rule Bill [Government of Ireland Bill] had been in force no Irish government could have, or would have dared to try to put down this rebellion.'

He wrote later that 'I have felt very bloodthirsty about the rebels since I saw the men they shot down in Stephen's Green & Haddington Road, and saw all Sackville Street in flames.' Fitzgibbon believed that 'College saved the centre of Dublin and the big banks, all of which have their head offices in or about College Green. The rebels thought we were far more numerous than we really were, and they were afraid to assault the place, which they could have had for the asking up to two o'clock on Monday, and at very small cost up to two o'clock on Tuesday.'

With the introduction of the Government of Ireland Act (1920) the country was partitioned into 'Northern Ireland' and 'Southern Ireland', with a House of Commons and a Senate of Southern Ireland set up in Dublin. This political arrangement was short-lived, however. Following the War of Independence and then the signing of the Anglo-Irish Treaty, 'Southern Ireland' became the Irish Free State in December 1922.

On 21 May 1921 an election was held for the House of Commons and Senate of Southern Ireland. Republicans, however, treated it as an election for the second Dáil Éireann. Sinn Féin, headed by Éamon de Valera, won 124 of the 128 'House of Commons' seats, with the remaining four won by unionist candidates. Gerald Fitzgibbon was one of these, as was Ernest Alton, who had been commanding officer of the OTC during the Rising. The Sinn Féin members refused to take their seats, and on 28 June 1921, when the parliament was opened by the Lord Lieutenant of Ireland, Viscount Fitzalan of Derwent, only Fitzgibbon, Alton and the two other unionists were present. They elected Fitzgibbon as speaker (chairperson) and then adjourned without setting another date for meeting. However, on 14 January 1922 Fitzgibbon and Alton were present at the meeting in the Mansion House, Dublin, at which sixty-four pro-Treaty Sinn Féin TDs, along with the four unionists, voted to ratify the Anglo-Irish Treaty. Fitzgibbon was subsequently elected to the Constituent Assembly of the Irish Free State in the election of 16 June 1922, considered an election to the third Dáil Éireann.

In 1924, when nearly all the senior judges in Ireland were forced into retirement, Hugh Kennedy, chief justice of the Irish Free State, recommended Gerald Fitzgibbon as a judge of the Supreme Court. Despite the fact that Kennedy was a nationalist and Fitzgibbon a unionist, Kennedy believed Fitzgibbon to be a man of excellent legal ability.

Fitzgibbon accepted the role and was open to working with the new Irish government; but because of the close relationship that soon developed between the government and the Catholic Church he began to come into conflict with Kennedy. In 1935 he declared that the Constitution of the Irish Free State contained provisions for its own amendment which allowed the suspension of the most basic human rights. By then he had developed a deep dislike for the new Irish state. He was involved in a minor way with the drafting of the Constitution of Ireland in 1937, but in 1938 he was obliged on grounds of age to retire from the Supreme Court. He died in Dublin in 1942, aged seventy-six.

Captain Ernest Alton, the 42-year-old *de facto* commanding officer of Dublin University OTC during the Rising, was later awarded the Military Cross for his actions in 1916. He subsequently recorded that, after the arrival of the 5th Leinster Regiment on Tuesday 25 April,

> our duties as guards were continued even when troops occupied the College in force on Wednesday. To detail the multifarious tasks that we had to discharge that week would be tedious. Anxiety was at an end as regards the safety of the College and the neighbourhood by Thursday, and officers, who had hitherto slept little and washed less, began again to appear more like their former selves. After the first two days we were reinforced by members of the O.T.C. who were now able to enter, and our duties were to some extent less anxious. On the following week Major Harris took over command. A rumour had got about that he had been killed, so we were particularly delighted to see his genial face again.

Ernest Alton then became involved in politics. After sitting briefly in the House of Commons of Southern Ireland, and being present on 14 January 1922 at the meeting in the Mansion House during which the Anglo-Irish Treaty was ratified, he was later elected to the Constituent Assembly of the Irish Free State, i.e. the third Dáil. He served as an independent member for Dublin University until the end of the eighth Dáil in 1937, when the university constituencies were abolished. He then became an independent senator for Dublin University, serving in the second Seanad (1938) and third Seanad (1938–1943) but did not contest the elections for the fourth Seanad. By 1943 he had been involved in politics for a total of twenty-two years. A nephew, Bryan Alton, son of Ernest's brother Norman, was also a senator, a member of the eleventh Seanad (1965–69) and twelfth Seanad (1969–1973) for the National University of Ireland constituency. A surgeon by profession, Bryan was also Éamon de Valera's personal doctor.

Ernest Alton was professor of Latin at Trinity College from 1921 until 1942 and subsequently provost of the university (at the same time that his fellow-veteran of the Rising, Arthur Luce, was vice-provost) until his death in 1952 after a short illness. Ernest Alton was seventy-eight years old when he died, and he is buried in Deansgrange Cemetery.

* * *

After the arrival of reinforcements at the college during the late afternoon of Tuesday 25 April 1916 Prof. John Joly was sent as a scout to Butt Bridge to see if it was occupied by the rebels. When he reached the bridge he decided to press on further to see if there were any rebels in nearby Liberty Hall. Though the building was empty when the *Helga* began shelling it the following morning, Joly wrote in *Reminiscences and Anticipations* that two shots were fired at him from one of the building's lower windows. 'I saw the smoke, so there was no doubt whence the shots came.'

That night Joly was back on sentry duty inside the college. The next morning he nearly opened fire on an OTC scout party who were returning after a mission outside the college. He held his fire when he realised the group were wearing khaki, while a sentry in another building nearby actually fired at the group. No one was injured.

On Thursday the 27th Joly noted that the OTC Medical Unit was dealing with a large number of civilian casualties who were being brought into the college for treatment, while – with hunger now becoming a serious issue among citizens – the British army authorities were commandeering food and making it available to the people of Dublin. (The insurgents did the same in the areas they controlled.) Among the civilian casualties brought in, Joly remembered that after a horse-drawn ambulance stopped outside the college a woman was lifted out.

> The stretcher dripped with her blood. A glance showed that death was not far from her. It was a face without hope. A shocking wound was hers. Shot through the lower part of the abdomen, the infernal bullet used by the Sinn Feiners [Joly is suggesting it was a dum-dum bullet] had done work which must surely be fatal. They tried to plug the wound. A little later she was brought on to hospital, where she died. This woman had done no wrong. She was probably seeking food for her six little children when death met her. There will be no one to sing her sorrows in modulated verse. The guilty 'Countess' may possibly one day evoke the strains of the bard. But this woman's anguish of farewell to her little children will be absorbed unnoticed save by these poor words in that great total of human sorrow which the mind cannot evaluate or even conceive.

The same day Joly spotted two men dressed in civilian clothes trying to enter the college, having pressed themselves into a group of returning soldiers and trying to hide in the crowd. When confronted, one of the men, who was found to have a bottle of whiskey, claimed to be an old soldier and began shouting that the other man was a bad character. This other man swore he had never seen the first man in his life. Joly was concerned that this might be a ploy to gain access to the college for the purpose of reconnaissance, and he separated the men and placed them under guard. He later found that, after being sent up to headquarters for questioning, both men had been released.

The following day Joly was involved in a mission to secure 'vital supplies' for the soldiers in Trinity College – namely cigarettes. On Friday the 28th it was discovered that a tobacconist's shop opposite the college was open for business. (The men guessed that this had something to do with the shop being next-door to a police station.) Joly later recalled:

> On this becoming known, a deputation reached me from some of the Tommies to the effect that I would confer a great favour on them if I would buy them 10 ounces of cigarettes. They entrusted me with a one-pound note. I was pleased with this mission, for as janitor I discharged very unpopular duties. There was no conceivable excuse they did not urge to get out of barracks, and I pitilessly listened to none of them. One poor lad who had escaped by another gate ... was carried in on a shutter drunk! Tommy is a forgiving creature. I got the cigarettes, and returned absolved and popular.

Joly cycled home that night for the first time since the beginning of the Rising, after obtaining a pass, though he had been urged not to go for his own safety. Although he was frequently challenged at barricades and check-points, he survived the trip, and after washing and changing his clothes he returned to the college the following day, Saturday the 29th, spending his last day on sentry duty at one of the college's entrances. The city was very active, and he saw large numbers of prisoners under escort coming and going.

That night, with Captain Alton, he went to the top of the look-out tower at the fire station in Tara Street and looked out over the city.

> The view northward was sublime and terrible. Acres of flame and red-hot buildings stretched across the middle distance. The lurid light, reflected on rolling clouds of smoke, rose and fell as roof and walls toppled over. Fresh fires appeared to be springing into existence at a point to the north-east, and it really looked as if we were witnessing the wholesale destruction by the devouring flames of the entire northern side of the City ...
>
> There can be no doubt that the accurate fire maintained from the College was an important factor in the salvation of the City. The Bank of Ireland (formerly the Irish House of Parliament) was otherwise unprotected, but no hostile being could have approached its doors. Its whole front was in view of the College. The sentries, which in ordinary times never cease to guard its doors, were absent, but the building was safe. An attempt was, in fact, made to take possession of its roof, but it was frustrated. The many important and stately buildings – banks, insurance offices, business premises – of Dame Street and Grafton Street were protected from the Rebel or from the looter in the same manner. The whole length of Westmoreland Street was kept clear by the College rifles; and even the strongholds of the enemy in Sackville Street were assailed from the northern end of the College. Regarding the position as a whole, the grounds and buildings of Trinity College filled the

function of a loyal nucleus, dividing the forces of the Rebels and keeping open to the troops some of the principal thoroughfares of the City.

After the Rising, Prof. Joly returned to his academic work. He attended the Balfour Educational Mission to America in 1918 as a delegate of Trinity College. The following year he was the first person to be elected to fellowship under the modified method of election, something he was always very proud of. That same year, because of his age, doctors insisted that he give up cycling. He compromised by starting to ride motorcycles, soon ending up with a Harley-Davidson. However, after an accident near Mallow in 1925 left him badly bruised he promised to start driving a car. Apparently, though, he always thought that cars were 'sissy' in comparison with motorbikes.

Meanwhile Joly became president of the Royal Dublin Society, warden of Alexandra College, a governor of two Dublin hospitals, and one of the most active Commissioners of Irish Lights. He published nearly 270 papers and several books during his lifetime and was awarded medals by the Royal Dublin Society and the Geological Society of London as well as several honorary degrees from universities in Europe and America.

John Joly died in 1933, aged seventy-six. He is buried in Mount Jerome Cemetery and is also commemorated beyond the planet Earth: in 1973 a crater on Mars was named in his honour.

* * *

As we have seen, OTC cadets were not active solely inside the grounds of Trinity College; in fact some never came within sight of the college throughout Easter Week and instead served alongside British army soldiers elsewhere in the city. Two such cadets were mentioned by Monk Gibbon in his memoir *Inglorious Soldier.* Gibbon was making his way to Portobello Barracks after leaving his sister's house.

> At that moment a cadet in the uniform of the O.T.C. – an undergraduate in Trinity – came by on a motor bicycle. I stopped him authoritatively. The one pip on my sleeve [a diamond-shaped badge, insignia of a second-lieutenant] allowed me to do that. 'What's happening in Dublin?' 'There's been some kind of a rebellion.' 'Are you sure?' 'Absolutely.' 'Turn round.' I got on the pillion of his motor cycle. 'Now drive me to the nearest barracks.'

After arriving at Portobello Barracks, Gibbon 'dismounted, thanked him [the OTC cadet] and he rode away again quickly in the direction from which we had come.' Gibbon encountered another cadet during the evening of Saturday the 29th. With Major Francis Fletcher-Vane he went out of barracks as far as Kelly's corner.

> A youth in a rather curious and unorthodox uniform – khaki jacket, but white collar and badgeless cap – had been stopped on his motor bicycle by

Surgeon Sub-Lieutenant Gerald Keatinge from Terenure, far right, aboard HMS *Poppy* (Rachel Keatinge)

the picket. He maintained that he was a member of the O.T.C. who had been holding Trinity College against the rebels since Monday. He had been searched and amongst his possessions was a small piece of equipment of solely personal significance, more appropriate to a votary of Venus than of Mars [evidently a condom]. I saw them showing it now to Vane, and it drew from him the brief comment, 'Disgusting!' A call was put through to T.C.D. and the youth's story established.

But a cadet who served outside Trinity College and who perhaps had the most interesting story to tell afterwards was seventeen-year-old Cadet-Sergeant Gerald Keatinge, who later wrote an account of his experiences. He had served in Portobello Barracks during the Rising, had taken part in the raid on Byrne's shop with Captain Bowen-Colthurst and was subsequently attached to the Ulster Composite Battalion at Amiens Street Station. After the Rising, in November 1916, he became a surgeon sub-lieutenant with the Royal Naval Volunteer Reserve and went on to serve on the sloop *Poppy* (meaning that he would have worked alongside Eric Murray, a former cadet-corporal who had also served with the OTC during the Rising before going on to become a surgeon sub-lieutenant aboard the same ship).

Silver Cups Presentation group, Trinity College, Dublin, 5 August 1916 (Paul Guéret)

Chairman:

Sir MAURICE DOCKRELL, D.L.

Committee:

W. L. Burke.

E. Tenison Collins.

Henry Dudgeon.

Charles Gamble.

M. B. Mathews.

Robt. Mitchell.

F. Thompson.

L. A. West.

Hon. Sec. & Treas.:

Lewis H. S. Beatty.

Waller & Co., Printers, Dublin.

PROGRAMME.

PRESENTATION

TO

The Dublin University Officers' Training Corps

TO BE HELD IN

THE PROVOST'S GARDEN.

TRINITY COLLEGE GROUNDS,

ON SATURDAY, 5TH AUGUST, 1916,

AT 3 O'CLOCK, P.M.

Silver Cups Presentation programme (Bryan Alton)

PROGRAMME.

1. Inspection of the Corps by the Chairman, Sir MAURICE DOCKRELL, D.L.

2. Presentation of Silver Cups to Commandant of Officers' Training Corps, who will, on behalf of the Corps, formally hand over the same to The Provost of Trinity College.

3. Presentation of Special Commemorative Replica to :—
   Rev. J. PENTLAND MAHAFFY, D.D., C V.O., *Provost of Trinity College.*

4. Presentation of Swords to the Officers of the Dublin University Officers' Training Corps.

5. Presentation of Special Silver Replicas to :—
   Major R. W. TATE, *Commandant.*
   Major G. A. HARRIS, *Adjutant.*
   Captain E. H. ALTON, *Officer Commanding Infantry.*

6. Presentation of Silver Replicas to Members of the Officers' Training Corps.

7. Presentation to ladies who rendered assistance in College during the Rebellion.

8. Presentation to the Chief Steward, College Officials and others.

By kind permission of the Commandant and Officers of the Dublin University Officers' Training Corps, there will be a Musical Selection by the Band of the Officers' Training Corps.

Tea will be provided after the Ceremony by Major R. W. Tate and the Officers of the Corps.

GOD SAVE THE KING.

Silver Cup presented to Cadet David Beckett from Co. Mayo, for service with Dublin University OTC during the Rising (Pat Beckett)

When the war ended Keatinge obtained his BA in 1919 and married in England in 1920. He obtained his MA from Trinity College in 1923 and shortly afterwards was working as an obstetrician and gynaecologist in Derby Hospital for Women. After the Second World War (in which he lost a son), Dr Keatinge moved to London in 1951, where he lived for another thirty years until his death in 1981, aged eighty-two. His daughter, Moira Watson, recently recalled that he

> got on very well with people, loving the gift of putting them at ease. He had a great deal of energy, combining obstetrics with general practice. This involved many night calls. He ran a surgery at 8.30 a.m. to 5.30 p.m. with a ½ day 'off' on Wednesday. He would be out all day doing visits ... He was also on the staff of the Women's Hospital where he operated twice a week. In his spare time he learnt Spanish & started a Spanish society during the Spanish Civil War ... Never idle, he was very good company & a natural raconteur.

A total of six regular army instructors attached to the OTC, ten OTC officers, three honorary OTC members and 148 cadets were active in helping to defeat the Rising, either at Trinity College or elsewhere in Dublin. In addition, two civilian OTC employees assisted with helping to defend the college, along with twenty-one college employees and six more civilian women. Individual British army and Commonwealth officers and soldiers often made their way to the college, and it is known that seventeen army officers ended up serving alongside the OTC during the Rising, together with forty-nine other ranks, fourteen of whom were colonial soldiers, either Australians and New Zealanders, South Africans or Canadians.

The members of Dublin University OTC paraded in the grounds of Trinity College on 6 May and were reviewed by General Maxwell, with the British prime minister, Herbert Asquith, looking on. (He had come to Dublin to see the situation for himself.) On 18 May a committee of local businessmen was formed to come up with a way of thanking Dublin University OTC for protecting the area during the Rising. The committee raised more than £700 from public donations, and it was decided to purchase and present two large silver cups to the OTC, individual smaller cups to each member of the garrison and commemorative swords to the OTC officers, along with the 'OTC Commemoration Bed' in Sir Patrick Dun's Hospital. The presentation took place in the provost's garden on 5 August. (Of the smaller silver cups only 138 were issued, despite there being 262 OTC members, assisting civilians and individual British army and Commonwealth officers and soldiers involved in the defence of the college.)

* * *

While the OTC at Trinity College suffered no casualties during the Rising, many of those who had defended the college in April 1916 would not survive to see the end of the war. Nineteen-year-old Cadet William Allardyce from Rathmines, son of a tailor's cutter from Aberdeenshire and a mother from Dublin, was active during the Rising. He had entered Trinity in 1914, aged seventeen, having previously attended St Andrew's College in Booterstown, and in the autumn of 1916 he became a surgeon-probationer on the destroyer *Negro*. On 21 December the *Negro* was escorting the destroyer *Hoste,* which was experiencing steering failure, back to Scapa Flow when the weather suddenly worsened and the *Hoste* rammed into the *Negro*. The impact knocked two depth charges off the *Hoste,* which detonated between the two ships, ripping apart the bottom of the *Negro* and seriously damaging the *Hoste.* The *Negro* sank quickly, with the loss of fifty men, while other ships nearby managed to save some of the *Hoste's* crew before it tore in half and also sank.

William Allardyce was one of those who died aboard the *Negro*. He was still only nineteen, and with no known grave he is today commemorated on the Chatham Naval Memorial and also on the St Andrew's College and Trinity College war memorials.

William Allardyce was not the only member of his family to die in the war. His older brother, George Allardyce – also a former Trinity student – died on 18 May 1918 in Oxford, aged twenty-two, of wounds received while serving as a lieutenant with the 4th Battalion of the Australian Imperial Force. He is buried in Mount Jerome Cemetery. William Allardyce's two younger brothers died in the Second World War. Brigadier James Allardyce died of wounds on 18 October 1944 in York, aged forty-five, having served with the Royal Artillery, and is buried in Fulford Cemetery, Yorkshire. The youngest of the brothers, Captain Ransome Allardyce, a doctor with the Royal Army Medical Corps who had studied medicine in Trinity College, Dublin, was killed on 15 February 1942 after the fall of Singapore. He was one of the 250 staff members and patients murdered by the Japanese army during the Alexandra Barracks Hospital Massacre, bayoneted to death by a Japanese soldier, aged thirty-nine; he now lies in Kranji War Cemetery. The father of the Allardyce brothers, George Allardyce, outlived his entire family. His wife had died in 1911, and by 1944 all four of his sons had died in war. Their names are on the St Andrew's College war memorial. George Allardyce died in 1953.

Cadet-Corporal Maurice Ashley, nineteen years old at the time of the Rising, who was born in London but raised in Ireland, was the son of an excise officer from Dublin and a mother from Dundalk and lived in Drumcondra, Dublin. After the Rising he was commissioned into the 1st Royal Irish Fusiliers, landing in France on 8 June 1917, the day after the Battle of Messines Ridge, to join it in the trenches. The same year, on 23 November, he was killed in action, aged twenty. With no known grave, Maurice Ashley's name is commemorated on the Cambrai Memorial, Louverval.

Twenty-one-year-old Second-Lieutenant Arthur Vigors of the 7th Royal Munster Fusiliers, also a former student in Trinity College and a former member of Dublin University OTC, was born in Co. Kildare. The family soon afterwards moved to Belfast, where Arthur's father, a native of Co. Carlow, worked as a debt collector. The family had later returned to live in Blessington. After taking part in the defence of Trinity College, Second-Lieutenant Vigors was attached to D Company, 9th Royal Dublin Fusiliers and was sent with it to join the 16th (Irish) Division on the Western Front. On 8 September 1916, just after the Battle of Guillemont on the Somme, he wrote a letter to his cousin.

Second-Lieutenant Arthur Vigors – former cadet with Dublin University OTC – from Co. Kildare (from *Dublin and the Great War, 1914–1918*)

I have been very busy since & have no time to write. We have had a really warm time these last few days but not half as warm as the Huns got, they surrender in droves now driven mad by hunger and by our bombardments. Our guns never cease day or night. The 9th Royal Dublin Fusiliers made a successful attack not long ago; before going into action, just before dawn we were addressed by the R.C. Chaplain who gave us absolution, it was a most impressive sight and then he made one of the most stirring speeches I ever heard, there in the field he stood while the guns thundered and appealed to them to fight for the honour of Ireland, to uphold the traditions of their historic regiment and fighting race, while the men stood listening with bowed heads, it was a great sight. We attacked just after dawn and then all hell was let loose on us, we were stunned and dazed but still the Dublin men held on so cooly as if they were going down Sackville St. God knows we lost heavily, but we won our position and the cursed Huns ran. I will never forget the Artillery barrage the Huns put up; the earth was one mass of flame & smoke. The Irish Division has made a great name for Ireland. I don't exactly know how I escaped being hit, as we have only eight officers left now of the battalion.

The day after writing this letter, 9 September 1916, Vigors took part in the Battle of Ginchy, in which he was killed. He was twenty-one. His body was never recovered, and so with no known grave his name is commemorated on the Thiepval Memorial.

Arthur's mother had to suffer another loss when his older brother Charles – a captain with the 12th Cheshire Regiment and a recipient of the Military Cross and the Croix de Guerre – was killed on 18 September 1918, aged twenty-seven. Also with no known grave, he is commemorated on the Doiran Memorial.

Cadet Ernest Despard was a man with an interesting family tree. Aged twenty-seven in 1916, Despard was born in Abbeyleix and lived in Mountrath. The son of a civil engineer and justice of the peace from Dublin and a mother from Co. Wicklow, Ernest Despard was related to Marcus Despard from Mountrath, an officer in the 50th (Queen's Own) Regiment of Foot who befriended Captain Horatio Nelson, later famous for commanding the British fleet during the Battle of Trafalgar, while serving alongside him in the San Juan expedition of 1780 in present-day Nicaragua. Despard became superintendent of the Bay of Honduras until 1790, when – after marrying a black woman and trying to give freed slaves equal rights – he was ordered back to England. He later joined the United Irishmen and was arrested in 1798, remaining in prison without trial for three years until he was released in 1801.

In 1802 it was claimed that Despard was involved in a plot to assassinate King George III, and also that he had been planning to take over the Tower of London and the Bank of England before starting an uprising in London, an event that became known as the 'Despard Plot'. Despard was again arrested; this time, however, he was tried, and despite Admiral Nelson appearing as a character witness he was found guilty of high treason and sentenced to be hanged, drawn and quartered, together with six alleged fellow-conspirators. This was the last time in British history this sentence was handed down. However, it was not carried out; the sentence was commuted to hanging and beheading, over fears that such an extreme punishment would be met with public outrage. Marcus Despard was hanged on 21 February 1803 in Horsemonger Lane Gaol, London, aged fifty-two. An estimated 22,000 people attended his funeral, the largest public gathering in London until Nelson's own funeral after the Battle of Trafalgar three years later.

One hundred and thirteen years after Marcus Despard was executed, Irish rebels in the GPO would take shots at the statue of the man who had defended him, standing on top of Nelson's Pillar in Sackville Street, while not far away Ernest Despard was an OTC cadet helping to defend his college. (The insurgents may also have tried to collapse Nelson's Pillar with explosives. Between 7:10 and 7:20 a.m. on Tuesday the 25th four explosions, followed by clouds of smoke, erupted from the base of the pillar. It did not fall, however, and it was later claimed that they were not trying to destroy the pillar but were knocking down tram standards to obtain the wire.)

In October 1916 Cadet Ernest Despard was commissioned into the Machine Gun Corps (Heavy) – an early name for the Tank Corps. He landed in France on 26 June 1917, and when he was promoted to lieutenant later that year he was an officer in E Battalion of the Tank Corps. On 26 September he died of wounds received in action, aged twenty-nine, and he now lies in Dozinghem Military Cemetery.

Cadet Thomas Jones-Nowlan, twenty-five years old, a native of Dublin, lived in Kilcullen, Co. Kildare, at the time of the Rising. Commissioned in December

1916 into the Royal Dublin Fusiliers after being active in Dublin during the Rising, he died on 27 May 1917, aged twenty-six, while serving as a second-lieutenant with the 1st Battalion. Today he lies in Duisans British Cemetery at Étrun.

Cadet Joseph Malone also took part in defeating the Rising, only to die later on the Western Front. He was born in the North Star Hotel in Amiens Street, Dublin, which was owned by his parents; they appear to have had a family home also in Howth. Malone was nineteen at the time of the Rising. Educated in Blackrock College and Belvedere College before attending Trinity, he joined Dublin University OTC in November 1915 before applying for a commission in January 1916 and then again – successfully this time – in mid-April 1916. He was waiting to be called up for officer training when the Rising began.

After being commissioned as a second-lieutenant in September 1916 he was posted to the 9th Royal Dublin Fusiliers and in January 1917 was sent to join the 16th (Irish) Division on the Western Front. On 16 August, during the Battle of Frezenberg Ridge, Second-Lieutenant Malone disappeared during the fighting. On 23 August his eldest brother, John Malone, who was living in the North Star Hotel, received a telegram stating: 'Regret to inform you that 2/Lieut JJ Malone Dublin Fusiliers is reported wounded & missing sixteenth august. Further reports will be sent if received.' On 1 September he received a second telegram. 'Deeply regret to inform that 2nd Lieut JJ Malone Dublin Fusiliers previously reported wounded & missing is now reported killed in action august sixteenth. The army council express their sympathy.'

Joseph Malone was only twenty years old when he was killed. With no known grave, today his name is commemorated on the Tyne Cot Memorial. His eldest brother, John Malone, aged only twenty-one, now had to take care of two younger brothers and a sister, aged between sixteen and eighteen, both parents having been dead for some time.

Cadet-Corporal Frederick McElroy, a native of Co. Tyrone, was twenty years old at the time of the Rising. He spent part of his youth in Co. Wexford, where his father was a land steward on the Esmonde family's Johnstown Castle estate (the family may have lived in Rathlannon Castle, a small tower-house in the grounds), before enlisting as a private during the First World War. He later became a cadet-corporal in Dublin University OTC, took part in the fighting during the Rising, and in November 1916 was commissioned into the Machine Gun Corps (Heavy). During his time with the 7th Battalion of the Tank Corps he was awarded the Distinguished Service Order

for conspicuous gallantry and devotion to duty in attack. He drove the enemy back and captured two strongly-held craters. When his tank caught fire and had to be evacuated he remained inside in spite of the fumes firing his Lewis gun, and held the enemy back single-handed when they attempted to capture his tank, inflicting heavy casualties on them. When his crew, many of whom were wounded, were surrounded in a shell-hole he killed eight of the enemy with his revolver, and it was owing to his great courage and coolness that the tank and the crew were saved.

On 11 November 1918, the day the war ended, Captain Frederick McElroy was still alive, but he died five days later, aged twenty-two. He now lies in Saint-Pol British Cemetery, Saint-Pol-sur-Ternoise.

Cadet-Corporal Walter Varian, a 21-year-old student at the time of the Rising, was a native of Dublin and lived in Stillorgan. Both his parents were from Dublin, his father the proprietor of I. S. Varian and Company, the brush manufacturers. By 1916 Walter Varian had already graduated with a BSc, having entered Trinity College in 1911, aged sixteen. Commissioned into the Royal Munster Fusiliers in April 1917, he landed in France the following month to join the 2nd Battalion on the Western Front. He was killed in action on 30 March 1918 at Hamel, aged twenty-three, not long after the start of the German Spring Offensive. He now lies in Longueval Road Cemetery, while his name is commemorated on a memorial plaque in the Unitarian Church, St Stephen's Green, Dublin.

On 11 April 1918 Varian's father received a letter from one of his son's men, who was then recovering from wounds in the General Hospital in Stratford-upon-Avon, Warwickshire.

Sir,

With my deepest sympathy I enclose these articles possessed by your son W. O. Varian, 2nd Lieut., when he passed away. I can assure you that he died happy, I having held his hand when he departed. I found him lying in the trench, wounded through the right side and the left wrist. I bandaged him and was in the act of taking him to an ambulance but alas he died before I could possibly do so, saying, 'For God's sake, let me rest.' These were his last words. Some things which he possessed went to Batt. HQ. These I expect you have received by now. I would have forwarded the enclosed sooner but could not do so, for after three quarters of an hour I got a bullet through my left arm and have been in bed since I came to England, but I am getting well again and will be on leave in a short time. Your son commanded my section for quite a while in Batt. 2 observing section and I can assure you he was held in high esteem by all under his command. I have no more to say only that he died happy for a just cause, and I hope he has not died in vain. Again I extend to you my sympathy and to all his bereaved.

I remain, Yours,

W. Guerin, Private.

Cadet Thomas McFerran, born at Elton Park in Sandycove, Co. Dublin, was the son of a solicitor from Co. Antrim and a mother from Dublin. Eighteen years old in 1916, he had attended Campbell College, Belfast, before entering Trinity College, Dublin. By the time of the Rising his mother had died and he was living with his

widower father in Sandycove Avenue, West. Commissioned into the Royal Dublin
Fusiliers in October 1916, he soon transferred to the Royal Flying Corps. On 21
June 1917 Second-Lieutenant McFerran was killed in action during an air fight
near Beselare while serving in No. 1 Squadron of the RFC, aged nineteen. With
no known grave, today his name is commemorated on the Arras Flying Services
Memorial.

* * *

Some of the Trinity College OTC cadets who had been active during the Rising
would go on to die during the Second World War. Cadet-Corporal Robert Butler
was born in Kingstown (Dún Laoghaire). He was eighteen years old in 1916, the
son of a Trinity College librarian from Cashel and a mother from Queenstown
(Cóbh). (During the First World War Robert's brother, Lance-Corporal William
Butler, who had also served during the Rising with the 10th Royal Dublin Fusiliers,
was killed in action on 24 April 1917 and now lies in Duisans British Cemetery,
Étrun.)

   Robert Butler served as an officer in the Leinster Regiment during the war, first
landing in France on 4 June 1917. After the war he joined the British Indian Army
and is known to have served in the 72nd Punjabi Regiment in Bombay (Mumbai)
in the early 1920s. By 1930 he had been promoted to captain, and in the Second
World War he served in the Pioneer Corps. He died 6 August 1941, aged forty-
three. He appears to have died in South Africa – suggesting wounds or sickness
rather than death in action – and now lies in Pietermaritzburg (Fort Napier)
Cemetery. In Ireland his name is also commemorated on the memorial plaque in
Christ Church, Dún Laoghaire.

   One former Trinity College OTC cadet went on to die in police uniform
after the war. Cadet David Beckett was born in the village of Mayo Abbey, near
Claremorris, Co. Mayo, and raised in Castlebar. His father was a farmer and land
inspector, and his mother was English. He was eighteen and a student at Trinity
College in April 1916, when he was active as a member of the college's OTC.

   After the Rising, Beckett was commissioned into the Connaught Rangers and
joined the 6th Battalion in the trenches on 19 February 1917. Attached to the 2nd
Royal Irish Regiment for three months later that year, he then returned to the
Connaught Rangers and was still serving with the 6th Battalion when the war
ended. He finished the war with the rank of lieutenant and was demobilised in
August 1919. David Beckett's grandson Pat Beckett recently recalled:

> His time at Trinity was not talked about within the family so I could not
> get a lot of information from my father and aunt and the reason why is after
> WW1 my grandfather went back to Trinity to finish his schooling and while
> there he witnessed a murder committed by a Sinn Fein member. He [the
> republican] killed a gentleman because he talked to the British. He escaped
> to the roof of the building [but] my grandfather chased him and shot him

so the Sinn Fein were coming to kill him. So he and my grandmother left Ireland and came to Canada and that's why we are here. It was never spoke of because he thought the Sinn Fein would find him and kill him. He moved to Windsor, Ontario, Canada and became a Police Officer.

Now a constable with the Windsor Police Force, Beckett served for twelve years before he was involved in a two-car collision on 2 November 1937. A report later stated: 'Cst [Constable] Beckett was responding to a call about a traffic accident when a vehicle ran [through] a red light. It struck the patrol wagon, throwing him from the vehicle. The wagon rolled over him and killed him.' He died at the scene from multiple skull fractures, the first member of Windsor Police Force to be killed in the line of duty. He was thirty-nine years old.

* * *

While they suffered no casualties during the Easter Rising, the men of Dublin University OTC did not all survive the war. Out of the 3,042 staff members, graduates and students who are known to have served during the war (1,040 of these being former members of Dublin University OTC), 463 died during the war. Their names are all recorded in the Hall of Honour in the university's postgraduate reading-room.

While the reduction in the number of students resulting from the war caused a strain in the college's finances – it was obliged to ask the government for financial assistance and in 1917 was forced to open up College Park for the grazing of sheep – Dublin University OTC continued to exist until April 1922. After the formation of the Irish Free State, however, it was formally disbanded, after twelve years in existence.

This was not the last time an OTC was active at Trinity College, however. In 1930 the Irish Defence Forces established a new OTC for the reserve of officers, but it was disbanded before the Second World War. The O'Reilly Institute is now sited where the OTC headquarters once stood, and the adjoining parade ground has been largely built on. One hundred years ago, however, it was the training ground for those who helped to defend their college during the 1916 Rising.

9

Conclusion

With the surrender of the rebel command on Saturday 29 April 1916, one Irish officer in the British army would be given the job of travelling to the various remaining outposts around Dublin to let them know that the Rising was over.

Captain Henry de Courcy Wheeler was present when Patrick Pearse, accompanied by Nurse Elizabeth O'Farrell, agreed to end hostilities and surrendered to Brigadier-General William Lowe at the top of Moore Street. Wheeler, who was Brigadier-General Lowe's staff captain, was photographed alongside his commanding officer at this famous moment in Irish history.

Henry Wheeler was a 44-year-old officer in the 8th King's Royal Rifle Corps as well as a barrister and a justice of the peace. He was born in Dublin in 1872. Having previously lived in Sandymount Avenue and then Robertstown House, Co. Kildare, he was now living with his family at the Curragh Camp, where they moved when the First World War began. His parents (neither of them alive in 1916) were William Ireland de Courcy Wheeler, a former president of the Royal College of Surgeons and a justice of the peace for Co. Kildare, and Frances Shaw from Foxrock, Co. Dublin (a first cousin of George Bernard Shaw). Wheeler's younger brother, also William Ireland de Courcy Wheeler, served as a major with the Royal Army Medical Corps at Mercer's Hospital throughout the Rising and was later mentioned in despatches for his actions. Three other brothers served as British army officers during the war.

Immediately after the surrender Brigadier-General Lowe and Captain Wheeler got into a car and drove off towards the headquarters of Irish Command at Parkgate. When they arrived, Pearse was brought before General John Maxwell, commander of British forces in Dublin, and requested to sign an order to the various commandants throughout Dublin telling them to lay down their arms. After signing this, Pearse was brought to a sitting-room in the building, and Captain Wheeler was ordered to guard him. 'I was handed a loaded revolver with

Patrick Pearse and Nurse Elizabeth O'Farrell surrender to Brigadier-General William Lowe and Captain Henry de Courcy Wheeler (National Museum of Ireland)

orders to keep it pointed at Commandant Pearse, and to shoot should he make an effort to escape. This was a very responsible and serious order to obey and to carry out should it have become necessary. Pearse did not seem in the least perturbed and greatly to my relief, I was on this duty for only 15 minutes when I was sent for by General Lowe and another officer was sent to relieve me.'

Captain Wheeler was then sent to the Dublin Castle Red Cross Hospital to get James Connolly – who had been brought there to have his wounds treated – to countersign the order. Connolly added his agreement in writing to the bottom of the document. This was then brought back to Nurse Elizabeth O'Farrell, who had remained in Moore Street, and she returned with the order to the insurgents in the area with instructions to leave their positions and pile their arms at the Parnell Monument. That night Captain Wheeler personally took the surrender of eighty-four members of the GPO garrison at the Parnell Monument. He recorded all the names, which included those of Harry Boland, Michael Collins, Seán Lemass, Seán MacEntee, Seán T. O'Kelly, William Pearse, and Joseph Plunkett.

The next day Captain Wheeler, accompanied by Nurse O'Farrell, was instructed to travel around Dublin to the various outposts so that Nurse O'Farrell could pass on the surrender order to each commandant. For this they were provided with a car, a driver, and a sergeant-major from the 5th Royal Irish Regiment as an escort. With Wheeler unarmed, and Nurse O'Farrell flying an old white apron tied to a stick as a flag of truce, they set off through a city where occasional firing was continuing and snipers were everywhere.

After Nurse O'Farrell delivered the surrender notice to the Irish Citizen Army at the College of Surgeons – having to approach the building on foot because of firing in Grafton Street that stopped the car from coming any closer – they drove on towards Boland's bakery, headquarters of Commandant Éamon de Valera's 3rd Battalion. However, because of sniping in the area they were unable to go any further than Butt Bridge. Nurse O'Farrell again completed the journey on foot, but de Valera did not know her and insisted that he would surrender only if Commandant Thomas MacDonagh of the 2nd Battalion instructed him to do so.

Nurse O'Farrell returned to Captain Wheeler and they drove on to Jacob's factory to find MacDonagh. After dropping Nurse O'Farrell off at St Patrick's Park, beside St Patrick's Cathedral, from where she could walk on to Jacob's, Wheeler returned to Dublin Castle. Here he received a phone call to say that the Irish Citizen Army garrison at the College of Surgeons under Michael Mallin and Constance Markievicz had lowered the Tricolour above the building to signal that they were ready to surrender (having received the message from Nurse O'Farrell earlier in the day). He now made his way to the College of Surgeons.

Captain Wheeler, who gave evidence at the courts-martial of Mallin and Markievicz (as well as four others), later recorded that

> I was on duty on 30th April outside the College of Surgeons. A body of prisoners surrendered to me between 12.30 p.m. and 1 p.m. The prisoner [Mallin] and the Countess of Markievicz came out of a side door of the College. The prisoner was carrying a white flag and was unarmed but the Countess was armed. The prisoner came forward and saluted and said he wished to surrender and this is the Countess Markievicz. He surrendered and stated he was the Commandant of the garrison. I took over the garrison which consisted of prisoner, Countess Markievicz, 109 men and 10 women. I found them in the College and they laid down their arms under my direction.

A member of the Irish Citizen Army garrison, James O'Shea, also recorded the event.

> Major [sic] Wheeler came in accompanied by another officer. We were standing at ease. Commandant Mallin called us smartly to attention, gave us 'arms down, three paces backward, march,' turned about, drew his sword and presented it, haft first, to Major Wheeler. Major Wheeler asked Mallin were all his men here. When Mallin replied that they were all here, Major Wheeler was surprised as he thought there would be about two hundred. He then addressed us and told us to get blankets as we might need them. We were then formed in two's and marched out of the College.

This must have been an unreal moment for Captain Henry de Courcy Wheeler, for Constance Markievicz was his wife's first cousin. He had met her several times, and a daughter recently born to Wheeler's wife at the Curragh had been named

Kathleen Constance Gore de Courcy Wheeler, after Constance Markievicz, née Gore-Booth.

After arresting his wife's cousin Wheeler offered her the use of a car, but Markievicz refused and said she would march. Wheeler then asked her for her Mauser pistol. She handed it over – kissing it first – and then said, 'I am ready.' With Commandant Mallin she moved to the head of her troops and marched away with them. (Wheeler's account of her court-martial contrasts with that of William Wylie, who prosecuted her. Wheeler later recalled that at her trial she was defiant, and that at one point she said: 'I have no witnesses, what I did was for the freedom of Ireland, and we thought we had a fighting chance.')

Captain Henry de Courcy Wheeler
(de Courcy Wheeler family)

Captain Wheeler returned to St Patrick's Park to wait for the return of Elizabeth O'Farrell. When she finally arrived – several hours late – she was accompanied by Commandant Thomas MacDonagh as well as the Capuchin friars Father Aloysius Travers and Father Augustine Hayden. Together the group travelled to the South Dublin Union and to Jameson's distillery in Marrowbone Lane to organise the surrenders there.

That evening Wheeler was preparing to return to Boland's bakery with Nurse O'Farrell, but he was told to leave it until the morning. Then word came that Commandant de Valera and the 3rd Battalion of the Irish Volunteers had already surrendered. All the main insurgent outposts had now laid down their arms.

Captain Wheeler's daughter, Dorothea Findlater, later recalled that 'he hated fighting against his countrymen. He was put in charge of Connolly and told to shoot him if he moved. I remember asking him if he would actually have shot him. "I would not," he said and he meant it!'

Captain Henry de Courcy Wheeler never stopped trying to serve overseas but, because of his excellent organisational ability, the army would never let him go. Before the end of the war he had been mentioned in despatches, and was also later promoted to major. He returned to living in Robertstown House and went on to become friendly with both Éamon de Valera and Seán T. O'Kelly. On 28 April 1934 a turf-cutting competition, organised by Wheeler, took place on the Bog of Allen. Those in attendance included Éamon de Valera, now president of the Executive Council (head of government) of the Irish Free State, Seán T. O'Kelly, vice-president of the Executive Council, Seán MacEntee, minister for finance, and

Major Henry de Courcy Wheeler (*centre*) with President Seán T. O'Kelly (*right*) and (*left*) William Norton, Tánaiste and Minister for Social Welfare, in 1949. (*The Irish Times*)

Seán Lemass, minster for industry and commerce. Apart from de Valera, Henry Wheeler had arrested all of them after the end of the Easter Rising.

Wheeler greeted de Valera in Irish during his opening address. When the two men later spoke, de Valera said to him: 'I'm a lucky man. Any leader who surrendered to you was executed!'

Fifteen years later, on 29 April 1949, Henry Wheeler, now aged seventy-seven, was present at a ceremony in Áras an Uachtaráin to hand over some of the 'souvenirs' that had come into his possession after the Rising. (The handing over was to mark the formal separation of the Irish state from the British Commonwealth.) As well as Constance Markievicz's pistol Wheeler had obtained Michael Mallin's walking-stick (which Mallin gave to him when surrendering), a Singer sewing-machine that had been used to make uniforms in Liberty Hall, the Tricolour that had flown above the College of Surgeons (which had been raised by Sergeant Frank Robbins and David O'Leary of the Irish Citizen Army), and pistols and revolvers belonging to several of the leaders, including Patrick Pearse's pistol, which had been handed over when Pearse surrendered at the top of Moore Street.

Major Wheeler now handed over Constance Markievicz's Mauser, Pearse's pistol, four other pistols, an ammunition pouch, and a canteen or mess tin. They were received by Seán T. O'Kelly, now president of Ireland, who Wheeler had arrested thirty-three years earlier. Wheeler also noted that, while he had been Brigadier-General Lowe's staff captain in 1916, O'Kelly had been Pearse's staff captain.

In 1966, to mark the fiftieth anniversary of the Rising, Michael Mallin's walking-stick and the Singer sewing-machine were presented to the state by Major Wheeler's family. Along with the pistols handed over in 1949, they are now housed in the National Museum of Ireland.

Henry de Courcy Wheeler died in 1956, aged eighty-four. However, in 2011 his name reappeared in the newspapers with reference to the disappearance of another Easter Rising 'souvenir'. The *Westmeath Examiner* of 2 February 2011 asked readers if they could remember where they were over the Christmas holiday of 1988 and if so if they could recall coming across a Tricolour, thrown in the street, draped around the shoulders of some reveller, or lying in somebody's back garden. Richard de Courcy-Wheeler, a resident of Newry and a grandson of Henry de Courcy Wheeler, was looking for any information that might lead to the recovery of the flag, or at least some information about where it ended up. He was convinced that it was the one that flew over the College of Surgeons in Dublin. His father, the late Annesley de Courcy-Wheeler, was a general practitioner who lived in Pearse Street, Mullingar, from 1964 until his retirement in 1989. 'At some stage the county council put up metal holders at the level of the first-floor windows for mini Christmas trees,' he told the paper. 'Each Christmas my father placed a large Tricolour in the holder, and in 1988 the flag was stolen, part of some revelry around Christmas or New Year.' He was convinced that the missing flag was the actual College of Surgeons Tricolour. It has never been found.

* * *

After the surrender, other Irish officers in the British army began to encounter the rebel leaders. Lieutenant Joseph Ridgway was a 36-year-old doctor with the Royal Army Medical Corps. He was the son of a butter merchant from Waterford and a mother from Co. Armagh. He had obtained his BA and MD from the University of Dublin and had been commissioned in December 1915. He was staying in the Shelbourne Hotel when the Rising began and was away at the Fairyhouse Races that Monday morning. Just before the last race he learnt that the rebellion had begun, and so he returned to the hotel. The following day he made his way to Dublin Castle. He later recorded that

> during my stay at the Castle I was detailed to take charge of the wounded prisoners who were in a large bedded ward, and also to act as a special dresser for an important political prisoner who was in a small room by himself. There was an armed guard on duty at the door and on entering I saw in bed, a medium sized, stoutly built, bald, florid complexioned middle aged man with a bushy moustache.

He had sustained a bullet wound on the right leg causing a compound fracture of the two long bones (Tibia and Fibula) in their middle third. A few days later he was brought to the operating theatre where I gave him an anaesthetic and the late Mr. Kennedy of Merrion Square, and the late Colonel Tobin – honorary visiting surgeons to the Dublin Castle Red Cross Hospital – operated. Two aluminium rods were placed on each side of the leg to immobilise it, and were held in position with plaster-of-paris, a 'window' being left for dressing the wound. The patient was James Connolly, one of the leaders of the Rising.

Twice daily I dressed the wound and had little chats with him and so I naturally got attached to my patient. When dressing his leg one evening I said in a low voice: 'Is there anything I could do for you in a small way?' He looked surprised and on my repeating my question, he said: 'Yes, I would like to get a message to my wife.' So far as I now can recollect he was given notepaper, an envelope and a pencil and a message was sent and a reply came back. I was aided by one of the V.A.D. [Voluntary Aid Detachment] ladies who were giving their services to this Red Cross hospital.

One afternoon later I was instructed to take over the medical charge from 2 p.m. to 6 p.m. I had been working in the casualty room. On leaving it and on crossing the front hall an orderly saluted and handed me a telegram. I casually opened it and this is what I read: 'Officer Commanding Dublin Castle. The execution of James Connolly is postponed. Asquith.' I put the telegram in the left hand top pocket of my tunic and went to tea. On meeting the officer who had detailed me for duty, he asked if everything had been quiet in his absence and I said yes, and then I handed him the telegram. He read it and looked alarmed, and asked me if I had mentioned its contents to anyone and I assured him I had not. He seemed relieved, and said, 'This should have gone to G.H.Q.'

It was said that when General Maxwell, the General Officer Commanding the troops, read the telegram from the prime minister, he at once declared he would resign if a reprieve was granted to any convicted political prisoner. As this would have caused a sensation at that critical stage of the Great War his wish was granted. Later, as I sensed that events might occur in connection with the medical duties, which might be unpleasant, I obtained permission to rejoin my unit, so I came gladly out into the sunshine of a glorious spring morning.

While Lieutenant Ridgway managed to escape from any 'unpleasant' medical duties, another Irish doctor in the Royal Army Medical Corps was not so lucky. In 1916 Captain Herbert Vernon Stanley was thirty-two years old. A Dubliner, he had joined the Royal Army Medical Corps several years before the war, and he went on to serve in Gallipoli before returning to Dublin.

Based at the Dublin Castle Red Cross Hospital during the Rising, Captain Stanley had accidentally sent Nurse Elizabeth O'Farrell to the guardroom of Ship Street Barracks after she had finished travelling around Dublin with Captain Wheeler to secure the various surrenders. Because of her services, an order had been issued that Nurse O'Farrell was not to be treated as an ordinary prisoner. When Stanley learnt of his mistake from Wheeler the two captains went looking for her, only to discover that she had been sent on to Richmond Barracks. Stanley managed to secure an ambulance and, accompanied by an assistant matron, he and Wheeler travelled to Richmond Barracks. When they arrived they were horrified to learn that Nurse O'Farrell had already been sent on to Kilmainham Jail in preparation for her deportation. The two captains and the assistant matron rushed to the prison, where Wheeler threatened to court-martial anyone who attempted to deport the nurse. When he threatened to get the general officer commanding troops in Dublin if Nurse O'Farrell was not handed over, she was quickly brought to him. The four then returned to Dublin Castle, with Captain Stanley apologising that he was to blame for the mistake. Father Aloysius Travers later recorded that Captain Stanley

> said it would be a consolation if one of the priests would drop into the 'Sinn Féin' ward in which the other prisoner-patients were, and say a word to those in it, and let their friends know that they were alive ... I was permitted to go round to each bed and speak to the patients. Some of them said they would be grateful if I would send them prayer-books. Captain Stanley said he would distribute them with pleasure if I sent them; and he did very kindly distribute the books which were sent ... Captain Stanley showed himself, all through, a Christian and humane man, and James Connolly spoke to me of his very great kindness to him, although Stanley was politically and in religion at variance with the prisoners.

Nevertheless Captain Stanley, as a medical officer, was appointed to oversee the executions in Kilmainham Jail. Years later he spoke about this to Edward Gerrard, who had served as a second-lieutenant in the Royal Field Artillery in Beggarsbush Barracks during the Rising. Gerrard recalled:

> About April, 1935, when I was in Aldershot, our Medical Officer was Colonel H. V. Stanley, R.A.M.C. He said to me, 'I was the Medical Officer who attended the executions of the first nine Sinn Féiners to be shot. After that I got so sick of the slaughter that I asked to be changed. Three refused to have their eyes bandaged' – I can't remember who the three were – anyway, he said that there were three – 'they all died like lions. The rifles of the firing party were waving like a field of corn. All the men were cut to ribbons at a range of about ten yards.' That is what he said to me.

It was a Dublin man who had to declare, after the first nine executions in Kilmainham Jail, that each insurgent leader was dead after being shot by firing squad. Captain Stanley was awarded the Military Cross for his actions during the Rising. He stayed in the army after the war and rose to the rank of colonel. He appears to have died in Surrey in 1960, aged seventy-seven.

* * *

When the fighting in Dublin finally ended, the task of counting the dead and wounded began. The Rising had resulted in the deaths of approximately 134 British forces personnel, including British army, Royal Navy and IAVTC as well as RIC and DMP policemen; approximately 387 more were wounded. If the police figures are deducted (seventeen killed and thirty wounded), Irishmen made up 35 per cent of the British military fatalities during the Rising (41 out of the 117 military deaths) and 29 per cent of the wounded (106 out of 357).

Some of the other Irishmen who were wounded in British army uniform before the end of the week included 31-year-old Lance-Corporal Patrick Sarsfield Murphy of the 5th Royal Irish Lancers, a pre-war regular soldier from Dublin and former London policeman who 'received GSW [gunshot wound] to neck below left ear with exit wound on fourth cerebral vertebra' on 27 April before being taken to Dublin Castle Red Cross Hospital. He survived, but the wound later contributed to the onset of epilepsy, memory lapses and partial loss of eyesight, which meant that shortly after Murphy returned to the Metropolitan Police in London after the war he was forced to retire on medical grounds.

Private Samuel McDonnell of the 8th (King's Royal Irish) Hussars, a 45-year-old veteran of the Anglo-Boer War from Castleblayney, Co. Monaghan, who had worked in the GPO sorting office for a time before the war, was also wounded during the Rising, as was a fellow-soldier in the 8th (King's Royal Irish) Hussars, Private John Mullally. Also a pre-war regular soldier, Mullally was thirty years old and a native of Ennis, Co. Clare. A veteran of India and the Western Front, he was wounded in the face and hands during the Rising and was discharged before the end of 1916 after developing pulmonary tuberculosis.

Sapper (i.e. Private) R. F. Cripps of the Royal Engineers, with links to Ballincollig, Co. Cork, was also wounded during the Rising, as were Gunner Thomas Toole from Dublin of the Royal Field Artillery and Corporal Charles Mills of the Royal Army Medical Corps, linked to Dublin. *Unarmed Persons Shot by Rebels* noted that Mills was wounded on 26 April 'while sitting beside driver of a motor ambulance which was trying to recover body of an ambulance [man?] in Charles St. The fire was so heavy attempt was abandoned.'

Lastly, 24-year-old Corporal Anthony Meenehan of the Connaught Rangers, a native of Knockglass, Ballinrobe, Co. Mayo, was also wounded. An RIC policeman before the war, he returned to the RIC afterwards and then went on to join the Royal Ulster Constabulary after its formation in 1922. When he retired he was the last serving RUC policeman to have previously served in the RIC.

Among the other Irish soldiers in the British army who were killed during Easter Week 1916, Private William Mulraney of the 8th (King's Royal Irish) Hussars was killed in Dublin on 26 April. He had enlisted in Dublin and had already served on the Western Front by the time of his death. William Mulraney is buried in Grangegorman Military Cemetery.

Major Percival Acheson of the Army Service Corps died on 29 April 1916, possibly of wounds received on the 24th. A 57-year-old officer who lived in Grange West, Fermoy, Co. Cork, he had been born in Southampton in England but was the son of a merchant from Co. Wexford. Today, Percival Acheson is buried in Castlehyde Church of Ireland churchyard, Fermoy.

Finally, twenty-year-old Lieutenant Philip Purser of the Army Service Corps, born in Birmingham (though his father was from Co. Westmeath) and raised in Dublin, died of wounds on 30 April 1916. In 1914 he had been discharged from the 1st County of London Yeomanry (Middlesex Duke of Cambridge's Own Hussars) after only twenty-six days' service because of poor health, but he persisted and finally succeeded in obtaining a commission. He served briefly in France in 1915 but was evacuated because of a heart condition and so was posted to permanent home duty. After the Rising began in Dublin he acted as a despatch-rider for higher command. He was shot in the abdomen on 29 April while returning from a mission to Kingstown (Dún Laoghaire) and died of his wounds the following day.

On 19 May 1916 Philip Purser's father, William Purser, wrote to the War Office to say:

> I beg to express my thanks to you and to Lord Kitchener for the sympathy conveyed in your letter of 17th inst. in regard to the death of my son, Lieut and acting adjutant Philip A. Purser A.S.C. who was shot by the Sinn Fein rebels on 29th ... My son, aged 20, may possibly have been the youngest adjutant in the service. I am informed that at the time of his death his C.O. had sent to H.Q. a very strong recommendation for his promotion to a Captaincy. My son volunteered to carry dispatches from the Curragh to Dublin on 'Easter Tuesday.' He was 'held up' by the Sinn Feiners en route but got through and delivered his dispatches in safety. He got through by guessing the pass word of the day, 'Liberty,' used by the Sinn Fein party! This was one of the most remarkable incidents during the recent rebellion.

Philip Purser was buried in the grounds of Dublin Castle. His grave was later lost or forgotten and was rediscovered only in May 1962. His body was exhumed and reinterred and today lies in Grangegorman Military Cemetery.

* * *

The Irish Volunteers and their comrades lost sixty-four killed during the fighting and an unknown number of wounded. However, those who suffered the most were the non-combatants: the ordinary citizens whose lives were destroyed by the fighting. 254 Irish civilians are known to have been killed during the Easter Rising and a further 2,217 injured.

Elsewhere around the country other Irish regiments of the British army had been involved in defeating the Rising. The 3rd and 4th Leinster Regiment and the 4th Royal Irish Regiment had all been sent to Limerick to deal with the rebellion there, while the 3rd Connaught Rangers had been despatched to defeat the rebels in Enniscorthy. Many members of the Irish National Volunteers had also mobilised around the country to assist the police until the military arrived.

The commanding officer of the 3rd Connaught Rangers was Colonel George French of Newbay, Co. Wexford. His son Lieutenant-Colonel Maurice French was killed during the Second World War on 14 November 1943, aged forty, while serving as commanding officer of the 2nd Royal Irish Fusiliers during the Battle of Leros. Maurice French today lies in the Leros War Cemetery, as does another of his officers, Lieutenant Hugh Gore-Booth, a nephew of Constance Markievicz, née Gore-Booth, who also died during the Battle of Leros on 11 November 1943, aged thirty-three.

In 1916 the damage to Dublin and its people was also assessed. The bulk of the destruction was centred on Sackville Street and the surrounding areas, which made this part of Dublin look like the shattered city of Ypres in Belgium. Artillery and raging fires had blasted and burnt the area into a pile of charred rubble. The fighting and fires had caused damage elsewhere in the city, but the majority of the estimated two hundred buildings destroyed during the Rising were in this zone. Ultimately the cost of the damage was estimated at £2½ to £3 million (taken at 1916 value). Furthermore, the destruction of so many shops and business premises was a serious blow to the Dublin economy.

Among the citizens of Dublin, 100,000 people – a third of the city's population at the time – were soon in receipt of public relief. Some had no place of work to return to, while others had lost everything they owned, including their homes. Also, the Rising had taken place during the first anniversary of both the Second Battle of Ypres (which began on 21 April 1915) and the V Beach landings at Gallipoli (25 April 1915), meaning that in late April 1916 hundreds of Dublin families were mourning the loss of family members the previous year.

It is perhaps not difficult to understand the anger directed at Volunteer Paddy Joe Stephenson during the Rising, as recorded in his account of the fight for the Mendicity Institution. 'Out on Usher's Quay we made for Church Street Bridge and the Four Courts. Nearing the corner of Bridge Street one of a group of women standing in a doorway called out: "There is two of them. The curse of God on you, it's out in Flanders you should be, you bastards – fighting the so and so Germans. Be God if I lay me hands on you I'll tear the guts out of you".' This was by no means an isolated incident, and the wives of British army soldiers – known locally as 'separation women' – as well as other Dublin women told the rebels on several occasions what they thought of them. On the first day of the Rising, at the McCaffrey Estate near the South Dublin Union, Lieutenant William O'Brien of the Irish Volunteers and his detachment of four men were on the receiving end of verbal abuse from army wives. One Volunteer told them to 'Go to hell' at almost the same time that the column of the 3rd Royal Irish Regiment approached from Richmond Barracks. This prompted the women to run, but one of them shouted back at the rebels, 'Yez'll bate it now, me boyos. Here come the military.'

At the same time another group of separation women began insulting the insurgents in the GPO. However, these women soon turned their anger on each other, much to the rebels' amusement, with two even pulling out each other's hair. After Colonel Hammond's troop of lancers had been fired on from the GPO and had retreated to barracks an old woman tried to stop a young newsboy from giving one of the fallen soldiers' rifles to the insurgents in the GPO. She tried to take it from him, but he hit her on the head and she fell down screaming. When a rebel party was sent from the GPO to barricade Lower Abbey Street at the junction of Sackville Street an angry mob gathered and shouted at them as they worked.

Over near the Four Courts, Volunteer Patrick Kelly had to draw his revolver to protect himself from local women. He had stopped a British army soldier who was trying to walk through a rebel area, only for onlooking women to begin abusing him verbally before marching towards him. The women then demanded that the soldier disarm the rebel but, unarmed, the soldier decided to simply walk back the way he had come, and the situation was over.

Even when the English soldiers of the 59th (2nd North Midland) Division set off from Kingstown towards the Royal Hospital in Kilmainham on the morning of 26 April they were supported by local people. Women – both servants and the ladies of the houses – came out with tea, sandwiches, fruit, chocolate and sweets for the advancing columns while thanking them for coming to help or giving them what information they had about rebel activities. Some citizens even gave the soldiers maps and binoculars. Later, when Colonel Ernest Maconchy, commanding officer of the 178th Brigade, rode to Mount Street Bridge, he too was cheered by some local people.

However, a few English officers were suspicious that local people might actually be rebel sympathisers and were trying to poison them, and so orders were passed among the 2nd/5th and 2nd/6th Sherwood Foresters to reject all gifts. Later, when the fighting began around Mount Street Bridge, it is reported that at one point people came out of their houses in Percy Place with sheets to carry the British army wounded back inside and away from danger, while after the battle had ended the soldiers were given tea and food by celebrating local people from Power's Court, just off Mount Street. At the same time eighteen-year-old Volunteer James Doyle encountered a hostile crowd near Merrion Square after escaping from Clanwilliam House.

After the insurgents attacked Dublin Castle and the wounded began arriving at the Red Cross Hospital there, one VAD nurse working at the hospital later wrote, as recorded by Max Caulfield in *The Easter Rebellion*: 'My only conscious sensation at the moment was of a burning desire to go out and have a shot at the rebels myself.'

Some people even got in harm's way in order to insult the insurgents. When the Irish Citizen Army troops were retreating from St Stephen's Green to the College of Surgeons a group of angry people, some hurling rotten vegetables, others armed with iron bars and hatchets, assaulted them as they ran while at the same time the British army machine-gunners were firing down from their positions on top of the Shelbourne Hotel. Sergeant Frank Robbins of the Irish Citizen Army took aim at the leader of the mob – a young woman who had been jeering him in St Stephen's Green the previous day – but was stopped by a Lieutenant Kelly, who tugged on his rifle. Robbins tried again to take aim, but Kelly gave him a direct order not to fire. The woman fled but continued to shout at Robbins once she reached a safe distance and had rejoined the angry crowd.

Elsewhere the people of Dublin often warned the military or the police about rebel positions, or insisted on being allowed to go about their daily business, regardless of rebel activities. One such woman refused to be prevented from walking home by her normal route and successfully climbed over a rebel barricade in Sackville Street – falling twice in front of a laughing crowd – before marching away and cursing the rebels.

* * *

For all the anger directed at the insurgents during Easter Week 1916, and for all the support initially shown towards the British army, both sides are known to have performed acts of kindness during the fight, as well as committing terrible acts of cruelty.

While some soldiers in the British army are known to have obtained supplies for prisoners in Richmond Barracks after the Rising, or otherwise treated them with decency – as well as providing safe escorts for civilians around the city during the fighting, and opening up food stores to the public when access to food became an issue – others are known to have mistreated the rebels, been physically violent towards them, and even attempting to shoot them after they had surrendered.

On 27 April 1916, when Daniel Doyle, a 46-year-old court crier from Upper Liffey Street, originally from Co. Wicklow, lifted his hand to wave to a friend he was shot dead by a British army sniper, who thought he was preparing to throw a grenade.

Max Caulfield records in *The Easter Rebellion* how a soldier posted on the roof of a house in Lower Mount Street went insane under the pressure of the close-quarter urban combat that he and his comrades were having to endure and went on a killing spree, indiscriminately shooting people who were simply walking by. Nearby a 29-year-old Dubliner, Charles Hyland, a dental surgeon who lived in Percy Place and who had earlier helped to carry wounded soldiers into Sir Patrick Dun's Hospital during the Battle of Mount Street Bridge, was also shot dead by a British army sniper. He was the son of Charles Hyland Snr, manager of the Gaiety Theatre. All civilians in the area had been warned to stay indoors, but Hyland had ignored – or had not heard about – the order.

After the Rising, Private Henry Wyatt of the 5th Royal Irish Lancers, a 22-year-old Dubliner, was sentenced to five years' penal servitude for the manslaughter of Robert Glaister, a 45-year-old engine-room artificer with the Royal Navy. A native of Silloth, Cumberland, Wyatt had previously enlisted in the 7th Royal Inniskilling Fusiliers in April 1915 and after being fined for eighteen days' absence in June that year was tried by district court-martial for an unspecified offence, given 140 days' hard labour as punishment, and then immediately discharged in January 1916. He subsequently re-enlisted in the 5th Royal Irish Lancers and on Friday 28 April 1916 was on sentry duty outside the Northern Hotel in Amiens Street when he shot Robert Glaister twice, ultimately killing him. Witnesses said that Wyatt had asked Glaister to halt, which he did, and then Wyatt shot him; Wyatt claimed that Glaister ignored the order to stop. Today Robert Glaister lies in Glasnevin Cemetery.

On the other side, the insurgents are known to have treated their British army prisoners exceptionally well, with Michael O'Rahilly putting himself in harm's way to take care of his prisoners inside the GPO and then rescuing a wounded soldier during the subsequent fighting in Moore Street. They are known to have also provided food to the civilian population where possible, and were joined from time to time – or at the very least assisted and provided with information – by many Dubliners who supported their cause.

However, some rebel hands were also blood-stained. On 25 April, in response to the looting in Sackville Street, Captain W. J. Brennan-Whitmore of the Irish Volunteers asked for permission to arrest and shoot two looters in order to set an example, but James Connolly would not allow it. Other civilians, however, were killed by insurgents during the fighting, and *Unarmed Persons Shot by Rebels* records that on Monday 24 April alone eight civilians were killed and fourteen more wounded by the rebels. Those killed included a Mr Dunne of High Street, who was 'shot by rebels for not getting off the street'; Michael Kavanagh of Queen's Square, 'shot for taking his lorry from barricade near Shelbourne Hotel in Stephens Green,' Michael Kelly of Clanbrassil Street, 'shot by a rebel on footway outside his own door,' 43-year-old John Armstrong, a mason-bricklayer of Great Longford Street, 'shot on Earlsfort Terrace for not moving on,' a man who the authorities believed to be a Mr E. Kane who was 'shot for refusing to assist in erecting a barricade at corner of Cuffe St. and Stephens Green,' and L. McNally of Lower Clanbrassil Street and fifteen-year-old Eleanor Warbrook of Fumbally Lane, both shot and killed in Fumbally Lane on 24 April 1916.

A letter from Prof. J. Pope of Trinity College to the provost, John Mahaffy, which the DMP later had in its possession, recorded that on 24 April 'a young girl was shot opposite General Post Office. A man in green uniform opened the door of the Post Office & called out something to the crowd; he then raised his hand with a revolver in it and I heard a shot and a young woman of about 17 or 18 cried out and fell. She was shot through the left breast and died.'

Among those who were wounded by the rebels on 24 April the two most serious cases were those of John Lysaght and Doreen Carphin. Lysaght, a 45-year-old engine fitter from Co. Limerick now living in Upper Kevin Street, 'went outside his door to bring in his child. A Sinn Feiner held a revolver to his head which he knocked aside. Another Sinn Feiner then bayoneted him, inflicting a very severe wound.' Lysaght was later treated in the Adelaide Hospital. Eight-year-old Doreen Carphin from Rathgar was 'shot by Sinn Feiners from Stephens Green, while passing Unitarian Church near College of Surgeons. Her father & mother both had their clothes pierced by bullets.' She was later treated in nearby Mercer's Hospital.

Among others who were killed or wounded by insurgents and mentioned in *Unarmed Persons Shot by Rebels*, one man was wounded while attempting to enter the building where he worked, several more were wounded while driving along but were not first told to halt, while on 25 April fifteen-year-old James Kelly of Phibsborough Road was 'alleged shot for refusing to join rebels.' He later died, and the report noted that this 'information was given by his brother, who afterwards declined to give any further assistance in the matter.' (This report also states that, 'regarding the persons who gave information to the Police where the persons were killed, nearly all these people refused to allow their names to be mentioned through fear of their business being injured or perhaps their lives endangered should their names become known.')

On Tuesday 25 April, when Volunteer Martin Mullen was attempting to join his comrades inside Boland's bakery, he was stopped outside the building by a group of soldiers' wives who abused and spat at him. Mullen tried to push through them, and the women called a passing postman to help. The postman was subsequently shot by insurgents inside Boland's bakery.

Mirroring the way in which two British army officers were killed in the Guinness brewery by their own forces, on Thursday 27 April an Irish Volunteer in Boland's bakery went insane and shot and killed a comrade who was on sentry duty, Peter Macken, a well-known Dublin city councillor. This man was subsequently shot by another Volunteer.

On Friday 28 April, while the rebels were attempting to withdraw from the GPO to Great Britain Street, they began breaking into the houses in nearby Henry Place in search of cover. Living at number 11 Henry Place was 45-year-old Thomas McKane, a foreman of works, originally from Co. Monaghan, together with his wife, 44-year-old Margaret McKane from Co. Carlow, and the couple's fourteen children. Having witnessed someone shot two days earlier and their body thrown up on a British army barricade, the McKanes had not gone outside their front door. They were hungry and were in the act of praying when the rebels began breaking into houses all along their street. When Thomas McKane heard the rebels banging on his door he picked up his youngest child and began leading his family towards a back door, trying to get them out of the house to safety. An insurgent then smashed one of the front windows with his rifle, but the weapon went off accidentally. The bullet tore through Thomas McKane's shoulder and narrowly missed the baby in his arms but hit his sixteen-year-old daughter, Bridget, in the head, killing her instantly.

The McKane family almost suffered another calamity after Margaret McKane, hysterical following the death of her daughter and the wounding of her husband, ran out of the house towards the barricade of the Sherwood Foresters in Moore Street, apparently attempting to get a priest. The soldiers told her to stay back but she kept running forward, and one soldier fired a warning shot. She was again ordered to stop, but she did not listen. Finally one private asked his officer whether he should fire on her or not. The officer told him to lower his rifle.

* * *

After the Rising the insurgents who were identified as being under the age of eighteen were simply told to go home. However, along with those who had actually taken part in the Rising, many known republicans and members of Sinn Féin – the majority of whom had nothing to do with the Rising – were rounded up and interned. In total, 3,509 people were arrested immediately following the event, with 1,424 of these being released without charge within two weeks. Of those who remained in custody, 187 were court-martialled, and 90 of these were sentenced to death. However, only fifteen of the death sentences were confirmed, and between 3 and 12 May 1916 fourteen men were shot by firing squad in Kilmainham Jail and a fifteenth in Cork Detention Barracks.

It quickly became obvious that the speed with which the courts-martial had been conducted, and the speed with which the executions were taking place, would be devastating to Home-Rule nationalism and could only result in a sharp increase in support for republicanism. (The actions of Captain Bowen-Colthurst and of the South Staffordshire Regiment at North King Street had already seriously damaged the British army and government's reputation in Ireland.) After the first three executions on 3 May the leader of the Irish Party, John Redmond, told the British prime minister, Herbert Asquith, that 'if any more executions take place in Ireland, the position will become impossible for any constitutional party or leader.' Asquith got in touch with General Maxwell, 'military governor' in Dublin under martial law since his arrival in Ireland on Friday 28 April, to impress upon him that 'anything like a large number of executions would ... sow the seeds of lasting trouble in Ireland.' Even Edward Carson, who had earlier offered 50,000 UVF men to help defeat the Rising while it was in progress, called for leniency. In the House of Commons he stated that 'no true Irishman calls for vengeance. It will be a matter requiring the greatest wisdom and the greatest calmness in dealing with these men. Whatever is done, let it be done not in a moment of temporary excitement but in a moment of deliberation.'

But still the executions continued. On 11 May, with thirteen men having now been shot by firing squad, John Dillon of the Irish Party, also speaking in the House of Commons, warned that 'you are letting loose a river of blood and, make no mistake about it, between the two races who, after three hundred years of hatred and strife, we had nearly succeeded in bringing together.'

The following day Seán Mac Diarmada and the badly wounded James Connolly were the last two insurgents to be shot. Connolly's execution in particular outraged elements of Irish society and marked the beginning of a change in public opinion.

It was these executions that gave Pearse his 'blood sacrifice', and it was the British response to the Rising, rather than the Rising itself, that ultimately paved the way for a growth in support for an Irish republic. Sinn Féin, a financially struggling nationalist party in 1916 that promoted passive resistance and the Austro-Hungarian 'dual monarchy' political system, which had absolutely nothing to do with the planning or carrying out of the Rising, was mistakenly identified with the rebellion by the authorities. As a result, republicans flocked to the party, and its support grew enormously. The founder of Sinn Féin, Arthur Griffith, would later say that 'Sinn Féin did not make the Rising, but the Rising made Sinn Féin.'

Captain Stephen Gwynn, a 52-year-old officer with the Connaught Rangers from Rathfarnham, Co. Dublin, and also an Irish Party MP, returned to Ireland from the trenches not long after the Rising. In his book *John Redmond's Last Years* (1919) he wrote:

> When I came home from France a few weeks later, a shrewd and prosperous Nationalist man of business said to me with fury: 'The fools! It was the first rebellion that ever had the country against it, and they turned the people round in a week' ... They were given the death of rebels in arms, to which no dishonour attaches. But a fatal mistake was made in suppressing all report of the proceedings of the court-martial on them, and this mistake was to be repeated indefinitely. Ireland was made to feel that this whole affair was taken completely out of the hands of Irishmen – that no attempt even was made to enlist Irish opinion on the side of law by a statement of the evidence on which law acted. Day by day there was a new bald announcement that such and such men had been shot.

Despite being blamed by history for the fervour with which the executions were carried out, General Sir John Maxwell, afterwards remembered by republicans as 'Bloody Maxwell', appears to have completely disliked his role in the event. Catriona Crowe, head of special projects at the National Archives, stated in an interview in 2014 as part of the television documentary 'A Sovereign People: The Story of the Irish Revolution':

> General Maxwell was the man who gets the blame for the 1916 executions. Now, his personal papers are in Princeton University, and this is contemporary – he is writing these letters every night from the Royal Hospital,

Kilmainham, where he's staying, headquarters of the British army, to his wife in England right through the period when he's overseeing the executions. He clearly doesn't like the executions, and at one point he says, 'Of course none of this dreadful stuff would be happening if we had stopped the Ulster Volunteers back when they started to get going. Home Rule is on the statute books. It must be implemented. It is the law. And it is the job of people who work for armies to uphold the law.' So it was quite fascinating to sit there and look at these letters and think, My goodness, he thought quite differently to the way we might have imagined.

In an article about Maxwell's personal papers, 'Imperialists at work and play: The Papers of General Sir John and Lady Maxwell', Letitia Ufford of Princeton University, New Jersey, wrote that 'even during the difficult days of the uprising, Maxwell, while praying for an end to the death sentences which he found himself imposing, sympathised with the plight of the Irish: "The poverty and improvidence in Dublin is appalling – my old Wassa bazaar not in it with the slums of Dublin. It is a disgrace to the British race!!"'

Between 1,400 and 1,800 insurgents were interned in prisons and camps in England and Wales. However, after Herbert Asquith was replaced by David Lloyd George as British prime minster in December 1916 the release of internees began, and they started returning home to Ireland from Christmas onwards. In June 1917 an unconditional amnesty was finally declared, and any insurgent who was still imprisoned at that time was finally released.

Having left Ireland as rebels, the insurgents now returned to cheering crowds as heroes. The following year the British government's attempt – ultimately unsuccessful – to impose conscription in Ireland, coupled with war-weariness, was the final nail in the coffin of 'Home Rule'. In particular the Conscription Crisis – as it became known – was hugely important in generating a further increase in support for Sinn Féin and for republicanism. In the 1918 general election Sinn Féin won 73 seats, unionists won 22 seats, and the old Irish Party was essentially wiped out, winning only 6 seats.

A year later, in 1919, the War of Independence began, and within three years Britain would be forced to agree to a truce with the IRA and bring about the creation of the Irish Free State. In many ways the Rising was the beginning of the end of forty years of constitutional nationalism and peaceful struggle, and it placed violence and the gun firmly back in Irish politics as a seemingly effective way of bringing about swift reforms. As Stephen Gwynn noted after the Rising, 'the Parliamentary Party [Irish Party] brought to Ireland a post-dated order for Home Rule, liable to an indefinite series of postponements; Sinn Fein by a week's rebellion secures that Home Rule shall be brought into force at once.'

One Irish soldier in the British army who experienced the drastic way in which public opinion began to change after the Rising was Private James Keogh of the 6th Royal Dublin Fusiliers. A Gallipoli veteran, he was not involved in the Rising but in early 1917 received news that his young wife had died in Dublin. He was given leave to return home for the funeral, during which he walked with his two young children and the rest of the mourners behind his wife's coffin. On reaching the church, however, the priest refused to allow Keogh (who was in uniform) to enter. His grandson recently recalled: 'The next time my grandfather James Keogh entered a church was for his own funeral. He died in February 1957.' He was buried in Grangegorman Military Cemetery, where many Irish soldiers who were killed while serving in the British army during the Rising also lie.

* * *

After the Easter Rising the Irishmen in the British army were still serving in the trenches during Christmas 1916 when the first rebels began returning home. In June 1917, when the amnesty was finally declared and the last insurgents were released, the men of the 16th (Irish) Division and 36th (Ulster) Division were fighting in the Battle of Messines Ridge in Belgium.

Among those who had been in the trenches at the time of the Rising many Irish soldiers were deeply upset and angered by the actions of republicans in Dublin. At the same time that the Rising was taking place in Dublin the 16th (Irish) Division was gassed and then attacked by the German army in their positions at Hulluch, near Loos, on 27 April 1916. On the first day of the attack the division suffered 442 casualties, and by the end of the battle two days later a total of 538 men in the division had been killed, along with 1,590 more wounded, most of them casualties from gas. A stream of letters and telegrams would soon be making their way to more homes in Ireland.

In those three days on the Western Front the 16th (Irish) Division lost more men killed than all the British army, rebel and civilian fatalities of the Rising combined.

Germany tried to capitalise on the Rising for propaganda purposes. On 1 May 1916 German soldiers raised a placard facing an Irish battalion across no-man's-land that read *Irishmen! Heavy uproar in Ireland. English guns are firing on your wives and children.* Other placards called on Irishmen to desert the British army.

Irish soldiers generally ignored these, but one group crawled out into no-man's-land to capture a placard, while in response to another German sign other Irish soldiers reportedly began singing Irish songs in defiance of the Germans, along with 'Rule, Britannia'. The 9th Royal Munster Fusiliers raised an effigy of Roger Casement above their trench; it annoyed the Germans opposite their position and was soon shot to pieces.

The Monica Roberts Collection in Dublin City Library and Archive, part of the Royal Dublin Fusiliers Association's archive, contains many letters of thanks sent by Irish soldiers in the trenches to the Band of Helpers for Soldiers, a voluntary group set up by Monica Roberts and her friends during the war to provide small gifts to men at the front. After the Rising many of the letters began to mention it, and – while the men were also worried about families in Dublin and hoped they were safe – the soldiers were generally outraged that the Rising had taken place. These men – especially the thousands of Irish National Volunteers who had enlisted in the belief that they were fighting for Home Rule – felt it was a betrayal of their suffering and sacrifices in the trenches. Private Joseph Clarke of the 2nd Royal Dublin Fusiliers wrote on 11 May 1916:

> I was sorry to hear of the rebel rising in Ireland but I hope by the time this letter reaches you the condition will have changed and things normal again. There is no-one more sorry to hear of the rising than the Irish troops out here – it worries them more than I can explain. Their whole cry is, if they could only get among them for a few days, the country would not be annoyed with them any more. Some of the men in this Battalion are very uneasy about the safety of their people and one or two poor fellows have lost relatives in this scandalous affair. We just have had some men returned off leave and they tell us that Dublin is in ruins. It is awfully hard to lose one's life out here without being shot at home. The Sherwood's [Sherwood Foresters] lost heavily but I expect the Rebels got the worst of the encounter. We of the 2nd Battalion, the Dublins [Royal Dublin Fusiliers], would ask for nothing better than the rebels should be sent out here and have an encounter with some of their 'so-called allies,' the Germans. I do not think anything they have done will cause any anxiety to England or her noble cause. We will win just the same. These men are pro-German pure and simple and no Irishmen will be sorry when they get justice meted out to them, which, in my opinion, should be death by being shot.

Private Christopher Fox of the same battalion wrote on 12 May 1916: 'Those Sinn Feiners are a lot of murderers they [*sic*] sooner Ireland gets rid of them they better they have brought a nice disgrace on the Old Country I can tell you they boys out here would like to catch a few of them and we would give them a rough time of it.' In another letter, dated 31 May 1916, Fox writes that 'I am glad to hear all the trouble is over in Dublin. I would like to have a few of those rebels out here, I can tell you I would give them 2 oz. of lead.'

The *Drogheda Independent* of 13 May 1916 published a letter from a Driver P. Nulty, written on 4 May.

> Sir, kindly give me a small space in your very popular and very widely circulated journal to say that the local men at the front regret very much the disturbance in Dublin, and are thankful that it did not spread to Drogheda. Every one is quite aware of its origin. Engineered by the Sinn Feiners, who are the Huns of Holy Ireland, they have been a considerable time on the Kaiser's Pay Roll, and the Apostle of Kultur will not help to defend them at their trials which they don't deserve at all. John Redmond's work of years is now flung to the winds; truly a very fitting response to his loyalty to the

country. Hanging is the only means to adopt. Shooting at sight of every known member of the Sinn Fein society might be resorted to with success, a price being put on their heads. If they want to fight let them come out to face their friends the Huns. We will be very pleased to return to Ireland and look after its affairs in a manner becoming a country belonging to the British Empire. Thank God! We have a Navy and Ireland is not yet a Hun Colony and never will be. Jim Connolly, known as the Kaiser of Dublin, did not wear an imperial moustache like his All High Pay Master. The All Highness and Supreme Bully of Potsdam has tried to create war in the Land of Saints and Scholars as he is not able to put a thorn in the Allies side. All the men from the town heartily agree with the measures taken to stop the rebellion and even that if it comes to shooting down of our own countrymen it would be carried out to the letter. Dublin will give you some idea of what Ypres is like when you see it. Sackville Street will speak but is only a midge compared with the destruction of sacred edifices in France and Belgium. I may close, but I say that there are societies in Ireland who need to be kept under observation, as the last affair is a disgrace with a blot on the memory of those who have made the supreme sacrifice, as Irish soldiers have done since this war began, and are every day and night sacrificing life and limb, and the pro-Germans of Ireland live comfortably. Let us hope that pro-Germanism will cease with the destruction of Sackville Street. I now close, dear Mr Editor, thanking you for past kindness and wishing your valuable paper further success.

In *John Redmond's Last Years,* Stephen Gwynn wrote: 'That was a long tour of trenches, some eighteen days beginning on the 29th of April, and throughout it papers came in with the Irish news. I shall never forget the men's indignation. They felt they had been stabbed in the back.'

But despite how most Irish soldiers in the British army responded to the Rising, some officers and politicians began to doubt their loyalty, or at the very least worry about it. While the higher command continued to trust Irish troops – almost certainly because Irish regiments had fought hard against the insurgents in Dublin – some lower-ranking officers and politicians began to grow wary of them. If republicanism was replacing Home-Rule nationalism, perhaps nationalists in the trenches would soon sympathise with republicanism too?

Private Tom Barry from Killorglin, Co. Kerry, serving with the Royal Field Artillery in Mesopotamia (Iraq) at the time of the Rising, would later become a prominent member of the IRA during the War of Independence and the Civil War. He admitted in his memoir *Guerilla Days in Ireland* (1949) that 'I went to the war for no other reason than that I wanted to see what war was like, to get a gun, to see new countries and to feel a grown man.' After hearing about the Rising, however, he felt that 'thus, through the blood sacrifices of the men of 1916, had one Irish youth of eighteen been awakened to Irish nationality.'

There were certainly others like Tom Barry, and there are several accounts of some men of the Royal Munster Fusiliers, the 6th Connaught Rangers and the 7th Royal Irish Rifles being referred to as 'Sinn Féiners' in the years after the Rising, suggesting that some soldiers in these units had subsequently become republicans. (It must be noted, however, that the authorities referred to nearly every type of Irish nationalist as 'Sinn Féiners' at the time.) But despite the concerns of some, the generals continued to trust their men, there were no mutinies and no increase in the number of courts-martial, no one deserted or

Connaught Rangers cap badge
(Author's Collection)

provided information to the enemy, and no one refused to continue to fight in the war; even Tom Barry saw it through to the end. In many cases, news of the Rising made men more determined to fight for their cause.

When the German army launched its Spring Offensive on 21 March 1918, its last all-out attempt to force the allies to the negotiating table, it is possible that it specifically targeted the British Fifth Army, which contained the 16th (Irish) Division, thinking that Irishmen would now stand and fight for Britain. They were wrong, and on the first day of the battle the 6th Connaught Rangers, consisting of roughly 520 men (and one of the battalions said to possibly contain some 'Sinn Féiners'), fought back against two German divisions. It suffered nearly 300 men killed and wounded on that day alone, as a result of which losses the battalion was ultimately disbanded.

When they finally began coming home after the war, Irishmen in the British army were facing a new Ireland. At least 32,000 of them – former members of the Irish National Volunteers – had enlisted in the hope of securing Home Rule for Ireland; now, by 1918 or 1919, Irish people wanted a republic. These soldiers had left Ireland years earlier as heroes to cheering crowds; now they were returning to angry mobs as traitors.

While some would ultimately join the republican cause during the War of Independence, and therefore find a new acceptance at home, most would just try to get on with life. But the changed country they had returned to never made this easy. By the 1920s half the estimated 100,000 First World War veterans who returned to Ireland were unemployed (compared with one in ten in Britain), 30,000 of them in Dublin alone. By 1919 Sinn Féin controlled many local authorities, and laws were passed in Munster that prevented local councils and Poor Law boards from hiring ex-soldiers. While republican employers would not hire ex-soldiers, neutral employers – not wanting to upset the republicans in their employment – often did the same.

In Britain, ex-soldiers could avail of the 'King's National Roll', an employment scheme for disabled veterans, and there was also a well-financed housing project. In Ireland the former scheme did not exist, while the Irish Free State government would contribute nothing to veterans' housing. (The reason behind this was explained in February 1922 in a report by the Local Government Board, which stated that 'there is grave danger of serious trouble in rural areas over this matter. A most undesirable class of ex-soldiers are getting those lands, while I.R.A. soldiers are walking about unemployed.') As a result, only 3,600 houses financed by the British government were built in Ireland, and their rents were higher than in Britain.

Sellers of the British Legion's poppy emblem were sometimes attacked, poppy depots were destroyed, and veterans were often assaulted by republicans during Armistice Day marches. Some veterans received threatening letters, others were physically removed from dances or hospitals, while some even had their homes burnt down. Worst of all, several were murdered by the IRA during the War of Independence. In his article 'Nodody's Children?' Michael Robinson wrote:

> At least eighty-two ex-servicemen were murdered prior to the Anglo-Irish Treaty, and between January and April 1921, almost a third of all civilian casualties at the hands of the IRA were ex-soldiers. Citing newspaper reports of the killings, Peter Hart and Jane Leonard demonstrate that many ex-servicemen were killed because they were suspected of being informers who had passed on information to the British army. For example, there were several examples of the murdered men's bodies having informant signs attached to them. Despite this suspected affiliation, however, the R.I.C. vehemently denied that some of the men had partaken in such activities. After the killing of a one-armed veteran in Limerick in 1921, one policeman reported that 'it would seem that the ex-soldier must be with the I.R.A. or be regarded as the enemy.'

For nearly a hundred years after the end of the First World War the view would remain that Irish First World War soldiers were traitors to Ireland: that they had fought for the wrong nation in the wrong war. The few attempts to soften this harsh view came in the form of trying to remove 'blame' from an Irishman for having enlisted: he was under age, he was conscripted, he only went for the wage because he had no other choice. Meanwhile the story of a rebellion against British rule by republicans in Dublin during one week in April 1916 dominated the history books.

The figures show that the Easter Rising was carried out by, at the most, about 1,400 rebels. These men and women account for 14 per cent of the 10,000 Irish

Volunteers who had broken away from the Irish National Volunteers in August 1914. Before the split the organisation had numbered approximately 190,000, meaning that the rebels who carried out the Easter Rising represented about three-quarters of 1 per cent of the total armed, uniformed and organised nationalists of Ireland at the time. As Prof. Diarmuid Ferriter of University College, Dublin, recently described them, the rebels of Easter Week were 'a minority within a minority'. Meanwhile the story of 200,000 Irishmen in a world war that lasted over four years – at least 35,000 of whom never came home – became a footnote in Irish history.

* * *

It is worth concluding with a few paragraphs showing how complicated Irish history can be, which will hopefully show that the truth is not always black and white.

Some people have associated Irish nationalism exclusively with Catholics, while Irish Protestants and the British establishment are seen to be similarly synonymous. In a short autobiography Cadet-Sergeant Gerald Keatinge of Dublin University OTC recorded that 'Protestants in general were proud that they were citizens of the British Empire but so were many Roman Catholics. There was, indeed, a tradition of service in the Armed Forces among many working people as well as the gentry.' It was not unusual in 1914 for an Irish Catholic to regard himself as an Irish person and as a citizen of the British Empire. Similarly, Diarmuid Coffey, a Dublin member of the Irish Volunteers, wrote in September 1955 that

> the outbreak of war had brought in all sorts of people who were or had been Unionist in sympathy but who saw in Redmond's attitude a nationalism with which they could be reconciled. I think that subsequent events have so overlaid the events of that time that the attitude of a very large number of the Irish Unionist Landlords, such as Cheevers, Taaffe, Powerscourt, Dunsany, Pollard, Urquhart, has been forgotten. It really seemed at the time as though there was a chance of uniting nearly the whole of Ireland except the Carsonites, into a body ready to accept a very considerable degree of Irish self-government and to work together for a United Ireland. The mass of the people seemed to think that England was for once engaged in a righteous war and at least not to oppose those who wanted to join in. The Unionists seemed to be ready to meet the people half way.

Following in the tradition of Theobald Wolfe Tone and Robert Emmet, Sir Roger Casement – one of the sixteen republicans executed following the Easter Rising – was a Protestant, as were most of the significant figures in the Howth gun-running in July 1914: Erskine Childers, Alice Stopford-Green, Mary Spring Rice, and William Gibson, Baron Ashbourne. Put simply, religion did not dictate a person's 'Irishness' in 1914.

On the other side of the divide Edward Carson, the leader of Ulster unionism, was a Dubliner who, despite his political views, also considered himself an Irishman. Similar to the way in which Irish Catholics could also consider themselves citizens of Britain, in 1914 the idea of being both a unionist and an Irishman was not an unusual one. Carson was educated at Wesley College and Trinity College and also spent his summers visiting Castle Ellen near Athenry, Co. Galway, where his mother, Isabella Lambert, came from. Here he played the local game of hurling on what is now the local GAA pitch at Carnaun, and then brought the game to Trinity College, where it became quite popular. In 1877 Carson is recorded as playing hurling in the grounds of Trinity College, and two years later it was the Irish Hurling Union in Trinity College – which included Edward Carson – that drew up the first code of rules for the modern game, later adopted after the formation of the Gaelic Athletic Association in 1884.

Another paradox of the time surrounds Patrick Pearse in 1915. In December that year he wrote (anonymously) that 'the old heart of the earth needed to be warmed by the red wine of the battlefields.' He was not talking about the planned Easter Rising, however: he was talking about the First World War. This pro-war comment was dismissed by James Connolly as something written by a 'blithering idiot'. Connolly also disliked the fact that the Irish Volunteers were courting one empire in an attempt to defeat another. The 'gallant allies in Europe' that the Proclamation of the Irish Republic refers to was Imperial Germany, which by 1916 had ignored Belgian neutrality and steamrolled through the country, subsequently invaded France, and invented poison gas and the flamethrower.

Another myth is that many of those who enlisted were under age and lied about their age, not knowing any better. In the 1916 Rising, however, the youngest combatants to die were all on the rebel side. Sixteen-year-old James Fox of number 74 Thomas Street, a member of Fianna Éireann, was killed during the Rising, as was fifteen-year-old Charles Darcy of number 4 Murphy's Cottages, Gloucester Street; he was a member of the Irish Citizen Army. The youngest of all was fourteen-year-old John Healy of number 188 Phibsborough Road, a despatch messenger with Fianna Éireann. It can be argued that it was British soldiers who shot these boys down, but it was Irish republicans who let them join the fight in the first place.

Along with the sixteen executions that took place at the end of the Rising, the British executed twenty-four republicans during the War of Independence. This makes a combined total of forty. In contrast, during the Civil War seventy-seven official executions were carried out by the Irish Free State, nearly double the number executed by the British in the revolutionary years 1916–1921. These were Irishmen executed by Irishmen.

Finally, following the outbreak of the Irish Civil War, thousands of Irish ex-British army soldiers enlisted in the new National (Free State) army, so many that by May 1923, 50 per cent of the army's 53,000 soldiers were former members of the British army, along with 20 per cent of the force's officers.

* * *

Perhaps the greatest unknown fact of modern Irish history is that thousands of Irishmen served in British army uniform during the Easter Rising and fought against the Irish Volunteers and the Irish Citizen Army. It might be less complicated to view the rebels as Irish and the military forces as British, but this is simply not the case.

On the morning of 24 April 1916 the 3rd Royal Irish Regiment, the 3rd Royal Irish Rifles and the 10th Royal Dublin Fusiliers were stationed in various barracks around Dublin. These three battalions contained 1,541 men between them, which means that – even allowing for a third of them to have been away on leave – approximately 1,000 Irish soldiers in British army uniform were involved in the fighting in Dublin as soon as the Rising began. By the following day the 3rd, 4th and 5th Royal Dublin Fusiliers, the 5th Leinster Regiment and the Ulster Composite Battalion had arrived from elsewhere around the country. Between them these additional units contained thousands more Irish troops. Prof. John Joly later referred to the Rising as 'that worst of all forms of strife, civil war.' He saw it as a conflict of Irish against Irish.

However, perhaps some acceptance of Irish involvement on both sides of the Rising can be found in some of the final words of three of the executed rebel leaders. Commandant Thomas MacDonagh, commanding officer of the 2nd Battalion of the Dublin Brigade, Irish Volunteers, who was executed on 3 May 1916, wrote his last letter in Kilmainham Jail at midnight on 2 May. In it he stated:

> My money affairs are in a bad way ... I ask my brother Joseph MacDonagh and my good and constant friend David Houston to help my poor wife in these matters ... I ask my friend David Houston to see Mr. W.G. Lyon, publisher of my latest book, Literature in Ireland, and see that its publication may be useful for my wife and family. If Joseph Plunkett survives me and is a free man I make him, with my wife, my literary executor [Plunkett was shot the day after MacDonagh]. Otherwise my wife and David Houston will take charge of my writings. For the first time I pray that they may bring in some profit at last. My wife will want money from every source.

The friend that MacDonagh mentions, 62-year-old David Houston from Co. Antrim, had lectured in botany at the Royal College of Science and then in 1910 came to teach science in Patrick Pearse's school, St Enda's. In 1915 MacDonagh wrote in another letter that 'my friend David Houston, the founder of the Irish Review, a splendid man, has been shocked by the Lusitania affair into going in to the British Army.' The British army would not have accepted Houston at his age, but he might possibly have ended up in a Volunteer Training Corps unit such as the 1st (Dublin) Battalion of the IAVTC. Whichever it was, Thomas MacDonagh in his last letter spoke highly of a man who, only a year earlier, had sought to join the British army.

Michael Mallin, in his last letter to his wife, wrote that 'I find no fault with the soldiers or the police,' before asking her to 'to pray for all the souls who fell in this fight, Irish and English.'

And when Commandant-General James Connolly, commanding officer of republican forces in Dublin in 1916, was asked by Father Aloysius Travers to say a prayer for the men about to carry out his execution, Connolly replied: 'I will say a prayer for all brave men who do their duty according to their lights.'

* * *

The story of the Easter Rising has never been fully told. The story of one Irish aspect of the Rising has always been forgotten.

Edward Gerrard, a Dubliner, served as a second-lieutenant in the Royal Field Artillery in Beggarsbush Barracks during the Rising. Today on his headstone in Cruagh Cemetery at Rockbrook, Co. Dublin, is the Latin inscription *Ex umbris et imaginibus in veritatem* – Out of shadows and phantasms into the truth. And the truth of the Easter Rising is that Irishmen fought, sacrificed and died on both sides.

Acknowledgements

With sincere thanks to

Belvedere College; Clongowes Wood College; Connaught Rangers Association; Irish Defence Forces Military Archives; Dublin City Library and Archive; Imperial War Museum (London); Manuscripts and Archives Research Library, Trinity College, Dublin; National Archives, Dublin; National Archives (London); National Library of Ireland; Public Record Office of Northern Ireland; Royal British Legion; Royal Dublin Fusiliers Association.

Yvonne Altman-O'Connor, Bryan Alton, Gareth Baillie-Stewart, George Banks, Oliver Beck, Pat Beckett, Helen Bell, Ken Bergin, Carolyn Bowers, Mr and Mrs Robert William Boyles, Pauline Brereton, Eddie Brittain, Reanna Broome, Tom Burke, Catherine Butcher, Brian Callum, Clive J. Carter, David Cassells, Damien Cawley, Jim Charters, Cecile Chemin, Mary Clark, Fiona Clyde, Mary Conefrey, Graham Corble, Nicole Coroner, Mario Corrigan, Julia Craig-McFeely, Nigel Curtin, Barry Dalby, Lynn Davidson, David Davin-Power, William Donnelly, Margaret Doyle, Vincent Doyle, Peter Ellis, Carmel Flahavan, Michael Goodbody, Maggie Goss, David Grant, Noelle Grothier, Paul Guéret, Charlie Hadden, Ian Harris, Mark Hifle, Michael Holland, Barry Houlihan, David Hutchinson, Diane Jakubans, Emma Jones, Anthony Kearon, Rachel Keatinge, J. Kiernan, Mike Lynch, Stephen Lynch, Sylvia McClintock, Aonghus Mac Domhnaill, Yvonne McEwen, Brian McGee, Patria McWalter, Paul Malpas, Kate Manning, Helen Masterson, Chris Mathews, Rachel Mathews-McKay, Jane Maxwell, Walter Millar, Ursula Mitchel, Mike Mitchell, Richard Moles, Tom Molyneux, Brodnax Moore, Ciara O'Brien, Dáithí O'Callaghan, Pam Orme, Anne Palmer, Kimberley Pearce, David Power, Denise Reddy, Lucille Redmond, Charles Rigg, Debra L. Rooke, Nancy Rosborough-Barnett, Betty-Jane and Bob Smith, Orna Somerville, Tony Storan, Sheron Sweeny, Chris Tangoniner, Jimmy Taylor, Alison Tomlin, Emer Twomey, Robin Vivian, Cyril Wall, Mandy Wand, Doreen Watson, Moira Watson, Iris Weir, Anthony Wheatman, Andrew Whiteside, Mel Wilcox, David Wraith, Catherine Wright.

Bibliography and further reading

The 6th Connaught Rangers: Belfast Nationalists and the Great War, Belfast: 6th Connaught Rangers Research Project, 2011.

Barry, Tom, *Guerrilla Days in Ireland,* Cork: Mercier Press, 2011.

Barton, Brian, *Secret Court Martial Records of the 1916 Easter Rising,* Stroud (Glos.): History Press, 2010.

Bourke, Joanna (ed.), *The Misfit Soldier: Edward Casey's War Story, 1914–1918,* Cork: Cork University Press, 1999.

Boyle, John F., *The Irish Rebellion of 1916: A Brief History of the Revolt and its Suppression,* London: Constable, 1916.

Burke, Tom, 'Fancy the Royal Irish captured Moore Street: Attitudes to the Easter Rising of Irish soldiers serving in the British army in Dublin,' *Irish Sword,* vol. 28 (2012).

Burrows, Brig.-Gen. A. R., *The 1st Battalion, the Faugh-a-Ballaghs, Irish Fusiliers in the Great War,* Aldershot: Gale and Polden, 1926.

Caulfield, Max, *The Easter Rebellion,* Dublin: Gill & Macmillan, 1963, 1995.

Coogan, Tim Pat, *1916: The Easter Rising,* London: Phoenix (Orion Books), 2005.

Cooper, Maj. Brian, *The 10th (Irish) Division in Gallipoli,* Dublin: Irish Academic Press, 1993.

Cooper-Walker, C. A., *The Book of the Seventh Service Battalion, the Royal Inniskilling Fusiliers, from Tipperary to Ypres,* Dublin: Brindley and Son, 1920.

Cullen, Clara, *The World Upturning: Elsie Henry's Irish Wartime Diaries, 1913–1919,* Dublin: Merrion, 2012.

Denman, Terrence, *Ireland's Unknown Soldiers: The 16th (Irish) Division in the Great War, 1914–1918,* Dublin: Irish Academic Press, 1992, 2008.

Dispatch of General Sir John Maxwell, *London Gazette,* 21 July 1916.

Doherty, Richard, and Truesdale, David, *Irish Winners of the Victoria Cross,* Dublin: Four Courts Press, 1999.

Dooney, Laura, 'Trinity College and the War', in *Ireland and the First World War,* Dublin: Trinity History Workshop Publications, 1988.

Enright, Seán, *Easter Rising, 1916: The Trials,* Dublin: Merrion, 2013.

Falls, Cyril, *The History of the First Seven Battalions, the Royal Irish Rifles (now the Royal Ulster Rifles) in the Great War,* Aldershot: Gale and Polden (for the Regimental Committee), 1925.

Ferguson, Stephen, *GPO Staff in 1916,* Cork: Mercier Press, 2012.

Fletcher-Vane, Sir Francis, *Agin the Governments: Memories and Adventures of Sir Francis Fletcher Vane, Bt,* London: Samson Low and Marston, 1929.

Fox, Sir Frank, *The Royal Inniskilling Fusiliers in the Great War,* London: Constable, 1928.

Foy, Michael T., and Barton, Brian, *The Easter Rising,* Stroud (Glos.): History Press, 2011.

Geoghegan, Brig.-Gen. Stannus, *The Campaigns and History of the Royal Irish Regiment, 1900–1922,* Edinburgh: Blackwood, 1927.

Gibbon, Monk, *Inglorious Soldier: An Autobiography,* London: Hutchinson, 1968.

Goodbody, Michael, *The Goodbodys: Story of an Irish Quaker Family, 1630–1950: Millers, Merchants and Manufacturers,* Dublin: Ashfield Press, 2011.

Grayson, Richard S., *Belfast Boys: How Nationalists and Unionists Fought and Died Together in the First World War,* London: Continuum, 2009.

Gwynn, Stephen Lucius, *John Redmond's Last Years,* New York: Longmans, Green, 1919.

Hanna, Henry, *The Pals at Suvla Bay: Being the Record of 'D' Company of the 7th Royal Dublin Fusiliers,* Dublin: E. Ponsonby, 1917.

Harris, Henry, *The Royal Irish Fusiliers (the 87th and 89th Regiments of Foot),* London: Cooper, 1972.

Hegarty, Shane, and O'Toole, Fintan, *The Irish Times Book of the 1916 Rising,* Dublin: Gill & Macmillan, 2006.

Hittle, J. B. E., *Michael Collins and the Anglo-Irish War: Britain's Counterinsurgency Failure,* Washington: Potomac Books, 2011.

Holmes, Richard, *Tommy: The British Soldier on the Western Front, 1914–1918,* London: Harper Perennial, 2005.

Jeffrey, Keith, *The GPO and the Easter Rising,* Dublin: Irish Academic Press, 2006.

Johnson, Lt-Col. F. W. E., *5th Battalion, Royal Irish Fusiliers, in the Great War,* Uckfield (Sussex): Naval and Military Press, 2004.

Johnston, Kevin, *Home or Away: The Great War and the Irish Revolution,* Dublin: Gill & Macmillan, 2010.

Joly, John, *Reminiscences and Anticipations,* London: Fisher Unwin, 1920.

Jourdain, Lt-Col. H. F. N., and Fraser, Edward, *The Connaught Rangers* (vols. 1–3), London: Royal United Service Institution, 1924–28.

Kipling, Rudyard, *The Irish Guards in the Great War, Vol. 1: The First Battalion,* London: Macmillan, 1923.

Kipling, Rudyard, *The Irish Guards in the Great War, Vol. 2: The Second Battalion,* London: Macmillan, 1923.

Kostick, Conor, and Collins, Lorcan, *The Easter Rising: A Guide to Dublin in 1916,* Dublin: O'Brien Press, 2000.

Lowe, William J., 'Who were the Black and Tans?' *History Ireland,* issue 3, autumn 2004.

Lucy, J. F., *There's a Devil in the Drum* [1938], Uckfield (Sussex): Naval and Military Press, 2001.

Lytton, Sir Henry, *Secrets of a Savoyard,* London: Jarrolds, 1922.

Lytton, Sir Henry, *A Wandering Minstrel,* London: Jarrolds, 1933.

McCance, Capt S., *History of the Royal Munster Fusiliers, 1861 to 1922,* privately printed, 1937; reprinted Cork: Schull Books, 1995.

McCann, B. P., 'The diary of 2nd Lieut Arthur V. G. Killingley, "A" Company, 4th Battalion, Royal Dublin Fusiliers, Easter Week, 1916', *Irish Sword,* vol. 20, no. 81, Summer 1997.

McCarthy, Cal, *Cumann na mBan and the Irish Revolution* (revised edition), Cork: The Collins Press, 2014.

MacDonagh, Michael, *The Irish at the Front,* London: Hodder and Stoughton, 1916.

MacDonagh, Michael, *The Irish on the Somme,* London: Hodder and Stoughton, 1917.

McGarry, Fearghal, *Rebels: Voices from the Easter Rising,* Dublin: Penguin Ireland, 2011.

McGarry, Fearghal, *The Rising: Easter 1916,* Oxford: Oxford University Press, 2011.

McHugh, Roger, *Dublin, 1916,* London: Arlington Books, 1966.

Murphy, David, *Irish Regiments in the World Wars* (illustrated by Gerry Embleton), Oxford: Osprey Publishing, 2007.

Norway, Mrs Hamilton, *The Sinn Fein Rebellion as I Saw It,* London: Smith, Elder, 1916.

O'Brien, Paul, *Blood on the Streets: 1916 and the Battle for Mount Street Bridge,* Cork: Mercier Press, 2008.

O'Brien, Paul, *Crossfire: The Battle of the Four Courts, 1916,* Dublin: New Island, 2012.

O'Brien, Paul, *Field of Fire: The Battle of Ashbourne, 1916,* Dublin: New Island, 2012.

O'Brien, Paul, *Shootout: The Battle for St Stephen's Green, 1916,* Dublin: New Island, 2013.

O'Brien, Paul, *Uncommon Valour: 1916 and the Battle for the South Dublin Union,* Cork: Mercier Press, 2010.

O'Donnell, Comdt P. D., 'A short history of Portobello Barracks', *An Cosantóir,* February 1969.

O'Farrell, Mick, *50 Things You Didn't Know about 1916,* Cork: Mercier Press, 2009.

Orr, Philip, *Field of Bones: An Irish Division at Gallipoli,* Dublin: Lilliput Press, 2006.

Orr, Philip, *The Road to the Somme: Men of the Ulster Division Tell Their Story,* Belfast: Blackstaff Press, 1987, 2008.

Record of the 5th (Service) Battalion, the Connaught Rangers, from 19th August, 1914, to 17th January, 1916, Uckfield (Sussex): Naval and Military Press, 2002.

Richardson, Neil, *A Coward If I Return, A Hero If I Fall: Stories of Irishmen in World War I,* Dublin: O'Brien Press, 2010.

Rickard, Mrs Victor, *The Story of the Munsters at Etreux, Festubert, Rue du Bois and Hulloch,* London: Hodder and Stoughton, 1918.

Robinson, Michael, 'Nobody's children? The trial and tribulations of Great War veterans in the Irish Free State', *Scoláire Staire,* vol. 2, issue 2, April 2012.

Ryan, Annie, *Witnesses: Inside the Easter Rising,* Dublin: Liberties Press, 2005.

Samuels, A. P. I., and Samuels, D. G., *With the Ulster Division in France: A Story of the 11th Battalion, Royal Irish Rifles (South Antrim Volunteers), from Bordon to Thiepval,* Uckfield (Sussex): Naval and Military Press, 2003.

Shilaro, Priscilla M., 'Colonial land policies: The Kenya Land Commission and the Kakamega Gold Rush, 1932–4', in *Historical Studies and Social Change in Western Kenya,* Nairobi: East African Educational Publishers, 2002.

Sinn Fein Rebellion Handbook, Dublin: Weekly Irish Times, 1917.

Stephens, James, *The Insurrection in Dublin,* New York: Macmillan Company, 1917.

Taylor, James W., *The 1st Royal Irish Rifles in the Great War,* Dublin: Four Courts Press, 2002.

Taylor, James W., *The 2nd Royal Irish Rifles in the Great War,* Dublin: Four Courts Press, 2005.

Townshend, Charles, *Easter 1916: The Irish Rebellion,* London: Penguin Books, 2006.

Ufford, Letitia W., 'Imperialists at work and play: The Papers of General Sir John and Lady Maxwell', *Princeton University Library Chronicle,* vol. 51, no. 2, winter 1990.

Wells, Warre B., and Marlow, N., *A History of the Irish Rebellion of 1916,* Dublin: Maunsel, 1916.

White, Gerry, and O'Shea, Brendan (illustrated by Bill Younghusband), *Irish Volunteer Soldier, 1913–23,* Oxford: Osprey Publishing, 2003.

Whitton, Lt-Col. F. E., *The History of the Prince of Wales's Leinster Regiment (Royal Canadians), Vol. 1 and Vol. 2,* Aldershot: Gale and Polden, 1924.

Willis, Clair, *Dublin, 1916: The Siege of the GPO,* London: Profile Books, 2009.

Willoughby, Roger, *A Military History of the University of Dublin and its Officer Training Corps, 1910–1922* (Special Publication No. 1), Cork: Medal Society of Ireland, 1989.

Wylly, Col. H. C., *Crown and Company: The Historical Records of the 2nd Battalion, Royal Dublin Fusiliers, formerly the 1st Bombay Regiment,* London: Arthur L. Humphreys, 1925.

Wylly, Col. H. C., *Neill's 'Blue Caps': The History of the 1st Battalion, the Royal Dublin Fusiliers,* Dublin: Maunsell, 1924.

Yeates, Pádraig, *A City in Wartime: Dublin, 1914–18,* Dublin: Gill & Macmillan, 2011.

Archival sources

Arthur Aston Luce's Recollections of Easter 1916 (Trinity College Manuscripts and Archives Library, IE TCD MS 4874)

Corporal Mein's 'The Sinn Féin Rebellion' (Trinity College Manuscripts and Archives Library, IE TCD MS 4873)

Elsie Mahaffy's account of the Easter Rising (Trinity College Manuscripts and Archives Library, IE TCD MS 2074)

Employment of Military Forces – Irish Rebellion (code 53 (G)) – Disturbances in Dublin (National Archives, London, WO 32/4307)

Gerald Fitzgibbon's letter to William Hume Blake, 10 May 1916 (Trinity College Manuscripts and Archives Library, IE TCD MS 11107)

Gilbert Waterhouse's 'The Sinn Féin Rebellion' (Trinity College Manuscripts and Archives Library, IE TCD MS 4875)

Grants of compensation to dependants of Volunteer Training Corps (National Archives, London, WO 35/69/4)

Henry Ernest Cruise, letter to Richard Cruise (Bantry House/Estate Collection, University College, Cork, MS 2553)

Judicial Division (National Archives, London, CO 903/19/2)

Monica Robert Collection: Clarke, Joseph (Royal Dublin Fusiliers Association Archive, Dublin City Library and Archive, RDFA/001/01)

Monica Robert Collection: Fox, Christopher (Royal Dublin Fusiliers Association Archive, Dublin City Library and Archive, RDFA/001/14)

Police reports of persons killed or wounded by rebels (National Archives, London, WO 35/69/1)

Recommendation for pension for the widow of an officer in the St John's Ambulance Brigade killed in action (National Archives, London, WO 35/69/1)

Report on execution of rebel prisoners by firing squad (National Archives, London, WO 35/67/2)

Robert N. Tweedy's letter to Edith Sophia Tweedy, 7 May 1916 (Trinity College Manuscripts and Archives Library, IE TCD MS 7533/3)

Unarmed persons shot by rebels (National Archives, London, WO 35/69/1)

Unpublished sources

Grant, Charles William, 'Autobiography of Charles William Grant'
Keatinge, Gerald Fitzmaurice, 'Some Experiences of a Cadet during the Irish Rebellion of Easter Week 1916'
Stephenson, Patrick Joseph, 'Heuston's Fort: the Mendicity Institute, Easter Week, 1916' (National Library of Ireland)

Military service records

Aldridge, Sgt John W., Royal Dublin Fusiliers, 15582 (National Archives, London)
Barry, 2/Lt William Roche Brereton, Royal Dublin Fusiliers (National Archives, London, WO339/54104)
Barton, Capt Charles Erskine, Royal Irish Rifles (National Archives, London, WO 339/2985)
Barton, Lt Robert Childers, Royal Dublin Fusiliers (National Archives, London, WO339/56863)
Battersby, Lt John A., Royal Irish Rifles (National Archives, London, WO339/45902)
Beckett, 2/Lt David Duke, Connaught Rangers (National Archives, London, WO 339/67915)
Bowen-Colthurst, Capt. John Colthurst, Royal Irish Rifles (National Archives, London, WO374/14934)
Bowie, Stoker Neil, Royal Navy (National Archives, London, ADN188/1121/115175, BT377/7/85315)
Boyle, Lt John Kemmy, Royal Irish Rifles (National Archives, London, WO 339/43888)
Brophy, Sgt Peter (alias Byers, Sgt Peter), Royal Dublin Fusiliers, 4907 (National Archives, London)
Burke, Lt H. C., Royal Irish Regiment (National Archives, London, WO 339/93544)
Burke, Capt Richard Edward Walter, Royal Irish Regiment (National Archives, London, WO339/51161)
Burnison, Pte Joseph, Royal Irish Fusiliers, 23825 (National Archives, London)
Byrne, Pte Denis, Royal Dublin Fusiliers, 25884 (National Archives, London)
Byrne, Pte Michael, Royal Dublin Fusiliers, 25743 (National Archives, London)
Calvert, 2/Lt James Howard, Royal Irish Rifles (National Archives, London, WO339/41747)
Campsie, Lt Peter Alexander, Royal Field Artillery (National Archives, London, WO 339/67227)
Carroll, Pte Edward, Royal Dublin Fusiliers, 1126 (National Archives, London)
Carroll, Capt James Francis Joseph, Royal Dublin Fusiliers (National Archives, London, WO339/9378)
Carrothers, 2/Lt John Samuel, Royal Inniskilling Fusiliers (National Archives, London, WO 339/67178)
Clarke, Cpl Joseph, Royal Irish Fusiliers, 23439 (National Archives, London)
Connolly, Lt William Patrick, Royal Dublin Fusiliers (National Archives, London, WO339/34281)
Conway, Pte Patrick, Royal Dublin Fusiliers, 22711 (National Archives, London)
Cope, L/Cpl Edward, Royal Dublin Fusiliers, 18795 (National Archives, London)

Coroner, Pte Joseph, Royal Dublin Fusiliers, 25001 (National Archives, London)

Cox, L/Cpl Thomas, Royal Dublin Fusiliers, 25477 (National Archives, London)

Craddock, Pte Cecil Graham, Royal Dublin Fusiliers, 25303 (National Archives, London)

Craddock, 2/Lt Cecil Graham, Royal Dublin Fusiliers (National Archives, London, WO339/73098)

Crockett, 2/Lt Charles Love, Royal Inniskilling Fusiliers (National Archives, London, WO339/1254)

Davies, Lt Douglas Joseph, Royal Dublin Fusiliers (National Archives, London, WO 339/72649)

de Burgh Daly, Capt Ulick, Royal Dublin Fusiliers (National Archives, London, WO 339/17344)

Despard, 2/Lt Ernest Richard, Tank Corps (National Archives, London, WO 339/64706)

Dobbin, Lt William Leonard Price, Royal Irish Rifles (National Archives, London, WO339/55777)

Dolan, Cpl Martin, Royal Dublin Fusiliers, 23828 (National Archives, London)

Dunn, 2/Lt James Acland, Royal Dublin Fusiliers (National Archives, London, WO339/55281)

Dunne, Pte Dominick, Royal Dublin Fusiliers, 24580 (National Archives, London)

Earls, Lt Arnold Longfield Lloyd, Royal Irish Regiment (National Archives, London, WO 339/46819)

Elliott, Lt Lawrence Rory, Royal Dublin Fusiliers (National Archives, London, WO 339/51044)

Ennis, Pte Peter, Scots Guards, 10404 (Scots Guards Archives)

Esmonde, Capt. John Lymbrick, Royal Dublin Fusiliers (National Archives, London, WO339/27293)

Esmonde, Lt-Col. Laurence Grattan, Royal Dublin Fusiliers (National Archives, London, WO 339/23099)

Fenelon, 2/Lt Louis Martin, Royal Flying Corps (National Archives, London, WO 339/112649)

Ferguson, Pte Henry, Royal Inniskilling Fusiliers, 17803 (National Archives, London)

Fletcher-Vane, Maj. Francis Patrick, Royal Munster Fusiliers (National Archives, London, WO339/13388, WO339/13389)

Fryday, Pte Neville Nicholas (Library and Archives Canada, RG 150, Accession 1992–93/166, box 3313-54)

Fryday, Pte W. F. (Library and Archives Canada, RG 150, Accession 1992–93/166, box 3313-55)

Gamble, CQMS Robert, Royal Irish Regiment, 2G/7 (National Archives, London)

Goodchild, Pte Edward, Royal Irish Regiment, 6428 (National Archives, London)

Grant, Lt Charles William, Royal Dublin Fusiliers (National Archives, London, WO339/52138)

Griffin, 2/Lt Gerald, Royal Dublin Fusiliers (National Archives, London, WO 339/76822)

Hadden, Lt Addison Barnes Perrott, South Irish Horse (National Archives, London, WO 339/69802)

Handley, Cpl Edward, Royal Dublin Fusiliers, 8248 (National Archives, London)

Hare, Sgt Henry, Royal Dublin Fusiliers, 6745 (National Archives, London)

Hawe, 2/Lt John Atherton, Royal Dublin Fusiliers (National Archives, London, WO339/47803)

Hawkins, Sgt Frederick, Royal Inniskilling Fusiliers, 27863 (National Archives, London)

Henchy, 2/Lt Alphonsus Alexander Watson, Royal Dublin Fusiliers (National Archives, London, WO339/53757, AIR76/221/4, AIR221/6)

Holmes, Maj. Philip Armstrong, Royal Irish Regiment (National Archives, London, WO 339/47950)

Jeffares, Capt. Richard Thorpe, Royal Irish Rifles (National Archives, London, WO 339/31057)

Jones-Nowlan, 2/Lt Thomas Camney, Royal Dublin Fusiliers (National Archives, London, WO 339/67947)

Kearns, Lt John, Royal Irish Rifles (National Archives, London, WO 339/48108)

Kelly, Lt-Col. Philip Edward, Royal Irish Fusiliers (National Archives, London, WO 339/7190)

Kennedy, Lt Thomas James, Royal Inniskilling Fusiliers (National Archives, London, WO 339/32233)

Killingley, Lt Arthur Victor Grevatt, Royal Dublin Fusiliers (National Archives, London, WO 339/70424)

Leahy, Lt Daniel O'Mahony, Royal Dublin Fusiliers (National Archives, London, WO339/13099)

Leatham, Maj. William Stanley Balfour, Royal Irish Rifles (National Archives, London, WO339/49598)

Leslie, Lt Walter Edward, Army Service Corps (National Archives, London, WO 339/64737)

Long, Lt Eugene Joseph, South Irish Horse (National Archives, London, WO 339/69803)

Luce, Lt Arthur Aston, Royal Irish Rifles (National Archives, London, WO339/34651)

Lynch, CSM Christopher, Royal Dublin Fusiliers, 25573 (National Archives, London)

McCammon, Lt-Col. Thomas Valentine Plaisted, Royal Irish Rifles (National Archives, London, WO 339/46427)

McCammond, 2/Lt Cecil Robert Walter, Royal Irish Rifles (National Archives, London, WO339/51001)

McCammond, Lt-Col Walter Edwin Carson, Royal Irish Rifles (National Archives, London, WO339/18029)

McCarthy, Pte Maurice, Royal Dublin Fusiliers, 8016 (National Archives, London)

McClintock, Lt-Col. John Knox, Royal Inniskilling Fusiliers (National Archives, London, WO339/89388)

McClughan, Capt. John Charles, Royal Irish Rifles (National Archives, London, WO339/30487)

McConnell, Lt A. E., Royal Irish Rifles (National Archives, London, WO 339/68829)

McDermott, Capt. Alfred William, Royal Dublin Fusiliers (National Archives, London, WO339/41235)

McDonnell, Pte Samuel, 8th (King's Royal Irish) Hussars, 30233 (National Archives, London)

McElroy, Captain Frederick William, Tank Corps (National Archives, London, WO 339/64740)

Mackay, 2/Lt George Frederick, Royal Flying Corps (National Archives, London, WO 339/57672)

McKee, Lt William Dickson, Royal Irish Rifles (National Archives, London, WO 339/29344)

MacNamara, Capt. Charles Rawdon, Royal Dublin Fusiliers (National Archives, London, WO 339/69112)

Malone, 2/Lt Joseph James, Royal Dublin Fusiliers (National Archives, London, WO339/61855)

Merry, L/Cpl Martin, Royal Dublin Fusiliers, 25197 (National Archives, London)

Molyneux, 2/Lt Ernest Thomas, Royal Flying Corps (National Archives, London, WO 339/61858)

Mooney, Lt Harold Lorcom, Royal Army Medical Corps (National Archives, London, WO339/11866)

Moran, 2/Lt William Aloysius, Royal Garrison Artillery (National Archives, London, WO 339/67235)

Morgan, Capt. Samuel Valentine, Royal Irish Rifles (National Archives, London, WO339/21471)

Morton, L/Cpl Nathaniel, Royal Irish Rifles, 250 (National Archives, London)

Mount, Lt William John, Royal Dublin Fusiliers (National Archives, London, WO 339/44296)

Mullally, Pte John, 8th (King's Royal Irish) Hussars, 6836 (National Archives, London)

Mullan, Lt Charles Seymour, Royal Garrison Artillery (National Archives, London, WO 339/50408)

Murphy, Lt Norbert, South Irish Horse (National Archives, London, WO 339/69804)

Murphy, Pte Patrick Sarsfield, 5th Royal Irish Lancers, 6396 (National Archives, London)

Murphy, Capt. William, Royal Irish Fusiliers (National Archives, London, WO 339/11302)

Neilan, Lt Gerald Aloysius, Royal Dublin Fusiliers (National Archives, London, WO339/26261)

Nolan, Pte Edward, Royal Dublin Fusiliers, 24910 (National Archives, London)

North, 2/Lt Francis Wilson, Royal Irish Regiment (National Archives, London, WO339/33640)

O'Dowda-Wade, Lt Joseph, Royal Dublin Fusiliers (National Archives, London, WO 339/51187)

O'Meara, Lt Harold John, Royal Field Artillery (National Archives, London, WO 339/59260)

O'Neill, 2/Lt Frederick, Royal Dublin Fusiliers (National Archives, London, WO339/47198)

Palmer, Capt. Lodge Stephen Norman, Royal Dublin Fusiliers (National Archives, London, WO339/11485)

Peirce, 2/Lt Bernard John McFarlane, Royal Dublin Fusiliers (National Archives, London, WO 339/64752)

Pinion, 2/Lt Eric, Royal Irish Rifles (National Archives, London, WO 339/57738)

Plunkett, Capt. Edward John Moreton Drax (Lord Dunsany), Royal Inniskilling Fusiliers (National Archives, London, WO339/93962)

Preece, Sgt George Reginald, Royal Dublin Fusiliers, 25437 (National Archives, London)

Price, Cdt James Chermside, Royal Military College (National Archives, London, WO 339/92688)

Purcell, 2/Lt William Frank, South Irish Horse (National Archives, London, WO 339/69806)

Purser, Lt Philip Addison, Army Service Corps (National Archives, London, WO339/13301)

Ramsay, Capt. Alan Livingstone, Royal Irish Regiment (National Archives, London, WO339/15968)

Rosborough, Maj. James, Royal Irish Rifles (National Archives, London, WO339/27301)

Rutter, Lt William, Machine Gun Corps (National Archives, London, WO 339/69947)

Scallan, 2/Lt Richard Talbot, Royal Garrison Artillery (National Archives, London, WO 339/66850)

Sheehy, Lt Eugene, Royal Dublin Fusiliers (National Archives, London, WO339/47808)

Smyth, Pte William, Royal Irish Rifles, 5762 (National Archives, London)

Stanley, Capt. Herbert Vernon, Royal Army Medical Corps (National Archives, London, WO339/22345)

Stein, 2/Lt John Francis, Royal Irish Rifles (National Archives, London, WO 339/55779)

Swan, Sgt William, Royal Irish Rifles, 5208 (National Archives, London)

Varian, 2/Lt Walter Osborne, Royal Munster Fusiliers (National Archives, London, WO 339/76283)

Vigors, 2/Lt Arthur Cecil, Royal Munster Fusiliers (National Archives, London, WO 339/35126)

Walsh, Pte Richard Henry, Royal Dublin Fusiliers, 25620 (National Archives, London)

Warmington, Capt. Alfred Ernest, Royal Irish Regiment (National Archives, London, WO339/10916)

Watchorn, Pte Abraham, Royal Dublin Fusiliers, 25026 (National Archives, London)

Watson, Pte Frederick, Royal Dublin Fusiliers, 19200 (National Archives, London)

Weir, Lt Charles, Royal Irish Rifles (National Archives, London, WO 339/44468)

Weir, 2/Lt John Horace, Royal Flying Corps (National Archives, London, WO 339/64765)

Weldon, Lt-Col. Anthony Arthur, Leinster Regiment (National Archives, London, WO 339/8390)

Wheatman, Pte Robert, Royal Dublin Fusiliers, 25649 (National Archives, London)

Wilson, Lt Leslie, Royal Irish Fusiliers (National Archives, London, WO339/43897)

Wilson, Capt. Thomas Joseph, Royal Dublin Fusiliers (National Archives, London, WO339/35133)

Wolfe, Pte John Joseph, Royal Irish Rifles, 5594 (National Archives, London)

Witness statements, Bureau of Military History

Balfe, Richard (WS 251)

Barton, Dulcibella (WS 936)

Barton, Robert C. (WS 979)

Bratton, Eugene (WS 467)

Broy, Éamon (WS 1280)

Burke, James J. (WS 1758)

Byrne, Joseph (WS 461)

Byrne, Tom (WS 564)

Byrne, Vincent (WS 423)

Coffey, Diarmuid (WS 1248)

Colgan, Patrick (WS 850)

Corrigan, William P. (WS 250)

Cosgrave, William T. (WS 268)

Curran, M. J. (WS 687)

Daly, Francis (WS 278)

de Brún, Seosamh (WS 312)

Desborough, Albert George Fletcher (WS 1604)

Doyle, Gerald (WS 1511)

Folan, Peter (WS 316)

Galligan, Peter Paul (WS 170)

Gerrard, E. (WS 348)

Good, Joseph (WS 388)

Grace, Seamus (WS 310)

Handley, Edward (WS 625)

Henderson, Frank (WS 249)

Holland, Robert (WS 280)

Holohan, Garry (WS 328)

Kavanagh, Seamus (WS 208)

Keane, Patrick (WS 1300)

Keating, Pauline (WS 432)
Kelly, Daniel (WS 1004)
Kelly, Patrick J. (WS 781)
Kennedy, Seán (WS 842)
Knightly, Michael (WS 833)
Laffan, Nicholas (WS 201)
Mannion, Annie (WS 297)
McDonagh, John (WS 219)
McDonnell, Andrew (WS 1768)
McDonough, Joseph (WS 1082)
Meldon, Thomas J. (WS 734)
Mitchell, Albert D. (WS 196)
Molony, Helena (WS 391)
Murphy, William (WS 352)
Nugent, Laurence (WS 907)
O'Connor, James J. (WS 1214)

O'Connor, Joseph (WS 157)
O'Connor, Pádraig (WS 813)
O'Donoghue, Thomas (WS 1666)
O'Shea, James (WS 733)
Prendergast, Seán (WS 755)
Rankin, Patrick (WS 163)
Ridgway, J. C. (WS 1431)
Robbins, Frank (WS 585)
Rowan, James (WS 871)
Saurin, Charles (WS 288)
Scollan, John J. (WS 318)
Spillane, Michael, and O'Sullivan,
    Michael J. (WS 132)
Tannam, Liam (WS 242)
Thornton, Frank (WS 510)
Tobin, Liam (WS 1753)

Index

Note: illustrations are indicated by page numbers in **bold**.